With the Publishers Compliments

THE NATURAL HISTORY OF THE

CHRISTIAN RELIGION

PUBLISHED BY

JAMES MACLEHOSE AND SONS, GLASGOW,

Publishers to the University.

———

MACMILLAN AND CO., LONDON AND NEW YORK.

London, - - Simpkin, Hamilton and Co.
Cambridge, - Macmillan and Bowes.
Edinburgh, - Douglas and Foulis.

MDCCCXCIV.

THE NATURAL HISTORY

OF THE

CHRISTIAN RELIGION

BEING A STUDY OF THE DOCTRINE OF JESUS
AS DEVELOPED FROM JUDAISM AND
CONVERTED INTO DOGMA

BY

WILLIAM MACKINTOSH, M.A., D.D.

GLASGOW
JAMES MACLEHOSE AND SONS
Publishers to the University
1894

PREFACE.

THE attempt made in this volume to trace the origin of Christianity to the common religious instinct, working under the influence of natural forces and amid historical conditions, is not the first of the kind which has been made, and probably, or rather certainly, will not be the last. When, in accordance with the demands of modern science, the supernatural element is rejected, a problem is presented to the theologian which cannot be put aside—which urgently demands attention. For Christianity is there, a great historical fact, in its origin the most epoch-making which the world has seen ; a fact, therefore, which must be accounted for, one way or another, by the way of natural development, if not by the way of the supernatural. Attempts in this direction, made at a time previous to the rise of what is called "modern criticism," could only be partially, if at all, successful. The volume which is here placed before the public could not possibly have been written until the new criticism had so far done its work, and may be regarded as an outcome of that great movement. In saying this, however, the writer is of course aware that the materials for such a work are scattered everywhere in abundance, not only in books devoted to theological criticism, but also in the great body of general literature.

In recent years many well-known works bearing on the natural origin and verity of the Christian religion have appeared in this country and on the continent. Of these the most recent, so far as known to the writer, is the notable and masterly work of Professor Edward Caird on *The Evolution of Religion*, published after the present volume was all but ready for the press. Being thus nearly related in point of time, the two books might be expected to exhibit phases or sections, more or less allied, of present-day theological thought. But it will be found that between the two there is no affinity, except, perhaps in the general result, so that theologically they neither admit of comparison nor lend support, unless it be undesignedly, to each other. In dealing with the religious problem, they proceed upon independent lines, and follow a quite different mode of treatment. For, while Professor Caird's mode is mainly, if not wholly, speculative and philosophical, that here adopted is mainly, or rather wholly, critical and historical ; the history, be it observed, being such as is arrived at by submitting the canonical records to the ordeal and sifting of modern criticism ; these, in fact, being the only two modes in which the question can be approached.

With consummate literary skill, and a perfect command of philosophic thought and idiom, Professor Caird seeks to show that the simple teaching, the intuitive utterances of Jesus commend themselves to, and coincide with the profoundest moral views of modern philosophy. Now this fact (admitting it to be a fact) is deeply interesting, and cannot but be very satisfactory to every thoughtful Christian ; for it affords as high a confirmation as can be expected of the substantial truth of our religion. But even if so, the question still remains, "How did the ideas of Jesus arise and evolve themselves in his mind ? How did he advance beyond the wisdom of the ancients, Jew and Gentile ?" Or, to put it differently, "How did he anticipate or discount the highest flights of modern thought ?" Plainly it could not be by any form or faculty of mysticism, for which, as Professor Caird incidentally remarks, the large claim has been made, that " it is the great means whereby a religious principle supple-

ments the defects of its own imperfect development, or antici-
pates the results of a more advanced stage than it has yet
attained." For, even if this questionable claim be allowed, no
tendency to mysticism is at all discernible in the teaching of
Jesus. Was it then, as some will say, by supernatural illumination that Jesus rose to that height? or was it rather by
the reaction of his mind upon the inherited and environing
conditions, social and spiritual, peculiar to Judea in his day?
The latter is the alternative which this volume has been
written to establish.

W. M.

March 14, 1894.

NOTE.—*The effect of the anti-supernatural theory of divine action
upon the orthodox dogma is summarily and somewhat abruptly indicated in the beginning of the third chapter of this book; and should
the reader wish to see a more detailed and qualified statement on this
point, he may be referred to the Appendix, which may best be read
immediately after Chapter second.*

CONTENTS.

PREFACE, - - - - - - - - - - - - pp. v–vii.

CHAPTER I.

INTRODUCTORY, - - - - - - - - - pp. 1–18.

The theological situation—Object of this book—Natural origin of Christianity—Successive stages of religious development—Miraculous element imaginary—Ultimate object of the "higher criticism"—The mythicizing tendency—Anti-supernatural theory of the universe—Method of procedure—Necessity for a fresh statement of critical results—Weakness and inconsistency of the Protestant position—Alliance of the churches against scepticism—No middle way.

CHAPTER II.

THEORY OF ANTI-SUPERNATURALISM, - - - - - pp. 19–55.

Prehistoric period of Christianity—Basis of negative and positive criticism—Impossibility of miracle—Various views on the subject—Newman—Kuenen and Huxley—Duke of Argyll—Archdeacon Wilson—The supernatural inconsistent with the idea of development—Scientific theory of the divine action—The human element—Two objections to the scientific theory—Statement of the anti-supernatural position—Further discussion of the second objection—Introduction of Christianity not a breach of continuity—No new element added to human nature—The phenomena no exception to common law of the universe—Tendency to trace religious revolutions to the direct action of the divine power—Hesitating statements of many writers—Difficulty of removing supernatural element from evangelical narrative—Free treatment of records necessary—Conjectural element—How far legitimate—Historical value of the Gospels.

CHAPTER III.

JESUS SIMPLY A TEACHER, - - - - - - - pp. 56–83.

Consequences of the anti-supernatural theory—Jesus simply a teacher, but in the widest sense—Regarded by the Church as a Redeemer—This idea at variance with his teaching—Exceptional utterances—No supernatural inspiration—Jesus made no claim to such —His teaching appealed to moral nature of man—His relation to his age—His genius—His teaching practical, not speculative—Relation of religion to philosophy and to science—Doctrine of Jesus autosoteric— Came not to destroy, but to fulfil.

CHAPTER IV.

RISE AND GROWTH IN ISRAEL OF IDEA OF KINGDOM OF GOD, pp. 84–132.

Relation of Christianity to Judaism—The Exodus—Israel's adoption— Mythical element in the history—The Mosaic law—Idea of the covenant —Hopes of the nation—The prophets—Their adaptation of legend and chronicle—Their principles—Their method—The Messianic prophecies —Prophetic interpretation of the national calamities—Opposition of the prophets to polytheism—Their attitude towards ritual—Their conception of moral government—Their hopes for the future—The idea of a Messiah—Idea of Son of God—Idea of suffering servant of God— Influence upon religion of the Messianic hope—The exile—The Levitical code—Its influence upon religion and national life—The book of Daniel—The Pharisees—Development of theological thought in Israel —Idea of immortality.

CHAPTER V.

TRANSFORMATION OF THIS IDEA BY JESUS, - - - pp. 133–157.

Barrenness of the four centuries preceding Jesus—Religious thought paralysed by idea of visible Kingdom of God—John the Baptist—Contrast between ideas of Kingdom of God held by John and by Jesus— Novelty of the idea taught by Jesus—Far-reaching nature of his doctrine —Its relation to the religion of Israel—The necessity of self help— Help from without not excluded—The forgiveness of sins—Autosoteric nature of his doctrine—His attitude to the Messianic idea—The central truth of Christianity.

CHAPTER VI.

LEGAL OR PHARISAIC IDEA OF RIGHTEOUSNESS AND OF THE RELIGIOUS RELATION, - - - - - - - pp. 158–173.

Tendency to formalism in religion of Israel—Reaction of Jesus against doctrine of Pharisees—The Essenes—Jerusalem the head-

quarters of Pharisaism—Minute regulation of Pharisaic life—Tendency
to encourage hypocrisy—Tendency to multiply ceremonies—Rise of
learned castes—Absence of sympathy and charity—Exaltation of external conformity—Pharisaic view of the Sinaitic covenant.

CHAPTER VII.

EVANGELIC IDEA AS TAUGHT BY JESUS, - - - - pp. 174–214.

Righteousness of the heart—Originality of this idea—Symmetry of
doctrine of Jesus—His moral courage—His ideal of humanity—His
conception of the divine character—Source of his religious insight—
Avenue by which he may have reached his conception of divine love
and forgiveness—His conclusions verifiable by others—His soteriological
doctrine the new element introduced into religion—Renovating power
of his gospel—Necessity of the new ideal of humanity and the new conception of God—Doctrine of divine fatherhood distinctive of teaching of
Jesus—Independent of Greek philosophy—Self-originating character
of divine love—Influence of this idea upon spiritual nature of man—
Absence of dogmatic element from teaching of Jesus—Educative influence of belief in divine forgiveness—Restatement of the distinctive
feature of doctrine of Jesus—Dependence of Christian ethics upon new
view of religious relation.

CHAPTER VIII.

HOW FAR THE DOCTRINE OF JESUS WAS ORIGINAL, - - pp. 215–225.

Minor importance of this question—Comparison of Jesus with his
predecessors—Doctrine to be regarded as a whole—Originality only
relative—Recognition of latent elements—Result of his personal genius
working on prophetic lines—Possible connection with the Essenes—His
superiority to the prophets.

CHAPTER IX.

THAT JESUS CLAIMED TO BE THE MESSIAH, - - - pp. 226–246.

Relation of the Messianic hope to the new religion—Early uncertainty of Jesus as to his own Messiahship—His doctrine independent of
Messianic ideas—Beginnings of his Messianic consciousness—The outer
warrant—Suspense and hesitation—Declaration of Peter at Cæsarea
Philippi—Its effect upon the mind of Jesus—Difficulties involved in the
denial of the Messianic consciousness of Jesus—Development of that
consciousness—Confidence in his own doctrine—Perception of his
spiritual superiority—Assumption of the Messianic rôle—Influence of
the belief in his Messiahship upon his disciples—Origin and growth of
this belief—Reciprocity between Jesus and his disciples.

CHAPTER X.

His Journey to Jerusalem and his Death there,   -   pp. 247–256.

Reasons for the journey—Effect of his appearance upon the priests and Pharisees—His mental attitude in presence of danger—His own conception of the influence of his death—Sublimity of his heroism.

CHAPTER XI.

The Christophanies,   -   -   -   -   -   -   -   pp. 257–297.

Shock to the disciples of the crucifixion—Their rally—Orthodox explanation—Objections—Manifestation only to a few—Discrepancy of the narratives—Uncritical attitude of early Church—Self-contradictory conception of the risen body—Resurrection not necessary to vindicate God's supremacy—Faith of the early Church must be accounted for— Suggested explanations and objections to them—The Vision-Theory— Reasons for its rejection—Involves an expectation of his resurrection— Its frequent occurrence and sudden cessation—The 500 brethren— Vision-Theory does not necessarily invalidate the Christian faith—But belief in the resurrection explained apart from the Vision-Theory— Detailed consideration of the mental condition of the disciples—Revival of their faith in Jesus—Clearer perception of his Messiahship—Senti- ment of adoration—Conviction of his imperishable life—Feeling of his spiritual presence—Expression of this feeling in language of the senses —This explanation not open to objections to Vision-Theory—Compari- son of Galilean brethren with Greeks at Mykalê—Literal interpretation of their figurative language—Conformity with Jewish ideas of the Messiah.

CHAPTER XII.

Mythical Transformation of Evangelic Tradition,   pp. 298–328.

Impulse given to the mythicizing tendency by the belief in the resurrection—Exaltation of the life of Jesus—Supernatural elements introduced—Analogous cases—Question of time—Growth of myth— Materials—Objections to the mythical theory—Desire to strengthen the authority of Jesus—External and internal evidences of Christianity— Desire to certify religious doctrines—All discussion suppressed in early Church—Parallel with other religions—Mythical tendency at work during life of Jesus—Absence of any central authority—Both gain and loss in admission of supernatural element—Belief in the second advent —Origin of this belief—Its influence—Summary of the tendencies which promoted the mythical process—Not specially a legend-loving age— Mythical process filled in details of life of Jesus—Educative value of the myth.

CHAPTER XIII.

RELATION OF MYTH TO DOGMA,   -   -   -   -   -   pp. 329–340.

Sense in which Jesus fulfilled the prophets—The ideal Israelite—Identification with Jesus—The dogmatic process—Relation of myth to dogma—Relation of dogma of Paul to doctrine of Jesus—Conversion rather than development—No dogma in Old Testament or in synoptic Gospels—Its origin in mind of Paul—His probable collaborateurs—His defects—His genius—His service to Christianity—Functions of myth and dogma.

CHAPTER XIV.

CONVERSION OF ST. PAUL, -   -   -   -   -   -   -   pp. 341–367.

Importance of Paul's influence upon Christianity—Causes of his conversion—His own view—His previous religious experience—Effect of contact with disciples of Jesus—His mental conflict—His apprehension of the doctrine of Jesus—Association of his new view with the person of Jesus—His vision—His conversion sudden only in appearance—His perception of the universality of Christianity—Anticipated by Stephen—Universalism of Christianity not derived from universalism of Roman Empire—This element inherent in doctrine of Jesus—Different views on this subject—Paul's conversion a perfectly natural phenomenon—Distinction between the alleged visions of the disciples and that of Paul—Value of his testimony as to the others—Distinction between the spiritual experience of Paul and that of the first disciples.

CHAPTER XV.

HIS DOCTRINE OF ATONEMENT BY THE DEATH OF JESUS, pp. 368–412.

Paul's Pharisaism—Effect upon his mind of the new doctrine—Sense of personal obligation to Jesus—Difficulty of reconciling the death of Jesus with his Messiahship—Idea of atonement—Relation between doctrine of Jesus and that of Paul—Paul's knowledge of the facts of Jesus' life—His apparent inconsistency—His exaltation of the death of Jesus—Need for a sensuous representation of a spiritual truth—Conversion of the autosoteric into a heterosoteric process—Influences tending to this—Paul's declension from the doctrine of Jesus—Pædagogic value of Paul's dogma—Its anti-legal spirit—Atonement the central principle of the dogma—Its relation to modern ideas—Its particularism—Distinction between the religion of Jesus and the Christian religion—Confusion in Paul's scheme of doctrine—Hellenistic and Jewish ideas—How far the former influenced Christianity.

CHAPTER XVI.

PAULINE DOGMA AS INVOLVED IN THAT OF ATONEMENT,   pp. 413-440.

Doctrine of atonement involves superhuman nature of the Messiah—Ascent to the idea of his divinity—Motive principle of the dogmatic development—Pauline anthropology—Literal meaning of Paul's language—His soteriological doctrine—Justification by faith—Criticism of the doctrine—Paul's modifications of it—Difficulty of defining the relation between the Law and the Gospel—Paul's responsibility for Antinomianism—Dissatisfaction with his own dogmatic system—Final view of the relation between Jesus and Paul—Practical influence of the Pauline dogma.

CHAPTER XVII.

CONFLICT BETWEEN JEWISH AND GENTILE CHRISTIANITY,   pp. 441-464.

Opposition to the Pauline dogma—Jewish and Gentile Christians—Points of agreement and of difference—Difference in the spiritual experience of Paul and of the other Apostles—Difference between his and their views of the atonement—His conception of Christian liberty—Exclusiveness and intolerance of the Jewish Christians—Dissensions in the Church—Vacillation of Peter—Paul's rabbinical use of the Old Testament—Epistle to the Hebrews—Distinction between Paul's view and that of the author of that epistle—Inconclusiveness of both their arguments—Schism averted—Irenical tendency in books of New Testament—Mutual concessions—Substantial triumph of Paulinism.

CHAPTER XVIII.

POST-PAULINE OR GNOSTIC PERIOD, -   -   -   -   - pp. 465-490.

Rise of Gnosticism—Dualistic theory of the universe—Its tendency to foster both asceticism and licentiousness—The deutero-Pauline epistles—Their modification of Paul's doctrine of justification by faith alone—Gnosticism partly an exaggerated reaction against Judaism—Development of the Pauline Christology—Gentile tendency to polytheism—Revival of dæmonism among Gentile Christians—Derogatory views of the person and work of Christ—Christianity removed from the practical into the speculative sphere—Gnosticism partly an exaggerated development of Pauline ideas—Reaction against Gnosticism—Relation between pre-Christian Hellenism and deutero-Paulinism—How far the deutero-Pauline epistles were intentionally anti-Gnostic.

CHAPTER XIX.

THE FOURTH GOSPEL, -   -   -   -   -   -   -   - pp. 491-577.

Relation of the fourth Gospel to the Gnostic heresy—Two main theories as to date and authorship of the Gospel—Internal and external evidence—Self-referent character of the discourses of Jesus as given in the fourth Gospel—Identification of Christ with the Logos—Opposition of the Jewish Christians to the doctrine of the divinity of Jesus— Attempt of the fourth Evangelist to solve the Gnostic problem—His combination of Pauline Christology with the Gnostic doctrine of the Logos—Other traces of Hellenistic influence in the fourth Gospel— Difference between the Alexandrian doctrine of the Logos and that of the fourth Evangelist—Use of the word Logos in the Apocalypse—Its use in pre-Christian Jewish literature—How far the Logos of the fourth Gospel is derived from that of Philo—Development of the Paulinistic Christology into that of the fourth Gospel—Necessity felt by the Evangelist for a new gospel—His motives in composing it—Unhistorical character of the fourth Gospel—Its attempt to supply the deficiencies of the others—Its treatment of the miracles and discourses of Jesus— Considerations which might make such procedure seem justifiable to the author—His idealization of the person of Christ—The self-testimony which he makes Jesus bear—No trace in the fourth Gospel of any growth in the consciousness of Jesus—The miracle at Bethany—The cleansing of the temple—Date of the crucifixion—Indifference of the Church to all discrepancies—Uncritical reception of the fourth Gospel —Artistic realism of the work—Other circumstances tending to secure its reception as genuine—Anonymity of the work—Genius of the author —His universalism—Influence of the fourth Gospel upon the Church— Doctrine of the Holy Spirit.

CHAPTER XX.

CONCLUSION, - - - - - - - - - pp. 578–589.

Further development of Christian doctrine—Difference between Pauline and Scholastic dogma—Analogy between the histories of Christianity and of Islam—Treatment which has been given to the historical data—In what sense Christianity is of divine origin—Justification of the attempt to present an anti-supernatural explanation of Christianity.

APPENDIX.

APPLICATION OF THE THEORY OF ANTI-SUPERNATURALISM
TO THE CHRISTIAN DOGMA, - - - - - - pp. 590–607.

The anti-supernatural theory involves the rejection of the cardinal Christian dogmas—Jesus only a man—His sinlessness only relative— He had no miraculous powers—Explanation of his "moral therapeutic" —His alleged prophetic utterances—His alleged resurrection—Question of immortality.

CHAPTER I.

INTRODUCTORY.

IN the agitated and uneasy state of theological opinion, which has prevailed during a great part of this century, the revered ideas and traditions of the past have been thrown into the crucible to be recast, or have been submitted to tests previously unthought of. In view of this fact the question is often asked, "What does it all mean? To what is it all tending?" As the tendency of modern criticism is to reduce, or entirely to get rid of the supernatural element of Christianity, this vague question, expressive of general bewilderment, may be translated into another and more specific question, viz., Whether Christianity can be accounted for on the supposition that there is no such element in it? In this latter and more specific form, this question is undoubtedly the most urgent in the whole field of present day theology; and it is manifest that, to be of any scientific or other value, negative or positive, any attempt to answer it, such as is to be made in this volume, must be thorough, *i.e.*, it must do full justice to the supposition from which it starts, and carry out that supposition to its consequences without faltering or reserve.

So conducted, the discussion may have one of two results —either it may discredit the supernatural theory of Christianity, or it may go far, in the way of a *reductio ad absurdum*, to demonstrate the untenableness of the anti-supernatural theory. Each reader will have to judge for himself, according to the impression made by the discussion upon his mind, to which of these alternatives it has led him. In any case it will do somewhat to put the latter theory to the touch, and bring the reader face to face with difficulties which, by being evaded or kept in the background of thought, produce an uneasiness and perplexity that distract the mind of the Church, and go far to shake the authority of Christianity and to impair its influence.

The writer is persuaded that the prevalent drift toward anti-supernaturalism can never be arrested until the case for it is fully and fairly stated, and is found to break down. The wriggling efforts of the usual apologetic sort to arrest or retard this drift will continue, as heretofore, to be unavailing. It may indeed be that the case for anti-supernaturalism, so far from breaking down, may prove to be good and valid. But even should it be so, the Churches may be expected to look upon the discussion with candour, and even with favour, provided it be also found, that, discharged of the supernatural element, Christianity may yet remain a valuable possession of humanity, a religion fitted to guide and allure men to the higher life. To arrive at such a result, would, it will be confessed, be an immense relief to all who have the interests of religion at heart, and are able to form an intelligent estimate of the modern phase of the religious problem.

It is not, of course, in the power of the author, to limit the circle of his readers, but he may be permitted to say, that this volume is not intended for those who find support for their spiritual life in any of the popular orthodox forms of Christianity. Nothing can be further from his intention than to unsettle the beliefs of those who can honestly make this avowal. He would even deprecate its perusal by any such. But some risk of this kind must be run, unless we choose to proceed upon the maxim (acted on by orthodox Mahometans, as well as by orthodox Christians, and, indeed, by the orthodox of all denominations) of abstaining from every attempt to revise the doctrines which have come down to us as a heritage from our forefathers.

The volume has been written partly for the comparatively few who take an abstract interest in the ascertainment of truth in the religious sphere, but chiefly for the many whose belief in Christianity, by contact with the inquiring or sceptical spirit of the age, is already unsettled, and who find, in their quest of a religion, that the antagonism, real or apparent, between science and the orthodox forms of Christianity makes it impossible for them to be satisfied with any of these.

The pale of orthodoxy may fairly be held to include all professors of Christianity who accept of its miraculous elements, or regard the New Testament in part, or in whole, as a specially inspired volume. At the present day, the confessional differences between the various sects go for very little, and have little or no significance for the spiritual life. The insistence upon these differences is chiefly calculated to perpetuate the existence of rival organizations ; to maintain the *status quo* in the relative strength and distribution of the sects; and to delay for another generation the impending crash of the several dogmatic systems, by which the mind of Christendom has been dominated for so many ages.

More than a century has elapsed, since one of the leading spirits of the time, a devout believer in the miraculous nature of Christianity (Dr. Johnson), gave it as his opinion that "all Christians, whether Papists or Protestants, agree in the essential articles, and that their differences are trivial, and rather political than religious." Few at that time shared in a sentiment so candid and sensible. But in the interval, the thoughts of men have widened and advanced so far, that now there are multitudes in the leisured and better educated classes throughout Christendom who are wholly unable to accept of Christianity as a supernatural system. Of these, many have entirely renounced the Christian profession. But others, and perhaps the much greater number, claim to be Christians still, because they feel that the orthodox form of Christianity is an accident, and that Christianity is identified with a profound truth, more or less underlying all the creeds, which appeals to man's inmost nature and supplies the necessary aliment to his spiritual life. And though the immediate object of this volume is not so much to prove the truth of Christianity, or to indicate wherein its essential truth lies, as rather, to trace its historical genesis, yet the writer is persuaded that its essential truth will best appear, incidentally or inferentially, in the course of such an inquiry.

The title of the volume will suffice to show that it is written on the lines of the great critical movement which has gone on in theology for the greater part of this century, and that it will be largely negative in its scope. At the same time, the writer wishes it to be understood from the first that, by intention at least, the volume is constructive, and, in the larger sense of the

word, even apologetic. This will be readily recognized by
some, if not by all, of its readers. Indeed, had the views of
the writer been merely negative, offering nothing in place of
what was removed or discarded, he would have hesitated to
lay them before the public. But he is encouraged to do so
because he believes that, by abandoning indefensible positions,
and, in particular, by dissolving the connection of Christianity
with miracle of every kind, it may be made to present a
stronger front to the world ; that when this just cause of
offence is removed, the intellect, which has been stigmatized
as a "universal solvent," will cease to be aggressive and
capricious and become friendly in its attitude.

With this conviction he will attempt to show that Christianity took its rise in a great spiritual and religious movement
among the Jewish people, or in a great transformation of
Jewish ideas effected by Jesus, and spreading from him to
his disciples ; and to find in that movement and in certain
favouring circumstances and historical conditions, without looking beyond to any supernatural or transcendental causes, an
explanation of the whole relative phenomena. He will treat
Christianity as an outgrowth of the human mind, and, therefore, as in no sense miraculous, but yet as a revelation of the
divine in so far as it has brought to light the true secret, the
idea, and the goal of humanity. He believes Christianity to
have been founded, proximately, in the great religious experience which befell Jesus in its purest form, and was reflected
in his life and teaching. He believes that that experience
was transmitted and propagated to the minds of his disciples,
not, however, in its pure and original form, but through the
medium of the impression made by the personality of Jesus
on their emotional nature ; and that that impression, acting
on their imaginative and ratiocinative faculties, was what gave
to Christianity the mythical and dogmatic construction which
is presented to us in the New Testament and in the creeds of
the Churches.

There are three propositions, the truth of which will be
made to appear in the following pages. First, that Judaism
and Christianity denote the successive stages of one long
evolution of religious thought and sentiment. The underlying
fact of a grand religious movement is the key to the whole
following discussion, a fact without which the literature and

history of Israel and of the early Church would be an insoluble enigma, a fortuitous development.   Secondly, that the phases of this long evolution in its decisive moments have been largely recorded in the form of myth and dogma, so that a miraculous aspect has been imparted to the evolution, which in itself went on naturally and rationally, or according to the laws of our spiritual and social nature.   And, thirdly, that the myth and dogma have mingled as important factors in the evolution itself.

By the first of these propositions it is not meant that the evolution dates its origin from Judaism, but rather that it reaches back to a long anterior time.   Few great thoughts which have dawned upon the minds of men have been lost ; and the salvage of one religion in its decay and senescence may have formed the stock with which another has started on its course and entered upon its new career.   If it be the case, and no one can doubt it, that Christianity was rooted in the religion of Israel, and was the heir of all that was best in it, there is little less certainty, though it has been disputed, that the religion of Israel was under deep obligations to that of Egypt, that is, to the most ancient civilization of the world ; so that the religious development, which has culminated in Christianity, was coeval in its origin with the earliest dawn of intelligence.   The evolution of the religious principle has had as many illustrations as there have been historical religions in the world.   Theologians have undertaken to trace the origin and growth of religion as illustrated by that of ancient Egypt, of China, of India, of Scandinavia, and even of Mexico and Peru.   But it may be remarked generally that in all these cases the evolution turned aside into a terminal, or stopped short of the higher reaches of religious thought.   There was much common to all of them with Judaism and Christianity, but it admits of being said, with every appearance of truth, that these latter began where those others left off.   And the higher development in the exceptional cases of Judaism and Christianity was probably due to a new ethical impulse, which gave them a fresh start.   The predominance of the ethical element kept them upon the right line of development, or enabled them to regain the line after every temporary divergence.   Thus it was that Christianity arose by the self-assertion of the moral nature in Jesus, and that the Reformation of the sixteenth century was due to a similar cause in the mind of Luther and his predecessors.

The miraculous element which, according to the second of the above propositions, runs through the records of the great evolution, is traceable to the imagination of the peoples, or of individual writers, during a period in which the direct intervention of the divinity was called in, without scruple, hesitation, or misgiving, and at the dictation of pious feeling, to explain everything that was out of the common course. The religious movement as it went on from age to age created for itself a miraculous history, just because it knew not how otherwise to place itself on record. Underlying the miraculous records of the Old and New Testaments there is the secret history of that great, non-miraculous religious movement which was of secular duration and ran through many stadia. This movement, as presented in the records, is woven into one with historical events. Men who were conscious of the movement, or took part in it, moulded the history, so as to make of it a vehicle and a sanction for the religious idea. So far as this was done consciously it was owing partly to the fact that the historical sense was not developed in their minds, and partly to the fact that the religious interest largely predominated. And it is obvious that by this treatment both the history and the idea would be made to suffer. The history was veiled, not to say distorted, and the idea came to no pure or adequate expression. The historical records do not so much show the phases of the religious evolution as rather the religious standing of the writers who compiled them as a vehicle for the utterance and propagation of their own religious ideas. From which view of these documents arises a most important inference for theological science. The mixed nature of the documents determines the ultimate aim and object of what is called the " higher criticism," as applied to them. This can be nothing short of tracing and following out the course of the underlying history, and of discovering, if not exactly, yet approximately, how those who took part in the salient or creative periods of the movement—or rather, perhaps, how those who came after conceived of these as periods of special divine interposition, and handed down the memory of them in narratives which imparted to them their miraculous colouring. We can only hope to discover *approximately* how this took place, because our sources of information are too scanty to admit of exact knowledge, and also because of the possible variations in the development of human thought and action under given conditions.

Once admit the rationale of the myth and its function in shaping the history of religion which we shall have an opportunity of explaining, and we may be prepared to find it everywhere as a never absent feature of the history in all its stages, an invariable element of the literature which the religious movement called forth. Men, who, like the Israelites, regarded all events as evidences of the direct operation of God in the world, would seek to represent the national fortunes generally, as illustrations of divine action, more palpable than they really afforded. And this endeavour, unconscious no doubt, would be a source of many mythical narratives which had no direct bearing on the religion. But any stir or movement in the religious life of the people would call the mythicizing tendency into its most lively action. When such was the case, the annalist or historiographer would have recourse to the supernatural factor to explain it. Only when the religious life of the people was flat, commonplace, or stagnant, would the record become prosaic, and decline into plain, unvarnished history. But at an epoch-making period, the mythicizing tendency would revive, and seek not only to represent the epoch itself, as something marvellous and preternatural, but also to revive and colour the history of preceding times, so as to make of them a prophecy of the new power, which had entered into the national life, and so to establish a certain unity between the past and the present, such as befitted a divine revelation.

In adopting the anti-supernatural theory of the universe, the writer must not be understood as questioning that a divine power moves in all nature and in all history, but only as denying that such a power moves in a sphere beyond and outside of nature. Granting that there is a supernatural element common to all phenomena, he denies that, in any phenomena whatever, physical or spiritual, there is such an element over and above what is common to all alike ; or that there are certain classes of phenomena, which are supernatural in a sense and to a degree which other classes are not. Further, in denying the specially supernatural character of Christianity, he is far from denying the existence of a great mystery in its genesis and constitution. "Geheimnisse sind noch keine Wunder."

It is only the situation and nature of the mystery that are shifted. For it seems to him to be a thing much more mysterious, much more inaccessible to the human understanding, that a divine idea, which commends itself as such to reason and conscience, should work itself out through the uniform operation of natural and psychological law, than that it should do so through the occasional operation of some supernatural and exceptional agency. Through the operation of natural laws, the supreme power whose will resides in these laws, or is identical with them, brings to pass results so marvellous, so unexpected, so much apart from ordinary routine, that men regard them as the work of a power which is above law, and proceed to construe and interpret them on that hypothesis. This is the dogmatic or symbolical construction of the mystery, which is not thereby enhanced, but, on the contrary, reduced, that we may not say degraded, to the level of human comprehension. No doubt, it may be said that, if the presence and action of a divine power, working out its own ends, through the operation of natural laws, be not denied, it does not much signify where that action is placed, or how it is conceived of; but the writer agrees with those who contend on the contrary that, in the presence of modern scientific thought, it has become a vital necessity for religion to acknowledge divine action only in the form and through the medium of natural law, physical and spiritual, and to have it understood once for all that the supernatural aspect, given in Scripture to divine action, is only the naïve representation of its natural, but recondite character, the form in which it presents itself to the unscientific mind.

The reader need not expect to find in the following pages anything of the nature of a history of the nascent Church, nor of a "Life of Jesus": for which, indeed, in the strict sense of the word, existing materials are far too scanty; though, during the last half century, many works with that title have been placed before the world. The author proposes to enter as little as possible into historical and exegetical details. He will pass lightly over many points which are largely discussed in such works as those just mentioned, or he will altogether omit them, because of their collateral and subsidiary character. He will also avoid, as far as possible, all points in regard to which, as it seems to him, historical and literary criticism has arrived at no very definite result : not by way of making out a special and one-sided plea for the views which he holds, but by way of confining attention to the broader aspects of the subject, and of dwelling fully on those particulars on which the genesis and early development of Christianity, which it is his object to trace, seem to hinge. Even these it is impossible to discuss within the compass of a single volume, without taking for granted the reader's acquaintance to some extent with the general results and methods of modern criticism. The writer, however, will not presume upon such acquaintance more than he can help, but endeavour, as far as possible, to write in a manner intelligible to the general reader, especially avoiding the details of textual exegesis, and even of literary and historical criticism, except in so far as these may be necessary to elucidate the line of argument.

The work may be said to consist of two parts, the one negative, and the other positive, which, however, pass and repass into each other without being divided by any line of demarcation. As the former is wholly, or largely, a summing up of certain results which have been pretty well established by the literary and historical investigations of the present century, it contains comparatively little that will be novel or fresh to the well-informed reader. But there is a necessity to place, even before such a reader, much that he is familiar with, in order to present a comprehensive view of the subject, to define the writer's standpoint, and to clear the ground for the positive sections of the inquiry. And it is hoped that these latter sections may be found to contain so much of a fairly original character as may, to the competent judgment, justify the writer in laying his views before the public.

He believes that the results of modern criticism are here applied, in a way never before attempted, to the solution of the problem indicated in the title ; and also, that the general results of that criticism may receive confirmation, when it is seen that they really do yield such a solution. While he admits that, on many of the critical questions to be touched upon in the following discussion, the last word has not yet been spoken, he may at least say that his general estimate

of the results of Old and New Testament criticism is the
best approximate which he has been able to form.   There
is an evident intention and endeavour on the part of apologists to belittle, or restrict and narrow these results.   And
if, against his will, the writer may be thought to have erred
on the other side, it may yet be seen that the general
validity of this discussion is not dependent on the absolute
correctness of all its details.

He is strongly persuaded that some such work as that
here attempted is called for by the state of modern criticism,
in order that its results may be placed before the public in
one connected view, and were it only to state the case
which it seeks to establish against the supernatural origin
and constitution of Christianity.   Provided the case be a
weak one, the fact will, by such a connected view, be made
to appear in a clearer light than it can be by any detached
portion of the evidences ; while, on the other hand, if the
case is a good one, the mere attempt to present such a
connected view cannot fail to throw light upon many obscure passages in the great evolution of religious thought of
which Christianity is the outcome.   There are many passages
in that evolution, the obscurity of which for the critical,
that is the reasoning and inquiring mind, is not dissipated
by the copious infusion in the primitive records of the
supernatural element ; and as little is it relieved by any
treatment or interpretation, however modern, of these documents which leaves that element standing.

It is not without a trembling sense of responsibility that
the writer ventures to place such a work as this before the
public.   But he is emboldened to take this step by the
consciousness that he is actuated by concern for the interests
of religion, and by the conviction that these interests are
better served, in this age especially, by a creed which,
scanty as it may seem, yet rests upon an appeal to reason
and experience, than by one embracing articles which, however endeared to us by old and tender associations, yet rest
upon a foundation of questionable solidity, and give occasion
to so much scepticism among men of thought both in
Catholic and in Protestant countries.

This is the main consideration which justifies a work of
this kind.   But a minor, though still important consideration

is, that the supernatural element disguises the nature of Christianity and is the source not only of endless diversity of opinion regarding its doctrines, but also of interminable feuds between the various Churches which are agreed in accepting that element. It was the element to which the early Church had recourse to explain to itself whatever was phenomenal or mysterious in its own experience ; and by retaining it in their view of Christianity, theologians of all schools and of all ages have had at their disposal an unlimited choice of conjectural possibilities by which to reconcile all discrepancies in the records, and to smooth away all the difficulties which their several views present to the critical judgment.

Catholic and Protestant alike can avail themselves of these possibilities, so that the controversies between them can never be settled. It may also be confidently affirmed that Protestantism can never be able to hold its own, and still less to turn the apologetic position of the Roman Catholic Church, until it abandon the supernatural ground, which has hitherto been common to both. With its historical prestige, the Catholic Church will always have the advantage in controversy with any rival which clings to the supernatural element. For, if the admission be made that Christianity was given to the world by supernatural revelation, the presumption will always be strong, that this element takes part in its development as well as in its origin ; and in the growing clash and hubbub of opinion, the presumption will wax stronger and stronger, that to preserve the benefit of Christianity, there must be somewhere a power in the world invested with the prerogative of infallibility, adapted " to smite hard, and to throw back the immense energy of the aggressive intellect," and in the absence of all other claimants, the Roman Catholic Church will hold the field. This position so ably and acutely maintained by Newman and other Catholic controversialists is impregnable.

Considered as a supernatural system, Christianity is so expansive, so plastic, and, so to say, unstable ; capable, i.e. of being shaped into such diverse forms by the breath and impact of human opinion, that if men have to determine what they should or should not believe, some final, outward and official authority seems to be a necessary adjunct of the system ; necessary, that is, if change is to be resisted, doubts to be resolved, and unity among its adherents to be preserved. The importance and the difficulty of preserving unity in the faith began, as may be seen in the canonical epistles, to be early felt (cf. 2 Cor. xiii. 11, Phil. ii. 2, Eph. iv. 3, etc.); and this feeling had much to do with the rise of the episcopate ; with the convocation of ecumenical councils ; and with the establishment of the Roman primacy : that is to say, with the whole course of ecclesiastical history.

This craving for a central authority has descended to modern times, and menaces the stability of the Protestant Churches. It was what lured Newman and many others into the Catholic Church, whose claim to having the seat of authority within itself, besides the force which it derives from historical prestige, is also, as already said, indefinitely strengthened by the fact that practically there is no other claimant in the field. And it can hardly but be admitted, that for Newman, starting as he did from a belief in the supernatural origin and dogmatic character of Christianity, secession was the natural and logical consequence. Scripture could not furnish the rule of faith which he craved, for it creates more controversies than it settles ; and men, whether educated or uneducated, who trust to private judgment, are able to find in it whatever they bring with them to its study. Besides, it can hardly be thought that God would first grant a special revelation of His will, and then stultify Himself by leaving men, with the book of revelation in their hands, as much at a loss as ever. The hope that this state of things can ever be remedied by the study and exegesis of Scripture argues a very sanguine state of mind.

Indeed, it seems to the writer that Catholic theologians have every reason to be satisfied with the present state of the controversial situation, as it is set forth, for example, in Mr. Gladstone's *Vaticanism* and the replies to it, and may abide the issue with perfect complacency. Besides refusing to make use of the great weapon which science has put into its hands, Protestantism, in the very process of shifting the seat of authority from the Church to the Scriptures, had to rely upon the authority of the Church in receiving the books of the New Testament as authentic, and so involved itself in a radical inconsistency, which cripples it to this day in its conflict with

Catholicism, and is amply sufficient to account for the counter-Reformation that began almost before Luther was in his grave. The progress of this reactionary movement has since then "slowed" considerably, but has never ceased to make headway, and may yet, not improbably, recover, as by a spring, the ground which it has lost. Many of us may scoff at the idea that, in an age of general and growing enlightenment, the Catholic Church can ever regain its power, resume its old intolerance, and once more become a danger to the State ; but even science itself is no safeguard against such a catastrophe, until the community is converted by it to the anti-supernatural theory of the universe, and ceases to be overawed by the Church's claim to supernatural powers.

It may be observed in general that, when a controversy is carried on for centuries on any subject of pressing and practical human interest, without reaching, or even tending to reach a consistent and satisfactory result—a result so commending itself to reason as to command universal assent—the reflection is obvious that the question or subject requires to be looked at from a point of view above that to which the disputants have been able to rise. And applying this observation to the matter in hand, the modern theologian hopes to obtain such a commanding view of the theological field by discarding entirely the miraculous element in the genesis and constitution of Christianity. But the Protestant Churches are as little disposed as the Catholic Church itself to follow him in this step. In his *History of England*, Mr. J. R. Green hits the nail on the head when he says that "the real value to mankind of the religious revolution of the sixteenth century lay, not in the substitution of one creed for another," or, let us say, of one authority for another, "but in the new spirit of inquiry, the new freedom of thought and of discussion, which was awakened during the process of change."

The Protestant Churches themselves never really broke away from authority, and never adopted what was really the only alternative principle—the principle of free and unfettered inquiry. On the authority of Scripture, they adopted the supernatural theory of Christianity, though the Copernican system had already given a shock, felt by Melancthon, and no doubt by many others, to the supernatural idea generally. From that shock the supernatural idea has never recovered. Every advance in science since then has only added to its shattering force, though orthodox Protestantism to this day refuses to recognize the fact.

Manifestly, the controversy hitherto waged between the Catholic and the Protestant Churches has been one not of principle, but of detail ; and the leaders, both of Catholic and of Protestant thought, are becoming more and more alive to the fact that that controversy is of less pressing and of less fundamental moment than another controversy to which they are challenged by a common enemy.   Indications are not wanting of a disposition on the part of both Churches to unite their forces, and to occupy common ground against the assaults of scientific criticism upon historical Christianity.

A watchful observer of the signs of the times (R. H. Hutton, in his *Memoir of Cardinal Newman*) has observed that " there is something like an *entente cordiale* between the Roman Catholic Church of to-day and the various other churches—an alliance against scepticism."   It needs little discernment to perceive that the positions taken up, for example, by such representative men as Mr. St. George Mivart and Mr. Hutton himself, in regard to the place of Scripture in the Christian system, are all but identical.   Scientific criticism has compelled the former to surrender the infallibility of the Scriptures, which the Catholic Church, under reservation of its own claim to the interpreting power, had declared to be canonical, or regulative of faith.   Even with this reservation, he can no longer regard the Scriptures as infallible.   It has become evident to him that there are statements—doctrinal and historical—in Scripture, which, by no license of interpretation, can be made to square with reason and fact.   He has therefore, along with many of his co-religionists, and without expressed disapproval on the part of the heads of the Church, definitely abandoned the old position. According to the best knowledge of the present writer, Mr. Hutton's position is, that the Scriptures of the Old Testament are the " grand but not infallible literature of a divinely-instructed people," and the Scriptures of the New Testament the literature of the early Christian Church under divine guidance.   Both these representative men seem to unite in regarding the Church of the Old and of the New " dispensation " as the subject or depositary of special inspiration—a localizing of the supernatural influence so vague, so elastic, and protean, as to be very serviceable indeed to the orthodox apologist, but not less obnoxious to modern thought than even the theory of the inspiration of the individual writers. Union is strength; but it is not by the union of Catholic and Protestant on such terms that the cause of Christianity can be strengthened.

In giving up to almost any extent the inspiration of Scripture the Roman Catholic Church really gives up nothing so long as it retains the doctrine of its own infallibility—the power of setting Scripture aside or ruling its interpretation. But the Protestant Church, in questioning ever so little the infallibility or special inspiration of Scripture, renounces, though it may be unconsciously, every authority in matters of religion, except that of the purified reason or religious instinct, and commits itself, by a great act of faith, to the divine principle in humanity as the supreme judge of Scripture and the guide into all truth. Between that authority and this there is no real standing ground in common. The mediating theory of an inspiration which is at once special and partial does not rescue the authority of Scripture. For on this theory the difficulty confessedly remains (*Spectator*, September 7, 1889) of "discriminating between the many various elements in Scripture and the proper amount of authority to be conceded to the different parts of it." This difficulty of discriminating in a partially inspired volume between what is and what is not inspired is a difficulty the same as that which exists in discriminating (on the supposition that no part of it is specially inspired) between what is true and what is not. If inspiration is partial, those portions only can be regarded as inspired which in one way or another we have first recognized to be true. The ability to discriminate between the various elements of Scripture requires that there be a principle which stands above Scripture. And where can that higher principle be seated but in the fallible reason of man, which is the testing instrument, the paramount authority. With every deduction which may thus be made from the authority of Scripture the writer believes, nevertheless, that it will ever remain for all civilized peoples "the book of religion," as Mr. Matthew Arnold regarded it, the literary deposit of the best that men have thought on the religious relation. It is a fact, apart from any theory as to inspiration, that when we search the Scriptures we find in them much that stimulates our religious feelings and appeals to our souls in proportion as we ourselves are imbued with the religious sentiment.

Instead, therefore, of regarding Scripture as a specially inspired volume, or as the literature of a divinely or specially guided nation or church, the writer regards it simply as the literature of a great religious movement, which culminated at two points, or rather ran through two stadia—the prophetic and the evangelic. The peculiarity of the former was that it was accompanied by a sense of incompleteness, and by an expectancy of further development. The latter was the long deferred, much desiderated, yet sudden consummation of the preceding—sudden inasmuch as it first declared itself in the consciousness of one man, who, by the heroism and power of his testimony to the truth revealed to his mind, stood so conspicuous and alone, that when that exulting consciousness communicated itself, through intercourse with him, to his disciples, they ascribed it to the occult and mysterious power of his work and person, and forthwith proclaimed him to be the author and bringer of salvation, entitled to divine honours.

However willing, therefore, nay, anxious, to remain upon comparatively orthodox ground, the writer has never been able to reconcile himself to any of the so-called mediating schools of Protestant theology. These always appeared to him to have originated in the illogical and futile endeavour to effect a fusion of ideas which are mutually repellent and exclusive, but are made by mere trick and dexterity of language to pass and repass like dissolving views into each other in such a way as to mask their inherent antinomy. While the mediating schools of theology, as distinct from the liberal schools, seek to assert at any price the supernatural character of Christianity, and dread that the abandonment of that would deprive it of its divine sanction, the position taken up in this volume is that all truth has the divine sanction, and that we can still be Christians while denying that there is anything supernatural either in the origin or in the history of our religion. A talented theologian in this country of the mediating school (Dr. Bruce) in his book on *The Miraculous Element of the Gospels* has admitted that the " value of the healing works of Jesus, as media of revelation, apart from their value as evidences of the divine origin of revelation, does not at all depend upon their miraculousness." " Take these works," he goes on to say, " as media of revelation and you may learn much that is of vital importance to Christianity, and be, in important respects, a Christian in faith and practice, while your judgment is in suspense on the whole subject of miracles." The position of the present writer cannot be better defined than by saying that he accepts of this remark, but extends it to the life and teaching of Jesus as a whole. He holds the significance of that life as a medium of divine revelation to be independent of a miraculous element, and that the revelation thereby conveyed is its own evidence.

To many it will seem to be unpardonable presumption on the part of any individual to assail a system of doctrine which has enjoyed the confidence of many generations, and furnished a stay to their spiritual life. But it is not so much the individual as modern thought and criticism which, through the individual, challenges the system. The writer's acquaintance with these, such as it is, has satisfied him that Christianity can no longer be safely left to rest upon the basis or hypothesis of the supernatural, and that its traditional or orthodox form is vitiated by the miraculous element which is essential to it in that form. The cause of Christianity, which he regards as the cause of religion, has already suffered much from being identified or made to stand or fall with a hypothesis which is no longer tenable. And with this conviction impressed on his mind, he undertakes to show that the genesis of Christianity may, like that of any other process, be explained on natural principles.

At this day there are, it is notorious, great multitudes of thoughtful Christians, who feel that their spiritual life has a sufficient stay in the simple, undogmatic teaching of Jesus, which is the common base of all the creeds ; but who, finding no help in the Pauline or orthodox dogma, do not trouble or concern themselves with it. Few, however, of those who are in this state of mind, are aware how much is involved in their position when consistently carried out—what a revolution it implies in the whole current of theological thought, or by what process of reasoning it may be, or needs to be, justified. For such persons we shall endeavour to make these points clear, and to show that the dogma which has no interest for them, is yet the form which the Christian idea has assumed in order the better to sway the will, to touch the feeling, to adapt itself to the intelligence of the general mind.

If in the following pages a thought should here and there be

B

repeated, let it be borne in mind that, in the course of the long secular development here to be traced, the same springs and principles of action may be expected to come into play at various points, and may require to be noted on each occasion ; that it may not be possible to dispose of a subject once for all when it first presents itself for consideration, and that the same remark or criticism occurring in a different connection need not be a mere repetition.   Further, it will appear that there are several decisive moments or stadia in the grand religious development which ended in orthodox Christianity, and that the writer has felt it necessary to devote to these an amount of attention which, to the hasty judgment, may seem excessive, but will, perhaps, be found on a closer acquaintance to be not more than proportioned to their importance.   He also trusts that his wish to avoid circumlocution will be accepted as his apology for his occasional, or, what may seem to be, his too frequent employment of technical theological terms.

CHAPTER II.

THEORY OF ANTI-SUPERNATURALISM.

LIKE other forms of positive religion, Christianity became a subject of history proper only when it began to take effect upon masses of men and to be an appreciable factor in their social condition. It had what may be called a prehistoric period, of which the memory or record was necessarily mythical, because the psychological laws which were in operation in its genesis were not understood, were not even thought of, by those who were the witnesses or reporters of its origin. With the few facts, which tradition or legend had preserved, the mythicizing fancy interwove supernatural elements to account for its genesis, and to bring it to that point at which it incorporated itself in forms of worship and of dogma, in institutions and in communities of adherents, and so entered as a visible factor into the stream of history. This mythical or prehistoric period was the period, first of its inception and genesis in the brooding, meditative mind of Jesus, and, next of its propagation to the minds of his personal followers and their more immediate converts : and this is the period with which we purpose chiefly to deal. The meaning and the truth of this preliminary statement and of others like it will appear gradually as we proceed in our discussion.

In few words, let it here be said summarily that the negative or "destructive" criticism which we propose to direct against orthodox Christianity, is based on the anti-supernatural view of the divine government, and that our positive but undogmatic construction of Christianity is based on the teaching of Jesus. In this section, we shall seek to define and to defend the anti-supernatural view, and to draw the inferences in regard to dogma which seem to flow from it. In several of the following sections we shall seek to show that the doctrine of Jesus is the doctrine of the absolute religion, or of that form of religion which answers to the religious idea ; and, also, that the path by which Jesus was led to his great discovery was by the way of historical development. In the remaining sections, we shall endeavour to trace the steps by which the dogma in its canonical form grew up out of the doctrine and the life of Jesus. The way is long and difficult : many of the steps are more or less conjectural : and some of the details may be doubtful and open to dispute, as of matters upon which the last word has not been spoken. But it is because, in spite of all such considerations, we have confidence in our general view, that we now venture to ask the attention of the public.

As we purpose to trace, step by step, the natural genesis of Christianity, that is, to show that it can be explained by natural causes, we must, at the outset, endeavour to point out our justification for an undertaking of this kind : a part of our task which will detain us for some time, but which, being necessary for the completeness of the discussion, cannot be altogether omitted or even summarily disposed of. Bespeaking, therefore, the reader's patience, we proceed to say, that this undertaking seems to us to be called for, because, with a large and ever increasing number of cultivated men, we hold that miracles not only " do not," but cannot happen. Not, we wish it to be observed, that we reached our view of the religious relation, or, let us rather say, of the nature of Christianity, by taking this as our starting point. For the genetic order of our thought was exactly the reverse, inasmuch as our view of that relation forced itself independently upon our conviction, and led us on to the position that miracle is impossible. But, without dwelling on this point, we confess that, as here stated in synthetic form, this assumption has all the appearance of an unwarranted begging of the whole question in dispute, and a summary setting aside of the claims of Christianity to be a supernatural revelation. This has been so strongly felt that, in order to avoid the appearance of a *petitio principii*, many even of those critics who deny the supernatural nature of Christianity, set out by admitting the possibility of miracle in the abstract, while maintaining that the alleged miracles of Christianity do not satisfy their canons of credibility. And no doubt this intermediate position has a certain air of judicial candour and of dispassionate consideration. But it cannot be concealed that this mode of treatment opens the door to endless controversy and gives no hope of a conclusive settlement. Just as in the interpretation of Scripture the acceptance of the miraculous element opens the door to discussions which lead to no result, so, in weighing the evidences of Christianity, to admit the possibility of miracle involves us in endless controversy and difference of opinion.

It is impossible to determine the amount of evidence which is necessary to prove the reality of an alleged miracle, or to say when it is that the presumption against such an abnormal occurrence is overcome. Minds of one class, especially those who have undergone a training in science, will demand an amount and species of evidence which, in the circumstances, is quite unattainable and out of the question. Another class of minds, especially those in whom the religious instinct has been strongly cultivated, will be only too easily satisfied as to the miraculous nature of Christianity, or indeed of any religious system in which they have been educated. To the latter it will always seem as if what is possible will, under certain conditions, and in emergencies of presumably supreme and universal gravity, be actualized; they will be ready to give the benefit of a presumption in favour of the Gospel miracles, and to accept evidence for them which is not much stronger than that which suffices to establish the occurrence of any not very common, but admittedly possible event—*e.g.*, to accept the narrative of the resurrection of Jesus almost as readily as that of his crucifixion. For such persons, indeed, the *reality* of the supernatural element in Christianity—the very thing which remains to be proved—may seem to be so probable in itself as to stand in need of little other proof. And when this broad ground is taken up, that element will come in everywhere to help the solution of the historical difficulty, to explain away every discrepancy in the records. With a little mystery here, and a little mystery there, every test of credibility will be satisfied, and the whole system will present itself to their minds with a fair show and a firm front; the weaker or missing links in the chain of evidence will be regarded as mere tests of faith;

and to make light of fundamental, no less than of superficial difficulties, will be regarded as a proof of the presence in their minds of a faculty of spiritual discernment, or of a faith that is above reason.   The supernatural element may, in fact, be compared to the grain of chaff which, according to the nursery tale, was demanded by the magician that he might give to the rope of sand the tenacity of a hempen cable.

In his *Grammar of Assent* and elsewhere, Cardinal Newman endeavours to show the *rationale* of such an attitude of mind towards the Gospel miracles.   He dwells upon the mystery which envelops all human affairs, but especially in the religious sphere ; upon the weakness and perversity of the human intellect ; its proneness to be led astray by false lights ; its inability to discriminate between the true and the false, and its irrepressible longing to attain to some certain knowledge of God.   From these and other such considerations, he infers the high probability that God will condescend to grant some direct and unmistakable revelation of absolute truth to mankind. And in the case of a religion calculated, like the Christian, to satisfy these longings, he further infers that, in order to convert the probability into certainty, and to establish the fact of its supernatural character, such an antecedent presumption needs only to be supplemented by some very slender extrinsic evidence—by an evidence which, apart from the intrinsic probability, would by no means satisfy the reason.

This may be taken as a rough description from memory of Newman's views on this subject.   What gives importance to these is, that they represent the views which are implicitly held by multitudes, and which enable them to put aside the scientific and critical objections to the credibility of the Gospel miracles.   Indeed, it is easy to see that to grant the possibility of miracle in the abstract, is to surrender the whole position to the orthodox theologian.   To say the very least, it is to place the supernatural character of Christianity among the things which cannot be disproved, and to throw the door open to a never-ending because resultless controversy between the scientific and the religious spirit.   For, as there is no prospect or likelihood of the scientific spirit abandoning its position, the controversy will come to an end, if it ever does, only when the religious spirit learns to accommodate itself to the scientific theory of the universe.

Nothing more need be said to demonstrate what an inconclusive procedure it is to rest the denial of the miraculous element of the Gospels, as Küenen in Holland and Huxley in this country are disposed to do, on the inadequacy of the historical evidence. When a critic like Küenen professes to believe, or not to dispute, the possibility of miracle in the abstract, and to be willing to leave that as an open and unsettled question, but at the same time shows himself very exacting as to the evidence for the miraculous element in Christianity as a whole, or for the miraculous works recorded of Jesus in particular, and declares that the evidence for these does not satisfy his canons of credibility, the likelihood is that, unconsciously to himself, there is an *arrière pensée* in his mind equivalent to the denial of the possibility of miracles ; at least, that is the impression which the rigour of his criticism will make on the minds of others.

Professor Huxley takes up much the same ground as Professor Küenen, and tells us that " No one is entitled to say *a priori* that any given so-called miraculous event is impossible," and that " Objections to the occurrence of miracles cannot be scientifically based on any *a priori* considerations." But to these propositions it may be replied, that the considerations to which he refers are not *a priori*, at least not in the sense of being metaphysical ; though, even if they were, they might yet be relevant ; neither are they *a priori* in the sense of being " unvermittelt," or independent of all previous knowledge or experience. Science itself has brought into view certain considerations which strongly imply the impossibility of any infraction of the immanent laws of existence—considerations which but for science would never have been heard of. Science has pushed its investigations into almost every department of existence, and in every one, physical and psychological, to which it has gained access, it has found that all occurrences, phenomena, and sequences bear invariable witness to the control of law and to the sway of order—that what is called divine action never operates irrespective of such order, or otherwise than naturally—*i.e.*, through, or in accordance with such order.

The inference is irresistible that the same thing holds true in those departments also, if such there be, which science has not yet invaded, and the tendency is fostered in the scientific mind to assume that every fact or event, however strange, and apparently exceptional or abnormal, admits of being subsumed under some general law or laws, either already ascertained or yet ascertainable. Of course, Professor Huxley admits this to the fullest extent. He says, " When repeated and minute examination (*i.e.*, science) never reveals a break in the chain of causes and effects, the belief that that chain never has been broken, and never will be broken, becomes one of the strongest and most justifiable of human convictions." This, in other words, is the belief in the universal reign of law ; or, which is the same thing, the belief that occurrences really abnormal or miraculous are excluded by a supreme necessity. But when this man of science defines nature as " the totality of all events, past, present, and to come," it seems to us that he really and unwarrantably seeks to beg the whole question as regards the so-called miracles of the New Testament, and contributes nothing whatever to its settlement. The definition may be, and, we believe, is in itself perfectly just. But then the very idea of miracle, as exemplified in the New Testament, and as evidential of the divine revelation, of which the Scripture professes to be the record, is that of an event or phenomenon, conceived of as outside the course of nature, and caused by the direct action of the power which is above nature. And the definition, by excluding the occurrence of such an event, involves an "*a priori* consideration," quite as much as the proposition that miracles are impossible, and indeed, as applied to the Scriptural narratives, is identical with it. In passing, it may be noticed that the ground occupied by Professor Huxley, though allied to that occupied by Professor Küenen, is yet not quite the same. For if the latter were satisfied with the evidence of any " so-called " miracle, such as the resurrection of Jesus, he would accept of it as an *actual* miracle or direct act of God ; whereas if Professor Huxley were satisfied with the evidence, he would still refuse to admit the miraculous character of the event, and rank it among natural phenomena.

Modern thought holds, in the form of a scientific conviction, what was matter of surmise or divination to a few of the leading minds in ages long past, viz., that the universe is governed by immutable laws inherent in the very nature and constitution of things—by laws which are " never reversed, never suspended, and never supplemented in the interest of any special object whatever." It holds that there exists a key to all phenomena both of mind and matter in laws of which some are hidden from us and remain to be ascertained. The key may not be complete in the sense of clearing up the mystery of existence ; but it is the key to all the knowledge which we shall ever acquire respecting that mystery.

It has been generally held that this view of the universal reign of law is fatal to any belief in the supernatural character of Christianity or of the alleged miracles of Scripture. But there is another view of this subject which seeks to evade this conclusion. This other view has been ably expounded by the Duke of Argyll in his widely read and classical treatise on the subject, and to his exposition the reader's attention may now be directed. The position or hypothesis from which he starts is, that the reign of law is universal, and that there can be no such thing as a violation or suspension of law. He believes that the so-called miracles of the New Testament were actual occurrences; but he does not admit that they were at variance with natural law. They were wrought by the divine power acting in accordance with laws, some of which are beyond our knowledge or beyond our reach ; a view of them to which he thinks that science itself can have no objections ; a sense in which " no man can have any difficulty in believing " in their supernatural character. " Ordinarily God governs it (the world) by the choice and use of means. . . . Extraordinary manifestations of His will—signs and wonders—may be wrought, for aught we know, by similar instrumentality—only by the selection and use of laws of which man knows and can know nothing, and which, if he did know, he could not employ." As man accomplishes his purposes by the selection and employment of the laws with which he is acquainted, the question is asked, " Is it difficult to believe that after the same manner also the divine will, of which ours is the image only, works and effects its purposes ? "

Now, upon all such reasoning we remark, (1.) That it seems to be much of the nature of an *argumentum ad ignorantiam.* It amounts in effect to this, that though we do not know the laws or the means by which the miracles recorded in Scripture could be accomplished, yet, for aught we can tell, there may be " *some law* " or laws, known to God, equal to their production.

(2.) The reasoning may seem to suggest a possible explanation of some of the minor and evidential miracles of the New

Testament, and of some remarkable departures from the ordinary course or concatenations of such, which we sometimes speak of as special providences—by two of which the Duke illustrates his meaning, viz., the marvellous preservation of the Jews as a distinct people, and the rapid propagation of Christianity ; but when this reasoning is made use of to explain the central and constituent facts of orthodox Christianity—such as the incarnation and the resurrection of Jesus—it fails altogether to diminish the difficulty which men have in believing such events, and for this simple reason, that the means by which such prodigies could be brought to pass are as difficult of comprehension as are the events themselves, when viewed as brought about independently of the use of means, and by the mere exercise of the divine will.

(3.) The reasoning is in flat contradiction to the tenor of all Scripture, which everywhere implies that the miracles were creative acts. As God said in the beginning, " Let there be light, and light was," so Jesus at the grave in Bethany said, " Lazarus, come forth ! and he that was dead came forth." Of means there is no mention, or rather they are excluded. Jesus speaks and it is done. His word of command gives voice to the exercise of his will. Beyond or besides that there is nothing more.

(4.) The analogy between human and divine agency, on which the Duke of Argyll insists, is very misleading and limping. The human agent, with all his faculties of invention and contrivance, belongs to and is part of the system of nature ; but the divine agent belongs to that system only in so far as he is immanent in the laws ; and as no power of self-arrangement or of self-adaptation to any special purpose is found to reside in these laws, they do not and cannot lend themselves to any such arrangement or adaptation on the part of the immanent power. And, on the other hand, if God be conceived as transcendent, His action in selecting and making use of laws for a special purpose is supernatural, just because, so conceived of, He is not in that system, but apart from and above it. So far as He is supposed to guide and control " the mutual action and reaction of the laws among each other," He does so from without the chain of natural sequence—*i.e.*, in a strictly supernatural manner. The clear conclusion therefore is, that divine action, however conceived, bears no analogy, except of the most general kind, to the action of man in " varying the results of natural law."

The hypothesis of such analogy stands or falls with a theory of the divine government of the world, which ontologically is very disputable—with the theory, viz., which represents God as selecting, combining, and, so to speak, manipulating laws that are the expression of His own will, and of which some are and some are not accessible to human knowledge. By this process God is supposed to effect purposes which these laws of themselves, without extraneous direction and control, could not effect—a position which to us appears to be quite untenable.

Finally, the proposition that unknown or unknowable laws may, by the power supreme, be brought into play in human affairs so as to effect extraordinary or unaccountable results such as those of which the Duke cites examples, is very doubtful or rather unthinkable. It is by the knowledge, explicit or implicit, of law that rational beings are enabled to direct their course in life ; and, therefore, so far as the guidance of conduct (or may we not say religion) is concerned, an unknown law is as good as no law, or can only operate mechanically so as to reduce men to the condition of puppets.

The Duke's theory seems to come near to that of Archdeacon Wilson (*Essays and Addresses*, p. 115), and of others, who assume that the affairs of man are "at once under the guiding control of Providence, as well as subject to uniform laws," and that the divine government may be "providential without being miraculous." In contradistinction to this doctrine our position is, that providence occupies no middle ground between the purely natural and the miraculous ; that God's control over human affairs is exercised solely through law ; and that law itself acknowledges no control. The uniform operation of law is the condition under which the human race, individually and collectively, works out its destiny and fulfils the divine purpose. Evidences for the occasional manifestation of laws that are not in constant operation exist only for the devout imagination. We use, no doubt, a true and a beautiful expression when we speak of God's "perfect providence." But its perfection consists solely in the unerring certainty with which law, moral and physical, takes effect. A bound is thus set to the errancy of the rational and reflecting subject ; a powerful motive is supplied to a life of conformity with law, and a corrective influence is seen to act constantly upon human conduct, so as " to bring good out of evil, and render those who think only of their own passions and purposes, executors of the will of heaven." Neither with nor without disguise, neither secretly nor openly can providence encroach on human liberty. To be consistent with its own action in endowing man with a will of his own, it must leave room for the exercise of freedom and permit of an element of imperfection and of evil, of negation and perversion in all human affairs.

To represent, as we are here doing, the sphere of providence as confined within definite and immovable limits has been characterized as " senseless cruelty " towards the large masses of religious men, who find comfort in the thought of providence as something over and above the reign of law, or as a vague and unrepresentable selection and marshalling of laws known and unknown, by a power which is above law and called into action by the prayer of faith. But the cruelty (which is only apparent) lies in the fact that the divine law executes itself in complete disregard of human misapprehension and perversity, and thus occasions a cruel disappointment to the wilful or illusory expectations of men. Instead of humouring their wilfulness or their illusions, it holds on in its undeviating course till it effects their disillusionment and enforces compliance. And so it is that when evil men in ignorance or forgetfulness of the law of retribution hope to escape the consequences of their deed, they cannot fail to be cruelly disappointed. And even pious men when they expect by means of faith and prayer to extort extraneous aid directly from above, must also be disappointed when they find that the expected aid does not fall responsive.

But there is no cruelty chargeable against those religious teachers who point out the true method of the divine government according to which God never departs from His laws, so that he who sets himself in opposition is crushed by their weight, Matth. xxi. 44 ; whereas, he who conforms to their requirements discovers in them the soul and purpose of divine goodness, Ps. xxxi. 19. The limitation of providence which we here allege is the explanation of the slow advance of humanity, and of the many puzzling questions which crowd upon the man who attempts to trace the progress of the race through the intricacies of its history ; through the forward and backward movements of its civilization. From what has just been said of providence, our views of the nature of prayer may be inferred. Without anticipating what may yet be said on this subject, we content ourselves with stating here, that according to our general view prayer is the act by which we surrender ourselves to the will and enter into the idea of God propounded by Jesus, and verifiable, as will yet be shown, in the experience of his disciples.

From the orthodox point of view on which the Duke of Argyll somewhat doubtfully takes his stand, Christianity is regarded as a revealed system in the making or unfolding of which natural and supernatural elements are combined in certain indeterminable proportions ; a great historical develop- ment, of which events or facts, not miraculous in themselves, it may be, but requiring the intervention of a miraculous hand, form a large part. But can that be called a development in which such elements are incorporated and are necessary for carrying it on ? All true development comes from within : it is the unfolding of a germ, it is rooted in the past. A process or evolution which depends on extraneous agency is mechanical, not organic, and just by the interference of supernatural agency ceases to be in any proper sense a divine work. For it represents God as adopting a finite manner of working ; as acting the part of a joiner or carpenter, mortising and dovetailing one piece with another, or of a chemist who by scientific and artificial processes is able to form compounds which are nowhere to be met with in the realms of nature. The religious instinct, the germ of which Christianity is the long deferred but ripest fruit—required, no doubt, like other germs, certain favourable conditions for its development ; but these conditions were given in the operation of natural laws, and in the universal frame of things, of which the germ itself is part : so that any force or action extraneous to that is out of the question. If it be said that the elements of human nature and the conditions under which they operate are not sufficient to account for Christianity, and that something more was necessary, this is what we refuse to believe. It is true that the Christian *dogma* implies the supernatural. But the question arises whether the dogma is essential to Christianity ; may the dogma not be an excrescence ? May Christianity not have a power independent of dogma : may not the power which it seems to derive from the dogma be unreal and illusory, and more than balanced by compensating weakness ? May not the truth which lies at the heart of Christianity be altogether in the doctrine of Jesus, from which the dogmatic element, as will be shown, is wholly absent ? What we purpose to prove is, that the supernatural element did not enter into the development, but that the faith in that element grew up side by side with the development as its explanation and was introduced into the record of it.

To the above view or theory of the relation in which God stands to the universe, may be opposed another view of it, which to us seems to be more legitimate and more in accordance with empirical and scientific observation. Of this other view, if we may claim nothing more for it, this at least may be said, that it is not *more* idle or fanciful than the preceding. And though it will necessitate a short digression, we shall here state briefly what it is. According to this view, the divine causality is absolute in the sense of its being immanent and all pervasive in the universe. Divine action is not transcendent so as to admit of the selection and manipulation of laws ; but it is absolute both in its scope and character ; immutable, irresistible, and invariable. A casual, precarious, finite, variable, and contingent element enters the universe only with the appearance upon the scene of man, the rational and reflective creature, whose action is yet limited and conditioned by the absolute ground of itself, and of all besides. Man it is, to whom it is given to make a selection of instruments, and to discover and draw forth by selection and combination all the hidden possibilities and properties of the elements, physical and spiritual, of nature ; and in his character of finite factor, to act as the deputy and lieutenant, the minister and interpreter of the Great First Cause. The pure outcome of the absolute causality of God, unvaried by finite action from without, is the earth with the vegetable and animal kingdom, and at the head and summit of it, man himself in his natural condition, carrying within him the germ and promise of the future. Whatever raises the earth above its natural or prairie value is due to human action, which clothes the earth with new beauty and covers it with monuments of adaptive skill. And so too, whatever exalts and elevates man himself above his natural state, which is only a little higher than that of the brutes, is also due to the exercise of his finite intelligence, conditioned and limited by that same absolute ground. His morality, his civilization, and his religion are self-developments of that divine germ within him, which is the highest product of the purely absolute action of God ; and contains within it the possibility of all that is higher in humanity and of its approximation to its divine source. A position in the universe is thus assigned to man, second only to that of God Himself, whose fellow-worker he is ; a position not accidental, but indispensable, and essential to the accomplishment and perfecting of the divine purpose.

It is through the instrumentality of this His progressive creature, man, that the work by which God manifests His otherwise unutterable thought is still in process. And in every event of human history, there is thus at once an element of divine necessity and of human finitude, by which latter is meant that variableness of man's action which results from his imperfect intelligence, and the relative or restricted freedom of his will. It is by both of those elements, indissolubly combined, that the divine purpose in creation, which is a postulate of human thought, is worked out. And this combination, be it observed, belongs to the natural, not to the supernatural order of the universe. Or if we prefer to have it so, let it be said that the order of the universe is the natural supernatural, by which is meant, that the divine or supernatural element is never and nowhere absent, but also not more present in the spiritual than in the physical life, in the religious than in the secular and political sphere of human history. And be it further observed, that this theory of the universe for which we have now pleaded on comparatively abstract grounds, is also that one of the two which answers best to the great outstanding facts of human experience.

Humanity is manifestly endowed with certain capacities, and placed in a vast and intricate universe, so as to be exposed to endless contingencies or vicissitudes of good and evil ; and according to this theory, it is in the play and interplay of these capacities and of these contingencies that the course of human history and the lives of individuals are determined. We may think or believe that providence plays a part in the affairs of men over and above that of the action of law in redressing the evils of existence, and in swaying the course of history to a better direction than it would otherwise take. But it is hard, or rather impossible to verify this belief. Ever and again we are forced to admit that the ways of providence are mysterious, an admission that there are facts and events which do not bear out this belief, but rather seem to run counter to it, a phrase by which we seek to set aside the logic of such facts, and to throw a veil over the unverifiable nature of the supernatural theory.

In dealing then with the claim of Christianity to be a supernatural system, we prefer to keep to the popular, Scriptural, and unevasive definition of the miracle, as a suspension of the laws of nature, or, better still, as an autocratic act of divine power, regardless of these laws, and independent of the use of means. Of any alleged event of this kind we deny the possibility. We hold that God governs the universe by immutable laws, and that He neither does nor can act except through such laws ; for they are laws which obviously do not imply a power of self-arrangement for any special purpose, and therefore do not lend themselves to any arrangement, such as seems to be required by the supernatural theory, on the part of the absolute power of God, which is immanent in them. Clearly the prerogative which the Duke of Argyll claims for God, of selecting the law by which He effects His purposes, is a prerogative which He can exercise not through the system of law itself, but only from outside or from above the law, and independently of it.

To enter fully into a defence of this position would be out of place here. But we may briefly dispose of two objections, which, if we may judge from the reliance placed upon them by recent distinguished apologists, must appeal powerfully to the popular theological feeling in this country. The first of these is, that this modern view of the divine government involves a denial of divine freedom, that it restricts and limits God's action, or, as it has been expressed, "makes the world His prison." It has been urged that we cannot deny to God that liberty of action which we ourselves enjoy. Can He, it has been asked, who has endowed His creature, man, with this gift, not Himself be possessed of it? It is forgotten, that while, in a comparison between man and the inferior creatures, the gift of freedom, or the power of choosing between two or more competing courses, is a prerogative of the higher nature of the human race, it may, in comparing the race with the creator, be a mark and badge of its imperfection and finitude. While the very most that can be predicated of man is the *posse non errare*, the *non posse errare* is the predicate of God. The great order which He has established, He has established once for all; an order so perfect that even He cannot alter or deviate from it without confessing to the *posse errare*. Indeed the objection, which we have been considering, is founded on an entirely sensuous and empirical conception of the relation in which God stands to the universe, and it is seen fairly to break down when we keep before us the true or scientific view of that relation, which is, that the universe, or the laws which obtain in it, express fully and absolutely the mind of God, and therefore admit of no exception. To say with an eminent living theologian (Fairbairn, *Studies*, p. 3), that "the universe is but a poor and inadequate expression of the divine thought," is a wholly misleading idea, and involves a thoroughly anthropomorphic conception of God. Confessedly, a man's work, æsthetic or moral, always and of necessity falls short of his ideal; but to transfer this shortcoming to the work of God, is the very essence or principle of anthropomorphism. What should be said is, that the law which obtains in the universe is the perfect and adequate transcript of the divine will, the perfect reflection or manifestation of the divine nature, the necessary and therefore invariable rule or mode of divine action. The true philosophic position is neither that of the optimist, who says that this is the best possible world; nor that of the pessimist, who says that it is the worst possible; but that it is the only possible world.

That human action, while modifying and to some extent controlling the course of events, is yet limited by the divine law is certain, but in no sense can God be said to be limited by a law which is the exact expression of His will. While acting in invariable accordance with that law God exercises the most absolute liberty, and it is not conceivable that He should act otherwise. The solitary apparent exception to these propositions, on which so much theology has been made to turn, is only apparent. Divine liberty is not limited by human perversity. The goodness and perfectness of God's creature, man, consists in the possibilities of good in his nature. These possibilities may not be realized: they even involve the possibility of evil. But in any case, the law under which man is placed, and for which God is responsible, is good in the sense that it "makes for righteousness" and for the general welfare, and that sooner or later it will work itself out.

There is yet another objection to the view of the divine government here advocated, which has some claim to scientific value, and which, if we may judge from the reliance placed upon it by apologetic theologians, must, as already said, appeal powerfully to popular theological feeling. This objection is founded on the hypothesis that there must have been certain points in kosmical evolution at which the resources of creative energy were called into play ; such, for example, as the formation of the world, the dawn of life, of consciousness, and of reason or conscience. The hypothesis is, that by no stretch of the evolutionary principle can we hope to account for the superinduction of organic existence upon the inorganic, or for the awakening of consciousness in the unconscious forms of existence. The elevation of existence at these and other points to a higher level can, it is said, be explained only by the influx of miraculous or creative energy ; and therefore there are occasions or conditions under which God may interfere by direct action in the process of evolution, in order to produce results which could not be produced by the medium of natural causality. And just such an occasion may have been the introduction of Christianity, in the discussion of which, therefore, we are not entitled to deny the possible presence of a miraculous element.

To admit the premiss in this reasoning is to abandon the anti-supernatural position, which, therefore, it is necessary to state here in few words conveniently placed to our hands. (Compare Dr. van Bell, *Tijdschrift*, 1888, p. 135.) The anti-supernaturalist denies *in toto* any such thing as a transcendent activity of the divine power ; and while he maintains that the divine action is wholly immanent in the things themselves, he also denies the possibility of any immanent activity outside of, apart from, or supplementary to that aboriginal, omnipresent, and ever-working immanence which takes shape and form in the nature, purpose, and constitution of the universe. When language, which implies the contrary, is employed, it is not scientific, but popular, and presents the action of God, not as it is in itself, but in a form which is symbolically approximate, and is also justifiable in so far as it may be helpful to the infirmity of human intelligence, and adapted to a state of intellectual pupilage. But the religious man who aims at scientific truth of conception is one who cultivates the thought that God, who is infinitely far off, is at the same time mysteriously nigh in the inmost depths of the human soul. Here, indeed, for him is the grand antinomy of thought which faith has now, more than ever, to resolve. The divine principle is the base and ground of all existence, and, in the unity and immanence of its action, is adequate to the production both of mind and matter, and of all the forms they assume, and of all the changes they undergo. Corresponding with this oneness of divine action is that oneness of mystery which envelops all existence. In no case, however common and familiar, and therefore, as many think, intelligible, can we penetrate the mystery of causation or of sequence any more than we can understand the origin of matter or the dawn of life. And at no point is it permissible to call in the idea of an exceptional exertion of divine power, whether immanent or transcendent, supplementary to that which is eternally operative. It may be long before the theological mind becomes familiarised with this scientific, anti-supernaturalistic conception of the divine relation to the universe. But until this conception is embraced, theology will remain, as it now is, in a deadlock, with no possibility of advance in any direction whatever.

That now given is the definitive, uncompromising, and for ourselves satisfactory reply to the advocates of miracle in all its forms. Still there are those who, while satisfied with the doctrine of natural and orderly evolution as a general principle, yet, as we have seen, postulate the presence of a supernatural factor at certain points in the great evolutionary procession. For the sake of such persons, of whom there are many, we may for a moment quit our uncompromising position, in order to point out to them that, even if their postulate be granted, it does not bring them much nearer to the conclusion that a like supplemental factor is required to account for the origin of Christianity. For it is at least conceivable that the action of immediate divine causality might be admissible in those other cases, but not in this latter. To take but one example, it might be said, from this lower point of view, that the awakening of conscious intelligence was a postulate of law itself, absolutely indispensable to the constitution of the kosmos, necessary for the manifestation of that infinite power which is the underlying ground of all phenomena, and whose resources were not exhausted by the appearance of inorganic nature or mere animal life. It is conceivable that the impulse of the eternal ground of existence to unfold, to utter, and manifest itself, may have evoked the exercise of a creative power to furnish the world with rational beings as the media and instruments of a more adequate and perfect manifestation of itself. But for such beings the world would have fallen short of that perfection which we ascribe to all God's works as the mirror of Himself, and would, to the eye of the Eternal, have presented an incompleteness like that of the truncated cone, or, rather let us say, of a stage on which the actors never appeared. Many of its hidden forces would never have come into play, its beauty would have been wasted for want of the seeing eye, its resources never unfolded, its capabilities undeveloped for want of the cunning hand, the combining intellect, and the inventive imagination of the rational finite being. It is conceivable, therefore, that an exercise of immediate causation on the part of God might be admissible at this point ; but that anything of the kind might cease to be admissible when the world was furnished in all its parts, when the higher stage was laid, when all the actors were in their places endowed with specific capacities of action and development, and when all nature, including human nature, was set forward in its course. The whole body of law, which lay ideally in the divine mind, might then come into full operation, and no conceivable motive or necessity could then remain for further interference on the part of God ; unless we regard as such the orderly action of laws in which His power and will are immanent—of laws which are immanent in the world and represent His presence there. Even, therefore, if we admit the operation of a creative energy—the incursion of a miraculous element in the origin of the human species, we need not admit the possibility of the same in the genesis of Christianity or in aid of the development of that religious principle which is inherent in human nature and part of its original equipment.

For we may remind the reader that the object of Christianity, as of all religion, is to raise humanity towards its ideal state, but that that state is determined and fixed by the human constitution, and must be conceived of as attainable through man's exercise of his own God-created capacities. An ideal state which postulated the incursion of an extraneous power for its realization, would not be the ideal proper to humanity, but one that was capriciously and arbitrarily presented to it. To speak more generally, the law to which the creature is subject, not being imposed upon it from without by arbitrary fiat, but being immanent and constitutive of its very nature, a departure from or suspension of that law, however momentary or infinitesimal, would involve the absolute subversion of the creature.

By those theologians who postulate an exertion of miraculous or creative energy for the dawn of life, or more generally for the introduction of higher forms of existence, it is admitted that these higher forms after their introduction lose their miraculous character and become with pre-existing nature subject to law ; but so far as we can perceive, there is no indication that by the introduction of Christianity there was thus naturalized in human life any divine or spiritual energy which did not belong to it, in germ at least, before that event. Man is still man within the area of Christendom. And as we know of no power or faculty which man ever possessed being lost to him by a fall, as little do we know of any such having been added to him by the regenerating influence of Christianity. Whatever change has taken place upon human life by this means has been the result, as we hope to show, of new ideas which have revealed themselves to man through the exercise of his spiritual faculties. The germ of all that is highest in religious development was present in man from the moment that the God-consciousness, or the knowledge of good and evil was kindled within him ; and we may be sure that there is nothing true in orthodox Christianity which may not be traced to that source. The only development of which humanity is susceptible is that of its germinal original endowment ; and if the human species were to go beyond that, it would cease to be human. To suppose that in the middle of a process of development a new and supernatural element may be thrown in to carry on the development to

a height, which it could not otherwise reach, is against all
analogy. A germ works itself out ; a development runs
through all the stadia of its course ; but a new element
would mean a new species. And if history and observation
tell us anything, they tell us that there have been good
men who never heard of Christianity, and that many who
have believed in Christianity have remained bad.

In theological language the added or supernatural element
in the inner life goes by the name of divine grace : and
according to Mr. R. H. Hutton (*Contemp. Review*, April, 1889),
" Grace is a life poured in from outside." We may misunderstand Mr. Hutton's use of these words, but we take
them to be a blunt, but certainly expressive definition of
divine grace in its orthodox acceptation ; as a dæmonic
influence which enters into the life whether of individuals
or of the Church at large. Such an acceptation of the
word " grace," however vaguely it may be held, can hardly
be distinguished from the crassest form of supernaturalism.
We do not object to the use of the word to denote the
beneficent action of the *Nicht-Ich* upon the *Ich ;* that is
to say, the action upon us of all the circumstances and
conditions of our lives, including the forces and influences
amid which we are placed by Christianity. The *Ich* itself
or individual consciousness is a creation of the *Nicht-Ich :*
the last and greatest of its creations, because it has the
distinction of enjoying a certain independence of the *Nicht-
Ich*, a certain spontaneity of action on the exercise of
which its subsequent history or growth depends. The *Ich*
derives much, or rather all, from the *Nicht-Ich ;* only not
in the direct form of a new life. For a new life could only
be poured in at the expense of that very independence
which is the distinctive quality of its nature. And this
limitation of the action of the *Nicht-Ich* is important,
because it preserves the idea of individual responsibility
and of the identity of consciousness through all the flux of
the circumstances and forces which tell upon us. No
analogy drawn from the physical life gives us any warrant
for supposing that spiritual life may be poured in from
outside. Nutriment from without is converted into living
tissue only by the selecting and assimilating action of the
vital forces within the organism itself. When, therefore, Jesus

is made to say, John vi. 63, " The words which I speak unto you, they are spirit and they are life," such language must be regarded as only figuratively and remotely true. His words do indeed nourish the spiritual life and minister to its growth ; but only by the interposed action of the spiritual life itself accepting his words and surrendering itself to their influence. His words are not the whole cause productive of that effect, yet it was this identification of the word with the life, initiated by St. Paul and consummated by the fourth Evangelist through his *logos*-idea, that threw the glamour of mysticism over the whole subject of the religious process, and kept the true and scientific view of that process for many ages altogether out of sight. According to the teaching of Jesus, as we shall yet see, the spiritual life is not poured into the soul but is kindled or awakened in it by the revelation to the inward eye of the grace of God, or by the operation of those beneficent forces and influences upon us which go by that name. The difference between the two views may not seem to be great, but it marks the difference between the natural and the supernatural theory.

But to return. Even on the principles of evolution there is confessedly a difficulty in explaining the entrance of life and consciousness into the world-system. It is inconceivable how living matter should proceed from matter not living ; or how the most rudimentary forms of life should be evolved from any form whatever of mere matter under any conditions however unusual, and however different from those now existing. The gap or interval, however minute in appearance, is felt to be immense and far too wide to be bridged and surmounted by the process of evolution, which follows the method of insensible and infinitesimal progression. The gap, indeed, seems to be impassable because we cannot trace or discern the presence of any germ of life in inorganic (or what to us seems inanimate) nature. On this account, the origin of life seems to be inconceivable in itself, and suggestive or postulant of a special act of creation. But there is obviously not the same difficulty in conceiving the development of higher forms of life out of those that are lower ; or the evolution of moral and intellectual powers out of the instincts of the lower animals ; inasmuch as in these latter there is a certain germ of intelligence plainly visible. And still less difficulty is there in conceiving or believing that the spiritual renovation effected by Christianity has been brought about without any special interposition. For, in the very lowest types of humanity, the moral and spiritual faculties and religious instincts are not absolutely awanting, but germinant; so that, even if, as Dr. A. R. Wallace thinks, man's moral and intellectual powers have originated in an act of creation; yet, such an act being granted, we cannot postulate a further creative act for the introduction of Christianity.

Having thus endeavoured to justify our general position in regard to the impossibility of miracle, we wish before quitting this part of our subject to emphasize the statement that there is no reason to suppose that the phenomena presented by Christianity form any exception to the common law of the universe or to the fixed order of nature. Modern science does not admit that there is any presumption in favour of such an exception. The presumption is altogether the other way. For if every other department of things terrestrial and human is governed by immutable law, it is antecedently improbable, or even incredible, that the supremacy and immanency of law should cease at the threshold of the religious department. The unity which the mind postulates in the world, without and within us, forbids such an idea. If the law physical and moral, corresponding to the two forms of existence, did not extend on every side; if the unseen power could not accomplish its highest ends except by departing from the common order and having recourse to an exceptional, unconformable and high handed interference with the autonomy of nature; in what other light could this fact be regarded except as a sign of finitude and weakness, a confession that divine wisdom had encountered a contingency for which provision had not been made in the original draft or constitution of things, and that the defect or oversight had to be remedied by a sort of after-thought—not less an afterthought, though part of an eternal purpose. The conception of a universe carrying within itself its own law, which, however obscure or latent for unnumbered ages, yet, without fail comes forth into adequate operation as new emergencies and new conditions arise—this surely is a higher conception than that of a universe for which a new law, or a supplemental and epicyclical mode of administration is requisite at some particular crisis ; and in which room is left, or occasions emerge for the direct intervention of some power which is conceived to be above law ; or for the operation of what has been called " a third kind of law."

It may be affirmed in general with regard to all the great world-historical revolutions in the religious sphere, that they have been accompanied by a tendency on the part of those who were caught up in them, to trace them to the immediate hand and will of God ; to fill up blanks, and to throw light on obscure passages in the history of their origin and growth, by alleging the presence and operation at certain points of a palpably divine power. From the nature of the case, as already pointed out, the faith thus generated in the supernatural element cannot be overthrown by merely assailing what has come to be regarded as the historical evidence. This can only be done negatively by calling in question the possibility of miracle in any case whatever, and positively in the way to be here attempted, viz., by tracing step by step the sinuous course of the religious development according to the operation of natural psychological laws. In this inquiry, therefore, we assume the impossibility of miracle in the full and scriptural sense of the word ; on the ground that this assumption, even if it be a begging of the question, is not an idle or groundless assumption, but one that is based on the scientific study and observation of the universe. At the same time we do not rest here or depend solely on this " *a priori* consideration," but are compelled by a logical necessity to inquire further, how in the case of the gospel miracles, the faith in them could have gained a footing in the minds of men without having the fact of their occurrence as a base of origination. And if we succeed in this inquiry and discover such an explanation, we may then turn with some confidence to the believer in the possibility of miracle, and put it to him, whether, even though for him miracle be possible, it does not, by the law of parsimony, cease to be credible, when the faith of it in the early Church and its establishment in tradition may be accounted for otherwise than by the supposition of its actual occurrence.

Against this mode of reasoning we do not know that any objection can be taken except by falling back upon the idea to which Cardinal Newman gives expression in his *Apologia*. Referring to the medicinal oil said to have flowed from St. Walburga's tomb, he makes the observation, that "in a given case, the possibility of assigning a human cause for an event does not, *ipso facto*, prove that it is not miraculous." If by these words Cardinal Newman meant that a certain divine action is mysteriously present in all natural development, this is what none but a materialist will call in question. But if the meaning be, as we rather think it is, that events and phenomena which can be accounted for by natural causes and human agencies do not exclude a special divine or miraculous interposition, his words breathe the concentrated spirit of the apologist, whose first and only aim is not to discover truth, but to defend a position already occupied. They seem to be connected with that yearning for a mystical view of the universe, or with that idea of angelic and subordinate agencies serving to supplement the scientific view of the physical and spiritual world, which from first to last dominated his thought. To this purely fanciful, and (in spite of the horror with which he would have regarded such an imputation) really gnosticising idea, he seems early to have surrendered himself, first, that he might be at liberty to interpret literally the figurative language in which the Old Testament describes natural phenomena, and ultimately to meet the draft of Roman Catholicism upon human credulity. But whatever be the explanation, the judgment expressed in the above words seems to us to go far to justify Carlyle's well known contemptuous estimate of the brain of this man of splendidly subtle intellect and rare literary genius. His dialectic is so powerful that his theology is assailable only in its assumptions, that is to say, by a method too radical for the ordinary Protestant controversialist to apply. The words of his which we have quoted, contain a proposition which can pass muster with the most acute minds, when they are dominated by an orthodox bias. We have observed that another eminent apologist (Dr. Wace, *Nineteenth Century*, May, 1889, p. 719) has adopted it, even while at the same time, somewhat inconsistently, quoting with approbation "the fixed rule of philosophizing, according to Newton, that we should not assume unknown causes when known ones suffice."

There is no doubt that the origin and history of Christianity are provisionally, or perhaps we should say approximately,

accounted for on the supernatural hypothesis, inasmuch as
miracle supplies an apparently sufficient explanation of it—
provided, indeed, we admit that the hypothesis of miracle,
which is sufficient to explain everything, can be said to explain
any phenomenon in particular. But, without dwelling on this
proviso, we say that orthodox theologians are able, to their own
satisfaction, to account for every phenomenon, and to explain
away every difficulty—literary, exegetical, and historical—by
the hypothesis of a supernatural factor, which, from its very
nature, admits of being drawn upon to any extent. But if
Christianity can be accounted for on the opposite hypothesis—
i.e., by calling into view the spiritual forces and the progressive
nature of humanity, then the supernatural idea will disappear
from human thought and lose its sole remaining foothold in
the human mind. For no one can possibly think of importing
the supernatural element into Christianity, unless it be absolutely indispensable—unless without it no sufficient reason can
be shown for the faiths which Christianity has generated and
for the effects it has produced.

Many great writers, philosophical and theological, of the
present century have, on this question of the supernatural in
Christianity, spoken hesitatingly or ambiguously, or in a way
which has been characterized as " *schillernd* "—a predicate for
which we know of no equivalent in English, and which we can
only paraphrase as a fusion or interplay of contradictory ideas,
effected by a species of literary legerdemain. The truth
seems to be, that in their laudable but mistaken apprehension
for the safety of religion, these writers have endeavoured to
reserve the impossibility of miracle as a covert and esoteric
doctrine. But we conceive that the interests of religion involved are too grave to be thus treated, and that this doctrine
should be avowed, and become by its open advocacy a factor
in the common life and thought of man. A great thinker
(Goethe) has said, " Aus einem thätigen Irrthum kann etwas
Treffliches entstehen " (" An erroneous belief may form an impulse to worthy conduct "), but so far as this is true, it is true
only so long as the error commands the assent of the intelligence of the age ; and it is only a doctrine which is in harmony
with fact that can permanently and universally benefit society.

In its negative aspect, then, scientific criticism sets aside the
supernatural factor in the religious as well as in all other

departments of human life. No miracle has ever happened, nor can happen, whether in the origin or in the history of religion—whether as evidential or constitutive of it. The idea of infallibility, whether in a church or in a book ; the idea of special inspiration, considered as a species of dæmonic possession of the human spirit by the divine ; the idea of divine grace considered as a " life poured in from outside," must alike be discarded. Positively, the assertion of scientific criticism is that all the changes which take place in the human mind, or within human experience, are evolved by psychological necessity, and in accordance with man's own nature. To say, with some apologists, that the influence of the invisible in the visible world is exercised in accordance with laws which, though unknowable by us, do in fact regulate and determine the action of the divine power, is quite irrelevant and beside the mark. The influence exerted by that power must needs be limited by laws, which regulate the nature of the finite creature ; and in religion the divine Being can only operate upon us objectively through the common law of our nature, and subjectively through the idea or conception of himself, which has broken in upon our minds in the contemplation of ourselves and of the other works and existences by which we arrive at a knowledge of the divine Contriver and Author of all. We regard the supernatural as only the naïve and provisional account of Christianity, congenial indeed to the thought of the age in which it originated, and to a theory of the universe which is now obsolete, but irrelevant to the thought and science which have been growing in consistency during the past three centuries. And if this be so, it follows that the New Testament, which gives a supernatural complexion to the origin and nature of Christianity, cannot be accepted by us as a close, satisfactory, authentic, and matter-of-fact record, but only as an approximate, and it may be ideal, mythical, or symbolical record of it.

Arrived at this turning point in the discussion, we are reminded that there are multitudes at this late time, even among educated and scientific men, who do not admit with us that the general question as to the supernatural is conclusively or definitively settled, but are disposed to think that the evidence and reasoning on both sides, negative and affirmative, are pretty equally balanced ; yet even for persons in this state of suspense, our discussion may not be without interest ; for without committing themselves in the meantime to one view or the other, they may regard our theory as to the genesis of Christianity as constructed on the basis of the supposition that there was nothing supernatural in the facts themselves, and that this complexion was given to them by the early tradition, and passed from it into the evangelic records which have come down to us. It is evident that if on the basis of this supposition we can satisfactorily or approximately account for the great faiths and facts of Christian history, it will go far to destroy whatever faith may yet survive in Christianity considered as a supernatural system. There will, as already remarked, be no inclination to import a miraculous element into events which can be otherwise accounted for. Let the admission even be made, that the scientific objection to the miraculous element of Christianity is balanced by the historical evidence in its favour ; yet if it can be shown that the faith of the early Church in that element (which in point of fact constitutes that evidence) can be explained otherwise than by its reality, that element will cease to be credible. But in either case, *i.e.*, whether we regard the miraculous element as conclusively or only as hypothetically set aside, it is evident that in dealing with the primitive records which represent that element as everywhere present, pervading and determinant, something more than a sound exegesis and hermeneutic will be needed to extract from them the proximate facts regarding the origin and development of the Christian system. We have only to make the attempt to find that we cannot effect the removal of the supernatural element, as if it were a mere appendage or external fixture, so as to leave the residuum standing as it was. That element is, so to speak, chemically combined with the history, and can be discharged only by a process which involves a change or dissolution of the entire fabric, or, if this be thought to be an exaggerated representation, let us say rather that it is an element woven like a strand into the texture of the history, so as to be removable only by a general disturbance and dislocation of the evangelical narrative.

This consequence is most distinctly apparent in dealing with the fourth Gospel in which the discourses which form the bulk of the narrative must be dismissed along with the miracles which form their text and illustration. There are, however, so many grounds for questioning the historical value of the fourth Gospel, that it can hardly be said to furnish a good example of what we are saying.   But our remark holds true of the more historical synoptic Gospels.   The introduction into these of supernatural elements implies such an empiric-dogmatic bias in the apprehension of the facts, and consequent metamorphosis of them, that we can hardly venture to say with certainty, even of one utterance reported of Jesus, that it proceeded from him in exactly the form of words in which it there appears.   We can feel the ground secure under our feet, only when we accept as his the gnomic and parabolic form, and general spirit of the teaching ; the new and original spirit, which is undoubtedly traceable to him, being necessarily supposed to have created for itself the succinct and inimitably luminous form so level to popular taste and intelligence, which is characteristic of his teaching.   The freshness of the ideas may, indeed, have communicated even to those who received them first hand from the great original, a power of masterly, popular, vivid expression akin to that of the master himself.   But there need be no hesitation in ascribing to Jesus whatever sentence or parable keeps upon the line of his teaching, and is a true utterance of the new spirit which he breathed into the world.

The moment, however, we undertake to show that Christianity arose and took its present shape without being ushered in or accompanied by events which can in any sense be called miraculous or supernatural, the very attempt requires that we adopt a somewhat free treatment of the records, in order to feel our way to a reconstruction of the general outlines, and to catch the significance of the salient facts which we still regard as historically authentic.   To deny the supernatural nature of the life and work of Jesus, and yet, with the majority of liberal theologians, to apply the usual verbal or textual exegesis, as sufficient to extract from the Gospels the actual data which underlie the history, is manifestly a halting and impotent procedure which cannot possibly lead to a satisfactory result, and amply accounts for the unprogressive, see-saw, distracted, and resultless course and condition of so-called liberal theology.

In saying that modern theology, even of the more liberal school, is "unprogressive," we say so not unadvisedly.   In the endeavour to bring the Pauline system of doctrine into accord with the growing thoughts of men (which is the inspiring motive of the system building), the theology of the last three hundred years has indeed produced many variants of that system in long, or, let us say, exhaustive succession, but not one of these can be said to have made any real advance to the end at which all of them have aimed. This is widely felt at the present day, and it has begun to dawn upon the theological mind, that the obstacle which blocks the way to that accord is the supernatural element which is common to all alike. What progress there has been, is not towards a variant of the Pauline dogma satisfactory to the reason, for that is an impossible result; but towards the discovery that in theory the absolute religion, as taught by Jesus, is of utter and undogmatic simplicity, the only difficulty of which lies in the practice of it. In this qualified sense, we admit the progressiveness of modern theology, but in no other—in the sense, namely, that it is making progress towards its own extinction.

In our view the religion of Jesus cannot be gathered from the Gospels or from the New Testament at large by textual criticism, however searching and however minute ; but by a higher criticism which may be called hyper-exegetical ; by a process more resembling the deciphering of a palimpsest, or the recovery of the history of ancient nations by the unearthing of their long-buried, long-forgotten monuments. We write with the conviction that, in a very short period of exceptionally active religious excitement, partly the cause and partly the effect of the report of the resurrection of Jesus, his sayings and doings were vermicularly overlaid by pious credulities and mythicizing fancies more effectually than were those ancient remains by the dust of ages. It is true that we have no means of weighing and judging probabilities in a matter of this kind by analogy or by comparison with what has taken place in any other corresponding case ; but, whatever may be said to the contrary, and in spite of the principle which Neander employed to reconcile the many apparently conflicting data, viz. that Christianity while supernatural in its origin was natural in its development, we agree with the Roman Catholic in thinking that the religion of Jesus would have been preserved from such a fate had its origin been supernatural ; and that the same divine spirit, which presided over its birth, would have watched over the channels of its transmission. Whereas, if it arose in the way of a natural development, it would necessarily be subject to all common vicissitudes; and we see nothing improbable in the supposition that its records may have been overlaid and transformed to almost any extent by frequent revision. But even so, the loss is not irremediable. For though the monuments, to which reference has just been made, were buried out of sight, yet, by what seems to be a common law, viz. that no thought perishes, the germs and principles of civilization of which they were the product and expression survived and continued to work among men. Even so we may suppose that the principles of the religion which Jesus enunciated continued under symbolic form to operate in the world. We have thus a sort of test, however delicate of application, to distinguish in the records between the pure and simple expression of these principles and those accretions which render them obnoxious to modern criticism. The endeavour to draw this distinction is bold and difficult; but it is forced upon us in spite of ourselves by the slow but irresistible advance of the human mind. And if we can thus ascertain the principles from which the great historical movement started, we shall be the better able to trace the course by which it gradually assumed the symbolic orthodox form. What in our view gives importance to the attempt, is our belief that the few principles to which the teaching of Jesus gave prominence, constitute to this day, under the disguise of symbol and dogma, the preserving salt of Christianity.

As we do not unreservedly accept the synoptic, or, let us say, the canonical data for the genesis of Christianity, it follows of course that in this inquiry we must proceed to some extent by the way of conjecture, which may be defined as an inference from the known to the unknown, and that many will consider this acknowledgment as sufficient to condemn our entire undertaking. We may, therefore, observe that conjecture in the sense now indicated may have every degree of probability from the very lowest to the very highest or the most absolute certainty. It is resorted to, and in the most wholesale manner, as might easily be shown, by orthodox theologians in all their attempts to harmonize the Gospels; and it comes largely into play also in all attempts to harmonize the canonical records generally, whether with what is called the profane history of the times or with the results of modern science. Every one who is acquainted with the methods of apologetic theology must be aware that it is a tissue of more or less doubtful probabilities. We do not urge this fact as an objection to apologetic theology, but only as a reason for not objecting to the employment of conjecture in this essay. A conjectural element must of necessity enter into the attack as well as into the defence of orthodoxy; and the only question is, on which side upon the whole the conjecture is the least violent, on which side the greater probability lies, or on which side the understanding encounters the least resistance.

In all critical and historical and even to some extent in scientific investigation, conjecture has a sphere of its own within whose limits it may render important services in the elucidation of truth. Our readers must determine for themselves whether we observe or trangress these limits, and whether our use of this instrument be legitimate or the reverse. Every canonical fact or datum of which we make use may, when taken separately, admit of a construction different from that which we put upon it; for that is only to say, that one conjecture or probable construction may be met by another or counter-conjecture. But the question is, whether the *natural* construction, as a whole, which we put upon Christianity is or is not sufficient to account for it; or, to put it differently, whether there is not a likelihood that the miraculous element was introduced into its annals by men who, under the conditions of the then existing culture, could not possibly understand or explain it otherwise, rather than that that element was actually a factor in its origin.

In one of the *Present Day Tracts*, Dr. Cairns says that " the genesis of systems is part of history; and if history by the application of its ordinary methods cannot explain the Christian religion, as it does all others, on mere natural principles, it must recognize a miracle." But this, it is manifest, is to lay down an impossible condition for the explanation demanded ; for the simple reason that the ordinary methods of history cannot in this case be brought into play. The ordinary and, indeed, the only method by which modern historians arrive at an approximately con-

clusive knowledge of long past events, is by the collation
comparison and questioning of the various, oftentimes discordant contemporaneous accounts of them.   But of the
origin of Christianity we have substantially and really only
one account, viz., that contained in the first three Gospels,
which represents or reflects the tradition of the early church.
And an observation may be made here, much the same as
that made by Hermann Grimm with regard to Vasari's
Lives of the Florentine Artists.   He says that Vasari is
the only one to give us information about many things;
and all comparison being out of the question, we can
never be sure whether he invents the things, or writes upon
reports which have a more solid foundation.   Something of
the same kind has been observed of the account which
has come down to us of the Punic wars, respecting which
no record has descended to us from Carthaginian sources.
But more close to the point is what is remarked in the
Nineteenth Century, October, 1887, by Mr. Justice Stephen.
" It does now and then happen that it is possible to show
(as by the discovery of documents not previously known),
that the accepted version of a story is false, and that the
true account of the matter is different.   But in regard to
the history of Christ this cannot be done, because all
memories of the time and place have disappeared."   It
can at the most be shown that the " accepted accounts of
many particular occurrences bear the well-known marks of
legend as distinguished from genuine history"; and hence,
if we endeavour to recast the life of Jesus we are thrown
upon conjecture, or that mode of reasoning which consists,
as has just been said, in passing from the known to the
unknown.   Hence, too, considering the nature of the problem before us, and the limitation of our sources of knowledge,
it would be unfair of the reader to demand at every point
or step a degree of probability and a precision of statement,
of which the subject and the means for its treatment at
our command do not admit.   He should be prepared to
find that there is a tone of indecision in many of our
remarks, and that the obscurity which rests on some
points is not wholly lifted.   It is not to be expected that
every detail in our construction should carry conviction;
but the intrinsic consistency of the whole may come near

it. Our construction is not like a chain, of which the weakest link determines the strength of the whole; but like a building, whose solidity is not materially impaired by the presence in it, here and there, of a defective stone.

Let it be observed, moreover, that our employment of conjecture is restricted ; not arbitrary nor fanciful; not atomic or opportunist in the sense of being without any fixed principle except that of assailing the orthodox position in detail. On the contrary, our conjecture will be found to be systematic in form, guided and suggested throughout by a certain view of the religious relation and of the springs and principles which it sets in motion. In its material aspect that relation was made known to mankind by Jesus, when he proclaimed the paternal character of God and the supreme value of the soul and the inwardness of the religious life. Taken by itself, this view of the relation favoured, if it did not solicit, the doctrine of supernaturalism, or so to speak, of a paternal government of the world as opposed to the constitutional. But modern science has irresistibly conducted or is conducting us to the formal or ideal aspect of that relation by which all that is supernatural is discharged from it. According to this aspect of it, the religious instinct is drawn out, the religious relation is maintained, not by any objective divine agency whether prevenient or subsequent to faith in the soul of man, but simply by the power with which the evangelic idea of that relation, as revealed by Jesus, appeals to the soul of man. Of this we shall have much to say as we proceed.

Let it be borne in mind, further, that what we here primarily attempt is neither a historical nor a literary criticism of the books of the New Testament ; nor an explanation of the genesis of these books, such as modern criticism has made us familiar with : but mainly an investigation of the genesis of Christianity itself, of which these books contain an account, proceeding on the basis of the supernatural and, therefore, not satisfactory to the scientific conscience. The very nature of this investigation obviously requires us to relinquish the idea of a close adherence to the Scripture record. We subscribe heartily to what Dr. Bruce says, that "it is the miraculous element in the Gospels which chiefly raises the question as to their historical trustworthiness. Eliminate that element and hardly a doubt would remain ; the residuary words and deeds of Jesus would be welcomed as proof that in Judæa there once lived a sage and philanthropist of unparalleled wisdom and goodness." The effect of these words is that, apart from the miraculous element, the gospel history would satisfy us, not only that the man Jesus had really lived, but that his doctrine showed him to be a man of unparalleled wisdom and goodness. This comes very near to saying, that the miraculous element is unessential to the history, and that the doctrine of Jesus carries in itself an evidence of its truth. But Dr. Bruce does not trust to this evidence, and feels it necessary, as he says, to occupy "the platform of the substantial historicity of the Gospels," inclusive of the miraculous narratives. Now we do not say that this somewhat Janus-like position is untenable, but only that we hold a very different position. It seems to us that to leave the supernatural element standing in the Gospels, as Dr. Bruce proposes, is to abandon all genuine historical criticism and to perpetuate the historical confusion. To remove that element, on the other hand, is to leave nothing standing beyond the general outline of the life of Jesus, and his ethical and religious teaching in its main form and substance. The Christian phantasy, which imported the supernatural element into the history, was capable also of modifying to some extent the forms of expression, but would hardly be tempted to alter the general scope of the teaching: nor can it be credited with the creation and invention of a style so marked and individualized in character, so congruent and helpful to the spirit and substance of the doctrine. There is, therefore, every reason to believe that many of the discourses of Jesus are reproduced all but verbally in the synoptic Gospels, though there is internal evidence that the order and arrangement have undergone much alteration ; attributable, there is little doubt, partly to the uncertainties of the oral tradition and partly to the literary discretion of the compilers of the Gospels. And there is a pervading unity of spirit and of purpose in the teaching of Jesus which puts into our hands a test of the genuineness of each separate utterance ascribed to him.

The objection may here suggest itself, indeed, that, by admitting the presence of a revising, mythical, and embellishing element in the Gospel history, we make it impossible to discriminate between what is real and what is fictitious ; we allow the hitherto solid structure of Gospel history to dissolve in our hands, and create a prejudice against every attempt to construct an approximately genuine theory or history of the origin of Christianity from the primitive records.

Something of this kind has been said by Grote and others of the legendary history of the early or so-called heroic ages of Greece. The works of Homer, it has been said, throw no light whatever upon the ages to which they refer ; and their whole historical value lies in conveying to us indirectly and undesignedly a vivid picture of the thinking and acting of the age to which the poet himself belonged. Now, it may be true, by the same rule, that, according to the theory of Volkmar, some of the elements of Gospel history really reflect and embody the beliefs and experiences of Christians of the early age in which they were compiled. But it is a manifest exaggeration to say, as Volkmar inclines to do, that the Gospels are a history of the Christian community under the veil of a life of Jesus its founder. The doctrinal teaching of Jesus, and his life as illustrative of that, as described in the Gospels, have a truth and a value quite independent of, and separable from the supernatural aspect under which he is presented to us : they contain elements, moreover, which we cannot possibly account for, except by tracing them to him, or to a great spiritual movement of which he was the head and centre. The Gospels owe, if not their only, yet their main value to that system of thought which is incorporated in the direct and parabolic teaching of Jesus ; and to the record which they contain of a life, which, in its general features, and independent of miraculous events, proves the height to which human nature may rise, and which the miraculous colouring serves in some measure to obscure.

Arrived now at the point of applying the foregoing remarks on the supernatural to Christianity, the question may suggest itself, whether a high expediency may not counsel a policy of reticence or reserve on this subject. Among the cultured and even the scientific classes there are many who have discarded, so far as they themselves are concerned, all belief in the supernatural character of Christianity, but are yet of opinion that, for the sake of the great masses of mankind, it is, and ever will be, necessary to present Christianity as a special message direct from heaven, or as a divine institution for human salvation; and that it would be dangerous to all the higher interests of society to dispel the illusion, lest the moral and religious ideas, the registered wisdom and experience of many ages, imbedded in Christianity, should become the sport of the vulgar, sceptical intellect; and lest with the warrant and sanction derived from their higher origin, they should also lose their legitimate salutary influence upon men's minds. But all such politic considerations, and the scruples to which they give rise, seem to us to savour of a somewhat low and time-serving expediency, and are here set aside, because we believe that Christianity carries its authority within itself, and that to know the truth and to see things as they are is good for man in the end. It is also very questionable whether an esoteric treatment of this or any subject is feasible, or can be long successful in the age upon which we have fallen, when every true thought is able to publish itself through a thousand channels and to become a common possession.

Whatever we may fondly wish, we must bow to the necessity of the case. We may rest assured that in his pursuit of spiritual truth, man must drop the cut-and-dry notion of a *deus ex machina*, or of a supernatural revelation, for, that on such easy terms, the race cannot hope to reach its goal on any of the great lines of its endeavour. But in lieu of that notion we have our finite reason, which, being itself spirit, has the idea of absolute spirit, or simply the pure idea germinant in its consciousness. The whole development of ethical and religious thought depends upon this idea, which, floating before the human soul, draws man's thoughts upwards to itself. And this grand fact is explanatory of much in the history and evolution of religion. For the idea has a twofold aspect, or rather a twofold mode of action, of which the one seems, but only seems, to undo the work of the other. Through popular feeling and imagination there is a tendency in the idea at every stage of its development to incorporate itself in ritual and myth, in symbol and dogma : that is to say, in some positive form or system of religion, as, *e.g.*, in Judaism and Christianity. And the idea for which the symbol and dogma are thus created becomes in time corrosive of these, when the reflection grows to a head that they do not fully or adequately represent it. When this has taken place, the same mental activities proceed at the bidding of the idea to create some more adequate symbol, which, in its turn is set aside by the solvent power of the intellect, which, as distinct from the reason, has the important function of bringing all thought and action to the test of the idea. And this process goes on till, in this age of advanced thought, the idea is aiming to find its full expression by assailing the supernatural theory of the divine government: the discovery having dawned upon the human mind that nature itself is the only true and absolute symbol of the divine. The unique place which Jesus occupies in the development of religious thought lies in this, that in him and in his doctrine the idea reached the purest possible, though finite and practical, or, let us say empiric expression: of which expression it only remains to his followers to find the scientific form and to draw the consequences in thought and practice. As for the dogma of the early Church we shall see that it was no true development of the thought of Jesus, but mainly a sensuous representation, or plastic metamorphosis of it, dictated by pious feeling and imagination: a view of the dogma which in part explains its tenacious possession of the mind of Christendom and the power of its appeal to this day to the common heart. But that it performs a pædagogic function is the most that can be claimed for it.

CHAPTER III.

THE FUNCTION OF JESUS AS A TEACHER.

IF that theory of the divine government which has now
been set forth be accepted, its logical and necessary consequence is to make havoc of the orthodox dogma concerning
the person and the functions of the founder of Christianity.
It is no longer possible to regard Jesus as an incarnation of the divine Being, who wrought miracles, and
by his death made atonement for the sins of men, and
rose again from the dead, and afterwards ascended into
heaven in the presence of his disciples; but as one who by
nature and from first to last was a member, pure and
simple, of the human family—a link of the human chain
just as any of ourselves are : having all the properties of
human nature, but those of no other : as one whose nature,
faculty, and character, were to the same extent with those
of other men the product of his ancestry and of his
surroundings ; and whose life and work went to determine
and to influence the life and history of succeeding generations.
What he did was to impart to men a higher view of their
duty and of their relation to God, and to die as a martyr
to the truths which he proclaimed. In a word, we set aside,
in virtue of our general principle, the so-called " central facts "
of Christianity, whether as constitutive of our religion or
evidential of its truth. Just because these are professedly
supernatural we can regard them not as facts at all, but as
mere accretions, or, as we shall yet more particularly see, as
a vestment woven for the spiritual substance of Christianity
under the stimulus of the spectacle or memory of a life,
which apart from such facts was sufficiently wonderful in
itself. Along with the so-called facts we also set aside the

doctrines of mediation, propitiation, and intercession, which stand or fall with the facts.   It is impossible for us to believe that Jesus altered God's relation to us, or restored it to what it once was—which is the only meaning we can attach to such offices and functions—but only that he altered our views of what that relation really is : that he was one of that select band of religious teachers who have from age to age brought the thoughts of men nearer to the truth of things : and the very greatest of them all.   Like others of that small and sacred band, he was a teacher not in the narrow sense of the word, but in its widest sense.   He certified his doctrine and rendered it impressive to the minds of his disciples by illustrating it in his own person and conduct, and so enlisting their sympathy in its behalf.

We have said that Jesus was a teacher in the widest sense of the word, and it is necessary to bear this in mind.   No doubt it is to his teaching in the narrower sense, as preserved to us in the synoptists, that we must primarily look for the definition of that ethical ideal and that conception of God which are the constituent and elementary principles of his religion.   And it cannot be questioned that he was possessed of an unrivalled gift of terse and pregnant utterance, and could adequately interpret into common language the facts of his own experience, which were at once the source and the result of his religious insight.   But the thought which he endeavoured to communicate to his disciples as the medium of imparting impulse and influencing life was communicated in part at least through his own manner of acting and suffering, or through the life which he led, quite as much as by the form and substance of his oral teaching.   Not merely did he address the intellect of his hearers or appeal merely by word of mouth to their moral and rational nature ; but over and above this, by his evident superiority to the common weaknesses of humanity, by his patience under contumely, by his deep tenderness and forbearance, by his singleness of purpose, by his zeal for the temporal and spiritual good of others, by his serene confidence in the love of God, which no strait or danger could disturb ; by all these traits of character, we say, he imposed on imagination, enlisted sympathy, awakened enthusiasm, and gained for himself personally the devotion of all who were sensitive to spiritual impressions.   That

principle of love, which according to him was the fulfilment
of the law, and the moving principle of God's dealings with
men, became a reality for the disciples by virtue of the
supreme exhibition of it in his own life of self-sacrifice. He
embodied and exemplified in his own conduct and character
the very truths which he taught, the self-sacrifice which he
inculcated. In the conflict which he provoked with the
accredited teachers of his people, he had the opportunity un-
sought, but forced upon him, of exhibiting without intermission
all the highest qualities of his nature, and especially those
passive virtues which entered so largely into his rule of life,
and were so new comparatively, even in name, to the ancient
world. By personal fidelity to his own rule he stamped the
beauty and the obligation of it upon that small circle who
were the witnesses of his career, and afterwards went forth, in
the persuasion that such a life was eternal, to spread the
knowledge and the practice of it among men. By the exhibition, faultless to all human judgment, of his own transcendent
ideal in the conduct of his own life, he exercised that truly
dæmonic faculty of impressing the minds of his immediate
followers, and charged with intenser power that attraction
which the ideal of itself always exerts more or less on human
hearts.

In that concrete and living form his great ideas became
luminous to the humblest intellect. However slow of heart,
his followers could not fail to see in him the living impersonation of the graces which he inculcated. In fact his teaching
did little but throw light on his life, and help them to
appreciate the beauty of that. And it would not be wrong
to say that his discourses were but the exponents of his own
experience, and interpreted his own example, helping the
disciples to gather the lesson which it conveyed and to understand and become alive to what was passing under their eyes :
the lesson of whose import, just because it was passing
before them, they were apt to miss or overlook. It may be
truly said that his life was but the object-lesson by which,
unintentionally we believe, he impressed his doctrine upon his
disciples.

We say unintentionally, for, while intent on being true to
his own ideal of righteousness, Jesus exerted over his disciples
an imposing and commanding influence, which was probably

undesigned on his part, as it was probably unconscious on theirs. The manifestation of the higher life as a means of swaying the minds of his disciples and drawing them through the sympathetic forces of their nature into fellowship with himself may never have entered into his thoughts. There is certainly no trace of conscious self-manifestation in the synoptic Gospels, if perhaps we except Matth. xi. 28, 29, a passage whose perfect beauty, for reasons elsewhere given, does not convince us of its authenticity. The probability is that the exhortation to learn meekness and lowliness from his example was only the interpretation of what the disciples had been made to feel, put by them afterwards into his mouth. For we can hardly help thinking that this idea of conscious self-manifestation on the part of Jesus, though it is a leading one and architectonic in the construction of the fourth Gospel, is foreign to the simplicity and self-forgetfulness of the mind of Jesus, as well as untrue to nature, and constitutes an essential and fundamental blemish in that work of splendid genius. Still we hold that the personal influence of Jesus, though unconscious on both sides, was of magical efficacy. It appealed to the higher nature of the disciples with a force which his mere teaching could never have exerted.

The man whose mind is thoroughly made up, as was the mind of Jesus, to a certain course of conduct, to brave death and all possible extremities in following it out, is thereby endowed with superhuman strength, and naturally takes the lead and acquires ascendency over those who hesitate and live in doubt. The spectacle of such a man submitting without visible effort, and with a foregone determination, to the yoke of righteousness in its sternest aspects, and enduring hardship and mortification without a murmur, and facing the prospect of a cruel and ignominious death without shrinking, was sufficient to inspire awe for his person and to lend authority to his words. These remarks will indicate what is meant by saying that Jesus was a teacher in the wider sense of the word, and that his power as such was greatly, or rather mainly, due to his personal qualities ; to the illustration in his conduct of the doctrines which he taught. Apart from his personality, his discourses would have led to little or no practical result, and he could never have " laid his mind " so effectually upon his disciples, nor have imparted to them that initial impulse which carried them on, step by step, and enabled them to give a new start to the religious history of mankind. Plato's ideal had many points of contact with that of Jesus, but then it remained a mere ideal : it, so to speak, "abode alone," not mingling with nor acting upon the springs of life ; whereas that other, by the sympathy which it awakened, sank deep into human hearts and brought forth much fruit (John xii. 24).

That we do not take an exaggerated view of the impression made upon the disciples by the personality of Jesus, or by the faultless illustration in his person of the high ideal which he had kindled in their minds, may be inferred with some probability from the analogous cases of Zoroaster, Buddha, and the better authenticated case of the great Chinese sage. The last of these was, perhaps, the most unimpassioned and unemotional of all the great men who have made their mark in the religious history of the world, and yet Dr. Legge says that "one of the most remarkable things connected with him is the impression which he made on his disciples. Many of these were among the ablest men in China of their time, and yet with them originated the practice of speaking of Confucius as the greatest man that ever lived. He won their entire admiration. They began the pæan which has since resounded through all the intervening ages, nor is its swell less loud and confident now than it was 24 centuries ago." This historical fact is one of a group which renders it credible that by sheer moral grandeur Jesus too may have made a profound impression upon his disciples, and that the tradition to that effect was not a mere mythical creation, but a reminiscence of an actual fact which was indispensable, as will yet be shown, to the origin of the mythical history.

As a teacher the highest aim and function of Jesus was, by word and deed, to imbue those who listened to him with his own ideas, to make them look at things with the same eyes as he did, to raise them to the level of his experience, and to awaken in them a religious consciousness similar to his own, that they might live and act accordingly. It was that and nothing more. But the Christian Church, the community or congregation of those who felt and bowed to the influence of his teaching, and embraced the way of life of which he set the example, has always wished to see more in him than a teacher, even in the most extended sense of the word. In the primitive documents of Christianity, in the books of the New Testament, he is represented as something more ; and the Church ever since has striven to vindicate for him a rank presumably higher ; regarding it as a degradation or but a scant honour to think or speak of him merely as a discoverer or revealer of truth, and not as the very truth itself ; or to regard his revelation as aught else or aught less than a self-revelation. His doctrine has been esteemed as of secondary worth, as merely interpretative of his person and function, and as deriving from this circumstance its whole value and significance. By St. Paul and St. John, and by the orthodox generally, Jesus has been regarded as the Mediator of a new relation between God and man ; and by modern supernaturalists, as the Bearer of a new power into human life, or of a new life superimposed upon the natural or physical life of humanity, akin to the introduction of the vital principle into inorganic nature : so that his office or function as a religious Teacher has come to be regarded as quite subordinate and ministrant, only necessary to awaken men's faith and to gain their rational and voluntary co-operation in the process of redemption.

But what we insist upon is that the Church did not learn this from himself, and received no encouragement from his teaching to look upon him as a Redeemer. He gave no sanction to such a view of his office and function. He did not present himself to his countrymen as more than a teacher of righteousness, or, let us say, of religion ; and the impression made upon them was not owing to any such unfounded claim on his part. If this be a fact, as we shall now endeavour to render probable, it is important to bear it in mind, because, as already hinted, we wish in what follows to ascertain exactly, or as near as may be, the nature of those influences which he brought to bear upon those around him : how he made the initial impression upon his followers : how the disciples were prepared to retain their faith in him in spite of his crucifixion, and even on reflection to rise to the conception of him as a heavenly and divine being : in a word, how they were led to a point at which the dogmatic view of his person and office impressed itself on their minds.

Had Jesus ever presented himself to his disciples as their

Redeemer, in the orthodox sense of the word, we could, from our point of view, only have regarded it as a proof that he was labouring under a form of delusion : for we take it to be an utterance approved by the deepest reason of ancient as well as modern times, that "no man can save his brother's soul, nor pay his brother's debt," or as the Psalmist says, " None can by any means redeem his brother, nor give to God a ransom for him." But what we here call attention to is, that he did not in his teaching seek to impress his disciples with that view of his person, and that we have no reason for thinking that the impression which he made on his disciples during his lifetime was at all owing to such a claim. We see in the synoptic Gospels many grounds for the belief that he never claimed to stand in such a relation or to perform such an office to his fellow-men. Such a claim would have been quite at variance with the rest of his teaching.

The idea of the fatherliness of God which he so emphati-cally proclaimed seems to exclude the necessity of expiation or redemption by a third person. For who is there who has not many times felt the difficulty of reconciling the two doctrines ; who has not been conscious that the idea of fatherly love is troubled and perplexed when he is required to believe that it is conditioned by the sacrifice of another in his behalf ? This is a condition, besides, to which we find no allusion made where we might naturally expect to find it, had it entered into the thought of Jesus. We miss it, for example, in his form of prayer ; where, if anywhere, an allusion might have been expected to a fact which, if it were a fact, had been necessarily determinant of that consciousness with which he sought to imbue his followers. We miss it also in the parable of the prodigal son, in which we have the most touching representation of God's treatment of His penitent children ; and in which the unmediated connection between the son's penitence and the father's forgiveness is the point which forms the very nerve of the narrative and the centre of interest. The intention of the parable is to accentuate the principle that divine love in all its manifestations is absolutely unconditioned and unfettered, with the exception, if it can be called an exception, that the penitent adopt as the law of his conduct the principle of which forgiveness is the manifestation, and thus place himself in harmony with the divine will. Add to this, that had Jesus really thought himself predestined to make atonement for human sin: had such an idea been a substantive part of his teaching, it had necessarily been central and salient, and had given a tone and colouring to the whole of it. That he should, in that case, have allowed it to remain in the background, or have refrained from giving it a conspicuous and commanding place, is hardly conceivable. He must have done so by a species of " economy," which Roman Catholic theologians have found to be a useful idea in controversial straits ; but of which, so far as we can see, Jesus made little or no use.

Still it must not be overlooked that Jesus is represented in the New Testament as claiming for himself a redemptive function. We do not here take into account his teaching in the fourth Gospel, because, for reasons to be afterwards stated, we hold it to be a wholly unauthentic record ; and, also, because it does not represent Jesus as claiming such a function in the common or Pauline sense of the word. But it must be admitted that in the synoptic Gospels there are at least two utterances of his which may, with some plausibility, be interpreted in reference to himself as fulfilling the function of a Redeemer. On his fatal journey to Jerusalem he is reported to have said, " The son of man came not to be ministered unto, but to minister, and to give his life a ransom for many " ; and at the institution of the last supper he is represented as speaking of his blood as being " shed for many for the remission of sins."

Now, were we to regard these exceptional sentences as genuine utterances of Jesus, we could hardly but regard them also as the germs from which the dogma of the atonement was subsequently developed by the Church. But it is by no means certain that the evangelists have, in either instance, given an exact reproduction of the words of Jesus ; for it must be borne in mind that both of these sayings were placed on record, not before, but after the dogmatizing tendency had set in ; not before, but after St. Paul had written his great epistles : and we may, therefore, with some confidence attribute words so isolated in the Gospels to the colouring process which the teaching of Jesus underwent in the course of its transmission by a society in which the ideas of atonement and expiation, as applied to his death, had, by independent links of association, become prevalent. So long as we credit Jesus with sobriety of judgment, our guiding principle of criticism, viz., the rejection of the supernatural element, forbids us to regard these sayings as genuinely his. We must regard them, as we do many other sayings attributed to him, as reflections on the part of his disciples touching his death, put by the mythical tradition into a form of words spoken by himself. It is more than likely that the dogma would seek to authenticate itself, or to be reflected in the life and teaching of Jesus ; just as, in almost all cases, ideas prevalent in the time of a historian are apt to colour and transform his narrative of past events. It is manifest that by attributing to Jesus, in the prospect of his death, words and sayings expressive of their own reflections with regard to that event, the disciples adopted a means of stamping these reflections with irresistible authority, besides placing the character and work of Jesus in a transcendent and peculiarly affecting light. Jesus might declare with truth that he esteemed it to be his aim and mission in the world "not to be ministered unto, but to minister " ; for these words do but express, in forcible and popular terms, that intense enthusiasm for the highest interests of humanity, and that resolved devotion of himself to the good of man, of which he, as well as the greatest of his disciples (Phil. ii. 17) was conscious. We have, therefore, no ground to doubt that these words were uttered by him, but the remaining words, "and to give his life a ransom for many," unless they were added in the course of oral transmission, were in all probability a marginal gloss or dogmatic expletive, which in the course of time became incorporated with the text.

A similar result may be arrived at in regard to the words used by Jesus when he instituted the last supper. These words are reported in much the same form by all three synoptists, and the concurring testimony of St. Paul is supposed to confirm their historical character. From St. Paul's account in the first epistle to the Corinthians of what took place on that occasion, we can see that there existed even in his time much diversity of opinion as to what had actually been said and done in that upper room, as well as to the nature and intention of the usage itself which had grown up in memory of it; just as we at the present day are far from agreed as to these points. We can hardly accept of St. Paul's testimony as to the expressions used by Jesus on the occasion, seeing that we are told by him that he claimed to settle doubts in regard to the usage which had grown up in connection with them, not because he had had communication on the subject with those who were present at the institution, but because he had received a communication in regard to it from the Lord himself (1 Cor. xi. 23). Not only is this the plain meaning of his words in 1 Cor. xi. 23, but, taken in connection with his emphatic averment that the gospel which he preached was not after man, but came to him by revelation of Jesus Christ, every other meaning is excluded. What remains to be said of this averment will be reserved till we come to speak of the Pauline epistles.

We are tempted to suppose that the apostle had seen the necessity of placing the seal of his apostolic authority upon one of the various forms of the tradition respecting the last meal which Jesus partook of with his disciples, by way of settling disputes, of repressing the irregularities which had gathered round the usage, and of utilizing it as a bond of union between Christians, inasmuch as, by its very nature as a visible rite, it was better fitted for that purpose than any mere abstract formula or symbol of belief. It was quite in the manner and fashion of the great apostle to regard the outcome of his own matured reflections as a revelation from the Lord. That he should have seen in the rite a confirmation of the dogma ; that he should have cast the tradition into a form in harmony with it, and also that his version of the incident should have been incorporated in the evangelical tradition, was only what we might expect.

We submit, therefore, that there is no unimpeachable authority for saying that Jesus in his teaching gave countenance to the ideas of atonement and expiation ; that he either regarded himself or encouraged his disciples to regard him as a Redeemer in the dogmatic or supernatural sense. If he gave any ground to his disciples for so regarding him it was not intentionally by anything which he said, but unwittingly, by the imposing grandeur of his character, by his claim to be the Messiah, and by the heroism of his death. The great and manifest object of all his ministry was like that of other

E

religious teachers, such as Buddha and Zoroaster, to teach and induce his disciples to redeem themselves, and to rouse them to the effort necessary to their self-elevation spiritually and morally.   This is the only sense in which we can regard him as a Redeemer.   In other words, we regard him simply as a great teacher, and it is necessary to explain our meaning in so saying.

In the first place, it is to be observed that, consistently with the denial of the supernatural element, we cannot admit that he was qualified for the teacher's office by supernatural illumination or special inspiration.   We cannot admit him to be an absolute authority in morals or religion, or admit, indeed, that there is any such authority except in the collective reason and conscience of man, however fallible these may be, and however difficult to ascertain their verdict amid the clamour and conflict of strange and discordant voices.   We can accept of even Jesus as an authority only in so far as his doctrine and example appeal to reason and to conscience. By disowning the supernatural element at this point we preserve the supremacy of these as the sole and ultimate arbiters in the religious sphere.   To admit the presence and action of that element at any point in the genesis and history of Christianity is, as we have seen, to set Christianity at variance with the requirements of modern science ; and, we may here add, to introduce into human life an insufferable and bastard dualism, of which, in modern times, the spirit of intolerance, the papal claim to infallibility, and the conflict between Church and State (even in its most constitutional form), are the necessary manifestations ; the last, a conflict in which no modus vivendi and no pragmatic sanction can do more than effect a temporary lull.   But even to limit the presence of a supernatural element (as some apologists seem inclined to do in the last resort) to the point of which we are here speaking, i.e., to regard Jesus as being entrusted with a divine commission to reveal the truth, is to lay an embargo on human reason, and to make way for another authority sufficient by its weight to crush the authority of reason and conscience.

A recent apologist of Protestantism, as against Roman Catholicism, has taken up the position that the authority of Jesus is co-ordinate with that of conscience ; for this, we suppose, is what he means when he says that Jesus is an authority "in the sense that conscience is," whereas "the Church is an authority only in the sense that law and legislature are authorities" (Fairbairn). The same position is, we think, taken up by Volkmar, one of the most advanced among German theologians ; but this position is of the nature of a compromise, which will neither repel the Catholic attack, nor satisfy the true idea which underlies Protestantism, and, indeed, every revolt against the authority of mere tradition. That idea is, that human reason is the very highest authority to which the ultimate appeal must be made in religion as in all else, and that all other or outward authority, including that of Jesus and of the Church, must verify or approve itself to this which is within us, *i.e.* to the collective reason of humanity. And it is our belief that the interests of religion, or, let us say, of Christianity are not imperilled by such an avowal : for that the great ideas of Christianity, as having their authority in themselves, can dispense with an infallible Founder and a miraculous history ; and that the Founder, though not infallible, still retains our veneration, because the doctrine which he taught does appeal to our reason, while he himself becomes not less, but more lovable and more marvellous, by the recognition of his simple humanity.

As now our fundamental principle forbids us to admit that Jesus could derive his doctrine from any special or abnormal source, so it is of great importance for this inquiry into the origin of Christianity that we are able to affirm that he advanced no claim of the kind ; that he never asserted nor implied that his knowledge of divine things was reached by direct, unmediated communication from God, rather than by the ordinary channels through which truth reaches the minds of men ; or that he was favoured with a species of inspiration, which put him in infallible possession of the truth and left no room for error or misconception. It is of great importance to be assured of this, because, as already said, we wish to ascertain the initial steps by which Jesus made an impression on the minds of his disciples. It is well to know that, whether intentionally or unintentionally, he did not seek to impose upon the minds of men, as other teachers have done, by claiming to be inspired or to stand in direct communication with God. He did not profess to derive his doctrine through such a channel ; and the awe which he inspired, the authority with which he spoke, was not due to the effect which such a claim has often had, when confidently advanced and supported by the accident of favouring circumstances. The words attributed to him, which seem most nearly to approach to such a claim, are those of Matth. xi. 27 and Luke x. 22 : " All things are delivered unto me of my Father ; and no man knoweth the son but the Father, neither knoweth any man the Father save the son, and he to whomsoever the son will reveal Him." These words have been supposed to indicate the belief that he enjoyed as his exclusive privilege a knowledge of divine things, in consequence of the peculiar relation in which he stood to God. And they bear such a close resemblance to the general tone of discourse attributed to Jesus in the fourth Gospel, that they are commonly cited to prove that even the synoptists have preserved a specimen of the use by Jesus of a style of self-assertion quite different from anything which is elsewhere ascribed to him by them, but eminently characteristic of the discourses ascribed to him by the fourth evangelist. And this solitary, or all but solitary, instance of the kind is supposed to prove the genuineness of the Johannine tradition, in spite of its apparent discordance with the synoptic. But to us it has always seemed as if this fact pointed to quite the opposite conclusion, and tended rather to throw suspicion on the genuineness of this portion of the synoptic record. The teaching of Jesus as preserved in this record we regard as the most important and authentic portion of the narrative ; and we do not rashly or willingly call any part of it in question. But we must confess that the close resemblance of the above passage to the general tone and spirit of the fourth Gospel, together with the contrast which it presents to the rest of the synoptic discourses, and its isolated position in these, seems to warrant some suspicion as to its authenticity.

At the same time we admit that, while the words under consideration (Matth. xi. 27) are appropriate to the idealized or dogmatic Christ, something like them may have been uttered by the historical Jesus. He might say that no man but he, the son, knew the Father, because he was conscious that he alone, of all living men, was possessed of the true conception of the divine character and of the true ideal of humanity. He knew enough of contemporary Judaism and heathenism to be satisfied of this ; and much as he may have been indebted to the ancient lawgivers and prophets of his people, profoundly versed as he was in their writings, yet he knew that his own insight into divine things went far beyond theirs.   In virtue of such a consciousness he could say that he had come to fulfil the law and the prophets ; and we shall yet see how much turned on this consciousness of his own higher insight ; how, in fact, it underlay his whole ministry ; and how it is conceivable that he may, in some form of words, have claimed an exclusive or unique knowledge of the Heavenly Father, and have laid stress upon the fact.   However great the obligation under which he lay to the prophetic line, he may yet have been fully conscious of the presence of those new elements in his teaching which harmonized, unified, and sublimated all that he owed to his prophetic predecessors ; and these were elements for which he could most readily account as in some sense a revelation of God to his soul : as, indeed, all truth may be regarded in that light.   They existed for him, not as mere intellectual notions, but as certitudes which formed the very base of his spiritual life, so that he felt himself to be at one with God.   The gulf between the finite and the infinite seemed for him to be so bridged that he could regard himself as in some mystical sense a son of God as well as a son of man.   But we cannot rest here : perfect candour requires that we go a step further, and say, that if Jesus claimed a special and supernatural derivation for any part of his doctrine, we cannot, in that case, feel constrained, even by the deepest reverence which we entertain for his person, to accept of such a claim on his authority.   We could only regard it as one proof among others that even in the province of religion, or bordering on it, he partook of that fallibility of judgment which is common to man ; or, let us say, of that tendency common to the age, as well as to much more recent times, to refer to a supernatural origin facts, whether of consciousness or of observation, which we cannot understand or explain.

It was an instance of fallibility, analogous to that which he betrays to the inquiring modern spirit, in his unquestioning belief in diabolic possession, in the verbal inspiration of Old Testament scriptures, if not also in the certainty of his own second coming, all remnants of Jewish ideas by which his mind was dominated, showing clearly that he was not free from error even in the province of religion, and too seriously enunciated by him to admit of being explained away as mere accommodation on his part to Jewish modes of thinking.

If we examine his teaching we shall find that even in his most emphatic utterances Jesus appealed to the reason and conscience and to the spiritual instincts of his audience. He demands belief, not because he says a thing, but he says it and expects it to make an impression on men's minds, and to gain their assent, because it carries in it its own authority; because it awakens a secret consciousness of its truth in those whom he addresses ; because it only needed to be uttered to obtain the assent of honest hearts open to conviction. He does not enforce the belief of his doctrine by declaring it to be the word of God, but he leaves it to be inferred that it is the word of God, because it appeals to the conscience. Nothing can be more evident to those who enter carefully into the spirit of his teaching, than that for him the nature of man was, in modern phraseology, autonomous, that all duty was regarded by him as enjoined in the first place by our own highest nature, and only secondarily considered as having the sanction of God, because He is the author of our constitution.

In this respect he differed widely from the prophets of former ages, inasmuch as they—satisfied that the truth which appealed to their souls had come to them as a communication from without, from another spirit distinct from their own, which seemed to come upon them by sudden and intermittent illapse (see Jerem. xiv. 8)—sought for the most part* to impose it on the minds of others, as by an ex-

* We say here "for the most part," because all through the Old Testament the words of inspiration often take the form of an appeal to our rational nature. In the Psalms (xciv.-xcvi.) and in the Prophets generally (Isa. xliv.) there are splendid instances of this description. It is one of many instances of his bias in favour of Greek thought when Dr. Hatch, p. 158, says that in contrast with Greek ethics the earliest Christianity "rested morality on a divine command." The fact that Jesus, at the bidding of his own nature, dared in certain cases to set aside the statute, is a practical proof that he at least did not do so, and when St. Paul says that the Gentiles are a law to themselves, it is an implicit proof that he did not do so either. Whatever, in the popular language of the New Testament, may seem to say the contrary, the thought that morality has its foundation in human nature is deeply imbedded in

traneous authority not resident in the truth itself. Whereas Jesus, from the circumstance that he enjoyed the calm, un-intoxicating, unecstatical, uninterrupted possession of the truth of God, and felt that the revealing spirit "abode" with him, recognised it as his own spirit, as a spirit which belonged to him as man, and in common with other men.

We remark the resulting difference between the teaching of Jesus and that of the ancient prophets in the absence from the former of all those formulas which occur with ceaseless iteration in the latter, and were the prophetic way of clothing with divine authority the voice of the oracle within themselves. The appeal of Jesus passes between his own higher nature and that of those whom he addresses, and the "authority" with which he was felt by the multitudes to speak, was derived from the inward assent and testimony of their own consciences (Matth. vii. 29). It was the "answer" of the conscience which clothed his word of wisdom with authority, just as the answering faith of the listening crowds often invested his word of command with healing virtue. Its power of calling forth this response was the marvel of it in either case. The truths which were invested with this authority, which had this power of commending themselves, may be regarded as elements of natural religion, which ordinary men might appreciate and recognise the force of, though only the religious genius might be able to excogitate and discover them. Of such elements it was that the doctrine of Jesus specially consisted; of truths which appealed to the moral and religious instincts of men: of some such especially as were at variance with the current notions of the time; of such it was that he constructed a religious system sufficient to satisfy the spiritual wants and religious yearnings of men, to make a profound and permanent impression on the con-duct of those who embraced it, and to promote their ascent to an ever higher level of the religious life. We say nothing here of the weight imparted to his doctrine by the seal of truth which was impressed upon it by the manner of his life and death, for of this we shall elsewhere have occasion to speak.*

Christianity, and shows itself especially, if indirectly and collaterally, in St. Paul's polemic against the obligation of the statutory law of Israel.

* That the authority and impressiveness with which he spoke may have

According to our view, Christianity as a specific form of religion took its rise, as we have already said, in the brooding, meditative mind of Jesus. His mind was the laboratory in which his inherited Judaism was liberated from certain elements of error and imperfection, and entered into combination with new elements supplied by his depth of insight into the nature of the religious principle, or of the relation subsisting between God and His rational offspring. In him singular reverence for the past and its wisdom was combined with absolute independence of judgment. Not at all infected with the presumptuous and immodest desire to dissent from pre-existing beliefs merely because they were established in the minds of the community, his was yet no merely receptive and passive, and still less a yielding nature, easily "subdued to the moral element" in which he lived ; but resting on a basis of its own, enabling him to withstand and vanquish ideas and tendencies which shocked or did not recommend themselves to his religious instincts. His prepossessions were all in favour of time-honoured beliefs, inherited from the fathers. These beliefs were among the conditions which helped to make him what he was, and of these he retained to the last his regard for not a few which do not admit of being verified, and which we now look upon as mere Jewish superstitions or "extra-beliefs."

been aided by the tone of his voice and his novel and awe-inspiring modes of speech, seems to be a legitimate inference from his habitual use of the Amen (verily) with which he prefaced his more emphatic utterances. The word was expressive of that certitude and depth of conviction which, when it reveals itself on the part of a speaker, is wont to have an imposing and subduing effect on the hearer. But it was not merely expressive of his own deep conviction, it was also a call to his hearers to regard the assent which they gave to his teaching as an absolute authority over their conduct. As if he had said, "You feel the truth of what I am now speaking, hold to it then in all earnestness." He thus encouraged the rising of the higher moral sense within them. He used the word to show that he appealed to that as the authority within themselves for the truth of his doctrine. According to the synoptists he used the word singly, whereas the fourth Evangelist makes him use it in a duplicated form. This is a minor difference between the synoptic Gospels and the fourth. But it is deserving of notice because it confirms the general observation, to be afterwards illustrated, that the fourth Evangelist sought to outdo and to go beyond the synoptists in their delineation of the life and teaching of Jesus.

The historical conditions amid which he appeared do not adequately explain how he became the teacher of a better form of religion than that in which he had been educated, and how he created a new epoch in the history of religion. These conditions were substantially the same, so far as we can discern, for multitudes of his contemporaries ; but he alone of all these multitudes showed any fitness for this enterprise. The fact can only be explained logically by falling back on the hypothesis that he was a great religious genius, or by crediting him with a great personal endowment and native force of character. Of no man in history could it less be said than of him, that he was the creature of his age ; and as little could it be said of that period of time that it would have been much the same, and have formed a turning point in religious history, had he not appeared. The course of the world's history did indeed flow on in the same direction as before for several centuries ; the change which he effected was confined to the small, obscure, but ever extending circle of those who yielded to his influence, and may all therefore be traced back to him as its fount of origin. Indeed, the rise of Christianity is a crucial instance to prove the theory that the advance of humanity along its many lines is due to the appearance from time to time of supremely gifted individuals : to the truths which they bring to light ; to the infection of their example ; or to the loyalty, veneration, and sympathy, which they rouse in the great masses of mankind. A general progressive illumination, unmarked by any salient or original discovery, may proceed from the explication or better understanding of some great principle previously divulged ; and results may flow, or deductions be drawn, which were not at first seen to be involved in it. But there have been great crises in human history and great revolutions in human life which have manifestly been due to the appearance of some towering genius, whom for a time his age could not understand and could but slowly overtake. Such, we believe, was preeminently the case with Jesus ; and we should have to say that it was true of him even if it were true of no other. That there are the greatest differences in the personal endowments of individuals, and that, even when to all appearance the conditions under which individuals grow up are the same, the resulting characters are very disparate, is what all must admit ;

this fact is also so universal that we must regard it as due to the operation of general laws.

It is to the operation of these same laws, and not to the action of any special providence, as the Duke of Argyll thinks, that we trace the rise and propagation of Christianity. If indeed we look merely to the deep and perhaps growing corruption of the ancient world, we may be tempted to regard the rise and rapid growth of Christianity as an abrupt and miraculous phenomenon in the world's history. The marvel is that a religion which inculcated a morality so severe should have had such a ready reception under such circumstances. But it should not be forgotten that, in historical fact, and by a sort of necessity, that corruption, such as it was, was accompanied by a growing consciousness of the prevailing evil and of the need of reformation ; and that this consciousness was in itself a preparation for the Gospel, or indeed for any religion which offered itself as a remedy for the evil. The higher life which revealed itself in Christianity was in reality a continuous development of that consciousness of evil which had grown up and become more pronounced in the Jewish and Gentile world. That consciousness was a manifestation of the good still latent, but struggling to assert itself in humanity. At the same time that consciousness, however acute, does not necessarily pass into a better life. It is often most acute in those who are unable to extricate themselves from the evil, and therefore continue still in their sin. A great step has yet to be taken by some strong son of man to react against the evil and to reach the level of a higher life. There is nothing improbable in the idea that an upward movement might begin in the mind of a single individual, whose consciousness of the evil was not only acute, but who by his depth of insight discerned the true and only remedy for it. And this was what actually took place in Christianity. Originating in the silent depths of the soul of Jesus, the great revolution in human life spread gradually from him as its centre, taking effect upon a few receptive spirits through intercourse with him, and communicated by them to a larger circle.

We can see that the question often discussed, Whether the moral condition of that age was or was not favourable to the rise of a pure religion ? is too general in its scope to be simply or categorically answered. It is conceivable that even the exceptional immorality and superstition of an age might, by reason of their tendency to provoke reaction, be favourable to the introduction of a better time. If credit may be given to the Roman satirists and to the Christian apologists (who followed the lead of St. Paul, Rom. i.), we should say that the Gentile nations (not to speak in the meantime of the Jews) were in the state here supposed. But the views of such writers are almost certainly exaggerated, and call for many qualifications, to which Dr. Hatch (Hibbert Lectures, 1888, p. 141) seeks to give expression. Adopting the conclusion to which a well-known German scholar has been led, he says :—" The age in which Christianity grew was in reality an age of moral reformation. There was the growth of a higher religious morality, which believed that God was pleased by moral action rather than by sacrifice. There was the growth of the belief that life required amendment. There was a reaction in the popular mind against the vices of the great centres of population," all preparing the minds of men to receive Christian teaching. Now, that there is a large measure of truth in this estimate of the age, we do not doubt ; yet we suspect that the reaction against the prevailing immorality and grossness of superstition was not very vigorous, or very widely diffused ; that it lay more in theory than in practice ; and that the belief in the necessity of amendment had no great influence upon the life. No doubt there were here and there individuals among the Stoics and Cynics of extraordinary virtue, standing out from the general level. But the signs of better things were confined in a measure to the schools and to the cultivated and literary classes. The great mass of the people, in the centres of population, seem to have been in a deplorable state of moral corruption ; and it is a notable fact, which, as is well known, has put its mark on the language of Rome, that it was just in these centres that Christianity gained its earliest and greatest triumphs. The "fulness of the time" at which Jesus came was due, we suspect, to the *widely felt* decay of faith and virtue, and to the proved failure and hopelessness of all attempts at self-reformation ; and it was only through some secret of power peculiar to the gospel that any great and general progress in morality was brought to pass. What that secret was may perhaps be made to appear in the following pages.

Of the circumstances and more intimate surroundings of the

life of Jesus, up to his thirty-third or thirty-fifth year, we know absolutely nothing ; and we may surmise that all before that was a period of much self-discipline, of self-questioning, and of meditation on religious problems. We may suppose that the religious society into which he was born, and the religious views in which he had been educated, did not satisfy his religious instincts ; that he yearned for something better ; and that in his quest for that he passed through some great spiritual crisis, some unique religious experience, of which his teaching was the mere exponent. The length of time which he spent in obscurity, on which the tradition throws no light and which furnished no augury to his parents or brethren of his future career, suggests the idea that he may have risen slowly to become what he was when he made his appearance on the stage of public life ; and that it was a probationary or disciplinary period of prolonged mental conflict and suffering and self-struggle.

To this view it has been objected, that such mental struggles leave scars in the life, tokens of past conflict and suffering ; indications of a personal acquaintance with sin ; reminiscences of painful experiences of frailty and of division in the members, to which St. Paul confesses ; the ground-swell of a storm that is past ; of all which Jesus exhibits no trace. But in his case all such indications may have vanished, because his victory was complete, his doubts solved, and his resolution irrevocably taken before he showed himself to the world.

That Jesus took little or no interest in merely speculative or abstract truth is very apparent. He did not trouble himself to find any dogmatic or philosophical basis for what was new in his doctrine ; and we may venture to say that he was the least speculative of all the great teachers of whom history has preserved a record. To be satisfied of this, we have only to compare him with Buddha, Zoroaster, or even with Confucius and other great men who figure in the history of religion. But perhaps there is no better proof of the absence from his mind of this speculative bent than the fact that he does not seem to have had any theory or opinion as to the origin of evil—the problem which, above all others, has exercised a fascination upon all great speculative thinkers. At least he made no use of any such theory, as Paul did afterwards ; and not a single utterance of his can be cited to show that he considered men to have lost a faculty or power which they ever possessed. He was satisfied to accept of evil as a great and patent fact or phenomenon of human life ; and his primary object was to show men by his teaching and conduct how moral evil might be eliminated from the lives of individuals by a hard and continuous struggle against adverse influences and conditions outward and inward. His whole teaching gathered round this point and bore exclusively on practice : in one word, his was a soteriological doctrine, explanatory of the method by which men might deliver themselves from the evil around and within them, and rise to the level of a better life, and approach the ideal of humanity. It was with men individually that he dealt, for he saw distinctly that before his doctrine could take effect on society, or on the world at large, or, let us say, on the Jewish people, it had first to take effect on the individuals composing it. His prefatory announcement, indeed, respecting the kingdom of God, suffices to prove that he sought to enlist individuals in a cause, which is much greater than any mere personal aim ; and his parables show that he did not overlook the reflex effect of the transformed society on individuals ; but it is with the effect of his doctrine on these latter that we have chiefly to do, in considering the genesis of his religion. The method of self-denial and self-devotion, which he inculcated, was one, we may be confident, which he had first proved and practised for himself, and then offered as a guide and help to his disciples, because he had found it to be the only method by which he or any man could attain to the higher levels of the religious life, and to that inner harmony in which true blessedness consists. He had seen that whatever else might be doubtful or obscure, *that* was the true method of life, the present duty of men, laid down to them by the very constitution of their nature ; *that* by which alone the possibilities within them might be developed, and the prophecy of better things fulfilled.

That there was no metaphysical element in the doctrine of Jesus is affirmed by E. von Hartmann, whose authority on such a point we may accept. And if he be right in defining the religious man as one who forms his life upon some metaphysical basis, we should be driven to the conclusion that the title of Jesus to be regarded as a great religious teacher rests upon a very slender foundation. Indeed, E. von Hartmann seems to think that by his remark, that Jesus never reflected on the immanence and transcendency of God, he has demolished the significance of the doctrine of Jesus for the present age. It would have been nearer the mark and more relevant, perhaps, had he said, what is probably true, that Jesus believed in the Old Testament miracles, or even in the miraculous nature of his own works of healing (though this latter is not quite so certain). But to all such observations the reply is, that the soteriological doctrine of Jesus stands on independent ground ; that it is but a statement of his personal experience, on which he does not theorize or speculate ; and that the unspeculative, unmetaphysical character of his doctrine is, negatively, that feature which has given to it its permanent hold of the human mind. The method which he propounded for the salvation, or the true education of man, is valid for all time, no matter whether the metaphysical relation of God to man and to the universe be (or be regarded as) that of transcendency or immanency or of both combined. In any and in every case man must, as we shall find that Jesus taught, maintain a struggle with himself in order to rise toward his ideal, and derive courage to persevere from faith in the propitious nature of the divine order. In all ages, too, the adequacy and necessity of this method will be verified in the spiritual experience of those who seriously put it in practice. In this method there is no mystery : " all is plain to him that understandeth." The mystery, which will always remain insoluble, is that depth of insight and of moral conviction, that strength of independent will and judgment which enabled Jesus to set aside the accredited teachers and highest authorities of his people, resting, as they apparently and by general confession did, upon the inspired records and traditions of the revered past. But this is a mystery of the same kind as that which resides in all development and growth.

We may here turn aside for a moment to say that many of us view, with not ungrounded jealousy, the claim of metaphysics and speculative philosophy to be the arbiters in religious or theological questions. It appears to be a sufficient reason for such jealousy, if there were no other, that speculative thinkers have not yet settled among themselves, and are not likely soon to settle, by their methods, what is absolute truth. That is true of metaphysical reasoning what Newman seems to say of science, that " its hypotheses rise and fall, and it is difficult to anticipate which of them will keep their ground." Yet in the face of this obvious reflection, we have seen in our own time curious attempts made by professedly orthodox theologians to effect a compromising alliance between speculative theories and the practical doctrines of Christianity ; and not the least strange thing of all in this reference is to find that the same theologian from whom we have just quoted has himself indulged in the same doubtful game. In his *Apologia* Newman tells us, without apology, or, so far as we know, recantation, that in one of his writings he " attempted to place the doctrine of the Real Presence on an intellectual basis—viz., the denial of the existence of space, except as a subjective idea of our minds." Could a better example be well given of the desperate shifts to which men will resort in defence of a foregone conclusion ? In the treatment of theological questions the speculative thought of past ages no doubt plays, and rightfully plays, an important part. The history of philosophy is a great storehouse for the elucidation of Christian dogma ; but no system of philosophy can lay claim to finality, and we cannot venture to shape our religious opinions by any current system. Eventually theology and philosophy may flow together, but meanwhile they must hold on their independent courses. With science, or the knowledge of the phenomenal, the case is somewhat different. For in a certain sense science, strictly so called, can lay claim to finality. For " science moves but slowly, slowly, creeping on from point to point," and never recedes from a point once gained. Year by year, century by century, it arrives at well-ascertained results, which can never be overturned or set aside ; and the grand general result is that the universe is governed on constitutional principles, by inflexible and unvarying laws, to which Creator and creature are alike subject. Every sphere into which the torch of science has been carried has yielded confirmation to this result, and it may confidently be predicted that every further advance of science will do the like. The presumption that there is no exception to the reign of law in any department of mind or matter is so overwhelming, that if the truth of Christianity were bound up with the reality in it of a miraculous element, it would stand on most precarious ground. We may dismiss at once every form of religious belief which is at variance with a single well-ascertained scientific fact. For in this age we have got beyond the stage of thought at which it is possible to believe that what is false either in philosophy or in science may be true in theology.

Further on, when we come to consider more particularly the teaching of Jesus, it will fall to us to show that a dogmatic or unverifiable element is entirely absent from his doctrine ; but in the meantime we would simply observe that the implicit recognition in his teaching of human autonomy, together with the absence of dogmatic elements, is as much as to say that his method of deliverance from evil is autosoteric—in plain terms, a process of self-elevation, or of self-extrication, or of self-redemption from evil—a process which can be carried out only by that struggle of man himself with his own lower nature, of which the cross is the symbol. Recognizing in himself, and in mankind generally, the presence of a higher nature in germ akin to the divine, or, as we should say, of an ideal nature representative of, or in subtle organic sympathy with, that universal order which is one with the will of God ; of a principle, therefore, to which as being common to man he could appeal ; he could not but also recognize the obligation lying upon himself and upon all men, to acquire for it the preponderance over the lower nature, of which he was also conscious. The obligation was involved in the very existence of that ideal principle, and the consciousness of that obligation also involved or was presumptive of the possibility of its fulfilment. He had found, no doubt, by experience that that preponderance of the good over the evil, and the gradual extinction of the latter, could only be secured by an earnest struggle ; and this fact, which had disclosed itself to his consciousness as a necessary law of human life was the centre round which were grouped all the elements of his teaching, whether theological or anthropological. And yet further, this same fact furnished him with the sole test which he could apply to the current popular beliefs. He questioned no inherited belief which did not come into collision with that. He did not seek to interfere with such, except in so far as they jarred with convictions which were drawn from experience, and were therefore more valid than tradition, and not to be surrendered at the bidding of any authority, however sacred or revered. Current ideas were suffered by him to stand side by side with these convictions, and were left there unsuspectingly until a time should arrive when the latter should cast those forth, and show their own right of survival by their capacity of entering into harmonious combination with the new theory or system of thought, by which the naïve or traditional theory was superseded. It may even be that his reverence for the ancient belief was so great, or his interest in his method so absorbing, as to keep in abeyance even that tendency or craving for inward unity of thought which is so congenial to the human mind, and also to prevent him from venturing upon ground where the facts of his consciousness did not form a certain guide.

That human consciousness may thus assert itself, and be the guarantee of facts or laws which lie beyond the area of traditional beliefs, that it may even form the nucleus or inception of a new synthesis of thought, is what is meant when we speak of the pioneering office of genius. What we say is, that the distinctive doctrine of Jesus rested on facts of his consciousness, and was therefore independent of any recognized theory; but like every doctrine resting on fact, and giving a true reflection of fact, it was capable of entering into combination with and finding a place for itself in the true theory of the universe, whatever that might prove to be. This is our reply to the assertion, which has been made by Von Hartmann and others, that we moderns can no longer honestly claim to be Christians since we have adopted a theory of the universe, a scheme of divine government different from that of which the doctrine of Jesus was an outgrowth. We meet this assertion by simply denying that the distinctive doctrines of Jesus, which are the central principles of Christianity, were an outgrowth or appendage of any theory of the universe, or can, with any propriety, be said to stand or fall with any such. We hope that this will appear more distinctly further on, when we have determined wherein the specific doctrine of Jesus consists.

As a mere statement of facts of consciousness, as it abode in the mind of Jesus, his doctrine was independent of any theory. Had the religious process as inculcated by Jesus been heterosoteric (*i.e.* carried on by help from outside), as it afterwards became in the hands of St. Paul and the early Church, the assertion made by Von Hartmann and others would have been valid; for in the hands of St. Paul the religious consciousness, as articulated by Jesus, adapted and allied it-

F

self to the existing or accepted theory of the universe, and just because it did so, was fitted to exert the greater influence upon the mind of that and many succeeding ages ; but for the same reason, *i.e.* just because it is allied and conformed to an exploded theory of the universe, it is now, *in that form*, losing its hold of the human mind and falling into discredit. Whereas the method of Jesus, in its purely autosoteric and undogmatic form, will survive under every revolution of human thought, and will compel the world to own itself Christian, because that name is derived from him who was the first to become distinctly conscious of that experience and to impart it to the world.

With these general and preliminary remarks on the function of Jesus as a teacher, we proceed now to observe that as (with a qualification to be afterwards made) he did not profess to be more than a teacher, so he did not profess to teach an absolutely new religion or to propose an absolutely new system of thought and conduct. He resembled most other, or, we may perhaps say, all other great founders of religion before and since in that he professed only to reform that religion in which he had himself been educated, and which was still believed in by those around him. To prevent an erroneous apprehension of his aims and purposes he said that he had come not to destroy but to fulfil the law, to fill it with a fuller and deeper meaning perhaps than even Moses himself or the prophets had found in it, or, we may say more generally, to bring into full light those views of religion which from early times had been struggling to find expression in Israel, views which had attained a very high form of expression in prophetic ages, but had lost their vitality and become inert under the rule of the priestly and learned castes.

His object was not so much to supersede the religion of Israel as to breathe a new life into it ; not merely to re-pristinate even the best thought of the past, but to restore it in a transfigured form, and to give heightened prominence to those very features of the religious idea which even the prophets had not been able to bring to full expression, and which had been all but forgotten and obscured by the commentators of later times. By the criticism which he applied to the records of preceding ages, and by his comparison of them with the ideas and usages prevalent in his own day, he was able to discern the deep significance of those very elements of prophetic teaching from which his contemporaries had fallen away, and to perceive the necessity of placing these elements in higher relief and making them more distinctive of his teaching. It is not improbable that the advance of evangelic doctrine beyond the prophetic standpoint could not have been made even by him but for the lesson which the intervening and non-prophetic ages conveyed to his penetrating eye. That he drew the lesson was an act of highest genius and insight, and was what entitled him to say that he came to fulfil the law and the prophets.

By this time it will appear, and it will appear more and more as we proceed, that we regard what are usually styled the central facts of Christianity, such as the incarnation and the resurrection of Jesus, not as facts at all, but only as quasi-historical, or mythical forms, in which Christian phantasy clothed the facts of Christian experience. For us, Jesus is the Founder of our faith, because he was the discoverer of the true relation between God and man, the originator of that organic environment, of that web of thought, of habit, and of association into which we are born, and which forms the starting point of the spiritual life of individuals within the Christian community. It will also be seen that though the alleged facts disappear under the sober, searching scrutiny of criticism and science, Christianity itself does not disappear or perish : inasmuch as the experience in which it consists still survives, and the specific consciousness which constitutes its essential principle is established in the system of human thought, and repeats itself from generation to generation, and operates to this day as the most powerful factor in the spiritual and social life of man.

CHAPTER IV.

THE GROWTH IN ISRAEL OF THE IDEA, "KINGDOM OF GOD."

JESUS entered upon his reforming activity by announcing that the kingdom of heaven was at hand, an announcement which, though it was prefatory to his teaching, must have been preceded in his mind by the discovery of the inwardness and blessedness of true righteousness, which, as we shall yet see, was the staple of his doctrine. In logical sequence, his view of the kingdom of God was derivative, an inference from his view as to the righteousness of God. But for convenience of arrangement we shall, at the risk of anticipating some of our remarks on the latter subject, first explain his views as to the former.

An announcement identical in terms had already been made by John the Baptist; but without adverting in the meantime to the significance of this fact, we proceed to say that by this announcement Jesus gave it at once to be understood by his audiences that between his doctrine and that which was current among them—that with which they were familiar—there was an unbroken continuity. The expectation of a divine kingdom which would realize the highest hopes of the people and remedy all the evils and disasters which had befallen the nation, had for many ages formed a great part of Jewish religion or Jewish faith; and both the idea and the expression had long been current. We might, therefore, without inquiring further into the origin and nature of this singular direction of the Jewish mind, content ourselves with accepting it as a historical fact, as a unique variety of national sentiment which was of happy consequence for the spiritual and religious progress, first, of the Jewish people, and then, through them, of

the world at large.   But this connecting link between the Old
and New Testaments—between the Jewish and the Christian
religions—is far too important to be dismissed with such a
summary treatment.   There is no better way of understanding
or explaining the relation which Christianity occupies to Judaism, or of placing in high relief the novelty and originality of
the doctrine of Jesus, than by tracing the rise and growth of
this idea, and observing the transformation which it underwent
in the thought of Jesus.   Like all great and fully developed
ideas, it had its roots in a far back time, and to trace its
history is the best way of getting to the understanding of it.
" The thought of the present," as has well been said, " cannot
be understood without reference to that of the past.   The
former is shaped by the latter both in the way of action and
of reaction.   What we think to-day is, to a very large extent,
the result or deposit of what men have thought before us ;
a heritage which we may scrutinize, test, and modify, or even
reject or abandon, but of which we cannot rid ourselves, or treat
as of no account."   Nothing could be better expressed ; and it
points out the method by which we may best approach the
doctrine of the kingdom of God, as it assumed its final form
in the teaching of Jesus.

There can be no two opinions as to the fact that Christianity
was deeply rooted in the religion of Israel—rooted in it far
more deeply and intimately, because organically and spiritually,
than in the somewhat mechanical way of which the supernatural theory gives the idea.   To see that such is the case,
we must go back to the commencement of the Jewish commonwealth, and trace the roots of Christianity, or, which is the
same thing, the roots of the idea " Kingdom of God " which
issued in Christianity, to that far distant time.   Like every
other religion, even the most rude and elementary, that of
Israel had a certain capacity of higher development.   In
combination with its theistic idea, its ethical elements gave
promise of a very high development.   But the mythical idea
of a covenant relation and of a national election, which was
intrinsic to it, or which, at least, entered deeply into its structure, and was the secret of its wonderful vitality, caused it, as
we shall yet find, to settle down into the Judaistic form, and
placed a limit to its capacity for a further advance.   In the
depths of their consciousness, the higher or prophetic minds of

the people were painfully aware that the " dispensation " under
which they lived was essentially, if not hopelessly, imperfect ;
and that another prophet, like unto Moses, was needed to lead
the people forth into a new land, not of promise but of fulfilment. They tried many times to burst through the limiting
barrier, and sometimes seemed, as in the case of Jeremiah
especially, to be on the point of succeeding ; but they were
unequal to the task, and Jesus it was who, greater than all the
prophets, burst the barrier, and set the religious idea free to
expand into its absolute form.

In order now to show the nature of his great achievement,
the work by which he laid the foundation of his new religion,
we must review the phases through which the religion of Israel
passed, till it arrived at that stage in which it presented itself
to him. Our remarks for this end, though they may seem to
be somewhat protracted, will be found not to be irrelevant to
the matter in hand; not to be a digression, but an integral part
of our subject. The details into which we shall here enter do
not profess to be exhaustive. For it is no part of our plan to
pass in review the history of Israel, or its religious thought and
usage, except in so far as these are supposed by us to lead up
to the thought of Jesus, or to have provoked the reaction in his
mind. We shall endeavour to show that the religion of Israel,
which attained its zenith in the prophetic age, had, by the time
of Jesus, gradually declined, and shrunk into a form which he
found it necessary to denounce and to supplant. And in
pursuance of this object, we shall leave unnoticed many topics
in the religious history of Israel which in themselves are of
interest, but for our purpose of only subsidiary or collateral
importance.

Many facts which have been brought to light in recent times
by the patient study of the monuments of ancient Egypt and
Assyria, leave little or no doubt that in the Book of Genesis
there are many allusions to personages and events of pre-
Mosaic times, which had lingered in the memory or literature
of Eastern nations, and were woven by a very free hand into a
consecutive narrative, so as to form a fitting introduction to the
Exodus from Egypt—the event which, whether mythical or
historical, real or imaginary, was the commencement spiritually
of the Israelitish people. To make this introduction more
complete and imposing, the writer or writers of the Book of

Genesis traced up an imaginary history to the creation of the world and to the first parents of our race; just as the Greeks invented links by which to claim a divine ancestry for their ruling dynasties: or just as genealogists in later times, for the glorification of certain families, have traced up their descent to the Norman Conquest, or to the beginnings of the modern era. Going back, therefore, to the Exodus as the commencement or starting point of the history of Israel, we have to remark that this great epoch-making event is wrapped in a deep obscurity, which cannot be dissipated even by the most critical study of the surviving monuments and records. It was probably an event without a parallel, or otherwise unheard of, in which a mixed multitude (Exod. xii. 38; Numb. xi. 4) was fused into a nation, born in a day (Isaiah lxvi. 8); or it was a crisis in what was already a national life, which left an ineffaceable stamp upon the character and history of the Israelitish race. We may readily believe that the shores of the Red Sea were on that occasion the scene of incidents of a very unusual character, such as are sometimes spoken of as a special providence. But of one thing we may be perfectly certain, viz. that great, surprising, and eventful as these incidents may have been, they were not of that preternatural character which the Pentateuch ascribes to them. The principle, or hypothesis, on which we conduct this whole inquiry, is that nothing miraculous has ever occurred, whether in the secular or in the religious history of mankind. It may be that the fugitive and alarmed people did not, at the very time of the Exodus, understand the actual sequence of the events in which they took part, and may have seen in them the indication of an immediate divine interposition in their behalf. But more probably it was the poetical, mythical, and pragmatizing phantasy of succeeding generations which exalted the accompanying circumstances into the region of the marvellous. Unconsciously the fancy may have been stimulated by the desire to supply the place of actual knowledge, to gratify national vanity, to ennoble and render interesting events connected with the first appearance of Israel as a distinct people—events which may have been very commonplace in reality, or even humiliating, as one very ancient author * represents them to have been. Or, again, the mythicizing phantasy

* Manetho, 300 B.C.

may have been stimulated by the political intention of strengthening the bond of intertribal and national unity ; or yet more than all, by the felt necessity of supplying a historical foundation for that belief of a peculiar relation to God which had grown up of itself in the nation, and of which men of prophetic minds discerned the importance.   The few facts which lingered in the memory of the people were so moulded by popular fancy as to convey the idea that a divine power had interfered to rescue them from an alien and oppressive domination ; an idea which naturally, or rather necessarily, involved the associated idea that God had chosen them out of all the nations of the earth, and adopted them as a peculiar people, whom he meant, and, *ipso facto*, engaged to befriend above all others for the time to come.   This was an idea which might easily take root in the popular mind of Israel.

Of every youthful nation it has been said that it secretly cherishes the hope of being the chosen one to occupy the first place among the kingdoms of the future ; and we may suppose that the marvellous circumstances of the Exodus, in which the finger of God was seen, may have caused the springing up among the people of a hope of this kind, not secretly cherished but universally diffused and openly avowed, so as powerfully to influence the national fortunes.   It was an idea too which, from the combination in it of political and religious elements, was calculated to take a deep and tenacious hold of the mind, and to awaken an enthusiasm very different from the languid feeling which is all that a purely spiritual or religious idea usually excites.

A distinguished critic (Ewald) has said with characteristic dogmatism that " there are no myths in the Bible, the mythical element being heathenish or of heathenish tendency."   This dictum implies that there are no heathenish elements in the Bible, a position of a very disputable character, except for those who hold a theory of its inspiration more strict at least than that of its being " the literature of a divinely instructed people."   At the present day it is impossible to pretend that the records of the Old Testament are purely historical, or that a mythical element is altogether absent.   Recent archæological discoveries have demonstrated that some traditions, as *e.g.* those of the cosmogony and the flood, were originally common to Israel and other Semitic nations ; and the high probability is,

that the transformation which these have undergone in the Old
Testament was due to the ethical genius which developed itself
in Israel.   Other traditions, which were of purely Israelitish
origin, such as those connected with the Exodus and with
later events in Israelitish history, were probably the creation of
the people at large, recast by men of cultivated and prophetic
mind into a new form, stripped of whatever heathenish elements
they contained, and made the vehicle of the more advanced
moral and religious views, which had grown up in later times,
so as to recommend them to the more backward and conservative classes.   It is absurd to deny, in whatever sense, the
mythical character of the obviously unhistorical or preternatural
element of the records, merely because that element is shaped
so as to promote the moral and religious education of the
people.

In the sequel we shall have much to say respecting the
mythical process, but at this point we shall confine ourselves
to the observation that this process was an accompaniment,
not occasional only or adventitious, but under certain conditions constant and inseparable, of the course of religious
development in Israel.   That a mythical handling of history—
the charging it with elements of a supernatural and abnormal
character—was not an accidental or occasional literary exercise,
but permanent and inevitable under the circumstances of a people,
bent, as the Israelites were, on regarding their history as a
record of very special providences,—this is what we assert.
Even at the present day of scientific enlightenment, men of
highly cultivated minds, such as the Duke of Argyll, while sensible that things in general are governed according to strict law
and fixed order, yet explain the progress of civilization, and the
persistence of grand religious movements under apparently untoward conditions, by the hypothesis that the divine power
secretly impresses, when needed, a favourable direction upon
human affairs, by calling laws into operation which are beyond
the knowledge and the use of finite intelligence, or by what has
been called " directionism."   The fact of such complementary,
or epicyclical divine action, can, of course, not be demonstrated;
because, confessedly, nothing ever happens in open or perceptible contravention of the common law of the universe.   But the
reality of such action, as a permanent factor of human life, is
taken simply on trust by faith.   Is it, then, improbable that in

ancient Israel, when men had little or no idea of the uniform action of law, or laid little stress upon it, they should fly to the idea of divine intervention to explain all very uncommon, inscrutable occurrences, or marvellous turns in their national history—an intervention not exerted secretly, so as to elude sense and demonstration, but openly and palpably in the form of abrupt and manifest miracle?   The feeling or sentiment at work to suggest this idea was the same then as it is now—the feeling that God will interfere occasionally to keep the course of history upon the line of the divine purpose, which would otherwise suffer shipwreck ; to prevent hardships and injustices which would be inflicted under the rigorous and untempered sway of any law, however beneficent in its general operation—the feeling, in short, that *summum jus* may become *summa injuria.* And this feeling, we say, must have worked in Israel without intermission from generation to generation, so as to put its impress everywhere upon the records of their history.   It should also be remembered that the miraculous narratives of the sacred books, though they were no doubt literally understood by the masses of the people, especially as time went on, may not have been seriously meant by the authors.   The narratives may, in many cases, have been allegorical, concrete, or poetic representations either of spiritual experiences in the inner life of individuals, or of that secret action of the Supreme Power which the people of Israel believed to be constantly operating in their favour, and which the piously scientific imagination of such men as the Duke of Argyll believes to be statedly at work in human history.

We do not wish to be understood as asserting that, at each period or conjuncture of the religious development in Israel, individuals were prompted to invest it with a supernatural character by way of explaining it.   We conceive rather that at such periods religion became a great factor of thought, and that individuals who participated in the new religious experience and had risen, more or less consciously, to a higher stage of religious development, were prompted by the literary instinct to give expression to it " in psalms and hymns and spiritual songs."   The Book of Psalms does but preserve the echoes of various ages and stages of development, and hence the diverse spirit which it breathes.   But this was not all, for to such individuals their religious experience became the medium through which they viewed the present and the coming age, and they gave utterance to their view of both often in dithyrambic strains, whether of hope or of despair, as we find in the prophetic and apokalyptic books. And, finally, individuals were prompted by religious feeling to colour and revise in mythical dramatic form the traditions of the past, so as to make of these a vehicle of their thought and to find in them a prophecy or presentiment of the new ideas to which they had risen. It was thus that the devotional, prophetic, and historical literature of the Old Testament grew up; the past, the present, and the future were drawn together, and a certain analogy of faith was preserved in its pages. To the higher minds of Israel who held the common belief that the nation had been elect of God from its cradle it could not but appear to be a strange and perplexing fact, so far as this was perceived, that during the course of its history it had passed through many stages of ethical and religious development— from polytheistic to monotheistic worship—and had ascended from a very low to a comparatively high level of the religious life. And, to throw over this fact a thick but (as it has proved) not an impenetrable veil; to make the earlier stages an anticipation of the later; to efface the differences between them, and to help on the development, was the unconscious motive of the mythicizing process to which the records were subjected. This is the way that we account, for example, for the promises said to have been made to the fathers of the race, of which St. Paul long after made such account.

Old Testament history gives itself out for the history of an hundred generations. But we cannot suppose that it is merely a catena or an abbreviated summary of the myths that had survived of these ages. Legends there may have been, and no doubt were, of very ancient date which had undergone gradual changes as they passed from mouth to mouth. But in their extant or canonical revision, these myths, we conceive, were largely the work of a prophetic band, and were intended, more or less consciously, to conduce, under the attractive form and sanction of history, to moral instruction, to stir the religious pulse of the national life, and to be the means of popularizing the purer ideas which had dawned upon the higher minds of the people.

On the former of the two hypotheses, in regard to which

we said above that the preternatural character given to the Exodus might be accounted for, it is conceivable that the great leader of the people may have taken advantage of the emergency to promulgate, in the name of God, who was believed to have brought them out of the land of bondage with a high hand, the general principles or first outlines of that Code of Laws, moral and religious, civil and ceremonial, which was afterwards expanded by himself, and by a succession of prophetic men imbued with his spirit, who spoke and wrote in his name. If it be a fact, as there is no reason to doubt, that Moses was skilled in all the wisdom, esoteric and exoteric, of the Egyptians, there can be no difficulty in conjecturing the source from which he derived the code of rudimentary ethics which is laid down in the Decalogue. The scrolls and inscriptions which, in recent times, have been brought to light and deciphered, have demonstrated that long before the time of Moses the moral standard, theoretically at least, was very high in Egypt, as high indeed as that of the Decalogue. The great distinction of the Israelites—a very great one—was that their morality, even if it dated from their residence in Egypt, had the effect of soon refining and exalting their religious ideas, as was never the case in Egypt itself, where, curiously and inexplicably enough, a debased form of popular religion retained its place side by side with a high development, in some quarters or classes, of the moral sentiment. The great fame and reputation of the Hebrew legislator is sufficiently justified by the fact that he so clearly discerned the importance of ethical and religious principles as a means of giving stability to social organization ; that he took the highest results of the most ancient civilization which the world had seen, and laid them at the foundation of his nascent state; that he snatched the torch of human progress from hands which could bear it no further, and passed it on to those of a fresh and youthful race—of a race which he may have freshened and rejuvenated by this very stroke of high policy.

The literary and historic criticism, however, which has been brought to bear on this subject leaves little room to doubt, if it has not even demonstrated, that in its extant form the Mosaic law was the work of many men and many ages, being neither more nor less than a register of rites, observances, and ethical principles, which, as they became established in the moral consciousness and in the usages of the people, were naturally referred back to Moses himself as the source of their authority. No matter how naturally or how derivatively these elements of religion and those patriotic sentiments which differentiated Israel from the surrounding peoples were evolved, we can easily conceive that in an uncritical age, which received without suspicion the idea of supernatural action, they might be universally regarded as due to a special revelation, and that the higher and prophetic minds of the nation, divining their value from a political and religious point of view, might employ themselves in framing and moulding the history of their forefathers on that hypothesis. These were men who believed firmly in the close, personal, and discriminating super-intendence by Jehovah of all human, but especially of all Israelitish affairs, and also in the law of retribution, which, founded in the nature of things and in the universal principles of the divine government, the mythical phantasy delights, according to its wont, to picture to itself as an arrangement come to between God and man at a certain conjuncture of human affairs. It was imagined, and said, that such an arrangement or understanding, to which the name of a covenant was given, had been come to between God and Israel on Mount Sinai, and that the law there given amid thunder and lightning, as recorded in the Book of Exodus, was the summary of its terms and conditions.

The idea of retribution which could otherwise be expressed only in an abstract, and, to untutored minds, uninteresting, vague, and unintelligible form was thus touched with interest and translated into a form which was level and impressive. We may take it for granted that the idea of such a covenant binding both upon God and the people, and expressive of reciprocal obligations (even though the word may, as some critics maintain, be of late occurrence in Hebrew literature), must have existed in germ at least from the time that a distinctive law and the faith of a divine election became the spiritual possession of Israel. But it should be borne in mind that the covenant which was thus a creation of the mythical fancy would be felt to involve more than a legal compact between equals. In such a compact the arrangement is annulled if one of the contracting parties violates the conditions But the conception that God had entered into a covenant with Israel alone of all the nations of the earth would be regarded as a proof of His distinguishing favour for the people, whom He had thus singled out, prior to and independent of their fidelity to the terms of the covenant; of a purpose on His part to exalt the nation, which would not suffer itself to be defeated by any temporary aberrations and infidelities on the part of the people. Individuals or generations might on account of these suffer deprivation of the covenanted benefits, but the race would continue to be the object of divine favour, and if God should seem to withdraw His patronage for a time, He would visit the people again, renew His covenant with them, and restore them, as at the first He had adopted them, without merit or desert on their part, and grant them an unconditional amnesty for all past defections. Thus, it is said, "I will make a full end of all the nations whither I have driven thee, but I will not make a full end of thee" (Jer. xlvi. 28); "I will return and have compassion on thee" (Jer. xii. 15). And therefore it is that the covenant is so often spoken of as "everlasting," as a covenant which might be broken on the part of the people, but would still be valid on the part of God (Isa. xxiv. 5; Deut. vii. 9; 2 Sam. xxiii. 5, vii. 14, 15; Ps. lxxxix. 30-34). This was a collateral view of the covenant which in times of national degeneracy and backsliding would rise into prominence and have very important bearing, by sustaining the hopes of the better remnant of the people, though, as we shall yet see, it might also have an evil and morally relaxing effect on the commonalty.

Whether, now, this idea of a divine election and a covenant relation arose at the time of the Exodus, or was a subsequent creation of the mythicizing fancy, in either case it taught the people to count upon a high degree of national prosperity, and to expect that he who had brought them out of Egypt had a great future in store for them, towards which he would carry them triumphantly through every obstacle. The hope thus excited of a grand destiny would, without doubt, impart increased strength to that tenacity, endurance, and elasticity which have in all ages distinguished the people, would place them for many ages on a footing of equality with circumjacent tribes, more numerous, it may be, than themselves, and better skilled in the arts of peace and war; would enable them to recover again by heroic effort from disasters and reverses

apparently crushing and overwhelming, and not only to hold
their own, upon the whole, when contending with varied
fortune with their foes, but even to win for a brief period
for their narrow territory an almost imperial extension. But
this period of comparative prosperity was brought to an end;
this joyous outlook received a rude shock, first from the disruption of the tribes into two hostile sections, and afterwards
from the appearance on the political stage of the gigantic and
better organized monarchies of the East and West, by which
the nation was successively assailed and brought into subjection. Against these overwhelming odds its religious enthusiasm
was of small avail, and its political condition became one
of "chronic dependence" upon foreign powers. At the
most, it could only exchange masters, and by the very
necessity of the case, by the narrowness of its geographical
limits, it was condemned to occupy not merely a subordinate,
but a humiliating position among the nations.

During the period when this change was taking place, the
people could not but come to perceive that, except at rare
and shortlived intervals, their fortunes had falsified the expectations which seemed to be legitimately founded on their
covenant relation to God, and that, to all human appearance,
there was little to presage a better destiny in the future.
The "boundless hopes" on which they had "fed" gave way
to a more or less settled feeling of disappointment and despondency, and the alternative was, as it were, forced upon
them, either of abandoning the thought of being a peculiar
people and losing faith in the God of their fathers, or of
throwing themselves with the whole force and weight of their
souls on the hope of a better time to come, in which God
would do something by way of fulfilling His engagements,
and indemnifying them for the miserable realities of the past
and present. Only in the form of such a hope could their
faith in God survive. He had, as they firmly believed, given
them ground to rely upon His unfailing patronage and pro-
tection, and unless a revival of the national fortunes was in
store for them, their faith in Him would seem to be a mere
delusion. The alternative thus presented must have amounted
to what may be called a prolonged crisis in the national life.
The people could hardly but feel that they stood at the parting
of the ways, and the choice lay between this and that.

But men do not easily or with a light heart abandon a great hope, and, least of all, such a race of men as the Jews in all ages have proved themselves to be. And hence it came that, for the better part of the nation, or for the select spirits in it, the more tragic their present circumstances, the more tenacious did they become of their confidence in the ultimate issue. The feeling of disappointment in the present and the past turned to aspiration for the future, to the hope of a golden age to come, into which they threw their whole energy, and, in despair of all self-help, it seemed to them as if it was only by the manifestation of a divine power like that or greater than that which displayed itself at the Red Sea, that they could be delivered from the new bondage and oppression worse than that of Egypt, and that the faithfulness of God to His people could be and would be demonstrated. This faith is the very spirit of prophecy, the undertone which runs through it all and is often expressed, as in Micah vii. 15, "According to the days of thy coming out of Egypt will I show unto him marvellous things." Comp. Jer. xvi. 14, 15 ; Isa. xliii. 18, 19. But this faith, while it sustained the fainting heart of Israel, also generated or confirmed a mis-direction of the religious sentiment which we shall yet have occasion to explain.

It was in this period of crisis and suspense, of mingled despondency and aspiration, that the line of canonical prophets appeared—a band of men, the most remarkable for services rendered to the development of the religious idea of which history makes mention, or with which any nation, ancient or modern, has been favoured. We can, indeed, only contemplate the prophetic line with feelings of unmixed astonishment. So far as the discovery or rectification of religious truth is concerned, we must confess that the phenomena of the prophetic era seem to us to be even more marvellous than those of the evangelical era. Great as the shortcomings of the prophets may have been, they laid the ground for the final step in the development of religious thought, and prepared the way for Jesus, in a much deeper sense, than John the Baptist can be said to have done. Indeed, it is less surprising that Jesus should have "fulfilled" the prophets than that the prophets themselves should have arisen in ancient Israel and prepared his way. He did but put the finishing touch to the work of his predecessors in the prophetic office ; and this, though it was an immense advance upon their thought, was yet, as we shall see, not wholly beyond comprehension.

By way of general characterization we may say that the prophet of Israel was also a poet, but he was more than a poet. The range of his vision took in other spheres besides that which has been claimed for the poet, whose eye " glances from heaven to earth, from earth to heaven." He looked behind and before, to the past and to the coming age. He stood in full sympathy with those feelings of veneration with which the vague traditions of the olden time were regarded by the uncritical and unlettered age, yet he coloured and moulded these so as to make of them a vehicle and a sanction to his own higher religious ideas, transforming, yet more or less preserving, the traditions in their general outline. This was a treatment which he applied to the Mosaic and the pre-Mosaic tradition. The future again was for him an empty space, which, with a free hand, he furnished with forms and images, fitted to awaken and direct the aspirations of his people toward a better state of things. It was for this end that he thought out the grandly vague conception of a Messiah, and of a kingdom of God yet to come.

Modern criticism has gone far to raise a presumption that the Old Testament was in the main the product of what is called the prophetic age of Israel——the age in which this nation " suddenly blazed out into a splendour of productive genius, of which its previous history gave but faint promise, and of which its subsequent history showed but little trace." (See Address on *Progress*, by A. J. Balfour.) There is no reason to doubt that many of the books which compose the volume are the works of the great men of that age whose names they bear. But, in addition to these, the historical books which, so to speak, form the connecting links of the whole volume, probably received their canonical form from priest-prophetic hands. Underlying these historical books there were, we imagine, chronicles of a more or less legendary character, to which reference is occasionally made, as, *e.g.* 1 Kings xiv. 18, 2 Chron. ix. 29. In other words, there were myths below the canonical myth, myths frequently revised and much overlaid, moulded and recast many times by the religious spirit which was expanding and growing apace, fed and nurtured by the very history which it was employed in creating. Indeed, if we think of it, we may see that it could hardly have been otherwise. Perhaps the most conspicuous and remarkable feature of the prophetic books is the evidence they contain, that the authors, one and all, were possessed with the deep conviction that they occupied a platform of religious thought far above that of the great mass of their countrymen, and that, compared with their own thought, the notions and beliefs current among the people were but as the " chaff to the wheat." Now, what could be done by men of their ardent temperament but to recommend their own higher views to the unenlightened masses, in the only, or, at least, in the most effectual way open to them, viz. by moulding anew the ancient legends, by inlaying these with hints and foreshadowings of their own more advanced ideas, introducing into the bare chronicle a pragmatism which was all their own, using the legends as a vehicle for impressing upon the minds of the people the higher principles of religion, so gaining for these a share or partnership in that pious reverence with which the people regarded their ancient literature. A learned class would have little difficulty in carrying out such a process unchallenged among a simple and illiterate people, and we regard it as the only effectual means of accomplishing their design of educating the people ; because the attempt, by means of direct or polemical teaching to eradicate superstitions which had been engrained in the popular mind by long inheritance and tradition, must have seemed to be the most hopeless of all tasks. The better and more promising method for this purpose was to drop seeds of thought in favourable but unsuspected situations, and leave them to germinate silently and unobserved in men's minds. Not to dwell upon this point, and to take but two examples of what we are here saying, it seems to us that we may regard as such a seed of retrospective thought the well known passage (Gen. i. 26), " And God said, Let us make man in our image, after our likeness," words suggestive of ideas eminently counter to the polytheism current in the prophetic age. The polytheist knew nothing of an archetypal beauty and goodness, and therefore fashioned his gods after his own image. Whereas the monotheist conceived of God as the embodiment of his own highest idea, and therefore rose to the thought that God had created man akin to Himself. Another example of the same kind may be seen in Gen. xii. 3, "In thee (Abraham) shall all families of the earth be blessed," words not obviously in harmony with the idea of divine favouritism of which the ruder masses of the people believed themselves to be the objects, but eminently suggestive of a truly prophetic idea, (Ps. lxxii. 19, Isa. lx. 3, and Isa. xlix. 6) "And the Lord said, It is a light thing, that thou shouldst be my servant, to raise up the tribes of Jacob, and to restore the preserved of Israel : I will also give thee for a light to the Gentiles, that thou mayst be my salvation unto the end of the earth." Such progressive manipulation of chronicle and legend, under which the actual events of past ages were more and more lost sight of, was, we say, the most likely means of training the people to that purer faith to which the select portion of the people had risen by a more or less sudden bound, at a great crisis in the national history, to which we shall yet have occasion to advert. The consciousness of a higher religious standing, which is so conspicuous in the prophetic books, was, we imagine, rendered all the more acute, unacquiescent, and intolerant towards the older forms of Hebrew worship, by the comparative suddenness with which, in vivid contrast to these, it "blazed up" in the prophetic mind. The prophet was a man who stood in the van of the religious movement. He gave literary expression to his advanced views in the form of psalm, or prophecy, or apokalypse, and he also sought to gain over the lagging masses of the people by such a reconstruction or redaction of the current legends and traditions as would bring these into accordance with his own higher views, so as to make of them an instrument of popular education and religious culture. We shall yet have occasion to observe that the last and greatest of the prophets (for it is in that light that we regard Jesus) did not make use of any such instrumentality for the education of his disciples. On the contrary he, very emphatically, discarded the employment of it ; confident in the power of his doctrine to reach the hearts of men, he declined to seek any basis for it in the revered past. In the calm certitude of his conviction he even set the authority of the past at defiance, as may be seen in Matth. v.

But this observation does not shake our belief that the early legends, vague but time honoured, were adapted to moral and monotheistic purposes by prophetic men ; and it is by not taking into account the probability of such prophetic redaction that an ingenious theologian like Dr. Matheson can persist in regarding these legends of the pre-Mosaic time as historical authorities, and draw from them the inference that the spirit of the Hebrew people was more large and charitable (*i.e.* univer-salistic in tendency) before the law was given than it afterwards became.   He finds an evidence of this especially in the notices of Abraham and the patriarchs in the book of Genesis, those times of the "promises" of which St. Paul in his polemic against the Jews has made such ingenious use.   But this inference involves such a reversal of the course of historical evolution, that we have no alternative but to regard the data from which it is drawn as introduced into the early history by prophetic redactors of a later age, who had a fore-glimpse—as we know that Jeremiah in especial had (Jer. xxxi. 31)—of the coming collapse of the Mosaic system, and of the rise of a more spiritual system, the establishment of a new and better covenant.

The literary effectiveness of the prophetic band and their originality of style was the least of it.   The marvel in regard to them is their absolute and vivid conviction of the monothe-istic idea ; their deep insight into the principles of the divine government, by which the triumph of right was secured, and into the nature of the service which God requires, with their passionate zeal for national regeneration.   They were conscious that on such subjects they were charged with a momentous message to their countrymen, which burned as a fire within them, or lay as a burden upon their souls.   It was with them as afterwards with St. Paul, when he said, "Woe is me, if I preach not the Gospel."   And their grand concern was to disburden their souls and to deliver the message with effect. They were distinguished not only by their deep spiritual insight, but also by this, that they made no distinction between esoteric and exoteric doctrine, but entered boldly and hopefully into a dangerous conflict with the superstitions of the great mass of their countrymen, and at length achieved their purpose so far as to make their monotheistic view a common or national possession.

For this end they did not rely upon mere reasoning and dialectic, though of these they had an overpowering command. They resorted to the device of clothing their own highest thoughts with divine authority, and compelling attention to their words by reporting them as the words of God Himself, and by constantly prefacing them with the formula, "Thus saith the Lord." This formula they used, we may be sure, in perfect good faith, though it may be difficult for us to conceive how such a thing was possible. Just as orthodox Christians who are conversant with the idea of supernatural grace, and believe themselves to be the subjects of it, yet do not profess to distinguish between the workings of their own minds and the working of the Spirit of God in them ; so the prophets of Israel may have identified their own highest thought with divine inspiration, and have given out the one for the other. The reiteration of that formula by men of such manifest sincerity, whose transcendent genius enabled them to sustain a high level of thought and language worthy of their elevated theme, gained for their teaching the credit of coming as a message direct from God Himself. This effect is probably to be seen in the popular usage (reprehended by Jeremiah xxiii. 33-38) of speaking of the prophet's burden as if it had been a burden on the mind of God.

The pictures which the prophets drew of a splendid future form what are called the Messianic prophecies. They sought to revive the national spirit by producing in more splendid and spiritual form the hopes that were struggling and floating vaguely in the popular mind. It is only, indeed, from the remains of their writings which have been preserved in the Old Testament, that we can infer the existence and nature of such feelings. We believe that they stood in somewhat the same relation of action and reaction to the popular sentiment of Israel, as we shall yet find that St. Paul and his coadjutors did to the legendary tradition of the Christian church. Their writings are evidently addressed as to people familiar with the feelings which they express, and appeal to sentiments which were current, and at the most needed to be spiritualized. They entered deeply into the national aspirations, as well as into the national feelings of impatience, disappointment, and chagrin. The aspiration with which the people at large turned to the future was, as we may well believe, in the first place a patriotic, popular, and only semi-religious sentiment, which did not originate in the prophetic mind, but was taken up and adopted by the prophets, partly, if we cannot say wholly, in the interest

of the monotheistic faith, and of the higher morality which
were painfully and slowly evolving themselves in prophetic
circles, and perhaps among the people at large, under the
natural growth of thought and under the pressure of calamity
and disappointed ambition. It is not improbable that political
and dynastic interests may also have mingled in the prophetic
mind with these higher objects. Just as the great Roman poet
manipulated and embellished the Latin legends for the purpose
of glorifying the Julian family, as a means of securing for it
the veneration of the people, and contributing to the stability
of the imperial régime, so there is reason to suppose that men
of a prophetic spirit revised the legend of Israel, more or less
unconsciously, for a purpose still more world-historical.

While in all probability the people generally were inclined
to regard their election as an unconditional act of divine
partiality, and could not understand or explain to themselves
the apparent hesitancy and vacillation of the divine purpose,
the prophets gave emphasis to the idea that the law given on
Mount Sinai was, as we have already said, the summary of the
conditions by which the people might secure a fulfilment on
God's part of His covenant purpose (Exod. xix. 5, 6). While
the people in general might regard the calamities of the time
as the natural effect of the overwhelming forces which precipitated themselves upon their small but devoted country, the prophets, on the other hand, in view of the degeneracy of the nation,
made use of these calamities to awaken the moral sensitiveness
of the people, and traced them to that national defection from
the terms of the covenant of which they were partly the cause
as well as the effect. They proclaimed that the calamities
under which the people groaned had been brought upon themselves by their neglect of the covenant obligations ; and that
so far from giving ground to suppose that God had forgotten
the covenant, these calamities were rather a proof of the
contrary, viz. of His faithfulness to its terms. This is an idea
which is specially worked out and insisted on in the last book
of the Pentateuch, the work of a prophetic hand ; besides being
everywhere given expression to in the books which are named
after the prophets.

At the same time, the idea of a covenanted relation between
God and a single people, to the exclusion of all others, lent
an element of caprice and partiality to the Jewish conception

of the divine Being, from which even the prophets could not
entirely rid themselves, and which continued, as will yet be
seen, to act prejudicially upon their religious thought and
sentiment. The God who could show such favouritism could
also be thought capable of deviations from strict equity in
dealing with the favoured people and in carrying out the
stipulations of the covenant. In times of national distress
and calamity the prophets laid the blame in general upon the
people as not having fulfilled their part of the contract. But
there were times and moods in which the prophets inclined
to regard the miseries of the people as a proof that God
Himself was forgetful of His promises and unmindful of His
covenant obligations, and to cast blame upon Him, though in
a deprecating and apologetic way. A tendency in this direction often betrays itself in the Old Testament, but perhaps
nowhere so clearly as in Psalm xliv., which, with all its tender
deference, is little else than an argument with God to keep
Him steadfast to His promises. " All this (evil) is come upon
us ; yet have we not forgotten thee, neither have we dealt
falsely in thy covenant" (v. 17) ; "Awake, why sleepest thou,
O Lord? Arise, cast us not off for ever" (v. 23). The orthodox commentator can explain away this view of the psalm,
but for us the question is "What was the feeling of the
Psalmist himself, and what idea did it convey to his contemporaries?" and of this there can be no doubt. It would
be easy to show that this idea of divine favouritism has not
been altogether banished even from the mind of Christendom :
that our devotions are apt to degenerate into a suit to hold
God to His engagements, and that this is an all but inevitable
result when God's relation to us is conceived of as removed
from a natural to a supernatural basis. But this is a subject
which does not concern us here.

If not absolutely free from anthropomorphic views of God,
the prophets were at least emancipated from the coarser forms
of these views. They entered into a conflict with the idolatrous, polytheistic worship of the people, which could not
but be very protracted, as we know it was, because of its
peculiarly difficult and perplexing nature. It would, for example, be no easy matter for the prophets to demonstrate the
connection of the sufferings and calamities of the people with
their defection from the worship of Jehovah, the one true and

national God.   For the better and more enlightened portion of
the people the national disasters might stimulate the development of religious thought and come in aid of the prophetic
message.   But in all religious and political controversies, one
and the same condition of things can be plausibly explained
by each of the opposing parties in support of its own position.
And this would certainly be the case here.   There may, for
reasons easy to be conceived, be no very distinct indication in
the prophetic writings of the fact, yet there can be little
doubt that many false teachers might and did seek to impress
the people with quite another view, viz., that these calamities
were visited upon them because of the attempts made to put
down polytheistic worship, and to deprive the ancient gods
of the honours which they had from time immemorial enjoyed.
To the ignorant and superstitious masses this view would
commend itself, and it could be set aside, not by mere
reasoning against polytheism and idolatry, of which there are
splendid examples in the prophetic books, but only by the
slow operation of the greater fervour and intensity of devotion
which were distinguishing characteristics of the prophetic
band.

To justify the dealings of God with His people, and to
show that these dealings were not at variance with the terms
of the covenant, the prophets drew vivid and probably not
exaggerated pictures of national sinfulness and depravity.
The people had, it is true, the appearance of being very
religious.   There was no end to the multitude of their sacrificial and other outward services (Isa. i. 11).   There was no
cessation of these from the one end of the year to the other
(Ps. l. 8).   But this did not satisfy the prophetic mind nor
blunt the edge of prophetic invective, and it is easy to see
the reason.   In the first place, the predilection or liking of
the people for ritual and ceremonial betrayed them into acts
of idolatry, i.e., the worship of other gods besides Jehovah.
The worship paid to Jehovah was distinguished from that
paid to the gods of the nations, not so much by its forms
as by its moral character and requirements. The similarity
between them in point of form was apt in the case of the
sensuous and unthinking multitude to put out of sight the
difference in point of spirit, and to be a standing temptation
to the people, if not to apostatize from the worship of Jehovah,

at least to join in the worship of other gods; and this, in spite of, and perhaps even by reason of the impurities and sensuous excitement which were associated with the strange forms of worship. It is easy to see that such latitudinarianism of practice would tend, not only to degrade their idea of divine holiness, and to prevent the monotheistic principle, for which the prophets contended, from coming to full expression and universal recognition, but also to be an obstruction to the moral education and improvement of the people. Nay, more, even when the object of worship was the God of Israel the prophets had still occasion to be dissatisfied, and to inveigh against the people generally, because the latter gave all but exclusive attention to the outward form, and were oblivious of the inner and moral side of religion, trusting that they would atone for their moral deficiencies and conciliate the favour of God by the exactness and diligence of their ritual service.

The polemic which the prophets waged against confounding worship with religion, and against the merging of piety in the practice of form and ceremony, is of constant recurrence in their writings. They do not, indeed, denounce or condemn ritual in the abstract, but only the over-estimation in which it was held as a means of pleasing God, and the disproportioned attention which was devoted to it, to the comparative neglect of morality and practical religion. One of them (Jer. vii. 22) went so far, in depreciating the value of the outward services, as to declare in unambiguous language that such services had never been enjoined by divine authority. An unrecorded tradition to this effect may have been known to Jeremiah, or, perhaps, he may have been cognizant of the principle to which Macaulay (ii. 616) gives expression where he says, "A really limited monarchy cannot long exist in a society which regards monarchy as something (specially) divine." So regarded, monarchy tends to become unlimited or despotic. Even so Jeremiah may have perceived that the undue value attached to outward rites was in part, at least, the necessary conse-quence of regarding them as a divine appointment; and with the view of correcting the popular tendency in this direction, he may, in the power and logic of the prophetic spirit, have questioned the truth of the current tradition.

Isaiah and Amos speak of the ritual services in a tone bordering on contempt, as if they were all but useless and hateful in the sight of God, when disjoined from the practice of justice, mercy, and humanity, or offered in room of these. (See Isa. i. 13-15 and parallel passages.) It is hardly to be conceived that such language could have been used had the Levitical law in its canonical form been in existence ; and we are led to suppose, either that the prophets knew by a tradition still extant that the Law or Book proper of the covenant was all or nearly all contained in the Decalogue ; or that by deep spiritual insight they had discerned that moral duties were all that were essential to religion and distinctive of Jehovism ; that these possessed a paramount value, whereof no hint is given in the Levitical code, which draws no distinction between moral and ritual requirements, but places both as alike binding under the same directly divine sanction. The fact that the Decalogue is silent in regard to cultus is significant, and gives countenance to the conjecture that the cultus which in process of time was, as we shall yet see, elaborated as " a shield " to protect the religion of Israel from the inroads of heathenism, was in early times common to Israelitish and other forms of worship, and therefore formed a link of connection between them which was a source of danger to the purer religion. There seems to be little doubt indeed that the outward technical forms in which the religious principle expressed itself, were observed by Israelites and other peoples very much in common. They were, in truth, the natural forms which had grown up and taken shape in ages antecedent to the patriarchal and Mosaic era. And the prophetic idea was that these forms were subordinate to the practice of justice and morality ; that the law which was binding on man had nothing to do with cultus, and that it was only by being and doing good that man could please God. This definition of the mental attitude of the prophets towards ritual may be overdrawn, but we cannot read their writings without arriving at the conclusion that it comes near to the truth. Tried by the prophetic feeling, the Israelites were seen to fall far short of their covenant obligations, notwithstanding their great religiosity ; and from the prophetic point of view, the national calamities, so far from discrediting the terms of the covenant, were much rather confirmatory of them.*

* Much has been written on the relations which subsisted between the priesthood and the prophetic line. It has been made out that at many of

As popularly conceived, the relation between God and the people had originated in an act of arbitrary election, or as by the preference of a parent for a favourite child. The adoption and the privileges connected with it were supposed to remain in force irrespective of conditions ; or if not quite that, yet the conditional nature of the relation was apt to be left out of sight. The prophets were the *élite* of the people, the first to conceive of this relation as depending for its continuance, or for its renewal when interrupted, on the fulfilment of moral conditions, of which, as already said, the law was the summary. At least they were the first to give prominence to this idea, and to impress it on the minds of the people. They were the men who had discovered the great natural law, admitting of none but apparent exceptions, according to which the fortunes of men in the long run correspond to their character and behaviour, and national sins entail, sooner or later, national retribution. They were as much persuaded as the rest of their countrymen that God had entered into covenant with Israel, and even that its election had conferred upon it a character of indelible holiness ; but they were not blind to the fact that the covenant had not set aside in its favour that principle of the divine government. They perceived that this principle was still in operation under the covenant, and even with greater stringency and certainty of incidence than in the case of the less highly favoured uncovenanted peoples.

This note was powerfully struck, and with great artistic effect and impressiveness by Amos, the first of the canonical prophets, in his two opening chapters. After denouncing judgments by the mouth of God, upon the surrounding nations,

its critical moments, the history of Israel turned upon the conflict between them. It could hardly but be that the relations should often be hostile between the prophets who were the guardians of religion in its spiritual aspect, and the priests who were the guardians of its organization and its external forms and ordinances. It may be said in general that the priest-hood being hereditary and well organized, and having the guardianship of the outward forms as its distinctive function, represented the conservative or aristocratic party in the State ; while the prophetic line, having the spiritual interests of religion under its care, and being without organization, was desultory and occasional in its action, and represented the reforming and democratic party. But the details of the conflict as between parties are obscure, and in the text we speak simply of the conflict between principles.

north, east, south, and west of the Holy Land, he concludes by launching denunciations, in the same words, against Israel and Judah, as if God made no distinction between them and their neighbours, but treated all alike. Then, in the third chapter, as if to explain this—to the people strange and surprising—procedure, the prophet represents God as saying to them, "You only have I known of all the families of the earth; *therefore* I will punish you for all your iniquities"—"punish you," that is to say, not merely in spite of, but by reason of my election of you. And the note thus struck keeps sounding more or less distinctly through all the subsequent prophetic literature. Indeed in one passage, Ezek. xx. 37, it is clearly intimated that a position of peculiar exposure to penal visitation was in the bond of the covenant, involved in its provisions. The thought to which Amos had risen was this, that God had chosen the people not out of mere unmeaning partiality and caprice, but to train them to His service and make of them a holy nation; that were He to allow them to continue in sin with impunity, or to "wink" at their iniquity, as He is elsewhere said to have done with respect to the Gentiles (Acts xvii. 30; xiv. 16), His purpose in their election would have been frustrated. It was necessary they should be made to understand that the "august principle of the moral government of the world," by which sin and suffering are indissolubly united, was not to be set aside or relaxed in their favour, because they were a chosen people; but that, on the contrary, it would come out into more stringent operation in their case than in that of the less favoured nations, who knew not God, nor were known of Him.

The inference from such a view was, that Israel could be "redeemed out of all its troubles," and prosperity and independence restored to it only as a sequel to the general revival of religion and to the truly national observance of the terms of the covenant. While the national life as a whole fell far below the prophetic standard, there was a remnant of the people which, not content with the observance of the merely outward forms of religion, strove to comply with its higher requirements as set forth by the prophets. Sometimes the prophets indulge the hope that the existence of such a remnant would in some way serve for the salvation of the nation at large. This cherished hope was, as will yet be seen, of deep importance for the development of Jewish and of Christian thought, and may easily be accounted for. The idea which had grown up among the people that a covenanted relation subsisted between God and the nation, naturally implied or suggested a certain solidarity of interest, spiritual as well as temporal, between the individuals composing the nation ; a solidarity which ought to be suggested indeed by many of the common facts and experiences of social life, but which might have escaped notice until it was made prominent by the idea of the national covenant.

At other times the prophets express the feeling that salvation is not to be expected in such a vicarious way, and can be found only by means of a grand act of national repentance. But then the general moral elevation of the people, which seemed to be the necessary condition of such a result, was more than could be looked for. No elements were discernible in the great mass of the people to give the promise of better days. The situation outwardly and inwardly was too desperate ; corruption too deep-seated and wide-spread ; the hardness of the people's heart presented an insuperable obstacle. The feeling that such was the case is well reflected in the canonical histories of the people, in the compilation of which it is easy to see that the prophetic pragmatism was at work, to make it appear that the outward and political condition of the people was in close uniform correspondence with their moral state. The defections and relapses of the people are represented as being so frequent, their efforts at reformation so short-lived and resultless, that the prophets might well despair of producing the desired effect upon their minds, and be content if only there could be kept alive in themselves and in their country-men the hope and prospect of a time, yet distant, in which " righteousness and peace should kiss each other " ; and " the mountain of the Lord's house should be established in the top of the mountains." This consummation, however devoutly to be wished, was reserved for the " latter days."

Through all the prophetic writings there also runs the idea that the high destiny, which as the covenanted people they had in prospect, would be achieved not by human power, but by some happy catastrophe, by some great act or manifestation of divine power. This, we say, was the prevailing expectation, though at certain conjunctures even the prophets, in their impatience for the event, seem to have imagined that it was on the eve of accomplishment by human and even by non-Israelitish hands (Isa. xliv. 28, xlv. 1). But, in general, the hopelessness of any reforming movement from within, and the visible fruitlessness of their own ministrations caused the prophets to fall in with the popular expectation of some great divine event, which would give a new turn to the national history, and bring to pass a state of things in which righteousness should flourish, and the chosen people receive the promises. The hope of Israel, as it finds expression in the prophetic writings, is wavering, fluid, and variable, not to say contradictory. And in certain of these writings the great consummation is placed in some indefinite, not clearly explained connection with the advent of a Messiah, or anointed messenger of God, by whom it is to be effected or ushered in. Presumably, this messenger was to be a member of the royal line of David—the man according to God's own heart—to whom, as the chief instrument of the divine purpose, prophets and psalmists united in directing the hopes of Israel. Of this special form of the expectation we may say that it was the natural if not the inevitable sequel of the more general form. For, as the great dramatist says, "Such tricks hath strong imagination, That if it would but apprehend some joy, It comprehends some Bringer of that joy." It sees in some personal agency the possible removal of every obstacle. But, no matter in what form the event presents itself to the prophetic mind, the prevailing feeling is that the time for it is yet distant; unknown changes must intervene, exhausting to patience; the prophets' vision cannot penetrate the obscurity in which it is folded, it is for him an object of faith founded on God's past dealings with His people. There are no present signs of its approach, it is reserved for "the dim and distant future," and the cry, "How long, O Lord, how long," is wrung from the souls of the most hopeful.

In respect of the prolonged tension of feeling and of expectation here depicted the reader should beware of judging of its historical probability by applying to it the lines of the present. There is a time for everything, and the time for the growth of such a feeling is past. The conditions for it, as for much else that was once a living reality, are no longer in existence. This caveat need not be repeated, but it should be observed throughout this discussion, in which every step is explained by keeping in view the conditions which led to it.

There are few things more remarkable in history than the development of religious thought in Israel. Like other people, and fully as much as other people, the Israelites seem to have experienced great difficulty in realizing to themselves the existence and action of a divine Being, without organs, without shape or form. This ineptitude or incapacity does not, it is true, explain the origin of idolatry and of image worship, but it goes far to explain the tenacious hold which these had upon the people, even after the spiritual idea had dawned upon the higher minds among them. The prophetic line, and those among the people whom it represented, were those who rose above that debasing superstition, or, let us say, above that low level of religion. They regarded God as an object of purely spiritual worship. But it must have been, even for them, no easy matter to sustain themselves at that elevation.

And, however, we may account for it, whether as a makeshift in that difficulty, as an object for the soul to rest upon in its moments of devotion, or to meet that craving for a great deliverer from their national calamities, which their covenanted relation seemed to warrant, there grew up among them the conception of a Being akin to the invisible God, fit agent and minister of the unseen Power, whose image, more or less human in its features, they could behold with the inner eye of the imagination, but which, from dread of a relapse into idolatry, they did not dare to represent in material form. No longer to be satisfied with material representations in human form of the invisible object of their worship, but not yet able to rise to the pure idea, they had recourse to the intermediate thought of a God-like Being in human form, a divine man, round whom their imagination could play. This shadowy Being they called by various names, as Son of God, or as Anointed of God; not without a hope that in some hour of supreme need he might yet be revealed outwardly to mortal sense as a Messiah, as a Priest of more than human order, or as a mighty prophet like Moses, in the person of a member of the royal line of David. Some such Being, whom the feebleness or grossness of the human faculties rendered a necessity of thought, and who might be regarded as in some sense an integer of the divine nature, looms indistinctly in vague perspective in many passages of the Old Testament. For, not to speak of the Book of Daniel, which has yet to be considered, we may see the evidences and traces of such an idea in Isaiah ix.; and in Psalms ii., xlv., and cx., etc. Mr. Arnold's attempt (*Literature and Dogma*, p. 113) to break down the force of many of these passages by representing them as mistranslations of the original, is of very doubtful success. This is, for example, very evident in what he says of the last of these passages, "The Lord said unto my Lord, Sit thou at my right hand." The seat on the right hand of God manifestly implies a participation in His dignity, as in the case of the Lamb, Rev. xxii. 1, 3. The idea to which we are referring crops up in enigmatic language more frequently perhaps in the Psalms than elsewhere, because these marvellous utterances of devotion contain gleams of obscure thoughts which flashed into the minds of the singers in moments of meditation and rapture, but did not admit of being expressed, except in the indistinct language proper to emotion. The mysterious character which this prophetic idea imparted to many passages in the Old Testament produced a puzzling effect upon many who searched the Scriptures in a later age. We can see an indication of this fact in the tradition (Matth. xxii. 42 etc.) which represents Jesus as making use of the words in Ps. cx. to puzzle his Jewish critics : " How then doth David in spirit call him Lord, saying, The Lord said unto my Lord, Sit thou on my right hand. . . . If David then call him Lord, how is he his son? And no man was able to answer him a word."

There is another indication of the same thing in the narrative of Philip's meeting with the Ethiopian eunuch, Acts viii. 26-34. The question of the latter, " Of whom speaketh the prophet this? of himself or of some other man?" indicates a bewilderment of which many must have been conscious in reading the prophetic writings. Though not formulated anywhere in these writings, and though expressed in vague protean forms, the conception of this mysterious Being seems to have had a hold upon the Jewish imagination in later times, till in the minds of the disciples of Jesus it shot into distinct embodiment in the person of the risen Christ, and facilitated the development of the Christological dogma. For us it helps to explain the curious phenomenon that zealous monotheists, such as were the Jewish Christians, with St. Paul among the rest, could of a sudden learn to regard Jesus as a son of God, partaker of the divine nature.

If, as now said, the mysterious height to which the Messianic prophecies sometimes rise helps us to understand how the early Jewish Christians could clothe the risen Christ with divine attributes, it is more difficult to understand how the prophets themselves with their decided monotheism could entertain the notion of such a being, or what they really meant by it. The probability is that it grew out of the idea of the divine election of the people. Possessed by this idea the prophets could not fail to draw out its implications and to touch it to highest issues. The hopes of national greatness to which this election gave rise were boundless, and in the view of the national history and of the depressing circumstances which seemed to stand in the way of the realization of these hopes, the prophets might feel that these could be realized only under the leadership of a member of the royal family endowed with supernatural powers, or by the descent of God Himself in human form to conduct the nation to the predestined summit. To the exalted patriotic imagination of the prophets this might seem to be the idea to which the election pointed, and in moments of enthusiastic vision they might pen the mysterious words; for it has always seemed to us that many of the most splendid passages of their books, abrupt and unconnected with the context as they often are, were the utterances of momentary feeling on the heights of enraptured thought, of sudden risings out of the general despondency, or of guesses of the modes in which God would yet fulfil the engagements under which He had come at Mount Sinai.

Before quitting this subject we may observe that the singular feature of prophetic literature to which we have now adverted may perhaps be traced ultimately to a source more remote than the difficulty common to men of forming a spiritual conception of the unseen Power or than the situation created for the Israelites by their election. The records of primitive civilizations have made us acquainted with the fact that in the early ages of the world kings or chief magistrates of the State, besides being commonly regarded as priests or intercessors between God and man, were also "revered as themselves gods, able to bestow on their subjects and worshippers blessings which are commonly supposed to be beyond the reach of men. . . . The notion of a man-God, or of a human being endowed with divine and supernatural powers, belongs to that early period of religious history in which God and man are still viewed as beings of much the same order, and before they are divided by the impassable gulf which later thought opens up between them " (Frazer's *Golden Bough*). In ancient Egypt, and the East generally, the title of king seemed to imply divinity.

With this fact in view, we say it is not impossible that the idea of a mysterious personage in whom human and divine attributes were confusedly blended may have come down as a dying echo from the dim and distant past, and been caught up by men of prophetic mind to shadow forth their conception of the great Deliverer whom Israel's evil days seemed to call for. It is not an unreasonable conjecture that in the devotional and liturgical literature of the prophetic era we may have a reminiscence or survival of the early mode of regarding the royal line of Israel ; not a rude survival, but refined and brought into harmony more or less with the growing thought of the times. This conjecture will not seem improbable if we take account of the persistency with which ancient superstitions linger on, and colour the faiths of a more enlightened time. That much of the later faith of Israel had its root in the dark superstitions of prehistoric ages there can be little doubt. In regard to some of these it may be said that they were anticipations or embryonic forms of the purer faith ; of others, that they survived to colour and to blemish the purer faith, which had evolved itself in the course of ages in spite of them and alongside of them. But this is a conjecture which, though capable of being worked out, as indeed it has been in various directions, need not detain us here.

The belief in a coming Messiah was, so to speak, a secondary formation in the mind of Israel. The Messianic personage was the natural and imaginative embodiment of that divine aid and patronage of which the people had early conceived a confident expectation. This was the first step ; and this hope having thus assumed a personal shape, the person was next clothed with befitting attributes, and represented as a powerful and quasi-divine being triumphant over all the adversaries of the people. Sometimes he is addressed by the prophet in glowing, magnifying language ; sometimes he is represented as addressing the Israelites or the surrounding heathen in terms suitable to the various relations in which he might be supposed to stand to them. But the evolution of the Messianic idea was not completed in Old Testament times, but reserved for the time of the New Testament, when it took up into itself another idea which had grown up simultaneously with it in ancient Israel. This was that of the suffering servant of God, who is Isaiah's (chap. liii.) portraiture of the true or ideal Israelite who fulfilled all righteousness, or of that small remnant of the people for whose sake the nation was spared. (In which connection see the prayer of Abraham for Sodom (Gen. xviii.), in which there is a foreshadowing, or rather a prolepsis, by prophetic hand of this conception.) The ideal Israelite was a prophetic conception, quite distinct from the apokalyptic conception of the Messiah ; so that, intelligibly enough, the Jewish commentators have always regarded them as separate subjects ; the Messiah being possessed of godlike attributes, which raised Him above suffering, while the ideal Israelite, in the endurance of suffering, presented humanity in its highest perfection. But the possibility existed that the two conceptions might flow together, or be fused into one. And this fusion took place when the early Church afterwards saw in the great sufferer, who had entered into glory, the combination of both and the fulfilment of all prophecy. In this fulfilment, however, it may be permitted to *us* to see not the evidence of prophetic prescience, but the culmination of a great prophetic idea, in which a radical and fateful transformation of Messianic thought was silently, and, as it were, authoritatively effected.

Were we to permit ourselves to be guided in the interpretation of the prophetic books by the light of subsequent events, we might put upon much of their language a spiritual meaning beyond or different from that which it literally and primarily suggests. But undoubtedly it was a divine and miraculous interposition which much of it led contemporaneous readers to look forward to. When Isaiah said, " Behold your God cometh with vengeance, even God with a recompense, He will come and save you ; " or again, " Awake, awake, put on strength, O arm of the Lord, awake as in the ancient days. . . . Art thou not it which hath dried the sea, the waters of the great deep, that hath made the depths of the sea a way for the ransomed to pass over?" what could his countrymen be led by such language to think but that the prophet was pointing forward to some great miraculous event? And so too Jeremiah, when he spoke of a new covenant, if he did not himself expect that it would be heralded by some demonstration grander and more imposing than that at Mount Sinai (which when we consider the depth and keenness of his spiritual insight seems possible), yet assuredly this was the expectation to which his language would give rise in the sensuous-minded and uninstructed masses of the people. Nay, the probability is that such an expectation was devoutly cherished by the prophetic mind itself. For what else could find vent in that ejaculation of the Psalmist, " Oh that the Salvation of Israel were come out of Zion," or in that cry of the prophet, "Oh, that thou wouldest rend the heavens and come down"? It may be said that these are figures of speech, the language of poetry and of vague longing. But the longing or expectation which they express in their literal acceptation was for Israelites, the children of the covenant and heirs of the promises, the logical sequence, the all but inevitable deduction from their national theism and their national history. For according to the way of thinking common to people and prophet, the transcendency of God was so absolute that He was regarded as the sole actor in all mundane affairs, while men were but his instruments more or less passive ; so that, especially in times of sore calamity and national despondency, hope could best revive or be kept alive in the form of an expectation of some such providences as took place at the Exodus. Indeed we may say that a hope not unakin to this is so natural to man under a sense of his weakness in presence of the great forces of nature and of the great power of evil, that it does not wait for the prompting of special considerations and conditions. The hope of divine help conceived of as "poured in from outside" is as common to us of the present day as it was to the Israelites of old. The hope of divine help, miraculous or sub-miraculous, can only be held in check or corrected by the scientific ideas of divine operation and of human autocracy of which there was not a thought in Israel.

In proportion now as the language of prophecy gave countenance to such an expectation, would its protest and denunciation against the formal religious observances when disjoined from moral conduct miss their intended effect : the effort at national reform would be tacitly abandoned, and the people, content with a lower aim, would fall back upon a provisional and interim form of religion, *i.e.*, the more studious cultivation of religion on its outer or ceremonial side. This result of prophetic teaching, uncontemplated but inevitable, would be fatal to all immediate strenuous moral effort, and make the people satisfied with doing less than their best. But two ends of not doubtful advantage would thereby be served. The cherished forms of worship being practicable and comparatively easy of observance would serve to keep up the show of regard to the divine will and give a religious air to the common life. At the same time, as we shall yet see more particularly, they would erect a wall of separation between the chosen people and the Gentiles, and keep the former apart and separate as a seed which could lay claim to the fulfilment of the promises.

These remarks bring us down to the time of the exile, or Babylonish captivity as it is called, at which the last object just mentioned—the maintenance by the Jews of their separate and corporate existence—became of paramount importance, and could not but be recognized by the chiefs of the people as a matter of life or death for the religion of Israel. The great danger which assailed the nation during this period was, that being deported from its native seat in the sacred soil of Palestine; from the scenes which, even to this day, strengthen the faith of the stranger in the great events associated with them, it should give way to the tendency towards idolatrous services by joining in the worship of its conquerors, and adopting their social usages. The ten tribes of the northern kingdom had apparently yielded to this temptation, and had become so completely amalgamated with the peoples among whom they dwelt as to have disappeared as a distinct people. We may take it for granted, in the case of these tribes, that this process, if not completed, was rapidly going on ; and that, warned by this catastrophe, either actually accomplished or visibly impending, the leaders of the southern tribes in Babylon may have felt that this tendency had to be met and counteracted ; and the method by which this was to be done may have readily suggested itself to their minds.

We have already adverted to the fact that the forms of worship practised by the Israelites in their native land were originally in a great measure identical with those of the heathen around them. But we may reasonably conjecture, or take for granted, that in the course of ages these forms had, in accordance with the religious genius of Israel, and in obedience to its moral and æsthetic instincts, differentiated themselves from the original forms that might still be retained by the non-ethical religions of the neighbouring nations. This process would as a matter of course go on gradually, silently, continuously and unconsciously, more especially after Israel had grown great and built for itself the magnificent temple of Jerusalem. The differences in form thus created may have been minute, yet when we consider the tendency of religious parties to attach importance to trifles, we may believe that minute and unessential as these differences may have been, they might yet give countenance and encouragement to that feeling of selectness and apartness which was founded on the ancient legends of the nation. The conscientious and punctilious observance of such differences, while it would erect a barrier against anything like syncretism of worship, would also earn for the people either the ridicule or the hostility of their neighbours, and would thus become the badge of their faith, and the test of their fidelity to their national God, and on that very account be regarded as the matter of prime importance in religion, more so even than the usage and practice of a higher morality in which their superiority would be less conspicuous and not so easily maintained.

Then it could not fail to be observed that the differences of form and ritual, in so far as they prevailed, acted as a restraint upon the Israelite, and made it less easy and natural for him to participate in the worship of other gods. The sinfulness of latitudinarianism was thereby kept present to his mind, and the difference in the object of his worship was made more impressive and more palpable by the difference in the form. In order therefore to apply an absolute check to idolatrous tendency, it was only necessary that there should be introduced into the existing forms, and in the line of previous development, new features or details which would partially modify, but not go the length of essentially altering or obliterating, the customs or forms which had been long in use. The motive for doing this had, as we see, grown up out of the circumstances in which the exiled Israelites were placed, and there were men among them, such as Ezekiel and afterwards Ezra, by whom this was felt and acted on.

There is every probability that the Levitical code as engrossed in the Pentateuch was compiled at this time, and that it was compiled for the very purpose of elaborating the ritual and making its distinctive features more prominent, so as to create such a chasm between it and the worship of other gods as to make conformity with both all but impossible. The only thing further necessary to ensure success to this procedure was to invest the code with indisputable authority, and this was done by incorporating it with the law of Moses in the Pentateuch, and so stamping it with that divine sanction which all regulations attributed to Moses had from time immemorial enjoyed. If we may judge from what we are told of the easy faith which Josiah and his subjects gave to the Mosaic authorship of the copy of the law found in the temple, there would be little difficulty in obtaining credit for the improved and enlarged or Levitical ritual. It was brought out under the editorship of a priest party, from which the people were accustomed to receive the law as its custodiers and interpreters, and to whose authority in matters of ritual they were accustomed to bow. The authors of the compilation could easily persuade themselves that they were justified in referring it back to Moses, and editing it under his name, seeing it was carefully framed in the spirit of his legislation.

From what has now been said, it will be seen that we do not wish to convey the impression that the Levitical code was imposed upon the people by a concerted stratagem on the part of its compilers, to which the people generally were not privy. The compilation was a necessity of the situation in which the exiles found themselves. On the one hand there would be on the part of many a disposition to conform to the religious usages of the conquerors among whom they lived, which, if indulged, would end in the abandonment of their own religion : an effect which was probably far advanced, if not an accomplished fact, in the case of the ten tribes. But, on the other hand, there would be on the part of the more enlightened and devout, especially in the priestly caste, an instinctive feeling of loyalty to the ancestral religion prompting them to resist and counteract this tendency, and so to avert the calamity, as it doubtless seemed to them, of denationalization and absorption among the heathen. There were devout and clearheaded men who understood the situation, and saw that it was only by securing the strict observance of the distinctive ritual that this calamity could be averted ; men who may therefore on that very account have believed in all sincerity that revision of the ritual had the sanction of Jehovah. To this belief they gave practical effect by the compilation of the Levitical code, which probably did little more than elaborate and define the distinctive usages of Israel as then observed ; besides claiming for them, even to their minutest details, divine sanction and authority. And it is to this code principally, and to the circumstances that called it forth, that we have to trace that modification of the religion of Israel which goes by the name of Judaism. And the respect which this code enjoyed, however questionable in some of its effects, was what gave to Judaism its tenacity and power of self-assertion and resistance, over against the unsettling and encroaching influences of heathenism.

After the return of the exiles and the resettlement in the Holy Land, the effect of the revised ritual and of the regulations referring to social intercourse with the outside populations which were then enforced was prodigious. The stop, which was thus put to mixed marriages and to participation by the Jews in the worship of other gods, effected somewhat forcibly and mechanically what the high and spiritual teaching of the prophets had failed to accomplish, for it was what mainly established the monotheistic principle in the minds of the people. The cross-fertilizing influence of Persian ideas may have contributed to bring about this desirable result, but undoubtedly the result was due in the main to the new ritual and the more stringent social regulations laid down in the Levitical code. Up till this period of their history the Israelites had shown in their intercourse with other peoples a certain geniality of disposition and a certain impressibility that might be called excessive, a proneness to adopt alien customs which, as we have seen, was a source of danger to their religion, but the new ritual and new regulations tended to isolate them from the people among whom they dwelt, and created a barrier against an inexclusive and sympathetic contact with them. This, according to our view, was the purpose for which the ritual had been revised and enlarged.

There is no doubt a very prevalent tendency among religious men to adopt an elaborate ritual in the worship of God, but over and above this tendency, we hold that the motive now referred to operated at this conjuncture for the revisal and elaboration of the Jewish ritual ; and the ritual in its new form had a further effect, probably not contemplated nor foreseen by its authors, for it was calculated in a great measure to undo or neutralize whatever influence had been exerted by the teaching of the great prophets. This arose from the fact of its placing for the first time the moral and ritual observances of religion on an equal footing in faith and practice. The reverence which up till this time had been tacitly and freely paid to ritual as a becoming usage approved by experience and recommended by tradition was now authoritatively claimed for it, as regulated by the same divine will and placed under the same sanction as that on which the Decalogue rested. A formal and statutory character was thus impressed upon religion in its principles and its manifestations alike.

We see that the effect of the Levitical law was partly beneficial and partly injurious to the interests of religion, and that its publication and enforcement are quite sufficient to account for the remarkable transformation that passed upon the Jewish people at and after the time of the captivity. The injurious and deadening effect upon the national character was not, like the other, immediately apparent, and not even, it may be, sensibly developed for some ages. For notwithstanding the identification in theory of worship and religion which, as being of its very essence, the Levitical code brought about, yet in practice the monotheistic principle which established itself contemporaneously in the minds of the people sufficed, as in the instance of Mahometanism, for a time to sustain the religious life at a high level and to give reality and substance to the forms of worship. There are not a few passages in ecclesiastical history to show that a deeply earnest and devotional spirit may be nourished for lengthened periods in connection with an elaborate ritual which in the long run, especially when its divine enactment is emphasized, absorbs the interest of the worshipper and tends to efface from his mind the distinction between religion and worship, and finally to reduce morality to quite a subordinate position and to throw the ethical aspects of religion into the background. It is to the period accordingly of which we now speak, the period during and subsequent to the exile, that the historical critic now assigns a great part of the psalter, incomparably the finest manual of devotion which any religion, not excepting the Christian, has produced. The psalms contributed by this period may be regarded as the first fresh utterance of the monotheistic principle on its establishment in the popular mind, of its first full swell through the life of the nation, as the first accents of a devotion uttering itself under forms understood to be expressly sanctioned by the living God.

To the same heightened feeling of devotion in the national mind may also perhaps be ascribed the institution of the synagogue, which was no doubt due in part to a felt necessity for the more frequent enjoyment of emotional worship than was supplied by the centralized system advocated by the Deuteronomist and adopted by the Levitical law. To the exaltation of this same feeling or craving may also be attributed in part the heroic effort by which, under the leadership of the Maccabees, the Jews shook off the Syrian yoke. And in connection with our subject—the origin of Christianity—a product as important as any, of the heightened veneration of the Jewish people for the forms of their worship, was the book of Daniel.

By the most competent critics this book is believed to have been composed in the midst of the Maccabean struggle, for the purpose of rousing the energies of the people to maintain the struggle and to bring it to a successful issue. With this in view it gives a vivid and realistic but wholly imaginary picture of the heroism displayed by youthful Jewish confessors of a former age, and confidently predicts the final triumph of the Jewish people over all their enemies, not so much by virtue of their own courage and devotion as in consequence of a divine intervention in their behalf. It mattered little to the men engaged in that terrible struggle whether the events ever happened which the book records. Enough that it set before them a noble picture of patriotism and of fidelity to the God of their fathers, and that it was calculated to awaken the same spirit in themselves, besides that it encouraged the hope of victory over their enemies by the same means. The question as to authorship and authenticity gave them no concern, and the book was secure of a place in the canon. Welcomed at first, we may suppose, by the intelligent few as a pious, and, for the time, useful invention, it would be received without suspicion as an authentic narrative by the people at large, and having served its purpose by nerving the nation to its conflict with Antiochus, it would ever after be revered as a book whose sacred origin was not to be questioned.

The work is a sort of historical romance, with an apokalyptic sequel. This sequel is composed in imitation of the prophetic books of the canon, and though in a literary and ethical point of view very inferior to these, it is yet in many respects as interesting as any of them, in consequence of the great influence which it exerted on the Jewish mind and of the relation in which it stood to the origin of Christianity. It affected to be written in an age much prior to the Maccabean and to predict or symbolize events which by that time had taken place and were known to its readers as matters of history. By this simple expedient of antedating its composition and converting history into prophecy, it gained credit in that uncritical age for its prediction of events yet future. The seeming fulfilment of predictions which were penned after the events was accepted as a guarantee for the fulfilment of predictions which were actually such. The book thus became a powerful agency in awakening faiths and hopes which, by their intensity and by their adaptation to popular tastes and aspirations, were eminently calculated in the revolution of times to secure their own accomplishment. It also lent vividness and massiveness to the object, hitherto vague and shadowy, of Jewish longing, by specializing it as the establishment upon earth of a kingdom which would supplant the great monarchies of the earth, to which it would bear a family resemblance, while differing from them in respect of the righteousness of its rule and the pre-eminence in it of the Jewish element. Being written after the Levitical law had long been in existence and had taken full effect in moulding the popular mind, the book displays a certain hard and mechanical tone in its religious sentiments, and gives new emphasis to the circumstances which, in previous books of prophecy, had been more or less implied, viz., that the kingdom would be set up by a great and apparently abrupt manifestation of divine power.

And, lastly, it is remarkable for this, that it distinctly connects or identifies this manifestation with the advent of one who is styled the Son of Man, the Messiah, or Anointed One of God.   For the writer of the book, *i.e.* for the prophet whom he personates, as for Jeremiah, the time of the advent is yet distant, reserved for the latter days, many weeks of years must yet elapse before the set time arrives, but he writes also with a deep conviction that the time, though distant, will yet surely come and not tarry.   An imposing air of certainty is even communicated to the event by the fixing of its date.   It would take us out of our way to discuss the much agitated question as to the determination of this date.   We shall only observe that, if, as seems likely, the author starts from Jeremiah's oracle regarding the seventy years, and, because that oracle had not been fulfilled to the full within these years, converts them into seventy weeks of years, the date predicted approximates to the actual date of the composition of the book itself, and must have been expressly intended to excite the hope of an accomplishment of the prophecy within the experience of the generation then living, and engaged in terrible struggle with Antiochus.   That the book was written with the express intention of animating the Jews in that struggle is, of course, carefully kept out of sight, but the intention is betrayed by the very observable fact that its vaticinations, which, under the disguise of peculiar forms, are comparatively distinct and historical down to the Maccabean age, become vague and irrelevant to the course of subsequent history, just as might be expected in an apocalypse written in that age.   It cannot be denied that the entire conception and plan of the book is exceedingly bold and original, eminently calculated to inspire the Jews with that confidence in the issue which ensured the success of their revolt, to make a deep impression upon the mind of succeeding as well as contemporary generations, and to give an impulse to the creation of that apocalyptic literature, several specimens of which, dating both before and after the Christian era, have survived to our time.   These have a value chiefly for the testimony which they furnish to the prevalence of the Messianic expectation in the century preceding the birth of Jesus.

This peculiar species of literature may be said to have been indigenous to the soil of Judaism, and to be an exclusively Jewish product.   It had its origin in the existence among the Jews of the expectation, founded in their early history, of a great future, and of a great leader to bring that future to pass. The tendency to forecast the nature of that future and to assign a date to the appearance of that leader could not but act irresistibly as a stimulus to the imagination, especially in times of great national humiliation and distress; and once the example of such a form of literature was set by the remarkable book of Daniel, it was followed by many works of a similar class though of inferior talent in the century and a half before the birth of Jesus, and the impulse thus given continued to operate in the succeeding century, during which the political situation had not altered for the better. Conceivably too, the impulse may have been strengthened during the latter period by the desire to present a different fulfilment of Messianic hope from that which Christianity offered. It even becomes a question, as will yet be seen, whether the book of Revelation in the New Testament canon, which belongs to the same class of literature and has largely influenced the course and character of Christian thought, is not in the main a Jewish production subjected to manipulation by Christian hands. The apokalyptic tendency could not, it is evident, exist in full force in the Christian consciousness, according to which the kingdom of God is not future but present, not visible but spiritual, affording no field or scope for apokalyptic emblems. But though Christian faith and sentiment might not be able to originate and carry out an apokalypse of the ages to come, yet, as Jewish works of this kind were in existence, and were, as is known to be the fact, held in respect by Jews and Christians alike, Christian feeling might seek by interpolation and otherwise, to adapt them to Christian requirements. This, however, is a subject to which we may yet have occasion to refer more at large.

So far as can be made out by the application of literary criticism the book of Daniel must have been written not much before the middle of the second century B.C., while the conflict with the Syrian monarchy was going on, and much about the time at which the Pharisaic party began to take its rise among the Jews. That the appearance of the book, or rather of that phase of Messianic expectation to which it gave expression, may have caused the segregation of a small and select section of the people who adopted its views, and were afterwards known as Pharisees, is not improbable. But in any case it is that book of the Old Testament which best represents their spirit; and in after times they were the custodiers in Israel of its main ideas. The thought of an extraneous interposition which was emphasized in the book of Daniel far more than it had been in the great classical era of prophecy, was calculated to draw away attention from that moral regeneration which had been insisted on by the great prophets as essential to the nature of the coming time, and consequently to impart a formal and unspiritual character to the religious ideas connected with it. Grounding on the notion of a kingdom of God after the pattern of earthly kingdoms, the Pharisees and the people whom they led, could only conceive of religion as conformity to definite law and external usage, such as befitted a visible institution. By punctilious attention to legal and ceremonial observances they hoped to secure for themselves a full participation in all its privileges. For them the kingdom in prospect lost its ideal character, and became unmoral in its conception. The hope of a great outward manifestation was, as we have already remarked, fatal to all higher moral effort, because it disposed men to be content with doing less than their best, and with the practice of formal services which, in their inmost hearts, they knew to be utterly worthless, because standing in no relation to the inner life, and having no tendency to effect an improvement in the social state. The habitual practice of such services was productive of that hollowness and hypocrisy of character with which the Pharisees were chargeable. And yet further, the combination of political aspiration with religious sentiment was another fatal circumstance, inasmuch as the former was sure to become the predominant and all but exclusive element, and to lend a mercenary character to the religious feeling. Religious services under these conditions partook of the nature of legal transactions by which men stipulated for the favour of God. And just such was the character impressed on the religion of the Jews by the prevalence among them for centuries of the presentiment of a divine interposition, such as that, or greater than that, which was believed by them to have laid the foundation of their State. Indeed, we may affirm, that owing to this outlook the religion of Israel was alloyed from the first with a legal and mercenary spirit, tempered only by the prophetic spirit which engaged in a long but losing battle with it, and was at length extinguished by the triumph of Pharisaism.

According to this view the Pharisaic spirit was not an accidental phenomenon of Judaism, but rather the final and inevitable outcome of the idea, fundamental in the religion of Israel, and dating back to the very earliest time, of an arbitrary and sovereign election of the people. This assumption, while it strung up the energies of the people at certain critical moments of their history to a point not to be otherwise reached perhaps, was yet attended with this baneful effect or drawback, that it had an inherent tendency to throw into disuse the spiritual instincts of the people, as if God had Himself taken their spiritual interests into His keeping. It imparted a heteronomous aspect to morality and religion, and so involved the practical consequence that conformity to the requirements of both became formal, mechanical, and unspontaneous. The prophetic spirit of a former age had been little else than a protest against the tendency in this direction. But the protest had been to little purpose, partly, no doubt, because the prophets were never able to emancipate themselves wholly from the very tendency against which they protested. Being inherent in the religion of Israel from the beginning, and therefore constant in its operation, this tendency was sure, in the long run, to prevail against a protest, which, however vehement, was not thorough, but was directed only against a symptom while it spared the root of the evil. Prophecy touched its highest point when by the mouth of Jeremiah it announced the outpouring of a new spirit to be the great event or manifestation to which the people had to look forward. But even for him this was an event which was to *befal* the nation at some distant time, to come upon it from without, to be, in short, heterosoteric. And it is not to be wondered at that prophecy had so often to complain that it had laboured in vain, and spent its strength in vain; or that, when, exhausted by its ineffectual effort, it expired, the thought of that new spirit should have dropped out of the popular mind, and there remained only the longing for some great act of God to secure the pre-eminence of Israel among the nations; just affording an example of the disposition common to our race, to seek in external circumstances that true good which can only be found within.

We have said that in spite of the identification of worship and religion which the Levitical Law brought about, the con-

temporaneous establishment of the monotheistic principle sufficed for a time to sustain the reality of the religious life.   But
we have now to observe that in the course of time the co-
ordination of the ceremonial with the moral and spiritual
service could not fail to eat out the heart of religion, and to
reduce it to a mere outward show.   This result reached its
climax in Pharisaism, for that must be our conclusion, unless
we are to suppose that the terms in which Pharisaism was
spoken of by Jesus were greatly exaggerated, his picture of
it a mere caricature.   And we have a voucher for the fairness
and accuracy of the truth and fidelity of his language in the
fact that his description of Pharisaism is just what we might
expect as the inevitable outcome of the confusion of form
and substance, of worship and religion.   In the earlier and
better ages of Israel the spirit of a true devotion found expression for itself in ritual transactions, and so long as such
a spirit continued to inspire the ritual, religion fulfilled its
hallowing and elevating office ; but the tendency towards a
mechanical observance of the ritual when unchecked, caused
religion itself to degenerate into a dead work, uninspired by
devout sentiment and powerless over the life of the worshipper.
This was what had happened with the Pharisees of the time of
Jesus, and with the people generally, so far as the influence of
the Pharisees extended.   The spirit had fled from their legal
observances, and their religion was left a *caput mortuum*.   A
constitutional weakness or congenital taint may, for long, consist with a display of vigorous vitality in the animal frame, but
is apt to reveal itself at last in premature decay or in some
disease of a malignant type.   The malign principle in the
religion of Israel was the Pharisaic spirit, from which, even in
its best days, it was never altogether free.   When that spirit
came to a head in the age of Jesus the religion had run its
course, and could do no more for humanity.   What was then
needed was a new departure—involving the radical elimination
of that inherited taint—which, as will presently be seen, it
received at the hands of Jesus when he substituted the evangelical for the legal principle as the moving spring of the
religious life.   And it may be safely asserted that no step
in the spiritual advance of humanity has so nearly answered
the idea of a new creation, or of a radical reconstruction of
pre-existing elements of thought in the religious sphere, unless,

indeed, we except the rise of the monotheistic principle in Israel.

We have now seen how the mythical idea of a covenanted relation between God and the people of Israel became fixed in the minds of the latter, and how, owing to the actual course of their later history, there grew up among them the hope of a kingdom of God upon earth, in which all their disasters and disappointments would be redressed, and the covenant be amply fulfilled. The hope of such a kingdom formed a great part of Israel's religion, standing to it in somewhat the same relation as the hope of a future life does to Christianity. But before advancing to the consideration of Christianity we must briefly direct attention to other aspects of the religious life of Israel : to the development of its theological thought, which was concurrent with the growth of that hope, and intimately associated with it.

It has already been mentioned incidentally that the monotheistic idea was evolved in Israel slowly and painfully, because retarded by many cross and refluent movements of thought, having to contend and force itself into recognition against the prejudice and inertia of the inherited polytheism. An obstinate battle of varying fortune had to be fought for this purpose. So much can be gathered with distinctness from the historical books of the Old Testament, though these do not record the actual course of events, but only as they appeared to the monotheistic party at a later time after the battle was won or victory was in prospect. Until this point was reached, *i.e.*, until the monotheistic principle was established or nearly so, there could be no such thing as any true advance in theological thought ; but, being reached, it became a starting point for ascertaining the character of the one true God and of His relations with men. For the monotheist, God was an all-powerful Being, limited neither by the existence of other gods nor by a fate behind and before all. But this power was at first unmoral, that is, arbitrary, capricious, and vengeful, a power controlled no more by inner than by outward force. At least, such a conception of God was in accordance with the idea of the national covenant. That idea grew up naturally when Jehovah was merely the national God : that one, out of the unknown multitude of gods, who had chosen Israel for his " portion " and " the lot of His inheritance." But even when

I

the higher faith had grown up, that there could be but one God, supreme over the nations of the earth, Israelites could not or would not abandon the idea, so flattering to national vanity, that He had preferred them to all other nations, and singled them out as objects of His special favour.   Yet the incongruity of such an idea with the character and even the dignity of such a Being could hardly escape attention.   And at a later period, when the monotheistic principle had established itself firmly in the mind of the nation, and leavened its thought, some explanation of this obvious incongruity was felt to be necessary. Rabbinical research has shown that for this purpose the theory found favour that God had offered His Law, His Book of the Covenant, to the other nations of the earth, but that Israel alone had accepted its yoke, and that God's election had fallen upon Israel only after it had proved itself worthy by accepting His offer.   Historical evidence in the Old Testament of the existence of such an opinion there was none, and even if there had been, it was far from really explaining the apparent incongruity.   But it had a certain show of reason, which served, as may be seen in many similar cases, to stand for an explanation. Besides this popular idea, which ministered to national pride, there was the truly prophetic idea that the election of Israel was for no superior worth of its own, but a mere act of God's sovereign pleasure, an act, however, which had in view the ultimate elevation of the other nations of the earth.   Passages to this effect, or pointing in this direction, are too numerous for citation, and furnish the first faint indication of a tendency towards universalism, or the denationalization of the religion of Israel, a tendency which, not being, perhaps, wholly palatable to national taste, the prophetic redactor has sought to warrant by introducing anticipations of it into the record of pre-Mosaic or patriarchal times, as a necessary and likely means of over-coming the prejudice of Jewish exclusiveness and assumption (Gen. xii. 3, xviii. 18, xxvi. 4, "The Lord said to Abraham (and to Isaac) . . . in thee shall all families of the earth be blessed"). And the same idea is taken up by psalmists, and prophets, and apostles in later ages, to explain as economical the apparent preference shown to Israel. The conception of God is gradually purified by the elevation of the moral sentiment. The thought of God as an arbitrary, partial, vindictive Being gives way to that of a righteous and impartial

Ruler, and of one who is merciful as well as just, deeply interested in the welfare of Israel indeed, seeking to train the nation to the love and practice of righteousness, but also anxious for the spiritual welfare of other nations (Book of Jonah), not offended merely by insults offered to Himself, His name, and His worship, but much more by the injustice perpetrated by man against his brother man, who is God's child and offspring. It dawns also upon the prophetic mind, not steadily perhaps, but fitfully, that He is not merely a just and righteous Being, careful of the true welfare of His children, but even tender and gentle in His treatment of them, patient of their infirmities and backslidings, sparing them in His anger, and grieving to punish. He pleads with Israel as a husband whose affection cannot be vanquished even by national faithlessness, or as a father whose fondness is only stirred by the rebellion of his sons. He implores them to reason with Him, and He threatens, only that He may escape the necessity of executing judgment. Comp. Ps. xviii. 35, Hosea xi. 8, Micah vi. 3, Jer. xxxi. 20, Book of Jonah. Yet it must be confessed that even the prophetic hold of this higher conception was wavering and unsteady, as is conspicuously apparent in the psalter, where the old popular, or, we may say, heathenish, and prophetic sentiments follow each other in baffling confusion, in irreconcilable juxtaposition. Not a reader but is surprised, if not pained, to see that the breath of vengeance and the breath of mercy blow by turns through those wonderful compositions, which were probably among the last, and were in some respects the greatest products of the prophetic spirit.

But the development of religious thought in Israel went on in other departments besides that of the strictly theological. The Covenant was represented as being made with the nation at large; it dealt with the people as a whole, and this was an important feature which could not be let go, because, while it brought the individual into no immediate relation to God, it seemed to secure a participation in the benefits of the Covenant to every individual without distinction. But in the later prophetic age the claims of the individual were recognized, and his personal relation to God was brought into prominence. The idea of individual responsibility emerged in addition to that of the nation at large, and the idea of a personal immortality took its place side by side with that of a corporate or national immortality.   In regard to this last, it seems as if the early Hebrew legislator had felt that he could make nothing of the strange and distressful views of a future life which had been elaborated in Egypt, and had therefore left all such out of sight.   The fact that his code was for civil life may also have had something to do with this apparent oversight, or there may have been, as we are inclined to think, a collateral religious life and system of belief which his code of law did not touch upon, but took for granted.   For the literature of a people does not always, or necessarily, reflect the full volume of its life.   But be this as it may, the effect of this omission in the early literature of the Israelites was to concentrate their thoughts in the long run on the possession and enjoyment of the Holy Land by themselves and their posterity, and to cause them to find contentment in the present service of God, and in the present sense of His favour.   It was only when that possession became insecure and disappointing that the people turned in upon themselves ; and the hope of a future life, which could never have been quite extinct in Israel any more than elsewhere, received a more and more pronounced expression in its literature.   The faint presentiment grew into a struggling faith, as may be seen in the prophecies of Ezekiel, in a few of the psalms, and in the book of Job, until, in the apocryphal book of Wisdom a firm belief in immortality is expressed for the first time without any sign of misgiving on the subject.

CHAPTER V.

THE IDEA OF THE KINGDOM OF GOD, AS TRANSFORMED BY JESUS.

AFTER this review of Jewish thought and aspiration, we feel, when we place it in the light of the New Testament, the incompleteness and imperfection of it all. But we also feel that we stand on the very threshold of Christianity, and that another step will carry us into another and higher region of thought. And yet, between the taking of that step, which disclosed the larger horizon, and the date at which the more creative and purely Jewish period of prophecy had run its course, an interval of about 400 years elapsed. For, if we except the contribution made to Messianic doctrine in the apocalypse of Daniel, and in a few of the psalms, the canonical writings, which are now generally assigned to this period, made little or no real or substantial addition to Jewish theology. As to the apocryphal literature belonging to this period, the greater part of it bears an unmistakable and undiluted Jewish character; but part of it, especially the book of Wisdom and Ecclesiasticus, affords indications that the faith of Israel, at least among the Jews of the dispersion, was beginning to be touched (as we know from other sources that it was) by Hellenic influences; and if, by this process, the religion of Israel was to some extent, and in some circles, denationalized, we may consent to regard it as a preparation for the universalism of the Gospel. But it has to be taken into account that the advance thus made was probably not felt in Palestine itself, and was literary and academic, rather than popular or practical, and above all, that in the absence of that new principle which the Gospel was afterwards to supply, the elements of Hellenic thought were too disparate and too far apart from the thought of Israel to admit of a living fusion. In the hands of the great Hellenist of Alexandria the semblance of such a fusion was only given by an unstinted use of the allegorical interpretation of the sacred writings, which was too visionary and too artificial to take hold of the general mind.

The rabbinical literature, which seems to have had its rise in this same uncreative period, was purely Jewish in its character, and was mainly occupied at its best with matters of ritual, with comments on the canonical Scriptures, and in working out into rigid and fantastic forms and conclusions the spiritual and poetic ideas of the prophets. The result of all this literary activity was to confirm the national religion in that deadness and formality towards which, as already shown, it had an inherent, obstinate, and ever-besetting bent. By means of the synagogal services and addresses, which stood largely if not entirely, no doubt, under rabbinical influence, the theology which thus grew up established itself in the popular mind, and remained, as will yet appear, to exert a powerful influence upon the dogmatic constructions of St. Paul. But Jesus was the heir of the prophetic ages pure and simple. The "basis in himself" had no affinity with distinctively synagogal doctrines, Pharisaic or rabbinical: these touched only to repel him (Matth. xvi. 6, "Take heed," he said to his disciples, "and beware of the leaven of the Pharisees and of the Sadducees"). And the elements of thought which combined in his mind to produce the new synthesis of religion, were all more or less present in germ at least and by anticipation in the prophetic writings.

We have, therefore, to explain to ourselves as we best can that great hiatus in the prophetic line, that comparative blank or arrestment of creative thought just before it received its final consummation, and made its great advance in the Gospel. This curious circumstance may be accounted for by the tenacity with which the idea of a visible kingdom of God upon earth had laid hold of the Jewish imagination. This idea, as will yet appear more distinctly, paralyzed religious thought, and placed an embargo on its further development. No doubt this idea had possession of the mind of Israel even in prophetic times. But in that creative and productive period the idea was fluid: the elastic vestment with which the spiritual thought was clothed admitted of its expansion; whereas, in the sub-sequent or intermediate period the idea hardened and stiffened into an inflexible dogma by which thought was strangled, and before another and further step could be taken, there was needed a man of religious insight and of superb spiritual force to rend that inelastic band, to discard that sensuous dream, that fiction so alluring and fascinating to the vulgar mind, and to conceive of that kingdom as an empire of the spirit : such a man, indeed, as only comes once in many ages, once, it may be, in an æon. It almost seems to us as if such a man might have appeared any time during these four hundred years, were it not that the historical conditions which were requisite for the success of his work may also have been necessary for the production of the man himself. Certain it is that in that long interval no man had the moral courage, or the spiritual insight to liberate the imprisoned spirit of prophecy. As water may, for a space, retain its fluidity after the freezing point has been reached, so generation succeeded generation without a man to stir the moral atmosphere or to speak the needed word, though the age called for it and the conditions were present. For here we may alter the common proverb and say, " *C'est le dernier pas que coûte.*" But at last the man did appear, and the word was spoken when Jesus proclaimed that the kingdom of God was within men. In these words he drew together the two separate lines along which the thought of Israel had travelled, and from their contact or point of convergence, there diffused itself a new light over the whole field of religion. The principle thus propounded was the manifesto or watchword of his religion, and the hour in which he first uttered it witnessed the birth of Christianity.

It has been often said with a truth that cannot be disputed, that Christianity was rooted in the religion of Israel, or that the one was a developed form of the other. But, as we proceed, we shall see that it was a development partly by way of recoil or reaction. The prophetic or creative period of the old religion had passed away, and instead of being followed by a period of epigonism, or of feeble reproduction, as it might have been, it was followed by a period in which the legal element, which prophecy had not surmounted, was taken up and pushed to a one-sided extreme, until to the searching eye of Jesus it betrayed its radical defect. From this he recoiled, or he reacted against it, and took up anew the forgotten spiritual element of prophecy, and gave to it (in his doctrine of

the evangelical relation) its full development. The recoil and
the development were but different aspects of his work.

The great achievement of John the Baptist, which formed
his title to be considered the forerunner of Jesus, was his
renewal under altered conditions of the prophetic protest.
He reacted against Pharisaic formalism, and called back the
attention of his countrymen to the absolute necessity of a
righteous life. He did not cease to look for the consummation
which Israel desired in the establishment upon earth of a kingdom of God ; but he recognized its spiritual character in so far
that it could only be inherited by a righteous nation, which,
however observant it might be of the rites and ceremonies of
religion, would not consider them to be of primary value, or
even of a value co-ordinate with the moral and spiritual duties
of religion. He showed how much he subordinated the former
by making absolutely no allusion to them in his preaching.
What he did was to call upon men to repent, and to change
their lives by way of qualifying themselves for the coming
kingdom. The outer manifestation of the kingdom was for
him a certainty, a necessity ; but it was not all nor nearly all ;
the external event was to go hand in hand with a spiritual
revolution in the nation and in the individuals composing it.
He told the crowds which listened to him that it was not
enough for them to have Abraham for their father, and that
their entrance into the kingdom of God would, in no sense, be a
mere right of birth or thing of privilege, but had to be qualified
for by a better mode of life, by fruits meet for repentance, by
works of humanity, of justice, of honesty, of beneficence, and
brotherly kindness, and generally by the adoption of a higher
standard of morality for the visible life and conduct. We
know now that the requirement of right and virtuous conduct
can be satisfied only when there is a corresponding disposition,
and that there is reality in the outer life only when it is a
reflection of the inner life. But John did not enter upon this
idea, and he fulfilled his part by preparing the way for the
more searching and spiritual doctrine of one who was to come
after, and by rousing men to the necessity of a more strict
conformity to the divine law in the overt form of their lives.
Hence his preaching was intensely earnest in its tone but
narrow in its range ; and however startling it may have been
at a time when the rites and ceremonies of religion almost

obliterated from men's minds the obligation of the higher cult, yet, like that of the prophets, it failed to go to the root of the evils of the age, and only attacked the symptoms, and could never have laid the foundation of a religion fitted to make a permanent impression on the world.

Perhaps we should not be far from the truth if we affirmed that he only gave prominence to duties which were generally recognized as such, but were practically forgotten without offence to the conscience ; that he laid emphasis on duties whose obligation no one could seriously question, but which the men of that generation did not lay much to heart. He had a keen discernment of the low moral condition into which, in spite of their religiosity, the people had sunk, showing itself in laxity of life and conduct, and in a disregard or violation of many social duties. But he did not trace these evils to their deep lying source, and he did his part by urgently denouncing them, and calling men to amendment of life as the means of restoring a better social state, and so preparing for the advent of the kingdom of God.

The prime and indispensable aim of all moral and religious teaching is to rouse the better will from that semi-torpid languid state which allows the immediate natural and uppermost inclinations to have their way without let or hindrance, to a state of active and resolute exercise. Now this tendency, which John's teaching no doubt had to a certain extent, was in a great measure counteracted by the expectation to which he gave countenance, as the ancient prophets had given, of a supernatural interposition by which a better state of things morally and religiously might be established.

John preached the necessity of repentance, indeed, or amendment of life, as a means of preparing for the expected event, or even of hastening it on. But still he spoke of the event, and taught his countrymen to think of it as a thing which would come to pass, irrespective of individual or national amendment, so that they would naturally regard it as the cause, rather than as the effect, or even the accompaniment of a higher national life. They could hardly but be encouraged by his doctrine to trust that this event, when it did come to pass, would turn to their advantage as children of the covenant and heirs of the promises, and thus to continue their attitude of expectancy, instead of exchanging it for one of energetic moral action.

Such teaching might not be wholly without effect ; it might operate beneficially by awakening the hope of better things, and stirring up the minds of men to put the house of their souls in order.   But that better state of things could never be inaugurated until men began to be acted on by quite another understanding, viz., that the kingdom of God—the supreme good connected with that expression—was not a thing to be waited for, or to come upon them from above, but a thing which was to spring up from within.

That the Baptist, notwithstanding the depth and force of his moral feelings, still looked for the establishment of the kingdom by means of a great visible manifestation, and that to that extent he shared in the carnal and worldly ideas of his countrymen, and in their tendency to " seek after a sign," is evident especially from the message which he sent from his prison to Jesus, " Art thou he that should come, or do we look for another ? "   He doubted whether Jesus could be the Messiah, notwithstanding the excitement caused by his teaching and the power of his doctrine, because he had inaugurated no new order of things, and had either wrought no miracle any more than John himself, or perhaps because the miracles which he was reported to have worked were not sufficiently notable or stupendous enough to mark him out as the promised Messiah.   In Jesus he recognized a teacher greater than himself, a teacher come from God, the very ideal of a religious teacher, worthy it may be in all respects to be regarded as the Messiah, except in the one respect that his teaching was accompanied by no great signs and wonders from heaven, nor by the establishment of a divine monarchy ; in fact, he expected that the Messiah would be something more than a teacher, and that teaching would be the least of the Messiah's functions, instead of the highest and greatest, as it was in the case of Jesus.   For the same reason that Judas betrayed his master, John seems to have doubted his Messianic mission.

And we may sum up our estimate of him by saying that the prophetic spirit was renascent in him, the main distinction between him and the prophets being that for him the divine event or manifestation, which was to make all right for Israel and to satisfy its expectations, was near at hand, had come within a measurable distance, and might fall within the experience of that generation, while *they* had seen it as a far-off vision, as an event not to happen in their age but at some distant period, and after the lapse of many years.   It has been conjectured with much probability that John calculated on the nearness of the time, because, in his opinion, the misery and humiliation of Israel under a foreign yoke had reached their climax, and the hour of Israel's necessity would prove to be God's opportunity.   Many passages in the prophets seemed to warrant the expectation that God would arise for the salvation of Israel in a day of extreme calamity.   And such a day could not but be thought (by a man like John of fervid patriotism and deep moral earnestness) to have arrived at that time of national degradation.   He had not been able, any more than the prophets, to disenthral himself from the sensuous expectations of his countrymen, and from the beliefs which clustered round the idea of their covenant relation with God.   And whatever immediate and apparent response his protest against the formality and unsound moral condition generally of his contemporaries may have called forth, it was doomed, like that of the prophets before him, to make no permanent impression, had it not been taken up by a mightier than he.

We have the concurrent testimony of the synoptic Gospels that Jesus began his work by calling on his hearers to "repent, for the kingdom of heaven is at hand," an announcement identical in form with that of John the Baptist.   From this circumstance some recent writers have drawn the inference that the doctrine of Jesus was a mere continuation or repetition of John's.   By way of making out that whatever is novel in Christianity is due to Paul rather than to Jesus, that Paul rather than Jesus is the founder of our religion, they have even gone the length of saying that there was nothing novel or distinctive in the doctrine of Jesus.   But this thesis receives no support from the announcement with which Jesus broke silence.   The *expression* "kingdom of God" was not new in the mouth of Jesus any more than it was in the mouth of John, but the *idea* which the former expressed by it *was* new. There had been a longing in many hearts for some better social state than had yet been seen, and men had vaguely pictured out to themselves some such state, but no one had ever come within sight of the idea which Jesus had laid hold of.

In the mouth of a Jew the words "kingdom of God" expressed his conception of the *summum bonum*—of an idea common to all nations in one form or another, congenial we may say to every human heart. In so far as the idea of righteousness was embraced in the Jewish form it might be a higher conception than that of any other people, but in so far as the kingdom was conceived of as restricted to the Jewish nation, it was a mean, selfish, and disennobling conception—a reflection of the strange contrasts in the Jewish character which have made it an enigma in history. The element of righteousness in the idea was the preserving salt, the redeeming ingredient which needed only to be accentuated and spiritualized as it was by Jesus to destroy its particularism and convert the particularistic into a universalistic idea. Jesus broke ground by his announcement that the kingdom of God was at hand, but his whole subsequent teaching showed that the kingdom which he had in view was different in nature and in its mode of coming from that of which John and all preceding teachers had spoken. And it will appear more and more as we proceed that the opening words of Jesus, though identical in form with those of John, were entirely different in spirit and intention. In employing the formula of John to convey a new meaning Jesus did but follow an instinct common to all religious reformers, to bring out to popular apprehension the continuity of the new with the old and pre-existent beliefs, to gain the general ear, to facilitate intelligence, and to avoid offence while awakening attention.

For John the kingdom of God was a visible system or institution, differing in some respects no doubt, but in many, perhaps in most others, resembling the kingdoms of the world. John expected that it would come with pomp and outward demonstration, so that men would at once and without difficulty recognize it for what it was, not less than if it had been seen to come down from God out of heaven like the holy city, the new Jerusalem of the Apocalypse. But for Jesus it was an invisible or rather an ideal kingdom, which would come, when it did come, "without observation," *i.e.*, unobserved by many, without visible show or circumstance, a kingdom which would have its place and power "within men," and would work secretly in the hearts of men and propagate itself by infection or sympathetic contact as by a sort of leaven from soul to soul. By some avenue of insight or meditation or experience he had made the discovery that the only possible kingdom of God was the reign of righteousness in the souls of individuals and in society as composed of individuals ; that it could come into existence or manifestation only in so far as righteousness prevailed ; that it actually did already exist wherever righteousness did prevail; in short, that it consisted in a state of mind and a manner of life, and could be approached or laid hold of only by means of a resolute and energetic surrender of individuals to the will of God. He had seen plainly that the fleshly passion of the Jew for national supremacy even were it gratified would only aggravate the real evils of his lot and enhance the moral distempers of the time ; that the greatest evils under which the people groaned were self-inflicted, and could not be remedied by external agencies, that, under every change of circumstance, even were it such as might tax divine power to produce, enough would still remain to debar them from true blessedness.

According to Jesus the kingdom of God was identical with the reign of righteousness; the one did not form a complement to the other as John and others believed, nor did they admit of being separated in thought as if they were distinct phenomena. These negative determinations are evidently conveyed in that notable counsel, to "seek first the kingdom of God and His righteousness, and all other things shall be added." The full meaning of these words may be best brought out by a slight change in their arrangement, as thus, " Seek first the righteousness of God and His kingdom shall be yours, and all other things besides shall be added to you." The true kingdom of God, the only kingdom deserving the name, that good thing which you ignorantly seek, whose nature you misconceive, will be found in seeking the righteousness of God. If that righteousness become the main object of your pursuit, if the search for it become your ruling passion, the kingdom is yours already, yours of necessity, yours *ipso facto*, just as he also said that the kingdom was theirs already in possession who were poor in spirit and pure in heart. This was a thought which John never reached, and as little did any of the prophets before him. To us it may seem self-evident, and it has passed in substance as a common-place idea into the thoughts of men. But to the men of that day it was novel, hardly intelligible to any, and no doubt offensive to many. The thoughts of the Jewish people had for ages been running in quite another direction, towards a kingdom in which righteousness of a sort might indeed prevail, but towards a kingdom which had other and more attractive attributes, which would not only satisfy many other longings besides the love of righteousness, but longings which were the reverse of righteous, into which the idea of righteousness hardly entered, and between which and the love of righteousness it would have puzzled them to trace any very obvious connection. The expectation cherished by the Jews could not be satisfied with a spiritual revival which could only begin in the self-reformation of the individuals composing the nation. A consummation to be thus attained seemed, apart from its difficulty, mean and inadequate compared with the expectation of a grand national renovation based on their covenanted relation to God, an "all too simple fare" for men who had long been "fed on boundless hopes."

The ideal nature of the kingdom of God is defined materially by its identification with the reign of righteousness, but formally by that saying (Luke xvii. 20, 21), "The kingdom of God cometh not with observation : neither shall they say, Lo here ! or, Lo there! for, behold, the kingdom of God is within you." According to these latter words the kingdom has its seat in the hearts of men, hidden there and invisible like everything that is truly great in human life. Jesus might mean that it is within men, i.e., within all men in the limited sense, that their lives are conditioned consciously and unconsciously by God-ordained and spiritual laws. And probably the more adequate and correct rendering of the words is that the "kingdom of God is among or in the midst of you," which we may understand as referring to the objective presence of the kingdom, in the fact of that divine order which is the expression of divine wisdom and goodness or of that "tendency which makes for righteousness." In the spiritual world objectively considered there are certain laws which obtain eternally, and which condition the life of man even when he does not take cognizance of them or reflect on their existence, or even does what he can to thwart them. But when these laws disclose themselves to his consciousness and are accepted by him as the guide and rule of his life, they acquire a new potency and a new significance. In that case the kingdom of God may be said to come or to spring up in the heart, and its laws through being recognized and reflected into the consciousness, unfold a power of changing the life which they did not previously exert. This is what is involved in the words of Jesus, what the words suggest to the modern mind. And an analogous instance will show that what takes place here by the revelation of spiritual law to the consciousness takes place in other spheres of thought and being, or, we may say, universally.

There is an electric force which under its proper laws has always been in existence, operating from the beginning throughout the universe, and conditioning the physical life of man, though unknown and unsuspected by himself. But an immense difference for the life and environment of man has been created in modern and recent times by his discovery of the existence of that force and by his application of it to his own use and benefit. Even so the discovery of spiritual laws and the application of them to the guidance and government of human life may be compared or almost said to amount to the rise of a new kingdom in the midst of men, and is calculated to put a new face on society. Simply by their disclosure to human consciousness they are fitted to make all things new and to revolutionize human affairs. The kingdom of God had in a sense, as we see, been always present, always operant among men in God's world, only it had been latent; its existence like that of other forces had not been apprehended, because men had not the eye to see it; they did not know where to look for it. And what Jesus did was to take away the veil that hid it from them. He did not create it, or lay its foundation, or bring it into existence. He only disclosed it to their eyes, he apprized them of its nature, taught them where to look for it, that it was in the midst of them, that it was nearer than they thought, and he showed them the way to become members of it; a service this so great no wonder that the church learned to revere him as the Head and Founder of the kingdom itself. And yet in the very fact that this kingdom, consisting as it does in the rule of spiritual laws, was always present, there lay the possibility that it might disclose itself, or, to use the language of Jesus, might draw nigh to men at any moment. Centuries before his day the idea of such a kingdom dawned upon a man of prophetic spirit, and was dimly but strikingly expressed by him (Deut. xxx. 14), where he says that the word of God, which we may understand of the gospel of the kingdom, or of the righteousness of God, with which St. Paul (Rom. x. 6) brings it into connection, was not hidden from men nor far off from them, but in their mouth and in their heart to do it. The obvious meaning of which language is that the higher and hidden life of righteousness being near at hand may at any moment disclose itself, as no doubt it often has done, sporadically to individuals here and there in all ages and countries. But the secret having found no adequate utterance, and having left no record of itself, always died upon the lips of the initiated few, and went no further until it was plainly translated into speech and uttered into life by Jesus, and by him laid as the foundation of a new, self-propagating, self-perpetuating society.

Let no one object, as many do, to the idea here presented of the kingdom of God, that it is too abstract and modern to have been entertained by Jesus, or that he shared in the expectation common to John the Baptist and the Jews generally of a visible and concrete manifestation of the kingdom of God. To us it appears that the negation of this Jewish idea is the very element and measure of the novelty of his doctrine. There is no evidence whatever that he expected the kingdom to exist in a massive or institutional form, or to be identified with any outward or visible state or corporation. He probably expected that the movement which he sought to inaugurate would spread by the extension of the reign of righteousness over society at large, leaving existing social aggregates and organizations much as they were. His simple, unfigurative, and fundamental proposition with regard to it was that this kingdom was within men, *i.e.*, spiritual and ideal ; and this proposition must be held to control the interpretation of all his utterances with regard to it, whether made by himself or by disciples in his name. That his thought dwelt exclusively on an ideal kingdom, or, as it is less properly styled, an invisible kingdom, is shown by the notable proposition just quoted, whose authenticity is guaranteed by the fact of its being reported as his by men to whose ideas on the subject it ran counter. And a certain presumption is also lent to this view by the fact that one at least of his predecessors in the prophetic line came near to him in this direction. The thought of Jeremiah was so engrossed by the effusion of the new spirit which he foretold, that he was comparatively indifferent to the preservation of the national life and the maintenance of the temple service. Wellhausen says of him, that he did not expect that his way of thinking could ever become the basis of a national life, and that "instead of the nation, the heart and the individual conviction were to him the subject of religion." For Jesus the kingdom of God existed already in every individual who aimed at conformity with the will of God. It might exist under many forms of government, it might arise without creating disturbance to any existing institution. In becoming members of it men became as a salt, a light, or a leaven in the earth, terms all of them expressive of a force which works secretly, silently, and unobtrusively. This purely ideal nature of the kingdom is also expressed by St. Paul where he says that it is "righteousness, peace, and joy in the Holy Ghost" (Rom. xiv. 17). And the circumstance that the personal followers of Jesus and even Paul himself, for a time at least, clung to the idea of a second advent and a new earth is for us a proof, not that Jesus had given encouragement to such an idea, but that inherited Jewish notions retained a hold of their minds in spite of his teaching, or that the natural tendency to let go or exchange the pure idea for a sensuous embodiment of it was too strong for them, and prevented them from entering fully into his thought. For such reasons we are disposed not to accept as genuine any language attributed to him which is, or is supposed to be, inconsistent with this idea, however abstract or modern the idea may be.

Than this saying of Jesus none more profound or far-reaching has ever been uttered. It comes near to saying, or rather it is identical with saying, that God himself is within us, a saying which has been often muttered in the philosophies both of the old and the modern time, but which no philosophy has had the boldness or the strength to stand or to fall with. It amounts to this, that human nature is potentially divine, that the God of whom we should stand in awe is not the God above us or the God around us, but the God within us; and that when we pray to Him it is but our higher nature in its weakness communing or pleading with our higher nature in its ideal strength, deep calling unto deep. When it was first uttered it declared the futility of the Jewish expectation that the kingdom of God was to come upon men from without; and for the present time it declares the futility of saying that the grace of God is "a life poured in from outside," for, as Jesus elsewhere explained it,

K

" Not that which entereth the mouth defileth (or purifieth) the man, but that which cometh out of the mouth." The tendency to seek a sign or symbol of the divine presence in the universe is ineradicable in human nature, or, we may say, an ultimate principle in it. The grand error is that men look for an outward sign in past historical events, or in some present day experience, instead of looking for the sign within themselves, in that higher nature which exists ideally in every man. This was what Jesus taught his disciples to do, but his thought was too great and too deep for the apprehension even of St. Paul, the chiefest of his apostles, and hence this greatest of his followers thought he had found that symbol, or shechinah of the divine presence, in the embodiment of that ideal nature, in the person of Jesus himself, where it has stood for his disciples to this day so as to interfere not a little with that spiritual worship of which One alone is the object.

The great revolution which Jesus sought to effect in the mental attitude of his countrymen, and which he more or less imperfectly succeeded in effecting in the case of his few disciples, is clearly intimated in his language concerning John the Baptist as recorded in Matth. xi., where he says, " All the prophets and the law prophesied until John." The meaning of these words is, that prophetic men had seen the kingdom of God as afar off; they regarded it as a thing not yet present, not yet possible, but reserved for future manifestation or for the latter days, and devout men, like Simeon, were taught by their prophecies to wait for it as the " consolation of Israel." John again represented a point or period of transition. He was more than a prophet, notwithstanding that the least in the kingdom of God was greater than he. It seemed to Jesus as if John had advanced beyond the prophetic stage, as if the word of the kingdom had trembled on his lips, but that he was not able to utter it. John had a presentiment of the approach of the kingdom as of something just about to be revealed, about to come into existence. He had a faint glimmering of its true nature, but he could not grasp it firmly, he could not reach or express it fully. This was reserved for Jesus to accomplish. And while he adopted the formula of John to begin with, that the kingdom of God was at hand, his whole subsequent teaching implied that it was already there. In Matth. xii. 28 and Luke xvii. 21 he says so, in so many words, and he could mean nothing less when he declared that it was already in possession of the poor in spirit.   Not only had the kingdom of God, objectively considered, been always present ; he could say of it, subjectively considered, that it had come at the time he spoke, because he had discovered it and divulged to his disciples its true nature, because he himself was in the midst of them a living proof in his own person that the new era had begun, and because they themselves, through sympathy with him, had begun to be conscious of its presence, to submit to its rule, and to enjoy its blessedness.   We may here mention that we do not suppose that the various expressions which Jesus uses with respect to the proximity or presence of the kingdom of God, viz., that it was at hand, that it was (already) come, that it was in the midst of them, betoken any growth in his view of its nature, any maturing of his thought in regard to it.   They are but varied expressions accommodated to the occasion, or to the audience, of the one idea, which was essential to his doctrine.

This doctrine was that the kingdom of God was not a thing to be waited for in the expectation, which the Jews entertained, that it would drop down upon them from above without effort of their own, for it was already in the midst of them ; yet so, we have now to add, that, to be enjoyed or taken possession of, it had to be sought for and striven after, to be laid hold of, or, to use his own words in the discourse just referred to, to be " taken by violence," to be seized by force,—emphatic language employed to give point to the antithesis between the attitude of men's minds towards the kingdom of God before and after the time of John.   In fact, the doctrine of Jesus may be described as a summons to men to forsake or relinquish their passive and expectant attitude for an energetic, resolute, and impetuous entrance into the kingdom.   And simple as this summons may appear to be, it is enough, when received and acted upon, to change the whole aspect of religion, the whole character of the spiritual life, and may we not also say, the whole course of human history.   These great effects may be expected from it, because by the removal of a heterocratic bandage from the human will, it allows the whole force of that will to deploy and set itself free.   When carried out to its full and legitimate consequences, this doctrine will yet discharge the supernatural element from the religious life, and substitute the power of the idea for the power of a hyperphysical agency upon the heart.

It appeared, in our remarks on the religion of Israel, that its watchword was " wait," wait for the great event which, as the elect people of God, you have in prospect. The attitude of expectancy thus imparted to the Israelitish mind, was the inevitable effect of their mythical history, or of their election and covenant relation, by which it was suggested to them that their final salvation would be an arbitrary sovereign act of God, like that which had been manifested in their election, and in no sense an act of their own. The watchword of the religion of Jesus was just the opposite. It was, " Wait not." Wait not for any event whatever. The kingdom of God is already come, it is in the midst of you ; you have only to lay hold of it, to take it by violence (Matth. xi. 12), to enter it by storm. Formally considered, this injunction was distinctive of the religion of Jesus over against Judaism : it demanded a complete change of mental attitude towards God and the spiritual world. It implied that God was a being of infinite good will, who placed no obstruction in the way of man to the highest good, but left the attainment of it in man's own hand, so that man had only to will, that he might, with the full consent of God, enter into possession of the highest bliss.

Taught by an experience of which we have no record, Jesus had gained a distinct and luminous apprehension of the truth, of which many in all ages have had glimpses, and of which the modern mind is rapidly getting a firm hold, that " for the individual there is no radical cure outside of human nature itself for the evils to which human nature is heir," that " within ourselves deliverance must be sought," and that " God says to each of us, If thou wilt have any good, take it from within thyself." He asserted the freedom of the human will as few teachers have ever done. He took for granted that there is a power intrinsic to the soul of man to react against the evil, to disengage itself from the chain by which it binds him, and to break that causal nexus by which one sin draws another after it. His own experience had inspired him with the confidence that man, at the bidding of the ideal, has a power within himself to lay the cross upon his strongest inclinations, to practise self-renunciation, to enter the strait gate, to make righteousness the first object of his pursuit, to subjugate the tendencies of his lower nature, and so to become a member of the kingdom of God which, for him, was equivalent to the highest conceivable good. From such a conviction as this, the immediate inference was that there was no need to wait, or to look as John and the Pharisees did, for any higher good, or for a miraculous manifestation of any kind from heaven, for that all true help could in the last resort come only from within in the form of self-help : not from the God above, but from the God within us. Jesus was no iconoclast, and with that reverence for the past which was conspicuous in him, he might still retain the belief in which he had been educated, that a messenger from heaven was about to appear on earth ; but it was still more clear to his mind, with the clearness and certitude of experience, that men ought not, and needed not, to wait for the appearance of such a messenger, for that every man had the key to the kingdom of heaven in his own hand: that by applying that key he might be a Messiah to himself as well as to others by persuading them to do the like for themselves. It was only "an evil and adulterous generation" which insisted upon "a sign from heaven" to announce the presence of the kingdom, or waited for a celestial messenger to inaugurate the reign of righteousness—adulterous perhaps, because, while professing to long for the kingdom of God, it had an eye to a kingdom which was not of God.

To avoid misapprehension, however, let it be carefully noted that the autosoteric,* or self-saving, self-helping process to which Jesus sought by his teaching and example to animate his followers, does not exclude help from without, according to the laws of our nature. In illustrating this proposition we glanced in a former passage of this discussion at the philosophic idea of the Ich and the Nicht Ich. According to this idea the

---

* The writer of this volume has adopted the terms "autosoteric" and "heterosoteric" from E. von Hartmann. But the idea expressed by the term "autosoteric" was expounded by the writer in a sermon on "The Renovating Power of Christianity," published some years before he had read von Hartmann's "Krisis," where the word occurs, and where it is denied that the term can be applied to the Christian system of religion. The idea that the term did, on the contrary, describe the religious process, not indeed as it appears in the Pauline dogma but as taught by Jesus, was the outcome of the writer's own reflections, not to say experience, and was what led him to alter his view of the Genesis of Christianity and to produce this work, of the many imperfections of which, considered as a presentation of that view, no one can be more aware than himself.

germ of the better nature within us requires to be developed, the law of our being to be fulfilled, through the trial of contact with the good and the evil around us, the good having been reinforced in Christian lands by the light of truth, of which Jesus, as we believe, gave the highest and purest expression ; or by what Mr. Arnold calls "the secret and the method" of Jesus. But, not to go back upon that idea, and to use a less abstract if less adequate illustration, we say here that the auto-soteric doctrine must be qualified, if qualification it can be called, by observing that there are forces inherent in the universal order ; God ordained, independent of the will of man, which yet come to his assistance when he fulfils his part ; that is to say, when he places himself in line with them, or when, by self-denial and self-discipline, and the control of his uppermost tendencies, he adjusts his action to their operation, and so avails himself of their aid. Whereas, when a man expects by mere force of will, or by the act of faith, to call into operation some force which is above nature, and which would not come into operation except for this act of his, this is the simply heterosoteric view, which was not known to Jesus.

The forces here referred to may be said to be conveyed to us through the social environment, that is, through our organic connection with the race of which we are members ; and admittedly they form an indispensable help to the individual who is intent on self-discipline. Apart from them, indeed, such discipline is neither practicable nor conceivable. But, however favourable the social environment may be, there is need, in the last resort, for an act or decision on the part of the individual himself to bring it to good effect, and to render it helpful to his discipline. The influences which radiate from society, even when it is Christianized, being partly good and partly evil, affect men differently, and there must be a certain elective affinity by which the individual assimilates the good in the formation of character; which affinity consists in a determination or habit, however unconscious, of the man himself. In this sense it may be said that the existence of such influences does in no way clash with the autosoteric character of the doctrine of Jesus.

But, besides the injunction of self-denial and self-abnegation, Jesus also inculcated the great doctrine of the forgiveness of sins, and it may be thought that this doctrine is at variance with what has now been said as to the autosoteric character of his teaching. To show, therefore, that such is not the case, a few remarks upon this doctrine will here be necessary, though the subject is one which will afterwards engage more of our attention.

Forgiveness of sin is an expression used by Jesus to denote the most salient or central phenomenon of the religious life. It is the interpretation, from a theistic point of view, of a profound experience of man's inner life, or of a law of that universal order through which and through which alone, God acts. According to this law it is, that for every individual who truly and resolutely turns from sin, and makes it his main aim to conform to the ideal requirements of his nature, his involuntary lapses and shortcomings cease to weigh upon his conscience, and to cause division or schism in the soul, and from being a source of intolerable self-reproach and discouragement, become a spur and stimulus to a better and ever better life. The relief thus experienced from that distressful and debilitating feeling, and the momentum thus imparted to the spiritual life, cannot but be traced by the devout theist to an act of oblivion and of grace on the part of God. That is the light or the aspect under which this fact of the inner life presented itself to Jesus, and was presented by him to his disciples ; and as it is with his point of view and his manner of thought that we have here to do, we need not trouble ourselves to ask if there be any more pure, more abstract, or philosophical explanation of the fact. Of the great practical value of such a view of it there can be no doubt. For a man thus to identify the working of his own higher or ideal nature with the presence of God within him, or to connect it with the thought of the God above him, the effect will be to lend intensity to his reverence for the ideal, and to impress him with the necessity of being true and honest, and of making sure that his sense of relief does not rest upon mere self-delusion and conceit. Possessed by the conviction of the placability of God, the mind, unfettered by the haunting fear of a divine Nemesis of treasured wrath and of the arrears of guilt, and thus, " at leisure from itself," resolutely addresses itself in spite of the physical and social consequences of past sin which remain, and in spite of the persistence of contracted habits, to persevere in its endeavour after the better life, and finds its reward in a sense of growing conformity to its own higher impulses.*

According to a theist, then, such as Jesus was, this great and crowning fact of the inner life is a proof, that, in consideration of the honesty and sincerity of the individual, God, who looks to the heart and the intention, takes the will for the deed, which is what is meant by divine forgiveness. There is here nothing supernatural. The belief in divine forgiveness is not awakened by supernatural illumination, nor is forgiveness itself imparted by any supernatural act of God. The man simply takes the verdict of his own conscience as the verdict of heaven. Just as the sinner feels, by the constraint or law of his own nature, that he is an object of divine condemnation, because he is condemned by his own heart, so the penitent, who turns from his sins, feels that divine condemnation is lifted from his soul, because his own heart has ceased to condemn him (1 John iii. 21), " If our heart condemn us not, then have we confidence toward God." We see, then, that divine forgiveness is not to be understood as importing any heterosoteric element into the spiritual renovation of the individual, or as in any sense implying the influx of an extraneous divine power into the stream of life. Being ever at hand for the penitent to lay hold of, it is rather the condition, or system, under which the individual is placed for carrying on the self-educative, self-redemptive process. And we shall only add that in its theistic aspect, as taught by Jesus, the doctrine of forgiveness is not, like a theorem of Euclid, demonstrable by pure and abstract reasoning, nor like a historical fact, to be established by the evidence of human testimony ; but it is an idea, or suggestion, which verifies itself practically in the experience of individuals by the beneficent influence which it exerts on their life and conduct, and by its enabling them to carry on the struggle with their lower nature. Apart from this struggle, the doctrine of forgiveness, however firmly believed, becomes a dead letter, or worse, an injurious

* If any man, without conscious reference to the Divine Being, and out of pure reverence for the ideal, places the latter before himself as the aim of his pursuit, and devotes himself in all sincerity to its realization, though ever falling short of it, the name of a religious man can hardly be denied to such a man, seeing that whether he know and confess it or not, the ideal is really the presence of God within him. But of such a man it is doubtful whether he can properly be called a Christian.

narcotic. In illustration of this statement, we may quote the striking language of Dean Stanley in his *Eastern Church* :— " In Christianity is forgiveness for every, even the greatest sin ; a doctrine, which, according to the manner in which it is presented to us, is, indeed, the worst corruption, or the noblest boast of the Christian religion. It may be the hateful Antinomianism, which, in the Protestant Church, has taken shelter under the Lutheran doctrine of " justification by faith alone " ; in the Roman Catholic Church, under the scholastic doctrine of priestly absolution. But it may also be the true doctrine of the gospel, the reception of the prodigal son, of the woman who was a sinner, and of the thief on the Cross, the doctrine that the divine forgiveness is ever at hand as soon as man turns to be forgiven." The law of divine forgiveness could not but be recondite and difficult of apprehension, owing to the circumstance that its manifestation in action is contingent on that moral and spiritual effort to which human nature is so averse. It could only reveal itself fully to one who strove towards perfection, and to secure *de facto* to his higher nature that supremacy which belongs to it *de jure*. And how few are there of whom this can be said. But we shall yet endeavour to show in the case of Jesus, how such a doctrine could dawn upon the mind of humanity, and also, that when received on authority, such as his, it would, by the infusion of hope, be calculated to rouse the soul from its state of moral inertia, and put new vigour into its effort, when already engaged, but hopelessly and unsuccessfully, in the Christian struggle.

We repeat, therefore, that the doctrine of Jesus is autosoteric. The one great and special lesson which he enforced was the duty of self-abnegation, of self-extrication from evil, the pursuit, that is, of the ideal life, stimulated and sustained by the conviction of the divine forgiveness of our lapses and shortcomings. That for which the Jews professed to wait—the help of God— was, according to Jesus, already given, already provided, and freely laid to hand, viz., the law of the forgiveness of the sins that are past, so that nothing was wanting on the part of the individual, but that he should enter the strait gate, and take up the cross, which, considering that all other conditions were satisfied, was pronounced by Jesus to be a light and easy yoke. Here, for him, was the supreme proof of the goodness of God, and the supreme motive of our love to Him. It is observable, that he nowhere *insists* on the duty of believing in the mercy of God. He tells men simply to call God Father. It is, as if he took for granted, that when men engage seriously in the effort to conform to the requirements of their ideal nature, they will naturally and necessarily believe in God's placable character ; it seemed to him as if the consciousness of personal weakness which that struggle would bring to light, would make this view of God so welcome to the individual that it did not need to be enforced.

So much at present for the teaching of Jesus. We proceed now to observe that there is not in the synoptists a particle of evidence that he started with the belief that he was the predicted Messiah, but much to the contrary. At a future stage we shall endeavour to point out how that belief may, in the sequel, have grown up in his mind, and what an important service was thereby rendered to the Christian society. But at present we content ourselves with saying that his proclamation as to the presence of the kingdom of God was underlaid by the thought that a Messiah might or might not come, that come when he might, whether soon or late, there was no need for any individual to wait for his coming. Men could not tell when he would come, men could not hasten his coming ; the time was a matter which the Father kept in his own hands, a matter over which they had no control, and for that very reason alone, a matter of comparative or entire indifference. The first, the immediate duty incumbent upon all men, to which all else had to be postponed, was to exercise the power they had of entering the kingdom of heaven which was already open, of making themselves free of its privileges, and of securing the highest bliss of which their nature was susceptible, a bliss without which even the kingdom of their imagination, of their fondest hopes, would descend in vain into the midst of them. The true, the only kingdom of God was of such a nature that all might enter it without delay ; even while the Messiah deferred his coming it was open to all who made righteousness their first pursuit ; and its coming was not, in the first instance at least, an event of national consequence, but of individual experience, so that the social life of the nation could be elevated only by the elevation of the individuals composing it.

This certitude had, we doubt not, as already said, been conveyed to him by irrefragable experience ; it was a faith for him which could not be shaken. From the gnomic and parabolic form, as well as from the authoritative tone of his teaching, it may easily be seen that he was perfectly aware of the immense significance of his doctrine, and fully anticipated its great and permanent effect on human life. He not only understood the religious situation of the time and the hidden needs of humanity, but he also knew exactly the contribution which he was making to correct, to elucidate, and to exalt the religious idea ; and in the conscious possession of an all-important truth for the elevation of his kind, he knew himself to be greater than John and all the prophets, and, as the Gospels indicate, had no scruple in setting aside their words when they came into collision with his gospel, or in declaring that he alone knew the will of the Father. With all their depth of spiritual insight, the prophets had fallen conspicuously short of the highest truth for the guidance and elevation of human conduct. In attributing the disasters and decadence of Israel to its declension from righteousness, they had devised the means of making the national conscience more sensitive, and of awakening the people to a consciousness of their moral degradation; but in exhorting them to a better life as a means of reviving their political state and restoring their prosperity, they incurred the risk of involving, if not themselves, yet the great mass of the people, in the danger of considering national and individual prosperity as the great end and object of desire, and righteousness as only a means to that end, and not as an immediate object of desire for its own sake ; thus unintentionally and unconsciously removing the kingdom of God to a distance, and giving encouragement to that evasive tendency which was sufficient to account for the lapse of the people into formality and the mere show of religion. Could they, like Jesus, have recognized the truth that calamities might befall the nation, however righteous it might be, and that suffering and persecution might overtake it, not merely in spite of, but by reason of, its righteousness (Matth. v. 10), they might have reached the idea round which they fluttered, but on which they never fairly settled, that righteousness itself was the first and main thing to be possessed of, and that all else would be added to those who sought it for its own sake; not that even the reign of righteousness would necessarily be accompanied by outward prosperity, or inward happiness, either for the individual or the people, but that all else, good or evil, would minister to the higher good, to that inner harmony of the soul, and to that sense of reconciliation with God which are one and the same thing. This was what Jesus taught, and to this day it is the central truth of Christianity. We are Christians only in so far as we practically recognize and form our lives upon it ; it is, indeed, the practical recognition of this truth which to this day constitutes the strength of our religion, while, with the practical oblivion of it, the heart of Christianity grows cold under mere forms and garniture. Other teachers may have had glimpses of the same idea, but none ever apprehended it so clearly as Jesus did, no one ever displayed the same fidelity to it in life and practice, and no one ever exercised the same power of stimulating others to form their lives upon it. He alone divined the power of the idea, and used it as a lever to move the world.

A great, but somewhat prejudiced, critic has given it as his deliberate opinion that the words put into the mouth of Jesus by the fourth Evangelist, " God is spirit, and they that worship Him must worship Him in spirit and in truth," give expression to the most distinctive principle in Christianity. To us, it appears, that the better authenticated words of Jesus on which we have dwelt, " The kingdom of God is within you," or " in the midst of you," contain a deeper and more comprehensive truth, of which that other is only an inference ; and a truth, too, drawn from immediate and profound experience. The meaning of these latter words is large, viz., that divine laws were then, and ever are, operant in the world of nature and of spirit, even though men may be unconscious of the fact that the kingdom of God consists in the reign of these laws, and that it is by recognizing and conforming to them as the rule and guide of life that men become members of that kingdom in the plenary sense. We hold that this was the grand disclosure which Jesus made to the world, on which his claim to be considered the greatest of all the great founders of religion may be chiefly rested. What he said was true for all ages and for all countries ; but it became true in the highest sense when men rose to the knowledge or full consciousness of it ; and, indeed, it is only in the human consciousness that this truth did, or could, reveal itself. There was nothing but a dim foreshadowing of it, if even that, in any of the Hebrew legislators and prophets. These men did, indeed, discover many of the moral and spiritual laws that are operant in the world ; but to them the kingdom of God, so far as they had a conception of it, consisted of something more, of something beyond the operation of such laws, of something visible and external, of something not ideal merely, but real. Whereas Jesus proclaimed that there was nothing beyond this, nothing higher than this for man to look to. And though his view may not have been clearly apprehended even by his followers, yet enough of it was impressed upon their minds to spiritualize the thoughts of men, to refine the religious idea, to consign all rites and ceremonies, all external institutions and observances to a subordinate and merely ministrant office in the service of religion, and to elevate morality, *i.e.*, conformity to eternal, as opposed to mere conventional and temporary, national and traditional regulations, to its supreme place in religion. The disclosure of this to man was the achievement of Jesus, which gives him a unique place in the history of religion, a position more unique, let us say, than that of the discoverer of gravitation in the physical sciences.

CHAPTER VI.

LEGAL OR PHARISAIC IDEA OF RIGHTEOUSNESS, AND OF THE RELIGIOUS RELATION.

WE have now seen that to express his definite idea of a reign of righteousness upon earth, the term "kingdom of God" was used by Jesus in a manner accidentally, or by way of accommodation to a vague and indefinite idea, which had grown up in the course of Jewish history, and that it recommended itself to him as a means of indicating and preserving the continuity of his teaching with the religious ideas then current among the Jews. It is obvious that his announcement with respect to the kingdom of God, its nearness and its character, though it came first in order in his teaching, must, in the evolution of his thought, have been preceded by the discovery of the spirituality, blessedness, and all sufficiency of true righteousness. We proceed, therefore, to observe that what was important for all time, and essential to his work of reformation, was the new and fuller meaning which he gave to the word "righteousness." By so doing he may be said to have "set the current and to have formed the standard" of the coming age. To this point, therefore, we shall now direct special attention.

The prophets, the poets, and the sages of Israel had laboured to impress a higher character on the popular and traditional religion of their times, and in so doing had foreshadowed much of the teaching of Jesus. But the nation at large seems, even in the prophetic age, to have entered but little into their moral and spiritual elevation, and to have been slow to follow their lead and adopt their views. And after the age of prophecy the religion of Israel seems to have retained little trace of its influence and rather to have undergone a strange degeneration.

During this period, in which the synagogue rose and flourished, the doctrine of a future life and of a bodily resurrection sank deep into the hearts of the people. But it seemed as if, while the horizon of humanity was thus widened and expanded, the religious life at the same time lost in depth and earnestness; as if the people had sought to lighten and mitigate the new burden of responsibility thus laid upon them by emptying the law of its spiritual contents and reducing its requirement to that of a mere mechanical and, therefore, practicable service.

The external rites and ceremonies of religion owe their origin to a spirit of devotion, which seeks in them an expression for itself. But these very forms, originally expressive of a spiritual reality, are wont to be retained and practised as a mechanical substitute after the spirit has fled. It is conceivable, therefore, that in the early periods of the history of Israel there may have breathed through the forms of its religion a devout spirit which may have more or less disappeared for certain periods. In the long course of that history the growth may have been towards a more moral and spiritual conception of religion; but this general tendency may not have excluded great alternations, backward as well as forward movements. And if we accept the critical conclusion that the Psalter (to say nothing of the Book of Wisdom) was mainly the product of the exile and the post-exilian age, we should be inclined to say that the forward movement of what is called the prophetic age was prolonged beyond the limits of the latter; but there can be no doubt that for several generations before the time of Jesus a backward movement had set in. The vice of formalism, against which prophets had protested in vain (though not without some effect in the earlier post-exilian ages), revived in greater force, and with altered aspect, in the later ages of that period, despite the prophetic tradition, and called forth the protest of a mightier prophet than Israel had ever known.

The downward and carnalizing tendency exhibited by the religion of Israel during this later period was probably much promoted by the circumstance already adverted to, viz., that the ritual and statutory observances peculiar to it were what after all distinguished it most visibly and palpably from the religion of surrounding nations, and that on that very account the loyal Israelite (who knew nothing of the principles which now obtain in the comparative science of religion, and keenly felt the neces-

sity of keeping aloof from heathen practices) would seek to
erect and maintain a barrier betwixt himself and the worshippers
of other gods by punctilious, unswerving, and ostentatious
attention to the distinctive outward forms and usages of his
nation. At former periods of their history, when the rites and
ceremonies of Israel bore more of a family resemblance to those
of neighbouring nations, there might exist a feeling that these
forms were not of essential or paramount importance, and were
subordinate to the higher duties of morality and religion.   But
in the course of ages, when these rites and ceremonies were
stereotyped into distinctive and diverging forms, and the divine
imprimatur, moreover, was stamped upon them by the Levitical
code, there would grow up the feeling that their observance
was the true test of fidelity and constituted the true wall of
partition between the Israelite and the heathen.   The ceremonial side of religion would, by a natural tendency, rise in
importance, and its moral aspect would be thrust more and
more into the background.   To maintain distinction in the
former was so much easier than to preserve superiority in the
latter.   We have also to take into consideration that a people
accustomed in a hundred ways, and under every variety of
circumstance, to testify regard to the divine will by sacrifice
and other outward observance, would also be tempted to suppose that they might satisfy the moral and spiritual precepts of
religion by the merely outward observance of them also, even
when the heart gravitated to the forbidden evil.

When the Jew of those times spoke of righteousness—of
that manner of life and conduct which the law enjoined, it
was of quite another sort from that which Jesus, as we shall
find, sought to enforce.   That section of the people, indeed,
which in the New Testament is represented by publicans and
sinners, would feel themselves excluded from a kingdom to
which righteousness in any sense was the key.   Their lives
were, or were supposed to be, regulated by no rule or idea
whatever of righteousness, and the discourses of Jesus would
be felt by them to be a call to take an earnest view of life—
to renounce pleasure, or expediency, or self-interest, as their
rule of action, and to conform their conduct to a principle or
law which was divine, and independent of individual caprice,
or self-will, the best or only apparent examples of such conformity which they had hitherto seen being the Scribes and

Pharisees, who were regarded as models of the religious life, and as the accredited expounders of the law. But Jesus had to deal not with those only whose lives were thus framed on no ideal, but mainly with those whose lives were constructed on a false ideal. What he undertook was to challenge the false and evasive Pharisaic ideal: to break its authority, and to erect the true ideal or standard of life in its place. His primary object, no doubt, was to impart to his followers the doctrine which he had drawn from his own spiritual experience; but he could hardly broach that doctrine, or make any statement of it, however simple, except in language antithetic to that of the Pharisees. In a secondary sense, therefore, his teaching was eminently polemical and destructive in order that it might be constructive and truly creative, and rescue religion and morality from that tendency to degeneration into which the leaders of the people had fallen. He expressed this view of his mission, and sought to impress it on all who listened to him, in that striking sentence, which was the complement of his injunction, to seek first the kingdom of God and His righteousness; and which, along with it, must have been the refrain of all his teaching—viz., "Except your righteousness exceed the righteousness of the Scribes and Pharisees, ye shall in no case enter the kingdom of heaven." There was a danger that even publicans and sinners, the lost sheep of the house of Israel, if they were awakened to greater earnestness, might yet fall into the mistake of forming their lives on the Pharisaic model; and for their sakes it was necessary, as well as for those who had embraced the Pharisaic life, to declare with emphasis that such a life gave no title to the kingdom of heaven. He had to make manifest to men's consciences that the Pharisaic ideal was too low in its pitch, and too narrow in its range; and to place in contrast with it a better form of righteousness. To introduce a higher standard than the Pharisaic was thus a main object of his teaching; and even at the present day, it is by contrasting and comparing the righteousness which he inculcated with that which was taught and practised by the Pharisees, that we may best understand the real nature and the central principle of the former.

Whether the polemical and simply thetical elements of the teaching of Jesus were contemporaneous, or whether the polemical element only emerged after Pharisaic opposition had declared itself, it is impossible to tell. The synoptic Gospels do not afford us the means of determining this question, for it is quite manifest that in them the connection and order in which Jesus uttered his sayings are not preserved. These have unquestionably undergone a process of mixture and rearrangement, either at the hands of the Evangelists themselves in compiling their Gospels, or during the formation of the traditions from which the Evangelists drew their materials. But if we may risk a conjecture we should say that, as it was the dissatisfaction of Jesus with Pharisaic *doctrine* (and not simply with Pharisaic practice, as was the case with John), which prompted him to step forth as a teacher, a certain polemical element may have characterized his teaching from the first ; though it is natural to suppose that, towards the end of his ministry, the tone of polemical acerbity would become more pronounced and emphatic. Comp. Matth. xvi. 12.

We make no allusion here to Essenism. The Essene communities which flourished in Palestine at that time seem indeed to have observed a rule of life of a more spiritual kind, and otherwise favourably distinguished from the Pharisaic ; and it has been maintained or suggested by some writers, that Jesus may in early life have been a member of one of these communities, and been much indebted for his higher views to an acquaintance with their usages and tenets. There is no necessity to deny the possibility of his association with these fraternities, though no record of it, and no allusion to it, however remote, has been preserved in the Gospels. But no impulse, and no enlightenment, which Jesus could have derived from this quarter, could explain or account for his view of the better righteousness, which was the fulcrum of his teaching. Notwithstanding the many parallelisms between Essenism and Christianity, it is a great exaggeration to regard the latter as a direct development of the former. The differences between them are fundamental. The Essenes had none of the hopeful buoyancy of the religion of Jesus ; they did not even aspire to be the salt of the earth, but only to escape the evil that was in the world or coming upon it, by shunning contact and intercourse with it. The development of such a system could never have led to the freedom and hopefulness, the universalism and vitality, which are acknowledged features of Christianity. The aloofness from common life which these sectaries maintained,* the dualistic element of their system of thought, their asceticism, and the rigidity of their ritual and their sabbatism placed a wide interval between their standpoint and that of Jesus. And we may rest assured that his great advance beyond the popular and Pharisaic religion of the time cannot be accounted for by his acquaintance with their views and practice. We have, therefore, to explain the development in his mind in some other way.

Pharisaism we regard as only the concentrated spirit, the more rigid form or the "superlative" of the religion common among the Jewish people in that age ; the latter was but a mild or lax form of Pharisaic legalism, and formed the atmosphere which Jesus breathed in his earlier years. We conceive that he arrived at his evangelical standpoint in morals and religion, partly by an independent study of the old prophetic literature, and partly by the reaction of a profound religious instinct against the very system of legalism, through which it had, up to a certain point, been trained.

Jerusalem was the headquarters or stronghold of Pharisaism : in remote outlying Galilee Pharisaism only manifested itself in a modified form. Had Jesus never made an excursion beyond the limits of Galilee the probability is that the inherent vice of Judaism might never have revealed itself to his mind. But that was not the case. The synoptists, indeed, mention his final visit to Jerusalem as the only one which he paid to it during his public ministry : but in the years before he began to teach he must often have visited the holy city, and have had the opportunity of observing Pharisaism full blown and, so to speak, rampant. And these visits to Jerusalem may have had the same effect upon him, in opening his eyes to the true nature of Pharisaism—the orthodox Judaism of the day—as the visit to Rome had upon Luther, in opening his eyes to the scandals and abuses of the Papal system. The religious life in Galilee might not be very active or very spiritual ; but the distance between the outward show and the reality might not be very

---

* It may be that this fundamental defect in Essenism suggested the exhortation addressed by Jesus to his disciples, in Matth. v. 15, 16, " Let your light shine before men." Such an exhortation was not needed, as against the Pharisaism of the day. As against that, the exhortations of quite the opposite kind, in ch. vi., were directed : " Take heed that ye do not your alms before men," etc.

obtrusive ; and a loving charitable spirit might be able to hope the best, and to believe that the outward forms gave expression to an underlying spirit of genuine devotion.   In Jerusalem, on the other hand, the unreality was too patent to escape the penetrating eye of Jesus, and would produce a revulsion in his mind which would carry him on to the conception of a higher and purer service.

The confusion and co-ordination, in theory and in practice, of law absolute or spiritual, and law positive or statutory, the cause or effect of the unreality here referred to, was not confined to Judaism and Pharisaism.   It was, and still is in some measure, common to all nations and all religions.   It is, therefore, conceivable that a similar reaction might have occurred in other lands, as indeed seems to have been the case in India under the influence of Buddha.   And as bearing on this possibility, it may be remarked that the specially anti-Judaic aspect of Christianity, under which it is presented by St. Paul, was, as will yet appear, ultimately, that is, in the post-Pauline period, quietly let fall as something unessential or even misleading.   But probably the error in theory and practice, to which reference is here made, was carried out more systematically and to greater lengths in Judæa than elsewhere.   And the reaction against it which occurred there was also more emphatic and permanent in its results.   The conditions there were peculiarly helpful to such an issue.   The ground was there prepared.   The Hebrew prophets, with whose writings Jesus was familiar, had uttered and placed upon record a powerful protest against the ceremonialism and externality of the national worship ; only they had not sufficient mental force and insight to erect a barrier against it, and to enunciate with emphasis the distinctive principle of a higher cult.   But this was what Jesus was able to supply.   He inherited their thought, and started from the ground which they occupied ; and, in the announcement that the kingdom of God was within men, he effected a further and final advance, by which religion was raised to a still higher level.

The Pharisaic righteousness, to the consideration of which we now turn (under the guidance chiefly of Wellhausen), consisted in the ἔννομος βίωσις, the regulation of life, to its minutest details, by the statutory enactments of the written and oral law, which was believed to have been given by special privilege and illumination to Moses and the other ancients of the people.

By the punctilious observance of these rules and statutes, the Jew was supposed to show his respect for the divine will, and to conciliate the divine favour. This was the whole duty and the whole religion of those who "waited for the consolation of Israel." According to such a view, the autonomy of man's nature was wholly lost sight of. In all questions as to conduct the Jew was taught not to look within ; not to consult the inward oracle, his own sense of right and wrong ; but to have recourse to the law and to the testimony, as these were authoritatively interpreted by the scribes and teachers, and to these alone. No room was left for the function of conscience (indeed it has been remarked that conscience is a word " strange to the Old Testament ") or for an ideal of life, in the proper sense of the word. The conception of a better life than the actual or average one could hardly be said to have a place in Jewish thought. Conformity to the statute was a mere opus, beyond which there was no aim in life, no thought of elevating the individual character, of ameliorating the social environment, or of entering upon a course of self-discipline for the purification and improvement of the inner man. Attention was confined to the duties positively enjoined, while little or no regard was paid to the cultivation of the corresponding virtues. The statute by which life was regulated was satisfied by a mechanical routine and outward compliance, which being practicable to those who were versed in its terms, seemed to them to obviate all call and necessity for repentance and a change of heart, and to justify that self-righteous tone, and that superciliousness of sentiment and behaviour which characterized the Pharisees. When, through ignorance or inadvertence, the statute was violated, expiations were prescribed for every such occasion. It was only when the commandment was sinned against, " with a high hand," that is, with presumption and premeditation, that such expiations lost their efficacy, and the duties of repentance and restitution were supposed to come into force. But it is easy to see that the self-righteous Pharisee could easily explain away, to his own satisfaction, all such aggravations, and ascribe a venial and expiable character to every transgression of the statute, so that the duties of repentance, and of a thorough change of conduct, might be kept out of sight or evaded. The statute embraced the whole outward life, and enclosed it in a network of observances ; but the affections and sympathies of the heart might neither be exercised nor acted upon by its fulfilment. And whatever may have been the case in the best ages of the commonwealth, or whatever may be the case among the Jews of the present day, it would seem that the tendency to mere formal observance was fully developed among the Pharisees of the time of Jesus. The show of mere outward respect to the will of God which these expositors of the legal system were able to keep up, and thereby to mould the practice of the great mass of the people, lent to them that character of hypocrisy with which as a class they were chargeable, though, no doubt, individuals were free of this taint.

In the Mosaic Code no distinction was made between moral, civil, and ceremonial enactments. All alike were clothed with the same extraneous authority, and were held to be of equal obligation. And though in the earlier post-exilian period the effect of this co-ordination might be to give a moral pathos to ceremonial and social observances, the effect of it had grown to be the very reverse in the time of Jesus. Even the moral observances had in his time contracted a formal and mechanical character. On the other hand, there had been a growing tendency to expand the ceremonial requirements, and to swell their number by the addition of sacrificial, purificatory, sabbatic, and liturgical regulations, of which Moses and the prophets knew nothing. And we should not be far wrong perhaps if we affirmed that practically, if unconsciously, the ceremonial observances were practised as a sort of atonement in general for the breach and infraction of the moral requirements; just as the ritual and technicalities of worship are apt to be among ourselves, with this difference, however, that in Judæa this perversion received countenance from the example and teaching of the highest authorities in such matters, while it only lingers now as a survival or superstition among the unreformed and ill-instructed in Christian lands. The value thus attached, more or less unconsciously, to ritual and ceremonial services, was the motive for their multiplication, and gave rise to the feeling, which expressed itself in the question of the rich young man in the Gospels, " What good thing (more) shall I do?" For, however punctilious the ἔννομος βίωσις, and however close the network which it threw around the life, it could never altogether satisfy even the most inactive conscience; something more was still in demand, and that something was sought for in the prescription by authority of some new observance, to afford a means or opportunity of showing a more than commonplace devotion ; a tendency which we may see in the sectaries of the present day, in their efforts to outbid the more regulated and canonical observances of the established churches. A certain definite observance and rule of action thus came, in the course of ages, to be sanctioned or prescribed for every imaginable situation or emergency in life, and for every omission or neglect of duty. The observance of legal forms, *secundum legem agere*, became the great business of life; something of the kind had to be attended to every hour of the day ; all common offices had to be performed in a prescribed mode, so that practically no act of life was indifferent ; the middle space between what was lawful and what was unlawful, between what was profane and what was religious, between the clean and the unclean, ceased to exist, or tended with every generation to become more and more narrow. It was no trifle to keep in mind the computed 613 precepts of the written law, and the much greater number of the unwritten or consuetudinary law. And religion, as thus conceived, had to be studied like a profession and practised like any intellectual or manual occupation. Every religion, not excepting Christianity, has exhibited the same tendency to reduce itself to a mere bodily exercise, to remove the life from the jurisdiction of conscience, and to atone by stability and uniformity for the lack of spontaneity and vitality.

The endless multiplication of legal provisions, of which we have explained the cause and origin, had also the effect of throwing the direction of the people in religious matters into the hands of learned castes, the Scribes and Pharisees, who had made the law their peculiar study, and had also to some unknown extent elaborated its details. The acquaintance of these men with the provisions of the law gave them a " lordship " (Mark x. 42) over the great mass of the people, whose ignorance of the law was accounted as a " curse " ; and the study of these provisions, which thus became the employment of their lives, was also stimulated by the very convenient doctrine that in point of merit it was co-ordinate with their observance. One of the most liberal and enlightened of the Rabbins, near the time of Jesus, is recorded to have declared that a layman, *i.e.*, a man outside of these classes, and therefore unskilled in the law, could not be religious, inasmuch as such a man could not know what was sin and what was not, and therefore could not but fall into sin and contract uncleanness. Those classes, which had made the law their study, and knew its provisions, were the " wise and prudent " (Matth. xi. 25), who trusted in their superior knowledge, and it was they whom Jesus had in his eye when, in the spirit of true humanity, he thanked his heavenly Father that it was not to them but to the poor and ignorant, the babes and sucklings, that he had revealed the things of the kingdom. No words could better show his sense of the immense revolution which he hoped to accomplish in the religious attitude and judgment of mankind.

To any one who had the faintest tincture of the prophetic spirit, or, we may say, the faintest foretaste of the evangelic spirit, such regulations, by reason of their complexity and multiplication, could not but be burdensome and oppressive in the highest degree, and appear to be a superfluous and vexatious byplay of the religious life, an arbitrary and capricious imposition by a hard and ungracious master. But to the Pharisee they were easy and tolerable, because, for the weightier matters of the law—justice, mercy, and truth—they substituted observances which were less contrary to his self will. True they destroyed his spontaneity of action, and converted duty into a matter of calculation, but they appeased and soothed his conscience, and by supplying him with a ready answer to all questions of casuistry, they relieved him from the pain of that self-discipline which largely consists in the faithful and candid application of moral principles to the conduct of life.

These regulations laid a yoke upon the spirit, bnt not the yoke of true religion. Their observance only gave to life a religious air, by filling it with quasi-religious transactions, which were a ministry of the letter, but not of the spirit, of the divine law. It is true that, in the circumstances in which the people were placed, under the jealous suspicion and hostility of unsympathizing polytheistic nations, the open manifestation of punctilious outward fidelity to the law, could only be maintained by a great devotion, which, to do them justice, they seldom shrank from ; but their devotion was largely prompted by national pride and assumption, and by the desire to propitiate the God of their fathers. At bottom it was the offspring of fear, and of an uncharitable and mercenary, grudging and exclusive habit of mind. Under the influence of such mixed feelings, the Jews might be, and often were, blameless and devout in outward deportment, and imbued with a spirit of awe and reverence before the unseen Power ; capable of manifesting the depth and sincerity of their convictions by heroic martyrdom for the faith, while manifestly, or even ostentatiously, destitute of the finer sensibilities of the heart, of charity and sympathy, as well as of that sincerity, which consists in the harmony of the outward and inward life, and sheds a beauty and a grace over all. It was of a religion such as theirs that that aphorism of a great observer holds true, that they who give themselves up to it are apt to use it as a stalking horse, and to fall into hypocrisy.

The religion of the Pharisee failed entirely to discipline the individual will, and had no tendency to realize the idea of a more perfect society. His observances brought him into no sympathetic contact with other men. It has been said of him that he could see the wrongs of which the world is full, and have no desire and make no effort to right them ; that he could be brought face to face with suffering, and misery, and ignorance, and stretch forth no hand for their relief; he could see the man lying wounded on the road, and pass by on the other side. It has even been said, with a certain degree of truth, that, for the fulfilment (satisfaction) of the Pharisaic sense of duty, the existence of society was hardly required. And yet, further, it was hardly a recognized part of the Pharisee's righteousness to extend the spirit of law to the control of the inner life, or to make it his aim to contribute to the establishment of conditions more favourable to the growth of the kingdom of God. To do what was enjoined in the statute, but to consider the issue as the affair of God, and to leave it coldly in His hands was his mental attitude; and his strict legality was combined with a spirit of comparative indifference to all human, and even to all national interests, except the one interest involved in the coming of the kingdom of God, which, he believed, he could neither help nor hinder, neither hasten nor retard. This negation of all higher aim could not be wholly unfelt by the Pharisees themselves ; and hence they threw themselves with all the more enthusiasm on the faith that, provided they propitiated God by the painful, servile, and fruitless compliance with His statutory requirements, He would be constrained or compelled to work for them and to fulfil His promises made long ages before to the fathers. They expected that the kingdom for which they waited would be advanced and established, not by any works of theirs, but simply by some mysterious, sudden, and unknown work of God, which might be regarded in the light of an extraneous reward for their faith and patience ; but in no sense as the necessary result and outcome of their service.

The negative form of the Decalogue was the necessary result of the fact that, being a politico-religious code of morals, it could only prescribe the minimum requirement for securing the stability of civil life ; or it was, perhaps, yet more the result of the limited development in that age of the moral sense. Its very form helped to encourage the notion that all righteousness might be fulfilled by abstinence from overt transgressions, and from flagrant violations of the duties enjoined ; that a formal and mechanical observance of the statute would suffice to satisfy its requirements in its religious, no less than in its civil aspect ; and that God did not look too inquisitorially into the inner life, but was satisfied by the consecration to Him of the outward life. If men did not avow a belief of this kind in so many words, they at least lived and acted for the most part as if it was their belief. The leaders of religious thought and practice paid tithes of mint and anise and cummin, but omitted the weightier matters of the law. . They stopped short of the adulterous act, but allowed the eye and the imagination to rove abroad. And this strictness of outward observance had an imposing effect upon the people at large ; and put out of countenance those feelings of natural piety, and of a more spiritual religion, which could not be wholly extirpated. It was not easy for any one to call in question the sincerity of those solemn religionists ; to discredit their teaching and practice was a thankless and a dangerous task. Only one could venture to make the attempt who was above suspicion ; who had sounded the deeps of man's moral nature; who had discerned the utter worthlessness and pettiness of mere outward homage to the divine will, and was besides sure of himself ; ready to brave all, and to stake life itself in the conflict which he was sure to provoke. And just such an one was Jesus. From the first he set himself earnestly to challenge the errors of the Pharisees in doctrine and in practice ; to discredit their authority, to destroy their prestige, and to substitute a true ideal of righteousness for their false ideal. The outwardness and formality ; the negative and propitiatory character of the Pharisaic righteousness was what constituted that legality of service, which is opposed to the true evangelic service ; the one rendered mercenarily with an eye to reward ; the other rendered freely as an act of thanksgiving to the Author of all good.

Not the least doubtful effect of the co-ordination of the cere-monial with the moral ordinances in the Mosaic law, was that it opened up a sphere of religious activity, apart from the sphere of moral activity ; that is, a sphere of activity devoid of any direct practical aim or bearing on the inner life ; a sphere upon which the religious forces and emotions are apt to be wholly misdirected, as, indeed, was the case in later Judaism. Some-thing of the same kind has taken place also in orthodox or dogmatic Christianity; the only difference, and that a great one, being that, in the latter case, the separate religious, emotional activity has been made to revolve round the person of the ideal Christ, and, through sympathy with his person, has been kept in close and indissoluble connection with the graces and humanities of life, of which that ideal figure was the most resplendent example—the symbol of the most perfect life which humanity has been able to conceive.

The righteousness of the Pharisee involved the idea that his whole life ought to be consecrated to God, in the sense that no act whatever could be morally indifferent or merely innocent, but, by being performed in a manner prescribed by divine authority, should have a character of holiness impressed upon it. The effect of that idea was seen in that air of sanctimonious gravity which distinguished him. But the service which he actually rendered was that of the outer life only. It was a stipulated service by which he commuted for the unreserved devotion of his whole man. There was in it an evidence of the dread and aversion with which men are apt to shrink before the breadth and depth of the divine law as written on the heart and inter-preted by the honest and enlightened conscience. Ordinances which rest on mere authority give men an excuse for not scanning too intently the law of the spirit of life written within : enabling them to keep up a show of deference to the will of their divine Author, and to avoid the appearance of breaking away altogether from His will. There was no wonder that prophets should express more than a doubt of the divine authorship of such ordinances, or that Jesus himself should have declared that one at least of the Mosaic regulations had been given for

the hardness of men's hearts, and thereby have lent countenance
to the conjecture that in his judgment many other such had
been given for the same or other inferior considerations, rather
than for their intrinsic and eternal validity.   But the time was
come, he implied, when all that had been done by way of concession to human weakness or obduracy should be disowned or
rescinded, when it should be made known that religion should
be pure and undefiled, that righteousness should be its own
reward, and should be seen to be in itself the element which
constituted the kingdom of God, the perfect form of society on
earth.

  Let it here be observed that the characteristic features of the
Pharisaic spirit, as now depicted, were not entirely due to the
abuse or perversion of the Mosaic law, but were in some
measure due also to the intrinsic nature of that law itself, considered as the establishment of a covenant relation between
God and Israel, and as the summary of the mutual obligations
of these two contracting parties.   The law and the covenant
might be regarded as the manifestation of God's free and
distinguishing favour for Israel ; and so long as this aspect of
them was kept in view the effect would be to ennoble and
spiritualize the minds of the people.   But recent investigations
into synagogal theology, by Weber and others, have brought
out the curious fact that in the pre-Christian age this capital
aspect of the covenant was in a great measure lost sight of, and
that quite another construction of it had gradually gained the
upper hand.   The idea of an eternal law founded in the nature
of God and man, which the tradition of the Sinaitic legislation
tended to obscure, was dropped out of mind, and it came to be
thought that God had given the law from Sinai, in order that
Israel might have the means, not otherwise possessed, of dis-
playing its regard to God's will, and so of acquiring a claim
upon His favour.   Naturally it followed that the more precepts
the law could be made to embrace, or to imply, the greater
merit could the Israelite accumulate.   Hence arose the endless
multiplication of legal prescriptions ; hence, too, the idea that a
certain reward was annexed to the observance of each separate
precept, and that a meritorious act of this kind must precede
each proof of goodwill on the part of God.   It was with this
idea in his view, of the relation between himself and God, that
the Pharisee paid scrupulous attention to the letter of the law,

not merely to propitiate God, but even to lay God under obligation, and to make Him the debtor. The result of such ideas could only be the mercenary practice of almsgiving without charity ; of prayer without devotion ; of fasting without penitence ; and of a religion in which austerity and sanctimoniousness, ostentation, self-complacency, censoriousness, and hypocrisy were distinguishing features. The evangelical idea of the relation between God and man, which had begun to dawn in the prophetic age, was supplanted by the ultra-legal idea ; and it was, we believe, the settling down of this latter into its rigid Pharisaic form, with the fatal consequences now depicted, which called forth the indignant protest of Jesus. His sense of this crying evil was what prompted him to that great enterprise, which was to transplant, or, to use a Paulinistic expression (Col. i. 13), to translate his countrymen out of the legal into the new or evangelic religious relation, and so to spiritualize and raise the standard of life. And we hold this to be, next to monotheism, the greatest step ever taken in the development of religious thought ; enough, in fact, however imperfectly apprehended, to account for all that followed in the wake of his teaching ; for all that influence of Christianity upon human life, which has kept pace with the development of the moral sense, and with the growing complexity of the social relations.

CHAPTER VII.

THE EVANGELIC IDEA AS TAUGHT BY JESUS.

To the externality—the mechanical and mercenary nature of the righteousness affected and practised by the Pharisees—Jesus opposed the demand of inwardness and spirituality as being essential to the righteousness of God and constitutive of its reality. This is a conception which runs through the Sermon on the Mount, and all his teaching which has come down to us. He commenced his discourse on the mount by affirming the blessedness, *i.e.*, the membership in the kingdom of God, not of those who punctiliously observed certain outward and statutory forms, but of those who were imbued with certain inward dispositions, such as poverty of spirit, meekness, and purity of heart. But his doctrine on this point received its most gnomic and striking expression in that memorable saying of his, " Not that which goeth into the mouth defileth a man, but that which cometh out of the mouth, this defileth a man." " Those things which proceed out of the mouth come forth from the heart, and they defile the man." These words are an example of the literary or popular form of speech, inasmuch as they are charged with a meaning, and thrown out at an object or idea, to which they do not give full and adequate expression. They imply the comparative or absolute worthlessness of the regulations laid down in the oral and written law respecting meats and drinks, and, by parity of reason, are suggestive of the relative unimportance of many or all of those ceremonial observances, to which the people were taught by the Scribes to attach such value. If Jesus did not go the length of making a categorical statement to this effect, it was probably due in part to the necessity of proceeding piecemeal, and opening up his views by degrees; and in part to his anxiety to deal tenderly with a system under which, with all its defects, the religious sentiment had been nurtured in Israel. Only the more obvious and crying abuses of the legal system called forth his indignation, and drew from him such depreciatory utterances as the above, which admitted of a general and far-reaching application. Such sentences, and others of a like import, suffice to show that he recognized and laid stress on that distinction between moral and ceremonial requirements, which Scribes and Pharisees deemed of no practical consequence, or were careful to ignore: that he regarded mere bodily defilement as not involving the soul in impurity; and they led up, or came near to the principle, that there is no religious or moral obligation to avoid what does not defile the soul, or to practise what does not purify the life; and that such avoidances and such practices are neither binding on the conscience nor acceptable to God. Nor can it be anywhere gathered from his teaching, that he contemplated the possibility that ascetic practices and penances would afterwards be enjoined by authority derived from him.

The righteousness, then, which he demanded of his disciples excelled that of the Pharisees, in respect of its inwardness and spirituality. It was the righteousness of the whole man—of the hidden man of the heart, as well as of the outward deportment—making itself apparent on the surface of the life, but having its seat in the life below the life, or in that which constitutes the inmost self of the individual. According to Jesus, it is a man's disposition, the state of a man's heart generally, which decides his moral worth. The true value of an act is determined by the intention with which it is performed, and the motive which inspires it. The guilt of the overt and palpable form of evil is already contracted by the lusting of the heart, even though the deed, which is the natural consummation of it, may, for lack of opportunity, or from the presence of some inferior and countervailing motive, not be actually committed. This doctrine strikes at the root of evil, cuts off every evasion of the commandment, and attaches the stigma of affectation, insincerity, or hypocrisy, to all conduct which is not an index of the inner life of the soul. It also enlarges the sphere of religion incalculably, by bringing it into connection with this inner life, and placing the whole man under the horizon and surveillance of law. The doctrine is, besides, so radical and far-reaching, that it may be said to have involved all that followed in his teaching. Manifestly it tended to undermine the authority of the Scribes and Pharisees, because it proposed a standard which, while commending itself to the moral sense of the people, was more exacting than that which could be gathered from the teaching and practice of these men, and exhibited them as taking credit for a righteousness which only satisfied a lower standard.

We are far from claiming absolute originality for this—the fundamental and root doctrine of Jesus. For, not to mention the thinkers among the Gentiles, with whose ethical doctrines there is no evidence of his being conversant, we acknowledge that the prophets of Israel had said much that was like it— much that approached it, though never so distinctly, so consciously, so emphatically, or in forms of language so level and impressive to popular apprehension. The Law itself had said, " Thou shalt not covet," though not perhaps in the sense which St. Paul put upon it, as a prohibition of concupiscence in the mere conception. And a prophetic voice had said of God, that He " desired truth in the inward parts " ; and we can see the same thought of inwardness struggling to find expression in prophetic ages, only to be lost sight of again under the rule of the priestly and learned castes. Yet, as we cannot suppose that Jesus was guided to his deeper insight into the nature of righteousness by any special illumination, neither do we require to regard him as a mere repristinator or servile restorer of past thought. He reproduced it in a new and transfigured form, and gave heightened prominence and significance to those very features of the religious idea which had been forgotten or obscured by the commentators of intermediate times. If he was, as no doubt he was, indebted to the suggestive language of a prophetic generation long asleep, he was yet able, by native insight, to apply to that language a searching criticism, and by comparing it with the ideas and usages prevalent in his own day, to discern the deep significance of those very elements of the prophetic teaching which had been lost to view, and to reduce them to a definite and gnomic expression which the ingenuity or dulness of later theologians has never to this day been able wholly to obscure. This was a work of the highest genius, but one too which could never have been achieved except for the labours of preceding commentators—the happiest result of which may have been to reveal to the penetrating eye of Jesus the defects of prophetic teaching—the points at which the prophets had failed, not for want of fidelity, but for lack of discernment, to give forth a more certain sound. Simply by giving due, *i.e.*, absolute significance to elements which had never received a prominence commensurate to their importance, he brought into view the religion of the heart, and presented to the faith of man an ideal so plain that it could dispense with the aids of representation by symbol and ceremony, and find its legitimate and necessary fruit in a pure and ever purer form of the common life of man.

We may even venture to go further, and say, that it was necessary that that formality, to which there was from the first a natural tendency in Judaism, should develop itself into utmost rigidity, in order to disclose to the mind of Jesus its full remoteness from true religion, and to evoke in his mind that strong revulsion towards the recognition of the inward aspect of religion of which his whole doctrine gave evidence. It has been truly said that "flagrant evils cure themselves by being flagrant"; and in the light of this observation we may say that Pharisaism made Jesus possible. The religious instinct in him was strong enough, and luminous enough, not to be vanquished by the Pharisaic element into which he was born—to withstand the common tendency to throw the inner side of religion into the background, and to recognize and react against that flagrant evil. Or we may say that his doctrine, while it was a reaction against Pharisaism, was the development of Jewish religion in its best days, and that it emphasized a side of religion which prophets had recognized and embraced in their view of it, but had not fully mastered, or sufficiently accentuated. By supplying a remedy to this great defect, Jesus threw a new light over all, and effected a complete transformation of the religious idea. If this be a just view of what he accomplished, some may be inclined to dispute its claim to be regarded as a work of transcendent genius, seeing that the wonder is, that the idea of inwardness, after dawning on the prophetic mind, should ever have fallen into abeyance, or that a people who believed in God's knowledge of the secrets of men's hearts, should ever have forgotten that He could be satisfied with no homage short of that of the whole man.   Be this as it may, the inwardness which he declared to be an essential and distinguishing mark of true righteousness, came as a new element, to produce unheard-of changes in pre-existing thought and life relations.   His doctrine must have come upon his disciples with a shock of surprise—not, indeed, as being absolutely new to them, or to other men, for many had surmised or suspected it before his day ; but it was now for the first time recognized in all its significance for the higher education of man.   Jesus made the doctrine his own, and associated it with his person for all coming time, by being the first to lay emphasis on it as a *sine qua non* of morality, and assigning to it its proper fundamental position in the system of religious thought and practice.

We do not admit, either, that it detracts from the originality of Jesus, that many before him had forecasts of his fundamental ideas, or that he arrived at these by being specially inspired, or endowed with a nature above the human.   The minds of men are almost infinitely graduated in their several capacities, the difference in degree often seeming to pass into a difference in kind—a fact which is expressed by saying that one man has talent while another has genius.   It may be laid down as a general maxim, that the truth which can appeal to the common order of minds will disclose itself to some mind of exceptional discernment.   And it may be doubted whether there is a single truth relevant to human nature and its needs, which the human mind, by individual or collective effort, has not the power of excogitating for itself—not always, it may be, by syllogistic methods, or mere logical deduction from the accumulated treasures of the past, but sometimes by a vital and spiritual process and guidance, beyond that of the understanding—by the breathing of a new spirit and a fuller life into pre-existing forms of thought.   " The imagination," it has been said, " which shudders at the hell of Dante, is the same faculty, weaker in degree, which called that picture into being." And in like manner, we may say that the spiritual faculty, to which that great idea appeals, out of which Christianity has sprung, is the same (only weaker in degree) as that which rescued it from obscurity, and placed it fully before the human consciousness.   Besides the historical and extraneous conditions amid which Jesus appeared, we must, indeed, also take into account that depth of insight, and that fidelity to conviction which belonged to his personal endowment, before we can satisfactorily explain his discovery. Those conditions, as already said, were substantially the same for multitudes of his contemporaries, while he alone, of all these multitudes, penetrated to the nature of true righteousness. We may not be able to trace, with any approach to certainty, the path by which he rose to his grand convictions, but we may conceive that there were secret, unfrequented avenues by which that faithful heart and that pondering soul might arrive at them.

And yet, in propounding the necessity of the spiritual element, Jesus was not so engrossed or pre-occupied by his discovery as to go to the opposite extreme. He did not become one-sided, and overlook the importance of the outward fulfilment of all righteousness. It was the righteousness of the whole man which he inculcated, and for him the outward act, in its own time and place, was as necessary and as indispensable as the will and the inclination to do good. He said expressly, that men should be known by their fruits and judged by their deeds. He enjoined men to make the fruit good as well as the tree, and demanded that the whole man should be cleansed in act and thought—that there should be harmony between the outer and the inner life. For him this harmony was what constituted reality in religion and morality. Without it there could only be an unreal appearance of both. It was reserved for one of his disciples (the writer of the Epistle of St. James) to teach, if possible, with even greater emphasis, that the inner life, to be perfected, needed to be manifested in the outer life ; that the mere sentiment of benevolence, or even the will to do good, was unreal, unless translated into act when occasion offered. But this emphasis was called forth by a new phase of evil, even worse if possible than the Pharisaic—by a danger or tendency which attached peculiarly to the profession of Pauline Christianity—that is to say, the danger of religion running to seed, and exhausting itself by indulgence in mere feeling and sentiment, or in willing without doing. The evil to which Jesus sought more immediately to apply the remedy was the unreal *act* of goodness—an evil which had for long been growing in Israel, and was at last consummated in Pharisaism. Not that in theory or in doctrine the importance of the motive, and of the right disposition, was denied even by Pharisees, but that practically these were forgotten or put out of sight. It was, indeed, because there was a latent consciousness of the imperative value of these in the hearts of all men, that when, to emancipate men from the authority of Pharisaic doctrine and usage, Jesus appealed to their sense of the importance of the right disposition, and laid it down as a postulate and first principle of religion, he did not speak quite in vain to the men of his generation, and that his voice was not as that of one crying in the wilderness. And yet the interval was wide indeed between the standpoint, not merely of the Pharisee, but even of the prophet, who, in moments of spiritual elevation, could express the conviction that God desired truth in the inward parts, and hated the covetous thought and the adulterous look, and the standpoint of Jesus who declared the principial worthlessness of all righteousness which did not proceed from the heart, and laid down as a fundamental axiom, that no law was fulfilled if obeyed with reluctance, and no virtue genuine unless cultivated for its own sake.

By laying down that no good fruit could proceed except from a good tree, and no good act except from a well-disposed heart, Jesus passed sentence of condemnation upon all mechanical forms of religion, and on all merely outward discipline and legality of behaviour. And when we bear in mind that he had a firm faith in the inspiration of the Old Testament generally, and of the Mosaic legislation in particular, in which moral duties and ceremonial usages were enjoined as of equal obligation, and the negative was the prevailing form of the moral precepts ; when we consider the prescriptive right which Scribes and Pharisees had long enjoyed as expounders of the Law and the Prophets, it becomes evident to us that it must have required a prodigious moral courage—a prodigious force and independence of character, besides a profound confidence in the autonomy of his own nature, to take up, without loss of reverence, with a view of religion so novel, and in many respects so different from that of which he professed it to be the fulfilment. Indeed, the combination in him of the revolutionary with the conservative and reverential spirit—a combination common to him with other great founders of religion —only becomes intelligible to us by supposing that, like St. Paul afterwards, he may have considered all these legal regulations, and the negative form of the Decalogue, to have been given by way of concession, or accommodation, to a rude and ignorant people, and that to retain them in permanent force was only to keep the people from advancing to a more perfect and instructed state. By some such consideration as this, which is partly hinted at in what he says of the hardness of men's hearts, and of the necessity of putting new wine into new bottles, he could, on the authority of the inner voice, while still believing in the divine sanction of the Law of Moses, venture to proclaim that it must give place to a more perfect way, and declare that instead of thwarting, he was in reality carrying out the divine intention in its every jot and tittle.

To sum up now what we have said in the present connection, we repeat that we do not ascribe to Jesus the discovery of any religious truth, absolutely new and original, but only the enunciation of truths which were not theoretically denied; which all men rather were semi-conscious of—which existed in a latent, germinal state in the minds of all men—which many gifted men had given utterance to before him, though not with the same perception of their significance for human life—truths, in fact, which, by the great majority of men in all ages, and under all religions, had been practically forgotten, and indeed still are. He was not the very first, it may be, to discover that inwardness is an essential attribute of righteousness; but he perceived the full importance of this element, and insisted upon it with an emphasis and persistency which no former teacher ever exhibited. He saw and taught, in a way which could scarcely be misunderstood, that no deed could be really good unless it was prompted by, unless it was the manifestation of, a rightly-disposed mind; that the motive and intention were part of the action itself, and had to be taken into account in our judgment of it. And the same fineness of insight, the same penetrating quality of the moral sense, which gave him such a vivid perception of this principle, led him on to the further truth, that the spirit of love, of which he was conscious as the actuating force of his own life and conduct, was the general disposition or principle which guaranteed the rightness of all particular motives and intentions; and yet, further, that this love had God as well as our fellow-men for its object.

We can thus see how Jesus, starting from his idea of inwardness, might have risen to his ideal of humanity—*i.e.*, to

his doctrine of love to God and man as the supreme rule and
motive of human conduct, and how he might have perceived
that, apart from this principle, the regard paid to the will of
God, whether dictated by the fear of His displeasure, or by the
mercenary desire to conciliate His favour, must necessarily be
formal and outward—a mere show and semblance without
reality — a show which men might mistake for reality,
though even they do not accept for themselves the show of
love for love itself when they perceive that love is absent,
but which God who looks upon the heart cannot accept. We
do not conceive that Jesus reached this conclusion by successive steps of the logical understanding, but rather that it was
implicitly involved in the very first step by which he separated
himself from Pharisaic influence, and that it rose simultaneously
therewith in his consciousness. As little do we mean to say,
that the doctrine was an absolutely novel discovery of his, a
view of which none before him had ever caught sight. The
very words which he used to express his ethical principle had
been employed by prophetic penmen many ages before his day,
but he gave to their words a wider range. The two factors of
what he called the "great commandment" occur apart from
each other indeed in prophetic legislation (Deut. vi. 5, and
Lev. xix. 18); but it is evident from the context that the
"neighbour" whom the Israelite was enjoined to love as himself might be understood, and indeed was understood, as
restricted to one of the covenanted people. It was a sense of
this which suggested that question of the lawyer, "Who is my
neighbour?" (Luke x. 29). The very extension of the duty
of love to the stranger within the gate (Deut. v. 14) is a proof
that it did not extend to those that were without. The genius
of Hebrew legislation, if it did not forbid, was not favourable to such extension, and Jesus was quite justified in his
interpretation of the law (Matth. v. 43), "It hath been said,
Thou shalt love thy neighbour, and hate thine enemy." The
shield which protected the stranger did not cover the enemy.
Love of the latter was more than the legal spirit could venture
to demand, for that would only have had the effect of betraying
too sensibly its "weakness through the flesh" (Rom. viii. 3),
and have put too great a strain upon its authority. Hence the
bitterness of hatred and invective which, without any apparent
sense of incongruity on the part of the Psalmist, mars and

disfigures many of the most beautiful, and otherwise most evangelical of the Psalms. It is no apology for these to say that the enemy referred to was the enemy of God. The principle of hatred is of a spreading nature, and if indulged in towards the enemies of God and of righteousness, will soon extend towards one's personal enemies. It was reserved for Jesus to say right out, what no legislator, prophet, or psalmist in Israel had ever said, " Love thine enemy." The limitation of the area in which love was to rule was removed once for all, as by a new commandment, by his parable of the Good Samaritan. It cannot be affirmed, with the least show of truth, that the injunction of love sounded the central or dominant note even in the ethical scale of prophecy. There was much in wide contrast with it in the prophetic thought, whereas it is the key to the whole thought of Jesus. Through him it receives a clear, emphatic, and compact expression, absolutely consistent with all else in his teaching ; and to this extent, at least, we must acknowledge the originality of his ethical standpoint. The great commandment, as understood in Israel, enjoined unlimited love towards God, and in so far admitted of no correction ; and our only remark here is, that, as conceived by Jesus, the love of God was a supreme regard to His will, into which we throw the entire strength of our nature. The emotion or sentiment which enters into this determination of our will is ethical, inasmuch as it is devotion to God as the living Ideal, with the added sense that such devotion is agreeable to the nature of man, and therefore his delight.

Passing now to the conception by Jesus of the divine character, we shall find that his originality is still more pronounced and unquestionable ; though here too, of course, he was anticipated in much by the prophets and poets of his people. An unquestioning faith in God as a living, conscious, and intelligent Agent, had come to Jesus by inheritance, and been received by him as the indispensable and indisputable presupposition of all religion. He had also inherited the idea of God as a God of righteousness, who infallibly meted out good and evil to men according to their works. This view of the divine character is as powerfully and persistently set forth in the Old Testament as it permits of being, though perhaps, in the light of the New Testament, we may think that we miss there some of the finer shadings of the idea. And yet further, he might, and no doubt did learn from the prophets and psalmists, to regard God as a gracious and merciful Being. There are numberless passages in the psalter and in the prophets which, taken by themselves, seem to place this aspect of His character in the very strongest light.   It is often painted with indescribable pathos ; but this very pathos is apt to betray the want of full conviction : it is too much a matter of reasoning (Isa. i. 18 ; v. 4 ; xliii. 26 ; Micah vi. 3), as if the prophet needed to dwell upon the consideration to make sure of it, whereas Jesus has no difficulty and no doubt.   He assumes and takes for granted the propitious and placable character of God, and speaks of it with a confidence and childlike simplicity of utterance more impressive than the deep pathos of the prophets.   But that is not all.   It is observable in the Old Testament that the righteousness of God in dealing with the disobedient has a certain air of vindictiveness, and that the divine righteousness and divine goodness stand side by side as if they were incommensurable quantities, or they are expressed in terms which do not admit of being resolved into each other, *vid.* Exod. xx. 5, 6 : " God is a jealous God ; who shows mercy."   Readers are left in doubt how His attributes can be reconciled.   A problem was thus presented to believers in Old Testament times which evidently puzzled them sorely, and which to the last remained for them insoluble.   At most there was a slight indication of a solution in such passages as Ps. lxii. 12 ; xcix. 8 ; and Ezek. xxxiii. 11-20 : " O Lord, thou wast a God that forgavest them, though thou tookest vengeance of their inventions " ; " As I live saith the Lord, I have no pleasure in the death of the wicked."   But the full solution was given by Jesus in his invocation of God as the heavenly Father, and in laying that view of His nature at the root of his religion.   The meaning of this designation is that God exercises as a Father His mercy towards the penitent by forgiving them, and towards the disobedient by punishing them with a view to their correction and final salvation.   Punishment and forgiveness are alike the manifestation of a merciful design ; and His righteousness is ministrant to His goodness and beneficence, or rather they are fundamentally one.   This is the evangelical view of the divine righteousness as opposed to the legal view, above which even the prophets could never rise.   The righteousness of God is inflexible, but salvation is its goal ; and eternity of punishment has no place in the Christian scheme, whatever texts may be cited to the contrary. And as to the novelty of this view of divine righteousness there can be no question. There is, indeed, more than one passage in the Old Testament in which the prophetic spirit almost seems to touch it, as where the first of the canonical prophets, Amos, in the passage already quoted, represents God as saying, "You only have I known of all the families of the earth, *therefore* I will punish you for all your iniquities." But the mere idea of an election was enough to prevent the thought from coming to full expression, and receiving full justice, as we may see, *e.g.*, in that remarkable instance in Jeremiah xxx. 11, where God says, "Though I make a full end of all nations, whither I have scattered thee, yet will I not make a full end of thee." The righteousness of God is here recon- ciled to His mercy towards Israel by an act of favouritism and caprice. His righteousness attains its proper end in the full and final destruction of the heathen ; but it is relaxed in favour of the "remnant of Israel" (Ezek. xi. 13). In the fatherly character of God, on the other hand, as depicted in the gospel, there is no antagonism between His goodness and His severity, between His mercy and His judgment ; and in this respect we mark a clear advance of the evan- gelical doctrine beyond the standpoint of the law and the prophets.

It may be said, indeed, that a wavering is visible in the doctrine of Jesus respecting the divine character somewhat similar to that in the Old Testament. It has been said that the Gospels attribute "two contrary spirits to Christ," that even "his language is often the language of denunciation as well as of blessing"; and that he represents God as extreme to mark iniquity. Now to this the reply is, that the life of man has its deeply serious side ; that, while heavy afflictions may overtake the righteous, the wicked do not go unpunished, and that in God's dealing with mankind His severity is hardly less conspicuous than His goodness. So far as the teaching of Jesus does but reflect these two aspects of His dealings there is nothing in it to object to. But in so far as it goes beyond this : so far, *e.g.*, as Jesus seems to teach everlasting punishment to the wicked, we take this to be a proof, not that two contrary spirits breathe in his teaching, but that his words have been misreported. His disciples were very apt, under their terrible persecutions, to overlook the nuances of his language and to exaggerate his denunciations of his opponents ; to give an edge, borrowed from prophetic or rabbinical teaching, to his words. But the man who had such a vivid intuition of the divine character : who could represent Him as "kind to the unthankful and to the evil," could not but reject from his teaching all that conflicted with that conception. We are far from seeking to deify Jesus, or even to represent him as an absolutely perfect revelation of God, whether by his teaching or his conduct. But persuaded as we are that he was "not less eminent for his intellectual than for his moral greatness," we believe that he thoroughly apprehended his own great doctrine of the divine fatherhood, and that he would give no countenance to any ideas which were manifestly inconsistent with it.

If, now, it be asked, how Jesus was able to reach this new conception of God, and to take this step in advance of prophecy, and of the current theology, it may help us to an answer if we consider that in proportion as our moral ideas are purified and exalted, so also is our conception of God and of the relation in which He stands to us. Naturally, or rather necessarily, we ascribe to God the possession of the highest imaginable qualities of which we have any conception. Let the speculative thinker cavil as he may, the idea that the finite creature cannot possibly be furnished with capacities, whether moral or intellectual, "by a Being, who himself has none," will always command the assent of the majority of mankind. We can hardly but conceive of our Ideal as realized in Him to constitute His perfection. It is impossible that, on any other view, we could ever present Him to ourselves as an object of supreme regard. Now it is manifest that that love which Jesus recognized as the principle of all right conduct, and of the presence of which in himself he was conscious as the actuating principle of his own life and conduct, embraced the loveless and the unthankful in its regards ; and according to what has just been said, he could not but feel that love in God would have a like function or aspect even towards the evil ; that His dealings with them, even in retribution, would be a manifestation of His love and good-

ness ; and that His relation to them would still be that of a
father seeking by severity to correct and conciliate them.
Such is certainly the spirit of his teaching, and there is a
probability that he gave it a more full, repeated, and unqualified expression than is reported in the synoptists (Luke
vi. 35, 36).

It does not enter into our plan to portray that inimitable
character of Jesus, in which tenderness of feeling and depth
of sympathy were so intimately blended with a certain gravity
of demeanour and sternness of judgment, so as to account
for the deep impression made upon his disciples by his
personality. And as little do we propose to attempt a
detailed analysis of his teaching, such as may be found in
the works of Pfleiderer, Weiss, Keim, and other German
theologians. The remark, indeed, is an obvious one, that
Jesus did not seek to teach a complete or connected system
of morality or religion ; but was content to enunciate a few
leading principles, to suggest certain motives of action, and
to breathe a new life into his disciples. And it is our object
only to trace, so far as we can, the line of thought and
action by which he gained that deep insight into the nature
of true religion, which not only placed him in antagonism to
the Pharisaism of his day, but even carried him beyond the
prophetic standpoint ; and we may say here, what we have
elsewhere implied, that we believe him to have gained that
insight, not by means of logical deduction, or metaphysical
reasoning, or philosophical speculation, but by a method
which we may call empirical or practical. We imagine him
to have been endowed in a unique degree with the power
conferred by the clear intellect, the single eye, and the pure
heart, of interpreting the moral and religious instincts, and of
reading those secrets of the spiritual life which are common
to the finite and the infinite (1 Cor. ii. 9-12).

There is thus a dialectic by which the mind of man may
be supposed to rise from the inwardness of genuine morality
to the idea of God as the Heavenly Father, who is kind even
to the evil and unthankful, and seeks their good, even in the
suffering which He sends upon them. Not that we can indicate
with certainty, or clearly represent to ourselves, how, or by
what avenue, a religious genius, situated as Jesus was, could
reach this conception. " The spirit bloweth where it listeth

. . . but thou canst not tell whence it cometh, and whither it goeth." We are only concerned to show that there *is* an avenue by which such a conclusion might be reached by the human mind; and we may trust that whatever is abstractly accessible to all men may be reached by one or more of our species. We do not imagine that the conception of God would grow up in the mind of Jesus distinct from his ideal of humanity, but that both together would rise and take shape *pari passu*. His deeply devout and reverential mind would regard as essential to the character of God that spirit of good which could only be the result of an effort of self-sacrifice and self-development in the mind of man. His imagination would clothe the divine Being with the attribute of love in its reality, which only belonged potentially or ideally to the human subject. The speculative or scientific thinker may derive from other sources his view of the unseen power, which pervades and upholds all existence; but the religious mind rises to its last and highest knowledge of God from its knowledge of self; and the finite spirit, whether in Jesus, or in any other individual, could have risen to the thought that love to God was man's bounden duty, only by conceiving, at the same time, of love as the great moral attribute and moving spring of divine action. To say that love is due from man to God involves the confession that God is lovable; and *that* He can be only because He is love.

But dialectic is not the only avenue by which Jesus might reach this conclusion. He might also reach it by personal experience. By such dialectic as the above it was possible only to reach a somewhat vague and general idea of the divine fatherliness. But by personal experience he might gain a more distinct and definite view of it and of its culmination in the forgiveness of sin, as we shall now proceed to show. We have often seen it asserted that provided a law or principle has been practically ascertained and established, it is of little or of no consequence how or by whom it has been discovered. But whatever truth there may be in this maxim, it does not apply here in a discussion which is intended to show that the conviction of the absolute placability of God, which the distinctively evangelical doctrine, might be derived, not from any supernatural communication, but through purely human experience.

That men from the beginning and under every form of
religion have entertained a hope of the divine forgiveness of
their sins is a well attested fact.   Such a hope is so natural
that it hardly needs to be accounted for.   Wherever the moral
sense is awakened and the accusing voice is heard, men feel
that some hope of forgiveness is necessary to save them from
despair, or from casting off all regard to the will of God, and
to give them any prospect of a gradual approximation to the
ideal life.   In Israel the hope of forgiveness was a strong and
living principle, but it never rose beyond a hope, of which
perhaps the most classical expression is that of the Psalmist
(cxxx. 4), " There is forgiveness with thee, that thou mayest be
feared." In that hope there was ever an element of uncertainty,
because the feeling was never got rid of that some propitiatory
service, ritualistic, ascetic, or disciplinary was needed, that God
might forgive.   Without any undue pressure of the letter of the
Psalmist's words, it may be said that the effect of this was that
God could only be "feared" or reverenced, but not loved.   The
need of propitiatory service not only introduces an element of
uncertainty, but, however minimized, it tends to belittle the
divine placability, and to repress the outflow of the replying
love which is the instrument of joyful progress towards the
ideal.   The exquisite narrative in Luke regarding the woman
who was a sinner seems to show, not that forgiveness is the
recognition or reward of love, but that the much love is the
token and effect of the free forgiveness.   To be instrumental
in this way, divine love needs to be conceived of as absolutely
free ; free from all dependence on propitiatory service, and as
such it is presented in the teaching of Jesus ; free, be it said, as
the common air which men breathe, and firm as the earth upon
which men walk in safety without fearing that a false step may
cause it to slip from under their feet.

The question now before us is, by what experience Jesus
rose from that uncertain hope of forgiveness to that certainty
and confidence which breathe through all his teaching.   The
great difficulty of this step of thought will be felt if we bear
in mind that the physical and social effects of sin remain in
all cases as its penalty, and seem to show that it is never
fully forgiven.   And our reply to the question now put is,
that Jesus rose to his conviction, not merely by development
of that natural hope, but mainly by starting afresh from the

spiritual basis on which the true relation of God to man depends.

(1.) We may figure to ourselves Jesus as a man of the ordinary or average type, and suppose him to 'have perceived, as all of us in some measure do perceive, that his moral nature, the fact of his being able to form an ideal carried in it the obligation ; and if the obligation, then the possibility of his realizing or gradually approximating to his ideal. And yet when, feeling the attraction and owning the authority of that ideal, he proceeded with the attempt to realize it, he would be taught by experience in the first instance that the task was so arduous as to be almost impossible. To his sensitive conscience the arrears of guilt would gather on his soul and place insuperable obstacles in the way of his advance till they would bring him to the brink of despair. He would feel that he could reach towards the ideal only through a succession of failures and stumblings, shortcomings, and defections, and that his endeavour to propitiate God would bring him no nearer the goal. He would perceive that to make advance possible there was an absolute necessity that there should be forgiveness with God, or, as *we* should say, some divine law or order of which forgiveness was the popular expression, the sensuous representation, and of which all religions without exception have given to their votaries the hope at least.

And we can further conceive that a deeply serious and aspiring spirit like Jesus would as a last resource put this hope, this idea, to the proof ; that he would tentatively, or, let us say, hypothetically or provisionally place confidence in divine forgiveness as his encouragement to devote himself to the work of righteousness, to the realization of the ideal, or to the reduction to a minimum of that evil from which no human being is absolutely free. He would, by a great resolve, give up all attempt to propitiate God, and surrender himself to the thought that nothing of the kind was necessary. And thus endeavouring, he would find that his confidence in the absolute placability of God would help him to advance to the goal. To proceed in this manner would no doubt be to act upon a hypothesis, but like many another hypothesis in physical and social science, it might be verified by the results in his own moral nature, and become for him a conviction and a certitude as we know it was for Jesus. We hold that there is no improbability in this conjecture. There is a range within which "what is called truth is only the hypothesis, which is found to work best." And if it be found that a belief in the absolute clemency of God is what above all else strengthens the soul in its conflict with evil, no stronger proof of this view of the divine character can be desired or imagined.

Or, (2.) We may conceive of Jesus as a man far above the average type, as a man of quite an exceptional or even unique strength and grandeur of character, who would never give way to despair or succumb to the difficulty of reaching the goal, but would keep the goal in view, and strive towards it with his whole soul in spite of all discouragements which might arise from involuntary lapses and constitutional defects. In the words of the Stoic Cleanthes (quoted by Dr. Hatch, *Hibbert Lectures*, 1888) such an one might say,—" Even though I degenerate be, and consent reluctantly, None the less I follow thee." Persevering thus, it might at last dawn upon him that the consciousness of this wholeness of intention, this singleness of aim, delivered him from self-condemnation. And very justly so, inasmuch as the finite creature being imperfect must necessarily fall short of its own ideal, and cannot by any possibility perfectly fulfil the abstract requirements of the law of its nature. The most, therefore, that absolute justice can demand is that the individual should honestly and sincerely strive to fulfil that law. For as Goethe says, " Vollkommenheit ist die Norm des Himmels, Vollkommenes wollen die Norm des Menschen."

The integrity of the finite creature consists not in absolute sinlessness, but in the sincerity of his effort to conform to the law ; and the consciousness of such integrity is what gives him confidence in the presence of the higher powers, and procures for him the highest good, the approbation of his own conscience, the sense of harmony with the universal order, or peace with God.

This conduct with its accompanying reward is specified by Jesus (Matth. vi. 33) as the duty incumbent upon all men without exception. And in our view there may have been not a few individuals of our race besides Jesus, though none so much as he, who have set themselves resolvedly, in spite of the evil which clung to them and haunted their steps and marred their lives, to make righteousness the aim and object of their most strenuous effort, and who, while so engaged, have emerged

as by a spiritual law from the sphere or element of strict, vexatious, and self-defeating legality into a sphere in which it
seemed as if justice was tempered by mercy, but which was
really a sphere in which the highest justice prevailed.   In so
saying we cannot omit to observe parenthetically that this
aspect of divine mercy, in which it is seen to turn to justice,
is presented in 1 John i. 9, " If we confess our sins, God is
faithful and just to forgive us our sins."   For it is only by
identifying justice and mercy in the last resort that we can
attach the full meaning to this passage, and we have to take
into account the fundamental identity of these two in order to
reconcile the great doctrine that men are saved by grace, with
that other equally great and prominent doctrine, that they will
be judged according to their works.   But to return : Men who
have experienced that translation, of which we are speaking,
from the one sphere to the other, would, if in any sense theists,
as a matter of course see in their escape from self-condemnation a token of their deliverance from divine condemnation.
For this is just what is asserted in the profound words of one
who drank deeply into the spirit of Jesus, and might meta-
phorically be said to have leaned upon his bosom.   " If our
heart condemn us not, then have we confidence toward God "
(1 John iii. 21).   In the verdict of their own highest nature
such persons would recognize the verdict of God, who " is
greater than our heart and knoweth all things."   If a man's
judgment of himself be the judgment pronounced by his own
highest nature, it is a very great thing, and not a " small thing,"
and must coincide with the judgment of God.   St. Paul's
words (1 Cor. iv. 3, 4) are not opposed to this view when they
are carefully weighed.   And it is thus conceivable that Jesus
might have risen to his confidence in the forgiveness of sins
whatever of their penalties might remain.

Whether this or that other be the process by which Jesus
rose to this confidence we leave our readers to judge.   We ourselves give the preference to the latter supposition.   But one
way or the other he gained his great conviction by deep insight
and experience without any supernatural communication, and
communicated it as his message to men to encourage them in
their struggle towards the better life.   The sense of blessedness
achieved by self-surrender to the highest law of his nature, Jesus
as a theist could not but regard in the light of an obligation to

God, who had so tempered his nature as to make it capable of such an experience, or as a proof and token of the infinite placability of the Author of his being. From the level of morality he thus rose by means of his theism into the atmosphere of religion, and he taught his disciples to maintain with success their conflict with evil, not so much by engaging in the struggle with their own lower nature as by rising above themselves into fellowship with the All-Good. That conviction of the absolute placability of God and of peace with Him, which in him, and possibly in other strong ones of our race, might be the *effect* of righteousness (Isa. xxxii. 17), may in the case of the weak ones, when received on his authority, be their motive and encouragement to engage in the work of righteousness. Luther's hope would never have carried him to a successful termination of the mental conflict in which his sense of guilt involved him. Had it not been for the "nameless monk," who is said to have reminded him of the forgiveness of sin, he would have sunk under that struggle. The assurance which Jesus gained as the result of deep insight and supreme devotion, Luther had to accept, on his authority, to sustain him from the first in the conflict. It is not given to every man to discover this great secret of the spiritual life. Only such a man as Jesus was, and others of like moral fibre and like spiritual insight, have proved and come upon it, aud announced it with more or less impressiveness and authority to their fellows. The most that men in general can do is to verify it in their own experience after it has been revealed to them in gospel or in prophecy. The full antl final revelation of this secret by Jesus has put each of us in the way of verifying it for himself, and constitutes our common dependence upon him as our guide to the better life.

His great achievement was, that he placed himself in touch and intercourse with the divine, and was enabled to reveal the secret of that intercourse for the benefit and instruction of man. This is what gives him to this day a unique claim to the boundless veneration of his followers, and forms his title to be regarded as the "author and finisher of our faith," the Founder of Christianity. In this sense it was that St. Paul was profoundly sensible of the dependence upon Jesus of his own spiritual life, and after him such men as Augustine and Luther, and all who have entered into the mind of Jesus and have

N

sounded the depths of the evangelical principle. From the view here given it may be seen that the evangelical idea of righteousness is relatively a development from the legal idea ; and it becomes intelligible how, in the teaching of Jesus, no absolute distinction is made or contrast drawn between faith and works, between law and grace, as in the teaching of St. Paul; a proof of how much more profoundly and simply than the latter the former had apprehended and solved the great spiritual problem. We can also see that Christianity owed its origin to a greater than Paul.

The craving for forgiveness, which is father to the hope, and is as common as the sense of guilt, predisposes men to accept of the proclamation of a free forgiveness—the glad tidings of the gospel. But the freedom and unconditional nature of it is safe-guarded by this, that while that hope or craving commits men to nothing, and may be cherished while sin is indulged in without control, this faith can only be received into a pure conscience, into a heart which honestly endeavours to turn from sin without any secret hankering after it. By proclaiming divine forgiveness on such terms, by causing that trembling, impotent hope of divine forgiveness, which has been entirely absent from no religion, to pass in the hearts of his followers into a life-sustaining energy, Jesus may be said to have raised the thoughts of men, and to have brought a new power into the world for the lifting of human life. The revelation of his soteriological method, the gaining for it a place in human faith and practice, we take to have been his peculiar work as a teacher ; his contribution to the moral welfare and spiritual interests of men. And the success which has attended his work is to be measured by the degree of earnestness and hopefulness which his followers have exhibited in their conflict with evil.

In expressing this opinion as to the nature of our spiritual dependence upon him, we are far from intending to imply that Christianity is a simply soteriological system. It rests upon presuppositions common to Judaism and all other ethical religions, and embraces these within itself. But what is meant is, that whatever was new in the teaching of Jesus was directly soteriological and bore upon human deliverance from evil. Whatever changes he introduced into current religious thought proceeded from his soteriological doctrine.

Whatever in Judaism was inconsistent with that doctrine he may be considered to have set aside, but to have left all else standing. Time was required for his doctrine to show its range of effect in various directions. But simple as that doctrine may seem to be, its effect, direct and indirect, immediate and remote, has, we believe, extended to every department of thought and action.

The uncertain and fluctuating hope of divine forgiveness is, as already remarked, absent from no religion. But the service which a man is enabled to render by such a hope is apt to be servile and propitiatory. The effort to which it stimulates is directed to earn the certainty of forgiveness by the more diligent and unreserved discharge of duty ; an effort which, being necessarily unsatisfactory to the tender conscience, is apt to slip into Pharisaic and outward observance, and to prompt that question—"What more shall I do?" and thus to turn again the whole moral life into a propitiatory and legal service. On the other hand, Jesus inculcated the certainty of forgiveness, and encouraged every man who honestly desired deliverance from evil to believe in it with the most unhesitating confidence. This confidence he laid at the very foundation of his religion, thus showing that he recognized its full significance. He taught men to regard divine love, or that forgiveness in which it finds its culminating manifestation, as something which goes before and is the source and spring of all true service ; of a service, that is, which is rendered not in a mercenary spirit, to earn or make sure of divine favour ; but in the spirit of thankfulness for that unearned goodness of God which is always operating, but of which we can become fully conscious only by drawing upon it as a source of strength in running the Christian race. Between that merely legal service which we may render from the hope of forgiveness of our failures, and the evangelical service to which we are prompted by that conviction of the preventing love of God, the difference is immense : and it is to Jesus that men are indebted for setting that difference forth, and enabling them to effect the passage from the one to the other. As disciples of Jesus we at first adopt his view of the religious relation upon his simple authority, as that of a Master who stood far above us in spiritual might. And in so far, his teaching may be said to be dogmatic, but it ceases to

be dogmatic when it is afterwards verified in our experience.
(Compare John iv. 39-42.)

It will help to an understanding of the renovating power of
the gospel if we here advert to the fact that human life is
subject to a law of moral continuity, by which is meant a
tendency in the life of sin to wax more and more sinful, and
to continue in the downward course on which it has once
entered, and even to acquire momentum in that course. At
the same time this tendency may be retarded, or arrested,
or even reverted and turned back, and an upward direction
impressed upon the life, without a breach or suspension of
that indefeasible law. The possibility of this is explained by
the presence and function of that ideal principle in the
human mind of which we have spoken, the intrinsically human
faculty of conceiving and of being attracted by a better life
than that which *is;* by a life the reverse it may be of that
which we have hitherto led or grown to. This faculty may
long lie dormant, or torpid and inactive, but it has the life
in itself, as is the case with every other germ, and may
awaken as by a stirring from within by its own vital energy,
or by some call, or from an appeal addressed to it from
without, such as that which awakens the sleeper (Eph. v.
8). Except through this ideal principle no reaction or
revulsion from the life of sin can take place in human
experience. It is an upward force, the germ of a higher
nature in man, and may be the inception of an impulse to a
triumphant struggle against that gravitation to evil which is
the penalty which we incur, or rather which we aggravate,
by indulging in habits of sin. But this germ needs to be
developed ; it would be suppressed, or brought to the point
of extinction, or reduced to a state of hopeless torpidity, by
mere disuse, or by countervailing tendencies, unless it were
stimulated and roused into activity either by social influences
or by the consciousness of the sympathy of the unseen
Power to which we are accountable. These better influences
are probably never wholly extinct in any form of society
however depraved. But at the time of Jesus the social
influences, though not wholly adverse, were at least not
calculated to stimulate the endeavour towards a high ideal.
The better influences necessary for such a purpose had yet
to be created, and for the time their place was supplied to

the disciples by their intercourse with Jesus himself and by his doctrine that God, as the Father in heaven, was on the side of every better effort. By teaching that God is patient of human failure, that He freely forgives men their lapses, and cancels their arrears of guilt, he inspired them with the courage to engage and to prevail in the great struggle of their lives. Not that he brought down any divine energy to take dæmonic possession of their wills and to supplement their own powers ; for that would have been to encroach on their individual life : but simply that he communicated to them an idea of divine sympathy and goodwill which exalted them above themselves in conformity with the laws of their nature and without trenching on the sacredness of their rational life. That was the idea which Jesus had drawn out of his own deep experience and sought to imprint on the consciousness of his disciples ;—the idea by which he awakened in humanity what has been fitly called the Christian consciousness. This consciousness, which Jesus has brought as a new power into human life, consists in a new ideal of humanity and a new conception of God, which are really one and indivisible. And even if the absolute and speculative truth of either the one or the other be questioned, it can hardly be denied that in practice they have proved to millions of our race to be the source of comfort in trouble, of strength against temptation, and of direction in the conduct of life. Together they constituted the idea by which Jesus sought to raise his countrymen to a higher level of the religious life, not as if he expected that the mere acceptance of it in theory would serve as by magic to that end, but that the end would be gained if they moulded life upon it and if they engaged in the hard struggle, to which it called them, with their baser and lower tendencies. By his teaching and example Jesus corrected and simplified our notion of the religious life ; but, great as is the boon which has thus been conferred upon us, there is still the difficulty of acting upon that notion.

That new ideal of humanity and that new conception of God were alike requisite for the foundation of the new religion. For it is evident that had Jesus only acted the part of a legislator, and lifted the standard of human life, he would thereby have deepened in us the consciousness of sin, and filled us with heightened despair. The high ideal, it may be confessed, has an attraction over our hearts. We would fain do the good, if we could, and choose the better part of which we approve ; but the distress and misery of man is that the power of performance is not ours. Our higher nature, though it has the might of conscious right upon its side, is yet weak by comparison, and unable to assert itself against the established habit and entrenched position of our lower nature. Notwithstanding our better knowledge and our higher aspiration our hearts still gravitate towards that selfishness which is and must be the first and uppermost instinct of the finite creature. That love, which is the fulfilling of the law, will not come at the word of command. At the very commencement of our struggle to be better, to act from higher principles, we are sensible that our motives are mixed ; that the evil is present with us, and that we have sinned already ; that self is the spring of our actions, even in the effort to rise above self ; that "from a selfish motive we cannot become unselfish," and that the gravitation of the will towards evil is equivalent to the deed of evil ; that it is only from some inferior motive that we have it in our power to form or to reform our lives ; that the battle has already gone against us at the beginning, and that it is of no use to continue the fight after we have been vanquished. To meet this daunting obstacle, this sore discouragement in our advance towards perfection, Jesus imparted his new conception of the divine character. He taught men to believe in God's fatherly disposition, in His love and goodwill, in His perpetual forgiveness of the sins that are past, and in the favourable regard which He extends, after all our falls and shortcomings, to our efforts to rise again, to renew our pursuit of the ideal which beckons to us, and lays the force of an obligation upon us, and in our approach to which lies the true felicity of our nature.

We can thus see that the power of upward attraction, which naturally and universally resides in the ideal, however insufficient of itself, may be reinforced by that love to God which the doctrine of divine forgiveness as taught by Jesus is calculated to awaken. For of love it has been said, that it "gives to every power a double power above their functions and their offices" (Shakespeare), and in this sense it is, and in no other, that Christianity is a graft upon the stock of nature.

We have dwelt the longer on the doctrine of divine forgiveness, because the view of it now taken is essential to the anti-supernatural construction of Christianity, and before leaving this part of the subject we shall here yet further illustrate what has been said :——

(1) The calm assuredness with which Jesus announced this doctrine arose from his knowledge that it would find an echo in the human heart. For the man who repents and turns from his sins the remembrance of them loses its accusing power, and their guilt seems to fall away as belonging to a past that is dead and gone. To say, therefore, that God forgives the penitent is as much as to say that the man's self-forgiveness has the sanction of God. The counsel given to the penitent, by a deep seer into the secrets of human life, is " Do as the heavens have done ; forget your evil ; with them forgive yourself."

(2) Viewed as the gift of God pardon can in no sense be regarded as a partial or arbitrary act of divine sovereignty. It is not, as ultra-evangelicals seem to think, a whitewash applied externally to the pollution of the soul. It can only be dispensed according to fixed principles and the uniform operation of a divine law. Divine placability is in truth only an aspect of divine justice. For God to withhold forgiveness from the penitent would argue an unjust and vindictive temper. The same deep seer into human life (Shakespeare) has said, " Who by repentance is not satisfied is not of heaven nor earth. For they are pleased." True it is that our best repentance needs to be repented of. But that is only to say that at the best our repentance is imperfect, and that our sense of this should supply a motive for renewed effort. And we cannot conceive of a just God as rejecting the repentance of a necessarily imperfect being like man simply because of its imperfection. He accepts as sincere a repentance which acts as a stimulus to forsake our sins.

And (3) this leads to the remark that man's faith in divine forgiveness is the means of which the new life is the end. The penalty of past sin is that it makes sincere repentance hard and difficult. But when under the pressure of sin repentance begins to stir, as it does more or less in all men, a conviction of divine forgiveness on the part of the sinner flying from temptation acts as a rearguard to prevent the reviving sin from again overtaking and regaining its mastery over him.   In short, to take it upon trust that forgiveness waits upon repentance is our encouragement to repent, and infuses the element of hope into our struggle, otherwise hopeless, with our baser nature.

From a world-historical point of view, or from that of the science of comparative theology, the rapid rise, and the almost as rapid decadence of Buddhism furnish a demonstration that principles of morality, however pure and exalted, and the practice of self-discipline, however rigid, do not of themselves contain all the elements which are necessary to the permanent elevation of humanity, or to its power of self-retrieval after periods of moral degeneracy.   This power, so far as we know, the doctrine of Buddha has never exhibited.   To these elements a theology and an eschatology require to be added. The latter was adopted by Jesus into his doctrine from the thought of his time and country ; and the theology which he added to the thoughts of men he presented in its purest and simplest form by teaching (drawn from the well of his own deep experience) that God was the Heavenly Father, who overlooks the lapses and failures of His children, and sympathizes with their every effort to extricate themselves from the slime of evil.

In these remarks we have anticipated and answered the objection to the ethical ideal of Christianity which Mr. Herbert Spencer has formulated, and of which many before him have felt the force.   According to him, that ideal is only too high for common human nature ; its requirements of self-abnegation, of the love of enemies, etc., are impracticable, apt to drive men to despair and to the renunciation or slackening of all moral effort, and so to prove injurious to practical morality, seeing that " by association with rules that cannot be obeyed, rules that can be obeyed lose their authority."   And such, indeed, might be the effect upon individuals who looked only to the ethical ideal, and did not also include within the field of their thought the Christian conception of the paternal character of God.   But he that extends his view to this is elevated above himself by the feeling that God is on his side, and is encouraged to address himself to the achievement of what he would otherwise regard as unachievable. After every fall such an one rises again, and perseveres in pursuit however far he may come short, and however slow his advance. The apostle who entered most deeply into the thought of Jesus, and was most conscious of his own insufficiency, tells us respecting himself, that he forgot the things that were behind, whether they were his past failures or his past successes, that he might press on to the things before, to heights not yet attained by him : and his was no abnormal or solitary experience.

The doctrine of the Divine Fatherhood is peculiarly distinctive of the teaching of Jesus ; as distinctive of it as that of the better righteousness and of the ideal nature of the kingdom of God ; and all three are no doubt organically connected. Not that the doctrine had absolutely never occurred to human minds before Jesus gave expression to it. That it had dawned faintly in almost every ethnic religion is well known, and in a few passages of the Hebrew Scriptures God is spoken of as a Father. But the novelty of the doctrine of Jesus consisted in the emphasis and prominence given to the idea. In the prayer which he gave to his disciples as a model he taught them to address God as " Our Father in Heaven " ; and this formula was adopted by all his disciples as their distinctive mode of addressing the Deity (1 Pet. ii. 17). Then, too, the Fatherhood of God, as conceived by Jesus, was distinguished from the conception of it in the Old Testament by the note of universalism. Singularly, though intelligibly enough, some orthodox theologians, in the apologetic interest, have sought as much as possible to minimize the originality of this doctrine of Jesus. One able apologist, Dr. Bruce, has lately pointed to the beautiful words of Isaiah, " Doubtless, thou art our Father, though Abraham be ignorant of us, and Israel acknowledge us not," as indicative of the " general drift of the Hebrew Scriptures," in which, moreover, he finds only " a few traces of a legal spirit."

But surely it requires some vastly apologetic bias or partiality of judgment thus to efface the distinction between the legal spirit which predominates in the Old Testament, and the evangelical spirit which predominates in the New. It is undeniable, no doubt, that there are anticipations, many of them of the evangelical spirit, in the Old Testament, just as there are traces of a survival of the legal spirit in the New Testament. But the whole context of the passage in Isaiah, which Dr. Bruce quotes, has only to be read in order to see that the prophet is addressing God as the God of Israel as distinct from the surrounding nations, of whom it is said, that "Thou never barest rule over them; they were not called by thy name" (Isa. lxiii. 19). Even Jeremiah knows of God as the "Father of Israel" only. In a word, God is called Father in the Old Testament only because He had chosen Israel as His peculiar people, and had given His law to it alone. And even this law once given, this mark of His favour once bestowed, all God's subsequent dealings with the people of Israel are supposed to be conducted, as already pointed out, in a strictly legal spirit. Or, if other-wise—if God from time to time refrains from dealing with them in such a spirit—it is only out of regard to the mercy which He had sworn to the fathers from the days of old (Micah vii. 18-20; Ps. lxxxix. 28, 31-34). And this idea of a Divine Fatherhood restricted to Israel obviously excludes the idea of the Universal Fatherhood which is the doctrine of Jesus. The interval between the standpoint of Jesus and that of the prophets is, indeed, immense. Passages there may be in the writings of the latter in which the interval seems almost as if it were on the point of vanishing, or of being bridged across; but the decisive step by which the communication might have been established is never taken, the interval is never got over. This observation is borne out by the col-lateral and very noticeable fact, that the new covenant which Jeremiah foretells is represented as a covenant "with the house of Israel and the house of Judah" only (Jer. xxxi. 31).

As we have here touched upon a singular misapprehension by a distinguished apologist of the relation at one very import-ant point between the doctrine of the Old and the New Testa-ments, we shall take the liberty of making a short digression in order to point out a corresponding misapprehension, equally singular, by another apologist (if he can be regarded as such) of the relation between Christian thought and Greek specula-tion. In his *Hibbert Lecture*, 1888, p. 224, Dr. Hatch says, that "in many passages of the New Testament, and not least of all in the discourses of Jesus, moral conduct is spoken of as work done for wages," and he refers to such passages as illustrative of the " Christian Idea," by way too of contrasting this idea with the more purely ethical thought of Greece.   He does not take into account that when such passages occur in the discourses of Jesus especially, as Matth. v. 12, Luke vi. 23, Mark ix. 41, they lose their legal and mercenary colouring if they are interpreted, as they ought to be, in the light of his fundamental thought ; nor does he advert to the many indications that the reward in heaven is not future but timeless.   In this same connection Dr. Hatch makes the very questionable statement that in the New Testament punishment is vindictive, and not remedial; and both this statement and that other that punishment is external to the offender, and follows on the offence by sentence of the Judge, and not by a self-acting law, are instances of a superficial criticism which makes no allowance for the use of popular phraseology, or a criticism which needs to be qualified by the general principle laid down by St. Paul, Gal. vi. 7, " Whatsoever a man soweth, that shall he also reap."   That there are traces of the legal spirit not easily to be explained away in some of the canonical books of the New Testament, and especially in the book of Revelation, is not to be denied.   In regard to which last book such traces may fairly be regarded as evidences of an insecure hold on the part of the apokalyptist, of the evangelical spirit, or perhaps, as lending some support to the latest theory regarding the book, according to which it is an interpolated edition of a Jewish apokalypse.

A somewhat hasty perusal of Dr. Hatch's book has left upon our mind the impression that he is carried away by the brief he took in hand, viz., to show the extent of Greek influence on the Christian Church ; a task which naturally commends itself to the liberal mind.   But it seems to us that, besides misplacing the sphere in which that influence took effect, he also much exaggerates the importance of the data on which he relies to prove the dependence of Christianity on Greek speculation. So far as we have observed he makes no express or categorical statement of his views on the subject, but from the passage we have quoted, and many others of a like tendency, he seems to come near to the opinion expressed by Prof. Max Müller in his address to the Oriental Congress, 1892, that " Christianity is the quickening of the old Semitic (Jewish) faith, by the highest philosophical inspirations of the Aryan, and more particularly of the Greek mind." It may be thought by some that such an opinion is inconsistent with Dr. Hatch's views at other points, and with his general attitude towards Christianity. But our studies have led us frequently to observe that consistency is not a conspicuous virtue in modern theologians of the liberal schools, and we are sometimes tempted to guess at the deeper-lying tendency of their thoughts from incidental indications of it. There can, at all events, be no doubt as to Prof. Max Müller's opinion. Language such as his just quoted distinctly minimizes the great part played by Jesus in the origin of Christianity, the rôle which fell to him, or rather was marked out for him, by his consciousness of spiritual power and insight, as well as by his perception of the degraded state to which religion had sunk among his countrymen, and of the fact that the ultimate ground of that degeneracy lay in the legal spirit of the Mosaic institution. It is true that, provided we have in Christianity the absolute form of religion, and can verify it in our experience, it matters little by what channel it has come to us. But in our view simple justice requires us to acknowledge that it was Jesus who "quickened" Jewish faith by his profound and original apprehension of the religious relation. Apart from this great achievement of his, Christianity could never have come into existence, the "inspiring" influences of Greek philosophy notwithstanding. What Greek philosophy really did was to contribute, along with Jewish thought, to the building up of dogma, or of that system of thought which seeks to rationalize, that is, to explain the ultimate fact of the divine nature, the ground of the evangelical idea, as set forth by Jesus; which, just because it was an ultimate fact, admitted really of no explanation, but only of being verified, and that too not by philosophical speculation, but by the personal experience of those who surrender themselves to the influence of the idea. The moral element of Christianity was in great measure common both to Aryan and Semitic thought. But to Jesus belongs the undivided glory of rising from the legal to the evangelic form of the religious relation; to a height that is so far above the region of religious thought, whether Aryan or Semitic, that it is to this day with difficulty attained even by his professed followers. Greek thought, i.e., such of it as contributed to the building up of dogma is, like dogma itself, if not fallen dead at the present day, only of pædagogic, and therefore of vanishing value.

The later stoicism—a slowly ripened product of Greek thought, the best elements of which it had absorbed into itself—became for its professors, towards the end of the Republic and in the early days of the Empire, a religion parallel in many of its aspects to Christianity. But while its ideal of life was scarcely less lofty than that of the latter, it made no provision for the sense of human shortcoming. In its system it gave no place to the forgiveness of sin, or for anything corresponding to that, and it knew only of amendment for the future. Owing mainly to this defect the stoic's devotion to the ideal was not irradiated by any joyful emotion. The conflict with his lower nature, to which the ideal summoned him, had to be carried on in the gloomy watchful spirit of legalism without any foregleam of anticipated victory. He might be sustained in the conflict by the stern enthusiasm for duty, but this was a principle which failed to make life for him otherwise than hard and devoid of the sense of happiness. This was apparent even in the case of Marcus Aurelius, its greatest disciple, of whom it has been justly said by Archdeacon Wilson, that it "is difficult to see that he could have been a better man had he been a Christian," but that he might have been a happier man, inasmuch as his meditations everywhere show that he "found no happiness in his religion."

Roman stoicism gave no support or encouragement to the irresolute, desponding, conscience-stricken struggler. It knew nothing of the strength or joy which comes to a lower nature from being in conscious sympathy with a higher. It was "a religion only for the strong" and the self-reliant, for men like Cato, Epictetus, and Marcus Aurelius. A system so little helpful to common human nature, so unsatisfactory to common human cravings, could only survive for a time within a limited circle, and as a fact it soon ceased to have a separate following. But, on the contrary, the doctrine taught by Jesus of the Fatherhood of God, who forgives the greatest sins, charged religion with emotion, heightened for men generally by the interpretation which his disciples put upon his martyr death. It thus gained a permanent hold of the human mind, and created a bond of sympathy between his followers which served as a principle of organization and stability.

Turning back now (after this digression) to the doctrine of Jesus respecting the Fatherhood of God, we remark that the novelty of his doctrine consisted in attaching to it not merely the note of universalism, but also the note of prevenience, or, let us say, its independence of external impulse. Like that of an earthly father, the love of our Heavenly Father is founded in His nature ; it seeks our welfare from the first before we have done anything to deserve it, and persists after we have done everything to make it forfeit; and before all else, it is this view of divine love which trains us to the love of Him. In words which are striking in themselves, and remarkable for us from their close bearing on much which is advanced in this essay, it has been said by a living author that "divine pardon is not something to be waited for, or striven after, a blessing dependent upon something that must precede it, it has not to be created by us or by anybody else for us through the exercise of faith or offer of atonement, but it *is* already, and *has been* all along, original and fundamental in the relation of God with man; and one of the uses and aims of Christ is to make known and certify by revealing the Father, what, but for his revelation, sin-confused natures would never have guessed, having, indeed, surmised quite the contrary, and what, even with his revelation, they yet find it hard to entertain and rest in. By this man is preached unto you the forgiveness of sins." With some qualification, which need not be dwelt upon, of the latter part of this quotation, we can accept of it as a just representation of Christ's doctrine of divine placability and love. According to this view God is the spring of love, as He is the spring of life. To Him belongs the initiative by the supreme privilege of His nature; and that, which in Him, the Infinite, is self-originated, underived, and unbegotten, comes in the finite creature at the call or conception of that love after it has refused to come at the command of interest or duty. That we do not need to propitiate God's favour is the very essence of that conception. It is ours already without that and before that. God seeks and wooes our confidence before all our doings and deservings. He forgives to the uttermost. He is not alienated from us by our past failures, and He does not look with disfavour on our honest efforts, however feeble and uncertain, at repentance and newness of life. A conviction of this truth is our encouragement to aim at the ideal in spite of our constant short-comings, our Sisyphus-like failures, and our slow progress towards the goal. This conviction is, in fact, the highest help and encouragement which we can have with due respect to our rational nature, in our advance in the spiritual life : the strongest incentive in our effort to deliver ourselves from evil. It places us in the most favourable position for carrying on our spiritual conflict, it reinforces the attractive power of the ideal, which is common to all men, and makes it to prevail over the material and unideal forces of evil. Whereas, to suppose that our higher nature, which just consists in that ideal principle, can be reinforced by the supernatural and extraneous action of another spirit or presence within us, is to break down the hedge of our personality, to destroy the rational character of our moral discipline and development, and to reduce it to a semi-physical or mechanical process, and finally to revert, as nearly as may be, to the Pharisaic or Judaic idea, that the goal of humanity may be reached or brought near by a miraculous interposition ; an idea, which, it is to be feared, exercises a materializing and paralyzing influence upon much of the Christianity of the present day, and needs to be remedied by a return to the pure and spiritual doctrine of Jesus. At all events, we can hardly question the existence, or refuse to recognize the influence of this idea at the present day, when we find Keble defining the Church as " a supernatural body, separated from the world to live a supernatural life, begun, continued, and ended in miracles " ; and a living expert in theology of a kind defining grace as " a life poured in from the outside."

If a mystical element is essential to religion, no one can say that it is not provided in the doctrine of Jesus as now presented. The idea of the selfless, aboriginal love of God, which forms the centre of his doctrine, opens up a field in which mystical contemplation may lose itself for ever. But we are none the less inclined to think that, owing to its practical nature, the religion of Jesus does not give much encouragement to the otiose play of mystical feeling any more than to the use of vain repetitions in prayer, or to the practice of inordinate and " perpetual adoration," away from touch with the duties and charities of life.

Here, then, is the conclusion to which we have come— viz., that by his doctrine of the Heavenly Father, which was peculiarly his own, and by his doctrine of the forgiveness of sin, which, if not his own, was yet emphasized by him more than by the sages and prophets of Israel, Jesus may be said to have placed the relation subsisting between God and man not indeed upon a new footing, but in a new light. These doctrines, which are really one and the same, are but the theistic interpretation of a profound experience; the translation into the language of emotion and religion of a common but recondite law of human nature, viz., that, if we turn from our sins, the memory of them ceases to lie as a burden on our conscience, and from being an obstacle, becomes a stimulus to our upward progress. This law of our nature was viewed by Jesus as an indication of the will of God— the Author of our constitution—that our sins should not retain dominion over us; and that, instead of thwarting our efforts at self-deliverance from the evil, He sides and sympathizes with them. When so interpreted this law is what, above all else, rouses into activity the religious sensibilities of our nature, and forms our great encouragement to struggle against our downward tendencies, to cope with the difficulties which beset us in our ascent toward the ideal, and to begin anew after every failure. And it was, as we have endeavoured to show, not by illumination "from outside," but by an act of introspection, by the experience and observation of what took place within himself, that Jesus rose to this view of the religious relation.

We have now seen that both the ideal of humanity and the conception of God, which form the basis and the essence of the teaching of Jesus, might have been arrived at by a dialectical and an experimental process, starting from presuppositions or beliefs which, if not held by all men in common, were the inheritance of the Jewish people. The combined process which seems, under circumstances and conditions more or less favourable, to have gone on slowly for ages, may have been retarded; may have been interrupted or diverted into a wrong channel; may have lost ground and then regained it; and it is conceivable that at last a great religious genius like Jesus—profoundly versed in the records and traditions of his people, in which their religious ideas appear in many stages of development, in isolated, germinal, and often obscure and enigmatic forms of expression—might, by pondering and meditating over them, and above all by the fidelity and singleness of heart with which he lived up to whatever recommended itself to his moral and spiritual sense, at length bring that process to completion, and arrive at the pure ideal and conception which supplied the elements of the absolute religion, and be able by his clear exposition and illustration of them, as well as by his manifest devotion and sincerity, to imprint them indelibly on the minds of his followers.

Having thus endeavoured to determine the specific doctrine of Jesus, so far as seems to be necessary for our purpose, we may pause to repeat, what has been already said incidentally, that there is no dogmatic element in that doctrine except such, if such there be, as is involved in the religious sentiment itself : a proposition to which, in view of modern thought, we attach much importance. If, for example, the personality of God is presupposed in the teaching of Jesus, as well as in the most elementary form of the religious sentiment, and if it yet be unverifiable and dogmatic, we may still observe that this consideration does not block the course of this discussion, whose object is not so much to prove the truth of Christianity as to trace its origin and the sources of its power in human life. We may, however, deny the force as well as the relevancy of this consideration. We contend that the doctrine of Jesus was purely and substantially a statement of the facts of his own inner consciousness, drawn from his personal experience, in conscious touch and converse with the deep ground of his spiritual nature, and therefore capable of verification by all who partake of his nature. His doctrine was that God is fatherly and exacts no more of men than that they turn from their sin and endeavour in sincerity to live up to their ideal. By cultivating such a disposition, and making this their aim, men are restored to inward harmony, or unity, which is but another name for the pacification of their nature with the divine principle within them, or with that supreme power on which they feel their absolute dependence ; and this is a fact of experience or of consciousness which may or may not involve the personality of that power, but it is a fact which has a truth of its own quite irrespective of the conclusion to which we may come on that point. The doctrine of the forgiveness of sins, which is here the crucial point in question, is, as formerly concluded, a theistic interpretation of a profound human experience ; but, even if the interpretation be problematical, yet the experience itself, once made by the Founder of our faith (and no doubt by many others though more faintly), remains on record, an indication to all men, whatever their creed, that moral effort is not in vain. Yet the conviction is impressed on our minds by many considerations, that, for men generally, the higher graces of the Christian life can flourish only in the element of theism, in which the ideal serves as a warrant of divine placability, and humanity itself passes for a great family, of which God is the head.

Belief in divine forgiveness, as taught by Jesus, is a principal part of our moral education ; and we can see that its rise and growth in the soul has features in common with the educative process generally. When the moral consciousness awakens, and the sense of guilt deepens in the soul, there comes along with it a craving for the forgiveness of that power on which we feel our dependence ; or, which is the same thing, for the approbation of our own higher nature. There is thus, in the normal course, a predisposition to believe in that divine forgiveness which the gospel announces. We begin our spiritual training by receiving the announcement with docility, just as children receive whatever is presented to them by their parents and instructors. But our faith cannot always rest on mere authority. At this stage it is only preparatory and transient. We have yet to be men in understanding, to prove all things ; to hold fast that only which is true, and to make it our own by the verification of experience. At first we cherish belief in forgiveness merely to relieve our sense of guilt, but as the moral sense becomes more sensitive and enlightened we perceive that that belief is only a means towards the great end of our moral education ; that it is of service to man only when it takes part in the moral process, and goes hand in hand with the earnest endeavour to achieve the ideal of our nature, and reinforces our efforts to extricate ourselves from the evil. The thought dawns upon our minds that forgiveness itself is not the reward of our faith, but that the faith in it is our encouragement to cultivate that state of mind, and to observe that conduct, which are acceptable to God. And, when, being put to this test, our faith makes it sensibly less difficult to lead the spiritual life and to resist besetting sins, it no longer rests upon the authority of any teacher, but has its authority within itself, and stands in need of no other and no higher verification. We can then say, with a sense of certitude, " I believe in the forgiveness of sins," and we feel the truth of those profound words of the fourth Evangelist, " If any man will do the will of God, he shall know of the doctrine, whether it be of God." We shall know that our sins are forgiven, as Jesus has taught us, no longer because he taught us, but because we have the witness within ourselves. To trust in divine forgiveness, and to derive from it a stimulus and encouragement to the better life, is the highest homage and worship we can pay to God. And here is the point where morality and religion are fused into one, and where the difficulty of the question as to the relation between these two may be said to disappear.

We have now found what is the distinctive note or feature of the doctrine of Jesus. On the negative side it is, that in the conduct of his spiritual life man need not, or rather must not, entertain the hope of any divine help from outside. On the positive side, it is that man's help, under the given conditions, favourable or unfavourable, of his life, can only come from within ; that is, that within every man, as part of his natural endowment, there is a latent power, the divinest thing in him, by which he may with more or less success resist or overcome the opposing evil, innate or incurred, though for the most part with heaviness of spirit, as of a heart divided against itself and drawn in different directions, so that every task, however light, becomes a burden : a power, therefore, which needs to be quickened into joyful and victorious effort by the consciousness, with which Jesus inspired his followers, of the ever-placable God, who forgives the sins that are past and looks with favour on the feeblest efforts towards a better and an ever better life. We believe that whatever else Jesus may have taught, as, *e.g.*, his injunction of love to one's enemies, was either not so peculiarly his as this was, or that it was a deduction from this doctrine. The orthodox Christian may think that this is a very defective and circumscribed account of the doctrine of Jesus, but for us it is inclusive of all else. Nay, we do not assume that even this doctrine is absolutely his own in the sense of its being quite original ; it is, in fact, a doctrine which smoulders under all forms of religion and makes them to be religions; and we believe that a dim and inexplicit surmise of it has been as old as humanity itself, but that, by his luminous and heroic advocacy of it in word and deed, Jesus made it to pass into the minds of his followers, and to acquire for itself a footing there such as it never before had. We shall only further add, that this view of the factors of the religious process, caught up from the teaching of Jesus, appealing to our consciousness, and followed out to its consequences, was what first suggested to us a steadfast doubt as to the supernatural theory of Christianity, which gradually settled into the deep conviction to which this volume gives utterance.

It has been shown by us how, from the prophetic or Pharisaic level, Jesus may have wound his way upward and scaled the height of a new consciousness, the consciousness of a new religious relation, by the communication of which to his disciples he became the Head and Founder of a new society— of a new humanity. It has been pointed out, that the doctrine of the forgiveness of sins was a theistic interpretation of·his profound human experience. We say a theistic interpretation, because he who had that experience, and was the interpreter of it, was himself a theist ; and in discussing the genesis of Christian doctrine that is all we have to think of. But in passing, the remark may be hazarded, that an individual imbued with the pantheistic view of the universe might not only have had a like experience, but have also referred it to that unseen Power which moves through all existence and is the ground of our being, and also that he might have expressed his consciousness of that experience in language not materially different from what Jesus is reported in the Gospels to have used. In the inner forum of that consciousness the difference between theism and pantheism is of no account, and does not make itself felt. That experience may be acquired and enjoyed, as we have elsewhere had occasion to observe, undisturbed by any metaphysical question of the kind.

Whether there be a difference between Christian ethics and the ethics of philosophical or common reason is a question which, however answered, does not vitally affect our position. It may or may not be demonstrable that the practical or the speculative reason was able to forestall the ethics of the gospel. It is not so much new obligations as new motives, or new encouragements to the good life, that we find in the teaching of Jesus. Still, if it be asserted, as we think it may, that there are certain distinctive principles or maxims in

Christian ethics, to which the "unassisted" or ordinary reason was never able to rise and which it can even yet only take upon trust, or find a verification of in the experiences of human life, we would place the explanation or the cause of this higher ethical flight of the gospel in that new conception of the divine character, and of the religious relation, which, as already shown, the profound insight and experience of Jesus enabled him to form. It was by his fidelity to the light that was in him, and by his conscious determination to live up to that light, that he discovered the great evangelic principle of divine placability, and the forgiveness of the sins that are past. But this principle having revealed itself to his mind, what more likely, or what more necessary than that, in consequence, the moral horizon should be widened, and that the standard of duty towards God and man should be elevated. Thus, for example, the duty of love to one's enemies, which is peculiar, if anything is, to the spirit of the gospel, is a manifest deduction from the infinite placability of God towards the penitent. The believer in this latter doctrine cannot but recognize the duty of being merciful as God is merciful, and of cultivating in himself a love resembling His. By way of caution, however, and to guard against the appearance of inconsistency with what has elsewhere been said, let it here be noted, that while from the beneficent disposition on the part of God, we may thus infer the duty of a like disposition on the part of man, we cannot reverse this step of reasoning and infer that the procedure of love on the part of God must be analogous to whatever is incumbent on man. There may be duties incumbent on the Christian to which there is nothing correspondent in God. This duty of love to our fellow men is measured by our readiness to make sacrifices on their behalf. But it cannot be said that God's love is measured by any act or acts of sacrifice on His part. A man's inherited tendencies, his early training, his social environment and habits of indulgence, may have been such as to require deep and prolonged self-denial in order that he may choose the right, or persevere in his integrity. But the Infinite knows of no such conditions. The duty of self-sacrifice is imposed on the rational creature by the finitude, the imperfection, the discord, and the division of his nature. But just as we have found that the Infinite is exempt from the possibility of error, so He is also exempt from the necessity of making any self-sacrifice to gain any object or end of His government whatever. The notion that out of goodness or condescension He may do anything which is not a necessity of His nature is inconceivable. It is by the manifestation or assertion, not by the sacrifice or suppression of Himself, that He does us good. There is a sense in which it may be well and truly said that Jesus offered himself a sacrifice for man upon the cross, but this act of Jesus can in no sense be spoken of as an act of self-devotion or of self-sacrifice on the part of God.

CHAPTER VIII.

HOW FAR THE DOCTRINE OF JESUS WAS ORIGINAL.

FOR those who, with ourselves, give up the notion of special, *i.e.*, supernatural illumination, the much vexed question, as to the novelty and originality of the doctrine of Jesus, is one of minor and quite subordinate importance, of historical rather than of religious interest. But the historical interest is so great, and the question has been so much canvassed, that at the risk of some repetition, and of some interruption of the argument, we crave indulgence while we pause to give a separate statement of our view on this subject. We do not for a moment question that the doctrine of Jesus, especially on its more ethical side, was anticipated at many points by previous teachers, and that many of his views had been accepted by the better minds of antiquity. Viewing him as inspired only in the same sense with other great teachers, as separated from them only in degree, and as having access to no source of illumination from which they were cut off, we are not concerned to make out that he made absolutely new discoveries in the religious sphere, and are disposed rather to regard his doctrine as the outcome of a great development to whose absolute beginning we cannot ascend, and many of whose intermediate steps we cannot trace with any clearness or certainty. There may not be a saying of his, whether moral or religious, whether relating to man's duty and destiny, or to God's dealings with man, but had its counterpart, parallel or forecast, somewhere in the great body of pre-Christian literature, classical or oriental, prophetic or rabbinical. There may not be a petition in his form of prayer, nor a sentence in his Sermon on the Mount, which may not admit of being compared with some detached sentence of nearly equivalent meaning from Greek philosopher or dramatist, from oriental sage or Jewish rabbi. We may depend upon it that the most central and important truths, which are associated with his name or referred to his teaching, had dawned, however vaguely, however fitfully and partially, on many prophetic spirits before his day. While making this concession, however, we may still claim for the doctrine of Jesus the character of novelty and originality, unless, indeed, we go the length of denying that there can be such a thing in the evolution of human thought. For we may ask, with E. von Hartmann, who does his best to dispute the originality of the doctrine of Jesus, "What doctrine could be regarded as new and original, in respect of all mankind, even if it were so in respect to the individual or to a particular nation, and how little of novelty remains in the doctrines of the most celebrated teachers if we deduct from them all that has been uttered or foreshadowed in preceding ages?"

It will be seen that we do not seek to exaggerate the originality of the doctrine of Jesus ; but we would guard against the opposite tendency to depreciate or ignore it altogether. This latter tendency is fostered by the neglect or oversight of those aspects which differentiate the sayings and doctrines of Jesus from those of other teachers which bear a general resemblance to them. In many cases the parallelism is only superficial, or not so close as it appears at first sight. For an example in point take Jesus' version of the Golden Rule. The criticism may seem to be minute and microscopical ; but it cannot be altogether accidental or without significance that his formulation of that rule differs materially from that ascribed to Hillel, Confucius, and others. Theirs was, "Do not to others what you would not wish them to do to you." But his was, "Whatsoever ye would that others should do to you, do ye to them likewise." Now between that negative and this positive version the distinction is wide. It is a distinction not verbal merely, or accidental, but correspondent to that which obtains generally between the legal standpoint, which is common to all ethical-religious systems, and the evangelical standpoint : between the law which came by Moses and the grace which came by Jesus. So, too, the record has been preserved of many striking sentences by such men as Hillel, Gamaliel, Antigonus of Sochoh, and others, which show that they had glimpses of some higher form of religion than the mere mechanical observance of the legal statutes. And advantage has been taken of such sayings by Renan and Von Hartmann to prove that there was little novel in the doctrine of Jesus ; that in its origin Christianity was little else than Judaism ; and by Jewish scholars to show that the ethics of the gospel are the same as appear in the Talmud. But it has been well observed by Kuenen that these sayings, however they may be multiplied, present a strange contrast to the rigid legalism which was the essence and enduring characteristic of Jewish teaching. The Jewish doctors either did not perceive the full range and effect of the more spiritual view, or had not the courage and mental force to draw the proper inference from it—viz., the relative, if not the absolute unimportance of mere forms when the substance was present. That Jesus was able to do this places him on quite another plane from that occupied by all the Jewish teachers of that age.

Another striking example will suffice to show that there may be much verbal or superficial similarity between maxims or principles which are yet far from being identical or even approximate in practical tendency, and in general spirit. The passive virtues which are in a great measure common both to Christianity and to Buddhism are in the latter founded on a pessimistic view of life, the negation of all incentive to an active and hopeful effort to stem or remedy its evils. Whereas, in the former, these same nominally identical virtues take the form of resignation to the will of God, and are found to be consistent with the most strenuous remedial efforts. The difference here is great, and is fully accounted for by the fact that Buddha did not, but that Jesus did, proceed, as we have shown, to translate the ethical doctrine into the language of religion.

The reader should bear in mind that it is the doctrine of Jesus as a consistent whole which we affirm to be unique and novel. To assert that anything like the doctrine of Jesus as a whole, or anything approaching it, was ever promulgated before his time, is little short of an affront to human judgment. And even if we were to suppose that to construct that unity he applied an eclectic method to the religious literature of all ages and countries, with which he had somehow gained an extensive and profound acquaintance, he would still deserve to be regarded as the greatest religious teacher whom the world has ever seen, for what he put aside, and for what he chose out or emphasized from the mass of unrelated and undigested thought which had thus been presented to his mind. Viewed as a whole, his moral standard and his conception of God are widely separated from every doctrine which preceded it, as well as from all that could be gathered from acquaintance with the best which men had thought or written in all previous ages, unless he had brought with him an electric touch to fuse the dispersed and often discordant thoughts into organic unity. There must have been, what Goethe said of Carlyle, a "basis of his own," a central principle contributed by himself, some individuality of judgment and of insight, to guide him in framing and building up the system which goes by his name. And if it be asked wherein that basis, that principle lay, we reply without hesitation that it lay in his consciousness of the new or evangelic idea of the religious relation. This idea, though it may have dawned faintly on many minds, was never able to secure for itself an established residence in the thoughts of men till Jesus rose to the clear vision of it, and gave it forth to the world. It was emphatically his own. For elsewhere we have seen that Roman stoicism, the highest product of the religious spirit of Greece, missed or fell short of the idea of divine forgiveness which is essential to that relation, and that the Jews never could dissociate from it the idea of propitiation ; so that nowhere do we find this idea in its purity except in the teaching of Jesus. We say, therefore, that by the clear utterance of this idea he crowned the edifice of religious thought which had been the growth of ages. This he did consciously in respect of Jewish thought, and unwittingly in respect of Gentile thought. On the ground of this idea alone we rest the novelty of his doctrine; and the novelty is greater than it seems, for it is pre-eminently one of those ideas which have issues far beyond themselves. It left nothing standing as it was ; it gave a fresh significance to old truths, and revolutionized the religious sentiment of man. Simply by his view of our relation to

God, Jesus renewed our relation to each other, he gave a new complexion to human duty, and changed the current of human history.

A relative novelty is all that we claim for the doctrine of Jesus, and, if we consider it well, we shall perceive that nothing more than this can possibly attach to the moral and spiritual teaching of him or of any other man. For what is and must be all true ethical and religious teaching but the interpretation of moral and religious instincts, which are fundamental and germinant in all men. What can possibly distinguish the teaching of Jesus except its more developed presentation of the principles of natural religion? The highest claim which his teaching can possibly advance is that it is the purest interpretation of these instincts, the highest development of that religion. All true teachers have come more or less upon the same lines of thought, and the religion of Jesus is superior to other forms, only in so far as it contains elements of natural religion beyond what they do, or has taken into account and embodied elements which those others overlooked or but partially apprehended, and has pursued the intimations of the religious instinct beyond the point at which *they* stopped short. Strange, indeed, had it been, had other teachers not anticipated Jesus at many points, or not had transient glimpses of what he more steadily discerned, or not approached or come within sight of the elevation on which he stood.

The central principles of the doctrine of Jesus have been, we believe, more or less anticipated by all the great founders of religion who have appeared in various ages, and in various regions of the earth. They are the only principles by which religion can be raised above being a thing of mere ritual, and worship, and dogma; the religious nature of man profoundly stirred, and respect awakened for the higher instincts, as intimations of the will of God. But owing to their very nearness, their simplicity and spirituality, these principles are recondite, and apt to be misunderstood, overlaid, and perverted.

It is an accepted canon of historical criticism, not only that no great truth comes abruptly upon the world, but also that the man who perceives the full significance of an old but immature idea, and reveals its bearing on life and practice, is more entitled to the praise of originality than those are who have come upon the traces of it, but have not possessed the intellectual force or insight to bring it fully to light, and have failed to discover its important place in relation to the general system of human thought. History has many instances to show in which ideas have floated for ages in the general mind of humanity, and have exercised a sort of fascination, as if something might possibly be made of them, but which yet have remained little more than dormant in the limbo of fancy and of vague speculation until some more powerful mind, favoured by opportunity or by development in other spheres of thought, has discovered their true significance and thrown them into clear expression, and obtained for them a settled place in the fabric of human knowledge.

While, then, we regard Jesus as a most original teacher, we also acknowledge that it would be a great exaggeration to say that his teaching was absolutely original. It had been strange indeed, or rather wholly abnormal and unaccountable, had he made an absolutely new beginning, an absolutely new appeal to the religious instincts, or had suddenly opened up an entirely new vein of ethical or religious thought. We rather welcome the thought, that many of his ideas had suggested themselves to the higher minds of our race. That he had received into himself a rich inheritance from the past, and that his was an original, because it was also a receptive nature, is what we do not question. Our position is, that the ideas which underlie all his teaching, while they had germinated in many of the highest minds of our species, did in him alone coalesce and blossom into that ideal of humanity and that conception of God which he offered as an instruction to his disciples, with the express design of lifting their life, and laying through them the basis of a new religion and of a better form of society. Still, in considering the genesis of the doctrine of Jesus as a distinctive system, it must not be forgotten that we have not a tittle of evidence that he was in any way indebted for it to Hellenic, or even Judæo-Hellenic literature or philosophy. The diffusion of these, by their comparatively full development of the moral consciousness, and by the many elements akin to Christianity which they contained, may have materially prepared the way for its subsequent rapid propagation. But to say that such elements ever came from these sources into contact with the mind of Jesus, or contributed a factor to his moral development, is quite another thing. It has been said, and, we believe, well and justly, that he was " a Jew from head to foot," touched by no influences, acquainted with no literature, but those of his own people and country. His moral consciousness was formed by the teachings of the legislators and prophets of Israel, and by his acquaintance with synagogal and Pharisaic doctrine and usage, till it could stand erect in its own strength and lay its line of judgment on all alike, and recognize their defects and shortcomings. For it is often thus, that the pupil passes beyond the sphere of his teachers, and rises, above the system in which he has been educated, to a higher level of thought. The mental development of Jesus proceeded not by the discovery of any absolutely new truths, but by the fuller recognition of elements which were germinant in the moral consciousness of men, and by the emphatic prominence which he gave to elements which, till then, had lain in the background ; so imparting new significance to much, and revolutionizing the whole field of religious thought.

To be fair and candid, we must estimate the force and originality of the genius of Jesus, as we have done, by contrasting and comparing his doctrine with that of the accredited teachers of his own day and country. It is evident that he was profoundly versed in the prophetic literature of a former age, and that, to a large extent, this circumstance may account for his superiority to many of the notions prevalent around him ; the marvel being, that with such a splendid literature— the product of a high spiritual insight—in their hands, and read in their synagogues every Sabbath day, the Jews of that age could be satisfied with the doctrine of the contemporary teachers ; that he alone broke away from Pharisaic leading strings, and took up again the thread which had dropped from prophetic hands. At the same time, we feel that we are in a new atmosphere, even when we pass from the study of prophetic literature to that of the Gospels, and that the religious idea is nowhere presented by any of the prophets, or by all of them together, with the same purity and uniform consistency as in the teaching of Jesus. It would seem, therefore, that we are thrown upon the personality and religious genius of himself to account for the highly developed presentment of the religious principle which we find there.

There is, as we have shown, little or no indication that Jesus was indebted for his doctrine to Gentile speculation ; the parallelisms between it and this not amounting to much.   But that he was indebted to the remains of prophetic literature there can be no doubt ; and the question arises, by what avenue these latter may have been brought into contact with his mind? And we feel that we cannot summarily dismiss the conjecture that he did not stand quite alone in his reaction against the Judaism of his time, or in his reverting to the prophetic spirit of the earlier age.   We are confessedly ignorant of the more intimate conditions which called his native qualities into action. It may be that his religious views were formed under the influence and in the atmosphere created by a small group of kindred spirits, who, in his day, represented an unbroken succession, running back in slender and inconspicuous line to prophetic times, and preserving the tradition of that more spiritual religion, which, in the best times, would seem to have been confined to a small minority of the Jewish people ; to have disappeared from the synagogue, and to have died out of the hearts of the accredited teachers of the people.   If there was such a group or circle—the existence of which is antecedently not improbable—we need not look for it among the Pharisees, and still less among the Sadducees : and the only other section of the people being that of the Essenes, who certainly were dissident from the common Judaism, of which the Pharisees were the main representatives, the question arises, how far it is probable that such a group or circle may have existed within the Essene communities? Considering the distinctly marked element which these formed in the population, the number of their settlements scattered over the land, and the contact, at many points, of their doctrine and mode of life with the teaching of Jesus, it does appear to be a singular circumstance, not easily to be accounted for, that no allusion is ever made to them in the Gospels.   The observation, that they are never once named in the Talmud, does not afford a parallel to this omission on the part of the Evangelists.

The silence of the Talmudists was in all probability a calculated silence, expressive of their contempt for what they regarded as a miserable sect ; a contempt which would be heightened by the fact, if fact it is, as surmised by Lightfoot, that after the destruction of Jerusalem the Essenes went over in a body to swell the Christian Church.   The silence of the

Gospels has by some authors been construed into a proof or consequence of the close connection in which Jesus stood to these communities, as arising out of the desire of the Evangelists to conceal this fact, and affording ground for the suspicion that Christianity was little more than an expansion or modified form of Essenism. But the more likely explanation is that the Evangelists felt it necessary only to call attention to the opposition which Jesus encountered, and naturally took little notice of the countenance and help which he received, or of surrounding influences like those of Essenism which were more or less favourable to his enterprise. It may readily be supposed that the Essenes, not being actively opposed to Jesus, might be passed over in the tradition as being on his side (Mark ix. 40). The existence among the Essenes of such a hidden, obscure, and little-heeded band as we here suppose, has some probability given to it by the notices, preserved in the Gospels, of John the Baptist, of Anna the prophetess, and of the aged Simeon. The ascetic habit of John's life was strange to ordinary Jewish notions, and suggests his possible connection with the Essenes; while the prophetic gifts which these people affected to cultivate may account for the reputation which Anna enjoyed, and it might be said of them in a very special sense, as of Simeon, that they "waited for the consolation of Israel," inasmuch as they did not idly wait like the Pharisees, by merely conforming to the statutory ordinances of Israel, but sought by their system of self-discipline to prepare themselves for the coming era. Not that we attach much weight to such considerations, or think the hypothesis here made to be of much importance ; for, let the relation be what it may in which Jesus stood to the Essene communities, whether one of absolute neutrality or of relative dependence, we have shown elsewhere that in no case could it suffice to explain Jesus, or supply us, so to speak, with the equation of the man. But we cannot help the feeling that but for some such hypothesis as the above of the connection of Jesus with some group or circle of which no record has been preserved, Jesus would come before us as a man without father or mother, in the spiritual sense of the word, and as having spontaneously taken up the broken thread of prophetic tradition after it had, as a living tradition, been lost for ages. What we know of rabbinical literature hardly warrants us in regarding it as the conductor of that tradition. But it would be contrary to general analogy to suppose that continuity had been completely broken, or that an entirely new beginning was made, unless, indeed, we choose to regard Christianity as a renascence due to the material transmission into new conditions of the documentary memorials of a past age. As there were Reformers before the Reformation, so, we doubt not, there were Christians before Christianity took its place among established institutions; and we are disposed to regard its Founder as the successor of the prophetic line of Israel : as, in some measure, the last and greatest of the prophets who was able to complete their work and testimony, because he inherited their views from acquaintance with their writings ; and also, it may be, from his connection with such a small circle as we suppose, which had inherited through forgotten links a tradition of the spirit in which the prophets lived and wrote ; of which, too, by his commanding figure and imposing personality, he became the central and presiding genius, besides that he infused fresh life into the lingering tradition, and gave to it a new start and development. The records which have come down to us, if they do not encourage, can scarcely be said to exclude such a conjecture.

But even from this point of view, we still regard Jesus as a great religious genius who rose above his surroundings ; who had the faculty of gathering up all the straggling lights of prophecy into one focus, and transmitting them in new and concentrated power to the coming age; as one whose deep insight thus gained into the nature of God and man, enabled him to throw light upon the relation subsisting between the human and divine ; as one, moreover, who by his heroic character and his tragic end stamped the memory of his life and teaching in indissoluble union on the minds of his disciples, and sent it rolling onwards, to gather into itself all such cross fertilizing elements as could enter into combination with it, and so imparted a new impulse and character both of good and evil to human life and destiny. He was as little a prophet as he was a poet in the narrower sense of the word, for he was, more truly than John the Baptist, greater than a prophet. The struggle which characterizes the prophet was past for him before he showed himself to the world. He had entered into the full possession of truths to which to the end the prophets rose with difficulty, and he was able to proclaim in the most simple and axiomatic form, both by word and deed, what they could only express by symbolic action, or utter in dark sayings, in figurative language, and in detached sayings above the ordinary level of their thoughts. While they felt as if they were but the mouthpiece of a higher intelligence, and were carried out of themselves, he did but give utterance and articulation to the deep moral and religious instincts of his own bosom ; a reason why he spoke with such calmness and manifest depth of conviction as to carry his doctrine " with authority " to the hearts of his disciples.

From our anxiety to vindicate the relative originality of the *thought and teaching* of Jesus, it must not be inferred that we attach to these an undue or exclusive importance. We do, indeed, attach to them a very great importance, because we take for granted that all right action depends on right thinking, and because we believe in the power of ideas. But we are far from supposing that articulate speech is the only vehicle for the transmission of ideas, or that these are disseminated by discourse only. There is a medium more impalpable than language by which they pass from mind to mind, and they may stir the heart and move the springs of action before they reach the understanding. Ideas may be implied when they are not expressed, and may act upon minds which are not conscious of their presence, or are even repelled by the formal statement of them. But no matter whether it be explicit or inexplicit, the right view of things must be present in order to the right dealing with them. In Jesus himself thought and impulse to action were at one, and the thought, which he endeavoured to communicate to his disciples, as the medium for imparting impulse and influencing life, was communicated, in part at least, through his own manner of acting and suffering, or through the life which he led quite as much as by the form and substance of his oral teaching. His discourses would probably have made but a slight impression on his hearers, had he not also acted what he taught, amid circumstances which tested his sincerity to the utmost ; and so gained an influence on the sympathies of many witnesses.

P

CHAPTER IX.

THAT JESUS CLAIMED TO BE THE MESSIAH.

WE endeavoured to show in a former chapter that Jesus neither regarded himself as a Redeemer, nor uttered anything to encourage his disciples to regard him in that light. But we now advance to the remark, that it is no less certain to our minds that he regarded himself as the promised Messiah, and gave his sanction to that belief on the part of his disciples : differing entirely in this respect from John the Baptist, who, while he looked for a Messiah, yet declined to apply the name to himself. Undoubtedly, the belief in the Messiahship of Jesus, however it originated in the minds of his followers, must have exercised a prodigious influence, and have lent a force to his words and a sanctity to his person beyond that, which, but for it, they could possibly have had. It was, indeed, a circumstance, the importance of which can hardly be exaggerated. For it is universally acknowledged, that unless the Messianic faith had connected itself with the person of Jesus, and unless the accumulated sanctities of the old religion had thus been laid claim to by the new, the latter could never have maintained itself in face of the opposition which it encountered at the first, nor have found a soil prepared for its reception in so many hearts. The existence of the Messianic hope in Israel was fitted to be either an insuperable obstacle or a great furtherance to the teacher of a new religion, differing materially from Judaism, or running counter to the current national ideas ; an obstacle to the teacher who could not assert his claim to be the Messiah, a furtherance to one who could. It was the cause of determined unbelief in the mass of the Jewish people ; it lent ardour and enthusiasm to the faith of the disciples.

The most probable account of the origin in the minds of his disciples of this belief in the Messiahship of Jesus, is that he himself participated in this belief and gave it his sanction. The common, orthodox explanation of this remarkable circumstance is either that he was conscious of his Messianic character by virtue of his divine nature, or that he was favoured with some mysterious communication from heaven to that effect. As to this explanation and the data on which it is founded, we shall only remark that when examined critically, and apart from any preconceived ideas on the subject, the prodigies which are recorded in the Gospels as having attended his birth, and the voice and vision which accompanied his baptism, appear to be nothing but the pious fancies or inventions of the circle of early disciples, who were unable to conceive such a thing as an inner warrant, and could only imagine that the secret of his mission had been broken to him by some communication addressed to the outer sense. On the very face of them the records contain indications that no such prodigies occurred. Among these indications is the fact that these alleged prodigies left no impression on the dwellers in the districts where they are said to have occurred, and did not influence the treatment which Jesus afterwards received. They awakened no expectation of his future greatness, and were entirely forgotten, it would seem, even by his mother and other relatives (see Mark iii. 21). That no trace of any surviving memory of these events occurs in the narratives is enough to show that, like many other legends, the evangelical tradition grew up piece-meal, without regard to that unity and consistency which the pragmatism of real history requires.

But, indeed, any supernatural explanation of the Messianic consciousness of Jesus is wholly inadmissible, and we must seek for another more consonant to the general principles which guide us in this inquiry. And with this in view, we start from the unquestionable fact that he did not, from the commencement of his ministry, give himself out to be the Messiah. The synoptic narratives convey the impression that until St. Peter's confession at Cæsarea Philippi, Jesus never spoke of himself as the Christ, and was never acknowledged or recognized as such by his disciples. Of this " remarkable reticence " of Jesus at the commencement of his public life, regarding his claim to be the Messiah, the best explanation by apologetic theologians

which we have seen is, that " his conception of the Messianic
King was not that which was current among his countrymen ;
that the word 'Christ' did not mean the same thing to his
hearers as to himself, and that it was difficult to use it without
fostering opinions he did not share, and encouraging hopes he
knew to be delusive." Some exception might be taken to this
explanation, but it is ingenious, and from the apologetic point
of view, satisfactory enough. We shall, therefore, content ourselves with simply putting our own construction of the facts
over against it.

In our view Jesus delayed his claim to be the Messiah, not out
of reticence or any species of economy in his teaching, but rather
owing to the circumstance that he had for a time no absolute
certainty as to the fact. There is no evidence in the synoptists
that his "plan" was matured from the first ; or, when he
announced that the kingdom of heaven was at hand, that he
even considered the advent of a Messiah to be necessary for its
establishment. Indeed, his idea of the kingdom as being
within men, and as coming without observation, was somewhat
at variance with that of a Messiah, and that he should, in
the ardour and freshness of the former, overlook, or put aside,
the thought of the latter, even if it seemed to be implied in the
prophetic books of the Old Testament, is not to be wondered
at. What we do know with some degree of certainty is, as we
have already seen, that while many waited for the consolation
of Israel, for the advent of a Messiah, he felt that they had no
need to wait, but taught them to abandon the expectant
attitude, and implied that no messenger from heaven was needed
to give the signal for the inauguration of the kingdom. The
spirit of his announcement was that, come when the Messiah
might, there was no need to wait even for him. Men could
not tell when he was to come, they could not hasten his coming. It was an event over which they had no control, but they
might exercise, without delay, the power which they did have
of entering the kingdom of God ; it being present in the midst
of them, though no Messiah had as yet made his appearance.
In stepping forward with a declaration to this effect, he gave a
transcendent proof of his confidence in the self-sufficing
authority of the human spirit to itself—an authority before
which the most sacred and time-honoured beliefs had to bend
and give way.

His assumption, at a later period, of the Messianic character was an afterthought, for which we can account without derogating from his truthfulness, or from the sanity and sobriety of his mind, as also without the supposition of any supernatural authentication of it to himself. We conceive that, as the grand and fundamental significance of his doctrine concerning the kingdom of God made itself more and more felt by him, the thought might gradually suggest itself to his mind, that he himself might be the predicted Messiah. The fact of his clearly perceiving and distinctly announcing that the highest life of man did not depend on the advent of a Messiah, or on any outward manifestation, might disclose itself to him as a title to regard himself as the Messiah; not such, indeed, as his contemporaries looked for, hardly even such as prophets had imaged and yearned for, but oné who surpassed their hopes and would more than fulfil their expectations. The consciousness that he was the sole bearer to man of a vital truth which the whole prophetic line had missed, was enough to satisfy him that he could, without presumption, appropriate the title of Messiah to himself. He had discovered the perpetual presence in the earth of that kingdom of God, of which men hitherto had been unconscious or unobservant, and also the way by which men might become members of it; that a change of mind and not of circumstance was the remedy for human ills. No higher truths than these had ever been discovered; none more capable of creating a new current in the world's history, and of heaving the religious life to a higher level. Then, he realized to himself that, as sole depositary of these great truths, he occupied a unique position in the world; he could not but feel that the cause of humanity rested with him, and the thought might well suggest itself to his mind, that he might be the Messiah of whom the prophets spoke.

But to this inner warrant for such a thought came also an outer warrant. The effect of his ministry in elevating the mind and character of his disciples would lend force to the idea. That this was so seems to be implied in the answer which he gave to John's inquiry, "Art thou he that should come, or do we look for another?" He did not answer the question categorically, but, indirectly or problematically, in words which seem to show that he had weighed this very question in his own mind. " Go and show John again those things which ye do hear and see, the blind receive their sight and the lame walk," etc., *i.e.*, that John may see whether the works which I do do not fulfil, and more than fulfil, the words of the prophets, or whether their words should still lead him to expect a greater than me. The effects of his ministry, to which he thus drew attention, were what satisfied his own mind, and he appealed to them to satisfy the Baptist. The effects to which he pointed were the spiritual effects of his doctrine, and went far beyond anything which had attended the preaching of John himself. The Baptist had produced a great commotion, and awakened lively expectations, but he had left the minds of men unsatisfied ; on the banks of Jordan he had touched the consciences and reformed the lives of many besides Zaccheus, but he had brought the joy and bliss of " salvation " to no man's house. The least of those who had joined themselves to the company of Jesus was greater than the Baptist himself. For John's teaching sanctioned that passive attitude, the last obstacle to all true progress in the higher life which Jesus sought to remove, and which, when replaced by an energetic surrender to the divine will, admitted to the soul a new light and life, to which John's disciples had necessarily remained strangers. In his reply to John's question, Jesus placed before him the consideration which weighed with himself and which he expected also to weigh with the Baptist, viz., that the effects of his ministry were far greater than those which followed the ministry of John, who announced the advent of the Messiah ; and that they were worthy of the Messiah himself. He may have felt that, come when he might, the Messiah could perform no greater work than the spiritual effects which his own doctrine was calculated to produce, and that, in so far, prophecy found its fulfilment in him. And we may also suppose that the cases of moral therapeutic which accompanied his footsteps, however they may be accounted for, could not be altogether without effect upon his self-estimate, could not but lend additional likelihood to the suggestion that he was the Messiah.

Still, we can readily conceive that, strong as these warrants, outward and inward, for applying the prophecies to himself, may have seemed to him to be, he may yet have seen reason for suspense and hesitation before he could resolve to announce himself to be the Messiah. The signs of Messiahship were not all to be seen in him. Much of the prophetic imagery did not plainly or literally apply to him. The therapeutic wonders which accompanied his preaching were too insignificant and of too doubtful a nature to be thought worthy of the Messiah. They did not satisfy the Jewish ideas of " a sign "; perhaps they did not satisfy his own. No angelic vision, nor voice, nor communication of any kind from heaven had conveyed a message to him, or given him a warrant to assume the name, and undertake the Messianic rôle. His healthy and sober nature had preserved him from such an illusion. His warrant was mainly within himself— in his conviction of the infinite importance and significance of his doctrine, and in his consciousness of high resolve and moral power which quailed before no danger, and was equal to any act of self-devotion. It may also have gradually dawned upon him that much of the prophetic language was figurative ; that the notes of the Messiah, as they might be gathered from the Old Testament, were to be spiritually interpreted, and that so interpreted, they might refer to him ; that he had indeed raised the dead in sin and healed the sick of soul by rousing to life and refreshing their moral nature : an effect more admirable and more truly divine than if he had controlled the forces of nature, and called the dead to life again ; and thus forming a sort of outer warrant for his belief, that he was the only kind of Messiah which human needs required or admitted of.

Finally, whatever hesitation might still remain, it was removed, we believe, by the discovery which he made at Cæsarea Philippi, that the belief in his Messiahship had grown silently up in the minds of his disciples. It was not, we may be sure, out of mere idle curiosity, nor out of sensitiveness to human judgment, that Jesus, at an advanced period of his ministry, put the question to his disciples, " Whom do men say that I am, and whom do ye say that I am ? " For it is ever the mark of a strong man to be self-dependent, self-contained, and somewhat indifferent to the judgment which others may form of him. He may have put the question in order to stimulate the somewhat musing and sluggish minds of the disciples ; to importune or extract a confession from them which would reveal to them the state of their own feelings, and bring into full consciousness that of which they were already sub-conscious. The sequel shows, indeed, that the consciousness was already present, the utterance of it already upon their lips, and that the question was all that was needed to call it forth. But the still more probable explanation of the question is, that, in the persistent absence of any sign or communication from heaven, such as had, according to his devout belief, been given to the servants of God in other ages, there still lingered a faint doubt in his own mind as to his Messianic mission; whether, that is to say, he was justified in assuming that, vitally and supremely important as his doctrine was to the highest interests of men, the Messianic mission had indeed fallen to him. To remove the last faint shadow of such a doubt, before advancing further on the course whose fateful close he had begun to foresee, he may have desired to know, for the confirmation of his faith in himself, what impression had been made by his teaching and personality on the minds of others, especially of those who had been witnesses of his life and doctrine, and who judged him with the penetration which comes even to simple souls by familiar intercourse and loving insight. Obviously they had long attached themselves to him with little or no suspicion of his being the Messiah; they regarded him at most as "another" who had come in the spirit, and in more than the power, of John the Baptist. In view of the expectant state of the Jews at the time we must regard this slowness of apprehension on the part of the disciples as a proof of uncommon obtuseness and unaccountable stupidity, provided, indeed, Jesus did actually perform the great miracles recorded of him in the Gospels,* and when, at last, the truth did break upon their minds their late enlightenment could hardly have merited the encomium that

---

* If, like John, Jesus performed no miracles, the fact that John, notwithstanding that the people inclined to regard him as the Messiah, had apparently failed to effect anything great, and had declined the Messianic title to himself, may have acted on the disciples of Jesus as a caution against being rash in holding him for the Messiah, and may help to explain their "slowness" of understanding. But if, as the synoptists unite in telling us, Jesus wrought miracles, while John did nothing of the sort, this backwardness on the part of the disciples is utterly incomprehensible.

"flesh and blood had not revealed it to them" (Matth. xvi. 17). It was because signs and wonders had not been forth-coming, and because the work and influence of Jesus had been altogether of a spiritual nature that he could justly say that not flesh and blood, but the Heavenly Father, the divine principle within them, had revealed the truth to them as to himself. In fact, they had been led to a con-viction of his Messiahship along the same line of thought and by the same indications as those to which Jesus himself had trusted. The confession of Peter was a grand one, just because it was made in the absence of every external warrant and proceeded from spiritual insight. But what we have chiefly to remark in regard to it is, that it formed a great turning point in the experience of Jesus himself no less than of his disciples. The last shadow of self-distrust vanished from his own mind, when he perceived that the disciples had been led, unsolicited and unprompted, to the very same con-clusion to which he himself had been led. It was with him as with other teachers and leaders of men. His own mind grew clearer; he gained new confidence in himself and in his mental visions when he found them ratified, and, as it were, reflected back from the minds of others. One of the deepest thinkers of this century says that one's opinion and conviction gains infinitely in strength and sureness the moment a second mind is found to have adopted it; and we believe that this observation was exemplified in the experience of Jesus at Cæsarea Philippi. The conviction of his Messiahship, which thus established itself in the mind of Jesus, was not in the least shaken by the hostility and unbelief of the ruling classes, for he could not fail to perceive that the sensuous, carnal, and worldly expectations with which the Messianic hope was associated in their minds, closed them against all higher truth, and that the true Messiah could not but dis-appoint their expectations and excite their enmity.

It has already been shown that the whole teaching of Jesus was calculated to dissuade his disciples from trusting to or waiting for any illapse of another spirit, or any divine manifestation of an external nature; that he called upon them to believe in the presence of the kingdom of God without waiting for a sign from heaven, and to make good their entrance into it by an energetic surrender of themselves

to the divine will. Had he persisted, like John, in the traditional thought that the kingdom of God could only be
ushered in by some miraculous manifestation, the truly
spiritual worship of God would not have been introduced by
him, and Christianity would not have come into existence.
It was in harmony with the counsel which he gave to his
disciples that he himself was able to dispense with any outward communication, audible or visual, from the unseen world,
and to regard the office for which he felt himself qualified
to be one to which he was divinely called and commissioned.
This qualification was his highest warrant for undertaking
the Messianic office. On this warrant he felt himself entitled,
nay bound, to act. He had faith in it, and upon that faith
did he cast himself with his whole soul. The notion, which
has been thrown out by some theologians, that he accepted
or applied to himself the designation of Messiah only by
way of accommodation to Jewish tradition is a feeble and
misleading representation. Sharing, as he did, in the national
expectation of a Messiah, his assumption of the Messianic
name and office was the most energetic and sublime act of
his life. It must have been a resolution to abide and to
dare all the unknown hazards which such a claim involved.
To shrink from any of these would, he must have felt,
not only discredit his claim, but also undo all the effects of
his teaching on the minds of his disciples. Indeed it is only
by a determination to be true to an idea that we can hope to
verify it and transform it into a certitude. And the preaching
of Jesus consisted very much in calling upon his countrymen
according to their measure to do as he did; not to pray,
" Lord, Lord," for help that would never come, but to do
the will of God; to seek first the kingdom of God, and to
enter the strait gate. The man who in the strength of his
own moral convictions could revise the Mosaic law and set
aside various of its provisions (Mark x. 5), in spite of the
prestige of divine authority attaching to them, might also be
able to appropriate Messianic language to himself, solely in
virtue of the inward warrant. And the disciples who put
their Master's counsels into practice would thereby put his
Messianic claim to the proof and verify it to their own satisfaction.

We are aware that the views here stated differ materially

from those generally or universally adopted, on the point under consideration, by theologians of the more advanced schools. The rule for them is to deny the Messianic consciousness of Jesus, and to regard it as mythically attributed to him by his disciples after the belief in his resurrection had taken root in their minds. But it appears to us that, by assigning priority to the belief in the resurrection, they leave that belief unaccounted for. By getting rid of the difficulty of accounting for the disciples' belief in the Messiahship of their Master they increase the difficulty of accounting for the origin of their belief in his resurrection. They give up an intermediate step or term by which the disciples might have risen to this latter belief. Had the disciples to the end only regarded him as a righteous man, they could hardly have risen to that belief. For the blood of many righteous men had been shed upon the earth without having such a consequence. And from our point of view, the difficulty of explaining the rise of the Messianic consciousness in the mind of Jesus, and the communication of the belief to his disciples, is much less than that of accounting for the belief of these last in his resurrection prior to their belief in his Messiahship. For there is no more authentic utterance of Jesus in the synoptists than this, that he came to fulfil (the law and) the prophets. As a fact this is just what he did, and we may well believe that he had the clearest intelligence that such was the case; that he had completed what the prophets had left unfinished; that he had come up to the truth which they had only seen afar off; that he had touched the goal of prophetic thought, and brought to a close that religious development of which the expectation of a Messiah was a phase or factor. He knew that by the revelation of his "method" of self-redemption he had brought to men the greatest help they could receive in the process, and that therefore he was greater than the prophets, who had all stopped short of that point. And what is this but to say, that he knew himself to be in a spiritual sense the Messiah whom men longed for, though with a vague and carnal notion of his nature. The one consciousness seems to us to involve the other. And let it be observed, that he could believe in his Messiahship without thinking himself to be more than man. He may have believed in the supernatural idea generally, and in the inspiration of the prophets in particular, and yet have felt all the same, as we have already shown, that the attainment of the *summum bonum* did not depend on any supernatural aid; and even that the announcement of this very truth was a boon to man than which even the Messiah could confer none greater.

In an early part of this essay, it was stated that there have been two stadia in the great religious development which we are tracing. The first of these was the prophetic period which was accompanied in the highest minds by a sense of incompleteness; by a sense, as in the case of Jeremiah (xxxi. 31), that the religious relation was not yet raised to its highest point, though it yet would be. And with this feeling, there was conjoined a prognostic in the general mind of the appearance of some great personage to lead men forward to the height of attainment. Jesus now was conscious that he had come to that height; that he had arrived at the truth which had baffled prophetic insight; and how could such a consciousness exist in his mind without kindling that other, which yet was not another, that he was the expected man, the Messiah, for whom prophets had paved the way.

Our contention then is, that the belief of Jesus in his Messiahship was not part of his original consciousness, and did not hold possession of his mind from the first, but grew up slowly and gathered strength gradually. The inner witness of qualification, from which came the first suggestion of it, was confirmed by observation of the effects of his teaching on the disciples. He may have waived the thought of it, and put it aside for a time, and have entertained it cautiously, confining it to his own bosom, revolving it in his mind, and remaining in suspense until he found that a suspicion or presentiment of it had grown up in the minds of his followers. It is by this conjecture of a slow and gradual, and even laborious and hesitating development of this consciousness, that we may best explain the very singular fact that he deferred his entrance upon his public ministry to a comparatively advanced period of his life. In a form of words, which seems to indicate some feeling of uncertainty as to the chronology, St. Luke tells us, that at the baptism, or the beginning of his ministry, Jesus was about thirty years of age. But there are data in the synoptists which make it probable that his age is understated by that Evangelist. During more than thirty years then, Jesus remained in absolute unbroken seclusion, attracting no particular attention from his family or his fellow-townsmen ; doing nothing all these years to prepare them for the assumption by him of the office of a teacher : of the teacher of a doctrine, which from the very first startled all men by its manifestly novel and revolutionary character. Now, it seems to us, that no explanation of this long inaction and obscurity, this absence of any indication of his future career, is so natural, as that, before he offered himself as an instructor, as a teacher of doctrines calculated to challenge and offend the cherished convictions of his age and country, to unhinge the minds of men, to give a new colour and direction to their thoughts, and to " change their customs," he wished to be sure of himself, sure of his doctrine, sure of his vocation, and sure of his plan of action.

The step which he must have long contemplated, which he felt himself fated to take, because imposed on him by a necessity which he recognized as nothing less than the will of God, was yet a daring, and momentous, and perhaps a dangerous step, and he was in no haste to take it. Above all things, it was incumbent on him that he should be fully persuaded in his own mind ; that he should have a distinct perception of the requirements of his mission, of the goal to which the thoughts pointed which stirred in him, and of the means of success at his command ; as also, that he should be able to judge how far he could calculate on his own devotion, and on his strength of purpose to carry out the enterprise before him. Years of solitary communion with himself and with God may have been required to mature his ideal of righteousness, to settle to his own satisfaction its relation to the kingdom of God, and to loosen the hold which Jewish prejudice and Jewish misconception might still retain over his feelings after they had lost it over his reason and judgment. Without deep and prolonged meditation and self-questioning, and anxious study of the thoughts of past generations, as recorded in the sacred writings of his people, he could not have succeeded in coming " into the clear " on such points, and in drawing a distinct line of separation between the truth as revealed to his mind, and the half truth which had revealed itself to the legislators, prophets, and wise men of old.

Among the ancients of the people, the men of old time, of whom Jesus spoke with but moderate, not to say scant, respect (Matth. v. 21, 27, etc.), were included the prophets, no less than the jurists and rabbins of former generations. Not that he undervalued the services which the prophets had rendered to the cause of religion ; but that he wished it to be understood, that he did not attribute finality to their doctrine, that he was not satisfied with their teaching, and that he undertook to complete or fulfil what they had left unfinished. Nothing could better express his confidence in the absolute superiority of his doctrine, than his repeated use of that formula in the Sermon on the Mount, "Ye have heard that it was said by (to) them of old time : but I say unto you" (on the contrary). This is the language of a man who knew himself to be in possession of a wisdom never before uttered. The same confidence is conspicuous in the Amen, with which he prefaced much of his teaching. This "verbum solenne" was not used by him as an imposing form of language to force his doctrine upon the acceptance of his hearers ; on the contrary, he expected it to derive its authority from the power of his doctrine to call forth the Amen on their part. His doctrine addressed itself to their inmost hearts, to that sense of what was good and true, which was overlaid by the selfish-ness and conventionality of life ; and encouraged the hidden and unexhumed consciousness to rise and assert itself, to take that place in thought and conduct which of right belonged to it. No doubt this is true only of his use of the word as a preface to his ethical dicta, and it is not impossible that the compilers of the Gospels may have re-presented him as using it unwarrantably, as, e.g., in prophetic announcements to which the assent of his hearers could not in any proper sense be an Amen. But, at all events, the formula was characteristic of his mode of discourse and, when he did employ it, it was as when he stretched forth his helping hand to the paralytic, to encourage him to exert the strength which might yet be latent, though spell-bound, in his limbs. And it is not impossible even, that the disciples' experience or consciousness of the helping sympathetic power over the spiritual life, which resided in words spoken by Jesus, may have suggested to their imaginations the narratives of those miraculous healings in the Gospels, which, in sensuous form, served so admirably to represent the working of that power.

The growth of moral certitude in the mind of Jesus, and the ripening of his purpose to proclaim his doctrine, was not the less but rather the more spontaneous, not the less but rather the more an evidence of his religious genius—that it was slow, deliberate, and laborious. Before he could reach that certitude and that resolution the light of prophecy failed him, and left him to the guidance of the inner light. He could not be satisfied with merely copying the ancient prophets, and occupying anew the ground on which they had stood ; for, if for no other reason, it is plain to us, and how much more to him, that they were never able to disengage their own higher thoughts from the lower conceptions of morality and religion which were established in the popular mind and in the national institutions. To take but one example to illustrate this observation, let any one read the 58th chapter of Isaiah, where one may clearly see the timidity, the uncertainty, and the unsteadiness of step with which this greatest and most evangelical of the prophets advanced to the higher doctrine. In the opening of that chapter the prophet shows that he is distinctly aware of the radical defect in that form of righteousness which his country-men affected. He next places in contrast with it, in words which have all the marks of the noblest inspiration and of the deepest spiritual insight, the idea of a better righteousness and of a really spiritual service. But with what bathos does he sink in the two concluding verses of the chapter into the mere legal view, and into the gross ceremonialism of Sabbath observance—enjoining *that* as if it were an essential part of the better righteousness, and of the same rank in point of obligation. It seems as if the eagle soul of the prophet were unable to sustain its flight in that rarefied atmosphere in which he is soaring, and had suddenly dropped to a lower region ; or, as if he had not the courage to trust himself to a path along which few besides himself were travelling. If the two concluding verses be not an interpolation by some priestly redactor, we must suppose that the prophet's heart had failed him in his solitude, or that his grasp of the new was weakened by his reluctance or inability to let go the old, and that he bowed to the necessity of a compromise between the two. In proof now of the greater distinctness with which the higher view of righteousness revealed itself to Jesus, we might here refer to that far-reaching and suggestive declaration of his—that the Son of man is Lord also of the Sabbath day, and that the Sabbath was made for man and not man for the Sabbath. Manifestly these words express a conscious spiritual freedom never attained by the evangelical prophet. They furnish an evidence that in the view of Jesus the obligation of all statutory duties depends on their ministering to the spiritual weal of man, and that the spirit of man himself is the judge of this. But for an illustration even more striking of the difference to which we refer, compare with the dubious vacillating spirit of the prophet the courage and decision with which, on a trying occasion, Jesus stood his ground and declined to enter into compromise with the traditional doctrine. The embarrassing question was proposed to him, " Why do the disciples of John and of the Pharisees fast, but thy disciples fast not ? " *i.e.* (if we may read between the lines and supply the underlying thought), " Supposing your doctrine is better than that of John and the Pharisees, and you advocate and plead for a higher righteousness, yet why not retain in combination with it the customs of the fathers ? What harm can there be in those pious exercises which have aided and sustained the religious life of Israel in the past ? " We are told that Jesus answered readily in that proverbial form which a principle assumes only when it is the result of frequent experience and mature reflection. " No man putteth a piece of a new garment upon an old . . . . and no man putteth new wine into old bottles." These words show that he was so persuaded of the absolute superiority of his new doctrine, and of its sufficiency as a guide to the better life and the true blessedness, that he declined to retain aught of the old in the same piece with it, or to consent to any compromise as the disciples of John and the Pharisees wished him to do, and as Isaiah actually set the example of doing. This rejection of compromise manifests, on the part of Jesus, a clearness of vision, a distinctness and resolvedness of purpose, which he could not have learned from the prophets, and which may have cost him years of earnest thought and self-discipline before he could have reached it. It may also be observed that these words occur in all the synoptic Gospels, and that they express such a vivid sense of the distinctive novelty of the doctrine of Jesus, as well as of the antagonism between it and the older doctrine, as to contribute with other considerations to throw suspicion on the genuineness of the Judaizing words put into his mouth by Matth. v. 18, " Till heaven and earth pass, one jot or one tittle shall in no wise pass from the law, till all be fulfilled."

From what is said of the Baptist and his disciples, we see that he occupied very much the same ground, morally and religiously, as did the ancient prophets ; the same wavering and hesitancy between the new and the old ; the same distrust of the sufficiency of the former; and it may have been the clear perception of this difference, to many impalpable, between himself and the preacher of the desert, which induced Jesus to take his long deferred resolution, and to try the effect of his higher ideas. One thing is certain, that during the years which he had spent in obscurity, unsuspected and unnoticed, his thought had matured so far that he had arrived at his doctrine of the better righteousness and of the purely ideal nature of the kingdom of God. So equipped and furnished for his great work, his observation of John's teaching, of its deficiency and of its failure to accomplish anything lasting towards the establishment of a better rule of life, together with its want of any principle distinctive enough to effect the overthrow of Pharisaism, was felt by him as a divine call to step forth to public view, and to undertake the task which had proved too hard for the Baptist.

We have thus endeavoured to show that it was the irrepressible and nearly mature growth of the Messianic consciousness in the mind of Jesus which prompted him to inquire of his disciples, " Whom say ye that I am ? " He put this question not so much to bring *their* secret feelings to the point of utterance, as to remove the last vestige of doubt from his own mind ; and when his own thought came back to him, reflected from their minds, it was the last and highest confirmation which that thought could receive, and emboldened him openly to assume the Messianic rôle. But we proceed now to observe, that when the disciples perceived his approval and sanction of Peter's confession, the remains of doubt would thereby be removed in turn from their minds, and that a new authority over their faith and life would thus be communicated to his words and doctrine.

We have already pointed out, incidentally, how much depended for the establishment of Christianity on a belief in the Messiahship of its Founder. And we may here remark by the way, that it was of even more importance that this belief should arise in the minds of the disciples than that it should have taken possession of the mind of Jesus himself; for it is conceivable that such belief might have grown up in their minds, just as we have seen that other beliefs did, without having received any encouragement from their Master; and that, had that been the case, the effect would have been none the less. Still, it is our conviction, for the reasons just stated, that this belief grew up simultaneously in the minds both of the Master and of the disciples, and that it was this circumstance which gave it a · firm and conclusive hold upon the minds of both. Proceeding upon this view, the rise and progress of this faith in the first disciples manifestly form an indispensable link or item in the genesis of Christianity, and call for further consideration.

It has been shown that, regarded as the Messiah, Jesus appeared in a very different guise from what his countrymen had been led to expect. He presented himself only as a teacher, i.e., as the last and greatest of the prophets, who had come to complete or fulfil their work. But there can be no doubt that a deep impression of his Messiahship was yet made by his teaching on the minds of many who were sensitive to its power of appeal, even though they could not but be conscious that his office as a teacher did not satisfy the notion which they had hitherto connected with the Messianic office. With the freshness of thought imparted by his teaching to their minds there was also conjoined a spirit of boundless veneration and confidence towards Jesus personally, and both combined to carry them out of themselves, and for the time to make new men of them. There is a likelihood, moreover, that the exalted and enthusiastic feeling thus produced was much more powerful than can be gathered from the remarkably sober, unimpassioned, and objective narrative of the synoptic Gospels. It is conceivable that at a subsequent stage of their experience, when their appreciation of the character of Jesus was greatly heightened, the personal companions of Jesus may have upbraided themselves for obtuseness of feeling and of understanding, in not having more clearly discerned the majesty and greatness of their Master while he was still with them; and that this feeling of self-reproach may have coloured their reminiscences of that wonderful time—those days of the Son of man, which they may have often wished to see again (Luke xvii. 22), and may have had the effect of creating and disseminating among them an exaggerated view of their slowness of apprehension. The Gospels leave the general impression, that while the disciples, during their intercourse with Jesus, contracted a strong and genuine attachment to him, they had not been able, even while bowing implicitly to his authority, to enter much into the understanding of his doctrine, and had imbibed comparatively little of his spirit ; and that they learned to love and venerate him for qualities and conduct which they could not imitate. But in judging how far we may, on this head, rely on the representation of the Gospels, we must, as has just been hinted, take into account the natural tendency on the part of the disciples, after they had risen to a transcendent view of his life and character, to disparage their own previous insight. The operation of such a tendency would be, to put its mark on the tradition and to co-operate with other causes in impairing the strictly historical character of the records.

That the disciples, in the time of their familiar intercourse with him, did not adequately recognize the unique grandeur of their Master, nor sufficiently enter into sympathy with his plans and feelings, is likely enough. The greatness and significance of a phenomenon do not always impress us most powerfully when it is transacting itself before us, or passing under our eyes. But for all that there are various indications that the impression made upon them by his personality was profound. A proof of this may be seen in the fact, that so many men and women left their homes and their occupations to listen to his words and minister to his wants. The feeling of such persons towards him was truly expressed by the words which the fourth Evangelist puts into their mouths, " To whom shall we go (but unto thee) : thou alone hast the words of eternal life." The great majority of those who were attracted by his fame as a teacher and miracle-worker might be drawn to him out of mere curiosity, or passing wonder and emotion ; but there was an inner and smaller circle, represented by the twelve, but not limited to them, whose confidence, veneration, and attachment, he had completely won, because they felt in their inmost hearts that his words were the words of eternal truth and soberness.

. Another indication of the same thing may be seen in his occasional exercise of a power of moral therapeutic. In

another connection the opinion has been expressed by us
that his works of healing and exorcism were the effect and
consequence of that faith and confidence which the subjects
of them reposed in him.   The most probable explanation that
can be given of these apparent miracles is that they were, at
the first, wrought by him unintentionally and unawares.   In
the commotion or mental tumult caused by the approach and
presence of one whom they regarded with enthusiastic veneration, or (as has been strikingly and sensuously expressed in
regard to a widely different occasion) in " that mysterious
shiver, which always runs through one on the approach of
divine things or great men," some forgot their pains, or threw
off permanently, or for a time at least, their sense of impotence
and paralysis, or their feeling of subjection to evil influence ;
and when, by repetition of such cases, the fame and rumour of
his miraculous powers were spread abroad, it needed but the
touch of his hand, the look of his eye, his voice of command,
the rustle of his garment, or the passing of his shadow, to make
men feel the power return to their limbs : every fresh instance
of the kind would heighten the healing power of the imagination
thus set to work.   Now, we say that the energy of the faith,
which was the efficient instrument of these healing acts, was
one more proof of the depth of the impression which Jesus had
made on men's minds even before the last scenes of his life.

But nothing could more strongly indicate the depth of this
impression than the fact that a persuasion of his being the
promised Messiah grew up silently, without prompting, and
without acknowledgment in the mind of Peter and his companions.   Many things in succession contributed to lead up
to this impression upon the few who took to him.   His
doctrine appealed powerfully to their spiritual nature, and
attracted them to his person, and that attraction grew more
magnetic and commanding when it was seen that, in his own
life and conduct, he so perfectly illustrated his doctrine, en-
acting it, so to speak, and making it to live before them,
and clothing it, as it were, with flesh and blood, so that it
was no more a mere doctrine to be believed, but a person
whom they could love and sympathize with, an object which
appealed at once to their intellect, their feeling, and their
imagination, and thus laid deep hold of their whole nature.
Yet further, it has to be observed that the physical or physi-

ological effects, which seemed to accompany his footsteps, his miracles of healing and exorcism, which were really, as just said, the effects of the faith in him which had been previously awakened, were regarded by all spectators as the puttings forth of a miraculous power on his part ; and this belief, it will be allowed, would also form a factor in the cumulative evidence to their minds that he was the divine messenger whose coming was at that time the fondest dream of the nation. What other explanation indeed could be given of the powers physical and spiritual which he seemed to exercise, than that he was the promised Messiah. This was a suggestion that must have been ever present to their minds, only kept from breaking forth into confession and loud acclaim by the fact that Jesus himself remained silent. All that was needed to convert that secretly cherished and growing persuasion into a faith for which men might either live or die, was a word of encouragement from him. And this word was spoken at the critical moment, when Peter for the first time, and as spokesman for his fellow-disciples, openly avowed his belief that Jesus was the Messiah. " Flesh and blood," said Jesus, " hath not revealed it unto thee, but my Father, which is in heaven." To find that Jesus thus sanctioned that faith in himself as the anointed messenger of God, which had been growing up independently and undemonstratively in them, was a consideration to which their reverent and unquestioning confidence in his truthfulness, sobriety, and humility could not but lend decisive weight. The suspicion either of imposture or delusion in connection with one whose whole life and conduct afforded a complete guarantee for the honesty and moderation of his judgment, could not possibly enter their minds. By the time of the journey to Cæsarea Philippi they had learned to trust him so implicitly that they believed his word even when he bore witness to himself. *They* might, but they felt that *he* could not be mistaken, and that the claim made by him was no boastful, insincere, or unwarranted claim, but one which he could not disavow nor put away from him without being untrue to himself and to his mission, a view of his position, we may observe, the same as that which St. Paul afterwards took of his own when he said, " Woe is me if I preach not the gospel."

According to the view now given, there was a certain reciprocity or interaction between the mind of Jesus and that of his disciples, unenlightened and dependent upon him as they were. Both he and they, as we imagine, had been gradually, silently, and simultaneously drawing near to the conclusion that he was none other than the promised Messiah, notwithstanding some appearances to the contrary, such as the absence of many expected signs and indications, and the hostility and unbelief of the accredited teachers of the nation; and this conclusion became the firm conviction both of master and disciple when the discovery was made by them that it was shared in by both alike. According to the orthodox-dogmatic view, which is foreshadowed or represented in the fourth Gospel, there could have been no such mutual or reciprocal action between Jesus and his disciples, no development of thought in his mind, and, by consequence, hardly any such in the minds of his disciples, who are therefore represented in that Gospel as being taught by the Baptist and by Jesus himself from the very first to regard him as the Lamb of God and the Son of God. Such transitive action as there might be must, in that case, have radiated all from *his* side, while *they* were but the passive, unresponsive, unreciprocating recipients of it. Such a view, however, does not answer to the relation which we consider to have existed between him and them. We may well conceive that he may have owed little to them, but that little may yet have been a not unessential factor in his spiritual development. The reflection of his own light from their minds back upon himself was not without effect upon him, as was illustrated immediately after the incident, or eclaircissement at Cæsarea Philippi. The fact there ascertained by him that his teaching and life had impressed the minds of his disciples with the conviction of his Messiahship, besides that it put a complete end to his state of suspense, was an indication to him that a crisis or turning point had arrived in his life-work ; that his doctrine had made a deep impression on his Galilean followers ; that a change in his mode and field of action was now necessary ; that he could no longer confine himself to a private or circumscribed and secluded sphere, nor remain a dweller in a remote province, or a wanderer in outlying corners of the land. This was a discovery which guided him towards his destiny, and formed, we may say, a necessary step in the development of Christianity.

CHAPTER X.

At this point of time, therefore, he turned his face towards Jerusalem, and did not pause until he arrived, though not by the direct route, in that city, where, or in whose immediate neighbourhood, he spent the last days of his life. This change of venue was due, not as some have supposed, to the feeling that his work in Galilee had been a failure, but rather to the perception that it had succeeded so far but could not be carried further, or at least completed, except at the capital, which was at once the holy city of the land, and the headquarters of the system which he wished to overthrow. The orthodox explanation is, that he went thither to complete his work by his death ; the explanation of the mediating school of theology is, that in the confidence of his Messiahship he went to Jerusalem in the expectation of some great manifestation there, by which his cause would be signally advanced, and the kingdom of God visibly set up. Of these two explanations the former has much more the air of truth than the latter. There is no evidence whatever in support of the latter explanation, no evidence that he contemplated or sought to precipitate a sudden extension on a national scale of the better form of society, or that he looked for any sudden and brilliant manifestation of divine power in his favour. There cannot be a doubt that he did indeed contemplate, as the ultimate natural and possible result of his teaching, a renovated form of society, whose bond of union would be an affinity of spirit in its individual members. But his immediate, as opposed to his ultimate, aim, was to "lay his mind" upon a limited circle which, by the virtue of its new life, would gradually extend and enlarge itself till it should fill the world and embrace humanity. His unique distinction as a teacher of religion consisted in his having spiritualized the historical idea of the kingdom of God, in having removed from it every trace of sensuousness, and in having made a clear separation between the things of God and the things of Cæsar. We, therefore, reject the supposition that he at any time expected the sudden and visible establishment of the kingdom of which he spoke. Such an expectation would have been at variance with the slow growth and gradual development which his parables of the mustard seed and the leaven ascribe to the kingdom, and at variance also with the general doctrine of its inwardness and ideal nature.

The true and natural and only remaining explanation of his journey to Jerusalem is that it was laid upon him as a necessity—the same necessity as is felt by men in situations corresponding to that in which he was placed—the necessity of advancing along a path on which they have entered, and of making progress in prosecuting the work they have begun. Having gained the ear and impressed the mind of Galilee, he must have felt that nothing more could be done by remaining there ; the seed which he had sown there must be left to germinate. It was necessary that he should transfer the scene of his labours to Judea, and to Jerusalem, the civil and religious capital of the country, and to present his doctrine and his claims to the heads and elders of the nation in whom the established religion had its chief representatives. He had no alternative but to come forth from his comparative obscurity and show himself openly to the world. This was a necessity of the situation which by imaginative insight,—that creative faculty by which the dramatist passes beyond the limits of experience, and thinks himself into untried conditions,—the fourth Evangelist (vii. 3, 4) was able to indicate—" His brethren, therefore, said unto him, Depart hence, and go into Judea, that thy disciples also may see the works that thou doest. For there is no man that doeth anything in secret, and he himself seeketh to be known openly. If thou do these things, shew thyself to the world." The Messianic programme required that Jesus should now put his reputation to the proof, and justify his pretensions by confronting the priests and rulers in their stronghold in the capital. Nothing

further could be done by the desultory and indecisive skirmish-
ing which he had conducted against them hitherto. Were he
to allow it to be thought that he had now done all he could do,
all he meant to do, in the way of fulfilling his ministry and
authenticating his Messiahship, the spell which had been cast
around his person would be broken, the tide would begin to
turn in favour of the constituted teachers and of the established
order which had been assailed by him. An advance upon
Jerusalem was so obviously imposed upon him by the circumstances, that to shrink from it *in reality* would have been to
decline the post of danger, to avoid the rising storm, to confess
himself unequal to the cherished project of his life, and to
abandon the great enterprise which he had undertaken of
laying the foundation of the spiritual kingdom of God, *i.e.*, as
already explained of creating a new current in the world's
history, and lifting the life of the nation up to a higher
level. Or had he only *seemed* to hold back it would be
attributed by his disciples to lack of courage and to distrust
of himself and his doctrine. Were that idea to gain ground
he could no longer hope to work upon the people and to
retain his hold of their minds. To linger and tarry upon
ground already traversed would be to pause in his work, to
give proof of indecision, or of hesitation, which would cost
him his credit with the people and go far to undo the effect
of all he had hitherto accomplished. The sympathy of the
disciples would fall away, and the stream of the new life
which had begun to flow would be cut off and dried up.
Therefore, knowing full well the double danger—the danger
to himself if he advanced to Jerusalem and the still greater
danger to the disciples if he held back—he chose the former,
and went up, not knowing the issue, but resolved on prosecuting his work by teaching in the streets and temple of the
city, and making his doctrine more widely and publicly
known.

The appearance of Jesus in the streets of Jerusalem could
not but be felt by the priests and Pharisees to be a defiance
and a challenge, and by them his death was determined on
now, if not before. Their motives, indeed, for this determination have been otherwise explained. The words attributed
to Caiaphas by the fourth Evangelist, " It is expedient for us
that one man should die for the people, and that the whole

nation perish not" (John xi. 50), suggest another explanation, viz., the dread lest the pretensions of Jesus to be the
Messiah should, by the stir it was calculated to create among
the people, bring them into collision with the Romans. St.
Luke also says that the mob arraigned him before Pilate for
entertaining treasonable designs. But there is no indication
whatever that the dread of being compromised by his doings
was well founded, and the probability is that this dread, if
expressed, was only a pretext. The Roman governor was to
all appearance disposed to regard Jesus as a harmless
enthusiast, a species of pretender, of which, like the Romans
generally, he was perfectly tolerant. He declared publicly
and emphatically that he could find no fault in Jesus, and
no occasion for the secular power to proceed against him.
The likelihood therefore is that the priests and rulers only
gave out, and wished it to be believed, that they had a fear
of this kind ; it was only the ostensible motive for their
action, designed to cover their real motive, which was to
defend their own religious prestige, or, let us say, their
hierocratic authority. This was respected by the Romans,
but was assailed by Jesus, who had entered on a life and
death struggle with them, which could be ended only by
removing him out of the way. The offence which Jesus
gave at this time to the priests and scribes reached its climax
(according to the synoptists) when he drove the money
changers and the sellers of doves from the temple. It has
been well remarked by Pfleiderer that this incident had for
the rise of Christianity the same significance as had the
act of Luther, in nailing his Theses to the door of the
Church at Wittenberg, for the rise of Protestantism. It
was by arrangement, doubtful from the religious point of
view, of the authorities, that the dealers were admitted to the
temple, and the action of Jesus in expelling them could
not but be regarded by the former as an insult to themselves
which could only be wiped out by his blood. The different
version which the fourth Evangelist gives of the immediate
causes which led to the crucifixion will have to engage our
attention when we come to the consideration of his Gospel.

His death was now resolved on, and he, probably anticipating the worst, went voluntarily and heroically into the jaws
of death, knowing that for him there was no retreat and

no escape except by the abandonment of his great enterprise. Whether he had ever had the hope of a different issue for himself even from the commencement of his ministry is very doubtful. He had taken ample time, as we have seen, to survey the situation, to count the cost, and to estimate the forces of inertia and of evil which were ranged against him. He had also from the first the fate of the Baptist before his eye, and he knew that his own project was much more radical and revolutionary in a religious sense, and therefore more calculated to excite antipathy, than the Baptist's had been. At any rate it is plain that the hope of a safe issue, if it was ever entertained by him, was faint indeed from the time of his return from Cæsarea Philippi. Brought up as he had been in the belief that God had wrought great deliverances for Israel and for many of His servants in ages past, he might possibly have some faint hope that God would interfere at the last moment in his behalf. The words with which, according to St. Matthew, he expired on the cross, seem to indicate the abandonment of such a hope. But whether these and other words on that occasion are or are not authentic, it is evident that the persistent non-intervention on the part of heaven must have disposed him to contemplate the probable triumph of his enemies and a cruel death for himself. His long delay in assuming the teacher's office may also have been due to his not being able to discern the presence of conditions necessary for a successful prosecution of his purpose ; and it is possible that he may have finally undertaken it only when at last the disclosure was made to his ruminating mind that true success might spring out of apparent defeat ; that in suffering patiently the last extremities of pain and ignominy he might give such an illustration of his doctrine and of his devotion to the cause of God as might invest his death with a triumphant power over men's minds. The fourth Evangelist credits him with this thought in that famous passage, " I, when I am lifted up, will draw all men unto me." But if such words, or words of like significance, were ever spoken by Jesus, if he ever anticipated such an effect from his death, it certainly argued a most complete knowledge of the human heart and its springs of action : such a knowledge as could hardly have been gained by experience. For the power of suffering to stir the deeper and mightier sympathies of the human heart could scarcely be said to have been yet exemplified, and was something quite novel in the history of man. But this power, though unknown to that age, was a fact which experience rendered familiar to the early Church, so that the Evangelist himself may have drawn upon that experience to illustrate the super-human foreknowledge of Jesus; by representing the strange effect of his death as having been designed or at least fore-seen by him. We are inclined therefore to regard the mental attitude of Jesus on the way to Jerusalem as one of suspense and of uncertainty as to the issue. We cannot tell, indeed, how far he might be carried or what deductions he might draw from his belief in his Messiahship. He might be led, as just said, to expect that God would interfere in his behalf at the last moment, if not before. But his resolution was taken, like that of the three youths spoken of in the book of Daniel—a book which he had doubtless made his deep study —that, even if God did not deliver, he would yet, be the issue what it might, be faithful to his mission.

The result was what Jesus apprehended, and was not unpre-pared for. His enemies prevailed. The spiritual weapons which he wielded told with no effect upon insensible hearts, and were blunted against weapons which were carnal. His enemies replied to all his appeals by nailing him to the cross, and putting him to death in its cruellest and most ignominious form; and his spirit, which had striven in vain with human prejudice and perversity, winged its flight to the presence of the Eternal. In this last proof which he gave of the purity of his idealism, in the patience, calm fortitude, and unshaken resolution with which, when left without a sign from heaven, and without sympathy from man, he encountered, without flinching, his cruel fate, the grandeur of his character, and his fidelity to the principles which he inculcated, were more con-spicuously manifested than in all his life besides. And such, doubtless, would have been the immediate impression made upon the minds of his disciples by the closing scenes, had not fear for their personal safety, and grief at the calamity which had befallen their Master, as well as the demolition of all the hopes they had built upon him, deprived them, for the time being, of the ability to weigh or to feel the force of such con-siderations.

It was when Jesus had the near prospect of death before him that he is reported by the Evangelists to have said that he had come to give his life a ransom for many, and to shed his blood for the remission of sins. Reasons have already been given for the conjecture that such words, in their plain, dogmatic sense, could not have been uttered by him ; but we may take this opportunity for saying that there is an undogmatic sense in which some such words may have been used by him. They may have been intended by him to express, without circumlocution, the service which he hoped to perform to his disciples, viz., not that of redeeming them, but that of stirring them up to redeem or emancipate themselves from the power of evil. He may have hoped that the manifestation in his death of self-denying love, and of devotion to the cause of righteousness, which brought with it the consciousness of divine forgiveness, the pacification of their higher nature, would infect them with the same spirit, and rouse their moral energies to embark in the conflict with evil ; and with this in view, he might speak of himself figuratively, or elliptically, as if he were actually to pay the price of their redemption—the more especially as he may have anticipated that he would fall as a victim or bloody sacrifice to the task which he had undertaken. He knew that that saying of his, " He that loseth his life shall save it," was true of himself as well as of others. Indeed, he knew it to be true of others because he had found it to be true of himself. But it was of the very nature of such self-sacrifice to look beyond self, so as to include others in the field of one's vision ; or it was to lose sight of self, so as to find it again in the life of others. And by the time at which Jesus had now arrived, the duty of saving his own life had become as nothing—had become merged and lost sight of—in the consuming ardour with which he addressed himself to the duty which he owed to the " many "—the duty of drawing them into sympathy with himself by going on to the bitter end, and by obedience unto death. To his prophetic, penetrating eye, it may have been revealed that his death, as the culmination of his life, might have the same effect ultimately on the life and conscience of his disciples as if it had been accepted by God as a ransom and atonement, according to the idea currently connected with these terms by the Jewish people ; and we can partially under-stand how, in a moment of grave enthusiasm, such words may have fallen from him. And if it were so ;—if the idea of atonement was thus used by Jesus, figuratively or popularly, to foreshadow the effects of his death, the disciples could hardly fail afterwards to misunderstand his words, and to take them as a warrant for the dogma, according to which his sufferings were in a literal sense the price and penalty paid to God for human redemption, while *his* expectation was that his death would operate on the moral and rational nature of many in such a way as to draw them by sympathy with him into a like spirit of devotion, and so to deliver them from the burden of guilt and the tyranny of sin. The disciples, on the other hand, would naturally give to the process a mysterious and supernatural character by overlooking the intermediate link, and giving solitary prominence to the ultimate effect. A mystical or magical character would thus be imported into the religious process which took its start from his death, just as it may be imported into any process by the omission of a link in the chain of causation. If, then, we accept of the two apparently exceptional sayings of Jesus as genuine, we should have to regard them, not as literally, but as figuratively meant—not as scientifically accurate, but, in the language of Mr. Arnold, as popular and literary expressions thrown out at a great subject, which the hearers could hardly understand, or as language called forth by the highly-wrought state of feeling with which Jesus advanced to his impending death, and by his intense realization of the great results which he expected to flow from it.

Probably the disciples were never able to realize the full grandeur of the spectacle which he presented in submitting to death. Even we can realize it only by dismissing the idea of the supernatural from all connection with it. The probability in that case is, that with the prospect before him of an early and violent termination of his lifework, he would be painfully sensible that he had failed of its accomplishment ; that he had made no permanent impression on the minds of his disciples ; and that his apparent defeat and discomfiture was not only apparent but real. But this, if it were the case, would only have the effect of exalting our idea of the nobility and lofty idealism of his character. "To die in vain," it has been well said, is "the noblest death." And we may remember those striking words of St. Paul, "For a good man some would even dare to die ; but God commendeth his love toward us, in that, while we were yet sinners, Christ died for us." By reasoning of an analogous kind, we should say that if Jesus could have anticipated with confidence the effect which his death actually has exerted upon succeeding generations, it would render the heroism of it more intelligible, *i.e.*, more commonplace, and more within the compass of ordinary humanity. The hope of doing some great thing, of effecting some large benefit for mankind, is what has nerved numberless individuals to acts of heroic self-devotion ; but if the suspicion overtook Jesus, that he had failed of his purpose, that his premature death would be the frustration of all his work, obliterating all traces of it in the world, and leaving his disciples none the better for it ; and if yet he remained true to the call of duty, and hearkened simply to the voice of conscience, this does not diminish the lustre of his character—does not show him to be less, but rather to be more than his disciples took him for. Be this as it may, we may be sure that, by the time of his journey towards Jerusalem, Jesus felt that he had now taught all that he could teach by word of mouth, that he could do nothing more for his disciples in the way of mere verbal utterance, and that even what they had learned would be lost upon them, the impression of it effaced, unless he went further, and proceeded to fix it upon their minds, by showing that he was ready to die for it. And this final step he took as an act, at once of fidelity to the higher truth which he taught, and of supreme love for his disciples—two objects which for him were one and indivisible. And however dark the situation, however deep the gloom which had gathered round him, he may even have hoped, as Socrates is said to have done, that his disciples after his death would carry on the work he had begun.

Our steps here are necessarily halting and uncertain. For we do not wish to affect a confidence which we do not feel, and we trust that the reader will keep this in view. Various alternatives present themselves to our minds, none of which can be definitely dismissed, corresponding, it may be, to the feelings of doubt and suspense which, at this crisis, agitated the mind of Jesus, without, however, shaking his resolve to be true to his inward vocation. Were it not for that belief in his own Messiahship which we attribute to him, we should deem it doubtful whether Jesus ever anticipated the posthumous triumph of his doctrine and his cause. His original aim was probably a modest one, and his main concern may have been for his "neighbours" and his immediate followers, to instruct them in the way to the better life. But, on the other hand, that belief of his, founded, as we have seen, on the transcendent significance of his doctrine and on its powerful effect upon his disciples, may probably have enlarged his horizon and extended his view, even to those who were not of that fold nor of that generation. It is pretty plain, not only that the statutory requirements of the Jewish law had no place in the way of life which he pointed out, but also that he was fully aware of this fact; and that, therefore, he may have seen that his doctrine was the truth for all people, Gentiles as well as Jews. Indeed, he could not but be aware that the fundamental and commanding principle of his doctrine placed the individual in a personal relation to God, which was one and the same for every man, and made all extraneous, conventional, and sectional distinctions of no account. He that enters into the spirit of this doctrine will hold loosely to any of the sects or parties into which Christendom is divided; but he will attach himself to all in whom he recognizes the like spirit.

CHAPTER XI.

THE CHRISTOPHANIES.

WHATEVER the Master's state of mind or outlook, certainly the disciples were wholly unprepared for the catastrophe. They either could not or would not understand the warnings respecting his impending fate, which he had given them ever since the day at Cæsarea Philippi. They *would* know nothing, any more than would the Jewish rulers and rabble, of a suffering Messiah. For even if, as is now affirmed, the idea of a suffering Messiah was not wholly strange to Jewish thought, yet we can easily understand how the reality, when presented in the guise of poverty and mean estate, might be too much for faith to embrace. The disciples seem persistently to have put aside from them the possibility of any but a triumphant issue to the life and labours of their great leader. The Baptist, as we have seen, doubted the Messiahship of Jesus, because no mighty wonders, no great event of national importance, had accompanied his ministry ; but the disciples, on the other hand, confident of his Messiahship, persisted in the belief that some such event, some visible and striking manifestation of his divine mission, would yet come in due time. In fact, this expectation was an integral element, an unconscious stipulation of their faith in him, and no sign of coming disaster could shake their confidence. Almost at the very last they disputed among themselves which of them should be greatest in the kingdom of heaven, the establishment of which they looked upon as an imminent and all but accomplished fact. The mother of Zebedee's children in perfect simplicity, and with motherly naïveté, asked that her two sons should have the places of honour assigned to them on the right and left of their Master. It was with the confidence inspired by such expectations that the disciples accompanied him to Jerusalem.

The disappointment, therefore, caused to the disciples by the catastrophe, which involved, for the moment, the ruin of all their hopes, was all the more acute and overwhelming because of its sudden and total unexpectedness. It was what they had never looked for, never taken into calculation, and a feeling of stupor and amazement mingled with their feeling of grief and of blank despair. It came like a clap of thunder in a serene sky, and, for the time, their dejection was complete, leaving them, a few, defenceless in the midst of mocking and hostile multitudes, perfectly spiritless, and without a plan of any kind for future guidance. No dream was ever more completely dissipated, no waking to reality was ever more painful, no fabric of a fond imagination was ever, to all appearance, more suddenly and totally laid prostrate, past all hope of restoration.

If we place before us all the circumstances of the case, the painful situation into which the disciples were thrown by the unexpected, violent, and ignominious removal of one in whom, as in a being of higher nature, they had learned to place the most absolute reliance, and had found an object of unbounded veneration ; by intercourse with whom they had felt themselves brought into close proximity, as it were, with the unseen world, and elevated to a level of the spiritual life which was new to their experience :—it cannot but appear extraordinary in the highest degree that, without self-reliance, without the support of numbers, and without any quality or promise of greatness, they should yet have rallied from that profound fall, that shipwreck of cherished hopes, and have reunited after their dispersion, to form the nucleus of a society for which there was neither model nor programme ; which yet, gradually and steadily, in the midst of a hostile world, constituted itself, took shape and organiza- tion, and changed the face of human affairs. But so it was. For, there is nothing more certain in the history of man than that the state of panic and prostration into which they were thrown was of short duration ; that the small, and apparently forlorn band, which had lost its head and centre, speedily regained its courage, and, in the absence of all the ordinary motives of human exertion, began, with imposing energy and confidence, and with a freshness of enthusiasm which astonished the multitude and made head against all opposition, to proclaim its belief in the Messiahship of the crucified one, to disseminate its new-born faith, and to add rapidly to the number of its adherents.

The great question has here to be considered, how this change of attitude, this revolution of feeling, was brought about; what forces were in operation to accomplish it? Could we trust implicitly to the evangelical narratives of this remarkable and unique phenomenon, we should have to believe that the period of depression and despondency on the part of the solitary band of disciples lasted for little more than a single day, and that they were roused from their state of panic and consternation by the reappearance in the midst of them of their crucified Master; that their feelings of dismay and despair gave place to a feeling of more than their former confidence and hopefulness, in consequence of the bodily manifestation to their senses of their risen Lord. Such an experience, had it actually befallen them, would, we readily admit, be enough to account for all the effects ascribed to it: for their emancipation from their feelings of shame, disappointment, grief, and despondency; for the energy with which they defied the hostility of their countrymen, and addressed themselves to the herculean task of converting the world, and leavening it with the faiths and principles with which Jesus had imbued them; and finally, it would account for the universal prevalence in the early Church of faith in the fact of the bodily resurrection of Jesus, and for the rapid propagation of the Christian religion. We do not question that such a cause was adequate to the production of all these great effects. To the early Church, indeed, it seemed to be such an adequate explanation, that it was unhesitatingly accepted as a fact, which was confirmed by every fresh triumph of the gospel. Yet, while making this admission, we can hardly resist the feeling that the idea of the bodily resurrection of Jesus is more like a suggestion of human phantasy to account for that great revolution in the spiritual life than like a divine expedient to produce it. And to this, the usual (orthodox) explanation of the undeniable facts, which have a place and a significance in universal history, there are various objections of a more tangible kind, severally and cumulatively decisive. Into these objections we do not enter fully, but only so far as seems necessary for our general purpose.

First, then, the undeniable circumstance that this manifestation, whatever it was, was made not to all the people, but to a
select few (Acts x. 40, 41); confined to brethren (1 Cor. xv. 6)
and Galilæans (Acts ii. 7), *i.e.*, to those who already believed, or
were disposed to believe, seems to show, at the outset, notwithstanding all that has been said to the contrary, that the phenomenon was not objective but subjective, a creation of faith, of
imaginative expectancy, or of sympathetic longing.   Just as we
have already accounted for the works of healing and exorcism
ascribed to Jesus, not by the supposition of a power or virtue
proceeding from him, but by that of a hidden rapport between
the spiritual and bodily state of the subjects called into activity
by awe and veneration for the person of Jesus, so we shall
account for these apparent manifestations (Christophanies, as
they have been called) by the after-effect or revival, after the
rude shock which it had received from the catastrophe of the
crucifixion, of that profound impression made by the personality
and teaching of Jesus on the minds of his followers.

Secondly, the three narratives (for we leave the fourth out of
account) of these manifestations are so utterly inconsistent and
discrepant as to details, as not merely, as orthodox theologians
would have us believe, to serve an apologetic purpose by doing
away with the suspicion of collusion on the part of the Evangelists, but also, over and above that, to seriously shake our
belief of there having been any palpable and external fact to
account for their origin.   That, whatever conclusion may be
arrived at as to the general fact of the resurrection, the detailed
account of the relative circumstances is very unreliable, may be
inferred from a single observation which can scarcely be disputed, viz., that Galilee, and not Jerusalem and its neighbourhood, was the scene of the experiences which gave rise to the
tradition, so that we may unhesitatingly put aside whatever is
reported in this reference to have occurred in the neighbourhood
of Jerusalem.*   There are various indications in the Gospels,

---

* The chief proof of what is here stated is drawn from St. Mark's Gospel.
This Gospel is now generally admitted to be the earliest, as it is the briefest
of the series; and there is strong evidence, both external and internal, that
in its original form it ended with the 8th verse of the 16th chapter. The
twelve following verses were unknown to the earliest of the Greek fathers,
and are wanting in the best manuscripts. Obviously, too, they are not the
natural sequel to what goes before. The Christophanies in Jerusalem or its

survivals of the earliest tradition, lingering memories of the actual facts, which, disregarded or overlaid by subsequent accretions, point to this general conclusion ; and reasons can easily be imagined, which may have weighed with the mythical fancy, to make the capital and the vicinity of the sepulchre, instead of outlying Galilee, the scene of the occurrences. Another fact, less frequently adverted to, which points in the same direction, is the omission or suppression in the synoptists of all direct reference in narrative form to St. Peter's vision of the risen Christ, which St. Paul (1 Cor. xv.) has placed in the foreground as having the precedence among the Christophanies. This observation has made a deep impression, as well it might, upon the calmly judicial mind of Weizsäcker, the distinguished critic, who, with a complete knowledge of all that has been urged upon the apologetic side, has recently reviewed the evidence for the resurrection. He regards the omission as a proof that the legendary element has quite got the better of the historical element in the Gospel narratives, and explains it by the conjecture that the actual experience of St. Peter, on which so much depended, was not of such a nature as to satisfy the craving of the Church for a palpable, *i.e.*, objective manifestation.

To harmonize the several narratives, and to reduce all the details into one consecutive and consistent whole, is indeed impossible. It is a task which can be achieved to the satisfaction even of the most credulous and illogical only by an expenditure of ingenuity which is sufficient, when duly considered, to create suspicion, and by such unstinted use of hypothesis and conjecture, as is never resorted to except for the establishment of a foregone conclusion. It may be said, indeed, that this is a remark which applies to our own discussion of the subject. But there is this great difference, that our resort to conjecture

neighbourhood which they narrate render nugatory the injunction given to the disciples in verse 7, to go to Galilee to see the risen Jesus. The natural sequel, which is, therefore, left to be inferred, would be, that the disciples obeyed the injunction and hastened to Galilee to see Jesus. Instead of which they are represented as lingering in Jerusalem, and seeing Jesus without proceeding to Galilee. The Christophanies with which they are thus favoured are manifestly a synopsis of those which are narrated by the other three Gospels ; adopted, that is to say, into the tradition at a time subsequent to the composition of St. Mark's Gospel, to which it was appended by another hand.

is justified, or rather rendered imperative, by the critical necessity of getting rid of the supernatural element, whereas conjecture is resorted to by apologists to vindicate the presence in
gospel history of that element against which the scientific conscience has risen, and is still rising more and more in rebellion.

If it be true, as has been asserted, that there is no other
event of ancient history so well authenticated as the fact of
the resurrection, or, that " there is a greater weight of historical
evidence for that event than there is for almost any other
received historical fact," it may also be asserted that there are
not many other events of which the earliest or contemporaneous records are so conflicting. Theologians have indeed
sought to invalidate the significance of this observation by
saying that Christian faith only requires that the *general* fact
of the bodily resurrection of Jesus should be recognized, but
that whether this or that detail in the records of it should be
received is a matter not of faith but merely of opinion or
criticism. This is a very convenient refuge no doubt for the
apologist, whom it frees from much embarrassment, and from
a large " surplusage " of difficulty, but the conflict between the
narratives is such that the suspicion can hardly be resisted,
that even the general fact, in which all three agree with each
other (viz., that Jesus manifested himself to the disciples in
bodily shape), never took place. There is every probability
that, had there been an actual apparition, the relative circumstances would have been faithfully treasured up in the tradition,
and handed down with unvarying, or, at least, substantial consistency, though, it may be, with minor variations. Whereas,
on the contrary, the several narratives exhibit that discrepancy
of detail which is the unfailing characteristic of all mythical
cycles ; a discrepancy, moreover, which, though by no means
unknown in actual history, is little likely to occur, when, as in
this case, there were no conflicting interests, and all the narra-
tors were interested in the substantiation of the central fact,
provided there was clear evidence of its occurrence. Had
there been a fixed and well ascertained, or ascertainable
nucleus of palpable fact, the details would, in all likelihood,
have grouped themselves round it with some degree of consistency. But, in the absence of such a nucleus, the phantasy
was left to revel without control, and to exercise its liberty
without concerted plan, or any attempt to harmonize its

creations with others of the same cycle. Such an attempt, indeed, would have interfered too much with the mythopœic license, and have postulated in these creations an element of consciousness and concert which is foreign to their nature.

We hold that the many discrepancies which exist between the synoptic narratives of the resurrection form a very important though secondary objection to their historical value except in a very qualified sense. Nothing can well be more absurd than to say with a distinguished apologist, that these discrepancies just suffice to show that we are dealing with history and not with fiction. Discrepancy is an almost invariable feature of legendary cycles, and can hardly, in any case, afford presumption of the historical character of a narrative. The mere appearance of inconsistency, when it is cleared away, may create a prejudice in favour of a narrative; but if, when all is done, the inconsistency remains and is seen to be irreducible, no such effect is, or can be, produced.

The apologetic position is hardly tenable, that these discrepancies cannot be real, seeing they cannot have appeared in that light to the early Church, which, from its proximity to the events, must be supposed to have been better qualified to judge of them and of their evidence than we of so late an age can be. The denial of this position in an unqualified form, or as an absolute canon, is the very nerve and postulate of all modern historical criticism. The critical spirit was very little developed in antiquity. The easy credence which antiquity in general gave to what was abnormal or supernatural is a proof and evidence of this observation, and the strong dogmatic bias or interest within the Church rendered its members more uncritical, if possible, than those who were outside. Once satisfied, in the way we have yet to indicate, of the general fact, that Jesus had reappeared in bodily shape to his disciples, the early Church viewed all discrepancies of detail with ready indifference, and regarded all questioning of them (just as the rigidly orthodox do at the present day) as mere trifling, as proof either of a suspiciously captious and sceptical tendency, or of a spirit of reprehensible lukewarmness. We may even go further and say that, in the swing and ardour of that living movement, of that grand uprising of the spiritual life, any such investigation would have been, not unjustly, stigmatized as ill-timed. Above all things it was necessary that the spiritual truth should establish itself as a power in life under any forms which lay ready to hand, or which the age could best appreciate. But the critical spirit of the present time, which is prompted by the yearning for truth and reality, and for the sight of things as they are, demands that the foundations of our faith should be narrowly looked into, and it is certain that our faith can no longer be preserved, merely by shutting our eyes to the difficulties which beset it, or by a blind reliance on authority, and an undiscriminating acquiescence in traditional beliefs. For our part, too, we imagine that the truths which Jesus promulgated—the fundamental truths of Christianity—may now dispense with all such adventitious aids to faith, and not only must, but can recommend themselves to our minds by their intrinsic authority.

Thirdly, an essential peculiarity of these narratives is, that they require us to suppose that the apparition of the risen Jesus was that of a body without the properties of a body, of a body which, at will, could lay aside some and retain others of these properties; which was either penetrable or impenetrable, coming near, perhaps, to the idea of what St. Paul calls a "spiritual body," whatever that may mean. Sober criticism must regard such a body, in spite of the ingenious fancies of certain orthodox physicists, as a monstrosity, a self-contradictory conception. But the mythicizing phantasy proceeds in its creations without regard to those conditions which limit the possibility of things. Its activity is conditioned by ignorance or obliviousness of the order which universally prevails, and it deals by preference with objects and events which are exempt from the ordinary limitations of reality. Not being restrained or controlled by the idea of law, and moving in a sphere where natural law, physical and spiritual, has no consideration, it hesitates not to unite what is incongruous, and to reconcile the irreconcilable. In such a sphere anything whatever may happen, and nothing is incredible for him who believes in the existence of such a sphere. The power which is supposed to be above law may be invoked to explain away every inconsistency, and to account for every extravagance.

Fourthly, the attempt has recently been made to create a presumption in favour of this great miraculous fact of the resurrection, by asserting that apart from it there is "no evidence of the material laws and the physical forces of nature being controlled by the Supreme Power, so as to subserve spiritual purposes, and that it is the one event which puts us in possession of God and immortality." But this assertion does not commend itself to our judgment, for if there be no other proof of the supremacy in the divine scheme of the spiritual power, and of the subserviency to it of the material forces, we must conclude that no such providential arrangement exists. That idea is too important to be rested on a single fact in the world's history, a fact, too, which is without analogy and without precedent. Rather than believe that such a solitary fact has ever occurred, or that other facts of analogous description, if they do occur, are yet hidden from observation—involved in impenetrable obscurity, until revealed by the light of this one, or brought by means of it within the field of human vision—we shall more readily believe that there is some flaw in the evidence of the alleged fact itself.

But, leaving such negative considerations, we pass now to one which to many minds will seem to be more decisive of the question before us, viz., that the *faith* of the early Church in the reappearance of Jesus after his death may have sprung up and established itself in the creed, without the actual occurrence of the alleged fact, and that we can account for this faith otherwise than by supposing it to be in exact correspondence with the event which actually did occur to raise the disciples out of their despondent state. Some such explanation is necessary. For strong as may be our abstract, exegetical, and critical objections to the bodily reappearance of Jesus, we must yet admit that were there no other mode of accounting, first, for the sudden emergence of the disciples from their state of consternation and despondency; and, secondly, for the universal, immediate, and we may almost say, instantaneous belief of the Church in his resurrection, we should have to accept of it as a fact, however strange and unprecedented ; unless, indeed, we preferred indefinitely to suspend our judgment. The sense of the alternative thus presented to us, either of accepting the idea of a supernatural occurrence, or of providing some other conjectural explanation of the phenomenon, has had the effect of suggesting or calling forth various attempts at some natural explanation.

The first of these suggestions is, that the body of Jesus was snatched from the sepulchre ; whether by friends or foes, and for what purpose, is left uncertain ; and that advantage was taken of this circumstance by the disciples to spread the report that he had burst the bands of death, and manifested himself to them.   For this conjecture there is not a shred of probability ; for, even admitting the fact of the disappearance of the body from the tomb, it is yet a long way from this to the origination and currency of the report.   As the report passed into circulation almost immediately after the death of Jesus, it is not easy to see how, on the supposition now referred to, this could have happened without the connivance, more or less active, of the leading disciples.   The mere fact that the body of Jesus had, in some way unexplained, disappeared, could not possibly, in their despondent state of mind, suggest to them that he had returned to life again, and still less could it warrant them to give countenance to the report that he had shown himself alive to them.   Such a tissue of falsehood and imposture on the part of men who bore a principal share in the great moral and spiritual movement which followed, is so inconceivable, and so abhorrent to the mind, that all ingenuous men must dismiss it from their thoughts, and exclude it from the region of possibilities.

A second conjecture, which is that of rationalism, involves Jesus himself, along with his disciples, in the charge of imposture.   According to it, Jesus did not actually expire on the cross, but awoke in the tomb from that state of unconsciousness, and of suspended animation, which was produced by the lengthened torture of his sufferings.   He rose again, not from the dead, as was supposed, but only from the grave, and reappeared among his disciples.   But this conjecture, though it has had a " sort of fascination for many eminent theologians " and men of science, is not merely devoid of any support from the Gospel narratives, but, besides that it leaves much unexplained, is ludicrously inadequate to account for the great rebound in the minds of the disciples.   If, as no one doubts, the circumstances of the crucifixion are in the main historical, Jesus must have been in a fearfully exhausted and bloodless condition before his removal from the cross ; and how could his reappearance in that dead-alive state ever have restored the disciples' faith in him as the triumphant Messiah, or have presented him to their imagination as the conqueror of death.

How could the real state of the case have been concealed from the world at large, as it must have been, except by means of a conspiracy, and collusion between Jesus himself and his disciples—a supposition of which it is unnecessary to express an opinion ; it being morally impossible that one who was the author of the Sermon on the Mount, and who braved the most deadly danger in carrying out its principles into practice, could ever have lent himself to such a fraud. Evidently, too, whatever may have been the sequel—whether Jesus permanently recovered, or quickly succumbed under the effects of his sufferings on the cross—there must have been a deliberate and concerted suppression of the truth in the report which the disciples made to the world of what they had seen and heard. It is enough to say that men who could be guilty of such a fraud could not possibly have furnished the "foundation" on which Christianity was built.

For the reasons assigned, we reject both of these explanations. But as the Gospel narratives agree with the universal faith of the early Church in testifying that Jesus reappeared to his disciples after his crucifixion, it is impossible to get rid of the idea that some great fact underlay this belief, while, at the same time, the discrepancy of detail in the narratives goes far to render it probable that this fact was of a nature, more or less impalpable, so as to admit of various recital and various construction. And just such a fact is that which is dealt with by the so-called "Vision-Theory"—the explanation which is now generally accepted in critical circles, though it does not satisfy us. According to this theory there was nothing real, substantial, or objective in the apparitions, or Christophanies, recorded in the Gospels, but all was phantasmal, visionary, spectral, and subjective. The figure which presented itself to the senses of the disciples was a form or image imprinted on the retina, not by any external object, but by a reflex action of the brain or mind of the disciples—an image which, being impressed on that membrane from within, projected itself into outer space according to the laws of ordinary vision. Physiological observations have shown conclusively that such phenomena are of not infrequent occurrence, so that *a priori* there is nothing incredible in the supposition that something of this nature was what befel the disciples ; that, in the profound grief into which the disciples were plunged, in their anxious and half-despairing expectation of the return of their Master from the world of spirits—suggested to them, it may be, by words which he had dropped in their hearing, more or less disregarded at the time, but now recalled to memory as a sort of forlorn hope—this reflex power of the mind may, in Peter, in Mary Magdalene, or some other disciple, have come into play, and called up a vision to the eye ; and that, by the contagion of sympathy, the vision may have spread, as is usual in analogous cases, from one disciple to others who were in the same predisposed state. This is the " Vision-Theory."

Still, for various reasons, we do not accept this theory, to replace that of an actual apparition. This theory presupposes, in one or all of the primitive disciples, not indeed an ecstatic state of mind, or a proneness to hysteria, or some form of hallucination, of which there is no apparent sign so far as can be judged from the records ; but, at the very least, a state of expectancy, for which we have no evidence whatever, of some such event as the resurrection and reappearance of Jesus. If we may trust to what is narrated of the women who, more faithful than their male companions, remained in the vicinity of Jesus, when these forsook him and fled (to Galilee), there is even evidence to the contrary ; for they, we are told, prepared spices and unguents to embalm the body, and thus afforded a clear proof that they, and by consequence the others, had no expectation of an immediate resurrection. This fact alone, if it be allowed to stand, throws very considerable suspicion on the historical value of those passages in the Gospels which represent Jesus as declaring that he would rise again in three days. Indeed, it is hardly conceivable that he should have done so. He may have perceived that everything in the natural course portended a fatal termination to the work in which he was engaged ; he may even, in the conviction of his Messiahship, have entertained some hope that God would, as already said, interpose at the last moment, if not before, in his behalf (Matth. xxvii. 46); or failing such interposition, he might yet be confident that he would come again to finish his Messianic work on earth. All this we may believe, because we cannot tell how far his Messianic consciousness might carry him. But that he should have predicted his resurrection on the third day would have betrayed in him a lack of sobriety, a degree of fanatical enthusiasm which would lower him in our esteem, and of which we see no indication in his character as depicted in the Gospels.

What there is of probability in supposing that the disciples may have expected his resurrection on the third day, is mainly founded on what he is reported by St. Matthew and St. Luke to have said of the sign of the prophet Jonah. But few things can be more certain in this regard than that what Jesus said of this sign was neither intended nor calculated to give countenance to such an expectation.

It seems that the Pharisees demanded of him a sign from heaven in confirmation of his doctrine, and, in the Gospel of St. Mark, Jesus is reported as making the curt and peremptory reply, " There shall no sign be given unto this generation." These words admit of being understood as a concession that none of the works which accompanied his teaching were miracles in the strict sense of the term. More probably, however, they only meant that no sign from heaven such as the Pharisees demanded should be given to them. But the tradition, as represented by St. Luke and St. Matthew, was not satisfied to rest here. The early Church may have felt that a sign of some sort was necessary to confirm the claims of Jesus to be a teacher sent from God. Hence St. Luke, as its spokesman, represents Jesus as saying that the sign which he would give would be like that of the prophet Jonas, which consisted in the preaching of the prophet—a very different sort of sign from that which the Pharisees sought, and therefore quite in keeping with the spirit of his declaration in St. Mark, that no sign would be given.

By its appeal to the consciences of the Ninevites, the call of the prophet carried in it its own authority, and was a sign to them ; and such also was the sign which Jesus would give to his countrymen. This is the plain and obvious meaning in St. Luke's report of the language. But in St. Matthew's Gospel the revising, commentating hand has been at work, and the sign in the case of the prophet, which is the point of comparison between him and Jesus, is made to consist in his temporary imprisonment in the whale's belly, a circumstance which the Ninevites are never said to have had any knowledge of, and which could therefore have been no sign to them. And the report of St. Matthew contradicts that of St. Mark, both in letter and in spirit. For if Jesus here said that he would give the Jews a sign by rising again from the dead on the third day, this was just to give them the promise of such a sign as they did ask for, and in so far a distinct contradiction of what, according to St. Mark, he did say.

This revision of the words of Jesus is in many ways significant, and may easily be accounted for. We may suppose that, on separate and independent grounds (yet to be explained), it had become the fixed faith of the Church that Jesus had risen again from the dead on the third day. But when it was observed that the duration of his entombment, though not entirely agreeing with that of Jonah's imprisonment, yet nearly coincided with it, the early Church could not refuse the suggestion or reject the temptation to believe that the one was the type of the other. The reference to Jonah therefore was so altered as to make it appear that the sign of which Jesus spoke consisted in the miraculous portion of Jonah's history. In this way the deep and fine significance of his words, the true point of comparison, was put out of sight; a limping and irrelevant comparison was instituted in its place, and a proof apparently given of the prescience of Jesus. This instance is one among many which show how freely and arbitrarily the mythical phantasy dealt with facts and sayings which tradition had preserved; how prone the Church was to give a prophetic and supernatural colour to the simplest words of Jesus, and to adapt the obscure and poetical language of the Old Testament to the beliefs which had taken root in the minds of its members. We can, with much show of probability, even assign the independent ground on which the faith that the resurrection took place on the third day was founded.

Nowhere in the New Testament is it said that Jesus was observed by the disciples in the very article or act of rising again, and that the event took place on the third day, rather than on the day preceding, may have become the generally received belief of the Church, only after some hesitation and diversity of opinion. (Compare Matth. xxviii. 1, with Luke xxiii. 54, with Keim's remarks on the subject.) It is easy to conceive how this happened. The experiences of the disciples, which were interpreted by them as the manifestations of the risen Jesus, befel them, let us suppose, on the third day. In that case it was natural for them to think that on that same day he had also risen again, and this probability would be confirmed for them when it was discovered, as it would soon be, that there was prophetic language to countenance the supposition. In Hosea vi. 2 occur these words, "After two days will he revive us: in the third day he will raise us up, and we shall live in his sight."

That these words contain a prophetic allusion to the resurrection of the Messiah is far from apparent. But in the absence of any definite information or testimony respecting the exact time of its occurrence, these words of the prophet, which, whatever they allude to, were really meant to indicate a short period of indefinite duration, were understood of a definite period, and so understood, were quite sufficient to determine or confirm the belief of the disciples in regard to the date of the resurrection of Jesus. For it is observable that we have data for thinking that the third day was partly fixed upon in deference to some prophetic authority. Thus, in Luke xxiv. 46, the risen Christ is represented as opening the understanding of the disciples, that they might understand the Scriptures, and saying to them, "Thus it is written, and thus it behoved Christ to suffer, and to rise from the dead the third day"; and in 1 Cor. xv. 4, Paul says that Christ rose again from the dead on the third day, "according to the scriptures." The fact of the resurrection was to Paul's mind sufficiently proved by the various manifestations of Jesus to the disciples, himself included. But he can only appeal to the Scriptures of the Old Testament as an evidence of the day of its occurrence. The words of Hosea, which the Apostle probably had in view, were enough to satisfy him on this point, and it may be that the same words may have contributed to settle the doubts of the Church at large. But there is no proof that these words, any more than the words of Jesus respecting the sign of the prophet Jonah, had raised an expectation of the resurrection *before* those experiences of the disciples which seemed to prove that it had taken place. The application of the words to the event was an afterthought. No sooner was it believed that Jesus had risen again than the question pressed for an answer, "When did it take place? On what day, or at what hour?" And the passage in Hosea, most probably, was eagerly caught at, as seeming to give to a question, which there was no proper means of settling, an answer which, by reason of the Christophanies on the third day, the disciples were disposed to accept.

We repeat, therefore, that there is no reason for thinking that the disciples were in that expectant state of mind which, according to psychologists, is the condition generally present of phenomena such as those on which the vision-theory of the resurrection of Jesus is made to hinge.

As already observed, it is a notable circumstance or feature of the evangelic narratives that the disciples are not represented as having been present to witness the resurrection at the moment of its taking place. Had these narratives been mere inventions, the likelihood is that this would have been the thing represented, as affording the most simple and direct evidence of the fact. But the mythical phantasy was at this point controlled, by having to deal with an actual experience, yet to be described, of the disciples ; and it never departed from this fact so far as to represent the resurrection itself as an object of vision.

In the above remarks we have proceeded on the supposition that the Evangelists are historically correct in representing that experience of the disciples, whatever it was, as having befallen them on the third day after the crucifixion. But it may here be observed that this supposition is involved in some doubt. If the experience of the disciples, which they construed as a bodily appearance to them of the risen Messiah, befel them in the vicinity of Jerusalem, there is nothing to be said against its occurrence on the third day. But there are several indications, as many have felt, that these experiences took place not in that neighbourhood at all, but in Galilee,* probably near the sea of that name, amid scenes still warm with the thought of their Master, and from which the light of his presence had not yet faded. Mark xvi. 7, xiv. 28, Matth. xxvi. 32, have not without reason been regarded as surviving traces of an early tradition to the effect that the scene of the so-called Christophanies was Galilee, which was distant by a straight line of fifty or sixty miles from Jerusalem, and much further by the route which avoided Samaria. Now if, as seems to have been the case (Mark xiv. 50, Matth. xxvi. 56), the disciples fled to Galilee as soon as Jesus was apprehended by the Jewish authorities, and left him to his fate, the report of his cruci-

* See in connection with this point the very striking use which Chancellor Weizsäcker makes, in the very first paragraph of his great work, of the well-known passage in Tacitus.

fixion would take two or three days to follow upon their heels, and, allowing two or three days more for the paroxysm of their grief to expend itself, it may have been nearly a week after the crucifixion till the great recovery took place. And, if this be so, the inference is, not that the third day was conjectured to be the day of the resurrection, in order to synchronize it with the Christophanies ; but, on the contrary, that the conjecture was guided simply by the words of the Old Testament already referred to ; so that the Christophanies were made to synchronize with the prophetic language, and that, as a necessary consequence, the scene of these was transferred to the neighbourhood of Jerusalem. The true order and sequence of the events may have been too natural, too commonplace, and perhaps too humiliating to be retained in the tradition. And, in fact, the fabling fancy could make nothing of the merely spiritual crisis through which, as we shall yet show, the disciples passed, and therefore not only transformed it into a Christophany, but laid the scene or the scenes of it in the vicinity of the tomb, so as to place the resurrection itself *en évidence* immediately after its conjectured occurrence, to fill up the interval between the third day of prophecy and the mysterious occurrences in Galilee, and also to gratify Jewish-Christian feeling by representing Jerusalem rather than Galilee as the point from which Christianity started on its world-wide career.

To return to the vision-theory. Another objection to it may be drawn from the infrequent occurrence and sudden cessation of the phenomenon. Had Jesus actually manifested himself to the senses of the disciples, we could understand that he would do so only as often or as seldom as he chose ; and we could be no judges of his reason for presenting himself before them just so many times and no more. But if the apparition, as the vision-theory will have it, depended on the agitated state and conflicting emotions of the small band of disciples, we are entitled on physiological grounds, and by historical analogies, to expect that the phenomenon would continue to repeat itself until the agitation had gradually subsided, and a considerable time had elapsed.

But from the Gospels, as well as from St. Paul's enumeration of the phenomena, which latter must be accepted as the most authentic record which we have, it is apparent that such was not the case. St. Paul's enumeration, which has few points of contact with the synoptic narratives, is put forward as exhaustive; and from it we gather that the apparition was repeated only six times, his own being included in the number. His own experience was also the last in point of time, and was separated from the other five, it would seem, by a considerable interval. And if we take into account that it occurred not much more than two or three years after the crucifixion, there is a strong likelihood that the Evangelists have preserved the true state of the case, in so far as they represent all the rest as having occurred either on one and the same day, or within a day or two of each other. No doubt St. Luke, in the beginning of the Acts of the Apostles, says that Jesus continued to show himself to the disciples at intervals for forty days after his resurrection. But, account for it as we may, this additional record is hardly reconcilable with that of his Gospel: that is to say, if we are to be guided in our judgment by the ordinary laws of criticism. But even if we succeed in harmonizing this record with that of the synoptists, it is plain that the alleged Christophanies were few in number and abruptly terminated—a distribution of the phenomena which is far from probable, if it be not incredible, and suggestive of the idea, that they were not what they are by the vision-theory represented as being. Not to anticipate what has in the sequel to be said of the vision, which, as we believe, was actually seen by St. Paul, and of the contribution which his testimony makes to the critical inquiry, we may remark here that it is easy to account for the fact that his vision was not followed up by others of the same kind. Evidently he stood alone, cut off for the time from sympathy and intercourse with any community of believers. The conditions of propagation were thus in his case awanting; but the singular thing is, that phantasmal phenomena of the kind, if they occurred to the earlier disciples, should have ceased so abruptly in a community in which sympathy was rife, and mental agitation, as a producing cause, was kept up by the heat of numbers, and by the interactive friction of mind with mind.

Yet another objection to the vision-theory may be found in the observation that the occurrences represented as visions by that theory befel the twelve disciples and the five hundred brethren simultaneously. Notwithstanding the analogies to this detail which have been culled from Huguenot and Camisard histories and other sources, we hold it to be an insuperable objection to this theory. The simultaneity of impression made upon many minds favours the idea of an objective manifestation rather than that of the subjective vision-theory. But we hope to show further on, when we come to discuss the experience and the testimony of St. Paul, that it harmonizes with a view of the occurrences quite different from either of these; in other words, with the subjective, yet not visional character of these occurrences.

Finally, it has often been objected to the vision-theory, that, if the fact were such as it supposes: if the disciples had their faith in Jesus restored by an apparition which had no existence except for the inward eye; by a vision which, originating in the mind, had projected itself into outward space, through the reflex or reverse action of the mind upon the retina, the Christian faith would be ultimately traceable to what, after all, was neither more nor less than an ocular illusion. Now, we do not admit the entire justice of such a criticism, or the force of the objection to Christianity which is founded on it, for to us it seems that, if an illusion of the kind actually took place, the credit of our religion might still be rescued in this apparently compromising connection.

It could be supposed that the vision was not the cause, but the effect of a faith, already inchoate, in Jesus, his character and doctrine; merely the form in which the springing faith took possession of the minds of the disciples: that a mental crisis had supervened of such an extraordinary nature, that by the *rapport* existing between body and mind, it was accompanied by a physical phenomenon scarcely less extraordinary, and which, as was natural, so engrossed the attention of the subjects of it as to indispose or incapacitate them for attending to what was passing within them. The possibility of this *rapport* was unknown and unsurmized by St. Peter and his companions; and the relation between the physical and mental would necessarily seem to them to be the reverse of what we suppose. They were as men but half awake, or in a dream, who do not mark or understand the sequence of events, and are apt to transpose cause and effect. The fact is well known to physiologists, that our dreams often seem to lead up to, and to terminate in what is rather their exciting cause;

that, however protracted in appearance to our consciousness, they are often but of momentary duration, the beginning and end of them being coincident. Proofs and illustrations of this curious fact may be dispensed with here, as many such may be found in works treating of psychology. And if we bear this fact in mind, there will appear to be nothing impossible in the idea that the vision, to which the disciples ascribed the recovery of their faith and courage, may have been evoked in the very turmoil and struggle of their minds towards the new faith which was dawning upon them ; and that, in short, the vision was born of that to which it seemed to give birth.

But, when we have got this length, it still remains for us to account for the new faith itself which arose in the minds of the disciples, independent of, though accompanied by, or creative of the vision, and if we succeed in explaining the origin of that faith, then the vision, if it did ensue, will lose its primary place in the genesis of our religion, and sink to quite a secondary and subordinate, if we may not say, an unessential place, because it had no intrinsic or genetic connection with the faith. And following up the train of thought thus suggested, we may at length arrive at the conclusion that nothing of the kind may have occurred ; that there was no vision whatever, actual or apparent, in the case ; so that nothing remains to be gathered from the narratives beyond the fact that there was a moment in the experience of the disciples at which the conviction flashed upon their minds that Jesus was yet alive and present with them in spirit, and that the idea of the vision was subsequently called in as a literary, popular, or sensuous representation of a grand and, to the disciples themselves, mysterious crisis in their inner life. The points of difference between their experience and that of St. Paul on a similar occasion will have to be afterwards considered.*

---

* By way of accounting for the faith of the early Church in the resurrection of Jesus, it has by some been deemed sufficient to say, that that was a very credulous, legend-loving age, fond of the marvellous, such as the resurrection and reappearance of men from the dead ; and that it had no gift or talent for the sifting or weighing of evidence. Proofs of this feature of the age are to be found even in the Gospels, where it is said that when Jesus began to excite astonishment by his teaching and manner of life, his countrymen were

Meanwhile, with such a solution of the phenomena in our view, we go back to the state in which the disciples were plunged by the unexpected catastrophe of the death of their Master ; and we put to ourselves the question, whether it was not possible that they might, on rational grounds and in obedience to the higher instincts which had been awakened in them, resume their faith in their Master and regain their courage after that shattering blow had fallen, which, besides breaking for the time the spell which he had cast upon them, and thrusting them from that elevation of the religious life to which they had risen in intercourse with him, had overwhelmed them with consternation, and left them nerveless, dispirited, friendless, and forlorn in a hostile world. That they all forsook him and fled (Matth. xxvi. 56) describes the immediate effect of that blow : they were thrown by it into a state of confusion and panic, and deprived of the power of reflection and of receiving a proper impression either of the events which were passing under their observation or of the mental changes of which they were the subjects.

But after the first paroxysm of grief and fear was passed, reflection would come back, and would turn to nothing so naturally as to the behaviour of their beloved Master under those trying and appalling circumstances which had deprived them of all presence of mind and of all self-command. They would perceive that the fatal turn of events which had seemed to invalidate his claim to be the Messiah was really calculated, by his behaviour under it, to confirm that claim more than aught else which they had seen or known of him before ; that it had applied the severest test to his character, and that he

disposed to regard him as one of the old prophets, or even as John the Baptist come to life again, after being put to death by Herod ; that Herod himself was perplexed by the rumour, and that even among Christians a legend gained ground that when Jesus rose again the graves were opened and the bodies of the saints rose up and were seen by many in Jerusalem (Matth. xxvii. 52). But it seems to us that the prevalence of a weak and unreasoning credulity, while it might explain the propagation and persistence of a report concerning the resurrection, after it was once set in circulation, yet goes but a little way in reducing the difficulty of accounting for the origin of the belief under circumstances so unfavourable, and for the energy with which, from the very first, it animated the minds of the disciples. And it is this undoubted and most remarkable fact for which we try to account in the text.

had stood the test without flinching ; so that they had greater reason than ever to trust his word and to venerate his person. They would see that he had been faithful unto death to the principles he had inculcated, and that in his mouth these were not mere flowers of rhetoric, or words of course, or of temporary excitement, but words of truth and soberness, for which he was prepared to live or die. His nobility of character, his patience under injury, his splendour of devotion and fortitude would shine forth with new lustre, and make them feel that it was simply impossible to conceive of him as a blasphemer, an impostor, or self-deceiver—between which conception and faith in his Messiahship there was for them no intermediate position. They would remember that the fate which had overtaken him, though it had been too much for their courage, had not deprived him of self-possession or brought to light any flaw or weakness in his character, but had been met by him with calm intrepidity and unshaken constancy.

A living theologian of much insight has said that Christ transfigured the cross, and, by dying upon it, changed it to human imagination from being an ignominious and loathed instrument of death to be the symbol of life ; and he regards the suddenness and completeness of this change as one of the strangest and most certain of historical facts. Now that the cross has been glorified by the death upon it of its grandest victim is no doubt true ; but when we view the crucifixion in connection with the genesis of Christianity, we may regard it as a truth of still greater significance that the cross glorified the Christ. The spiritual sense of the disciples had been so far trained and educated by their intercourse and association with Jesus as to discern the hidden "glory" of the cross—*i.e.*, of the death of Jesus upon it. No act of his life " became him " or exalted him so much in their eyes, or so revealed his true greatness, as his death. It was not the Christ who, in the first instance, transfigured the cross, but the cross which transfigured the Christ. And this difference in the mode of viewing the matter is not without significance—the one view fitting in with the supernatural, the other with the natural construction of Christianity. At all events, the mode and spirit in which Jesus laid down his life was what above all else transfigured him in the eyes of his disciples and confirmed his claim to be the Messiah or the Christ.

To these considerations we have yet to add this, that the catastrophe, though it had come upon them unawares and taken them by surprise, had not been uncontemplated by him, but had found him ready and prepared, and that there had been much in his teaching that might have prepared them also for the issue. He had taught them that the enmity of the world might be incurred by the friends of God ; that the suffering of persecution for righteousness' sake might be the avenue to bliss ; that heaven might be entered through much tribulation ; that the loss of life might be the means of saving it ; and it was natural to suppose that what was applicable to them was no less applicable to him. Elements of thought were in this way supplied, from which faith might spring anew, and confidence in him and his doctrine be restored, in spite of that disastrous eclipse which he had undergone ; nay, possibly, all the more in consequence of it. They might perceive that, in all that had befallen, there was no reason for the renunciation of their faith in him. Current opinion among their countrymen went strongly, it is true, against the idea of a suffering Messiah. For though this idea, as distinct from that of the suffering servant of God, had been mooted in the synagogue, and had received countenance from at least one passage in the book of Daniel (which is, however, of doubtful interpretation), yet we may affirm none the less, as we have already done, that it had no such practical hold of the Jewish mind, as to overcome the prejudice otherwise excited against Jesus. And, indeed, it is plain that sufferings and distresses which the people themselves had inflicted on Jesus could not possibly, without a too manifest self-contradiction, be regarded by them as a note or proof of his Messiahship. Still, taking the claim made by Jesus to be the Messiah in connection with much of his teaching, it must have become evident to the disciples that that idea of a suffering Messiah was not abhorrent to *him* at least, and this observation must have gone far, after his death, to reconcile *their* minds to it ; the observation, we mean, that however strange and novel the idea may have been to them, as to the rest of their countrymen, it had nothing in it strange or deterrent to him, but had been accepted by him as indicative of one of the possibilities to which he had exposed himself in undertaking the Messianic office. This, we say, was an observation which would come to the aid of their reviving faith.

The crucifixion of Jesus was, as we have seen, a crushing blow to all those worldly hopes which the disciples had built upon their connection with him: to hopes which prevented the birth of the pure ideal in their minds. When all such hopes were crushed and gone, there would be an interval of blank despair, during which all would be cold and dead within them. But the mind of man is so constituted that it does not willingly surrender itself to despair; it does not easily or all at once give up a long and fondly cherished hope. The impression which Jesus had made upon the disciples had been too deep to permit of being effaced without a struggle, and we may be sure that their minds would react against the feeling of despair into which they had for a time been plunged, and begin again to hope against hope. Purified by that terrible disillusionment, hope would spring up anew within them. And the question would present itself to their minds, whether they could yet retain that splendid vision of holiness and immortal goodness in the death of all those carnal hopes with which, to their apprehension, it had hitherto been encrusted, or, had they to renounce both at once? Who will venture to deny that in that wreck of earth-born hopes that vision might disengage itself and stand forth anew in the light invisible, and that in that self-same hour it might seem to the disciples as if Jesus himself had risen again to view in more glorious state than ever, in a form no longer carnal, but spiritual?

At this point we may throw in two not immaterial observations. The first is, that if we may believe that the disciples might rise, by an act of the spiritual reason rather than by means of a visual or corporeal apparition, to the conviction that the crucified Jesus was alive in God, we are thereby delivered from the intolerable strain put upon our reason and our scientific conscience by the necessity of believing in a miraculous and wholly abnormal event as the foundation of our spiritual life. The other observation is, that if this great spiritual revolution in the minds of the disciples were to take place at all, it was in conformity with psychological principles that it should take place suddenly on the third, or some early day after the crucifixion, rather than at some considerably later period. For besides that spiritual revolutions, however protracted in preparation, often, if not always, come suddenly at the last, and seem to be the affair of a moment, we have to consider that, in this case, the conditioning circumstances were all present ; the flood was at the full, and if not taken at once, the conditions might have shifted and never have recurred. It was quite in the nature of things, therefore, that if the gloom which fell upon the disciples was ever to pass away, the period of its continuance should be brief and its dissipation sudden. This circumstance would render the event the more striking to the senses, but does not suffice to invest it with the character of miracle.

Our endeavour throughout this discussion has been to explain the genesis of our religion by reference to certain simple and well-recognized principles of human nature, or to analogous facts, taken in conjunction with what we conceive to be the critical deposit of the canonical records, and we pursue the same plan in elucidation of the great turning point in the history of Christianity at which we have arrived. Now, we do not proceed far in the history of religion before we learn that the human mind is endowed with marvellous elasticity, and that there are occasions on which, under the inspiration of an idea, it rises at a bound from the depths of despondency to the height of confidence in itself and in God. As by a flash from heaven, a new light covers the face of the world. And just such an occasion was it, we believe, on which St. Peter and his companions threw aside their doubts and regained confidence in their Master, which, now that he had signally illustrated his own ideal, was really identical with confidence in the truth which he taught. They accepted him at once as Messiah in a higher sense than prophets had dreamt of. They perceived that he had realized in his own person that idea of God's suffering servant, which they now felt to be a higher idea, morally, than any which they had hitherto connected with him, whom they had been accustomed to long for. To believe that though put to an ignominious death by the priests and rulers of the nation, he was still, as he had professed himself to be, the Messiah ; and that now, when he had been violently cast out from the earth, he had been caught up into heaven and passed into the presence of God, were one and the same faith. For it was simply impossible for the disciples to believe that he, who had so evidently walked with God upon earth, and had raised them by intercourse with him into the same fellowship, could be less than the Messiah, or be elsewhere than in the bosom of God.   The imposing authority which he had formerly exerted over them asserted itself anew in spite of the shock it had received from his crucifixion.   *Then* they had believed in him, expecting to find in him all the marks of the Messiah; which expectation made faith easy to them.   But *now*, in the absence of all such marks, they had discovered that he had other marks upon him greater than those they had asked for.

No more painful or more depressing situation can be conceived than that of the disciples when their Master was torn from their side.   But in his short yet intimate intercourse with them, he had prepared them for this hour, for this critical conjuncture, and it was soon seen that he had not laboured in vain.   The impression made upon their minds by his doctrine and personality survived the dreadful ordeal to which their faith in him was exposed.   His life and teaching had been one great appeal to their religious instincts, and these instincts being thus called forth and exercised by use, now asserted an authority above that of the priests and teachers of the nation.   The verdict pronounced by these latter against his doctrines and claims had no authority over men who had learned to recognize in him a higher authority.   The impression which Jesus had made upon them was that of a life manifestly hid with God : and the depth of that impression was shown by its power of self-retrieval after the shock it had sustained by his death ; in the case of Judas by his remorse and suicide ; in the other disciples by their advance to a higher view of his person than they had been able to take while he was with them in the flesh.   Purified from the dross of earthly ambition, their feeling of reverence was intensified into a sentiment of adoration.   The discovery that there was nothing more to hope for from him in the way of earthly honour and distinction, threw them with utter singleness of intention upon the spiritual benefits which he had conferred upon them. Forced by the catastrophe to accept his theory of the kingdom of God, and of the divine life, they took an immense step which involved a complete change in their religious views. While the worldly expectations which they had hitherto associated with the Messianic idea were demolished, they yet retained their faith in him as the Messiah.   In proportion as these expectations had dimmed their spiritual vision did the relinquishment of them seem to more than restore to them the Messiah whom they had lost. They saw him immediately in a transfiguring light, and his words came back to them with a new meaning and a new significance. The effect of his death was not to dishonour but to glorify him in their eyes ; and the ideal which his teaching and personality had . suggested to their minds became identified with himself in their consciousness, and fused into one with his image.

If, to reconcile the shame and humiliation of the cross with the glories predicted of the Messiah, the minds of the disciples leaped forward at this crisis, or in the sequel, to the idea of his second advent, by which all these predictions should be fulfilled, this was a thing which, situated as they were, so naturally followed their conviction of his exaltation into heaven, that it might be, but hardly needed to be, prompted by the apokalyptist (Dan. vii. 13), where he represents the Son of Man as coming with the clouds of heaven to receive everlasting dominion and glory. The disciples were satisfied that the triumph of righteousness was only deferred, and that, like Job, they and their Master would yet be comforted by receiving the reward of suffering and the fruit of righteousness. Yet, if their thoughts at this conjuncture did take this turn, we can see how little foundation there is for saying that " at first the disciples loved their Master because they believed he would realize their (Jewish) ideals, but that at last they loved him because they made his ideals theirs." It may be fairly questioned whether his ideals ever became theirs fully. They loved him to the last chiefly because of his grand soul-subduing personality ; it was for this that they gave him devotion and veneration. But never, even after the cross had revealed him in a higher light, did they fully understand and adopt his ideas as ideas. Such at least must be our conclusion, if we may judge from the broad fact that this hope of a second advent for so long retained possession of their minds, and that their ideas of Jewish privilege for so long presented an obstacle to the spread of Pauline universalism.

The crucifixion was to some extent the death of those worldly hopes, which were integral elements of the Messianic idea then current, and were still clung to by the disciples, in some measure, to the last. For a moment it seemed as if, with the extinction or disappointment of these hopes, the spell which Jesus had cast over them were broken once for all, and their faith in his Messiahship were irretrievably gone. But this state of mind lasted only for a day or two; the impression made upon them had been too deep to be effaced by a single blow, too entrancing and too inextricably bound up with their religious sympathies and spiritual instincts to be renounced without a struggle, without an energetic reaction of their minds against such a calamity. Between the " two pains, so counter and so keen," of faith and doubt, the struggle may have been severe. But, freed from the alloy of worldly expectations, the faith of the disciples would rise anew from its collapse, as by a natural and unobstructed buoyancy; helped, it may be, by the recollection that Jesus himself had never entertained such hopes, or only held them loosely, and that it had been no part of his teaching to excite such hopes in their minds, but rather the reverse. Not seldom, as we have seen, had he in their hearing, and for their instruction, muttered gloomy presentiments of the fate to which he was advancing; and so far was he from encouraging in them the expectation of a triumphant progress or a prosperous issue, that he emphatically damped all such expectations; and in the moment of their highest elation, when the conviction of his Messiahship had flamed up in their minds, he had begun from that time forth to show to them that he must go to Jerusalem and suffer many things, and be killed. According to the uniform testimony of the Gospels, he allowed it to be seen that he shrank from the fate which awaited him, but submitted to it as a necessity imposed upon him. The blessedness which he told them of was never of a kind which excluded suffering, and the way to life was through the shadow of death. When he spoke in this fashion the disciples could not understand what he meant, and were simply bewildered. The idea of a suffering Messiah, and of a blessedness of which suffering and death were necessary elements, were all but unintelligible to them. And it was only when suffering of the direst kind had overtaken both themselves and their Master that they recalled his words to mind, and better understood what he meant; and the fact that this fate had been foreseen and foretold by him was what came to the aid of their faith in that time of extremity. " If " (we may conceive them as saying to themselves), " if the presentiment of such a catas-

rophe did not shake his faith in himself and in his Messiahship, why should its fulfilment shake ours? Might not the
popular notion of the Messiah be a false one? Had not
Jesus, by the patient heroism and unresisting fortitude with
which he met his fate, revealed himself in a more glorious
light than would have been possible in a career of unchecked
triumph and success?" Their intercourse with him had, no
doubt, trained them to appreciate the higher moral beauty of
his character, and to see in the manner of his death a new
evidence of his Messiahship. As Peter was the first to
recognize the previous evidence, it is just what we might
expect when we find that he is represented as being also the
first of the male disciples to recognize this new evidence, and
to catch a sight of the risen Saviour; risen, that is, into a higher
beauty. Thoughts which require time for us to trace, and to
present in a succession, which may not, moreover, correspond
with the actual order of their sequence, may all have been com-
pressed into the feeling of a moment, or have risen simultaneously in the minds of the disciples.

To our notion, one great achievement of Jesus, one grand
result of his life and of his behaviour in death, was really this,
that he thereby impressed his disciples with the conviction that
his was a life in God, a life essentially immortal, so that when
he died he could not be holden of death—his death could only
be a passage from a mortal to an immortal life. His life had
been so manifestly divine that his disciples could not believe it
to be extinct, or to be less eternal than the life of God. The
crisis in their thought was brought on simply by the intensifica-
tion of a feeling which is common, or rather universal, among
men : of the reluctance which all men experience to admit the
idea that those whom we have loved and honoured have gone
clean out of existence when the band which connects the soul
with the body is dissolved. This reluctance grows and mounts
with our feeling of veneration and dependence on the being we
seem to have lost. When Jesus died, it was to the disciples
inconceivable that a life of such divine beauty should have
lapsed ; that a being so godlike, so victorious over the fear of
death, and so defiant of its terrors, should be subject to its
power. All that had been visible of him, all that was mortal
of him, had been consigned to the tomb ; but this undeniable
fact could not prevent the rising conviction that the spirit

within him had escaped, and soared into a new life in a higher and happier sphere. The sudden birth of this conviction in the minds of the disciples we hold to have been the true Christophany, the apotheosis of Jesus.

Admitting, however, that the disciples regained their confidence in Jesus in the way we have now pointed out, and became assured that he had passed into the divine presence, we have yet to ask, or to explain to ourselves, how it was that they and their converts became possessed by the further conviction that he had revealed himself in bodily shape to their eyes. In explanation of this curious, this fateful, world-historical circumstance, the consideration immediately presents itself, that the underlying spiritual fact, such as we suppose it to have been, was manifestly of such a nature that in order to pass into popular belief, and to adapt itself to ordinary, *i.e.*, rude, average intelligence, it had necessarily to undergo a process of deposition, *i.e.*, of transition from the spiritual to the material or sensuous form. There was a necessity that the spiritual idea which had suddenly sprung up and taken absolute possession of the few disciples should, in order to its permanence and transmission to the general mind, throw itself into the form of an outward historical event, which might incorporate and embrace details, in which consistency, as of minor importance, might not be observed. We do not mean to say that the disciples perceived this postulate of the situation, and knowingly threw their experience into this literary form ; but we mean to say that the situation was favourable to an interpretation of that experience which the disciples were otherwise, as can easily be shown, disposed to put upon it. In the delightful conviction that they had not really lost their friend and Master, who still lived and loved them ; in the ecstasy and tumult of soul produced by the inrush of that novel, far-reaching thought, they were hardly conscious, as one after another they were seized and caught by it, of what was taking place in their experience. The effect of that ecstatic state of mind, in making them unobservant of the changes going forward within and around them, was akin to that of the panic and consternation into which they had been thrown by the fatal turn of events which led to the crucifixion. There was little of voluntary or conscious effort in this supreme crisis and revolution of their thought. Just as has happened in many conversions in subsequent times, they were, or seemed to themselves to be, transported or carried out of themselves by a power which seemed to come upon them "from outside," or by an inspiration which, in reality, was but the outcome of past impressions now reasserting themselves; of impressions which had been made by the teaching and personality of Jesus upon their religious instincts, and had now revived after temporary effacement. Still more mysterious and inexplicable would the crisis appear to them afterwards to be, when they came to reflect on a moment of such immense significance.

It might even seem as if, unknown to them, Jesus had been spiritually present; or, as if their inner sense had perceived a real presence which their outer senses did not perceive. And when the words of Jesus which they could not formerly understand, and the presence which they could not fully appreciate, came back upon them with new power, it would seem as if Jesus had manifested himself anew, alive from the dead, and been present with them in spirit, if not in body. The impression received from converse with him had never been really obliterated, but only for a time suspended; the manner and heroism of his death, when they reflected on it, would do more than restore the ascendency which he had gained over their faith; and this restoration of their faith in him would be equivalent to a new manifestation of Jesus to their souls; to a resurrection of Jesus *in them*, which in the earthquake and upheaval might be confounded with one which had objective reality.

What then actually took place on a day or days immediately subsequent to the crucifixion was, not that Jesus rose again from the dead, but that the disciples, commencing with Peter, emerged suddenly, as in a moment, from the more than sepulchral gloom, into which they had been plunged by the death of Jesus, and in which it seemed as if the light of faith had been for ever extinguished. The faith which was latent in their very grief and despair flashed forth into flame, revealing Jesus to them in a new and purified light. It was as if Jesus had risen from the tomb and shown himself alive again. The effect of what they experienced was as great as would have been produced by the restoration of his bodily presence to the midst of them. In the perturbation and ecstasy of the moment, they were in the state, in which the soldiers on guard, who are mythically said to have seen the angel at the sepulchre, are represented as being ; (Matth. xxviii. 4) " as dead men," or as men who dream ; for whom the partition wall between the outer and the inner world has ceased to be.   Little accustomed as the disciples in their simplicity were to watch the workings of their own minds, to analyze their own sensations, or to retrace the steps by which they reached a conclusion, and little able to explain to themselves what had happened, they might, when they tried to recall and realize that mysterious crisis, suppose that Jesus himself had actually been present, unknown to them, as he is said to have been to the two disciples on the way to Emmaus, in some semi-spiritual, semi-corporeal shape.   For it is not at all unlikely that the mythical details, which have accumulated round the tradition of his resurrection, may, in this and other cases, only reflect in a sensuous or outward form, the moments or reminiscences of mental experiences which befel the disciples.

There is yet another consideration which may here be taken into account, viz., that what had *found* and electrified the immediate followers of Jesus was not so much his oral teaching as rather the living and moving exemplification of it in his own person.   During his lifetime, it was the spell of his personal influence which drew disciples and bound them to his side. Their intercourse with him, besides attaching them to his person, communicated to them somewhat of his own elevation of feeling, of his deep religious sentiment, and his sense of fellowship with the unseen world.   But this influence depended for its continuance upon his presence in the midst of them, and was apt to fade gradually away, if not to vanish suddenly, if he were removed from their company.   That that influence might be permanent it required to be exerted, not in the form of a memory of what he had been for them, but in the form of a sense of his abiding presence : of a conviction, that though he had vanished from their sight, by being caught up into heaven, he was in some real sort present with them still. We may therefore conjecture that, after his death, a sub-consciousness that such was the case may have fired a craving in their minds to have his presence restored and perpetuated among them, as the only means of maintaining that high condition of their souls, without which life thenceforth could hardly be tolerable.   For a moment or moments of spiritual elevation it might even seem as if that craving had been gratified ; as if Jesus had presented himself spiritually, if not bodily before them ; and to their mounting faith that moment of intense realization might ever after serve as a pledge of his abiding presence, and form the germ out of which grew in time their belief in his omnipresence and divinity, besides, in all probability, finding expression for itself in those farewell words attributed to Jesus in the mythical tradition : " Lo, I am with you alway, even unto the end of the world " (Matth. xxviii. 20).

The reader will at once perceive that the theory here propounded is not open to the objection, which is fatal to the vision-theory, viz., that while it is perfectly conceivable that a vision might befal Peter by himself, or James by himself, it is not conceivable that such a thing could befal all the twelve disciples simultaneously, and still more the five hundred brethren mentioned by St. Paul. For, on the other hand, it is quite conceivable that a wave of feeling, a thrill of conviction, as to the Messiahship of Jesus, and the risen life and spiritual presence in the midst of them of their crucified Master, may have passed over and agitated such a multitude when the impulse was given by the breathing words and burning emotion expressed by St. Peter, and communicated by him first to the interior circle of his brother apostles, and through them to the greater multitude. We have only to conceive that all the multitude consisted of Galilæans, predisposed as Peter himself had been, by veneration for the memory of Jesus, enhanced by the spectacle of the sublime devotion with which he had confronted his death, to catch up a higher conception of his character, and to take up again the hopes which they had built upon him, but had for a moment lost their hold of. That conception and these hopes when presented to them anew by Peter and James would come upon them as a revelation, or an illumination, which could, as already pointed out, only be described figuratively as a vision, or veritable and bodily manifestation of the risen Jesus. It would seem to themselves perhaps, or to others at least, to whom they spoke of it, as if Jesus, or their mental image of him had risen before them in a new transfigured aspect. The representation of the great experience could only transmit itself to others in a form more or less sensuous ; in which form it would rapidly, if not instantaneously, establish itself as historical fact in Christian tradition.

To account therefore for St. Paul's testimony to the vision of the five hundred brethren, our theory requires that a wave of emotion, a thrill of conviction, had passed over them ; a revival after eclipse of their former faith in Jesus, which, in being revived, became exalted and intensified; and that this inner change or process became for themselves, or for those to whom it was reported, identified with an outward and visible manifestation of Jesus to their senses.   We take the process or incident to have been an example of a phenomenon not unknown or unfamiliar to the classical nations of antiquity, analogous to those sudden (and simultaneous) impressions, generally of panic terror, but sometimes of quite an opposite character, which take effect on multitudes as on one man, and are attributed to the voice or other manifestation of a divine, or at least mysterious, presence.   In his fifth volume of the *History of Greece*, Mr. Grote calls attention to a phenomenon or incident of this kind which is typical, and by no means a rare or solitary instance in ancient history, nor without parallel in modern and more recent times.   Following Herodotus, Mr. Grote tells us that when the Greeks were about to advance to the charge at Mykalê, a divine Pheme (φήμη, fama), or message, to which a herald's staff, floating towards the beach, was the signal or symbol, flew into the Greek camp, acquainting it as by a revelation, sudden and unaccountable, that on that very morning their countrymen in Bœotia had gained a complete victory over the Persian host under Mardonius.   The anxiety which had previously prevailed among the Greeks was dissipated in a moment, and, filled with joy and confidence, they charged the opposing host with irresistible energy.   Such, adds Mr. Grote, "is the account given by Herodotus, and doubtless universally accepted in his time, when the combatants of Mykalè were yet alive to tell their own story."   Incidents of a similar kind have occurred in ancient and modern times, but we single out this one, because, as just said, it is typical.   And we remark upon it that the situation of the Greeks on the foreign strand at Mykalê, in the presence of a hostile force far superior in number, and strongly posted, was in the highest degree critical, and felt to be so by the Greeks themselves. They were, moreover, aware that their compatriots were facing

T

the still more powerful army of Mardonius in Bœotia, and that even their own victory, if achieved, would be of small avail, if Mardonius gained the victory on their native soil, in the heart of Greece. While these anxious thoughts weighed on every individual in the Greek army, the herald's staff, or some object resembling such a staff, was observed to be floating towards the shore on which they were drawn up ; and to men, who, under the influence of pious and anxious feeling, were on the outlook for signs and omens, this object seemed to be a prognostic or revelation that the battle had been fought and won by their countrymen at home. This impression shot like an inspiration or common spontaneous feeling through the Greek army, " effacing for the time each man's separate indi-viduality." The explanation of the simultaneity of the feeling is to be sought in the universal Greek habit of looking for omens, and in the anxiety which at the moment pervaded the army, predisposing every individual in it to receive the impression, which, according to Greek ideas, the herald's staff was in such circumstances fitted to give. It was a welcome omen which all could interpret, and at the moment nothing was thought of beyond this. But afterwards, when people began to reflect on it, the idea of a divine voice or influence, of which the herald's staff was only the outward and visible sign, was called in to account for the suddenness and simul-taneity of the impression which pervaded the army.

An idea or impression may thus arise and take possession suddenly of many minds, of which no man can tell the source. Under certain conditions a faith may thus shoot through a multitude as by an electric shock, presenting a phenomenon so bewildering and otherwise inexplicable, that men naturally seek an explanation of it in some mysterious and unknown force.

The situation of the five hundred Galilæans was similar to that of the Greeks at Mykalê, in respect of their being dominated and possessed by one common idea, and placed by events that had recently befallen them in the same mental attitude. They were all " brethren," *i.e.*, men who had enjoyed the benefit of intercourse with Jesus during his lifetime, who had listened to his teaching, who had been deeply impressed by his words and deeds, penetrated by one common feeling of enthusiastic veneration for his person, and of passionate regret that he

was now lost to view; united by one common idea that he
who had so manifestly walked with God on earth, could hardly
have fallen a helpless victim to human malice; all therefore
prepared, as one man, for some great and triumphant vindication of his transcendent worth and Messianic character.
The slightest impulse or signal from without would suffice
to change that passive and expectant state of mind into one
of energetic faith and action. And just such an extraneous
impulse was given, we may suppose, by the enthusiastic
declaration of St. Peter and the other apostles of their conviction that Jesus had passed from the cross on earth to the
throne in heaven. Such a declaration to minds so predisposed,
would act on them as a spark on explosive materials, or as the
"feather touch" which crystallizes water into the solid state.
This we believe to be the natural explanation of the simultaneous experience of the five hundred brethren. But this explanation not being recognized or thought of by the disciples,
they afterwards explained the seemingly mysterious occurrence
to themselves and others by the supposition of some intervening
divine agency; or more definitely, by a spiritual manifestation
of Jesus to their minds, which gradually grew to be regarded
as having taken place in the shape of a bodily manifestation of
Jesus to their senses.

Had there been no victory in Bœotia, the effect of the omen
in imparting victorious confidence to the Greek army at
Mykalê would have been the same; and so, even though Jesus
did not rise again, the *faith of that event* gave to his followers
the victory over the world; it became to them "a fact of their
consciousness as real as any historical event whatever, and
supplied a basis for the historical development" of the Church
and its dogma. The great critic, to whom we have more than
once referred, began his history of the Church by laying down
the dictum that this faith alone is the subject of history, while
the nature of the resurrection itself lies outside of historical
inquiry. We therefore regard the genesis of this faith as
belonging to what we have called the pre-historic period of
Christianity, and have treated it as a subject, not of historical,
but of psychological investigation.

According to our view then, the disciples of Jesus recovered
their faith in him by a mental revelation, an inward experience
or spiritual crisis; by a crisis so great as to stun their minds;

so sudden and unique as to appear to them to be mysterious and supernatural, the work of a divine and extraneous agent. But even were we to suppose that the disciples did not themselves believe that their assurance of the new life of Jesus was owing to an apparition of their crucified, but risen Master, there would yet exist the difficulty of explaining to others what had actually befallen them, the nature of their experience, and the grounds of their faith; the difficulty of unfolding the steps of thought or the evolution of feeling by which they had reached the conviction that he who had been trampled on and cast out from the earth had been caught up into heaven to the right hand of God, from thence to exercise authority over them, to be a law to their lives, and to come again on the clouds of heaven to be the Judge of men.

They could explain the great experience through which they had passed, the revolution in their consciousness, only in language which, literally understood, would seem to imply an outward manifestation of Jesus to their bodily senses. And this explanation would be accepted all the more readily because it would suggest a level and adequate cause for the otherwise inexplicable boldness and confidence with which these simple-minded, unbefriended men proclaimed their faith to a hostile world, and assumed the aggressive under circumstances which, but for some such experience, must, to all ordinary reason, have appeared to be dispiriting and discouraging in the highest degree.

It would thus come to pass that a crisis, which in its nature and its cause was rational and spiritual, would be transformed in imagination and general report into one which was effected by a cause at once supernatural and physical. What took place here is analogous to what took place with regard to the answer which Jesus made to the two disciples whom John sent to ask him whether he was the Messiah. According to the more historical narrative of St. Matthew, Jesus referred the messengers to his powers of healing the (possibly spiritual) diseases of men, as the credentials of his Messiahship. But St. Luke, in his version of the incident, makes it to appear that Jesus referred the messengers to the miraculous cures which he performed " in that same hour " in their presence, thus substituting or suggesting a literal meaning of his words for the figurative meaning. Just so it was that the first teachers of

Christianity, when, in addressing the people, they spoke of their great spiritual experience ; of the truth which had manifested itself to their consciences ; would of necessity employ language which might admit of being understood of a visible manifestation of Jesus in person to their bodily senses. The confidence with which they asserted, in the face of a sceptical world, that Jesus was alive again and had risen from the dead, could hardly be otherwise accounted for by the multitudes. The language in which these simple and uneducated men were able to express themselves was a rude instrument of thought. They were unacquainted with any dialect in which their thoughts, or rather their feelings, could be rendered intelligible to the minds of others who were not in the same mental condition as they were, or had not passed through the same experience. They were reduced to the necessity of expressing spiritual perceptions by means of figurative language, which was apt to be literally understood, and which so understood conveyed ideas wide of the reality, but yet sensuously representative of it.

Either they did not fully and clearly apprehend the movements of their own minds, and could not retrace the course of thought by which they had reached their convictions, or they were unable to carry others through a similar process, and to explain it in language which others could understand. That sudden flash of intelligence which had revealed Jesus to them in a new light, and thereby raised them out of their state of despondency, could only be described by them as a vision of the risen Jesus. To all inquirers they could only say, " We know that he has risen again, for we have seen him." They had seen him, indeed, with the spiritual eye, but they were understood as having seen him with the outward eye, and this acceptation of their testimony, while approximately or figuratively descriptive of their experience, saved them all the difficulty of further explanation. The words expressive of their belief ($\chi\rho\iota\sigma\tau\grave{o}s$ $\dot{a}\nu\acute{e}\sigma\tau\eta$) became a form of salutation, and the perpetual repetition of this form without explanation would help in some measure to favour the process. Still another circumstance which operated in the same direction may be seen in the fact that there were passages in the Old Testament which might be understood of a resurrection of the Messiah, and that the Jews of that age, as already noticed, perceived no great *a priori* objection to the report that this man or that had risen from the dead and been seen alive again.

Yet further, even if the immediate disciples of Jesus were aware of their inability to communicate to the minds of others those spiritual impressions of which they were profoundly conscious, except by the use of figurative language which admitted of a literal construction far enough from corresponding with the actual fact, yet it is conceivable that they might shrink from the responsibility of correcting the notions thus inadequately or unintentionally disseminated. The very proneness of their converts to adopt the notion of an actual Christophany might produce a fear in their minds that they themselves had been blind to the real nature of the mysterious experience which they had gone through ; and that they might arrest the diffusion of the new faith, if they were to raise scruples and misgivings as to the nature of their own testimony. Somewhat in the same way that many persons at the present day may be persuaded of the non-supernatural origin of Christianity, but dread the effect upon society if such a persuasion became general. Or again, it may be that, satisfied in their own minds of the claim of Jesus to be the Messiah, and of his risen life and ascension into heaven, they might think it of comparatively small importance how the like faith might be communicated to other minds.

If in looking back to that mysterious evolution of Messianic thought in the minds of the personal disciples of Jesus, on the hypothesis we have explained, we can, with all our psychological knowledge, hardly trace the process, and cannot but recognize its unique character and its surpassing gravity, we may well believe that the disciples in whom the evolution accomplished itself, were in no better position than we are to do so, while they were much more ready on reflection, and in their exalted state of feeling, to ascribe it without hesitation or suspense to some supernatural agency, which, at the time it was operating, they might not wot of. And when in that time of ecstatic feeling the converts still more readily took up the notion of such an agency to explain the occurrence, the calmer judgment of the original disciples could hardly be expected to stand out against the ideas of men, who, for aught they knew, might be channels of an inspiration equal to their own. And if so, it is not the first nor the only case in which the enthusiasm of the convert has swept aside the better knowledge and discretion of the master; and the interpretation of facts has given a new colour to the facts, and been accepted by those, who were themselves parties to their occurrence.

We have seen what an important part in the genesis of the faith was played by the Messianic doctrine. For us the doctrine which Jesus preached and illustrated has a truth of its own, apart from and independent of his claim to be the Messiah. But for the primitive disciples, who were Jews, it was otherwise. For them that claim was part of his doctrine, and but for that claim, his revolutionary doctrine might never have gained their assent. The Messianic doctrine had been the growth of centuries, and by making good his claim to be the fulfilment of that idea, Jesus became to his followers an object of absolute devotion. He that served himself heir to all the hopes connected with that idea, and was enabled by help of this personal distinction to launch his doctrine upon its world-wide career, had a claim to a higher authority than even that of the law of Moses; and in renouncing Jewish habits of thought and practice, the disciples seemed to have the countenance of Moses himself. By pointing to a Messiah, a prophet like unto Moses, the law had indicated a lurking consciousness of its own imperfection, and possible supersession. The faith of the better righteousness went along with the faith in the Messiahship of him who proclaimed it. And both faiths revived together in the disciples after the short eclipse they had undergone at the death of Jesus. According to Jewish notions the Messiah could not die, or if he could die, he could not be holden of death, he could not see corruption. He could die only to live again with a new, a higher and an immortal life. The moment, therefore, the disciples regained their confidence in his claim to be the Messiah, he was for them alive again. He had been as good as dead while they were in despair, but the revival of their faith was a rising of Christ in them, which they could hardly distinguish from the objective fact of a resurrection; which they could hardly but confound with it; or, if this confusion was not in *their* minds—if *they* were fully cognizant of the subjective nature of their experience, yet, in its transmission by the vehicle of language, it could hardly but pass into the idea of an actual bodily resurrection, of which they had been the witnesses. And at this day those of us who are

unable to regard the resurrection of Jesus as an actual historical
event stand beside the sepulchre of Jesus with the memorials
of his life and the records of his teaching in our hands ; and
have now, apart from the allegation of his bodily resurrection,
and of his Messiahship, to decide according to the answer of
our religious instincts, and to our much extended knowledge
of the divine order, how far the doctrine which Jesus taught
and illustrated contains in it the principles of true religion.

CHAPTER XII.

THE MYTHICAL TRANSFORMATION OF THE EVANGELIC TRADITION.

HAVING thus seen how the belief in the resurrection of Jesus took root in the mind of the infant Church, we proceed to remark that a starting point was thus furnished, an impulse given, to what is called the mythical construction, *i.e.*, the metamorphosis, the embellishment, or, in a word, the denaturalization of the entire evangelic tradition, including and probably beginning with that respecting the resurrection. For while the mythopœic process was stimulated by a belief in the simple fact of the resurrection, it is natural to suppose that the process thus stimulated and set agoing, would not only embellish the life of Jesus, but also in turn add detail and circumstance to the resurrection itself. The belief that the personal disciples of Jesus had been favoured with a Christophany would, of course, be vague at first and indefinite ; but, as time went on, a multitude of details not necessarily very consistent with each other would grow up around it, by way of dramatizing it, or drawing it out into separate scenes ; such, *e.g.*, as that he was not only seen again, but also heard to speak ; that he said this and that, that he partook of food, that his apparition was that of a real body, which admitted of being touched and handled, that the marks of the nails were visible, that he appeared and disappeared at will, as a spiritual being might be supposed capable of doing, that one of the disciples doubted at first but was afterwards convinced by the evidence of his senses ; and lastly, the cessation of these manifestations was accounted for by saying that he took his final departure from the earth by ascending in the presence of his disciples into the clouds. But the mythicizing process which thus supplied details to the vague belief of the resurrection so as to visualize it or make it representable to the fancy, performed a like service to the events of his lifetime also.   The tradition of these latter was, we believe, revised, moulded, and coloured, so as not only to visualize them, but also to exalt the person of Jesus, by exhibiting him as a wonder-worker, and by attributing to him such miracles as might form a lifelike vehicle of pathetic expression in dramatic form of the more or less common and normal phases of the great and varied religious experience to which Christianity had given rise.   This is evidently an important part of our subject, upon which it will be necessary to dwell at some length.

That much of ancient history has undergone a mythical transformation there can be no doubt whatever.   But it has recently been said that after being an object of dread forty or fifty years ago, the mythical theory in its application to gospel history no longer excites attention, but " has disappeared like water absorbed in the earth."   This observation is somewhat ambiguous.   It may mean that Christianity has survived the shock which seemed to be given to it by that theory ; which is true.   But if, as seems to be intended, the meaning is that the theory, as applied to the gospel records, is now discredited and thrown aside, the observation is only remarkable for its singularity and its disregard of fact.   For the theory did not originate with Strauss, and has not disappeared with him.   And if little, comparatively, is now expressly said of it ; if it has in a great measure ceased to be matter of discussion, the reason is that it is so established in the theological mind as to be substantially accepted, even by those who hold to the supernatural elements of Christianity, and applied even by them, within varying limits, to the critical study of the Gospel records.   In its application to these it has passed into the thoughts of many, and will not easily be dislodged.

By the manner in which Jesus had encountered and braved the last extremity of suffering, he had given a crowning proof of his greatness, had restored the disciples to faith in his Messiahship, after its momentary eclipse, and had satisfied them that, as Messiah, he had ascended into the " heavenly places," into a sphere which gave unfettered scope to their imagination.   Their faith, resuscitated, was more than it had been before the trial to which it had been subjected.   That the disciples should now regard Jesus with feelings of heightened veneration, and impute to him a greatness which, amid the common-place of his earthly life, and the familiarities of personal intercourse, they had never dreamt of, was inevitable. They would feel as if, while he lived and communed with them, their eyes had been holden so that they could not know him, as is said of the two disciples on the way to Emmaus. They would be amazed that they had not discerned his hidden glory when he was yet with them ; they might even reproach themselves for the slowness and obtuseness of their understanding, and what more natural than that they should seek to atone for their culpable stupidity by importing a marvellous element into acts and sayings of his which were quite within the compass of humanity, and by investing every incident of his life with a miraculous character.

This tendency, natural in their situation, was at the root of the mythicizing process ; but it is not necessary to suppose that this process owed, to the personal followers of Jesus, much more than its inception. They had been the witnesses of his earthly career, and their recollection of its incidents was probably too vivid and fresh to permit of their taking an active part in that process. At most they may have been passively implicated, by not interfering authoritatively to put a stop to it during their lifetime. But we conceive of it as being actively carried on afterwards, if not then, by their converts, who stood at a greater distance from the events, and knew of these only by reports which seemed to them not to do full justice to one whom they regarded as the Son of God ; by men, that is, who wished to see in his life the concrete embodiment of much of that new religious experience which they traced in some more or less indefinite way to that model life of his. For, it must always be kept in mind, that probably fifty years or still more elapsed between the close of that life and the final revision of any of the synoptic Gospels.

In all probability no part of the earthly life of Jesus escaped this mythicizing, metamorphic process. There were treasured up, in reverent remembrance, the outstanding facts of his life ; its general course or scaffolding ; the catastrophe of its end, and the substance of its teaching and doctrine, and a superhuman and miraculous character would be impressed upon all, so far as there was an opening for it ; so far as the tradition seemed to lend itself to or to invite such a treatment ; or even, in so far as it could be transformed into a vehicle to symbolize the salient and ever-recurrent features of the Christian life.

At many points of the evangelic history there are unmistakable traces of such a process. In the fourth Gospel a process of a somewhat similar kind is carried on under such thin disguise as to have escaped detection, only in consequence of the uncritical state of mind which characterized the early age of the Church ; and to have been screened from observation in later times only by dogmatic pre-suppositions which men brought with them to the examination of Gospel history. But reserving our remarks on the fourth Gospel for a subsequent section of this essay, we proceed here to say that traces of the mythopœic process are distinctly visible in the earlier Gospels ; as, *e.g.*, where the idea which appears in one Gospel in the teaching of Jesus in the form of a parable is in another Gospel made the basis of a miracle alleged to have been wrought by him (comp. Matth. xxi. 19 with Luke xiii. 7) ; or where a transaction, which in one Gospel proceeds on the ordinary level of human life is in another exalted into the region of the marvellous. In some few cases of this kind we can see the metamorphosis going on under our very eyes as it were, and can mark its successive stages.

It does not fall within the scope of this discussion to illustrate the various statements which are made in the course of it. But in illustration of what has just been said, we ask the reader to compare Matth. xxvi. 18 with Mark xiv. 13 and Luke xxii. 10. The incident here recorded presents, in Matthew's version of it, nothing of an unusual character. Jesus gives the name of the person in whose house he wished to partake of the Passover—a name possibly familiar to the disciples, though not preserved in the tradition. According to the other two versions he tells the disciples that by taking a certain route they would meet a man, of whom presumably they knew nothing, and whose encounter with them Jesus could foresee only by a supernatural prerogative. That is to say, that the later revisers of an ordinary incident have converted it into a miraculous incident. To mention only another instance of a similar kind, we ask the reader to compare Matth. ix. 20 with Mark v. 25 and Luke viii. 46. What actually occurred to the woman mentioned in these parallel passages was, that she felt

herself cured at the moment she touched the hem of the garment.   This is all that is said by St. Matthew ; but the explanation had suggested itself that the cure had been effected
by a virtue which went out from Jesus for that purpose ; and
as the report passed from mouth to mouth, Jesus was made
first to *feel* the going forth of this virtue, as we see in Mark's
account, and then to *say* that he did, as in Luke's account.   In
other words, the miraculous or materialized interpretation put
by popular fancy upon the incident is incorporated in the
narratives, and thrown into a dramatic form.   In these instances we have a hint or example of what no doubt took place,
by a uniformly operating tendency, in many other instances
in which we cannot trace the process, or see it taking place
under our eyes.   The conversion of the simple, non-miraculous,
incident into the miraculous fancy may, in many instances, have
been accomplished by the witnesses or spectators, all unconsciously, in the very moment of its occurrence ; or, if not that,
the transmutation may have taken place before the tradition
was committed to writing ; so that we have no means left, as
in the above instances, of proving or tracing the transition from
the one form to the other.   In either case, some event in the
life of Jesus, or some saying of his, indistinctly remembered,
or imperfectly understood, has served as a suggestion to the
religious phantasy, and has been by it made use of as a *point
d'appui* for a construction of its own.   Such suggestion may
have been of the most general and distant kind.   The thought,
that if Jesus had not really worked some imaginable miracle,
yet that he might have done so ; that it was not beyond his
power, or that it would serve as an illustration of his doctrine,
would be enough to set the phantasy to work.   The superhuman nature of Jesus having become a fixed idea, two results
would follow, which in this connection deserve to be borne in
mind.   In the first place, this belief would tend, in the apprehension of the Church itself, to transform the incidents of his
earthly life, so as to bring them into keeping with that belief,
and thus lead to a partial, unsuspecting reconstruction of the
tradition ; and secondly, the Church would suffer to pass, or
even deem allowable, any narrative that would help to impress
the like belief upon the minds of inquirers or unbelievers.   In
the latter case the end was good if the means were questionable.   But in truth, the mythicizing fancy, whether creating,

or only moulding its materials, acts more or less involuntarily and unconsciously; so that, what in a self-conscious and critical age might be immoral, will not incur such a sentence in an age in which faith controls or suppresses the play of the critical faculties, and in which the historical sense is, in a great measure, dormant and undeveloped.

We may feel a difficulty in conceiving, or in representing to ourselves the possibility of the wholesale transformation of the life of Jesus which is postulated by the anti-supernatural hypo-thesis, as having been carried out by the synoptic tradition, or rather by the Church at large, whose floating and protean beliefs the Evangelists may only have caught and fixed by placing them on record, besides summarizing and arranging them, each in his own way. But we shall not be staggered by this difficulty if we bear in mind that analogous cases in the religious sphere may be appealed to. It is hardly to be ques-tioned that the traditions regarding Zoroaster, Buddha, and other founders of religion have come down to us in a mythical or legendary form. It seems, indeed, as if there were some-thing in an active and excited state of the religious feelings peculiarly favourable to a process of this kind. Comparatively little tendency in this direction was exhibited in the case of Mahometanism ; but this was probably owing to the fact that the feelings to which the prophet of Arabia appealed were not strictly or purely religious or mystical, and that his revela-tions and the memorials of his life were committed to writing in the Koran during his own lifetime, by his own hand, or rather at his dictation—the effect of which was, from the very first, and ever after, to deprive tradition of its elasticity and its creative impulse, and to check or restrain within the narrowest limits the mythicizing proclivities of the faithful.

Against the mythical theory as applied to the criticism of Gospel history, the objection is often urged that the mythicizing process is a work of time, and can only be carried on in a society and amid circumstances separated by a considerable interval from the events on which it employs itself. Such an interval, it is said, did not intervene between the date of the events recorded and the record of them in the Gospels. Indeed the interval is almost reduced to none at all, if we take into account the testimony of St. Paul. This seems to be a very strong, and to many even an insuperable objection to the prevalence of a mythical element in the Gospels. But its force is very much impaired, or even totally destroyed, if we take into account the following considerations. St. Paul's testimony, on which so much stress is laid, is really confined, so far as it here concerns us, to the fact of the Christophanies mentioned by him in 1 Cor. xv., and to the general belief in the resurrection of Jesus founded upon them. Now, according to our mode of regarding them, these Christophanies were not mythical in the strict and proper sense of the word. They were only the materialization or externalization of a great spiritual experience, which actually befel St. Paul and the other apostles. And this externalizing process, while it imparted to that experience a supernatural character, was *not* a work of time at all but intrinsic to the apostles' mode of conceiving or interpreting their experience. When the apostles turned their reflection upon their experience, and sought to explain to themselves what had befallen them, they could only conceive or speak of it as a manifestation to themselves of the Christ or of Jesus come to life again. The reality of the manifestation was for them the main thing which could not be called in question or admit of doubt. Whether it was corporeal or spiritual, visible or invisible, was, if problematical, of no moment to them ; but to those to whom their experience was reported, it would naturally be regarded as having been visible and corporeal, so that there is nothing to hinder us from conceiving how this could be the general belief in the Church at the date of Paul's conversion, *i.e.*, two or three years after the crucifixion. Time was not required for the growth of such a belief. What, on the other hand, *was* a work of time was the operation of the mythicizing fancy upon the Christophanies, in the way of supplying details of time, place, and circumstance, so as to impart to them an air of " solid realism," and to present them pictorially or dramatically to the imagination. The same fancy was directed simultaneously, and in a like fashion, upon the events of the earthly life of Jesus, to exalt and supernaturalize them. But there is no evidence that either Paul or the original disciples took any part in this mythicizing process. As for St. Paul, we imagine that he was so much occupied with the dogmatizing process (in which, as we shall yet see, he took the leading part), that that other gave him little or no concern. Indeed, it is astonishing how entirely absent from his epistles is any reference (if we except that to the Last Supper) to the events of the life of Jesus ; and there is a presumption that his attitude in relation to that other process, so far as these events were concerned, was one of neutrality or indifference, if not even of impotence to check or control it. And we have already shown that by the time the tradition regarding the Christophanies was stereotyped by the synoptists, details had been introduced into it which were not in perfect harmony with the bare and simple facts to which St. Paul's statement was confined. We hold, therefore, that the earliest date to which St. Mark's Gospel, in its original form, can be assigned, i.e., about thirty years after the crucifixion, is also the earliest date at which we can be said to know anything approximately certain as to the state and progress of the Christian tradition ; not to mention that our knowledge thus acquired of the state of tradition at that early date is of a very uncertain kind, seeing that among critics there is hardly a doubt that St. Mark's Gospel, as extant, is a revision of its original form.

It is alleged, however, that even that space of time is too short to admit of the transformation of the actual facts by the mythicizing process. But to many, and of late years, we believe to an ever increasing number, it has appeared that too much has been made of this demand for time, as well as of the distinction which has been drawn between the circumstances under which the evangelical and other mythical histories got into currency. If in the case of Buddha, for example, it could be shown (which we rather think it cannot be) that the process began long after his contemporaries and companions were off the scene, the process must at any rate have begun in the face of an existing tradition which must have had an authority little short of that of the testimony of companions and eye-witnesses. The truth is, that the genesis of the myth under any circumstances is difficult to understand. The myth is a growth, and has the mystery and secrecy of all growths ; and it is much more likely to proceed apace in the midst of a tumultuous excitement produced by a great religious movement or spiritual experience which stimulates the imagination and the speculative faculties—an excitement whose source even those who are affected by it do not comprehend, but which they are afraid to undervalue—than after the excitement has subsided and the experience, though still propagating itself by sympathy, is yet

U

no longer so living and infectious or so apparently mysterious as at the first. Illustrations of these remarks might be drawn from the legendary history of St. Columba and other saints of the Roman Calendar. But enough has been said upon the subject.

In the case now of the Christian tradition, the mythicizing process must have received an extraordinary impetus from the belief in the resurrection of Jesus ; a belief, which, as we have seen, was floated into currency by the literal interpretation of figurative language used to describe the great spiritual experience or revolution in the thought and life of those who had enjoyed the disciplinary benefit of personal intercourse with him. This belief, indeed, was just the form in which that experience sought and found expression for itself, and devised the means of its own transmission to other minds. It was a belief which threw a new or retrospective light upon the earthly life of Jesus ; the resurrection being felt to be a master fact, which postulated an interpretation or construction in accordance with itself of that life, and of the catastrophe of its end. The belief of it stirred into activity the idealizing faculty, and suffused the actual facts of the life with a higher glory than was otherwise to be seen in them. And every touch or stroke by which the pious fancy could exalt the nature or function of the risen Christ found a ready acquiescence on the part of men who were possessed by that belief. To men whose entire thought was moulded by the moral and spiritual idea which had been impressed upon them by the teaching and personality of Jesus, it now grew to be a necessity, an intellectual delight, to illustrate that idea by embodying it on all sides, in words and actions which they ascribed to him.

Then too, there were ample and abundant materials ready at hand to help, to guide, and to facilitate the process. The Christian or evangelic tradition was, as already said, not a pure creation, evolved from human consciousness ; it was rather the filling up of the given outlines of a great life ; it was built up upon the scaffolding which that life supplied. Add to this, that the memory of the personal disciples was stored with many surprising proofs which Jesus had given of his power in the healing of bodily and mental ailments, in changing the life and calming the fears and passions of men ; and these, after the great crisis, would present themselves as exertions of more than human power, and would be talked of in terms that to those who had not witnessed them would suggest that he had actually raised the dead, and given sight to the blind, and multiplied the loaves and commanded the elements. And yet further, the historical and prophetic books of the Old Testament furnished a perfect mine of materials and suggestions for the mythical construction. Those who believed in the Messiahship of Jesus (and such were all who believed in his resurrection) were bound also to believe that he had excelled all the deeds recorded of Old Testament heroes, and that the Messianic prophecies had all been fulfilled in him ; so that, wherever possible, the highly figurative language of these would be applied to him in a literal sense. In many well-known cases, there is, especially in St. Matthew's Gospel, an evident endeavour to do this without much regard either to probability or to the facts of his history ; to make out the correspondence between prophecy and fulfilment to be much more exact than it was; even to give a prospective or prophetic meaning to language which was clearly retrospective or historical, and otherwise to set all the laws of sober exegesis at defiance ; and we cannot tell how far this tendency may have operated to alter the facts and tenor of his life. While in his answer to the messengers of John, Jesus spiritualized certain of these prophecies to make out their application to himself, the Evangelists and early Church, on the contrary, by ascribing to Jesus a fulfilment of them to the letter, obtained a confirmation of their belief in his supernatural deeds, and so gradually lost sight of the historical Jesus, and substituted as the object of their veneration, an ideal Christ of their own.

It has been well observed by M. de Broc, that the true knowledge of the past enables us to explain the present, and serves as a warning for the future. And applying this observation to the case before us, we may say, that if the early disciples of Jesus had been acquainted with the true course of the history of Israel, which modern criticism has approximately revealed to us, they would have been prepared to understand Jesus, and the great revolution in their thoughts and lives which he had effected. But having instead of such a knowledge only the popular and canonical view of that history, they failed to comprehend him, and explained him to themselves by regarding him as a living miracle, as a prodigy of the same nature as many others which embellished the national history in the past ; and thus it was natural, or, we may say, inevitable, that to use M. Arnold's expression, " The extra-belief of the Old Testament was transferred to the New Testament," and that the canonical history of the origin of Christianity became a mythical history. The miracles of the Old and New Testaments must stand or fall together.   The belief in the former, which prevailed in the age of Jesus, goes far to explain the belief in the latter.   Both cycles had their origin in very much the same principles.   And there can hardly be a more uncritical proceeding, or a more desperate shift on the part of apologists, than to retain their faith in the latter while making a sacrifice of the former.   Thus to assail parts of the orthodox system, while leaving untouched the basis of the system, viz., the supernatural idea, is enough to account for the sterility of much of the criticism of the current broad theology.

A recent writer (Dr. Cairns), whose orthodox bias is too strong to permit of his dealing candidly with theological questions, has pronounced it to be " the radical difficulty in the heart of the mythical theory," that, " if as that theory implies, Jesus was a mere man, or moralist, without miracle or ray of divinity," he could never have so " dazzled " the disciples as to make them " creators of himself."   From our point of view, the difficulty here said to be radical is only superficial or none at all.   We have already anticipated and solved it, in showing that by the majesty of his character, the elevation of his life, the authority of his teaching, and his occasional exercise of moral therapeutic, Jesus impressed his disciples, while still among them, with a belief in his Messiahship ; and we have only to add, that before the mythical process properly began, the impression thus made was deepened by the spiritual grandeur of his death, which crowning event made possible the belief in his resurrection, and so " dazzled " the disciples that an ideal colouring was imparted to all their reminiscences of his life.

Another apologist (Dr. Fairbairn) has objected to the mythical hypothesis, that it has the radical fault of making " the New Testament miracles echoes and imitations of those recorded in the Old."   According to this hypothesis, he goes on, " Jesus was arrayed in the marvels that had been made to surround the prophets.   What they had done, he had to do.

. . . But to this theory, it was necessary that the miracles of Christ should exactly repeat and reflect those of the Old Testament ; a difference in character and design was failure at a point where to fail was fatal. And here the failure was complete. The miracles of the Old Testament are mainly punitive, but those of Christ mainly remedial. The first express, for the most part, a retributive spirit, but the second are acts of benevolence." In illustration of this criticism, reference is then made to the incident recorded in Luke ix. 54-56, where the disciples ask Jesus, after the example of Elijah, to call down fire from heaven to consume the Samaritans who would not receive him into their village. But Jesus "rebuked the disciples and said that he was come not to destroy men's lives, but to save them." As Dr. Fairbairn seems to place reliance on this objection, we have given his words at length. But it fills us with surprise that such reasoning can satisfy the mind of a theologian so able and so ingenious. For, obviously, the Christian mythicist would be careful only to make it appear that Jesus had performed miracles as great as the prophets had, or greater, with some general features it might be of resemblance, but necessarily of quite a different spirit and character, and in harmony with the new spirit of his own religion. Only a blundering mythicist of defective insight and sympathy could have done otherwise. The skilful mythicist who was in sympathetic touch with the gospel could only attribute miracles to Jesus which exhibited a marked difference from those of the Old Testament, and were dramatically consistent with the distinctive spirit of his character and teaching. Dr. Fairbairn seems to forget that the mythicizing fancy was a play of the Christian consciousness, and was doubtless guided and controlled, even if unconsciously, by a deep insight into the distinctive nature of the new doctrine ; an insight which in default of other modes of self-explication, found vent just through the mythicizing faculty. Indeed, the passage referred to in St. Luke's Gospel is probably a reflection of the feeling which accompanied the mythical process of the incongruity of attributing to Jesus such punitive and retributive miracles as are of ordinary occurrence in the Old Testament. At the birth of those simple but beautiful creations of the Christian sentiment, the sense of fitness cannot be supposed to have been absent. To be just to the mythical theory, we must suppose that the phantasy in shaping these symbolical narratives was instinct with the Christian spirit, and knew its work, even though all unconscious, it may be, like every great original artist, of the rule which it followed. But though the Christian myths could not by any possibility have been a mere echo or reflection of those of the Old Testament, yet there cannot be a doubt that they were enriched and fertilized by acquaintance with those mythical cycles which had been the growth of many ages, and were now on a sudden call made to yield all that they suggestively could in the service and under the urgency of a higher idea and a grander enthusiasm.

The reverence in which the Old Testament was held by the disciples operated in two ways to colour the evangelic tradition. The disciples sought, on the one hand, to find in it anticipations or forecasts of all those events of the life of Jesus of which the memory was preserved by the Church ; and, on the other, to invest him with all those attributes of the Messianic character which had been traced in the Old Testament ; in both ways, suggesting the imposing idea that the life of Jesus was the fulfilment of one grand divine purpose which had been set forth in the ancient records of Israel, or, in the language of the apokalypse, that " the testimony of Jesus is the spirit of prophecy."

The same apologist of supernaturalism brings up yet another objection to the mythical theory, to which we may shortly advert, viz., that " it fails to explain why no miracles were attributed to the Baptist."   To this we reply, that a sufficient reason may be assigned for the omission.   The mythicizing phantasy shows a certain caprice in its choice of the events and persons around which it plays for which we cannot altogether account.   But it is, at least, conceivable that John's character, being less winning and attractive, and his work less distinctive and epoch-making than that of Jesus, had also less power to strike the popular imagination, to awaken sympathy, and to encourage that loving contemplation which is the soil best adapted for the springing of the mythical process ; and besides this, we have to consider that though some of the Baptist's disciples seem to have remained attached to his memory and doctrine, yet we may believe that the finest and most impressionable spirits among them, and those who were gifted with the deepest religious insight, joined themselves to Jesus, and enrolled themselves among his followers. John, moreover, always disclaimed any title to be regarded as Messiah ; and when one who did advance this claim made his appearance, there would be no disposition to magnify John's function, but rather to suffer his light to be extinguished in that of one greater than he. The situation thus created is well defined by the fourth Evangelist, where he makes the Baptist say, " He must increase, but I must decrease." John vanished from men's thoughts when Jesus began to occupy them. The religious phantasy did not play around his person, because he was not an object of supreme interest to the Christian community.

In this same connection Dr. Fairbairn, whom we take to be one of the most enlightened of our apologists, brings forward, in proof of the historical reality of the miracles ascribed to Jesus, what he calls their " miraculous moderation," the absence of all extravagance from the exercise of his supernatural gifts, the fact of his never being represented as using these gifts on his own behalf, or for hostile or defensive purposes, " his abstention from the use of his power being even more remarkable than his exercise of it." Now, if Jesus really was endued with miraculous powers and with redemptive functions, it is only what we had to expect, that he would exercise these powers in a manner consistent with his general purposes. In other words, the moderation referred to would hardly need to be accounted for, and we may freely admit that the manner in which Jesus is represented as exercising these powers is such as to raise a presumption in favour of their reality, though hardly so strong a presumption as Dr. Fairbairn's words seem to imply. But the marvel is that, supposing he did not really work miracles, the mythopœic fancy, in ascribing such works to him, should have observed these limits and proprieties. The real question for us is, whether, on our view, we can account for this moderation, this absence of extravagance in the synoptic myths, or for this congruity between the general conception of the character of Jesus and the particular deeds and sayings ascribed to him ? And to this question the reply is, that the mythopœist must be conceived of as instinct with Christian feeling—as steeped in Christian ideas ; one of which was that Jesus came not to be ministered unto, but to minister ; that his death was an atonement for sin, and that he could not save others except by the sacrifice of himself. Here was an idea which the mythical fancy would carefully observe, and seek to give effect to in its creations—an idea which would not only elevate the mythicizing impulse, but also drive off all childish and irrelevant fancies, such as those of the apocryphal Gospels. The silly and extravagant narratives of these Gospels are mere travesties, suggested to vulgar minds, who were in no wise touched with the moral grandeur of the theme; but to those who worthily appreciate them, all great ideas clothe themselves in noble and fitting forms of representation; and as we peruse the simple, restrained, and dignified synoptic narratives, while we do not regard them as literally true, we cannot fail to perceive that they are the fancies or creations of men who entered deeply into the mind and purpose of Jesus—how deeply is, we think, apparent most of all in the highly figurative narrative of the Temptation in the Wilderness, which may be reckoned as one of the most consummate of these creations. But we need not do more than refer to this.

The last objection to the mythical theory to which we shall here advert is drawn from the " solid realism " (to use the expression of Dr. Bruce), *i.e.*, the versimilitude or life-like appearance which unquestionably characterizes many or all of the miraculous narratives of the Gospels. This feature has been much commented on by apologetic theologians, and much importance attached to it. But it is now pretty generally understood to furnish a very weak evidence for the historical value of the miracles as a whole, as well as a very unreliable test for discriminating between the authentic and the doubtful miracles, where anything of the kind is attempted. This note of authenticity is impressed upon many works of pure fiction ; and it is felt, besides, that the loving contemplation of any subject whatever, whether commonplace or abnormal, confers an artistic power of describing it, of entering into its spirit, drawing out its details with sympathetic insight, and investing it with all the air of reality. In the case before us, this power would just exercise itself in imparting that very air of so-called " solid realism " to the idealistic touches and miraculous features which were given by popular fancy to the life of Jesus. This air of realism, which undoubtedly invests throughout the incidents, natural and supernatural, recorded by the synoptists, is reproduced in the Ammergau Mystery, where it makes a lifelike impression on the spectators ; but there, as here, it goes but a little way in substantiating to the critical mind the historical value of those incidents.

It may help to make the mythicizing process intelligible if we bear in mind that the early Church must have been unconsciously influenced by the desire, not merely to exalt the person of Christ, but also to strengthen and consolidate the credentials of the new faith. To the vast majority of its converts the Gospel probably came, not as an appeal to their spiritual instincts, but as a rule of life and a method of salvation dictated with authority by an infallible teacher; infallible because believed to have been raised again from the dead by the power of God; and it became necessary to confirm that authority, in every way that could be devised or imagined, against the inroads of scepticism and doubt. The marvels with which the life of Jesus was invested were strikingly calculated not only to enrich Christian thought, and to store the believer's mind with symbols and pictures of the new life in Christ, but also to serve as credentials of his authority, and so fitted to sustain believers on the heights of enthusiasm and the fulness of conviction. This latter was an object of pressing if not absolute necessity, because the early disciples must have felt in a peculiar degree what men have felt in all ages of religious exaltation, " How difficult it is to keep heights which the soul is competent to gain." No less truly than finely has it been said that " we cannot always burn with ecstasy, we cannot always retain the vision, and there are hours of faithlessness and of distrust in which we have to cling blindly to facts revealed to us in the vanished moment of inspiration " (Dowden). As in times of doubt, of temptation, and of despair, individuals sometimes fall back, as even Cromwell seems to have done, for strength and comfort on the moments of insight and of elevation to which they had themselves attained in the past, so when they were assailed by the sneers and cavils of unbelievers, or haunted by misgivings from within, the early Christians would feel the need of refreshing and redintegrating their faith by recalling their memories of the life of Jesus; and the more wonderful these memories were, the more would they be fitted to stay the wavering soul and to supply an objective foundation to a faith of which the subjects of it might at times be painfully suspicious that it was subjective in its character. If this need of the spiritual life might not act as a stimulus to

mythical inventiveness, we may at least conceive of it as predisposing the mind of believers to the ready acceptance of
incidents however miraculous.   In moments of great spiritual
illumination the early disciples, with St. Paul among them,
might be able to lay hold of the evangelical conception of
God ; but when the illumination grew faint they must have
felt, as we all do at this day, the need of some warrant or
authority for that conception ; and they were in a manner
driven to seek such authority in an exalted view of him who
had revealed it to them.   Their craving for such a warrant
could not be satisfied until they had exalted him to an equality
with God, and thus, no doubt, it became a motive of the
mythopœic process, and, as we shall yet see, of the dogmatic
process also.

At this point we are reminded of the great diversity of
opinion among orthodox theologians as to the relation subsisting between what are called the external and the internal
evidences of Christianity, or as to how these two branches of
evidence supplement and support each other.   By some the
internal evidences are regarded as quite subordinate, as satisfactory only from connection with the external evidences.   By
others the physical miracles, considered as credentials, are so
much undervalued that they are spoken of as " a deadweight
upon the gospel, making it more difficult to believe than it
would have been without them."   Between these two extremes
an intermediate position has been suggested, viz., that miracles
were wrought by Jesus, not to convince or convert unbelievers,
but to remove lingering or reviving doubts from minds which
had already responded to the inward and spiritual appeal of
the gospel, but were fearful of being the victims of illusion, and
desired to have some palpable guarantee of the faith before
surrendering themselves finally and unreservedly to its control.
A view this of the function of miracle which is at once interesting and plausible, because it takes into account the well-
attested fact of common experience in the religious life, that
periods of exaltation and of assured conviction are apt to be
followed by periods of reaction, and to decline gradually and
insensibly into a life of commonplace and doubt ; and because it
assigns to miracles a place in the general system of religion as
the divinely appointed remedy for this instability and fluctua-
tion of the religious life.   But to modern criticism it appears

that this feeling of insecurity, this dread of illusion, this craving for an outward guarantee, instead of having been met by the actual occurrence of miracles, *i.e.*, by a special and exceptional procedure of providence, was what prompted believers unconsciously to provide for themselves the desiderated confirmation of their faith by shaping the life of Jesus into a more and more miraculous form. It is, we admit, hard to conceive how in the early Church mythical invention could co-exist in an active state with the presence of doubt and misgiving, except by some such supposition as that of the existence within it of contrary currents of thought and feeling. But it is, at least, not difficult to understand how the craving for relief from agitating doubts and the dread of illusion might operate in securing an easy and ready welcome and reception to narratives of miraculous works, which were thrown into circulation by the more potent and affirmative forces of the spiritual life. The orthodox apologetic view of the relative value of the two kinds of evidence is supposed to find support in those words of Jesus in the narrative of the man whom he cured of palsy, " that ye may know that the Son of man hath power on earth to forgive sins, . . . arise, take up thy bed, and go unto thine house." But these words, instead of being spoken by Jesus, were more probably put into his mouth by the mythicist or the Evangelist, and addressed by him, as it were, " over the heads of an imaginary audience" to men of the Evangelist's own time. It was thereby suggested that if miracles for the confirmation of faith did not happen within the experience of the latter, they had happened, at least, under the ministry of Jesus, who by such means had satisfied for his contemporaries those very doubts which would be felt by men of the next and all succeeding generations.

If we may be justified in speaking of the motives for a process which went on unconsciously in the Church, we should be inclined to say that a principal motive which spurred on the mythical process was the unconscious desire to convert the probability of certain religious doctrines into a certainty. The so-called Christophanies marked the moments at which there suddenly rose up, for the first time in the minds of the disciples, the intense realization or certitude of the new life into which Jesus had ascended. But naturally, and by a common experience, these moments, as has just been pointed out, were succeeded by others of less lively realization ; by moments, that is, of incipient doubt and misgiving, and the desire to retain, or rather to recover the original feeling of certitude, acted as a stimulus to the pious fancy to exalt the work and character of Jesus, by way of strengthening the grounds of their faith in him.

Apropos of this remark, we notice that in *Literature and Dogma*, Mr. Arnold says, and says truly, that "the region of hope and presentiment extends far beyond the region of what we know with certainty," but that we may help ourselves in the conduct of life by taking an object of hope and presentiment, as if it were an object of certainty, and that so long as these extra-beliefs serve this purpose we may well hesitate to attack them. With the same "region" in his eye, Cardinal Newman maintains, in various passages, that the disposition to receive without cogent proof the objects of Christian hope and aspiration as if they were certain, is a test of the religious character and an evidence of saving faith. But "No," says the man of understanding, who takes reason as his highest guide, "no, I will retain my hopes and my aspirations, and derive from them what help I can in the conduct of life ; but receive their objects as matters of faith or certainty I shall not, until they verify themselves to my reason." The hopes and presentiments which were awakened in the first disciples of Jesus by their intercourse with him seemed to them to be verified by his resurrection. But now, when the only meaning which we can attach to the resurrection is the rising of Christ —the ideal man—in us, our hopes can only be verified by what we see when we look within and around us. When we perceive the beginnings of the life eternal in ourselves and others here, we may look forward with heightened confidence to the continuance of the same life hereafter. And it was perhaps from the perception of this that St. Paul (Rom. v. 4) could say that "experience worketh hope."

To take these words literally, and apart from the connection in which they stand to St. Paul's general system of thought, would be uncritical. But taking them thus for the present, they would seem to imply that the ground of Christian hope is not some doctrine placed ready to hand in a creed or formula, which we may take for granted on authority; but something which grows up within us as an experience of the inner life: and our religion can no more be a national affair, as it was with the Israelites of old, nor an affair of joint subscription to a creed, as it is with the orthodox churches of to-day, but an affair of the individual life and conscience. And we can recognize the ideal Church only as a voluntary association for mutual edification and common worship of men like-minded in the desire and effort to cultivate the higher life, of which Jesus set the example. This is a view, however, which we can arrive at by other lines of thought, and we do not need to rest it upon the doubtful interpretation of words incidentally used by the apostle in another connection. But to leave this digression, we proceed to remark that the mythopœic process was facilitated by the close and heated atmosphere in which it was carried on. All free discussion, all impartial or hostile criticism, was rigorously and effectually excluded from the Christian pale. Outside opinion was never allowed to penetrate within the barriers which the new faith erected round itself. To doubt or to hesitate was to lay oneself open to the charge of scepticism or indifference, and the dread of the entrance or encroachment of such a spirit was repressive of all real investigation or scrutiny of evidence. In the very intelligible lack of historical allusions to such a state of things in the early Church, our conjecture in regard to it is warranted by the observation of cases of an analogous kind, and a situation was thus created eminently favourable to the growth of the myth. Even in our own day we have witnessed the rise and establishment of a sect in the midst of us, claiming to be endowed with the gift of miracles and tongues, and there is a strong presumption that but for the repressive vigilance of the more critical questioning and scientific spirit of the age, this sect would by this time have been appealing to a body of miracles and legends little short of those with which the lives of Jesus, and of some of the mediæval saints, have been embellished. To a strong faith everything, even the impossible, is credible; and we can easily conceive how, in a community which owed its very existence, its separate life, to the passage of a great wave of religious excitement, its whole mental activity, its whole literary inventiveness may have been fired by the one purpose of exalting the object of its faith. If in any case we cannot trace all the steps of the process, we may yet know that there were tendencies and principles at work which sufficed to introduce mythical elements into the evangelical tradition, and that phenomena similar to those for which we contend have occurred in the development of other faiths besides the Christian, such as Buddhism, Zoroastrianism, and Confucianism.

Let a society in which a high and novel religion—at war with human passion and with established maxims and usages— forms the main and absorbing interest of life ; let such a society arise and consolidate itself amid conditions of an apparently adverse and untoward kind, and manifest a power to remodel and renovate the lives of its adherents. The existence of such a society will be a phenomenon of a character so exceptional and mysterious that the mythopœic fancy, which, as is seen in other cases, is at the service of religion, will inevitably be touched and quickened by it, and play around the circumstances, real or imaginary, of its origin, until there is given to them a definite and historical shape, in which the supernatural element will be an important factor ; and such, we believe, was the case in the Christian society. That a mythical process transformed the events connected with the origin of Christianity into a consecutive miraculous history may be paralleled, and rendered credible, not only by what has happened in the case of other religions, but by analogy with the manner in which apologists of the present day, whether of the orthodox or mediating school, starting from a belief in the inspiration or substantial historical value of Scripture, resort to the most hazardous and far-fetched methods and devices, hermeneutical and scientific, for the removal of difficulties. Just so the early Church, starting from a belief in the resurrection and divinity of Jesus and in his miraculous powers, placed no limit to its inventiveness and credulity in dealing with the tradition of his life.

In addition to what has now been advanced on this part of the subject, we should not omit to take into consideration, that even during his lifetime Jesus may have been credited with miraculous powers—with powers which he really seemed to exercise in the healing of disease and in the exorcism of evil spirits. When, therefore, narratives got into circulation after his death, of miracles wrought by him that passed far beyond these limits, such narratives might be regarded, even by the disciples, who, in his company, had witnessed nothing of the kind, as a mere play of the devout fancy—as innocent illustrations or sensuous descriptions of those spiritual powers which they had seen him exercise, or even of miraculous powers which he might have exercised had he been so minded—as narratives accommodated to the less spiritual apprehension of many of the converts ; and such narratives, when not challenged as fictitious or unauthentic, but allowed to circulate in a spirit of charitable or considerate indulgence towards neophytes of the less spiritual sort, would at length be accepted by the whole Church as strictly historical. The chain of evidence which certified their actual occurrence would seldom, if ever, be examined ; it would be enough if they seemed to be true illustrations of the spirit of Jesus and of his mode of action ; or if examined, it admitted in general of being so imperfectly scrutinized or tested, as to leave room for a certain degree of doubt in the minds of those interested, and the benefit of the doubt would, more or less uniformly, be given in favour of the marvel. No one, however strong his faith, independently of such supplementary narratives, would feel called on to question their authenticity. Such narratives would be felt to be poetically, if not literally, true ; and, while calculated to strengthen the faith, to give play to the emotions, to delight the imagination, and to aid the understanding of believers, not to disparage the office and character of Jesus. The attempt to draw a distinction between miracles which he did and miracles which he did not perform—to begin to make it a question of evidence rather than of faith, would, if made, have excited doubts, and possibly, in many cases, have extinguished enthusiasm and have arrested the spread of the great movement in the midst of its swing ; for the state of mind which prevailed in the infant Church no story would seem to be absolutely false which tended to exalt the powers of Jesus and to brighten the aureole which surrounded his person. The faith which befitted the hour was not pragmatical but unhesitating, provided only the alleged facts were true to the grand and central idea.

Without adverting to other considerations that might come in here, we should say, finally, that the unorganized state of the early Church—the absence of any central authority or court of appeal, and the rapid extension into foreign lands of a faith which, in its freshness and creative vigour, was naturally impatient of such authority as might, for example, be claimed by an apostolic congress—was also favourable to the mythicizing process. Anecdotes originating, no one knew where, and circulating simply by virtue of their congruity with the evangelic doctrine and spirit, could not be easily set aside or thrown out of circulation as unauthentic; no authority was anywhere lodged by which this might be done. The authority of the personal followers of Jesus, who had been witnesses of his life and conversation, could extend but a little way towards effecting this object, even if they regarded it as an object in itself desirable. The ferment in the Church was too active to be stayed ; the new spirit in its struggle towards self-consciousness and self-expression was too imperious to be resisted.

The early Christians generally having once surrendered themselves to the faith of the resurrection, there was no *a priori* objection to the occurrence of any miraculous work whatever, provided only it was in harmony with the wisdom and beneficence which characterized the life and mind of Jesus. The report of any work of which this might be predicated received credit as a matter of course and without examination. That such was the case we may see from a comparison of the fourth with the other three Gospels. The fourth Evangelist reports many works and sayings of Jesus of which, so far as we may judge from the synoptists, the other eye- and ear-witnesses knew nothing—works and sayings which it requires no little ingenuity to reconcile with those reported by the latter. But no one could venture at the time to deny that the apparent discrepancy might be accounted for by some such conjecture as that which is put forward at the present day, viz., that the fourth Evangelist was admitted to an intimacy of intercourse with Jesus, or had means and opportunities of observation, or a retentiveness of memory, or a receptivity for the highest mysteries of the faith peculiar to himself. The use of criticism in any proper sense of the word was in complete abeyance ; presumption was thought to be in favour of miraculous occurrences ; the evidence for such occurrences was never sifted, and the sufficient reason for accepting as true the report of any work attributed to Jesus was, as we have said, its conformity or fitness to the general idea which the converts had been led to form respecting his character and principles of action. The enthusiastic belief of the original disciples was enough to kindle the same belief in the minds of others, and to account for the propagation of the movement which resulted in the establishment of the Church. Consider-

ations such as these, which do not profess to be exhaustive of
the subject, make it possible for us to conceive that the
reminiscences of the life of Jesus, preserved by his personal
followers, may, in a very brief period, have gathered accretions,
and been rapidly moulded into that mythical form of which
we have three revisions in the New Testament.   All of these
are very wide indeed from the life which they profess to
depict ; and though not more truly noble and elevating in their
appeal to human sympathies, yet, owing to the presence in
them of the mysterious and supernatural element, more impressive to the imagination of men in whom spiritual instincts were
but feebly developed, as were most of those whose preparatory
discipline had been such only as the effete heathenism or the
rigid Judaism of the age could supply.   From which remark
it will be seen, that in our opinion there may be both gain
and loss in the identification of Christianity with a supernatural
system of religion.   The supernatural element, besides being
attractive to many minds, is, when accepted, unquestionably
calculated to give consecration and sanction to the moral and
religious truths which have been garnered in Christianity, and
to place them beyond the reach of cavil and the questioning of
the intellect.   But so far as this is an advantage, it is dearly
purchased by a corresponding loss ; the loss, namely, of the
prophetic spirit, of the deep personal engagement with religious
truth ; and also the loss which it occasions by throwing the
mind of the individual into the Judaic attitude of expectancy
and of passive longing for some immediate divine manifestation in the form of a secret reinforcement of the spiritual life;
or into what must be regarded as a position of false relativity
to God.   But above all, the great disadvantage of the supernatural element is that it is liable, nay certain, to fall sooner or
later into discredit ; and when that has taken place, the religion
which is bound up with it is also apt, for a time at least,
to share in its fall, and to lose hold of the human mind.

The mythicizing process to which we have now drawn
attention was carried on by the disciples, more or less unconsciously, in their endeavour to elevate their Master into a
greatness proximate to the divine, and into a complete and
faultless embodiment of that ideal which had been suggested to them by his life, and especially by its closing
scenes.   The tendency to do this was in their situation all

x

but irresistible. It has been said that " in every elevated soul there is a burning thirst for something more elevated than itself; it desires to behold its ideal in a bodily form, external to itself, that it may the more easily rise towards it" (Carlyle). This craving was powerfully active in the disciples of Jesus. The veneration which he had awakened in them knew no bounds, and in their effort to gain an adequate impression of his character, they naturally and inevitably fell into the habit of investing him in their imagination with those supernatural characters and powers, to his possession of which many incidents in his career seemed to point.

Having thus seen how the faith of the resurrection established itself in the Church, and supplied an impulse to the mythopœic process, we must here pause to call attention to another faith closely connected with that other, the effect of which was to aid materially in the same process. We refer to the faith that the risen Christ would come a second time, to establish the kingdom of God, and to begin his personal reign upon the earth before the generation then living should have disappeared. That a belief of this nature prevailed universally in the primitive Church is hardly less certain than that a belief prevailed in the resurrection of Jesus. It is even probable that for a time this belief was the more absorbing of the two, and that the apparition of Jesus to the disciples on the third and succeeding days was regarded chiefly as showing that he was already invested with the celestial form in which he should descend on the clouds of heaven to begin his reign. As time went on, however; as that generation of believers disappeared one by one from the earth, and there was no sign of his second advent, it was, we may be sure, a source of trial to faith, and a sore discouragement to the Church. But the faith in Jesus was too deeply rooted to brook denial; it survived this disappointment just as we believe that it will yet survive the loss of the supernatural idea which has hitherto been considered essential to its existence. The Church seems to have gradually given up the hope, and to have considered that the day of the Lord was deferred to an indefinite period (2 Thess. ii. 2).

But what interests us here is the question as to how this faith in the second advent arose, and whether Jesus had given to his disciples any reason to entertain such an expectation. In his great work on *The Apostolic Age*, Weizsäcker gives it as his opinion that the prediction of Jesus regarding his resurrection cannot be received as historical, while at the same time he is satisfied that the promise that Jesus would come again to erect the kingdom of God, is an essential portion of the oldest tradition. By which language we do not understand this author as intending to express the opinion that Jesus actually made this promise. For it would be inconsistent with the distinguishing and fundamental doctrine of Jesus respecting the spiritual nature of the kingdom ; and it is ever the mark and characteristic of genius, when it has laid hold of a great truth such as this, that it is " misled by no false fires." The intense conviction that the kingdom of God was purely spiritual was what emboldened Jesus, the promulgator of this truth, to regard himself as the Messiah in the true sense of the word. And we may be sure that he would guard this doctrine carefully against misconception. To the safety and security of this position his inmost nature bore testimony. And had he said anything to imply that his kingdom was of a mixed nature, partly sensuous or carnal, and partly spiritual, or had he admitted into his teaching anything predictive in the strict sense of the word, he would for us no longer occupy that unapproachable eminence which belongs to him as a teacher of religion. It is true that in Matth. xvi. 27, and elsewhere, he is represented as using language calculated to give occasion to a faith of a mixed nature. But we do not regard such lauguage as a genuine utterance of his, any more than John i. 51, which resembles it in spirit and intention, " Verily, I say unto you, hereafter ye shall see heaven open and the angels of God ascending and descending upon the Son of Man," and was probably built after the manner of the fourth Evangelist, upon hints of the kind in the synoptists. We therefore consider this extra and temporary faith of the primitive Church to be a survival of the inherited Jewish idea of the kingdom of God which the spiritual teaching of Jesus had failed to correct.

We conceive that this inherited idea asserted itself anew in the evangelical tradition of his teaching, in the form of a prediction uttered by him to encourage the belief that though apparently discredited for the present by the catastrophe of his death, it would yet be fulfilled in the experience of that generation. We conceive too that this faith did not arise at the very first along with that of the resurrection, but that it arose some time after that other faith in the visible apparitions of Jesus had established itself in the minds of the disciples. After a time, when these experiences had manifestly ceased, the question would inevitably arise, " Why does he not show himself any more ? Will he not come again to erect the kingdom for which we have been taught by the fathers to look ?" " Yes," the answer would be, " he will come again, not immediately, however, but within the lifetime of this generation. Ancient prophecy will yet be fulfilled. These manifestations of Jesus to a favoured few are only pledges of his final coming, when every eye shall see him." That a faith which expressed itself thus should quickly gain ground under the circumstances, and establish itself in the minds of men who already believed in the resurrection of Jesus, and in the Scriptures of the Old Testament, it is easy to imagine.

The prevalence of such a faith is enough to show how far were the personal disciples, and the early Church generally, from being indoctrinated by the spiritual teaching of Jesus ; but it was of immense temporary advantage to the Church, by inspiring it with the idea that the time of endurance would be short ; and so confirming the fidelity of its members to their profession. We have even reason to believe that it gave an ascetic tone to the Church of that time, and withdrew its interest almost entirely from a world which was soon to undergo a total change, and to pass under a different regiment. This effect still survives to some extent in Christianity, and, as placing it in antagonism to modern culture, has been made a subject of reproach to it, though, as we have already shown incidentally, this feature of religion receives no countenance from Jesus himself, who enjoined his disciples to give to Cæsar the things of Cæsar, and, in opposition to the Baptist, set the example of eating and drinking like other men.

The important bearing which this faith in the second advent must have had upon the mythopœic process is quite apparent. For while a lively expectation of the speedy occurrence of the great event was yet prevalent in the Church, i.e., for the first generation of believers, there would be no serious or systematic attempt to reduce the oral tradition of the life of Jesus to

writing, and this period of suspense would be favourable to the
mythopœic process, because the oral tradition would be quick
and elastic, not stereotyped, but open to incessant revision.
The faith, too, would prompt men to seek a justification for
itself in words spoken by Jesus, and to interpolate his teaching
with language which seemed to warrant the expectation of his
second advent. There may also be something in the idea of
Volkmar, that when through long deferment the hope of the
second advent became faint and languid, the Church, even while
it suffered predictions of that event to retain their place in
tradition, would yet turn back to the earthly life of Jesus, and
seek to invest it with a glory greater than had yet been seen in
it, by way of compensating for the failure of hope in that other
direction.

There were thus, we see, various tendencies at work to
promote the process of a mythical embellishment and metamorphosis of the actual reminiscences of the life of Jesus.
There was the tendency to exalt his character, to impart more
and more of a miraculous aspect to his life, to represent him
as performing marvels in no degree inferior to those recorded
in the Old Testament, and worthy of one reputed to be greater
than all the prophets. There was the tendency to make his
life a mirror or reflection of the new spiritual consciousness,
which was traceable to him ; an anticipation of that varied experience which the Christian community had gained in its
conflict with the hostile and unbelieving world. Before the
Gospels were written the community had witnessed the effect
of the new religious principle in the midst of opposing forces,
the resistance it had met, the impression it had made, and the
conquests it had won ; and this experience was a fund which
could be drawn upon to enrich the life and teaching of Jesus
with materials suitable to its character, and prophetic of the
needs of the coming age. There was yet further a tendency
to clothe the reflections of the Church upon its own marvellous
history, so far as it had gone, in the form of words and discourses put by it into the mouth of Jesus ; words which were
thus, in effect, predictive *post eventum*, after the manner of
apokalyptic literature. One critic, indeed (Volkmar), has gone
so far as to treat the Gospels not so much as a life of Jesus as
rather a history, whose elements have been drawn chiefly from
sources such as these. And though this is a manifest ex-

aggeration, yet there is a certain amount of truth in it, and much of the synoptic material (though how much cannot exactly be said) may be accounted for in this way. When we find an incident recorded in the Gospels which is vividly or symbolically illustrative of the situation and experience of the early Christians, or any saying ascribed to Jesus which they might have used in controversy with their Jewish countrymen, we may regard that incident or that saying as of doubtful or mythical origin : as meant to place on record an experience by way of preserving it for the benefit of the Church, and calculated to act upon the sceptical mind by its apparently apokalyptical or prophetic character. At the same time it is manifest that the relation in which Jesus stood to the Jews may have foreshadowed that of the disciples to their countrymen ; and that he may have spoken or acted in a way which we can suppose them to have done, so that the speculation here referred to is of doubtful value.

It goes but a little way towards explaining the legendary accretions of the life of Jesus to say, that that was a legend-loving age, and that the growth of legend was to be looked for. It is by no means clear to our mind that that was a peculiarly legend-loving age, and there is the fact that no legend grew up around the remarkable figure of the Baptist. Tendencies there were, no doubt, in that as in other ages, favourable to the growth of legend. But the mythical traditions of Christianity can be explained only by taking into account not only wants common to the human mind, which found satisfaction in them, but also pre-existing beliefs and peculiar circumstances in the situation of the early Christians. The impression which the primitive disciples received of the personality of Jesus during their intercourse with him was what gave the initiative, and caused those experiences which were interpreted as Christophanies. But it soon came to be a practical question—urgent, if unformulated and unexpressed—what was to compensate for the cessation of that intercourse ? what was to convey that impression to those who had not enjoyed that privilege, who had not seen and companied with him ? The impression had for this purpose to shape itself into language, and pass, by the instrumentality of words, into the general consciousness. The very alphabet of such a language had to be constructed. And no one capable of appreciating the nature of the problem thus

presented will be disposed to underrate its difficulty. It required the genius of a Paul, as will be immediately seen, after
prolonged meditation in the recesses of Arabia, and after much
experience of mission work and of the conditions of its successful prosecution, to reduce that impression to the form of dogma.
But the Galilæan disciples applied themselves to the easier task
of justifying that impression, and keeping it alive in their own
minds and in the minds of their converts, by exalting the
details of his life.   Any plain, matter-of-fact report of it would
have produced but a pale impression of the reality as it appeared to themselves ; pale in comparison with that which the
reality had made on eye- and ear-witnesses of it.   Hence the
necessity, or expediency, to which they unconsciously yielded,
of vivifying that impression by imparting a mystical and supernatural colouring to their report of it, *i.e.*, by submitting it to
the mythicizing process.

The perfect and consistent beauty of the Gospel narratives
throughout, and not least of the miraculous narratives, has been
universally acknowledged.   By many who cannot regard them
as strictly historical, they have been regarded as productions of
high literary genius.   One great sceptic expressed the opinion
that it is easier to conceive that the life had been lived than
that the story of it had been invented.   But it may help us
to conceive how such narratives could have been put together,
if we bear in mind that the outline of the record had been
given in the life actually led by Jesus, a life which, in comparison with the lives of other men, was of surpassing moral
beauty.   We may therefore apply here the observation of
Aristotle, that it requires no extraordinary genius to fill up
an outline with appropriate details which time reveals to us, or
helps us to find, and so to complete the picture.   The *time*,
which Aristotle postulates, was an important factor for the
filling up of that outline, because the ideal traits of the picture
required to be suggested by the results which, on a large scale
in the history of the Church, were in some sense a continuation
or a " filling-up " of that individual life.   The Gospel narratives were not thought out by any one mind, but were the
growth of many minds and many years.   Details were from
time to time added to the tradition, many of which were
not the belated records of incidents in the life of Jesus, but
registers of Christian experiences in the form of such incidents

—the explanation, probably, why they have lent themselves in all ages of the Church so admirably to homiletic use.

Before leaving this subject of the mythopœic process to which the records or reminiscences of the life of Jesus were subjected, we would briefly remark that though in vulgar estimation, and at first sight, the process may seem simply to pervert and falsify the history, yet in reality it is the process by which the past is exalted and glorified, the religious sentiment intensified, and feelings of awe, reverence, and devotion educated to a point which they might not otherwise attain. By the mythical transformation of its objects, the religious sentiment mounts from stage to stage, until at length it arrives at the conception of the pure Ideal or concrete image of the Ideal, and can dispense with the ladder by which it has mounted to that height. In the religious history of the past it has, in many cases, been one of the great educative processes of the world, by giving expression to the moral and religious aspirations, and clothing ethical ideas in forms sensuous but impressive, and presenting to men images of heroism and saintship greater than were furnished by the contemplation or achievements of actual life. Such has been the case especially in respect of Gospel history. While the mythopœic process, as we have pointed out, received its impulse from the belief in the resurrection of Jesus, its unconscious aim was to represent him as realizing in his person to the full that ideal of goodness and greatness which his life and resurrection had suggested to the minds of the disciples, and no obstacle or misgiving was suffered to arrest the process until the Church was satisfied that this goal was reached ; though, as we shall yet see, after the mythicizing fancy, in its unconscious action, had done its best, and exhausted its resources, a further and final advance had yet to be made in the same direction before the Church could be satisfied that the idealizing transformation of the life of Jesus had reached its predetermined goal. This advance was made by the fourth Gospel.

CHAPTER XIII.

RELATION OF MYTH TO DOGMA.

LET us here pause to offer a few observations, by way of summing up and further elucidating what has now been said respecting the mythical element of the Gospels, besides connecting it with the prophetic thought in ancient Israel, and preparing the reader for the dogmatic form into which, as we shall yet find, the religion of Jesus settled in the Christian Church.

I. We hold that neither the conception of divinity, nor the ideal of humanity, were ethically perfect in Israel. The teaching of Jesus was needed to supply the defects and missing traits in both; and when these were supplied by his life and doctrine, the Church advanced to a higher ideal, and proceeded to conceive of it as embodied in his person. Thus may Jesus justly be said to have fulfilled the prophets—first by exalting and perfecting their ideals, and then by the illustration of these in himself. In this fulfilment, however, we do not see the evidence of a prophetic foreknowledge of events which took place five or six hundred years after the prophets lived; for that would manifestly be a supernatural prevision. But yet, the correspondence between the prophetic embodiment of the ideal, and the general features of the life of Jesus as reported by the synoptists, is so close, that no sane person can regard it as purely accidental. We therefore explain the fulfilment to ourselves as due fundamentally to the evolution of that religious idea of which Israel and the early Church were the organs. In its Christian stage the idea was germinant in that of Israel, and the latter was anticipative or prophetic of the former. By a stroke of the imagination, the prophets gave to their ideal its concrete form in the suffering servant of God, while the Christian mythicist read his new ideal into the historic personality of Jesus. In words which have, if we remember, been used by some recent writer, but which, at all events, express the drift of our thought, " the prophets impersonated their ideal, while the Church idealized the person," thus between them completing the circle of thought.

II. By virtue of what has been called " imaginative insight," like that by which Plato divined the cruel fate to which a perfectly good man would necessarily expose himself, the prophetic spirit in Israel may have conceived that the ideal Israelite, were he to appear, would have to encounter the murderous rancour of his countrymen, and even to suffer death at their hands. It would also be the crowning glory of such an one (compare 1 Pet. ii. 20) to suffer wrongfully, without impatience, without resentment, and without abatement of his patriotism. In actual life no example of such transcendent virtue might be visible, but the thought of one such might be suggested to the idealizing mind of the prophet by the semblance of it in the spectacle of the innocent victims that were daily led to the altar of sacrifice in the temple. At least, it was certainly associated with that spectacle in the mind of Isaiah (liii. 7), as well as afterwards in the grandly speculative soul of the fourth Evangelist (John i. 29). But this prophetic idealization would also be associated with a thought of wider range. The facts of human life could not but reveal to Hebrew thinkers, no less than to the dramatists of Greece, the idea of the solidarity, for good and evil, of the family or the race. It was too evident to be overlooked by observant minds, that the sins and crimes of men were followed by sufferings on the part of the guilty person himself, and on the part of his kindred and children, however little these latter might have partaken of his sin. This law of the physical and moral world, affirmed in the Decalogue, and attributed to the decree of God (Exod. xx. 5, 6), entered deeply into the mind of Israel. And just as suffering, inclusive of the tendency to guilt, as the penalty of sin, was spread around, and entailed from generation to generation, so there was a remedial action of this same law of continuity— the converse of that other—which must also have engaged the mind of Israel. The inherited tendency to guilt did not fetter the will ; for a man was master of his fate, and might resist the tendency. An individual might put forth such a pre-eminent degree of moral energy, as not only to extirpate the inherited taint in himself, but also stem and turn back the advancing tide of evil. A life of such exceptional worth was supposed not merely to exert, by the power of sympathy, a natural influence on the surrounding society, but also to be of supererogatory value, and even to be endued with vicarious virtue, sufficient in the eye of God to palliate or atone for the sins of the society of which he was a member. For, let it be remarked, that though these theological terms are of comparatively recent origin, yet the ideas which they express were not unfamiliar in Israel. They were the ideas to which Isaiah gave popular and dramatic expression in his delineation of the servant of God, and were probably taking shape in his time in national thought, though they had not yet assumed that definite and dogmatic form to which they afterwards rose in the theology of the Synagogue. (See Weber's book on this theology.) And these same ideas remained in force to influence the mind of St. Paul and of the early Church ; being called in to explain the great revolution which flowed from the devoted life and death of Jesus; in which explanation, divested of its dogmatic element, we have to acknowledge a great world-historic truth, viz., that by his life and doctrine Jesus did weaken the forces of evil, and did introduce a new renovating or redemptive influence into human life. What St. Paul's teaching did was, as will yet appear, to represent this natural operation of the life and work of Jesus, under the form of a supernatural operation.

III. That Jesus was a pre-eminently righteous man—an ideal Israelite—was the impression made upon the minds of those who companied with him, by his whole personality—by the beauty of his character, by the grandeur of his spirit, and by the power of his doctrine ; and his cruel death, so far from undeceiving them, or convincing them that they had made a mistake, rather confirmed that immediate impression, and awakened in them the further faith that God had raised him from the dead. Their assurance of his resurrection was so vivid that it may have imparted itself to many who had not enjoyed the privilege of immediate personal intercourse with him ; but when, as must often have been the case, their testimony failed to overcome the prejudice against him to which his ignominious death gave rise, it was supplemented and confirmed by proofs drawn from the prophetic writings, that the servant of God, in whom the Messiah was now merged, behoved to die and to rise again in triumph. It has been well pointed out by Weizsäcker, that the recourse to this supplementary proof for these two events—the death and resurrection of the Messiah—formed the beginning of Christian theology, and that this proof from the Old Testament was subsequently stretched to other incidents in the Gospel history. In the multifarious records, prophetic and historical, of that revered volume, it was easy for the strong faith of the Church to find prophetic allusions to many other circumstances of the life of Jesus, till at length, by a pious adjustment of materials, from this side and from that, this proof was gradually drawn as a " net " over the whole evangelic tradition. This process does not exactly cover what is meant by the mythical process, but it certainly took part therein; and the mention of it leads us naturally to the consideration of the dogmatic process, to which we now turn.

Having endeavoured to show that the faiths which grew up after the crucifixion furnished a starting point, and an impulse to the mythicizing process, we proceed to remark that these same faiths gave rise also to the dogmatic process by which the " religion of Jesus " was converted into "the Christian religion." These two processes have, according to our view, a common source. They both spring from a tendency or habit of mind very intelligible in itself, but against which, in its various forms, all the best thought of modern times has protested, viz., the habit or tendency to explain the facts of experience, common or recondite alike, in whole or in detail, by assumptions which transcend experience, or by the action of forces, to the reality of which we cannot rise from the human consciousness—the starting point for all real knowledge. In the case of the early disciples of Jesus, the experience to be explained may be variously described as the sudden rise within them of the new hope, the transformation of their religious consciousness on the third day after the crucifixion, or the revival of their confidence in their crucified Master, with all that it involved. This great experience could for them be explained only by the supposition of some mysterious agency, or by the action of a supernatural element, which, in the concrete form of myth, or in the abstract form of dogma, they thought into their conception of the nature, life, and function of Jesus. The actual and rational cause of that experience was the new idea and the new conception which had been imparted by Jesus as new contents to the consciousness of his disciples. But this intermediate factor being overlooked, or at least not deemed sufficient to account for that experience, a mystical or supernatural cause was associated with it for that purpose, as will yet be seen more particularly.

Speaking generally, the myth may be said to have elevated the person and the work of Jesus into a supernatural region, whereas the dogma was the use made of the faith thus generated to give to the person and work of Jesus an immediate, causative, or genetic relation to the great inward experience or revelation of the spiritual life which befel the disciples, and was propagated from them to their converts. But, more particularly, the relation between the myth and the dogma may be said to be one of mutual interaction. The dogma is implicated or involved as a presupposition in the myth. As the supernatural, non-rational, or magical explanation of Christian experience, it entered as an intrinsic, but inexplicit element into the mythical record of the life of Jesus, and could never, for any period however brief, have been wholly wanting in the Church ; but in its separate, explicit, and developed form, in which it may have reacted upon the myth, it was mainly, at least in its initial shape, the work or creation of St. Paul, who has therefore properly and deservedly been called " the first Christian dogmatist," and who is certainly, next to Jesus himself, the greatest figure in the history of the Christian Church.

In addition to what has here been said regarding the relation in which the dogma and tradition stood to each other, there is the important consideration, that the dogma, like any other idea, had a self-evolving power, more or less independent of the tradition from which it took its inception, and that there would necessarily be a tendency in the tradition, while still fluid, to adjust itself to the dogma by mythical accretions as it settled into form. The most crucial illustration of such self-adjustment is to be found in the dating of the crucifixion, both in the synoptists and in the fourth Gospel. But our discussion of this point will be reserved for our remarks on the fourth Evangelist.

And here let it be remarked, that the dogma of St. Paul can hardly be regarded as a pure reflexion of the doctrine of Jesus, inasmuch as it took its form from the introduction and presence of the supernatural idea, which, as we contend, was entirely absent from the teaching and the life of Jesus. This idea prevailed universally during the whole period of the New as well as of the Old Testament ; and necessarily imparted to the historical and doctrinal elements of the records a character and colouring which did not properly belong to them. Carrying out the idea of evolution, Dr. E. Caird is naturally led to regard as " legitimate developments," the form given to the doctrine of Jesus by St. Paul and the fourth Evangelist ; but even this view of the later form of doctrine can hardly be received without protest, if we keep in view, what Dr. Caird himself admits, 2,235, that in some of the words of Jesus, his leading principles, viz., that self-realization is only possible through self-sacrifice, and that true progress is only possible by gradual development, are " more clearly expressed than they ever were by any one down to the present century, when they have become the key-note of all speculation." This seems to be an admission that neither in Pauline nor in post-Pauline doctrine, has there been any substantive development, but at most only a variation of the form, the infusion into it, not strictly legitimate, of supernatural elements ; in other words, the conversion of it into dogma. What development there has been, has been a development of the foreign and unreal supernatural element, brought about by the effort of faith and traditional belief to defend themselves against the objections of the intellect, by means of scholastic distinctions, not always intelligible, which again make new demands on faith. St. Paul did indeed retain in substance the doctrine of Jesus as to the religious relation, but he very materially changed it in form by raising it into the supernatural sphere, by taking Jesus out of the ordinary conditions of humanity, and representing him not as the teacher, but as the mediating instrument of that relation ; thus sacrificing the simplicity which we instinctively feel to be befitting to that relation, and giving to it a circuitousness and intricacy which did not belong to it as taught by Jesus. In our view, the forms which the doctrine of Jesus subsequently assumed in canonical literature, were not so much developments as rather conversions of the subjective form of the religious process as taught by Jesus into an objective form, so as to meet the exigency of an age in which the supernatural idea dominated the thoughts of men ; to invest the doctrine with extraneous authority, and to render it palpable and impressive to popular imagination. And here, let it not be thought, that in returning to the simplicity of the doctrine of Jesus, the Church will take a reactionary step or lose the benefit of its varied and manifold experiences, and of its inner conflicts in the long past. On the contrary, we imagine that by deliberately and explicitly discharging from the religious sphere, the super-natural idea which Jesus implicitly and undesignedly declared not to be essential, the Church will greatly purify and enrich its thought, and probably initiate a new era in its history.

It may now occur to the reader that, up to this point, nothing has been said as to the presence of dogma in the great evolution of religious thought, which we have been tracing. For this apparent omission the reason is, that neither in the Old Testament nor in the synoptic Gospels is there such a thing as dogma proper, or, as it makes its appearance, as will immediately be seen, in the Pauline and post-Pauline epistles. The supernatural element of Old Testament theology appears in the form of myth, but does not shoot forth or blossom into dogma ; and the cause of this is evident. The legal view of the religious relation, which is predominant in the Old Testa-ment, does not postulate or further the dogmatic process. For in that view there was, or there seemed to be, nothing mys-terious—nothing that seemed to call for explanation. The legal seemed to be the natural relation between God and His creature, man—analogous to that which existed between man and man, or to that between master and servant, modified by the idea of the election. The legal view prevailed even in the Old Testament view of the forgiveness of sin ; for both sacrifice and repentance were only legal acts—natural means enjoined and sanctioned by God to propitiate His anger, and to effect the restoration of the sinner to His favour. Here all was plain and intelligible ; and the same may be said of the teaching of Jesus. The evangelical relation which Jesus taught was grounded or resident in the nature of God Himself, and was only the explication of his new conception of the divine char-acter. No propitiation was needed to bring the relation to good effect. Repentance itself was not a propitiatory work but merely the opening or turning of the mind to embrace the divine goodness, which was never suspended. But then, to men accustomed, as St. Paul *had been*, and as all men naturally are, to regard the religious relation from the legal point of view, the evangelical relation could not but seem to involve a great mystery. It was not easy for such to understand or to believe that God could forgive without some propitiatory service, even though such unconditional forgiveness was the very nerve of the evangelical idea. The difficulty which thus presented itself was got over, as will yet be shown, by representing the propitiation as made once for all by God Himself—*i.e.*, by an atonement offered by Christ, as Son of God, upon the cross. The dogma sprang from the endeavour to show how the new or evangelical relation was established and adjusted itself to the prior or legal relation. In the main this was accomplished by St. Paul, who was profoundly conscious, indeed, of the evangelical relation, but could not rest, as Jesus did, without further explanation, in the simple idea of the fatherliness of God. In truth, the great Apostle was only in part *intellectually* emancipated from the legal idea ; and by a stroke of genius he laid hold of the person of the risen Messiah, as the historical vehicle for giving concrete form to his compromise between that and the evangelical idea. What is here said enables us to understand why there is no demand, either in the Old Testament or in the synoptists, for anything corresponding to faith in the Pauline or dogmatic acceptation, and how it is nowhere said, in either the one or the other, that the foolishness of God is wiser than men ; or that the things of God are foolishness to the natural man (1 Cor. i. 25 ; ii. 14). Jesus, indeed, is represented as thanking God that He had hidden the Gospel mystery from the wise and prudent, but had revealed it to babes ; but we have pointed out elsewhere that, if these words are authentically reported, they bear a different meaning from that which favours the Pauline view.

The propriety of styling St. Paul a dogmatist, as above, can only be disputed, as it has been, by attaching a limited and very technical signification to the term. We feel ourselves perfectly warranted in speaking of a Pauline dogma, and in regarding it as the formless, or, catachrestically speaking, as the raw material which the Church in all subsequent ages has sought to systematize, to elaborate, and more or less to rationalize. The dogmatic element was present in the Pauline doctrine before it underwent any process or manipulation of this kind. The dogma arose in the Apostle's mind, in his endeavour to trace a hidden and mysterious connection between the new relation to God, of which he had become conscious in the moment of his conversion, and the death and resurrection of Jesus. To him it seemed as if that relation, instead of being founded in the nature of God and man, had been established historically by these events. The transference of this relation from the natural basis, on which it rested in the teaching of Jesus, to the historical, *i.e.*, supernatural basis, on which it was placed by St. Paul, was what gave it the dogmatic character.

Before proceeding to define more particularly the unique and creative position occupied by St. Paul in the history of Christian theology, we may here notice that Dr. C. Weizsäcker, who holds a place second to none among living theologians, approves the suggestion that side by side with St. Paul there were collaborateurs, more or less independent of him in the creation of the dogma, such as Apollos, Barnabas, Andronicus, Lysias, and others ; that these men dogmatized in a more mild and irenical spirit than St. Paul ; especially, we suppose, in the anthropological and soteriological field ; that they sought to resolve differences between Jewish and Gentile converts ; and that they may have paved the way for the introduction of forms of worship, for which St. Paul did not provide, or for that catholic ceremonial which has been called a revised edition of the Jewish ceremonial, and which gave to Gentile Christians a substitute for their ancestral religious customs. This is both a highly probable and highly interesting speculation, inasmuch as it enables us to conceive that the dogmatic evolution was not entirely the work of one man, and that it might have assumed a form and system not materially different from those of the orthodox Church, even though Paul had never been converted. At the same time, it must be said, that documentary grounds for this surmise, however probable in itself, are almost wholly wanting ; and we shall here speak of St. Paul as if his was the mind in which exclusively the dogmatic process took its rise and determinate direction.

We conceive of the great Apostle as a man of imperial intellect and force of character, thoroughly versed in the thought and literature of the Jewish people, and initiated also to a large extent in the thought and literature of Greece ; not capable, indeed, of rising, like Jesus, above the influence of his age and training, but still one of the highest typical specimens of our race, who, being caught up as in a whirlwind into a state of rapt devotion and enthusiasm, by the vivid revelation of the unseen world, and the sudden disclosure to his mind of the solution of the great soteriological problem, for which many men in all ages and countries had been yearning, was seized with the desire to communicate, as he best could, the same light and fervour to the world at large. His defect as a thinker was, that he could not, like Jesus, distinguish between what was essential and what was accidental, between what was permanent and what was transient, in the inherited faith of Israel. What was new in the doctrine of Jesus he could assimilate only under the forms of thought which had received the consecration of ages ; and even when, to use his own language (1 Cor. xiii. 10), that which was perfect was come, he could not strip from it the vestment which was proper only to the imperfect form. His dogma, whatever else may be said of it, was, as will yet be seen, a compromise between the old faith and the new—a survival of the earlier faith, which the new faith, though at war with it, could not cast out from his mind. But against this apparent defect in St. Paul's apprehension there has to be set the fact that he was enabled, partly in consequence of this very defect, to render a great service to Christianity. For it is just possible that the doctrine of Jesus, in its simple, calm, and somewhat jejune form, could not of itself have maintained its place in the world, nor have supplied the generating principle of a renovated society. But St. Paul, by retaining in connection with it some of the inherited forms of religious thought, at points where the continuity with these might otherwise have seemed to be broken, and by casting it into the historico-dogmatic form, in association with the person and life of Jesus, was enabled to procure for it an entrance into men's minds, besides rendering it level and impressive to the average or sensuous understanding, and giving to it that hold upon human sympathies and affections which it has never lost. We may thus say that, by a stroke of highest genius, the Apostle made good whatever was defective in his apprehension of the doc-trine of Jesus, and rendered to Christianity an important, and for many ages an indispensable, though probably what may yet prove to be a temporary, or merely provisional service.

According to what has now been said, the myth and the dogma may be considered as allied literary forms employed directly for the sensuous presentation of the Christian idea, and serving indirectly to furnish a sanction to the same. In the Old Testament both of these functions were fulfilled by the myth alone, while in the New Testament they are fulfilled by the myth and dogma conjointly. The character and prevailing forms of a mythical cycle are determined by the memories, the feelings, the usages, the genius, and ambitions of the people whose creation it is. In Judæa now, under what may be called prophetic influences, a strong ethical and religious aspiration was, as we have seen, superinduced upon the purely national and patriotic feeling. Hence the deeply religious character of the mythical cycle which had its origin in that country. The Jewish people we regard as the guardians or subjects of a great ethico-religious evolution, which took place among them in the course of their history. And it is easy to see that many circumstances combined to favour the growth of a mythical cycle as an accompaniment or by-product of that evolution. To refer here to but one of these, we say that the necessity must have been instinctively felt at every stage of that evolution, of making secure the point attained ; that is (to use a rabbinical expression), of supplying a " hedge," or sanction for the great moral and spiritual principles which had revealed themselves to the highest minds of the people, but were apt to degenerate into mere routine or literality, if not to be set aside by the " corrosive action " of the sceptical intellect, or still more by the " sophistry of the passions." In Israel this " hedge " was supplied unconsciously by the mythical creation, and for many ages was of great practical value ; but in the end, as has been shown, it concentrated attention upon itself, so as to draw off the thoughts of the people from the spirit of the law, for which it should have been a " protective covering," and resulted in the growth of a rigid Pharisaic legalism. It has been shown that at the juncture, when this result had fully worked itself out, Jesus undertook to break down the " hedge," and to bring into view the pure idea. But the time for this great step was not fully ripe, and the need of a " hedge " was again felt, even for the new revelation, and was supplied by the Church gene-

rally in the form of the synoptic myth, and by St. Paul and
his coadjutors in the form of the dogma which taught men to
regard Jesus as a divine messenger whose authority could not
be disputed, and whose death and resurrection were represented
as factors in the great redemption. But we write with the
conviction that, in this late age, the "hedge" of dogma and
myth may be supposed to have served its purpose, and requires
now to be removed once for all, that the pure idea may stand
forth in the power of its own light, and be made to bear
directly on the mind of man.

CHAPTER XIV.

CONVERSION OF ST. PAUL.

NEXT to the death and resurrection of Jesus no event has exercised a more decisive or more permanent influence on the fortunes of the Christian Church than the conversion of St. Paul. We propose therefore to bestow upon it an amount of attention proportioned to its importance. For which purpose we shall have, in the first place, to consider this event in itself and the circumstances by which it was brought about, or which help to explain it. Further on we shall have to return to it again, in order to show how the Apostle's understanding of it entered as a factor into his construction of the Pauline or orthodox dogma; and yet again, to show how it helps to explain the Apostle's antagonism to Jewish Christianity, and his championship of Christian liberty.

The personal intercourse of the first disciples with Jesus had, as we have seen, suggested to their minds a higher ideal of righteousness than that of the Pharisees. Then came the glorifying effect of his death, which, through the impulse given by it to the mythicizing process, tended to identify him with that ideal—to present him as its living impersonation, and helped, with the Messianic idea, to ally him in their minds with the divine nature. The feeling of this special alliance was what found expression in the mythical history, with its implicit dogmatic element. By means of this same feeling the ideas with which Jesus had enriched the thoughts of his disciples were invested with a divine sanction, as well as with a power of quickening their sympathies. The achievement now of St. Paul consisted in drawing out this vague dogmatic element into an explicit and definite form, and finding in it a symbol or sensuous representation of the abstract religious ideas of Jesus, at once relevant to the naïve theory of the universe, which was seldom questioned in that or for many succeeding ages, and also fitted, for that reason, to bring these ideas into powerful touch with human life, so long as the minds of men continued to be dominated by that theory.   Considering, then, the important position occupied by Paul with reference both to the evidence for the resurrection of Jesus, and to the genesis and development of the resulting dogma, it will be necessary to point out how he came to occupy that position, and how he contributed to the construction of orthodox Christianity : in other words, how he was converted to the new faith.

When we reject the supernatural cause of this great turning-point in the Apostle's life we cannot regard it as the effect produced on his mind by the testimony of the original disciples to the resurrection of Jesus.   There is no doubt, at least, that for a time he gave no credit to their testimony, the time, we mean, during which he continued to persecute them.   It is conceivable, indeed, that the fortitude of the disciples and their martyr patience under persecution may at length have told upon him, and, convincing him of their sincerity, have overcome his disbelief.   But the spectacle thus presented to him was not likely to operate upon a man who, like St. Paul, felt himself capable of a like self-devotion to his own faith.   Like many persecutors, he was made of the stuff of which martyrs are made, and he may have seen no indication of a divine influence in the self-devotion of his victims.   Further, we have already shown that to supplement the evidential value of their own testimony to the resurrection of their crucified Master, the primitive disciples had recourse to certain passages of the Old Testament which seemed to contemplate the death and resurrection of the Messiah.   And it is evident from 1 Cor. xv. 3, 4, that, in dealing with his hearers, St. Paul borrowed or adopted the same mode of persuasion.   But it does not follow from this fact that the line of reasoning thus founded on the scriptures was the producing cause of his own conversion, any more than that it was what produced faith in the resurrection on the part of his predecessors in the gospel.   The presumption is that he was as little touched by their appeal to the Old Testament as by their own testimony to the resurrection.   And the probability is, that conviction was brought home to his mind from quite another source, very distinct from either of these, by which an end was at once put to his persecuting zeal, and a totally new direction was impressed upon his life. It has appeared that the deep impression made upon the first disciples by the personality of Jesus was what issued in their belief in his resurrection. But we propose to make it appear that in the case of St. Paul the initiative was given to faith by his experience or consciousness of the emancipating power of the doctrine of Jesus. In other words, the grand impression was made on the original disciples by the personality of Jesus and not by the principle which he represented. In the case of St. Paul, on the other hand, it was the principle taught and represented by Jesus which produced the revelation in his mind, and it was only mediately, though simultaneously, that the person of Jesus was glorified to his imagination, and all doubt as to the Messiahship and resurrection was removed from his mind. These two points being once established to the Apostle's satisfaction, we can easily understand how his mind might be predisposed to find allusions to them in the Old Testament, and to disregard all critical objections, whether grammatical or historical, to the soundness and value of the prophetic proof, of which, as being level and impressive to the average mind, he proceeded to make use in his great work of winning adherents to the gospel. We have yet, therefore, to point out what we consider to have been the efficient cause of St. Paul's own conversion.

As we are not entitled to suppose that Peter and his companions were rescued from their state of despondency by the Christophanies of which we read in the synoptists, so we are as little entitled to suppose that Saul the persecutor was converted by a like phenomenon into Paul the Apostle and Confessor. It is true that St. Paul himself regarded his conversion as wholly supernatural—as an act of God, quite independent of any will or predisposition of his own ; as much so, indeed, as his birth (Gal. i. 15). But we are obliged to take quite a different view of that great turning-point in his history, were it for no other reason than to preserve the continuity of his spiritual life, and to get rid, in his case, as in the case of the earlier disciples, of the intrusion of a non-rational and non-conditioned element. His experience was yet, we believe, in many ways different from the experience of the earlier disciples, just as his mental constitution and his previous training were different. He tells us himself that he had been a Pharisee, *i.e.*, instructed in Pharisaic doctrine, and trained under Pharisaic influence to the Pharisaic form of life. At the same time he had, at an early period, adopted a more spiritual interpretation of the law than was customary among these religionists. We may confidently infer that such was the case if we understand, as we are certainly entitled to do, that in the seventh chapter of the Epistle to the Romans he is describing or alluding to his own experience, not after, but before his conversion. or, we may rather say, before as well as after that event. What he there says of covetousness, and of the law in the members warring against the law of the mind, gives us the idea that his outward blamelessness, and his zeal for the law of God—in a word, the righteousness which he cultivated in common with other Pharisees, and of which he could and did boast, did not satisfy the demands of his own conscience. There still remained in him that restlessness of soul, that sense of an aching void in the heart, that vague yearning for something unattained or unattainable, which is an experience familiar to men, though seldom acute as in him. The likelihood is that, in his deep earnestness, he was seeking, as many like-minded in all ages have done, to reach forward to a spiritual ideal, and to terminate that inward strife between the evil toward which his mind gravitated, and the good of which he approved. His first and most natural effort for this end would be to hold on to Pharisaic methods ; to try the effect of a more and more rigid observance of the law, and of the traditional and conventional usages of his nation. But a glimpse of the higher ideal would be enough at any moment to destroy his satisfaction in such a course, and to rouse within him that persecuting zeal which he himself (Phil. iii. 6) significantly conjoins with the mention of his legal blamelessness. In contact with the disciples whom he persecuted, he had, we may believe, learned enough of the doctrine of Jesus to recognize in it a competing method of righteousness, which, just because it claimed to be a better method than that to which he had devoted himself (Matth. v. 20), and because it suggested that he was in the wrong way altogether, disturbed his peace—made him uneasy, by the introduction of painful doubts into his mind, and roused in him in revenge a spirit of intolerance. It was to give vent to this feeling, and to show his veneration and his fidelity to the law of God, that he " breathed out threatenings and slaughters " against those who professed to follow that other method. He had probably asked himself, as the young Pharisee is said to have asked Jesus, What more he should do to inherit the kingdom of God ? *i.e.*, what thing more than he had already done ; what more perfect compliance with the legal requirements—a question which must often have pressed itself upon zealous Israelites, and have played an important part, as we have seen, in the multiplication of the legal requirements—and he may have persuaded himself that, to persecute and extirpate the followers of him who was accused of making void the law, besides soothing the feeling of irritation and disquietude which they occasioned to him, would also be a supreme proof of devotion to the cause of righteousness. We imagine him to have been in their state of mind of whom the poet has said, they " thought more grace to gain if . . . . they wrestled down Feelings their own nature strove to own." He may have fought hard to stifle his own better instincts, and to acquire, like other persecutors, a higher merit in the sight of God, by doing violence to the more humane and charitable feelings, and by turning a deaf ear to the misgivings incited in him by his intercourse with the disciples, and by the glimpse thus afforded him of a higher rule than the Pharisaic. Agitating and torturing doubts as to the safety and rightfulness of such a course could not but assail his mind, and well might the heavenly voice, which but gave utterance to his own feelings, say to him at length, " It is hard for thee to kick against the pricks." A conflict so lacerating to conscience, and to all the higher nature of a man of Paul's scrupulous integrity and loving disposition, could not last. A moment came in which his passionate resolution to cling to the old religion, his obstinate hostility to the new broke down—a crisis in which the competing and better righteousness, which Jesus had taught and exemplified, disclosed its intrinsic superiority to his mind, placed him in an entirely new relation to God, and opened up to him the prospect of higher attainment, through the idea of that divine forgiveness which, if not entirely discarded in the Pharisaic doctrine, was at least inconspicuous and inoperative, crowded out in that complex and conventional directory of conduct.

According to the doctrine of Jesus, forgiveness stands in no relation to expiation of any kind, in which sense it is wholly unconditional. And it was by catching a sight of this doctrine, which involved an entirely new view of the religious relation, that Paul was converted, though, as will yet be seen, he did not clearly apprehend that it was so. To say, therefore, with Dr. Matheson (*The Spiritual Development of St. Paul*), that after the Apostle's conversion he fled into Arabia " to win forgiveness by personal expiation," is as much as to say that at his conversion he had not received so much as an elementary idea of the evangelical doctrine, the very essence of which is that it excludes the idea of expiation, whether by God or by man himself. The revelation to the Apostle's mind of the new relation was the point from which his whole subsequent development naturally and logically proceeded ; whereas, to say, with Dr. Matheson, that St. Paul's development proceeded from his " vision of Christ in glory," is the purest supernaturalism, depriving the Apostle's development of a rational, *i.e.*, a spiritual basis, and turning it upside down. To regard the vision of Christ in glory, in whatever sense, as anything more than an accompaniment or byproduct of the real conversion, and to trace to it the development of the Apostle's dogmatic and ethical views, is to throw the whole history into confusion. It is only by completely ignoring the results of critical investigation and by the lawless play of a tortuous ingenuity, exegetical and other, that an air of plausibility has been given to this hypothesis. To our mind, Dr. Matheson's eloquent volume is one of many which prove how little, even at this day, the spirit of modern criticism has told upon some of the best minds amongst us.

To the ardent, sanguine, and consequent mind of the Apostle, the Christian principle, of which he caught a glimpse, could not remain indifferent, but must exert either a repellent or an attractive force, and if attractive, it could not but take entire possession of his soul, and become the chief determinant of his inner life. Moreover, as the new idea was indissolubly associated with the person of the Crucified One, who, as was confidently reported, had been seen again by his disciples, it is perfectly conceivable that in the case of a man like Paul, constitutionally epileptic, or subject to some species of hysteria, the moral and intellectual crisis may have been accompanied by some vision, or apparition, or startling flash of light, which would be considered by him as identical with the vision to which the sect which he persecuted was accustomed to appeal. In this way, the spiritual movement which, as we have seen, had commenced independently in Paul's mind, just as it has commenced in the minds of many other men, was attracted by, or, we may say, taken up, or drawn into, that other movement with which he had been brought into close connection by his persecuting zeal, and against whose magnetic influence he had struggled with frantic violence, but in vain. For " Im Streit vollzieht sich derselbe Wesensaustausch, wie in der Liebe." We take the conversion of St. Paul to have been an exemplification of the strange, but not uncommon, phenomenon of a man yielding unconsciously, and in spite of himself, to the encroachment of ideas, which he endeavours and seems violently to resist.

There can be no doubt that the great crisis in St. Paul's life, if not, as he himself thought, produced, was at least accompanied by a vision of some kind or other, and it is necessary for us to determine, as far as we can, the nature of the phenomenon, and also the place which it occupied in the genesis and development of orthodox Christianity. There does not appear to us to be any good reason for supposing that Paul ever saw " Christ in the flesh," that is to say, Jesus in his lifetime, so that in his vision there could in no respect be a recognition of the personal appearance of Jesus. A sense of this seems to be indicated in the mythical narrative of Paul's conversion in the Acts of the Apostles, where he is represented as requiring to ask, " Who art thou, Lord ? " and as receiving the reply, " I am Jesus, whom thou persecutest." What we do know with certainty is that Paul himself *thought* he had had a vision of the risen Jesus. Beyond this all is uncertain, as any one must admit who has looked into the subject and compared the various accounts of his conversion. The result of such a comparison is to convince us of the impossibility of determining from these accounts what actually took place.

The several narratives of the incident given in the Acts of the Apostles (one of them by the author of the book, and the other two by St. Paul himself, *as there reported*), do not tally with each other, but differ considerably in various particulars, and are probably made up, to an indeterminable extent, of mythical elements. The differences in point of detail may seem to be very minute, and not inconsistent with substantial harmony; but certain it is that no two independent critics will agree as to how the several narratives may be combined into one consistent history.

In all three narratives it is said that Paul fell to the ground, while in one of them it is said that all the men with him also fell to the ground, but in the other two they are said to have remained standing. No mention is made of Paul's having seen any figure; indeed, it seems from all the narratives as if before or in the act of falling he only saw a great light, and as if his prostrate attitude and the blinding light would prevent him from seeing any figure whatever—a view which is confirmed by the circumstance that the men who journeyed with him, and who are said by two accounts to have remained erect while Paul was prostrate, saw no man. In one narrative it is said that they heard the voice, and in another that they saw the light, but did not hear the voice. These are some of the discrepancies, and if we try to remove or reconcile these discrepancies, we may best succeed in doing so by supposing that the apparitors saw the light, but no figure in it, and that they heard a noise, which they took to be the sound of a voice, without being able to distinguish the words —a combination of circumstances which suggests the idea of a flash of lightning and a peal of thunder, or some other natural phenomenon, which, by its sudden and awe-inspiring nature, may have helped, in the distracted and conflicting state of Paul's mind, to precipitate the crisis of his life. But the more probable explanation of these discrepancies is that the details of the one historic moment of the vision were all mythical; various representations of an event which in itself was mysterious and indescribable. For not only do the several narratives differ apparently or materially from each other, but what is more important to observe is, that they do not seem to bear out the authentic declaration of Paul himself, that he had seen the Lord (1 Cor. xv. 8). For in these narratives it is only said that he saw a dazzling, blinding light, and heard words spoken to him by some one, calling him by name, reproaching him for his persecuting conduct, and, according to one account, advising him of his mission to the Gentiles. It has also to be noted that, while different versions are given of the words uttered by the voice on the occasion, there is every appearance as if most or all of the words were supplied by a plastic imagination, seeking unconsciously to clothe the bare facts, whatever they may have been, with appropriate circumstance and colour. They may be regarded as the literary or dramatic interpretation which Paul himself, or the Church at large, or, lastly, the author of the Acts, put upon the divine purpose in so suddenly and marvellously calling him. In confirmation of this view it will be observed that in one of the narratives the words imputed to the voice give a striking description of the work to which Paul afterwards devoted himself, of the mission which dawned upon him, when he had time to reflect on his situation, and to construe the significance of what had befallen him. They might be an after-thought, put either by himself or by the annalist into an appro-priate form of words, such as genuine feeling or a clear intelligence seldom fails to suggest, expressive of that concep-tion of his mission, which afterwards unfolded itself to his mind, as marked out for him by the divine power which had called and converted him, and dramatically represented as spoken to him in the very moment of crisis.

Or, again, the words said to have been heard and uttered by St. Paul on the occasion may be explained by the reflex action of Paul's mind at the moment—an action which might affect the sense of hearing as well as the sense of sight. Here all is conjecture, and we do not pretend to decide between these two views. Whoever, indeed, seeks carefully to take all the data into consideration, and to reflect upon them, will hesitate to pronounce an opinion very definitely or very oracularly upon the subject. But these narratives taken by themselves, and still more when taken in conjunction with Paul's own authentic declaration, that Christ had been seen by him, along with his description of the vision as a revelation of Christ *in* him (Gal. i. 16), make the impression upon our minds that the whole phenomenon was subjective, and happened to himself exclu-sively ; that the figure which he saw, or thought he saw, was an unsubstantial fabric, a painting of the mind's eye ; and that the words which he is said to have heard, if heard at all, were heard by the inward ear.

One thing we may regard as conclusively settled, viz., that Paul's conversion was sudden and abrupt only in appearance—the natural sequel or issue of a process which had been going on in his mind, possibly from a time anterior to his acquaintance with the life and doctrine of Jesus. The probability is, that his intercourse with the disciples, however unfriendly on his part, had rendered acute that vague unrest, those unsatisfied longings, that sense of self-dissatisfaction which his zeal for the law had failed to soothe or to compose. The glimpse he derived from them of the higher form of righteousness disturbed his Pharisaic self-complacency, and introduced torturing doubts into his mind. To suppress these doubts and misgivings he resorted, as already said, to persecution of the followers of the new faith, which shook his confidence in the old faith; and offered himself as an eager, though reluctant and compulsory, instrument to carry out the behests of the Sanhedrim.

But a method, which appears to have been successful in the case of many religionists, like Queen Isabella, Maria Theresa, and Madame De Maintenon, failed in his case to silence his misgivings and to restore his mental composure. We suppose that the victorious elation of the disciples in the midst of persecution only exasperated that conflict by which his soul was torn and distracted, and it was the painful consciousness of this fact which clothed itself in those remarkable words of the voice which he heard with the inward, if not with the outward ear, " It is hard for thee to kick against the pricks." Hard, indeed, it must have been to a man of his sensitive and religious mind. In defying and resisting those inward remonstrances he could not but dread that he was fighting against God, a dread which we know from various notices in the Acts of the Apostles was not uncommon at that time of spiritual convulsion. A fine feeling of the situation in which St. Paul was placed may have suggested to the mythicist or the annalist the dramatic articulation of the voice. But we are disposed, on psychological grounds, to believe that the above words may have been audible to the inward ear of the persecutor in the very moment of crisis; that they rose within him as the expression of a feeling which, up to that moment, he had striven to keep down, but which now broke through his power of self-control, and came upon him as if given utterance to by a voice from without.

Not the least remarkable circumstance connected with the conversion of Paul is the fact, implied not only in the Acts of the Apostles but also in his Epistles, that he felt himself from the first called to be an Apostle to the Gentiles. This fact has been thought by many theologians, and among others by Baur apparently, to add much to the marvellous character of his conversion. The comprehension of the Gentiles in the kingdom of God was an idea so remote from all his previous modes of thought, so little indicated even in the teaching of Jesus, and so distasteful to those who preceded the Apostle in the gospel, that his faith in it, which seems to have been almost simultaneous with his conversion, has been looked upon as inexplicable, except on the supposition of a mysterious communication of it to his mind. Yet, if we consider it well, we shall perceive that even this faith was no abrupt or unmediated bound of thought. We cannot suppose that it broke away from all his previous experience, or stood in no continuity with his past way of thinking. To show that this was not the case, Weizsäcker advances the hypothesis, that, even previous to his conversion, the Apostle had been much occupied with the hope of the general gathering of the Gentiles into the Jewish fold, that his persecuting zeal was provoked by the idea that the rise of the Christian sect and its spread into the adjoining provinces was calculated to frustrate or defer this great object of Jewish hope, and that, on the instant of his conversion, the new faith disclosed itself to him as the true means of converting and gathering in the heathen world. Now, it may be, that some such hope, encouraged by prophetic hints, may have been entertained by Philo, and other earnest and aspiring spirits among the Jews of the dispersion. But theirs was not the hope of St. Paul ; they looked simply for an extension of the Jewish rite. But the hypothesis is, that St. Paul turned from Judaism to the Christian doctrine, because the latter seemed to open the prospect of a universal religion, in which the distinction between Jew and Gentile should have no place. He perceived in Christian doctrine some element, the absence of which in Judaism blocked the way to its universal diffusion. And it is to his perception of this element that we have to ascribe both his conversion, and his recognition of the universalistic tendencies of the new doctrine. In other words, we take his universalism to be a necessary deduction from the element, his perception of which was the immediate cause of his conversion. And we have to inquire what that element was.

Before his conversion he no doubt felt, in common with all the Pharisaic opponents of Jesus, that the new doctrine was calculated to "destroy the law," to "change the customs" delivered by Moses to the people, to annul Jewish privilege, and so to place all the nations of the earth on the same level of religious equality in the sight of God. This feeling was what

constituted "the offence of the cross" to the Jewish mind
(Gal. v. 11), and was the very nerve of Jewish and Pharisaic
opposition to the infant church.   For a man educated and
indoctrinated as the Apostle had been, it was at once a religious
and a patriotic feeling, and served, in a great measure, to
palliate his persecuting zeal, and to justify him in saying that
he had acted in ignorance.   But in becoming a follower of
Jesus, he must have been sensible that he could only be true to
the faith by accepting its consequences, logical as well as penal;
and it is only what we should expect from his thorough-going
character and sanguine temperament, that after his conversion
he should labour with all his might to give prominence to the
anti-Judaic universalistic aspect of Christianity, *i.e.*, to that very
aspect of it which had previously embittered his antipathy, and
that he should recognize the apostleship to the Gentiles as the
mission to which he was specially called.   The same effect was
not produced by the new faith on the minds of Peter and the
earlier disciples, because in them the exclusive and Pharisaic
spirit had not been so intensified, as it was in the case of Paul,
by his training in the schools.   They did not feel as he did the
irreconcilable antagonism between Pharisaism and the spirit of
Jesus; and the resultant form of their religion was a sort of compromise or amalgamation between the old and the new spirit.
But with Paul there could here be no compromise.   The
Pharisaic, or specially Jewish and exclusive spirit, was completely broken in him by his conversion, and forced to give way
to that of universalism, which was perceived by his clear intelligence to be the direct consequence or corollary of the doctrine
of Jesus.

There is then a probability that the grandeur of this thought
of universalism, or of the equality of men without distinction of
race in the sight of God, which was seen by St. Paul to flow
from the doctrine of Jesus, was one of the determining causes
of his conversion.   This grand idea may have flashed upon
his mind suddenly in the very crisis of his fate, and may have
inspired him with the consciousness of his mission.   Certainly
no greater thought than this has ever inspired the soul of man;
nor could Paul himself better indicate the significance of his
conversion than by speaking of it as a call or summons,
addressed to him by Christ in person, to devote himself to the
ministry of the Gentiles.   The fact that he was, or believed

himself to be, the sole depositary of this grand truth, imposed upon him the personal obligation to proclaim it to the world, and he could say, as he afterwards said, "Woe is me if I preach not (this) Gospel." The necessity thus imposed upon him was analogous to that to which Jesus himself bowed with awful joy in undertaking the Messianic rôle.

Yet it were a great mistake to suppose, as some have done, that the universalistic tendency of Christianity was a new character stamped upon it by the genius of Paul, and that had he not been converted to the faith, and had he not delivered his contribution to its development, Christianity might have settled down into a modified form of Judaism. This tendency, though, for reasons already glanced at, not emphasized or insisted on by Jesus himself, was evidently germinant from the first in his doctrine, and sooner or later the discovery was sure to be made by his disciples, that it was the very nature of his religion to burst the swaddling bands of Judaism in order to unfold its true character, and to enter upon a world-wide career of its own. Apart altogether from the reasoning of Paul upon the subject which, though laboured, is not always lucid, or as level to the modern mind as it may have been to the ancient Jewish mind, it must soon have become apparent that the central principles of Jesus involved the universalistic idea. Accordingly, if we may here trust to the evidence of the Acts of the Apostles, St. Paul's views were to some extent anticipated and given expression to by the proto-martyr Stephen, at whose death Paul was a consenting spectator, and whose dying testimony even may have reached his ears, and have helped, with other things, to direct his attention to this feature of the new religion. Many years ago it was pointed out for the first time by Dr. F. Baur, the great critic, whose investigation of the history of the early Church formed an epoch in the historico-theological domain, that Stephen was in this respect a precursor of St. Paul. The universalistic tendency was, indeed, an element so essential and intrinsic to the religion of Jesus, that only the veil of Jewish prejudice, not taken away even from his immediate disciples, could for a time have obscured it ; but it could not possibly have remained a secret to the more liberalized and open-minded Jews and Hellenists among its converts, to say nothing of its converts among the heathen. We are disposed to regard the account of St. Stephen, and the report of his speech, as a genuine fragment

z

of apostolic history, just because it contains a pre-Pauline, yet not very distinct or explicit testimony to the intrinsic universalism of the religion of Jesus. It seems to show what we might naturally expect—that the thought to which St. Paul gave clear expression had previously dawned darkly in the minds of still earlier disciples, because it lay in the very nature of the new doctrine. But thus much may be conceded to the honour of St. Paul, that his dialectical genius peculiarly qualified him to establish and to make plain to popular apprehension the anti-Judaic and universalistic aspect of the Christian doctrine, as well as to engage in the minutiæ of a discussion or controversy, which was not suited to the authoritative and peremptory tone with which Jesus directly addressed the religious instincts of his hearers.

The rise of the universalistic idea in the Christian community has been accounted for by saying that " the time had come when the human spirit was to make this momentous advance," that universalism was " the goal to which the history of the world had been tending for centuries," and that the universalism of Christianity " necessarily pre-supposes the universalism of the Roman Empire, and could never have become part of the general consciousness of the nations, had not political universalism prepared the way for it." In spite, however, of the great authority with which these propositions are advanced, and the general acceptance which they have met, we regard them as specimens of a sort of generalization in which the philosophy of history delights, but which must be received with much qualification. It is very doubtful whether the union of the Roman Empire was ever, as Dr. Baur says, " a bond of mental sympathy," or whether the different races of men could ever have been drawn together by any political movements whatever. It is the religious sentiment in its pure and spiritual form, as it exists in Christianity, that could alone have had force to bring the universalistic idea into full light. In the political sphere it is the selfish and ambitious principles of our nature which seek to force on a factitious universalism, which is really particularism ; whereas it is the principle of true humanity, as set forth in Christianity, that tends towards a real universalism. The distinction and glory of Christianity is, that it substituted a true and practicable universalism of freedom for the unreal universalism of slavery, which Assyrian, Persian, Greek, and Roman genius in succession had blindly and fruitlessly striven to impose on the world ; and it was through the influence of Christianity that the idea arose amid the ruins of these empires ; for there can be no doubt that the world-historical character and destiny of its religion was divined by the Church at a very early period, giving to its confessors and martyrs the feeling that they, and not their persecutors, were the true conquerors, and bracing them for the agonizing effort which was requisite for laying the foundation of a universal empire of the Spirit. The universalism of Christianity was grounded on the great principle of the Fatherhood of God, or, let us say, the brotherhood of man. That of the Roman Empire was grounded on no principle whatever : it was the mere outcome of party struggles and of political exigencies. Merivale says that the Romans " unconsciously formed their subjects into one nation." But the idea of universalism was an element of the Christian consciousness from the very first. And finally, " the bond of mental sympathy " among the Romans was not only weak at the best, but neither embraced all ranks within the Empire, nor any people beyond its limits. In the Christian Church, on the other hand, that " bond " embraced the whole human family without distinction, and was a mighty engine for the conversion of the world. The political and religious ideas were, in short, so little akin, that the one could scarcely have " prepared the way " for the other.

If, then, it be asked to whom the credit must be assigned of starting the idea of universalism, we reply that it belongs to Jesus, seeing that the idea is intrinsic to his doctrine. The miraculous element may be disjoined from Christianity, as we are now endeavouring to show, but the universalistic element is so constituent of Christianity as not to admit of being dissociated from it. In proclaiming the Fatherhood of God and the inwardness of righteousness, Jesus, without having to say so, laid the foundation of a universal religion. The fact that he regarded himself as the Messiah, and several of his sayings placed on record by the synoptists, may seem indeed to give some countenance to the allegation that he did not clearly realize or anticipate the universalistic range and tendency of his reforming efforts ; and, by way of showing that Paul rather than Jesus was the author of all that was new and distinctive in our religion, this allegation has been eagerly

made use of by many of the modern assailants of Christianity.
Of these assailants (outside the ranks of the materialists) the
most recent and most radical is E. von Hartmann. But,
strangely enough, Dr. B. Weiss, one of the ablest and most
recent of modern apologists, has adopted the view that " Jesus
was not fully aware of the universalistic tendency of his own
teaching and action   .   .   .   and that the Christian religion,
while intrinsically fitted and destined to become a world-wide
faith, nevertheless took its rise in the mind of a man who
deemed himself merely the Messiah of Israel, having it for
his vocation to set up in the holy land the theocratic kingdom
of Hebrew prophecy, embracing among its citizens all men of
Jewish birth, and as many from the Gentiles as were willing to
become proselytes."

The fact that Dr. Weiss has espoused this view may
probably have weighed with E. von Hartmann in pronouncing
his analysis of the doctrine of Jesus to be the best which has
come under his notice. At all events it is a point on which
he has the distinguished apologist on his side. But, in spite
of the assailant and the apologist, we hold it to be utterly
incredible that Jesus could have been unconscious of the universalistic drift and tendency of his doctrine. Dr. Bruce,
whose description of Dr. Weiss' position we have quoted, says
well (*Miraculous Element*, etc., p. 331), that the doctrines of
Jesus, viz., the doctrine of God as the heavenly Father, and the
doctrine of man as made in the image of God, "are the fundamental truths of a universal religion"; and " who can believe
that the man who could discover these two fundamental truths,
and perceive that they were fundamental, could not also understand their implications and consequences, especially one so
obvious as that of religious universalism ? " It may be said,
indeed, that the man who first discovers and states a principle
may not, and perhaps never does, perceive the remoter consequences which it involves. But it should be borne in mind
that the doctrine of Jesus related exclusively to that which is
universal and highest in man ; that so far as can be seen from
the synoptists, he exhibited by his conduct and practice a
marked disregard and disrespect for those particularistic rites
and forms, and for that claim to descent from Abraham, the
friend of God, which differentiated the Jews from all other
people ; and finally, that so far as his teaching was specially

addressed to his countrymen, it was polemical and antithetic ; but that so far as this polemical character was absent from it, his teaching might be taken to heart by all men, without distinction. We may, therefore, infer that in his view his Jewish countrymen were merged in the one common mass of humanity so far as religion was concerned. The universalistic, or, let us call it, the levelling character of his doctrine lay too near, too much on the surface, to be overlooked by him. The fact that St. Paul perceived the universalistic bearing of the doctrine so instantaneously on his conversion, inclines us to believe that this aspect of it could not have escaped the observation of him from whom the apostle derived it. The strength of Jewish prejudice, and the vanity of Jewish assumption, from which Jesus was free, were what blinded the Jewish Christians generally to the universalistic character of the new religion. And though Jesus did not, like Paul, give prominence and emphasis to this aspect of it, we may yet confidently regard it as an integral part of his system of thought ; for, as Prof. Butcher, speaking of Aristotle, says (*Some Aspects of the Greek Genius*, p. 235), " It is not unfair in dealing with so coherent a thinker, to credit him with seeing the obvious conclusions which flow from his principles, even though he has not formally stated them." It is upon such general considerations as these, rather than upon any doubtful appeal to particular expressions and incidents in the synoptists, that we rely to show that Jesus could not have been unconscious of the universalism of his doctrine.

But while we firmly regard the reasoning of Dr. Bruce on this subject as conclusive, we dissent from him when he proceeds, by way of confirming his judgment, to ask, " How could Jesus have had insight into these (fundamental) truths unless he had first had a vision of the kingdom of God, not confined to one land or nation, but cosmopolitan in character, opening its gates to all on equal terms." This question implies an inversion of the true order of the thought of Jesus. For, if the idea of a universal kingdom of God came *first* (*i.e.* before the other two fundamental ideas to which Dr. Bruce refers) within the sphere of the mental vision of Jesus, we must ask whence Jesus could derive the idea of such a kingdom, which evidently lies beyond the range of immediate consciousness. Few apologetic theologians at the present day will venture to say that he derived it from special or supernatural inspiration, were it for no other reason than that to say so would make all previous development of that idea in Israel of no account. As little could he have derived it from the prophetic scriptures of the Old Testament, in which, with many utterances indicative of a tendency towards universalism (which, however, did not go beyond the standpoint of the Jewish Christians of a later age), the kingdom of God was essentially particularistic: the enlargement, in a purified form, of the Jewish state. Failing this derivation, we should be thrown upon the hypothesis of Dr. Baur, that the religious universalism of Jesus presupposed, or was in some way derived from the political universalism of the Empire; in which case we should still have to inquire whence the idea of the divine fatherhood had been derived, to which the political universalism can hardly be said to bring us any nearer. But, in truth, the effect of this view of Dr. Bruce is, as already said, to invert and derange the genetic order of the thought of Jesus. Dr. Bruce seems here to have inadvertently fallen into a mistake similar to that which Carlyle corrects in his *Latter Day Pamphlets:* "Not because heaven existed did men know good and evil . . . it was because men felt the difference between good and evil that heaven and hell first came to exist." The difference between good and evil is perceived directly by the human consciousness, whereas the notions of heaven and hell are derivative. So we may suppose that Jesus obtained his view of righteousness directly from his consciousness, and all that he said concerning the kingdom of God came from that and after that, and probably contained little or nothing beyond that.

The nascent, but halting universalism, which is, undoubtedly, discernible in the prophets of Israel, was coincident with, and inseparable from their ethicizing of the conception of Jehovah. And we cannot help thinking that with his more advanced ethicizing of the same conception a fully developed and unqualified universalism could not have been strange to the mind of Jesus. We have endeavoured to show in a previous portion of this discussion that the insight of Jesus into the spiritual nature of man's true righteousness was what led up to his vision of the divine fatherhood, stripped of the particularism and exclusiveness which attached to it in the Old Testament, and both together revealed to him the kingdom of God open to all men as men, "apart from all external accessories," and "without distinction of race, customs, or religious forms of any kind." This we believe to have been the true order of his thought, so far as we may speak of a succession where the consciousness of all may have been simultaneous.

We say, therefore, that the idea of the all-embracing kingdom of God must have come upon Jesus, not first, but as a consequence of those others: a consequence so plainly and intimately connected with those others that he could not possibly have been unaware of the connection: a consequence so plain and intimate indeed that he might, without anxiety, and calmly, leave it with much else to disclose itself, as self-evident to the minds of his disciples. The doctrine of Jesus could not possibly have been confined within the narrow limits of Jewish exclusiveness. The new wine could not but burst the old bottles. The universalism of St. Paul flowed directly from the spiritual form of religion of which Jesus was the discoverer. The reserve or hesitation apparent in the synoptic language of Jesus, as afterwards in the conduct of the chief apostles, and in the attitude of Jewish Christians generally, may have been due to the imperfect intelligence or sympathy of his personal followers who reported his words. It disappears entirely in the language of St. Paul, as where he says (Rom. iii. 29), " Is He the God of the Jews only? Is He not also of the Gentiles? Yes, of the Gentiles also." To the Jews pertained, as the Apostle elsewhere says, the adoption, the glory, the covenants, the giving of the law, the service of God, the promises, the fathers, and the Christ. But not all these advantages together gave to them any exclusive or preferential claim to consider Him as their God. The universalism to which St. Paul thus gave emphatic utterance became, in the hands of the fourth Evangelist, one of the items or factors in a new revision of the life and teaching of Jesus. And it may be added, before passing from this subject, that an idea of such general human and philosophical interest could not be confined to the Christian community, but would find its way into the intellectual atmosphere and be caught up by thinkers like Seneca and Juvenal, and so pass, in a modified form, into the common thought of the age, which had, indeed, to some extent, been prepared for its reception by the teaching of the Stoics.

Having thus endeavoured to explain that call to the apostle-ship of the Gentiles which St. Paul thought he had received at the moment of his conversion, and its bearing on the universalism of Christianity, we now return to the more par-ticular consideration of that great crisis of his life. In reality, it was the result of the impression made upon his mind by what he had learned of the doctrine, life, and death of Jesus, from common report, or from the victims of his persecuting zeal. He himself declares, no doubt, that he received his knowledge of the gospel and his call to the apostleship, not from man, but by direct revelation from Jesus Christ. But we can easily understand how that should be his view of the matter. His intercourse with the disciples being of a hostile controversial kind, and his knowledge of their opinions being fragmentary and disjointed, he could hardly view these as the channels of the truth to his mind ; and the instantaneousness with which the scattered hints arranged themselves into one connected view of the religious relation, and brought a sense of deliverance to his mind, could hardly but present itself to his imagination as a supernatural experience. For, a super-natural character is imparted to any sudden revolution in the religious sphere, or indeed, to any phenomenon whatever, if we lose out of sight or are unable to supply some link in the chain of natural causation. But to us no link seems wanting to account for the crisis in Paul's life. We conceive of it as being preceded by a period, however short, of oscilla-tion in his mind between sympathy and antipathy towards that new view of the religious relation which had come to his knowledge by hints and snatches in his contact with the disciples. And it set in at the moment at which the attrac-tion, exerted upon him by those scattered hints, overcame or counterbalanced the repulsion or offence which they occasioned to his Jewish prejudices as being a death-blow to his view of Jewish privilege, and to the Pharisaic ideals which had given the bent to his mind.

In mental conflict with the new doctrine, he succumbed to its power, he was infected by its spirit. Up to this event-ful moment he had given no credit to the testimony of the disciples respecting the resurrection. Indeed, the claims of Jesus to be the Messiah were so much discredited by his igno-minious death that no amount of testimony would have satisfied the Apostle that Jesus had been raised from the dead, at least by a divine power. Not even the martyr-spirit of the witnesses, impressive as it was, sufficed to satisfy him of that; for probably he was even then of the opinion which he expressed at a later period, that a man might give his body to be burned without being a friend of God, and without giving thereby a proof of the truth of his testimony. He may even have been conscious that he could himself have witnessed unto death for the traditions of the fathers to which the alleged death of the Messiah seemed to be at variance. But his disbelief of the resurrection was dissipated by his sudden and independent perception of the unique grandeur of the life and death of Jesus, and of the perfect beauty of his teaching, as well as of its complete adaptation to the deepest needs and aspirations of his own soul. The vision, or phenomenon, which was the main content of his consciousness at the decisive moment, was a merely collateral result or by-effect, depending on his exceptional mental or physical idiosyncrasy. It was the form which the crisis or turning-point in his life assumed, or in which it asserted itself to his own consciousness—the channel into which it was directed by the current report, that the great teacher and martyr had risen again from the dead and showed himself openly to his disciples. And without anticipating too far what has yet to be said, we may here observe, that the indubitable occurrence of this startling phenomenon to St. Paul may have helped to confirm and to disseminate the belief already current in the previous apparitions, though, according to our theory, these were not really of the nature of visual manifestations, but only the popular explanation of the sudden and otherwise inexplicable dispersion of the cloud which had overcast the minds of the disciples at the crucifixion.

The distinction which we draw between the experience (the alleged visions) of the primitive disciples and that of St. Paul, seems to us to be not unwarranted. Our supposition is, that there was no vision of any kind in the case of the former, partly because there is no evidence that any of them were constitutionally subject to ecstatic or hysterical conditions. Such evidence as may be cited to prove that they were (as, for example, in the case of Peter, Acts x.) is either irrelevant or not reliable. Mental changes, however great, had no tendency, so far as we know, to excite the reflex action of their mental eye, or to conjure up visionary shapes or sounds to their bodily senses.   But from Paul himself we learn that *he was* subject or predisposed to such conditions.   In 2nd Corinthians, chap. xii., he tells us of visions and revelations which he had received ; of one occasion on which he seemed to himself to be caught up into heaven, to hear unspeakable words which it was not lawful for a man to utter, and not to know whether, when this took place, he was in the body or out of the body ; and, if we may trust what is reported of him in the Acts of the Apostles, he there speaks of having been in a trance, or ecstasy, in Jerusalem—from which, and other notices, we get the impression that such states were not infrequent with him.   That a man now liable to such peculiar states of mind should, in the greatest crisis of his life, in the moment of undergoing a sudden and complete revolution of his whole system of thought, while the report was flying that the author of the new thought had been seen alive after his martyr death, have had a vision similar to those of which he had heard so much, is what we should almost be prepared for.   It was a phenomenon of the same, or of a like species with others that befel him on other occasions, and therefore not unlikely to occur under such extraordinary circumstances.   The words of the Apostle (2 Cor. xii.) in describing his peculiar experiences are very remarkable.   They seem to indicate that he thought it possible that the spirit of a man might separate itself from his body, and have a vision for itself apart from his bodily senses.   According to the same notion, he might think it possible that Jesus could present himself to the spiritual perception, or to the senses of the disciples, without the intervention of an actual body.   For aught the Apostle could tell or know, Jesus might have risen again, and have manifested himself without being in the body.   That is to say, the manifestation might have a reality to the spirit which it had not for the bodily sense, and it almost seems as if the Apostle was himself doubtful as to the nature of these manifestations, and as to whether they were in any sense objective. No doubt it is the intention of the synoptists and the writer of the "Acts" to represent them as objective, but it by no means follows that Paul himself was confident of this.   Of one thing only was he absolutely certain, viz., that there had been a manifestation of some kind to him of the risen Christ, and such as to leave no doubt on his own mind as to the fact of the resurrection. Even if we put aside his description of the event as a revelation of the Son of God *in* him (Gal. i. 16), the secret doubt in his mind as to the nature of the manifestation seems to crop up, or to betray itself in those words of his just referred to, " Whether in the body, or out of the body, I cannot tell, God knoweth." This doubt he may have surmounted or got rid of by his incongruous conception of " a spiritual body " —a relic of a phase of thought with reference to the connection between body and spirit which we of the present day have outgrown.

It has been contended that Paul himself was conscious of a distinction between the vision which accompanied his conversion and his other kindred experiences, and that he considered the former to be of a more objective character than his trances and ecstasies. But the fact that the former was probably the first of the kind which he had experienced, that it had occurred at the most critical and decisive moment of his life, and had thus made a more vivid impression upon his mind, and completely swept away for the moment every vestige of waking consciousness, or rather every effort at introspection, is enough to account for the distinction which he may have drawn ; but it is a distinction to which we can attach no value, and which we cannot regard as either warranted by the facts, or authenticated by the judgment of the Apostle.

It is indeed very difficult, if not impossible, to pronounce what was the Apostle's own view as to the nature of his vision. There is much in his language to give countenance to the idea that he conceived of it as having been addressed to the spiritual senses only, and not to the corporeal. But this, again, is rendered doubtful if we take into account that in 1 Cor. xv. he enumerates six instances as an exhaustive list of these occurrences. A sudden, merely spiritual revelation of Christ was a common, not to say universal experience of the early converts, and something of the kind is a frequent experience even to this day. And if the Apostle conceived that no more was meant by the six Christophanies, it is hard to understand why he should have enumerated them at all, or have thought them worthy of being singled out as pre-eminently demonstrative of the resurrection.

Admitting, then, as beyond question, that Paul's conversion

was accompanied by a vision of some sort, as a by-product, we now go on to say, that this fact invalidates, to some extent, his testimony, of which so much has been made by the apologists of orthodoxy, as to the other five Christophanies which he enumerates in 1 Cor. xv.   We cannot, indeed, set aside his testimony as to the remarkable nature of the experiences of the earlier disciples, but we do not feel bound to believe that these experiences were, as he seems to have supposed, in the form of a vision such as that which befel himself, or were accompanied by such a vision.   It was doubtless natural, or inevitable, that he should be of this opinion.   The language which the earlier disciples made use of to explain the process or phenomenon by which they had recovered their faith in Christ, to make it intelligible to the popular mind, was necessarily figurative, but was understood literally by those whom they addressed, and by frequent repetition may have lost its figurative character, even for themselves ; or, if it could never altogether have lost its figurative character for them, yet, being firmly persuaded of the substantial truth and supreme importance of that which they sought to communicate, they might feel it to be inopportune and ill-advised to betray hesitation as to the mode of expressing it, lest to others doubts might be suggested as to its reality. · In one way or another, the figurative language employed must have reacted powerfully upon the view which men took of the occurrence.

The great mental experience now which had befallen the twelve attendants of Jesus and the five hundred Galilæans would be reported to St. Paul in its figurative and sensuous clothing, and acting upon his highly strung and peculiar mental organization, it would, as we have already said, contribute, along with the new religious ideas derived from the disciples with whom he came in contact, to conjure up an apparition in his own case which he would necessarily, and as a matter of course, regard as of the same nature as that which was said to have been seen by the original followers of Jesus.   Nor was he likely to discover that this was a hasty conclusion.   For, when, three years after his conversion, he went up to Jerusalem to see Peter, it is by no means likely that the conference of the two men would turn upon the nature of their experiences.   St. Paul's mind would be prepossessed with the idea that the experience of Peter and his companions had been the same with his own, and he would feel no curiosity upon the subject, nor think of scrutinizing the details. On the other hand, Peter had by this time, we presume, accepted the sensuous representation of that experience in place of the real explanation ; or, for the sake of convenience, he had adopted the figurative mode of describing it, and would naturally suppose that St. Paul in any allusion which he might make to a vision, might only be referring to a similar experience and employing that figurative style of expression which seemed to come naturally to all who spoke of that crisis of the spiritual life. St. Peter might thus, no less than St. Paul, be preoccupied by the idea that the experience of both had been the same, and might never think of coming to any understanding upon the real facts. At a later period, when St. Paul's relations and intercourse with those who were " of reputation " had become of a less cordial and confidential kind, he was still less likely in conference with them to be dispossessed of his preconception as to the nature of their experience. Meeting with an imperious, ardent convert, like Paul, who stood on his own independent basis in virtue of a private and separate revelation, and was possessed with the idea of a vision all his own, it is possible that even Peter when he conversed with this *enfant terrible* might be carried away by his enthusiasm, and regard the account of his vision as confirmatory of that popular notion of the experiences of the earlier disciples which had floated into currency by their own mode of reporting them. These various considerations help us to understand how St. Paul could place the purely spiritual experiences of the earlier disciples in the same category with his own, though they were materially different.

We can see, therefore, how the fact that Paul had, or believed that he had had, an actual vision of his own, by disposing him to receive without inquiry the reports concerning the visions of the earlier disciples, might impair the value of his testimony to the truth of these reports.

In reflecting upon this difficult subject we should bear in mind, that under the hands of men, who, like Peter and Paul, had undergone that great spiritual revolution, the difference between a visible and a spiritual manifestation of the risen Christ was apt to disappear.

To simple-minded men like St. Peter and his companions, unaccustomed to analyze their sensations, or carefully to draw the line between the outer and the inner world, that revolution might appear to be a self-presentation of Jesus to their spiritual sense, even though " their eyes were holden," that they did not actually see him, and even though it was only by the " burning of their hearts within them," and by the opening and enlargement of their understanding to the new faith, that they had perceived any trace of his presence (Luke xxiv. 16, 32). This inner experience was of itself a proof to them that he had been present in some mysterious way, and had really appeared to them, though, at the moment they wist not of it. Some such manifestation of the glorified Christ was the only intelligible explanation of the sudden inrush of the new faith, and seemed to warrant them in affirming, or at least not rashly denying, that Jesus had appeared to them. Were they to express doubts as to the *nature* of the manifestation, it might, to the minds of their converts, suggest doubts as already said, respecting the *reality* of the fact itself, which in the main was " most surely believed " or fully established among them, and seemed to constitute the indispensable foundation of that new life into which they had been born. To inquire too curiously into the nature of the manifestation might even appear to them to argue a trifling, if not a profane and captious spirit. In what specific sense the avenue by which the revelation had come to them was divine, was an inquiry not for a moment of perfect faith, but for a time like the present in which faith has to adjust itself to the scientific theory of the universe.

Let us pause here to emphasize the spiritual crisis which took place in the experience of St. Paul, as distinct from that which took place in that of the twelve and the five hundred Galilæans. In these latter it was a purely mental phenomenon, a sudden evolution of thought ; a revival, and, therefore, more than a revival of the deep impression which, during his lifetime, Jesus had made on their sympathies and religious instincts : we say it was more than that, because it shot out into a conviction that his life was immortal, that though put to death in the flesh he had risen into a higher sphere, and was alive again in the spirit. In the case of St. Paul, the crisis involved other elements. It consisted primarily in the revelation to his mind of the truth of the new or evangelical form of the religious relation which Jesus had taught, and involved in it a belief in the currently reported resurrection of him who had revealed that relation.   It was also accompanied in his case by something of the nature of a vision, of the reality of which, whether as a presentation to the outer or the inner sense, he had the most entire conviction.   This conviction of his did not, indeed, originate a belief that the earlier disciples had had a similar experience ; but it may have confirmed the belief, which had already taken root, to that effect, and have put the merely subjective or mental nature of that experience quite out of sight, and perhaps out of the memory even of those who had been the subjects of it.

CHAPTER XV.

WE now proceed to consider St. Paul's dogmatic construction of the religious relation, founded on the teaching, death, and resurrection of Jesus. And as the subject in itself is complex and involved, we crave the reader's indulgence for whatever prolixity or other defect he may observe in our treatment of it. We go back to the point which we have already touched upon, viz., that though by upbringing, profession, and conviction a Pharisee, yet there are indications in St. Paul's epistles that even before his conversion a new synthesis of religion had begun to declare itself in his mind. Whether it was from native bent and instinct, or from the study of Judæo-prophetic or Hellenic literature, or from the stimulus imparted to his thoughts by hints and rumours of the doctrine of Jesus, against whose subtle influence he could not bar his mind, even by placing himself in deadly antagonism to it, he seems to have differed from most of the Pharisaic name, by aiming at inward conformity to the divine law, and by a more spiritual, comprehensive, and exacting view of the range of its requirements. He speaks of the bann which the law had pronounced against covetousness as having laid hold of him, and impressed him with a conviction of sin to which he had otherwise been a stranger (Rom. vii. 7). And proceeding from this point he seems to have gained an ideal of humanity, a conception of the law and its requirements, more spiritual than was contained in the Pharisaic system. It is also quite clear that that mental conflict between the ideal and the real had begun in him, which, if not absolutely unknown to the Pharisee, or, indeed, to any human being, could not, by anything contained in his system of thought, be brought to a satisfactory issue. Pharisaism, in fact, was a system for evading or obviating that conflict.

The ceremonialism to which the Pharisees devoted themselves; their minute and scrupulous attention to law in its external aspect, which had no immediate ethical significance, offered a salve to the conscience. To a multitude of what may be called casuistical regulations they ascribed, as coming from the fathers, a divine authority not inferior to that of the Decalogue; thus practically making the law of no effect by crowding out its moral requirements. Their religious life moved in a routine of symbolical and statutory transactions, which formed no part of the actual business of religion. A system of this kind, which had no contact with the inner life, no relation to everyday matters, and no tendency to make men better, could not possibly satisfy a greatly earnest, thoughtful man like Paul, and it needed, as we have said, but a slight touch or impact from without to shake its hold over his mind; and that touch was given at the critical moment. True, the habit of reverence, which is characteristic of the religious tone of mind, the sanctity of inherited beliefs, and his native loyalty of heart, did not suffer him easily to renounce his association with the religious party in which he had been trained and educated. The struggle in his mind between the old which was waning and the new which was dawning was no doubt severe. The former had the sanction of the fathers and of the accredited teachers of the day; and the new, while as yet the character and life of Jesus had only a sort of fascination for him which he felt himself bound to resist, had no other sanction than that of his own moral and religious instincts. The patriotic and exclusive Jewish feeling, which was strong in Paul, threw all its weight upon one side; but the conflict was decided in favour of the other side by the pressing urgency, by the felt need of a personal and individual righteousness higher and better than the Pharisaic form of it, which had hitherto been his aim. After repeated, and perhaps long continued failure, it broke upon Paul's mind that his efforts to establish such a righteousness were vain, and that the only thing which could save him from throwing up the effort in despair, and deliver him from the deep-felt schism of his nature, was that new conception of God, and that conviction of divine forgiveness, to which Jesus had given prominence in his teaching. This conclusion was, we may be sure, the outcome of much inward debate ; and just because, under the influence of inherited ideas, he struggled long against it, would it, at length, all the more suddenly and violently break upon his mind as a revelation from without, and form a crisis, an abrupt revolution, a new starting point for his whole subsequent life.

Our explanation, then, of the Apostle's conversion is that it was occasioned by the moral and spiritual ideas introduced into his mind by contact and intercourse, though of a hostile kind, with the little band of men whom he persecuted. The very fierceness with which he strove against the spread of these ideas was a sign that they were gaining hold of him ; it was but the effort to arrest their growing mastery over himself, which he could only regard as a treason and a betrayal of all he had hitherto held sacred. This was the true secret of that hatred, akin to dread, with which he regarded these ideas. But he did not view it in that light, he did not perceive at the time that his mind was yielding to the influence of those very ideas ; or that an involuntary, elemental, and forlorn struggle, of which the issue was foregone, was going on within him against the power of ideas which appealed to his higher reason ; and he regarded it only as the working of his own deadly exasperation against the doctrine and person of Jesus. The crisis, therefore, when it did come, seemed to come abruptly and in despite of himself, as if it were a break in the continuity of his inner life, so that, when he reflected upon it, he could not but attribute the revolution in his feelings to extraneous intervention, to the vision or apparition which was only the by-effect or accompaniment of the crisis.

It will be seen that the explanation now given of the conversion of Paul differs widely from that given by T. H. Green, (vol. iii.). This writer considers that crisis in the life of Paul to have been brought about by the brooding of his mind on the death of one who was said to have been the Messiah, and to have risen again from the dead. The testimony of the disciples had not persuaded him of the fact of the resurrection, but a process of what can only be called imaginative, if not fanciful and abstract reasoning on the hypothesis that the resurrection was a fact had converted him to that belief. Mr. Green says, " The conception of a crucified Messiah . . . .

bearing the curse and penalty of the law," was felt by the Apostle to be "just what he wanted" to deliver him from the consciousness of being under the curse of the law. His sense of this was a proof to the Apostle that Jesus was the Messiah, and that he had risen again from the dead. But this explanation seems to us to be too abstract, too complex and indirect for the occasion. Some such hypothetical reasoning might seem satisfactory to the Apostle after his conversion, but could hardly be the cause of his conversion. And it appears to us that the facts require the more simple and direct explanation which we have given, viz., that when the Apostle was engaged in persecuting the disciples, entering their houses and haling them to prison, he would question them as to their faith, and could not but gather some knowledge of the doctrine of Jesus. A few hints, however straggling, broken, and fragmentary, would suffice to disclose to his nimble and penetrating spirit that what Jesus taught was a new view of the religious relation ; and this, at the conjuncture at which his feeling of the tyranny exercised over him by the Jewish or legal view of that relation had "come to a head," was just "what he wanted." The new or evangelical view of that relation, as distinct from or opposed to the legal view of it, recommended itself to his mind by its own intrinsic authority ; by its adaptation to his inmost needs ; by its instantaneous power of emancipating his soul from its internal conflict, and healing the inward schism. It had a verity of its own, independent of Messianic doctrine and Jewish preconceptions. It revealed itself to him as the true hope of man, by no hypothetical or doubtful chain of reasoning, but simply by its revolutionary effect upon his entire inner state; and it satisfied him, that he who had revealed it could be none other than the great messenger of God of whom the prophets had written.

When speaking of the doctrine of Jesus, we pointed out that it was his discovery of the evangelic view of the religious relation which satisfied him, that he himself, as the discoverer of that relation, was the promised Messiah. And our position now is that St. Paul, conscious of having derived this view, however mediately and indirectly, from Jesus, was satisfied that his claim to be the Messiah was well founded. The moment of Paul's conversion was just the moment at which, after much inward debate and misgiving, the evangelic view as taught by Jesus took absolute possession of his mind. As by a flash of inward light, he recognized the immense import of that new relation which formed the core of that teaching. The doctrine was so novel, so revolutionary in the religious sphere, of such startling range and gravity, and of such beneficent consequence to himself, that he readily believed all that the disciples alleged of the resurrection of him who had revealed it.

While the conflict still raged in his bosom between the two principles " so counter and so keen," it would seem to the vivid and excited imagination of the Apostle as if the conflict lay between himself and a personal enemy, between himself as the faithful champion of the traditions of the fathers, and that other whom he identified with the new ideas which were seething and asserting themselves within him. This personal and ghostly character which the conflict assumed to his imagination is not only made probable by many historical analogies, but also indicated by the words which shaped themselves out to Paul's imagination from the midst of the light which was above that of the sun at noonday : " Saul, Saul, why persecutest thou me ? "   In the moment of crisis, when the new ideas gained the upper hand, it would appear to him as if Jesus had wrestled and prevailed, and cast him to the ground. The light, the fall, and the voice were but the form into which his sense of mental illumination and of subjugation by one who was stronger than he had thrown itself. And when he afterwards reflected on that wonderful experience, it would seem to him as if the struggle which had gone on within him had been brought to an issue by an act of self-manifestation on the part of Jesus, by an act of condescension to him personally, if not on his own account, yet to him as a chosen instrument to transmit " the benefit " to others (Gal. i. 16). And yet further, it is easy to conceive that the relief at length experienced in his conscience, the pacification of his inner life by the termination of the struggle, or by his going over to the new ideas, would ever after be associated in his mind with the person of Jesus, who had taken the extraordinary step of stooping from heaven to bring it about, *i.e.*, to overcome that opposition to himself in the Apostle's mind which had otherwise been insuperable, and that the Apostle would ever after strive to repay this great and distinguishing act of condescension by magnifying the significance of the person and office of Jesus in connection with the idea of that new relation which was thenceforth to be the fulcrum of his spiritual life.

But, however persuaded the Apostle may have been that Jesus was the Messiah, a great difficulty must from the first have presented itself to his mind. The question could not but press itself, or be pressed upon him by those to whom he sought to impart his own faith, why it was that one who was the Messiah, the fore-ordained, long predicted, long expected messenger of God, whom alone of the race God had deemed worthy of being raised from the dead, should have been subjected to a death so cruel, to a fate so ignominious. For if, as has been recently asserted by students of rabbinical literature, the idea of a suffering Messiah was not quite strange or distasteful to the Jews of that age, yet the idea of his suffering a death so ignominious as that of the cross must have been peculiarly offensive and incredible. It is easy to conceive that even if, as an abstract idea, that of a suffering Messiah might not be disgusting to the Jewish mind; yet the concrete presentation of such an idea in the person of Jesus, who at once disappointed current Messianic expectation, and made himself otherwise obnoxious by his doctrine, would be sure to excite only contempt and unbelief.

Had St. Paul and the other early preachers of the gospel had no more to say in apologetic explanation of the death of Jesus than that it was a proof of his loyalty to the great and fruitful views which he propounded in his lifetime ; that he had brought it upon himself because he would not withhold his testimony to the truth, but elected to brave a cruel death in his effort to make that truth common property, and to leave it as his legacy to the world, his contribution to the elements of human welfare, for the guidance and elevation of human life ; it is very doubtful indeed whether such an explanation would have been satisfactory to the men of that generation whatever we of the present day may think of it.

The early disciples must have felt that both for themselves and for their converts some other, some further explanation was necessary. And it appears as if such explanation was not immediately forthcoming. For, from the first discourses of the apostles recorded in the Acts it seems as if they were at some loss to say in what light the crucifixion should be regarded ; as if they hesitated and could not at first make up their minds as to the construction to be put upon it. They speak as if it were a momentary triumph of wickedness, an event not accidental indeed, because determined beforehand in the divine counsels, but accomplished unwittingly by the hands of men (Acts ii. 23, iv. 28) ; an explanation which is evidently no explanation, because the same thing may be predicated of any wicked deed whatever, and therefore did not assign to this any distinctive character. The crucifixion was in fact a sort of puzzle to the disciples, which, however, did not shake their faith in him as the Messiah, and in the truth of his doctrine and the reality of his resurrection. On the contrary, their faith assumed the interim form of a belief that the offence of the cross would soon be removed by the reappearance of their Master in glorious state to the discomfiture and confusion of his enemies.

But we can see from the Epistles of St. Paul that long before the interim faith expired, the crucifixion came to be regarded as the very end for which the Messiah had come into the world ; as a death, not in the common order of nature, but of a wholly abnormal character, ordained indeed of God, and inflicted by the instrumentality and malice of men, but yet voluntary on the part of the sufferer, and expiatory of the sins of others in fulfilment of a grand redemptive purpose on the part of God.

The question therefore remains to be answered, how this view of the death of Jesus on the cross came to be adopted ; how it suggested itself to the mind of Paul and the other disciples. His great spiritual deliverance from the bonds of superstition and of legal thraldom had been brought about, as we believe, by the sudden alteration in his view of the religious relation ; but even if he himself was conscious that this revolution in his views had something to do with his conversion, it yet did not satisfy him as a complete explanation of that great crisis in his life. For if the doctrine of Jesus, by being conveyed to his knowledge, had sufficed to produce this crisis, there would seem to be no necessity for his death on the cross ; the idea that he had died as a martyr to seal the truth of his doctrine being one at that time of little or no weight.

That event could therefore only be regarded by the Apostle as a great mystery—"a mystery of godliness"—by which a great divine purpose was effected ; and what could that be, but to render an atonement for the sins of men ? The impulse in the Apostle's mind to exalt the person and office of Jesus naturally found furtherance and gave welcome to such a construction. Regarded in this light, the crucifixion seemed to supply a complete and satisfactory explanation of that newly-discovered relation, not as immanent and aboriginal, or founded in the nature of things, but as supernaturally effected by its means ; and the suggestion of atonement in connection with that event was not unlikely to occur to the mind of St. Paul, or of any other person familiar with the idea of sacrifice and of atonement by the shedding of blood. And this process of thought, however complex and far from obvious it may seem to us, might pass swiftly in the Apostle's mind, and make there an indelible impression.

To consider Jesus as not merely revealing the placable character of God, but as offering an atoning sacrifice, and, by the shedding of his blood, purchasing the forgiveness of sin, and the gift of a new spirit, seemed to exalt his function, and to make human obligation to him more palpable and personal. And it is easy to see that these two views respecting his function, though very different, might easily pass into each other— the less palpable into the more palpable idea ; which latter was not only more easily expressed, but was approved and recommended both to the Jewish and Gentile mind by the analogous, and to them familiar and inherited idea of animal sacrifice, and others of a cognate nature.

Profoundly sensible of his obligation to Jesus, the Apostle yet mistook the nature of that obligation. He conceived of Jesus, not as the originator of a great idea, but as the generator of a dynamic force in the life of man, as the source of a dæmonic rather than of a moral influence in the souls of believers. No doubt the power of the idea in the first age of the Church was such as might seem to warrant the view that the force which he exercised was dynamic. But the dogma in which St. Paul explicated this view was the cause of that collision with science, in which to this day Christianity is involved. Against this great drawback, however, we have to place the consideration that the Apostle's inferiority to Jesus as a thinker was what constituted his excellence as a teacher for his own time. His converts shared in his own incapacity to receive the truth in its free and absolute form, and the shape which it took in his mind recommended itself to them. This dogma has retained its sway to the present day among Christians, because it is the anthropomorphic equivalent of a pure truth which appeals to the heart and reason of men.

As to the relation subsisting between the doctrine of Jesus and that of St. Paul, our position may be briefly stated. The experience of the latter, which ended in his conversion, began with that same spiritual conception of the law to which we traced the development in the mind of Jesus. Both he and Jesus rose to the idea of the new religious relation by the same avenue, but with a difference which is not to be overlooked. (1) The experience of Paul was not self-evolved, but helped and brought on by the doctrine of Jesus, which was the exponent of an experience which in him was original. (2) The experience of Paul was accompanied by a state of mind, of which, from first to last, we see not a trace in Jesus, viz., a state of ecstasy, the very nature of which was that he lost the consciousness of what was passing within him. So that (3) the Apostle could only explain to himself what had passed by assuming that a power outside of himself and above himself had transformed his life and thought; that the new relation into which he had been transplanted, was due to some work of Jesus, which, according to Jewish ideas, could be nothing else than an atonement effected by his death on the cross. What had really happened in the moment of that translation was that the idea of the evangelic relation, as taught by Jesus, had suddenly appealed, or verified itself, to his consciousness by putting an end to that otherwise interminable conflict which had hitherto waged within him. One way or another, the Apostle was aware of his dependence on Jesus, but, as just said, he mistook or exaggerated the nature of his dependence, and explained his whole experience as the effect of an atonement, or, speaking generally, as "the pouring in of a life from outside."

The difference between the doctrine of Jesus and the doctrine of Paul is gross and palpable, so much so indeed that of late years it has been averred by distinguished theologians, among whom may be mentioned Holsten on the continent, and T. H. Green in this country, that the doctrine of Paul was not derived from that of Jesus. What gives some countenance to this proposition is, that in the Epistles of Paul there is, with the exception of what he says of the Lord's Supper, an utter absence of any reference to the teaching of Jesus and the incidents of his life. From which fact the inference has been drawn that St. Paul was "ignorant of the life of Jesus prior to his death, as detailed in the synoptic Gospels," and that his doctrine was only the interpretation which he put upon the death and resurrection of the Messiah. But as, by the time that the Apostle wrote his great Epistles, he had conversed with the earlier apostles, and no doubt with many of the first disciples, there is, to say the least, a huge unlikelihood that he could have remained ignorant of the leading events of the life of Jesus. It is hardly conceivable that he should not have taken care to inform himself as to the earthly life and teaching of one whom he adored as the Lord from heaven. His omission to do so would argue a state of mind so incurious and indifferent as to be unnatural and incomprehensible. That he never refers in his Epistles to the teaching of Jesus may be explained by the fact that in the death and resurrection of Jesus he saw a compendious illustration or symbol of the entire soteriological method as taught by Jesus, beyond which, in writing to believers who were presumably acquainted with the events of the earthly life of Jesus, he did not need to go. And we are led to the conclusion that the dogma of St. Paul is neither more nor less than the doctrine of Jesus as seen through a refracting medium, or as deflected by contact in the mind of the Apostle with the facts of his death and resurrection. It may even be said that by his claim to be the Messiah, and by his submission to death, Jesus himself, unconsciously and unintentionally, gave occasion to this deflection of his doctrine.

The conjecture may also be hazarded that St. Paul's silence with regard to events of the earthly life of Jesus was owing in some measure to the fact that there was little for him to say, and that little needed to be said upon the subject. The course of that life was probably diversified by few salient details ; and the doctrine, though pregnant and suggestive in the highest degree, was so simple as to admit of being summed up by the Apostle in his word of the cross and his doctrine of divine grace. We conceive of Jesus as going up and down, preaching the same simple doctrine, and impressing it powerfully on the crowds by the solemnity of his bearing and by his manifest sincerity and devotion, and, finally, by the pathos of his death. Variety was given to the tradition of his life by the mythicizing tendency of men who stood at a greater distance from him, and who sought to draw out and to explicate into dramatic effects the singleness of impression which its main features had made upon their minds.

Admitting to the fullest extent the difference between the dogma of St. Paul and the doctrine of Jesus, we none the less maintain the genetic relation in which the latter stands to the former. The most noticeable feature in the teaching of Jesus was the omission in it of all reference to the doctrine, at that time universal, of atonement or propitiation. This meant that, as far as he knew, these ideas did not enter into the religious relation. He did not feel that they were necessary to constitute that relation. He did not indeed repudiate or wage a polemic against them. He only ignored them or allowed them to drop out of sight. His doctrine of the Divine Fatherhood dispensed with them, or threw them so far into the background as virtually to set them aside. Placability was represented by him as of the very essence of the divine nature. God was ever ready, in spite of provocation, to welcome and countenance the faintest efforts on the part of the sinner to reconcile himself to God, to forget and cancel all his arrears of guilt. There might be a burden or penalty making repentance hard and difficult to the sinner himself; but they did not alienate the good-will of God, or dispose Him to avert His countenance from the penitent. This was the grand truth, the revelation of which to the mind of Paul resulted in his conversion. Up to that moment he had struggled and wrestled with such determination, we may be sure, as such a man is capable of, to propitiate God by the sedulous fulfilment of all legal conditions. But by painful experience he had been made to feel that the effort was fruitless, the task beyond his strength; and from the teaching of Jesus, conveyed to his knowledge in the roundabout way already pointed out, he learned that the effort was as unnecessary as it was fruitless, for that God was propitious by nature, and did not need to be propitiated. It was this doctrine, eagerly laid hold of, we may suppose, as a forlorn hope, which resulted in his conversion. But the strange thing at first sight is, that in order to explain to himself the great revolution in his inner life he re-introduced into his system of thought that very idea of atonement the abandonment of which had brought it about. A character was thus imparted to his entire way of thinking so materially different from that of Jesus as to lend some countenance to the idea that it had an independent origin.

By founding his dogmatic system upon the death of Jesus viewed as an atonement, he may be said to have rehabilitated the idea of atonement, and to have restored it to that position in the theological province from which it had been thrust by the great Teacher. But this curious fact—this apparent inconsistency—becomes intelligible when we observe that the idea of atonement, as it reappears in his dogma, is no longer what it was in the religion of Israel, but has undergone a capital transformation. The Apostle's mind was so possessed or, we may say, dominated by the inherited idea of atonement, which, in his view, had the seal and sanction of divine authority, that he concluded that it must, under all circumstances, retain a meaning and a place in the religious relation. And the problem for him evidently was to reconcile with that idea what Jesus had said as to the essentially propitious character of God; and this he accomplished to his own satisfaction by supposing that God had manifested this aspect of His character by providing, in the person of the Messiah, as the substitute and representative of men, the propitiation which was necessary. Forgiveness, in virtue of this atonement, was thus seen to be the free, unbought gift of God, without merit or desert of man. The whole work of propitiation was laid upon the God-provided substitute, so that nothing more of the kind was requisite; man individually and collectively was relieved of a task for him impossible; gratuitously established in the religious relation which Jesus had in view. No propitiatory service, moral or ceremonial, was thenceforth to be required of the sinner; the only service now to be demanded of him was the service of thanksgiving—the service of a soul inspired by love to manifest its grateful sense of the unspeakable grace of God in granting this great relief. The whole Mosaic ceremonial, whether of the nature of sin-offering or thank-offering, was absolutely abolished; for even that of the latter description which remained in force was no longer a statutory offering, but such only as the heart, in gratitude for the great deliverance, could render—the soul being now a law to itself, freed from all servile or legal restraint, and placed in full enjoyment of the liberty of a child of God. To the Apostle it seemed as if in this way the majesty of the law had been fully vindicated by the revelation of divine grace on the cross of Christ. He was satisfied that his construction of the doctrine of Jesus brought it into perfect harmony with that of Moses and the prophets, though to the Jews it might be a stumbling-block. He even believed that he had the authority of the Old Testament for adopting a view which reverence and gratitude prompted him to take, and that the words of inspiration weighed with him in adopting it (1 Cor. xv. 3). In this way he reconciled his inherited belief as to the necessity of atonement with his new belief that none was needed from man himself as a sinner.

The explanation of the ignominious death of Jesus thus arrived at would recommend itself to the Apostle's mind, first, because it would seem to show that continuity was preserved between the law which enjoined atonement and the doctrine of Jesus, which was exposed to the suspicion of discarding or ignoring it ; and, secondly, because it fell in with the Apostle's impulse to exalt to the utmost the person and function of Jesus. It presented Jesus to his mind not merely as shedding new light by his teaching upon the nature of the religious relation, but also as effecting a radical alteration upon it, as offering himself a sacrifice to improve the relation previously subsisting, or as fulfilling a condition necessary for its rearrangement or readjustment.

To most men the doctrine of Jesus, even as illustrated by his life and death, might never have appealed, until it had thus been placed in connection with the ideas of sacrifice and atonement which had come to them by inheritance from the fathers as essential to the religious relation. But even Paul himself and others, who might be of finer and of deeper insight, and had experienced the directly emancipating effect of the new conception of God and man, might yet be induced to give in to the same ideas, and so to slide down into a lower form of doctrine than that of Jesus ; not, indeed, by the mere spirit of accommodation and of opportunism, in order to secure a ready reception for the evangelic doctrine, but because these ideas as applied to the death of Jesus recommended themselves, as has just been said, to their own minds also, as a means of exalting the function of Jesus, and of preserving the continuity of the new doctrine with the old.

The view of the crucifixion thus obtained was fitted as no other could be to lend an absolute and permanent, instead of only a relative and historical, significance to the person of Jesus. It put a construction on his death the very opposite of that which superficially belonged to it, and attached to it a transcendent and supernatural character, besides affording the means of giving a clear, uncircuitous, and what might seem to be a sufficient explanation of that new moral and renovating power which had in some mysterious way been introduced into the lives of those who surrendered themselves to the influence of the gospel.

For St. Paul himself the connection between his conversion and the death of Jesus became obvious. By regarding the latter as an atonement he placed it in a genetic relation to the grand revolution in the state of his feelings, or to that sense of reconciliation with God in which that revolution had issued. The change in his own mind was the sequel of the propitiatory effect of that atonement, or of the change effected by it on the mind of God. The sensible change which had taken place in the Apostle's relation to God was regarded by him as a result produced, not so much by the disclosure to his mind of the gracious relation in which God had always stood to the sinner, as rather by the mysterious change which had been effected on the mind of God by the self-sacrifice of Jesus Messiah. The Messiah had both effected a change in God's relation to man, and also revealed it to the Apostle on the way to Damascus ; and by this revelation had effected a change in the Apostle's relation to God. Or we may say simply, that by a tendency natural to men, St. Paul had transferred to God the varying states of his own consciousness. He regarded the change from a state of alienation to a state of reconciliation—which, by virtue of the death of Jesus, had taken place in himself—as the reflection or the sequel of a change effected by the same great event on the mind of God. In other words, the revolution effected by the cross of Christ was for the Apostle not merely subjective, but objective. A view of the death on the cross, which has fired the thoughts of millions of devout souls for so many ages, may well have commended itself to the Apostle in his moments of rapture. It gratified his craving to intensify to the uttermost the sense of obligation under which he had been laid by him who had condescended on the way to Damascus to snatch him as a brand from the burning. That view of it might not, indeed, be obviously consistent with the eternal and essential fatherliness of God,* as taught by Jesus, and accepted from that source by Paul himself; but an objection, which has not proved insurmountable to many generations of believers, might not be insuperable to the Apostle. It might even seem to him that only by connecting the idea of atonement with the death of Jesus could he be justified in pouring forth and lavishing upon him the full flood of his reverence and gratitude; and here, as in other instances, the Apostle was little careful to reconcile conflicting ideas.

In order to explain yet more fully the dogmatic form into which St. Paul threw the doctrine of divine placability as taught by Jesus, we may take into account, not only the categories of Jewish thought, which continued, unknown to himself, powerfully to sway and to limit his thought after he seemed to himself to have broken away from them; but also the difficulty, common to men generally, and not least to the Oriental and Semitic mind, of embracing and holding a spiritual truth, such as that of divine grace and placability, in its naked simplicity, without the medium of symbolic form or sensuous representation. This was a difficulty which may have been much felt by Paul himself, or which, at least, he had to provide for in the minds of those whom he sought to imbue with the new doctrine. The violent and ignominious death of him whom he believed to be the Messiah, and to have been raised again from the dead, in token of the divine sanction and author-

---

* It is perhaps by way of meeting this obvious objection, and helping out the idea generally, that a Paulinistic writer says that Christ was fore-ordained (for this purpose) before the foundation of the world (1 Peter i. 20), and that the Apokalyptist speaks of Christ as slain from the foundation of the world (Rev. xiii. 8); as much as to say that the atonement, though accomplished in time, was part of an eternal purpose—an essential manifestation of the divine nature. But if these and other parallel passages were written with such an intention, they can only be regarded as a makeshift.

ization of his claims, besides being an event so mysterious as not to admit of being explained, except by the idea that it was undergone for sins not his own, also supplied just what was needed to give to his Jewish mind a firm hold of the gracious character of God ; an object or ground for the imagination to dwell upon ; a medium or proof of an idea which would otherwise only float vaguely in the mind. Instead of calling upon men, as Jesus had done, to believe in the forgiveness of sin, just because it is God's property to forgive, or because such a faith is indispensable to the development of man's moral nature, St. Paul pointed to the crucifixion as, in some sense, a ground and guarantee for divine forgiveness, even though, looked at more closely, it may seem to be an infraction of that very principle, and to compromise or place it in a doubtful light, as we have insisted, besides presenting to the understanding difficulties greater than those which it is designed to remove, though of a different kind.

One of these difficulties is experienced when we proceed to answer the question, whether the atonement was made for some of the human race, or for all without exception. This is a question which cannot be evaded : and the answer to it either way brings us face to face with overwhelming objections, both in relation to the character of God and to the requirement of faith. Whereas, the idea of divine love operating through the divine order, which is ever upon the side of the true penitent, if more difficult for the mind to apprehend, or vividly to realize, is at least consistent with itself and free from intrinsic objections. But here, as throughout this essay, it is our object not so much to criticize Paul's dogma as to account for its origin and genesis. And when we apply criticism to the Pauline dogmatic construction, it is intended only to show that that construction is not the necessary inference from the teaching of Jesus ; and to explain how it comes that, while the orthodox believer still clings to St. Paul's dogma, increasing multitudes of those who make religion a subject of thought, are falling back upon the simple, undogmatic teaching of Jesus, and cherish the feeling that, in doing so, they retain the substance of Christianity.

Placed in the light in which St. Paul learned to regard it, the suffering of death was seen to be worthy of the Messiah ; worthy even in proportion to its ignominy; fitted to exalt the

Messianic office, and to give a new and higher meaning even to those prophetic words which seemed to present the Messianic career as one of triumph. For here was a triumph indeed to those who could see it, achieved for men over the powers of evil. In connection with the sublime patience which Jesus had exhibited in the prospect and suffering of death, and with those doctrines of his, of which it was the supreme illustration, such a view might well be taken of it, and afford a satisfactory answer to that urgent question respecting the *cui bono* which must have suggested itself to the earlier disciples as well as to St. Paul, and which, had it not admitted of a clear and distinct answer, might have proved fatal to the further progress of the gospel. The same view explained how this righteous man was not saved by his righteousness, and how he might be a chosen instrument of God and yet be given over as a victim to human malice. His very innocence and sinlessness, it might be thought, was what, according to the principles of the Mosaic law, fitted and qualified him to expiate human guilt. The belief of the original disciples in his Messiahship had made them incredulous to the last as to the sufferings of which he warned them; but after he had endured the sufferings which he had had in prospect, the disciples could not but soon perceive that those characters of innocence and sinlessness which had formerly pointed him out to their spiritual apprehension as the Messiah, and been most of all illustrated in his person, were what also qualified him to atone for the sins of others. The traditional ideas of the Messiah and of the suffering " Servant of God " were thus made, by the course of events, to coalesce in their minds; and the image of a Messiah suffering, but triumphant in suffering, took possession of their minds, reconciling ideas, which in the Old Testament stood apart, as if mutually exclusive and repellent; and enriching the world with a new standard of humanity.

The difference between the doctrine of Jesus and the dogma of St. Paul may be formally defined by saying that the former was the simple, unreasoned utterance of the immediate intuitive moral and religious consciousness of the great Teacher, while the latter was the Apostle's reflection upon the former placed in the light of the crucifixion and resurrection; the form which the Apostle adopted to bring into palpable or sensuous expression the spiritual soteriological method as taught by Jesus and exemplified in the experience of the Apostle himself. It could not escape his notice that the method of Jesus was signally illustrated in the conduct and catastrophe of his life. Then the Apostle's belief in the resurrection naturally imparted a transcendent aspect to the person of the Teacher and placed him in an indefinitely causative relation to the soteriological process. The Apostle was thus led to convert the self-redemptive process as taught by Jesus into a heterosoteric process which ran side by side with that other and mirrored itself in it. This explanation at once of the difference and the correspondence between the teaching of the Master and of the disciple enables us to account for several remarkable facts. (1) It explains how it came to pass that notwithstanding the great metamorphosis which the doctrine underwent in the dogma, this latter yet retains or reflects so much of the spirit of the former. (2) It accounts in part at least for the rapid propagation of Christianity, inasmuch as the doctrine of Jesus was thus presented to the world in a popular form, level to the apprehension of the average man, and eminently calculated to call into play the mighty force of that devotional sentiment which is as widespread as humanity itself. And (3) it explains how a man, gifted like St. Paul, could yet be persuaded that he had "received" his doctrine from the Lord, in other words, that he had been guided in the construction of his dogma by the Spirit of God.

The doctrine of Jesus, gleaned by St. Paul, as we have seen, from the victims of his persecuting zeal, must have served to the Apostle as a canon, resting on the authority of Jesus, and verified by his own experience ; and when the correspondence between it and the interpretation, by means of Jewish categories, of the death and resurrection of Jesus, disclosed itself point by point to his reflection, it came home to him with the authority of a revelation from heaven. Cases of an analogous kind are to be met with in history. When Philo speaks of being sometimes overtaken by a divine afflatus or ecstasy he may be understood to refer to the joyful certitude produced in his mind by a crisis or fruitful fusion of his thought. And just such an ecstasy, falling within the experience of St. Paul, may have seemed to him to clothe his thought with divine authority.

2 B

We do not intend by anything which has been said to imply that St. Paul was the first of the disciples to connect the idea of expiation with the death of Jesus. There are many indications in the epistles of St. Paul, as well as in the Acts of the Apostles, if not also in the synoptists, that he was forestalled in this view by the earlier disciples, and that the Jewish Christians generally attached the same idea to the crucifixion. They did so indeed, but in a sense so different, that it led, as will afterwards be seen, to a conflict between the Jewish and Gentile sections of the Church, which came near to rending the Church in twain. But, without touching on this conflict here, we shall meanwhile confine our remarks to the development of the dogma in the mind of St. Paul.

The sudden somersault or transition in the mind of Paul from the purely spiritual and autosoteric views of Jesus back to the dogmatic and heterosoteric Jewish point of view is not without analogy in the history of religion. An analogous fact may be seen in the sudden transition in the mind of Luther from that solitary exercise of autonomy on his part which resulted in the Reformation to the heteronomous position which he afterwards adopted, and of which Protestant theology was the result. As might be shown in Luther's case, so in the case of Paul, there were powerful motives or considerations acting on his mind to produce this self-contradiction. There was, in the first place, the tendency to an anthropomorphic conception of God, to which his, as well as most other minds, was disposed. When a man contemplates the crimes and the inhumanities of his fellow-men, it requires a great effort of self-suppression to forgive and pity the wrong-doer ; and so he is apt to transfer a like necessity to the mind of God, and to suppose that in forgiving His erring children God requires to repress His feeling of righteous indignation, to put restraint upon Himself, and, in short, to perform an act of self-sacrifice—an idea and mode of expression of which even modern theologians make use. It is true that there is no such division in the divine being as there is in the finite, every act of God being the act of His whole and undivided nature, and that to think otherwise is anthropomorphic. Yet this is the conception of God which has embodied itself in the Pauline or orthodox doctrine of the atonement, and has given to that doctrine its hold upon the human mind. It is a doctrine which represents the truth, not as it is absolutely or in itself, but figuratively, symbolically, or approximately, and may have been the only form in which the truth could have been made level to the apprehension whether of Jews or Gentiles in that age.

Further, it has to be considered that St. Paul's mind was deeply saturated by the Hebrew or Jewish ideas on the subject of atonement. These were, that sin had to be expiated by suffering; that it was indifferent by whom the suffering was borne, whether by the guilty person himself or by some one connected with him, by family, tribal, or national ties; that the undeserved sufferings of the innocent were of expiatory virtue and of vicarious efficacy. Such ideas may have been suggested to the minds of people and prophet by the spectacle constantly presented to their eyes of dumb animals, some of them the very picture of innocence, devoted, according to prevalent sacrificial practice, as an atonement for the sins of individuals or of the nation at large. Or these ideas may have been derived from the observation that the penalty of sin and crime often fell, not upon the guilty, but upon the innocent, and so took end. By the powerfully poetic imagination of Isaiah this law or fact of common human life which had arrested the mind of Israel was dramatically presented or impersonated in historical or concrete form in the " Servant of God," whose voluntary endurance of suffering for sins not his own was the highest proof of his righteousness. The application of this same idea to interpret the intention and significance of the death of the Messiah must, we may be sure, have had an irresistible fascination for St. Paul, as well as for the other disciples. The tragic fate of Jesus Messiah would seem to him as to them to be the grandest exemplification of the constantly recurring phenomenon. For, if the idealized dramatic representation of this phenomenon by the prophet has ever since been regarded as a forecast or prediction of that world-historical event, we can easily imagine that the kindred spirit of the Apostle would catch up the suggestion in contemplating the same great tragedy.

The doctrine of the atonement in St. Paul's epistles has this in common with the Jewish doctrine, that it presupposes a certain imperfectness or shortcoming in the divine fatherliness : the presence in the divine mind of some obstruction to its complete manifestation, by the removal of which it may the more fully and demonstratively be established. To a soul like Paul's thirsting for righteousness, but yet conscience-stricken, laden with a sense of sin, and oppressed by a feeling of impotence, it might, we may think, have been as exhilarating to have the disclosure made to it, that in the nature of God there was no obstacle to the deliverance of the sinner from the power of evil, and that the very idea of divine fatherliness excluded any obstacle on the part of God, as that such an obstacle having existed it had yet been removed by an act of supreme self-sacrifice on the part of God. But the latter view would, in such a mind, evoke a pathos, an emotion which the other would not, somewhat in the same way as the symbolical or dramatic representation of a principle in the form of a historical event makes a more vivid and affecting impression than a mere naked statement of the principle itself. This may have been unconsciously felt by St. Paul, and may have conduced to his adoption of the dogmatic construction or interpretation of the crucifixion. The subjective obstacle to his hopeful pursuit of the ethical ideal—viz., his conception of God as an exacting Judge requiring to be propitiated, which had been removed as a weight from his soul by the insight which he had gained into the divine character—presented itself to his imagination by reason of that very pathos as an objective obstacle which had been removed by the self-sacrifice of him who had graciously stooped from heaven to confer and remonstrate with him on his insane behaviour. The idea of the cross, which was at once the instrument of the death of Jesus and the symbol of the soteriological process, as proclaimed by Jesus, fired the soul of the Apostle and became the great and almost sole theme of his gospel (1 Cor. ii. 2), an observation which, by the way, seems to justify, if anything of the kind is needed, our contention that the teaching of Jesus in the main was soteriological.

It is evident, too, that if we leave out of sight the dogmatic element of St. Paul's teaching, we find it anticipated at every point by that of Jesus, whose claim, therefore, to be the Founder of Christianity cannot be transferred to the Apostle. Thus, even if Jesus did not use the word "cross," as he is reported by the synoptists to have done—for we do not wish to make such a question turn upon the occurrence of a word—yet the idea, expressed or symbolized by it, of self-denial and self-abnegation enters as essentially and as pervadingly into his doctrine as into that of St. Paul. The only thing which by any possibility can be placed to the credit of the latter in this connection is that he has rendered that idea more pathetic and more touching by connecting it with the actual or material cross on which Jesus died. And there can be no doubt that the Pauline doctrine of the atonement effected visibly or "evidently" (Gal. iii. 1) on the cross, has a pædagogic value which it will retain so long, but only so long, as the supernatural idea retains its hold of the human mind.

The practice of atonement by sacrifice seems to have been universal, for unnumbered ages, throughout the ancient world; and to have approved itself to the human heart as the natural means of paying homage to God or of propitiating His favour. And though, according to our view, Jesus dispensed with it, as having no place in the religious relation, yet, by connecting the idea of atonement with his death, the early Church thought to conserve it as an approved means of quickening the power of sympathy, and of enlisting religious feeling on behalf of the moral and spiritual elements of the doctrines of Jesus. This is one mode of accounting for the Pauline doctrine of atonement; or we may account for it somewhat differently by regarding it as a concession to his Jewish feeling, a compromise between the doctrine of Jesus and the doctrine of the Pharisees; an indication that the Apostle, imbued as he was with the evangelic, universalistic spirit, was yet not able to emancipate himself so completely as Jesus had done from the influence of Jewish provincialism.

By exchanging the heterosoteric Jewish idea for the autosoteric, Jesus showed how completely he had emancipated himself, how near he went to putting an end to Jewish thought. He only did not separate himself entirely from it because his doctrine still rested on its religious presuppositions; and retained, in the act of exalting, its ethical and theistic ideas. The step which Jesus thus took was too far in advance for Paul to follow his lead. Indeed, the Pauline dogma was nothing but the very natural though unconscious endeavour, as we have already seen, to preserve continuity between the Christian and the Jewish idea of the religious relation at a vital point where continuity seemed in danger of being broken. The law had said that without shedding of blood there could be no remission of sins ; but Jesus had proclaimed in absolute terms, without respect to Jewish privilege, or to propitiatory forms of worship, the boundless love and good-will of the Heavenly Father towards His penitent children ; and the consciousness which he sought to awaken in his disciples was but the echo of that sentiment. To reconcile these two antagonistic positions, the Church, through St. Paul as its spokesman, declared the blood of him who made the announcement of the unconditioned placability of God to be of surpassing virtue; an atonement of universal efficacy; the ground of that free forgiveness which was the main element of the Christian consciousness. Of course, this proposition of St. Paul cannot be verified. The human consciousness may bear witness to the fact, that forgiveness may be confidently laid hold of by the true penitent without challenge from his own higher nature—the divinity within him. But to certify that such privilege is due, in any sense, to the blood shed on Calvary is wholly beyond the reach and faculty of consciousness. Clearly this is, in Arnold's language, an unverifiable or extra-belief.

We can see that, in his endeavour to free the Christian spirit from the Jewish particularistic limitations which clung to it, St. Paul made use, for this end, of Jewish materials and rabbinical modes of thought. His mode of ratiocination was that of contemporary Jewish theology, to which he had been trained in the schools, and which had become as a second nature to him. But it may also have been employed by him of set purpose, in order to convict Judaism out of its own mouth, and to turn its own weapons against itself. An artificial, hybrid, and somewhat incongruous character was thus given to his dialectic. In the construction of his dogma he proceeded upon the plan of arbitrarily retaining or discarding the Jewish categories of thought just as it suited his purpose, And it has been observed by Weizsäcker and others, that the same Apostle who did most to free Christianity from the limits of Judaism, also contributed much to preserve in it the Jewish spirit.

There is ever an *a priori* presumption, that a doctrine far in advance of an age will not be comprehended by the age, however clearly it may be stated ; and the fact that the Pauline form of doctrine took such hold of that generation may be regarded as a proof that it had retained or incorporated with itself certain elements of thought, inherited from the past, which did not properly belong to it; elements which were even at variance with its spirit, but which helped to overcome prejudice against what was novel, and by recommending it to the men of that age, invested it with such prestige as to recommend it to many subsequent ages. The doctrine of Jesus was but the expression of his deep and independent consciousness or conviction of the goodness of the Heavenly Father; of the love rooted in the divine nature; a love so self-subsistent that it did not need to be conciliated, but acted rather as an aboriginal impulse to conciliate all rational creatures, and to train them to the love and practice of goodness for its own sake, after the fashion of the divine. This mental attitude into which Jesus sought to bring his disciples was in strong contrast to that of the Pharisees, all whose religious services had for their aim to propitiate the goodwill of God, and to establish a claim upon his favour by conventional moralities and punctilious attention to statutory observances and expiatory rites. St. Paul's doctrine, again, is evidently a mean or compromise between the two. For, according to him, God has been propitiated, only not by sacrifice offered or observance practised by man himself, but by the self-sacrifice of one who was the divinely appointed substitute or representative of man. And now, man no longer needed to atone for his sin, but only to believe in the atonement which had been offered once for all upon the cross by his substitute; and so to enjoy the benefit of a work already accomplished, or, perhaps, to join in with a work already begun, and to build upon a foundation securely laid. The Apostle thus got rid or kept clear of the mercenary, or Pharisaic taint, and sought with true evangelic aim, if not by a wholly evangelic method, to awaken love and gratitude as the propelling motives of human effort.

From this point of view it may be said that, practically, the doctrine of Jesus and the doctrine of St. Paul amount to much the same thing; that the religious relation, which, according to Jesus, is immanent, is, according to St. Paul, brought to pass by the cross; or, that St. Paul represents God as placed, by means of a propitiation offered outside the human sphere, in the same relation to us as Jesus represents Him to be placed, apart from any transaction of the kind. But there is this great difference, that St. Paul's doctrine sacrifices the idea of the absolute goodness and unchangeableness of God, and obscures that feature of the divine order according to which the sense of forgiveness, even as of necessity, and irrespective of all other conditions, follows on repentance, and the harvest of good is assured to him who sows the seed of good. According to the same doctrine also, human redemption is effected by the somewhat mechanical, cumbrous, and artificial contrivance of introducing a third party into a transaction which lies properly between God and man, or between the higher or divine and the lower nature of man, *i.e.*, by the introduction of a supernatural element into the soteriological process. Finally, instead of relying, as Jesus did, on the intrinsic evidence of the doctrine which attributes boundless goodness to the divine nature, St. Paul points to the historical fact of the atonement made on Calvary—" He that spared not His own son, but delivered him up for us all, how shall He not with him also freely give us all things " (Rom. viii. 32). He points to the cross as the instrument of an act of self-sacrifice on the part of God ; an idea of which it is difficult for us to form a conception, seeing that in God there is no darkness at all—no lower nature to call for, or to afford the necessary condition for such an act—an objection to the Pauline view which is none the less conclusive because of its being simple and intelligible. It surely invalidates the absolute freeness and aboriginal character of the love of God as taught by Jesus, if it be said that a sacrifice of any kind whatever on the part of God, whether that of a third person or a self-sacrifice, was needed in the way of propitiating His love, or setting it free to act.

And here we may introduce our decisive reply to the allegation, which has frequently been advanced of late, that Paul is the real founder of Christianity, viz., that we recognize in the teaching of Jesus, simple as it is, an apprehension of the religious relation at once higher and more consistent with itself, in regard both to the human and the divine nature, than that of Paul. The former would conduct us to a spiritual height above that on which the latter has placed us. The faith which Jesus enjoined was devotion to the righteousness of God, that is, to the ideal of humanity.

Paul changed this into devotion to the person of Jesus, in whom he saw that ideal embodied. The same thing has been expressed by saying that the doctrine of Jesus was converted by St. Paul into the dogma concerning Jesus. The dogma which we thus owe to the Apostle is not, we have already admitted, wholly disparate from the evangelic doctrine, but rather a close reflection of it in symbolic form ; and has rendered a great provisional or pædagogic service to the religious idea. The abstract unembodied ideal, as presented in the teaching of Jesus and illustrated by his example, was not calculated to attract and attach the minds of the bulk of mankind ; and it was probably a necessity in the very nature of things that the personality in which that ideal was seen to be most adequately manifested, should be raised for the human understanding to the position of that divine nature with which the ideal is identical (Matth. v. 48).

But not the less on that account do we affirm that the dogma of St. Paul is a descent, a falling away from the doctrine of Jesus. Had Paul not been preceded by Jesus, he might (such is our opinion of his religious genius and his ethical intensity) have attempted, on the basis of an independent development of thought, to reform and revolutionize the national religion. But his dogmatic construction or modification of the religion of Jesus suffices to show that he was too much dominated by Jewish ideas to have effected his purpose, or at least to have done more than to found or originate a Jewish sect. He could never have reached the idea of the perfect and essential Fatherhood of God, or have thrown aside, as Jesus did, the ideas of sacrifice and mediation as unessential to the religious relation. He was not able to accept or apprehend the doctrine of Jesus in its simplicity, even when presented to him, or to incorporate it into his own system of thought, except through these foreign and irrelevant ideas. And the probability is, that in any form of religion which he could have originated, these would have been primary and essential instead of being secondary, interjectional, and instrumental, as in the dogmatic form which he impressed upon the reluctant religion of Jesus.

That God forgives sins freely, that with His consent we may leave our sins behind us and pass on to a better life, and that expiation for sins that are past is unnecessary, is a doctrine which men have much difficulty in accepting. They may have a strong feeling of their own sinfulness, but having no adequate conception of the nature of sin, they do not perceive that by its nature it is inexpiable, but imagine that some great thing has to be done, some great price to be paid, in short, some atonement to be made, whether by themselves or by another in their stead, in order to its remission. This is a universal idea confined to no age, ancient or modern, and holds a very conspicuous place in the Old Testament, underlying and pervading its whole system of thought. Yet the rationale of it is nowhere clearly or definitely stated, and in the synagogal theology the doctrine seems to be explicit that atonement may be made in various forms, singly or combined, according to circumstances, most conspicuously by sacrifice and other legal ritual observances, and also by penitence, by acts of an ascetic or purificatory character, by almsgiving, by restitution, and even by the supererogatory merits of the fathers. Many things might thus contribute to effect the sinner's forgiveness; many things had to be taken into account before the sinner could be satisfied of his being forgiven; feelings of great anxiety, lest some necessary thing had been omitted, were produced in his mind, and a consequent uncertainty as to his condition in the sight of God. It hardly needs to be added, that such a state of theological opinion must also have contributed much to fix and strengthen the mercenary and servile habit of religion in the Jewish mind.

But while letting go, as we have seen, the simple teaching of Jesus, in so far as it excluded *in toto* the idea of atonement, St. Paul yet removed all uncertainty from the believer's mind by his emphatic declaration that there was one and only one atonement for all sin whatever, and that it had been accomplished once for all upon the cross. It may, in this respect, be affirmed of the dogma of St. Paul, as of the doctrine of Jesus, that it is anti-Judaical and anti-legal in the highest degree. The Apostle may indeed be said to have returned, as by a circuitous route, to the point from which he started at his conversion, and the circuit thus made by him encloses the area of his dogma. But by his dogma he applied an antidote to that legal and particularistic spirit which was apt to pass over and to infect the Christian Church through its

Jewish members ; and we have mainly to ascribe it to him, that the Church was, if not completely, yet in a great measure saved from this danger.

For though, as has been shown, Jesus himself could not but realize the universalistic range and tendency of his doctrine, yet, whether because he felt a tenderness toward those forms of worship by which his soul had been nurtured, or because he deemed it inexpedient to alarm the feelings and susceptibilities of his disciples before they were at home in the true spiritual worship, the various utterances of his which bore upon this subject had a delphic and even conflicting sound, which left it doubtful whether in his view the rites and usages of Jewish worship were to retain their place in his new religion. The apparent conflict in his teaching on this point has, it is true, no existence for those critics who regard Matth. v. 18, 19, "Till heaven and earth pass, one jot or one tittle shall in no wise pass from the law, till all be fulfilled," as an interpolation ; and Matth. ix. 17, "Neither do men put new wine into old bottles," etc., as the index of his true position in regard to the law. And it can scarcely be denied that much may be said in support of such a criticism ; this especially, that Matth. v. 19 is, as much as can be, conceived in the spirit of Pharisaic legalism, whereas v. 20 is manifestly a strongly expressed depreciation of it, "Except your righteousness shall exceed the righteousness of the scribes and Pharisees, ye shall in no case enter into the kingdom of heaven." But in spite of this and other textual difficulties, we are not inclined to question the authenticity of vv. 18 and 19. For we must take into consideration that the new legislation may in a very true sense be regarded as a fulfilment of the older ; that in common with other founders of religion, such as Zoroaster, Confucius, and Mahomet, Jesus desired to represent himself as a continuator and reformer of the previously existing religion; and that he must have known well that he ran the risk of being regarded with suspicion as a setter forth of strange doctrines. These considerations make it by no means improbable that he would not only be careful not to run unnecessary risk, but also that he might make use of such a statement as that in vv. 18, 19 by way of soothing prejudice and allaying suspicion, even though he could unfold his new doctrine in all its aspects only by means of statements which to his countrymen would seem to be not very consistent with that other. Still, it must be confessed that the verbal exegesis of such passages does not help us much. Every one will be guided in his interpretation of these by general and extraneous or collateral considerations. We therefore content ourselves with repeating that it was reserved for St. Paul to give forth a certain sound upon this point. He it was who saw clearly, and made the Church at large to see, that through the retention of Jewish forms the spirit of legalism might insinuate itself into the Christian community, or even throw it back into Judaism, besides arresting the progress of the gospel among the Gentiles.

The Pauline dogma excluded the idea of propitiatory service on the part of man, and along with that the whole system of worship of which that service was the centre. The dogma did not absolutely dispense with atonement as the doctrine of Jesus did, but it was fitted by the very use which it retained of that idea to bring home to the minds of men in vivid, because in outward and historical form, that conception of divine love which excludes the need of all expiation on the part of the sinner himself; and to supply the great incentive to that heartfelt devotion of the life, the consciousness of which relieves the soul in a kingly manner of all painful anxiety as to the observance of outward forms, and constitutes the soul a law to itself. It thus set aside the law of outward ordinances and statutory observances more effectually even than the more pure and thorough doctrine of Jesus could do at that time, just because it put something massive and palpable in the place of these. And in this respect Paul may be said to have rendered a great and, under reservation, an indispensable service to the Christian Church. Not that in the creation of his dogma the Apostle had this last object primarily in view. The dogma was essentially the spontaneous growth of his mind; and if there was any semi-conscious calculation in it at all, it was primarily to meet the Apostle's own personal need, rather than to meet the need of the Church at large. He may have sought to maintain at initial intensity, or to charge with growing emotion, that aspiration after the ideal which had been fired in him by the revelation of Christ to his soul, by representing to himself that ideal as perfectly embodied in the person of Christ. For this purpose he turned not to the details of that earthly life of Jesus, as did the mythical fancy with the same end in view, but concentrated his thoughts upon the closing scene of that life, in which he saw in typical form a transcendent exhibition of all evangelical righteousness ; a transaction which appealed powerfully to the warmest feelings of his heart, and enlisted all his sympathies in behalf of the ideal. He may also have felt, and, no doubt, did feel, that what was thus a need for himself was no less a need for his fellow Christians, and that it was his bounden duty to preach the gospel in this form to all who would listen to him.

The idea of atonement is not only the real point of contact between Jewish and Pauline theology, as is obvious, but also the true centre, or rather starting-point of the latter in its career of development. A numerous school of modern theologians, indeed, would have us believe that the doctrine of incarnation is the grand doctrine, to which that of the atonement, and all others in the Pauline system, are subordinate ; but there can be no question that belief in the atonement was the genetic prius of belief in the incarnation and in the divinity of Christ : the centre out of which the whole dogma was evolved. These doctrines of the incarnation and of the divinity of Jesus are inevitable inferences from that of atonement, provided this is regarded as of objective significance and as an offering presented to God, which was certainly its significance for the mind St. Paul. Thence, it may be noted, that where incarnation is promoted to the central position in so-called orthodox doctrine, there is generally, if not invariably, a tendency to regard atonement only in its subjective aspect: to represent the work and death of Jesus not as the means by which God is reconciled to men, but simply as the means by which God reconciles men to Himself—a curtailment of its significance and value which we see little or nothing in St. Paul's epistles to warrant—and to regard his mission into the world as a sort of show-miracle, intended merely to *display* an ideal human life as a stimulus and object for imitation. This is a view of it, of which it has been well and strikingly observed, that had it been adopted by St. Paul, he would necessarily have made more frequent reference to the details of the earthly life of Jesus as exemplary to that of believers, which yet he seldom, or rather never, does : while his constant reference is to the death upon the cross as the ordained means of salvation. This same view of the death of

Jesus, as a mere display or manifestation of divine love, comes as near as can be to the idea of "a sign from heaven," a mere display, not indeed of divine power, such as the Jews demanded, but of divine goodness ; and throws an air of unreality over the great event, which is fitted to deprive it of all genuine influence upon the mind of the spectator.

There is truth, no doubt, in what Weizsäcker says, that St. Paul nowhere speaks of the wrath of God being removed by the death of Christ ; but only of the latter as a work of divine love, which does not permit us to think of there being any hindrance to its exercise in the nature of God Himself (2 Cor. v. 19). But to the omission of this link of thought in the writings of St. Paul we attach no decisive importance. In regard to the omission of this thought, we are disposed to say *sub intelligitur.* For, if the Apostle nowhere says that the wrath of God was appeased by the cross of Christ, he yet, in many places, speaks of His wrath ; and shuts us up to the inference, that it was appeased by that instrumentality. How little importance need be attached to this negative consideration, or to this omission on the part of the Apostle, is shown by the observation which Weizsäcker lets fall, shortly before, viz., that while the Apostle speaks of the death of Jesus as a sacrifice or offering for sin, he nowhere says, what is said in the Epistle to the Hebrews, that it had superseded, or come in place of, the sacrifices under the law, though no one can doubt, that this was his opinion, or that such a remark lay in the very line of his thought. The truth seems to be, that for the Apostle the wrath of God against sinners was a reality, to reconcile which with the fact that He had given His Son to die for them was a puzzle, to the solution of which the Apostle did not see his way. He probably believed that God's love had prevailed to that extent over His wrath at their sin. And if this be so, it seems to show that there was a certain dualism in his conception of the divine nature which he could not explain away. In the fourth Gospel and in 1st John the dualistic element is even more unmistakable ; and indeed this element is essential to dogmatic or supernatural Christianity in all its forms.

For St. Paul and the writer of the Epistle to the Hebrews, the death of Jesus on the cross was an atonement analogous to the ancient animal sacrifices, which they regarded as prefiguring it. As the Jews considered that the death of the victim on the

altar was graciously accepted in place of the sinner's who presented the offering, so the Apostle applied that idea to the death
of Jesus, and considered it to be the real expiation, of which
those others had been only types and figures. The analogy is
more fully and clearly expressed in the Epistle to the Hebrews ;
but it underlies the doctrine of St. Paul, and whatever the idea
of a subjective atonement may have to recommend it to the
school of modern theologians referred to, it does not cover the
idea in St. Paul's mind. He shared in the sacrificial idea,
common in the ancient world, viz., that God in his mercy
accepted the animal's life or soul in place of that which had
been forfeited by the sinner. It might have occurred to
men's minds, that God in mercy might have pardoned the
sinner without exacting such a worthless substitute. But the
men of the old world were unable to conceive of mercy being
extended to the sinner, unless God's displeasure with his sin
were first appeased by an offering, which would at least express
an acknowledgment of His right to punish. They could not
rid themselves of a certain dualism in the nature of God,
or resist the tendency to make an anthropomorphic distinction
between His mercy and His justice ; and the sacrificial or
expiatory idea, objectively considered, was needed to reconcile
the action of both for the benefit of the sinner. This idea,
under certain modifications, passed over into St. Paul's doctrine,
and remains to this day the substratum of orthodox theology.
He regarded the life which Jesus had surrendered on the cross
as the price which had been paid for the forfeited life of man.
Human redemption was for him the resultant of two divergent forces in the divine nature. And he was probably
inspired by his singular personal experience to draw wide
the distinction between law and grace. His zeal for the former
had made him a persecutor and a blasphemer; his conversion
was regarded by him as an effect of sovereign grace ; and the
development of this unreal distinction issued in all those dialectical subtleties which characterize his dogmatic system,
rendering it hard to be understood and susceptible of such
conflicting interpretations as to have exercised the ingenuity
of commentators, and to have made it the subject of theological
contention for nearly two millenniums, without any prospect
as yet of a definite settlement. But the modern idea of
divine unity, not numerical but spiritual, of which mercy and

justice are but different aspects to human apprehension, has overthrown this doctrine of atonement, and revealed to us that the distinction between the two so-called attributes exists only in the finite, but not in the infinite subject. By nothing, perhaps, is the purity of the religious insight of Jesus so much shown as by his omitting—that is, discarding—the idea of atonement from connection with divine grace and forgiveness, or, let us say, from the religious relation. That idea, on the other hand, was too strongly entrenched in the mind of St. Paul to be got rid of. Instead of discarding it altogether, the Apostle had recourse to the compromise, already attributed to him, of removing it out of the human sphere into a region of mystery, and making it, by a sort of gnostic treatment, the moment of a theogonic process. In his theology, indeed, atonement was in no respect as it had been in Jewish theology, either morally or ceremonially, an act of man himself accepted by God, nor was it a result produced in the soul of man by an act on the part of God ; but it was an act of God, not graciously prescribing or accepting an imperfect sacrifice on the part of man, but Himself offering a perfect sacrifice in the person of His Son, and transferring the guilt of the sinner at once and for ever to a holy victim.

From this point of view, we can see that Jesus was a pure idealist whom the age could not comprehend, while, on the other hand, Paul as a teacher remained in touch with his age by incorporating the doctrine of atonement with the teaching of Jesus, and so imparting to the religious relation a juridical and realistic character. The various attempts which have been made, by way of conciliating modern thought, to strip St. Paul's view of that relation of this juridical element, are but samples of what Jesus meant when he warned his disciples against pouring new wine into old bottles. They are but so many attempts to rehabilitate or rationalize conceptions that are out of date, and, by a veiled and modernized use of the allegorical form of interpretation, to make them square with the thought of the new era. All systems of thought, even the most diverse, whether in the moral or spiritual field, have certain points of contact, and by the exercise of an ingenious dialectic may be made to run together and brought into a certain degree, greater or less, of propinquity. But by no ingenuity, however specious, can the modern ideas of the religious relation be identified with those which underlie the dogma of St. Paul. The immense diligence and constructive power with which German theologians especially have sought to perform this feat have failed to convince us that St. Paul had the remotest forecast of modern ideas upon the subject. At the most, these theologians do but reverse the dogmatic process of St. Paul, and get back, as near as may be, to the doctrine of Jesus, of which they seek to give us the modern equivalent in grand and laboured philosophic form.

There is nothing more evident in St. Paul's epistles than that he was enthusiastically persuaded of the universalism of the religion of which he was the expounder. According to his mind this predicate belonged to it, because it placed the whole human race on an equal footing in the sight of God, and because it conferred its benefits on the Gentiles without requiring them first to become Jews. Before his conversion, the ground of his hostility to the religion of Jesus was that it took no account of Jewish privilege, and set those things aside on which Jewish privilege depended. And after embracing the new doctrine he did not forget this feature of it. The grandeur of the idea was probably one of those things in it by which it appealed to his mind, so as at once to attract and to repel him ; and he was far indeed from thinking that he had obscured or obliterated this aspect of Christianity by his dogma of the atonement. At a time when the supernatural idea connected with the person and work of Jesus gave no offence, and presented no difficulty to faith, there was nothing illogical in such a position. But had St. Paul lived at the present day, it is doubtful whether he could have proclaimed this doctrine with the same confidence in its universalistic character. No doctrine is fully entitled to that designation which does not appeal to the essential principles and instincts of human nature, and which cannot win its way to the hearts of men independent of authority, and assert for itself a place in the great system of human thought. We have endeavoured to show that by certain avenues of dialectic and of experience it is competent for man to rise, as Jesus did, to the conception of the Heavenly Father, who freely forgives our sins, and looks with benign and encouraging eye upon our every effort to extricate ourselves from the toils of evil ; but it is confessedly impossible for man, except by special revelation, to rise to the other Pauline and orthodox idea of God, as determined in his relations to man by the death upon the Cross of one in human form. This is a thought which can evidently be received only upon the authority of such a revelation ; and it is not easy to see how universalism can be predicated of this doctrine in an age like the present, when it is a thousand times more difficult to embrace a faith in the supernatural than it would be to submit to all the requirements of the Mosaic law. The mere fact that the preacher of the gospel invites all men, without distinction, to partake of its benefits, does not make it universalistic. No religion, however exclusive and non-proselytizing, has refused to enrol converts on its own conditions. But universalism can be affirmed of a religion only when the condition it demands is the acceptance of truths which appeal to the human heart as eternally true and valid : which rest not upon doubtful or irrelevant speculations, nor upon an obsolete theory of the divine government ; but are involved or implied in the very constitution of our rational nature. Our conviction is that the doctrine of Jesus may justly lay claim to this predicate of universalism, but only as enunciated by himself, and not as construed by St. Paul. By its strictly practical nature ; by its abstention from speculation and from the claim to inspiration ; by its bearing on the moral life, and by the fact that the evidence on which it rests is independent of a supernatural basis, " the religion of Jesus " may claim to be regarded as the absolute and universal religion. But the " Christian religion " as conceived and taught by St. Paul rested on the old, *i.e.*, the naïve, non-scientific theory of the universe, and having the supernatural as its presupposition, can retain its hold over those only who overlook that connection, or are content to separate what is permanent in it from what is transient, and who, like ourselves, find that the spiritual elements of Christianity have an absolute and independent value. We are not staggered in the judgment here expressed by the fact that St. Paul evidently regards universalism as a signature or note of his gospel. That claim in his day none would care to dispute. But it is only by the sacrifice in his doctrine of the supernatural which differentiates his teaching from that of Jesus that this claim can now be made good.

The distinction here drawn between the religion of Jesus and the Pauline or Christian religion, was first, we believe, distinctly recognised by Lessing. But as stated by him, it was only a surmise or divination, which could not be verified in the then existing condition of Biblical criticism ; whereas now a strong and growing presumption has been created in its favour by every advance which criticism has made since Lessing's day— and it is a distinction which commands our assent.* We hold that, unconsciously and unintentionally, St. Paul broke or fell away from the simplicity and universalism of the doctrine of Jesus, in his desire to preserve, as far as possible, the thread of continuity between it and the older form of religion, as well as to magnify the significance of the person of Jesus, and to main- tain, at its initial intensity, his own sense of obligation to him. While, in his teaching as preserved by the synoptists, Jesus makes no reference to his own person, in the Pauline doctrine he becomes all in all : a place is assigned to him in the Christian consciousness which he never claims for himself; a virtue is ascribed to his work in the soteriological process which did not belong to it ; and the spirit of his doctrine is clothed in a form which, by identifying it with his person, might seem to compensate for the withdrawal of his personal presence, and also render his doctrine more palpable and level to ordinary human apprehension.

They who have taken hold of the Fatherhood of God, of the unchangeableness of the divine law, and of personal responsibility as taught by Jesus, and even by Paul himself, will not easily be

---

* The surmise of Lessing has never, we believe, since his day, been lost sight of. One of the most eminent of living theologians has gone the length of saying that the simple doctrine of Jesus was "spoiled" by St. Paul's doctrine of the atonement. The writer of this volume takes this opportunity to state that the same idea forced itself upon him independently, at a time when he was comparatively little read in German theology, and when he was not aware that the distinction referred to had been drawn. It appeared to him that the soteriological doctrine of Jesus was complete in itself; at once more simple, more intelligible, and more satisfactory, than the elaborate dogmatic form into which it had been cast by St. Paul. Parenthetically, it may here be remarked that the true "Fall" in Christian doctrine lay, not as a fanciful theologian (Thiersch), and others after him have maintained, between the apostolic and the post-apostolic age, but between Jesus himself and his apostles ; or, according to what has just been said, between the religion of Jesus, and the Christian religion. This fall consisted in the conversion of the simple, practical doctrine of Jesus into the complex dogma of St. Paul, by which the whole subsequent development of Christian theology has been determined.

indoctrinated with the idea of atonement, by which the Apostle effected this conversion of the religion of Jesus into the Christian religion. The metamorphosis which the religion of Jesus thus underwent was very great, if not radical. In the synoptists, Jesus only appears to instruct men, by word and by example, to redeem or deliver themselves from the power of evil ; to whom therefore our gratitude and veneration are tempered by the consideration that, after all, he was but a member of a long prophetic chain, the product of a great religious movement going before, as well as a factor in the continuance and acceleration of that movement. But in St. Paul's epistles he is presented as the author of a redemption, of which we become partakers only by faith in him, *i.e.*, by means of some subjective relation to him, or by a certain ethical disposition, consisting in love to him and in imitation of his manner of life. A permanent and absolute significance is thus given in the religious life of man to the person of Jesus. By a single stroke his autosoteric doctrine is converted into one that is heterosoteric ; and our historical dependence on his teaching and example, into a metaphysical dependence on his work and person. That happy change in the sinner's state which, according to the doctrine of Jesus, is effected by the conception of divine love, animating and exhilarating the soul in its conflict with evil, is, according to St. Paul, accomplished by divine grace, considered as an energy or potency flowing from the person of Christ, and called into operation by faith in him, so as to act directly or magically on the human will. If, according to the Apostle's view, we can, in any sense, be said to save ourselves, it is by believing on Christ, by copying his example, and in this way qualifying ourselves to partake of his redemption ; so that human deliverance from evil is seen, in a sense, to be the joint work of Jesus and of the sinner himself—a process partly autosoteric and partly heterosoteric ; and the whole subject becomes involved, as theologians well know, in inextricable confusion, giving occasion to innumerable controversies in the Church, which do not seem to admit of settlement, and ever reappear in new forms.

The confusion in St. Paul's scheme of doctrine, which we here allege, and for the existence of which we may take these controversies to be the objective evidence, may be best accounted for, we say, by the fact that his doctrine is a compromise between the autosoteric and the heterosoteric point of view. Conspicuous in his writings there is a wavering between the two forms of doctrine ; an effort to qualify, by rationalizing, the magical influence of Christ, without seeming to deprive him of the sole glory and credit of man's salvation. When the Apostle presses upon his readers the study of the example of Christ, the sympathetic contemplation of Christ crucified, manifestly set forth by the preached word for this very purpose, it appears as if he trusted that this contemplation would operate upon the rational and receptive nature of man, and contribute to his emancipation from evil, and his edification in the moral life. But when he says, on the other hand, " I live, and yet not I, but Christ liveth in me," we may call this a mystical, coming near to a magical, view of the believer's life : a view of it which is further confirmed by the representation of a spirit proceeding from Christ, and taking dæmonic possession of the believer ; for this representation, if more fully carried out in the fourth Gospel, is not foreign to St. Paul's mode of thinking (Rom. viii. 11, 1 Cor. iii. 16).

In passing, we pause here to observe that it was a true instinct which, probably from the earliest ages of the world, led men to the thought that sacrifice and mediation of some sort were requisite to place the relation of men to God on its proper footing. This thought was inherited by St. Paul from the fathers ; but he also shared in a tendency, which the history of religions shows to have been frequently exemplified in the ethnic religions of the world—viz., to conceive of the mediating function as concentrated in some one individual, supposed to be participant both of the human and the divine nature. The true idea, which is at once more consonant to the teaching of Jesus, and to which modern thought inclines, is that this function belongs to the God in man ; to that divine principle which resides in every individual ; by surrendering himself to whose promptings all the discordant elements of his nature are controlled, and he is brought into the true reciprocal relation to God, so as to be able to say from the heart, " Not my will, but Thine be done." Looked at from this point of view, the difference between the religion of Jesus and the religion of St. Paul—between Christianity as a natural and as a supernatural system—may seem to be not very great, theoretical rather than practical. But be this as it may, it is necessary that the true theory should be recognized, in order to remove all ground of offence to scientific thought, and also to do away with the Judaic or passive habit of mind in the matter of religion.

To explain to himself and to others how the sufferings of the Messiah could atone for the sins of men, the Apostle adopted an idea for which he was indebted partly to a Hellenistic source, and partly to the current synagogal theology. According to the latter, it was a matter of indifference by whom the penalty of sin was borne, whether by the sinner himself or by some one more or less related to him ; the law was satisfied—the sin was expiated provided the penalty was borne. Then there was the Hellenistic idea of an archetypal man—a second Adam, or second head of the human family ; of one in whom the idea of humanity was realized, between whom and the human race there was such solidarity that he could represent it before God. Obviously, the kinship between these two ideas was such that the one could be incorporated with the other ; and the result was that Christ, as the archetypal man or second Adam, could expiate the sins of the race. Whether the assumptions thus made are or are not satisfactory to the critical modern mind is of no consequence. Enough that they commended themselves to the Apostle's mind. To him they seemed to afford a probable or rational justification of the doctrine of the Atonement. He therefore adopted and made use of them to explain and recommend that doctrine to his converts.

Be it observed that this idea of the second Adam was not, as Mr. Arnold would have us think, a mere literary fancy or sportive allusion ; but a link of thought essential to the Apostle's dogma. There are many casual indications in his epistles that he considered it to be essentially pertinent to his system of thought ; and there is one such indication in particular, in his view of the resurrection of Christ as the guarantee of the resurrection of believers. It could be so only because of the solidarity between believers and Christ as their representative, corresponding to that which exists between the head and the members of the body, so that the head, in its ascent, can be conceived as drawing the body after it. We here assume that St. Paul's idea of Christ as the representative man was not a mere coincidence with Hellenistic thought, but was adopted by him from that source. For it has, we think, been demonstrated by E. Pfleiderer (*Philosophie des Heraklit*) that the Apostle was well acquainted with Hellenistic thought, and even with its modes of expression.

We have here met for the first time with an indication of Greek or Hellenistic influence upon the religious evolution which we have been tracing, and as this influence becomes more and more patent in the subsequent stages, we shall here pause to express our general views as to the place occupied by such influences in the evolution. We are not at all disposed to question the fact, or to depreciate the importance of Hellenism (in which a fusion had already taken place between Greek and Jewish thought), considered as a factor in the evolution of Christian thought. On the contrary, we deem it to be an enhancement of the great position of Christianity, when it is shown that the two great branches of human thought—the Aryan and the Semitic, the Greek and the Jewish—coalesced in its growth. We imagine, however, that there is a tendency at present to overrate, as well as to antedate, the part which the former played in the process. And our appreciation of the service which Greek or Hellenistic thought has rendered is qualified by the following considerations :—

(1) It does not appear to have influenced the *genesis* of Christianity. There is, no doubt, a difficulty in conceiving how the Founder of our faith could altogether have escaped the touch of Greek thought, educated as he was in the land of Galilee, amid a mixed population of Greeks and Jews. There, as elsewhere in the countries overrun by Alexander, Greek influences had been more or less at work for more than two centuries. And it is barely conceivable that there could have been a corner of the land, or an interior circle in it, so isolated, so shut off from Greek thought, as not to have felt its power. But what we say is, that in the teaching of Jesus there is no clear indication of distinctively Greek ideas—nothing which might not have been evolved from Jewish thought alone. The evangelical idea, which was the centre of His doctrine, while it was a revolt against the vulgar Pharisaism of the day, was the development, or fulfilment, of the higher or prophetic mind of Israel. And it is evident that he did not, and indeed could not have drawn the idea from Greek inspiration. Not only had the Greek mind not

been able to rise to the height of the idea, but it had, to all appearance, missed and passed it by. The highest water-mark of Greek thought in that direction is probably to be seen in that idea of the Stoics, that there is no such thing as forgiveness for past failures, but only amendment for the future. We are not blind to the fact, that this doctrinal position of the Stoics displays a certain depth of insight into the process of the spiritual life ; but the undue emphasis which it lays on the legal aspect of the process is a stray or mis-leading note in it, and it falls far short of the deeper insight of Jesus, viz., that there is a moment in the spiritual life at which, while the physical and social penalties of sin remain, its oppressive and condemning power falls like a burden from the conscience ; and the remembrance of past failure, from being a drag, becomes a stimulus to the upward progress. That is a moment or crisis in the life of which thousands of Christians have been distinctly conscious, and of which Bunyan gives a striking picture in his dream. And all who prelimin-arily—after the manner of the educative process—accept of this fact on the testimony of Jesus, and honestly (Luke viii. 15) endeavour to prove and verify it in their own case, are His true followers. It is scarcely necessary to add here, that if the distinctive teaching of Jesus could not be derived from his acquaintance with the Stoic thought, still less could it be derived from the rival Greek school of practical philosophy, viz., the Epicurean. Nothing can be less in harmony with the ideal, practical doctrine of Jesus, than the " long-sighted prudence which contents itself with moderate and safe enjoy-ment," and that disbelief in providence inculcated by Epi-curus.

(2) If Greek thought had nothing to do with the genesis of Christianity, there can be no doubt, that in the construction of the dogma St. Paul was indebted in the second degree to Greek or Hellenistic speculation. Whether he derived aid directly from acquaintance with Greek and Hellenistic literature, or indirectly from the elements of Greek or Hellenistic thought floating at large in the intellectual atmosphere, matters not. To judge from abstract considerations, it is as improbable that St. Paul could have remained uninfluenced by Greek thought, as that he was uninfluenced by the teaching and the details of the life of Jesus. A man of intellect so piercing could not shut his

mind against an influence with which he could not but come in contact in his native Tarsus and in his journeyings up and down the civilized, largely Hellenized world. Professor Mahaffy (*Greek Life and Thought*) from his purely historical point of view, speaks of the Greek (Stoic) colour and training of St. Paul's mind, and says that there is "no mistaking" the influence upon him of Greek thought. In proof of this, he singles out the splendid period in 2 Cor. vi., where the contrasts presented by the Christian life are described by the Apostle in terms borrowed from the Stoic formulæ of the moral life. The Apostle may indeed have only taken a suggestion from that source by way of delineating his own experience of the Christian life. But if this does not affect the substance of his thought, it shows at least that he was not unacquainted with Stoic doctrine. And this is all the more likely, inasmuch as Tarsus, the Apostle's birth-place, was one of the chief seats of Stoic philosophy. So too, it has been demonstrated, we think, by E. Pfleiderer (*Philosophie des Heraklit*, pp. 295, etc.), that in 2 Cor. v. 1-9 the Apostle must have had the Hellenistic Book of Wisdom directly in his view : and that there are other passages in his epistles which show unmistakable traces of his acquaintance with this book, in which elements of Greek and Jewish thought had already coalesced. It may no doubt be said that Greek elements of thought may have exerted an influence upon him without his being conscious of it. But it is not improbable that E. Pfleiderer may have hit upon an important fact as throwing light upon the dogmatic process, when he suggests, that in Phil. ii. 6-11—a passage in which St. Paul's Christological doctrine advances a step forward, and takes a higher flight than elsewhere in his epistles (if perhaps 2 Cor. viii. 9 be excepted)—the Apostle had a remarkable speculation of Heraklitus directly in view. The number of centuries which intervened between the philosopher and the Apostle does not shake the value or impair the probability of this suggestion ; for the authority of Heraklitus, as a great master in philosophy, seems to have revived in that late or Hellenistic age, and it is not unreasonable to suppose that Paul may have been acquainted with his writings. Now, in his style of mystical, theosophic speculation, Heraklitus imagines that the Absolute may divest Himself of His high estate : may descend to a lower sphere of existence, and subject Himself to suffering and even to death: and having thus given proof of His virtue, may ascend in triumph to His original state. The parallel here to the passage in the Epistle to the Philippians is so close and striking that it can hardly be accidental, and renders probable the suggestion of a genetic connection.

(3) In a former section of this discussion, it was remarked that dogma proper was absent from the Old Testament ; and if, for the reasons then given, this be admitted, it might be supposed that the dogmatizing or speculative tendency which appears in the New Testament was, as Dr. Hatch (Hibbert Lecture, 1888) endeavours to show, *mainly* owing to contact with the speculative philosophy of Greece. But it seems to us that there is something of exaggeration in this view. It is true that Greek habits of thought did ere long become an important factor in the construction of the dogmatic system ; but in the initial stage even of this process the speculative tendency was spontaneous and independent, called forth by the singular situation in which the first disciples found themselves placed by the death of their Master, and by their belief in his Messiah-ship and resurrection. The dogma of the atonement, which was the starting point of the whole system, is really neither more nor less than an unverifiable speculation or hypothesis in regard to the nature and purpose of the death of the Messiah. It suggested or offered itself to the disciples as an explanation at once of the ignominious death of one whom they regarded as the promised Messiah, and of the great spiritual change which had passed upon themselves. And with this explanation upon their minds, they went forth to inculcate the faith of the atonement as the means of producing the same change in the minds of others. That is to say, the belief in the atonement, which was the *effect* produced on the minds of the first disciples by their own great spiritual experience, became, in the case of their converts, the *cause* of a like experience. And in passing we may remark, that this is the ultimate explanation of the historical fact referred to by Dr. Hatch, that from the end of the second century onwards—by which time the forward impulse given to Christianity by the contagious and assimilative power of the new life was exhausted—attention was turned to the creed rather than to the conduct, and that the intellectual rather than the moral element became the basis of union among its adherents. Moreover, it is evident that a speculation at once

so vague and so momentous as that of the atonement could not
fail to quicken the speculative tendency generally, and, *proprio
motu*, to call for further definition, which it received in the first
instance at the hands of St. Paul, and in which the influence
of Greek philosophy gradually made itself more and more felt
till it culminated in the fourth Gospel.

(4) The definition which Paul gave, as we have just seen,
to the original (Jewish-Christian) form of the atonement, by
which its incidence was universalized, may be traced either
directly to the universalistic tendency of the doctrine of Jesus,
or indirectly to the Apostle's contact with Greek (Stoic)
philosophy, in which the same tendency had made its appearance. Probably both may have co-operated to influence
the Apostle's thought. And this leads us to remark, that
wherever Greek influence is apparent in the dogmatic presentation, we find in general that there was between the Greek
thought and the thought of Jesus a certain kinship, which
renders it probable that both contributed to the formation of
the dogma. And it will be found, as we proceed, that the
unalterable bent given to the religious consciousness by the
personality and teaching of Jesus exercised a controlling
influence in the selection or rejection by the Church of those
elements, whether of Greek or of Jewish origin, which it sought
to incorporate with the growing dogma; and this same bent it
was which kept development upon the line of what in the end
prevailed as orthodoxy.

(5) According to Jewish notions, the perfect man was he
who fulfilled the requirements of the statutory law, ceremonial
or moral. The man who did so was said to fulfil all righteousness (Matth. iii. 15). But according to Greek notions, he was
the perfect or ideal man who lived or acted up to the inner
law of his being. This latter notion was involved in that
saying of Jesus, "The kingdom of God is within you," and
also in that other, that the righteousness of God surpassed
that which consisted in the fulfilment of statutory law (Matth.
v. 20). But it was through the Greek conception of the ideal
man that these sayings of Jesus laid hold of the mind of
Paul, or at least were explicated by him. The Apostle
recognized the Greek notion as the higher of the two, and
he proceeded to exalt the Christ, by representing him as the
embodiment of the human ideal. The ideal Christ supplanted

in the mind of the Apostle the historical Jesus, so that he was content to know nothing of Christ after the flesh. And as the notion of human perfection derived from Greek philosophy was embodied in Christ by St. Paul, so we shall yet see that the Logos-idea was derived from the same source and embodied in Christ by the fourth Evangelist. Christ thus became at once the ideal man, or second Adam, and the Lord from heaven (1 Cor. xv. 47). And it is from this point of view that we may best see how much Christianity in its dogmatic form was indebted to Greek philosophy.

CHAPTER XVI.

PAULINE DOGMA AS INVOLVED IN THAT OF ATONEMENT.

LEAVING these general remarks on the influence of Greek thought, we proceed to trace the logical sequence of the doctrine of the atonement. This doctrine, which has already occupied our attention, we regard as not only the centre round which the entire dogmatic construction revolves, but also as the point from which it starts. We hold that the process by which the religion of Jesus was converted by the Apostle into the Christian religion commenced from this point rather than from the belief in the resurrection, because it is conceivable that the latter might have been regarded merely as a divine confirmation, or historical authentication, of the teaching of Jesus, and the dogma might never have advanced beyond this point—that is to say, that the remission of sins might simply have been " preached in the name of Jesus "—a phraseology which we have already found to have been usual in the earliest days of the Church, but which falls far short of the dogmatic position. In saying, however, that the dogma took its start from the Apostle's faith in the atonement, we do not mean that it took shape in his mind as a logical deduction from that faith ; but that for him, with his Jewish ideas and modes of reasoning, it was inchoate or germinally present therein.

In the first place, the atonement involved a belief that the Messiah, by whom it was offered, was superhuman ; akin by nature to the divine. Whether or not it be the case, as some have insisted that, according to Jewish belief, the Messiah behoved to be divine, certainly the conception or estimate of the Messianic rank and position of Jesus must have been immensely heightened when he was regarded as Redeemer: as having, by his death, effected an alteration in the religious relation, and set free the love of God to flow forth toward His creatures.   In St. Paul's epistles he is presented as something more than human ; as not only made of the seed of David, according to the flesh, but as declared, or determined to be, " Son of God, with power, according to the spirit of holiness, by the resurrection from the dead "—a mode of speaking from which might be gathered that the relation between the Father and the Son was ethical only, though it tends, as it could hardly fail of doing, by the mere force of speech, to assume the character of a metaphysical relation.   Hence we find that the Apostle uniformly calls him " Lord," the name which in the Old Testament is kept sacred to God alone ; and in one passage the Apostle seems to go so far as to call him " God over all," though this rendering is doubtful, and it is everywhere manifest that the Apostle does not overlook the fact of a certain subordination of the one sharer of the divine nature to the other.

The two ideas now, of an archetypal man, and of a being so akin to God as to be entitled to a divine appellation, and yet, in some indefinite sense, distinct from the Father of all, were common in Hellenistic speculation, and not unknown in the theology of the synagogue, and were applied by the Apostle to Jesus as postulated by the redemptive function ascribed to him.   St. Paul saw in him a union of the divine and human natures, and to his practical mind that union involved a mystery which he simply accepted, because it seemed essential to the atonement ; but he made no attempt to account for it. And we may here observe that, to a large school of modern theologians, this position of the Apostle recommends itself by its very indistinctness.   They speak of the person of Jesus as being the meeting place or intersecting point of the divine and human natures; which and other like forms of expression convey no certain meaning, but recommend themselves to this class of theologians by reason of their very vagueness.   It was otherwise with the early Christians of the same age as St. Paul and of the age succeeding.   To them this union of the two natures in the person of Jesus presented a problem which called forth various attempts to explain it, though none of them may be satisfactory to the critical judgment.   Leaving out of view the extreme docetic doctrine, there is that of the apocryphal Gospels, and perhaps that of St. Mark, that the Spirit of God descended upon the man Jesus at his baptism, so as to endue him with divine power and wisdom, suggestive of an inspiration such as the prophets enjoyed, but of a higher and unintermittent kind, and of a virtue superadded to his humanity. Then there is that of his generation by the Holy Ghost, in the womb of the Virgin Mary, which may have been suggested by many incidents in heathen mythology, or by well-known expressions in the Old Testament. This is the explanation of the synoptic Gospels, which has been adopted and retained to this day by the orthodox Churches. But the highly speculative and creative mind of the fourth Evangelist could not rest without making an attempt to fix, in a unique, original, and distinctive way the exact relation in which Jesus stood to God, and to determine his place in the scale of universal being. Not satisfied with styling him the Son of God, like St. Paul, he calls him the "only begotten Son" of God—*i.e.*, not created nor adopted, but standing in a unique relation to God, specifically different from that of all God's other rational and spiritual offspring. But even this designation was too indefinite to satisfy the Evangelist ; for it was figurative, borrowed from or suggested by a simply human relationship, which was not archetypal, and therefore could not properly shadow forth that peculiar relation which he conceived to exist between God and man in the person of Jesus Christ ; and hence he seeks a nearer and closer determination of this relation, which he finds, as we shall afterwards see, in the application to it of the Logos-idea—an idea which was at once a gift of Greek philosophy, and led up to by previous developments of thought in the Church.

Whatever may have been the case with the Evangelists, the interest in speculative or theoretic completeness was very weak in the mind of St. Paul. It was a practical necessity which led him and the Church in its first stage generally to exalt the person of Jesus to the utmost. The belief that the Messiah had taken upon him the sins of men, and by the suffering of death had expiated their guilt, rendered him an object to the Apostle of the highest veneration and the most absolute devotion. The Apostle could not but feel that one to whom honour and homage, substantially divine, were due, must be divine ; and that that homage, which could not be withheld from him, would trench upon the divine prerogative, unless he was in some sense, and to some extent, partaker of the divine nature ; that but for this a significance would be lent to his person which would be distracting to the monotheistic sentiment. For this distraction is often felt to this day by Christian men, notwithstanding all that has been done to exalt and deify the person of Christ. The service rendered to humanity by atonement and redemption must have been felt by the Apostle to be too great for any but a being akin to God to render ; to be greater indeed than any other which men were accustomed to trace even to God. For what was life itself and all its enjoyments compared with deliverance from that load of sin, which, to the awakened conscience, makes life intolerable ; from the deep-felt schism within the soul, and from the dreaded hostility of the unseen power.

That the long-promised Messiah should, as Paul believed, have been commissioned to render a service to man so much greater than anything which had been expected of him, to effect such a massive and transcendent revolution in the religious relation, and that too at such a cost of suffering to himself, could not but immeasurably enhance the conception which had been hitherto entertained of the Messiah, and seem to justify the application to him of many mysterious and enigmatical sayings of the Old Testament, of which it was difficult to say to what they referred, whether to God or to some other being of a godlike nature. The theological idea was thus set in motion, and the exaltation of the person of the Messiah could hardly stop at any point short of what would appear to be an infraction of the monotheistic principle. Having ceased to regard him as a mere man, the Apostle could not but invest him with attributes which brought him near to divinity. His feelings of gratitude and obligation would allow no rest to his imagination at any point sensibly short of this. In a word, the thought of atonement, thus associated by him with the person of Jesus, was of such a nature that he and all who entertained it were under the necessity either of advancing till they arrived at this point, or of again receding from it, and falling back to the idea of the pure humanity. The former alternative admitted of a great development, and defined itself as that of orthodoxy. The latter was probably fallen into by many of the Jewish Christians, who gradually sank back into a sect, not separated by any distinctive principle from the rest of their countrymen, to disappear at last from record, because they could not follow the catholic development of the Christo-logical doctrine inaugurated by St. Paul. Besides many other traces of this process, which history has preserved, there is some indication of such a halt in the Epistle of St. James, the Judæo-Christian origin of which cannot be doubted; and which is remarkable for the very inconspicuous significance assigned in it to the person of Jesus, and also for its polemic against the doctrine of faith, and against the position which that doctrine necessarily occupies in Pauline or orthodox theology.

We have here arrived at a point at which we may direct atten-tion to what may be called the motive principle of the dogmatic development. In his *Apologia*, Newman, speaking of his transi-tion period, makes the following confession : " The feeling grows upon me that the reason for which I believe as much as our own system (the Anglican) teaches, must lead me to believe more, and that not to believe more was to fall back into scepticism." Now this very feeling of propulsion, this necessity for a consistent and exhaustive development of the germinal idea, must have prevailed, less consciously, it may be, yet power-fully, in the mind of the early Church. Beginning with the belief in the Messiahship, the atonement and resurrection of Jesus, it could not stop short till it had fixed his position at the very highest, and made him a member of the divine college. That section of the Judæo-Christian Church which, in deference to the inherited monotheistic principle, stopped short on the way to this point, fell back into Ebionitism, and finally ceased to be Christian in any recognized sense. This, at least, is our con-struction, and we think the likeliest, of this dimly seen pheno-menon. A forward movement was of the very essence of the dogmatic principle : an intrinsic necessity. The belief of so much compelled to the belief of more. To pause in the move-ment, or to hesitate in accepting the consequences of a step already taken, even to question the truth of any narrative which illustrated or magnified the powers of Jesus, was enough to open the door to scepticism, and to shake the hold of that which was already attained. " All or nothing " was the alterna-tive presented to the early Church. And the consciousness of this, more or less distinct, operated all through the dogmatic development. History has many illustrations to show of a like

2 D

process, the most conspicuous of which at the present day is to be found in the operation of the Protestant principle of free inquiry, which must be either carried out in its integrity or entirely abandoned.

We cannot refrain here from observing that the modern or mediating school of theologians in this country, while they shrink from denying the divinity of Christ, and the doctrines of atonement and inspiration, yet do not hesitate to go as far, short of this, as they possibly can.   They do not seem to be aware that the citadel of orthodoxy, when deprived by such tactics of its outposts and bulwarks, is left in an isolated and defenceless position; that these outworks were thrown up by the early Church because it instinctively, if unconsciously, felt them to be essential to the safety of the citadel itself; and that, after all that can be said to the contrary, the true and best working motto for the orthodox apologist may be that of "all or nothing"; and his most defensible position that of verbal inspiration.

Passing now to the anthropological department of the Pauline theology, we observe that the natural condition of the human subject, *i.e.*, his condition apart from faith in Christ, is therein made to correspond with the function of Christ as Redeemer; or to be such, so to speak, as to make room for the exercise of that function.   Man is conceived of, or represented, as so constituted by nature, or so formed by habit, as to stand in need of redemption; as unable to redeem himself, but yet as capable of being redeemed by Christ.   In other words, the natural condition of humanity is such as to supply a *raison d'être* for the atonement.   This is as much as to say that the atonement determines the anthropology of the Apostle no less than his Christology.   He was predisposed to adopt a certain view on this subject, partly by his own religious experience both before and after his conversion, and partly by the opinions with respect to it which were current in the Jewish schools of theology.   All the Apostle's endeavours to deliver himself from the oppressive sense of guilt and to reach the higher forms of righteousness had been in vain, though he had engaged in those endeavours with all the intensity of his nature; and this experience seemed to him to be a proof of the natural impotency of man; to postulate the help of a higher power, which he conceived of as derived from the atonement offered to God, and as the necessary foundation or preliminary to all effectual effort towards a better life on the part of man, and also as an explanation of that better success which attended his own efforts after he had come under the influence of Jesus. To account for that vexatious impotency, for that strange inability to approach the ideal of one's nature, he accentuated, or put a new meaning into the Mosaic narrative of the Fall, and drew from it, or put into it, the doctrine of original sin and of human depravity, while he threw into the background, or altogether ignored the idea of human liberty, which had been so emphatically, though not explicitly, presupposed in the teaching of Jesus.

It used to be said that Paul was the first who found such a meaning in the Old Testament narrative, and that the narrative itself contained a prophecy or early anticipation of the Apostle's doctrine, and was therefore divinely corroborative of it. But recent investigation has clearly shown that the Apostle's view of the sin of Adam, and of its effects, is not peculiar to him, but in a great measure derived by him from the teaching of the synagogue. The tendency towards evil had, according to that teaching, existed by nature in the human subject; but it was only in consequence of Adam's sin that it had gained a new and well-nigh irresistible supremacy over the tendency to good. (*See* Weber's *Altsynagogale Theologie.*)

This doctrine was merely reproduced in sharpened form by St. Paul, and incorporated into his anthropological system. It is an instance to prove that he construed his own experience, and sought to determine its connection with the death of Jesus, by means of those current theological ideas with which his mind was saturated. According to him no true liberty can be predicated of man in his natural state : it is an endowment which man has lost by the primeval fall, in which the whole race participated, in the person of its progenitor and representative. What is new in the Apostle's doctrine is that this liberty has been regained for men by the redemption purchased by Christ, who is conceived of as the second Adam, or head and representative of a new and spiritual election. The power and liberty to do good is the distinction of those who obey the call of the gospel, which the Apostle describes as a call into the glorious liberty of the children of God, of a restored humanity. "As by one man's disobedience, many (*i.e.,* all) were made sinners, so by the obedience of one shall many be made righteous." As humanity fell from the state of innocence and liberty in the person of its first head, or representative, so, by the grace of God, Christ became its second head, that in him Paradise might be regained, and all restored to their first estate on condition of faith in him.

We repeat here what has already been said, that we cannot listen for a moment to the notion of a great critic, that Paul did not really mean what he said in these representations of the fall and the restoration of man, or that they are merely figurative and literary expressions thrown out at a subject or fact imperfectly apprehended. Certain facts there are, no doubt, underlying the Apostle's views, such as those of the frailty of individual man, and the solidarity of the race, but the critic is not entitled to make use of such facts as if they exhausted the meaning of the Apostle. The plain interpretation goes much beyond such facts, and is also the true one; and we believe that the Apostle's language is seriously intended to bring out the actual function which Jesus discharged, and the relation which he occupied to the human family. That his language is not playfully and figuratively but seriously meant is fully borne out by its concordance with current thought, and also by his sweeping and pitiless denunciations of human depravity in the first chapter of the Epistle to the Romans, and elsewhere. The description of human depravity, in connection with the worship of idols, which is given in the first chapter of Romans, resembles so curiously, and in some points almost so verbally, the description of it in the 14th chapter of the Hellenistic (apocryphal) Book of Wisdom, that it helps to bear out what has already been suggested as to the Apostle's acquaintance with Hellenistic literature. But there is an exaggeration and one-sidedness in these descriptions, which we do not meet with in the teaching of Jesus.

The latter presupposes a seed of goodness in man, which needs only to be quickened; a spirit of goodness to which appeal may be made. And according to the best observation this is the true view. We may not be able to tell whether man has sprung from a creature in which there was no God-consciousness, for the beginning as well as the end of things is shrouded in deep obscurity. But wherever that consciousness has arisen, we hold that there has been good as well as evil in man. The good may not be very deep, or it may lie too deep, but still it

is there ; it may be little able to stand the test of temptation,
but still it is there ; between it and the most fearful evil there
may be but a step, but still it is there ; and if Paul did not
believe this, certainly Jesus did. The ideal humanity never
existed as a reality for so much as a moment in the primeval
state, but it exists as an inextinguishable thought in the heart
of man, as the divine germ in his nature, as the promise and
possibility of a divine life yet to be ; and the divine purpose is
that the good which is in man shall rise from the possible to
the actual in him.

This is the view of man's natural state implied in the teaching
of Jesus, and, to some extent, it seems to be implied also in the
doctrine of Paul as well, who, even when he speaks of the soul as
dead in sin, does not suppose it to be so dead, but that it may
hear the call to awake to righteousness (1 Cor. xv. 34, Eph.
v. 14). But the Apostle only seems to make this concession so
far as may be necessary in obedience to undeniable and palpable
facts, and because it is a postulate of the very preaching of the
gospel, which he makes no attempt to reconcile with his general
doctrine, and which, in fact, is irreconcilable with it. In those
passages in which he paves the way and lays the ground for his
dogmatic and heterosoteric views, he speaks as if men were
wholly given up to vile affections, and had entirely lost the
power of seeking or doing any good thing.

If it be said that such passages are written for a " polemical
purpose," the reply is, that with them the whole structure of his
dogma stands or falls. And whatever utterances of a contrary
signification may be producible from the writings of the impetuous, and sometimes not quite logical Apostle, there can be
no doubt that the Augustinian and Lutheran, or rather Calvin-
istic creeds, are the true expositions of the dogmatic views to
which the Apostle was driven by his construction of the death
of Jesus and of his own unique experience. We call his views
dogmatic because they were based on Jewish presuppositions
which were not verifiable, though to himself they appeared to
be unchallengeable and of axiomatic certainty. The circumstance that these presuppositions admitted of application to the facts of Christian consciousness, and that, being
so applied, they gave to these latter a transcendent and
mystical significance which seemed to justify and fall in with
the Apostle's feelings of devout reverence for the person of

Jesus, was enough to place them for him beyond the possibility of doubt.

A strong presumption in favour of the view now given of the Apostle's anthropological doctrine may be seen in the fact, that those schools of theology which seek to soften his view of human impotency and depravity have always been obliged to tone down or abandon the heterosoteric aspects of his doctrine. And in imputing a fundamental inconsistency to his dogmatic structure, we do not feel that we make an improbable or presumptuous suggestion. In such inconsistency we only see an example of what men of ardent genius are peculiarly apt to fall into ; an inconsistency between their theoretical and their practical views, which are oftentimes wide apart from each other, especially where an element of mysticism comes in. In his endeavour to persuade and influence the minds of men, the Apostle necessarily presupposes that they enjoy a certain freedom of action and a certain soundness of judgment in things spiritual; but in his endeavour to magnify the function and the work of Jesus, he is obliged polemically to take a view of human depravity which seems to deprive men of every vestige of freedom. So we have seen instances in our own day of men great in the literary world becoming so intent on a particular view of a subject, as unintentionally to be for the time oblivious of all nuances, sidelights, and qualifying considerations, and by excluding these from their field of vision to establish a foregone conclusion. The tendency this way is one main feature which distinguishes the literary from the scientific bent of mind. The history of literature has many instances to show of that one-sidedness which is lent to genius by its own intensity.

Turning now to the soteriological doctrine of the Apostle, we observe that the salvation of the sinner was conceived of by him as having the atonement as its necessary presupposition, as depending indeed on the appropriation by the sinner of the merit of the atonement, while faith was the appropriating instrument. In other words, the Apostle's great and distinctive doctrine of justification by faith alone was the logical, or, at least, the natural sequel of that other doctrine that the death of Jesus on the Cross was the sole and all-sufficient atonement for sin. In the Epistle to the Hebrews, and elsewhere in the New Testament, faith is spoken of in a very general way, as if it were a belief in the unseen in opposition to the materialistic view; but with Paul the object of the faith which justifies is the atonement of Jesus, and this is the use of the word to this day in strictly orthodox theology. It is a faith that the sins of the individual are atoned for by the sufferings of Jesus. The justifying power of this faith recommended itself to the mind of the Apostle, and proved itself to his satisfaction, because it seemed to be required in explanation of his own sudden and complete conversion; and, generally speaking, to secure the entire glory of man's salvation to God, who had provided the atonement; to exclude all plea of merit on the part of man, and to lay a foundation for that humility which differentiates Christian piety from that of the Jewish and Gentile world. The anxiety of the Apostle to secure such ends grew out of his own religious experience, for it appeared to him as if the grace of God had laid hold of him in the very height of his career of hostility to Jesus, so that his conversion was entirely due to an act of divine condescension, and the most he could claim for himself was that he had not "been disobedient to the heavenly vision," but had been a merely passive recipient of the grace of God. Nay, he would fain be more abject still, and strip himself even of the possible or seeming merit of a passive obedience, and minimize to the utmost his own part in the work of salvation; for there are some passages in which he comes near to imply that faith itself is a gift of God to the soul, a conviction impressed on the mind, as in his own case, by the presentation of irresistible evidence. That evidence in the case of Paul himself was the apparition of the risen Jesus, and in the case of other men the testimony of himself and other witnesses to the resurrection, or a witness of the Spirit of God to the soul.

In its plain and obvious meaning, faith is an intellectual or at most a fiducial persuasion of the atoning virtue of the death of Jesus; and to maintain that such a faith sufficed to procure justification for the sinner, fell in, as no other doctrine could, with the Apostle's purpose of claiming and asserting an absolute significance in the soteriological province for the person and work of Jesus, and of assigning to these a substantive, elemental, and exclusive value. But we cannot overlook the fact that this doctrine is hardly consistent with the inextinguishable idea of individual responsibility or with that other great doctrine which is common to the synoptic Jesus and to Paul himself, who states it early in his Epistle to the Romans as if he was anxious beforehand to guard the interests of practical religion against any inference prejudicial to them that might be drawn from his gospel : viz., that " God will render to every man according to his deeds " ; that He will acquit or condemn men, not according as they have or have not acquired by their faith a lien or claim upon the store of another's merits, but according to their own manner of life ; and that in His judgment of men He will take account of acts and habits of mind or of that character in which they are registered, and not of faith apart from these ; in a word, administer the law of the spiritual harvest, which is the true flaming sword which guards the gates of Paradise.

St. Paul would fain persuade himself that all who believed were children of the light and of the day (1 Thess. v. 5), as might no doubt be the natural result, the likely consequence. But he could not conceal from himself that faith might exist in some sense and in some degree without exerting or being accompanied by any purifying influence on the life and character, and hence he seeks to escape or to correct the dangerous consequence of his one-sided and extreme doctrine of justification by faith alone by means of supplementary doctrines which are hardly consistent with it, if they be not even glaringly inconsistent with it.

In many passages of his epistles it is implied, as well as insisted on by orthodox interpreters, that faith, the subjective factor by which the benefit of the atonement is appropriated, has a more extended signification than that of a mere intellectual, historical, or even fiducial persuasion which it naturally and primarily suggests ; and that it includes the adoption and practice of the soteriological method of Jesus, the acceptance of him practically " as the leader and true ruler of life," so that he is the justified man, the Christian indeed, who takes Jesus as the " highest authority, the principal guide in all spiritual and moral matters," and enters sympathetically into his spirit and manner of life. But it has to be observed that, by this extension of the word " faith," the atonement, if it be not indeed rendered superfluous, both in its Godward and manward aspect, acquires efficacy only when the contemplation of it acts on the gratitude of man for the love displayed by it, or for the removal by its means of an otherwise insuperable obstacle presented by the righteousness of God to human salvation ; and thus becomes an incentive and stimulus to a new life. And if this be conceded, it is plain that the practice of the method is the main or determining element on which the efficacy of the atonement is made to hinge, and that, however the idea of human merit may be excluded, it is not by the fact of an atonement.

There is thus little difficulty in criticizing the Pauline doctrine of faith, till it seems to dissolve in our hands ; but yet it is easy to conceive how the doctrine suggested itself to his mind and maintained its hold over his judgment. We have only to suppose the case of a man conscious of a process of moral deterioration and tormented by an accusing conscience ; or, as was the case with St. Paul before conversion, of a man thirsting for righteousness, but at the same time disabled and discouraged by the idea of a jealous, severe, and captious judge in heaven, from making the necessary change in his life ; it is easy to conceive that faith in an atonement made by a third person might at once pacify the conscience of such a man, and excite in him the feeling of a profound and enduring gratitude, and prove ever after a stimulus in the pursuit of righteousness. We can conceive also that such a man might thenceforth attribute the whole change that might subsequently pass upon him to the new persuasion or faith which had sprung up in his mind, and take no account of the preparatory steps in the process or of the previous mental state or disposition to which his faith had supplied the one additional element necessary to the vigorous and successful prosecution of the new life, and to the production of that inward satisfaction flowing from the consciousness of it. This oversight would, it is evident, be a mistake in theory which might involve grave consequences in practice. But we may take the opportunity of remarking that it would involve a mistake of an opposite kind, to say with Mr. T. H. Green (essay on " Faith "), that " the conflict between the law of the mind or reason and the law of sin in the members is the natural parent of the seemingly altered life that follows the acceptance of the gospel." In his essay on " Conversion " it is true, he remarks, and remarks well, "that the moral state which St. Paul describes in the seventh chapter of Romans is not a state of habitual indulgence in sin. It is a state in which the consciousness of sin is at its height, but the habit of wrong-doing at its minimum." In these words Mr. Green seems to imply that the heightened consciousness of sin was sufficient to carry the Apostle through the crisis of conversion without any breach in the continuity of his moral life. But to us the true view seems to be that the conflict to which that consciousness gave rise was necessary to his conversion as its preliminary process, and that the conflict could not have been brought to a successful issue except by the disclosure to his mind of the propitious character of God. This disclosure was "the natural parent" or proximate cause of the Apostle's conversion—the auxiliary ideal force, apart from which the law of the mind could never have gained the victory over the law of sin in his members.

Were all men now in the same mental or spiritual condition as St. Paul was before his conversion, there would be little or no practical danger in the doctrine of justification by faith alone. The danger lay in the indiscriminate presentation of faith as a panacea for all moral evil. What seemed to the Apostle to represent his own case was believed by him at the first to hold good in the case of all others. And with this conviction he began, with the untempered vehemence of his ardent nature, to proclaim his doctrine. A well-known utterance of the young Melanchthon seems to show that he also was impressed for a time by a similar conviction. But though experience and observation soon taught the Apostle, as it did Melanchthon, that something more than an intellectual persuasion of the evangelical doctrine was necessary for the renewal of the life; yet owing to a certain want of mental flexibility, which is a general accompaniment of the enthusiastic and sanguine temperament, the Apostle, instead of qualifying or withdrawing his formula, retained its use ; while by way of safe-guard, he extended the meaning of its terms so as to include devotion or self-surrender to the person and method of Jesus. By thus retaining his formula of the justifying power of faith, the Apostle was able, for controversial purposes, to present the gospel in strong contrast to the law and its works. But by the extension more or less of the principal term, his formula lost much or all of its paradoxical significance, inasmuch as faith, with such latitude of meaning, is presumptive, or, we may say, inclusive of the entire religious life.

It is obvious that in the supposed case of a person aspiring to a better life, but oppressed by a sense of continual short-coming, the simple persuasion of divine goodness, as inculcated by Jesus, might accomplish all that a belief in atonement could accomplish; and that, if the interposed idea of atonement had any advantage, it lay in this, that this idea was so impressed on the mind of the ancient world that it was easy to connect it with the death of Jesus, and to see therein not merely an affecting illustration of his great ideal of humanity, but also a proof of divine love more palpable and moving than could be seen in any other token of it whatever. But, on the other hand, the belief that an atonement had been made by the Son of God, which had such a magical and beneficial effect on Paul's mental condition, as well as on the minds of thousands and millions since his day, and especially on such men as Augustine, Luther, and Whitfield, may have, and no doubt has had quite a relaxing, and even indurating effect on the minds of others, strangers to the purifying and pædagogic discipline of life. Indeed, we may admit that a belief in the one form of doctrine affords no better guarantee than a belief in the other for the moral elevation of the believer. It is only when a man is laid hold of by either the one or the other, so as to receive from it an impulse or encouragement to put forth an endeavour after the good life, that it is ethically safe. But there is this ground among others for preferring the doctrine of Jesus, that much as he laid stress on the essential love of God, as a source of forgiveness, he nowhere advances any doctrine parallel to that of Paul respecting the alone justifying power of faith, nor one equally liable to be misconstrued by ignorance, or to be perverted by the "casuistry of the passions." The authoritative and impressive announcement of Jesus respecting the forgiveness of sins was in reality the good tidings from which the gospel derived its name. But it was good tidings to those only who received it into "good and honest hearts," who sought first the kingdom of God, and hungered after righteousness. To those who used it as an anodyne to conscience, or derived from it a comfortable excuse for the relaxation of moral effort, it brought no good, but rather the reverse. In a word, the belief in this doctrine has no moral value, except in so far as it is resorted to in order to quicken aspiration, and to render practicable the pursuit of the ideal, under the sense of perpetual shortcoming.

In his distinctive doctrine of justification by faith alone, St. Paul appears to have fallen into an error analogous to that of Socrates, of whom it has been said that he "resolved all virtue into knowledge or wisdom, and omitted to notice what is not less essential to virtue—viz., the proper condition of the emotions and desires, taking account only of the intellect." The Apostle made the whole method of salvation, the attainment of righteousness, to turn upon a special act of faith as its sole instrument, throwing for the time entirely out of sight the general state of mind, the soil in which such a faith takes root, and grows up, and, at the most, bringing in that state of mind apologetically, not as a preliminary or co-ordinate, but as a consequent of faith ; though experience and observation had told him, as it has told all ages of the Church since his day, that, by a sort of "mystery of iniquity," it is by no means an invariable consequent. There were representatives of the spirit of Antichrist then as now ; men who held the truth in unrighteousness ; who believed but did not obey the gospel of Christ; whose existence and nature were explained in the First Epistle of St. John, by saying "they went out from us, because they were not of us," *i.e.*, because their faith was not ours. Both John and Paul had had their attention riveted and arrested by the same, to them inexplicable phenomenon—a phenomenon quite inexplicable, so long as a paramount and exclusive position is assigned to faith as the subjective factor of religion. The fact was that the faith might be the same substantially in all cases, but the conditions might be different ; it might be an essential element in a new life, without being the all-sufficient determinant of that life. St. Paul's error consisted in overlooking the peculiarities of his own experience, and deducing from it a doctrine of universal application. A certain conviction had dawned upon his mind, and seemed to produce that great moral elevation in him with which it was concurrent ; and, with the customary precipitancy of a grand enthusiasm, he laid it down as a universal dictum that the same persuasion was all-sufficient to produce the same effect, and to bring others into the same moral atmosphere with himself.

To us it appears, then, that Paul not only laid down a soteriological theory differing in important respects from that laid down and exemplified by Jesus ; but also that he did not confine his deductive reasoning within the limits of that theory, but sought to escape the dangerous consequences by partial departures from it. The historian just quoted says again of Socrates that, in spite of his theory, no man ever insisted more emphatically on the necessity of enjoining the control of the appetites and passions, of enforcing good habits, and the value of that state of the sentiments and emotions which such a course tended to form. And the example of Socrates, whose dialectic was certainly not inferior to that of Paul, may incline us to believe that the latter may have fallen more or less unconsciously into a like happy inconsistency; that, in his eagerness to assert and exalt the power of faith in the soteriological process, he was betrayed into an exaggeration of statement, which could only be corrected by other statements amounting to a modification or withdrawal of his distinctive principle. That faith in divine goodness plays an essential part, both negative and positive, in the regeneration of the individual life, is as certain as a wide experience can make it; but that it is the sole instrument of a sinner's justification, or that divine goodness has been manifested in the offering of an atonement for man's sin, are statements which may well be called in question, even though they may rest on the authority of St. Paul, and of what has been regarded as the orthodox Church in ancient and modern times. The truth seems to be that St. Paul, under the desire to controvert Jewish legalism and to exalt the person of Jesus, took up the ground that faith in Jesus was the sole instrument of salvation, because this doctrine seemed to minimize to the utmost the part of man himself in the work of salvation, and left no room for propitiatory service. But that, on the other hand, under the influence of anxiety for the cause of religion and morality, he either used the word " faith " in the wider sense, which included the moral endeavour to form oneself on the pattern of Jesus, or simply enforced the practice of Christian graces as equally indispensable to salvation, without attempting to reconcile his different views on the subject.

One of the great difficulties experienced in the first age of the Church was to set in a clear light the relation between the new doctrine and the old : between law and gospel, between faith and works, the question involved in all these being radically the same. St. Paul was no doubt profoundly convinced that law did not occupy the same place as it formerly did, or was supposed to occupy. Practically, he felt that his own relation to it had, by his conversion, undergone a total change; but then there was the difficulty of theoretically defining wherein the change consisted, and of thereby enlightening the minds of his converts, and protecting them against the risk or danger of falling back inadvertently into their old relation to it.

The observation has been made, that it must have been very difficult for those whom he addressed clearly to understand the difference between the absolute significance of the law, which he vehemently denied, and its relative and pædagogic value, on which he as vehemently insisted; to understand how his doctrine, which seemed to " make void " the law, in reality " established " it.   There is neither presumption nor irreverence in asserting, that, with all his eloquence and power of dialectic, Paul did not succeed in making his meaning clear either to himself or to his readers; or in explaining that change in his position, of which yet both he and they were profoundly conscious.   We are entitled to say so when we consider how much men, who bow to his authority and believe in his inspiration, yet differ in their interpretation of his language on this point; and how puzzling his meaning is even when we bring the most teachable disposition to the study of his words.   The truth is, that we may say of Paul, as we may say of Luther, the greatest of his disciples, that his own mind was not clear upon the subject; that he did not clearly apprehend the rationale of the difference between the legal and evangelical standpoint, of which, however, he felt the reality.   He betrays the confusion of his thought by the very vehemence of his language, by the persistency with which he returns again and again to the restatement of it, and by the ambiguous sense in which he uses the word " law " itself.   So far as we can make out, by help of the thought which has been expended on the subject by the theologians of subsequent ages, what the Apostle would be at, was, as already indicated, to deny not merely the validity of the ceremonial part of the Mosaic law, or that of the law as a whole, moral and ceremonial; but the obligation of law generally, in its propitiatory aspect, or considered as a directory for earning or conciliating the goodwill of God; all propitiatory service being, by its very nature, grudging, mercenary, and servile; neither worthy of God to accept, nor of man to render, being neither spontaneous nor such as should flow from a due recognition of the absolute dependence of the finite upon the infinite. At the centre of the whole statutory law of Israel stood the idea of atonement ; the whole of it, moral and cere-monial, was coloured and pervaded by the idea of propitiation. And considering that, according to the evangelical view, God did not need to be propitiated, the legal service was really a misdirection of the spiritual energies ; a struggle against what offered no resistance ; a mere beating of the air. And further, that service, being ultimately traceable to the principle of fear, is not self-regulative in its demonstrations, but a mere calcula-tion of less and more, and is under the necessity of following some rule or statute laid down by external authority ; whereas the principle of love, which flows from the conviction that God does not need to be propitiated, but is fatherly and gracious in all His purposes with men, *is* self-regulative, and follows its own inward promptings, and acknowledges no outward rule, but enters into the enjoyment and exercise of true spiritual freedom. And so it comes to be felt, that love to God and man is a sufficient rule for all right action, and that external or statutory law is only for the lawless and the disobedient.

It seems to be the case that men in general cannot rise to a higher level of religious thought, except by combining the new ideas and forms of thought with the old ; and it may be con-fidently asserted that the dogma of Paul, respecting the atoning sacrifice of Christ, was, as already pointed out, an unconscious compromise, or concession to the legal spirit, against which the Apostle so earnestly contended. He did not clearly or thoroughly grasp the principle that God does not need to be propitiated. His own experience, indeed, had convinced him that such propitiation could not be offered by man for himself ; but the idea was too deeply engrained by his Jewish training into his system of thought to suffer him to dismiss it altogether; and he was led to take up the middle ground of atonement by a third party. As conceived by him, the atonement, besides that it did not seem to disparage the fatherly character of God, gave a mysterious explanation of the death of Jesus, and lent an absolute and permanent significance to his person ; and being offered once for all by one in man's stead, it delivered man from the necessity of rendering a mercenary service as well as from all uncertainty as to his relation to God. This dogma has much to recommend it, and has many features in common with the doctrine of Jesus ; but, in so far as any difference is apparent, we appeal from Paul the disciple to Jesus the Master, whose teaching is the pure echo of our deepest consciousness.

St. Paul in his literary character can hardly be acquitted from all responsibility for that tendency to Antinomianism which has manifested itself from time to time in the history of the Christian Church. His language in defence and in illustration of his soteriological doctrine comes at some points perilously near to the Antinomian doctrine : as, *e.g.*, where he says (Romans vii. 17-20), " If I do that I would not, it is no more I that do it, but sin that dwelleth in me," etc. Such language, however it may be explained, certainly produces a startling impression at first sight, and it can hardly be denied either that there is a colourable pretext for Antinomian teaching in Pauline doctrine, or that an apparent connection may be traced between the tendency that way and the heterosoteric character which St. Paul impressed on the soteriological method of Jesus. While the latter taught men by word and deed to redeem themselves, St. Paul represented men as capable of being redeemed, and *him* as invested with redemptive powers and functions. While Jesus sought to awaken and call into action those capacities by which we may rescue ourselves from the power of evil, St. Paul represented him as effecting our rescue by what he did and suffered on our behalf. From being an inward process, which takes place in each individual, the soteriological process was transmuted into an outward historical event in the life of another, who is man's substitute and representative. From being carried on in accordance with natural psychological laws, it was changed into a process which we may call magical, vicarious, and heteronomous. If it cannot be said that the work of Christ has, according to St. Paul, quite supplanted the inward process and deprived it of all reality, we may affirm at least that the central weight of human redemption has been removed by him from the sphere of the individual's life to that of our common representative. Such is the view naturally impressed on our minds by the perusal of the Pauline epistles, and it has given occasion to endless controversies between those in whom the dogmatic interest is paramount and those in whom that interest is subordinated to the more general interests of religion and morality. If in Paul's dogma the soteriological

doctrine is not merged in the soterological, we may say at least
that he has added a soterological doctrine of his own to the
soteriology of Jesus.

There is some appearance as if St. Paul himself had been
taught by experience and observation that there was something
not quite satisfactory in his dogmatic system ; that while it
might exalt the significance of the person of Jesus and keep at
a distance the propitiatory character of Christian worship, it
rather weakened the safeguards of the spiritual life of man.
And hence, while in moments of enthusiasm he styles the
redemption effected by Christ " complete," his language at other
times implies that it is not complete except under certain subjective conditions. We are, according to him, saved by faith in
Christ's work, and yet commanded to work out our own salvation. Except for this personal work, the work of Christ our
substitute is vain, so that, to all intents and purposes, the work
of Christ requires to be supplemented by that of the individual
believer himself ; in other words, the method of salvation is
partly autosoteric and partly heterosoteric. Jesus has achieved
complete redemption for us, and yet we have to labour and
struggle with fear and trembling as if all he has done for us
were nothing, and all yet remained to be done by us. Practically this is what it amounts to. Under the Pauline idea of
redemption there only remains the idea that the autosoteric
work of the individual, the inward process by which he
extricates himself from evil, has been made way for by a preliminary work on the part of Christ. The individual needs to
enter upon or join in with the work which has already been
begun in his behalf. The process in the individual is a continuation of the work and life of Christ ; or, according to the
Paulinistic Epistle to the Colossians, it is " a filling up " of what
is lacking in the latter. This is a view of the subject which is
fully satisfied by regarding Jesus as a teacher and an example,
and so a source of moral and spiritual influence ; but it does
not require that we should regard him as a redeemer in the
dogmatic and heterosoteric sense of the word. It seems,
indeed, as if the central idea of Paul's dogmatic system broke
down by his own showing and under his own hand, and that
in the end he returns to the autosoteric doctrine, which the
synoptists ascribe to Jesus. This apparent inconsistency, or
retreat from his ordinary position, on the part of the Apostle,

becomes intelligible when we consider that his dogmatic system
was the resultant of various heterogeneous elements and forms
of thought which existed together in his mind.   On the one
hand, there were certain patent and undeniable facts of the
ethical and religious life, such as those of human frailty and
individual responsibility : the tradition or reminiscence of the
life and teaching of Jesus, together with the sudden and mysterious revival in the minds of the early disciples of their faith in
him after his death.   On the other hand, there was the idea of
the bodily apparition of Jesus, to which that revolution was
ascribed, together with the view, then universally prevalent, of
the divine government : viz., that it resorted at certain points
to supernatural agency, whether in the processes of finite minds
or in those of external nature ; and lastly, there was the
inherited Jewish idea of the religious relation, into connection
with which all had to be brought.   The dogma resulting from
these heterogeneous elements could not be wholly satisfactory
even to Paul himself.   By his powerful and ingenious dialectic
he might slur over its defects and antinomies and conceal them
from his readers ; but in accomplishing this he could not always
keep within the margin of his system.   In his epistles we mark
an occasional shifting of ground, a certain jolt in the working
of the mechanism of his thought which threatens to throw it
out of gear ; and, to prevent or conceal this catastrophe, a
recourse here and there to ideas which are at variance with the
rest of his doctrine.

According to St. Paul, the faith of the disciple is the instrument at once of his justification and his sanctification : the subjective factor, which operates on the mind of God to put His
mercy and His grace in motion for the disciple's benefit; so
that, according to this view, the circuit of the soteriological
process is inundated by a supernatural, mysterious, and incalculable foreign element.   When once men have begun to
draw upon this element in explanation of the facts of the
spiritual life, there is no limit to which this may be done.   The
process may be carried on till no fact or function of that life is
left independent of the supernatural element, and the history
of religion becomes the history of one long, supernatural
intervention in human affairs.

A view of the spiritual life is thus arrived at, which, if it
deepen awe and enrich the religious sentiment, is yet at

variance with that autonomy which is essential to our moral nature, and presents to the human intellect a stumbling-block which more than outweighs the value of that energy which it communicates. At a previous point in our remarks we found that it was the faith or expectation of a divine manifestation which arrested or stagnated the religious life of the Jew; and we now remark that, so far as Christians entertain any expectation of this kind, or look for an access of any power, other than those which are personal to them, into the springs of their life, they just in so far fall back to the Jewish standpoint; and also that the Jewish element, which found expression in St. Paul's doctrine of the atonement, protended likewise into his view of the nature and operation of divine grace within the soul. According to the teaching of Jesus faith operates in a different way. It reconciles man to God by the conception of His fatherliness, and encourages him to aim at the ideal of his nature, in spite of every shortcoming. With every fresh experience of the help which he derives from that conception his faith mounts to an ever higher level; he feels more and more that he is "master of his fate," and asks for no sign from heaven, outward or inward, and for no power beyond or behind his own to aid him in his self-discipline. And thus his nature is lifted, not by any supernatural agency evoked by his faith, but simply by the conviction that, the Supreme Power of the universe being on his side, the ideal which beckons him from afar is within his reach. The grace of God resides in the constitution of the man himself, and in the great system of which he forms a part; while the supernatural aspect in which it is presented by St. Paul is only the colour put upon it by devout imagination—an indication that the Apostle slid down from the elevation on which Jesus stood to that lower level which the Church has occupied ever since.

In order to obtain a distinct, and for us a final view of the relation in which Jesus and St. Paul stand to each other, and their respective places in the development of religion, we have to consider the ground which is common to all ethical religions as such. These have all had their origin and growth in the effort more or less blind, more or less instinctive, to arrive at some such view of the invisible forces which rule the world as would best encourage and assist the human subject in his attempts to approach the ideal, and to soothe the gnawing dissatisfaction which is occasioned by the sense of shortcoming. They are all but experiments to discover the best conditions under which the spiritual life can be conducted. In his felt inability to rise towards the ideal, to heal the inward schism, or to disarm divine anger, man had recourse to acts of technical religion, to ritual practices, and especially to sacrifice, as a means to these ends.

Now what distinguishes the religion of Jesus, as it appears in his doctrine, is its entire freedom not only, as we have seen, from all speculative and metaphysical notions as to the nature of God or man, but also from all such makeshifts and substitutes as those just mentioned for the truly ideal life. He drew his conception of God entirely from the consciousness of his own moral and spiritual necessities and aspirations. The idea of the Heavenly Father, who forgives the sins of His penitent children, was a postulate of his own spiritual nature, and was all that was needed to stimulate and prosper his endeavours after the perfect life ; it was, as formerly pointed out, his theistic interpretation of the blessedness which accompanied such endeavours. But this simplicity of his doctrine, which was at once its crowning excellence and the seal of its truth, was in a great measure lost sight of by St. Paul. This Apostle's view of the life and death of Jesus, and of their relation to that higher life, which, in some mysterious way, they seemed to have the power of awakening in the souls of men, was by the Apostle determined, in the first degree, by bringing to bear upon them certain speculative and unverifiable ideas inherited from his Jewish training; and in the second and lower degree, by certain elements of Greek and Hellenistic thought, which recommended themselves to his mind as cognate and helpful to the former. The recourse which he had to such materials was enough to obscure, as by the interposition of a clouded medium, the fair form of the religion of Jesus ; but happily not enough to prevent it from shining through and revealing its features till the present day, as " in a glass darkly," and thus preserving its spirit as a living presence among men. If it be thought that the criticism which has been applied in the foregoing remarks to the doctrine of St. Paul is out of place in a discussion as to the origin of Christianity, let it be considered that criticism has not been our primary and immediate object, but has only been used to show that, on the one hand, his doctrine left an opening for dangerous misconstruction ; and, on the other, necessitated a correction or further development, which, as will yet be seen, it received in the deutero-Pauline period.

The relation of the dogma of St. Paul to the teaching of Jesus, both of which we have now, so far as it was necessary for our purpose, passed in review, is of deep interest and deserving of our closest attention.   That the difference between them is not one of mere form is very apparent.   Over against the simplicity and directness with which Jesus defines the method and the process of the new life, there is the complex instrumentalism which the Apostle brings into play.   Evidently, the dogma embraces elements which do not enter into the doctrine, and yet there is a certain congruity between them ; and they seem superficially to be parts or members of one scheme of thought, in such a way, that the parts of the one supplement or fit into those of the other.   We have en-deavoured to account for this by pointing out that the con-crete form in which the doctrine of Jesus presented itself to his personal followers in his person, death, and resurrection, served as a middle term, so to speak, or meeting point, in which the doctrine and the dogma converged and passed into each other ; and, also, that faith in his resurrection imparted a supernatural character to everything connected with him, besides suggesting the idea that a mystical action proceeding from his person had produced that great change in their feelings and sentiments of which his disciples were conscious.   We say, therefore, that the dogma was neither more nor less than the unfolding or explication by the early Church of the concrete form, and of that mystical action, in the light of the supernatural hypothesis common to the age, and of the inherited categories of Jewish and Gentile thought.   Or, confining our attention to the part played by St. Paul in the dogmatic process, we may obtain a slightly different view of what took place.   The Apostle never, we believe, saw Jesus in the flesh, and was, therefore, never acted upon by personal intercourse with him.   But, when the evangelic view of the religious relation, as taught by Jesus, broke upon his mind, and brought about his conversion, we may conceive of him as not being satisfied, as Jesus himself had evidently been, to rest in that relation as an ultimate fact of the religious consciousness, beyond which, and beneath which it was impossible to penetrate; but as seeking to rationalize his experience, and imagining that he had found an explanation of it, by applying to the death of Jesus the ideas of expiation and propitiation which had been the first and earliest thought of the ancient world on the subject, and had descended, through untold generations, to the Apostle's time. From this point of view, it may even be said, that St. Paul was the first rationalist, as well as the first dogmatist, of the Christian Church; or, that by one act of rationalism he laid the foundation of the dogma. This act of the Apostle was, in truth, rationalistic in a sense in which the so-called rationalism of modern times is not. The Apostle introduced the supernatural to explain experiences and facts which, however wonderful, were really natural; while modern rationalists have only endeavoured, oftentimes no doubt by absurd critical methods and expedients. to remove the supernatural element thus causelessly introduced, But, in the present connection, the important thing is to remember that, in whichever of these two ways the passage from the doctrine to the dogma was effected, the communication between them has always remained open, and has been traversed continually by multitudes ever since. In all ages of the Church there have been devout and earnest men, who, though trained to the belief in dogma, have yet returned in practice to the simple doctrine of Jesus. The possibility of this is to be explained by the existence in the human soul of the craving for the ideal life. Wherever this craving is sincere and strong it prompts and enables the man to effect this passage. It inspires him with the feeling to which the friends of Daniel (iii. 18) gave expression. He looks for help from God; but, if that help seems to be withheld, he resolves none the less to do the will of God. And this resolution becomes the habitual posture of his mind. The Christian neophyte, attracted by the Christian ideal, but, by experience, becoming alive to the apparently insurmountable difficulty of being faithful to it, naturally seeks at first to overcome the difficulty by obtaining, through the prayer of faith, that aid from above, the expectation of which the dogma seems to warrant; in fact, he regards the dogma as defining the method and the conditions under which the fund or treasury of divine aid or grace is administered. But when the expected aid fails to come; when, except at moments of enthusiasm, he seems to himself to be thrown upon his own resources, he next takes encouragement from the evangelical idea of the paternal character of God, to put his shoulder to the wheel, and to labour with patient perseverance in his Christian vocation. Nay, even then, when the power for a better life does seem to come, he still imputes it to the aid of heaven, regarding that aid as the source of the new strength, which seems to be imparted to his will. In other words, the dogma abandoned in practice retains its hold of the imagination, through which creative faculty the belief in external divine aid goes far to supply the lack of that aid, and has much the same effect as if that aid were given.

The prayerful struggle with God to incline Him to send down help turns to a struggle of the man with his own spirit to comply with the requirements of the gospel. The earnestness which exhausted itself in supplication for help from above converts itself into the earnestness of self-help ; the scope, which it finds at first in the form of petition, trains it to seek scope for itself in the form of personal action and engagement in the Christian struggle. And what is this but to say, that the dogma has a pædagogic use : that it serves for a time as a working theory of the Christian life, but is not its absolute rule or perfect method. Not that St. Paul framed his dogma by a far-seeing or deeply calculated policy to adapt Christianity to beginners, but that the dogmatic categories of atonement and propitiation satisfied his own craving for an explanation of the evangelic idea, while the doctrine that an infinite sacrifice for sin had been offered on the Cross satisfied the like craving on the part of his converts, by making the divine placability more vivid, more easy of apprehension, and perhaps more affecting. And it is possible, that owing to its value and place in religious education, the dogma, which is by nature plastic, may, in one or other of its many forms, endure indefinitely, as an introduction to the higher thought and practice of Christianity ; that, as according to St. Paul, the law was a schoolmaster under the Old Testament to bring men to Christ, so, under the New Testament, the dogma may remain in a period of long transition, as a propædeutic more or less indispensable to the truly ideal life—the struggle towards perfection. But when our object is, as here, to discover the kernel or central truth of Christianity, and to satisfy ourselves of its truth, we must look at it apart from the dogma. The views here expressed, which come near to saying that there is an esoteric as well as an exoteric doctrine of Christianity, may seem to be at variance with its spirit ; but it should be borne in mind that all the higher forms of religion incline to have these two distinct forms, and if we have to admit the same of Christianity, it cannot be helped, and all we can say is that the distinction, so far as Christianity is concerned, may be considered as one of those things that vanish away, being adapted to the immaturity of the individual and of the race.

CHAPTER XVII.

CONFLICT BETWEEN JEWISH AND GENTILE CHRISTIANITY.

THIS discussion might here be brought to a close. Having shown that the autosoteric doctrine of Jesus was converted in the mind of St. Paul into the heterosoteric dogma, we might take for granted that this great transformation was decisive of all that followed. For good or for evil, the Pauline dogma was now doomed to run its course; or may we not rather say, for good *and* evil, the remark being obvious that good and evil were both combined in it. It was inevitable that the system which St. Paul had outlined should be filled up; that the ferment produced by the idea should work itself out amid the strife of parties, and in collision with extraneous and alien elements of thought. It is therefore of less importance to show how this took place. But we must not shrink from proceeding till we arrive at the close of what may be called the creative (or, let us say, the canonical) period of the dogmatic development. With this in view, we proceed to observe that the Pauline dogma did not, without a struggle, establish itself in the faith of the rapidly growing Christian community—a struggle which, though it came near to rending the Church in twain, was yet, in the interests of unity, so tenderly handled in the canonical epistles, or alluded to in terms so vague as to have required the highest efforts of historical criticism to bring it fully to light. To the early origin of this struggle, which continued to agitate the Church far into the century and beyond it, the epistles of St. Paul bear testimony. The question at issue was whether or not Christianity could effect a separation between itself and Judaism, and achieve an independent position as a distinct and universalistic form of religion; as a dispensation of the spirit, and not of the letter. To effect this was an indispensable step towards the growth of a catholic Church; an object which, without anachronism, we may say that St. Paul had very much at heart almost from the first. For when he went up the second time to Jerusalem (Gal. ii. 1) to communicate the gospel, which he preached to them which were of reputation in the Church there, his aim was to provide, " lest by any means he should run, or had run, in vain "—*i.e.*, as Weizsäcker clearly points out, not that any doubts in his own mind as to the truth of his teaching might be dispelled by conference with men, who, he was conscious, could " add nothing " to him ; but that he might ascertain whether his apostolic teaching would meet with recognition on the part of the apostles of the circumcision, and so pave the way for the association, in one communion, of all believers, whether Jews or Gentiles. In becoming followers of Jesus the first disciples did not feel that they had ceased to be Jews. The only difference between them and the rest of their countrymen consisted in their belief that the promised Messiah had now come in the person of their Master, and by his death on the Cross had made atonement for the sins of the people. They did not, in consequence of this belief, renounce their allegiance to the law, or call in question a single word of ancient prophecy. As a fact, they continued as heretofore to observe the legal ordinances and to frequent the temple services. They were indeed exceedingly "zealous of the law," and seem to have enjoyed a reputation for uncommon piety. But when St. Paul went a step further, and, as we have already seen, defined the nature of the atonement to be such as to abrogate the law, and to render circumcision superfluous, he drew upon himself the charge of the rankest heresy and impiety. His antagonism to the law scandalized the Jewish Christians, no less than the unconverted portion of the people ; and there is much reason to think that those persecutors of him and his doctrine, of whom we read so much in the Acts of the Apostles, were many of them professors of the new doctrine ; men who felt themselves deeply compromised in the eyes of their countrymen by the extreme doctrine and practice of one of their number. These men sought to vindicate themselves by disowning St. Paul, denouncing his doctrine, and declining to have fellowship with his converts. Hence a spirit of discord and dissension within the Church, which threatened it with disaster. And had not St. Paul braved this danger, and thrown wide the portals of the Church for the admission of the Gentiles, it is not impossible that, in course of time, the greater mass of the Jewish people would have drawn the small community of Christians back into renewed unity with itself, and built the sepulchre of Jesus, as they had done for the ancient prophets, whom they had slain: and have waited patiently for the second advent as they had waited for the first. But this was not to be. The great spirit which moves through history had decreed that the idea of divine catholicity should be established once for all by the " casting out " from the Church of the Jewish or exclusive element.

Let it be here remarked that the turn of events in the early Church to which we are referring, viz., the admission of the Gentiles and the casting out of the Jews, was not so mysterious or inexplicable as it seems to have appeared to St. Paul. Placed at a distance from the events in question, and in the light of dispassionate criticism, the modern may discern the juncture and the sequence of those events better even than one who could say " *quorum pars fui.*" History has preserved cases on record in which religions have received a kindlier and fuller welcome in other lands than in that of their birth. And there are *a priori* considerations which would lead us to expect that, whatever might happen with individuals, the spirit of Christianity would be more purely and simply caught up by Gentile populations than by the Jewish people. Gentile habits of thought and conduct were so widely different from those of Christianity that when a Gentile did embrace Christianity he could hardly but feel that he had taken a great step, involving a complete break with his past life, and putting him on his guard against a revival of its influence. On the other hand, the kinship and historical connection between Jewish and Christian modes of thought were such that, as already said, in becoming a Christian the Jew might feel that the step was not a great one, and that he might, after a sort, still remain a Jew. There was thus a temptation for the Jewish-Christian to retain as much of his old faith and practice as he could possibly combine with his Christianity ; so to alloy the pure gold of the gospel, and even to slip back into his old way of thinking and acting, and once more to become a full-blooded Jew. This tendency goes far to account for the gradual disappearance of the Jewish section of the Church. The probability is that that section did not so much merge itself into the Gentile or Catholic Church as rather relapse into Judaism. At all events, it lost its vitality as a distinct section, and disappeared by degrees from record. But the episode in the history of the Church, viz., the conflict between the two sections which has led to these remarks, was so decisive in its consequences, and so instructive in itself, besides affording confirmation of our general views as to St. Paul's dogmatic definitions, that we shall now enter into details to show how the conflict arose and was ended.

The Christian community was recruited from the beginning by converts, partly from the Jewish and partly from the Gentile populations. And the beliefs held by these two sections of the Church were, or seemed to be, superficially very much the same. But we shall see immediately that, at certain central points, the agreement between them was not real, but superficial and verbal only : a circumstance which necessarily led to misunderstandings in conference, and to divergences in actual practice, which rendered abortive all approaches to union between the two branches of the Church. There are various indications that St. Paul was forestalled in his view of the atoning nature of the death of Jesus by the earlier disciples. There is, indeed, the authority of the Apostle himself for thinking that it was so. His language in Gal. ii. shows that, amid differences between him and them, a belief in the atonement was common ground ; and from 1 Cor. xv. 3 it may be inferred that the older disciples had derived this view of the crucifixion from the Old Testament scriptures, while he himself had received it secondhand from them, or by what he considered to be direct illumination from above. And though in Luke xxiv. 26, Acts ii. 38, and other passages belonging to the earliest period, or at least indicative of the belief of the Church from the beginning of the gospel, atonement is not distinctly expressed, yet the thought of it is not far off, and was sure to suggest itself ; so that remission of sins " in the name of Jesus " might easily become remission by virtue of the death of Jesus. Further, the Jewish section of the primitive Church seems to have concurred with the Gentile section in regarding Jesus as a Son of God no less than as a Son of David. At least, there is nothing in St. Paul's polemic against his Jewish opponents to lead to an opposite conclusion ; and if the

Apokalypse represents an early and prevalent phase of Jewish Christian thought, the somewhat dubious and halting Christology rises at times to a level with that of St. Paul, and even to that of the fourth Evangelist. But this is a view of the Apokalypse which has been very much shaken by recent criticism, so that we cannot build any conclusion upon it. We know, however, that in the rabbinical literature of the 2nd century, Jewish Christians are reproached as apostates, because they had departed from the monotheistic principle of Judaism, so far as to regard Jesus as a divine being. Yet it is probable that the tendency on the part of the Jewish converts (involuntary, nay, inevitable, and even commendable, as it no doubt was), to retain their former habits of thought in connection with their new faith, may have interfered, in the minds of many of them, with that conception of Christ which was essential to Pauline Christianity, and may have inclined them towards those Ebionitic views of Christ's person into which many of them seem ultimately to have fallen. It may be that, from the very first, their Christological view was not sufficiently clear and explicit to conquer their Jewish habits of thought and to place them securely on the Paulo-Christian level. But, on the whole, we seem to be justified in concluding that no material difference of opinion as to the work and person of Christ existed visibly between the two sections of converts, or that the differences which did exist were overlaid or kept out of sight by the use of terms which were common to both. Yet a difference between the Pauline and Jewish-Christian conception of Christ, all but fundamental and insurmountable, which otherwise might not for long have betrayed its presence, soon came to light in the practical conduct of life, or in the soteriological department of the dogma.

It was inevitable that the first disciples, the moment they took up the idea that the death of Jesus was an atonement for sin, should ask themselves the question, How far did the efficacy of the atonement extend, and what were the conditions for participating in its efficacy? Their answers to these questions could not be doubtful. They had, as we have shown, arrived previously at a belief in the Messianic office of Jesus, and their view of his death as an atonement presupposed that belief. Their idea of the atonement was therefore necessarily controlled by that of his Messiahship, and the fact that the

Messiah had come of Israel, and belonged to Israel, was calculated to intensify their conceit of national privilege, and to
deepen the prejudice of exclusiveness in their minds. It can
easily be understood how, as it is said in Acts xxi. 20, the Jews
who believed in Jesus, and thus added a new article to their
creed, should, on that very account, be the more "zealous of
the law." The verse seems to imply that this was a common,
if not universal, characteristic of Jewish believers. They were
prone to persuade themselves that their new faith demanded of
them a strict observance of the old law, and that the atonement
was limited to the Jewish people, and to individuals of other
nationalities who conformed to its requirements. They not
only continued to observe the rites and ceremonies to which
they had been accustomed, but they maintained that the
Gentiles could enter their communion and share in their privileges only by undergoing circumcision, as the sign of the
covenant, and so taking upon them the yoke of the law. The
born Jew could not easily be persuaded to admit those who
refused to pass under that yoke to the same platform with
himself. He could not be made to understand how a system of
divine appointment could be of transient obligation. He had
always believed that the punctilious and universal observance
of the law was the very goal of the national history, and that,
apart from circumcision, the practice of all the virtues was of
no avail in God's sight. He regarded the antinomism which
St. Paul preached as a species of libertinism, against which
his religious feelings and his moral sense rose in rebellion.
He knew of no other law than the written or oral law of Israel,
and had been scrupulously trained to look to that for the
guidance of his conduct, and to regard the Gentiles, who were
without that law, as having no proper directory of moral
conduct, and therefore unfitted to enter the kingdom of God.

Owing to their previous habits of thought, the Jewish
Christians could hardly be expected to apprehend the simple
doctrine of Jesus. Their doctrinal position was one of transition between the old and the new. Recent researches into the
theology of the synagogue, by Weber especially, have brought
out the fact, to which Old Testament theology also bears
witness, that the ideas current in Judea respecting atonement
were vague and complex in the highest degree. The offering
of sacrifice, though the most striking, was by no means the

only method of atonement.   According to the nature of the offence, it required to be conjoined with penitence on the part of the offender, and with numberless performances of a ritual-istic kind prescribed by usage and statute.   And above all, the notion prevailed, that when, as might often be felt to be the case, the personal performances of the sinner did not suffice to atone for his past sins, the supererogatory merits of righteous men might be imputed to him, or thrown by the Supreme Judge into the scale in his favour.   The religious life of the Jewish people was powerfully swayed by these ideas, and when con-verted to the faith of Jesus as Messiah, it was inevitable that they should regard the great atonement simply as the highest instance of vicarious suffering : or as a means of expiating sin supplementary to all the other means appointed or sanctioned by the divine law and by prophetic authority, so that these latter still remained in force and their observance still obliga-tory.   The sufferings of Jesus were placed by them on a footing with the sufferings of other pious men—expiatory, like theirs, of sins, though of higher value.   His sufferings had added to the fund of merit accumulated by the prophets and righteous men of former ages for the benefit of the Jewish people, and formed a new "advantage" (Rom. iii. 1) to all of Jewish faith and Jewish extraction.

The new consciousness of the primitive disciples was of the nature of an instinct, or of a sympathetic attachment to Jesus. The new principle which had come into their lives existed in the form of an unthinking, absorbing devotion to his all-subduing personality ; and manifested itself chiefly in their endeavour to mould their lives upon his: a devotion of which, simple-minded, earnest men, without abstract theories or preconceptions, are quite susceptible.   They did not so much receive his doctrine as believe in his person ; and had the cause of Christianity rested solely on men whose chief or sole qualification was devotion of such sort, it might never have come to more than a form of Judaism, and we should now have had a Jewish sect instead of the Christian Church.   The novelty of Christianity, as such men conceived of it, would not have been distinctive or specific enough in principle to effect its disjunction from Judaism, and to give to it a secure and independent position. They and their converts would have continued in theory and practice to combine the new faith with the conceit of Jewish privilege and the obligation of Jewish rites and usages, and the gospel would never have been preached in its freedom to the Gentiles.

Had Paul reached his faith in the great atonement by the same avenue as the early disciples, he would probably have limited its virtue (by which is meant its area of incidence, and its degree of efficacy) just as they did. But though, from the moment of his conversion, he, no doubt, regarded Jesus as the Messiah, yet it was through a distinct channel, viz., that of his own prior experience, touched and illuminated by what of the teaching of Jesus had reached his ear, or had been conveyed "without the word" to his heart and understanding. He was thus led to apprehend the death of Jesus as an atonement, without viewing it, as those others did, through the veil of Jewish prejudice. There is nothing *a priori* improbable in this remarkable circumstance. Jesus was under the necessity of recruiting his company of followers from the population of Galilee. These recruits were, it may well be supposed, more or less well-meaning men ; but they were probably also slow of understanding and dull of apprehension ; and it is conceivable that, while *they* missed the supreme significance of his doctrine, notwithstanding their intimate intercourse with him, a few straggling hints of it might be sufficient to stimulate and illumine the mind of a man prepared, like St. Paul, for its reception, by keenness of intellect and previous experience.

From that source a new element of thought which had escaped the observation of the primitive disciples, and of which they knew nothing, had entered the mind of Paul. It was the simple and far-reaching idea which had distilled itself from all he had heard of the life and doctrine of Jesus, viz., that God was by nature propitious and did not need to be propitiated ; which had delivered him instantaneously, and as by volcanic energy, from the fruitless and maddening attempt to propitiate God, and broke through the limitations and prejudices which circumscribed the thoughts of the earlier disciples. This idea was what emancipated him from the sense of legal bondage, and revealed to him the principle of evangelical freedom, besides discovering to him the foundation on which an all-embracing religion might be reared. And this same idea continued powerfully to influence his thought. The immediacy with which it appealed to his reason gave to it an absolute significance, and set authority and tradition aside as by some higher right, like that which Jesus himself claimed when he set aside the law of the Sabbath. Jesus claimed that right as the Son of Man, *i.e.*, in virtue of that true humanity which spoke out in him (Mark ii. 28). And St. Paul felt in like manner that it was the true humanity in himself which answered to the appeal made to it by that evangelic view of the divine character which flashed upon him in his moment of anguish and despair.

It may indeed be questioned, in the name of the thought and accumulated experience of the present time, whether even he penetrated to the full consequence and understood the full range of the new doctrine. For a moment, never forgotten by him, he rose to the vision or contemplation of the new conception of God, and stood upon the height which Jesus securely and permanently occupied. But the dogma which he proceeded to construct is a proof that it was only for a moment. If the view taken in these pages of the origin of his dogma be generally or substantially correct, even Paul himself departed or fell away from the pure and simple doctrine of Jesus, or from that idea of the religious relation which had been the cause of his conversion. We can easily understand how the idea of atonement might be too strongly entrenched in the Apostle's mind to be dispossessed even by his deeper insight. It was the means which, from the earliest time and for untold ages, the ancient world—Jewish and Gentile—had made use of to propitiate God, and to restore the sinner to a sense of His favour. The worshipper of old had a dim conception that the act of sacrifice was a solemn acknowledgment that nothing less than the dedication of himself, soul and body, was the debt which he owed to his Maker, and he had hoped that that acknowledgment would be mercifully accepted as a partial, in place of a perfect, discharge of his debt. In such a practice lay a germ or dim presentiment of the purest form of religion, but which, just because it was only a germ, had to be done away when that which was perfect was come. But the idea had too powerful a hold upon the Apostle's mind for him to get rid of it entirely. He felt that it must still have a place and a function in the new religious relation which had disclosed itself to his mind, and he proceeded to incorporate it in his view of that relation. The historical fact, for fact it is, that disciples of such undoubted devotion and common intelligence as Peter, James, and John, and their followers, committed the mistake of thinking the observance of the Jewish law as in some way conducive to salvation, and did not perceive the incongruity of such an idea with the doctrine of their Master, contributes a presumption that another disciple of equal devotion and of greater depth of spiritual insight might fall into the lesser misapprehension of transferring the atoning function to that Master, biased as that other was by the desire to magnify the work and nature of him who had stooped from heaven to pluck him as a brand from the burning.

The persistent and latent power over the Apostle's mind of the evangelical idea to which his conversion was due, showed itself in this, that the atonement with which he overlaid it was made by him to answer to that idea so far as range and scope were concerned. He represented the atonement as of such absolute value that, instead of supplementing, it superseded all other forms of atonement and rendered them superfluous. He made it to be the one only and sole expiation for human sin. The legal conception of the religious relation was thus set aside ; law itself was made of no effect ; all men were placed on a footing of equality in the sight of God ; privilege was abolished ; and the distinction between Jew and Gentile, between clean and unclean, was effaced. The Apostle saw no inconsistency between the propitious character of God and an atonement which was made, not by man himself, but by God, in the person of man's representative. It seemed to him that one fate had overtaken all legal services, whether of expiation or of thanksgiving. The propitiatory element which was present in both alike was condemned. The service of the Christian was to be a service of pure thanksgiving, from which the propitiatory element was discharged ; a service of undissembled love and thankfulness for the atonement, which was God's supreme and unspeakable gift to man.

We see that both St. Paul and the earlier disciples were agreed in attaching the character of an atonement to the death of Jesus. But there was this difference between his view of it and theirs, that he laid greater emphasis upon it than they did, or than the Jewish Christians generally were disposed to do. While these latter maintained their faith in the Messiahship of Jesus, *in spite* of his ignominious death, he became the Messiah

for Paul *in consequence* of it.   While *they* spoke of his crucifixion apologetically as at most a culmination of sacrificial
worship, which sanctioned or even glorified the sacrifices and
other ceremonial observances of the law, *he* went the length of
regarding it aggressively, as superseding and abrogating all other
sacrifice, together with the whole system of ceremonial service,
and especially as doing away at once and for ever with the
propitiatory element of man's own conformity to the divine will.
The distinction thus pointed out between the view of St. Paul
and that of the earlier disciples gives meaning to those passages
in which St. Paul speaks of *his* gospel as something apart and
distinct (Rom. ii. 16 ; 2 Cor. iv. 3, xi. 4 ; Gal. ii. 2 ; 2 Thess.
ii. 14).   There is indeed every reason to believe that there was
more than a merely nominal distinction between the gospel,
which was powerful for the conversion of the Gentiles, and the
gospel which retained the allegiance of the Jewish Christians ;
between the gospel of the uncircumcision and the gospel of the
circumcision.   It was by the preaching of the former that
Christianity advanced to its universalistic position in the world.
The Jewish leaven might continue to work in secret ; but
Christianity became a great power of God in the world by the
labour of men who did their best to expel that leaven from the
Church.

The new conception of God and of the religious relation,
which, as we have contended, was the real cause of St. Paul's
conversion, opened his eyes to many things ; and among others
to this, that the Gentiles who had not the law were " a law to
themselves," and that to have the spirit of love awakened in
them, was all that was needed to give them a clear discernment
of the indelible characters of the law written on their hearts,
as well as an impulse to an ever growing conformity with it.
And this one thing needful for their moral life, he found in
"the word of the Cross," or in the doctrine of atonement, offered
for human sin by the self-sacrifice of the Son of God.   The love
awakened by the contemplation of that great manifestation of
divine love, seemed to him to supply a new rule and a new
motive for human conduct, fitted both to enable the Gentile
Christians to dispense with all other law, and also to emancipate Jewish Christians from the burdensome observance of
their own statutory requirements.   When St. Paul found that
statutory observances were no longer necessary to his own

spiritual life, or to the maintenance of his communion with God he boldly set them aside, and taught others to do likewise. He had the conviction that the truth which had set himself free, was by its very nature a charter of freedom for all men without distinction. For no man, it has been said, "was ever yet convinced of any momentous truth, without feeling in himself the power, as well as the desire, of communicating it."

From that new rule and that new motive there evolved itself, in the mind of the Apostle, the idea of human, or rather Christian liberty : an idea which, so far as we can gather from the synoptic reports, had not been clearly or explicitly expressed by Jesus in his teaching. At the most, he only taught it indirectly, by the more or less frequent exercise of it in his own person, as, e.g., by claiming for himself and for men generally, the lordship over the Sabbath day ; by setting aside the Levitical regulations as to divorce, and by his apparent non-observance of Jewish ritual generally. This absence of any express reference to religious liberty, either was, or seemed to be, an omission in his doctrine, which the fourth Evangelist, with St. Paul in his view, could not fail to supply in his hyper-ideal report of the teaching of Jesus : " If the Son shall make you free, ye shall be free indeed." " The truth shall make you free" (John viii. 32-36). But it was St. Paul, who, having felt himself enfranchised from his bondage to the statutory law, and released from the necessity of any propitiatory service whatever, was the first to utter the idea. His sense of enfranchisement he explained to himself, by regarding the atonement on the Cross as complete in itself, and as superseding all other propitiations, as well as the law which enjoined them. And it was what he had in view, when he declared that he was called in the moment of his conversion to the apostleship of the Gentiles, who had not the law. His clear and vivid perception of the principle which differentiated the doctrine of Jesus from that current among the Jews of his day, gave him courage to proclaim with unhesitating confidence that legal and traditional observances interfered with Christian liberty and were no longer binding ; and that the death of Christ was the medium of a universal benefit, comprehensive of Jew and Gentile alike. He was thus qualified from the moment of his conversion to be the Apostle of the Gentiles ; and in that qualification he recognized a special call. Renan, indeed, gives it as his opinion, that St. Paul, no less than the other apostles, preached the necessity of circumcision in the first period of his ministry; but that he felt himself compelled, with a view to the success of his work among the Gentiles, to admit many of them, " surreptitiously," into the Church without insisting upon their submission to that rite; and that by degrees he came to consider it, and ritual generally, as useless, and even as derogatory to the merits of Christ. Looked at from the standpoint of ordinary historical pragmatism, this view has much to recommend it. But certainly it is not the view which the writer of the Acts of the Apostles took ; and what is more decisive, it is not the view which may be gathered from St. Paul's own account in the Epistle to the Galatians i. 12-16. And though the singularity of the Apostle's conversion is much enhanced, when it is regarded as the sudden revelation to his mind of his distinctive, and universalistic gospel, yet we are disposed to adopt this view of it, in preference to that, which is otherwise the more likely, both because it has the authority of Paul himself, and because it harmonizes best with the view we have taken of his conversion. The same critic is also of opinion, as might be expected, that it is historically inaccurate to say, that St. Paul advanced a claim to apostleship from the time of his conversion ; for that the conviction of his apostleship took possession of his mind slowly, and only became fixed after the great success of his first missionary journey. In view of St. Paul's own expressions, this opinion also is very doubtful ; and it may be dismissed as of little material consequence, though, like the other opinion just referred to, it somewhat reduces the marvellous nature of the disclosure made to the mind of the Apostle.

With the existence in the Church of fundamentally different views as to the nature and extent of the atonement, it was inevitable that misunderstandings should arise between its different sections. We have shown that the national feeling of exclusiveness was apt to be intensified in its Jewish section. There are various indications in the New Testament, and especially in the Acts of the Apostles, that there was a minority in this section, which, with deeper insight into the principles of the gospel, yet out of a natural feeling of piety, retained their inherited usages without seeking to impose them on the Gentile converts. But this considerate and moderate position was soon found to be untenable, because it did not supply a *modus vivendi* when the Jewish and Gentile communities came together. And, moreover, the rigid and conservative party in the Jewish section became more and more intolerant of the greater freedom enjoyed by the Gentile converts, and sought to impose legal observances upon them. By insisting upon their own historical right and their national privileges, they succeeded in over-ruling the more liberal, or mediating and temporizing party, among their Jewish brethren, as we may see in the case of Peter himself at Antioch. The relations between the two sections of the Church became more and more strained, especially after the unsuccessful effort made by St. Paul, as recorded in Gal. ii., to prevail upon Peter to live as did the Gentiles, and to assert for himself the same liberty as these latter enjoyed. We call St. Paul's effort unsuccessful because, though Renan believes that he did prevail upon Peter to adopt the more liberal practice, Weizsäcker shows, by a fine analysis of St. Paul's language, that such was not the case. The probability is that the zealot party which, at that crisis, prevailed against the better judgment of St. Peter, gradually gained the upper hand in the Jewish section of the Church, which, for the greater part, and in course of time, would relapse into Judaism, and fall away from connection with the Christian community. It was to counteract the tendency in this direction, and to prevent the Gentiles from being overborne and carried away by these zealots, as many of them seem to have been (Gal. iii.), that St. Paul emphasized his distinctive doctrine and sought to establish the free universalism of the gospel, by his broad principle of justification by faith alone, without the works of the law. It was probably with the same end in view that the Apostle, while in the interests of practical religion he covertly and virtually qualified this principle, yet never seems to have withdrawn the formula. To call the latter in question was left for another apostle, viz., St. James (ii. 14-26).

It would seem, indeed, as if the line of thought and action adopted by St. Paul in this matter went far to enhance the danger of schism and dissension in the Church. The idea of Christian liberty, as expounded by him, was at once a weapon for conquest and a cause of strife. In his uncompromising zeal and his enthusiastic devotion to the pure idea, he not only

admitted the Gentiles to gospel privileges without requiring
from them obedience to the law ; but he also insisted that the
Jewish converts should descend from their assumed position of
privilege and consent to occupy the same platform as the
Gentile converts, that so there might be equality between them,
and that the two sections might form one community of
Christians, not divided by difference of usage.   He goes near
to imply that to attach value to the Mosaic observances was
tantamount to a dishonour of the gospel, and to a denial of
Christ (Gal. v. 1-4) ; that to submit to circumcision and to
persevere in the practice of legal rites involved a forfeiture of
the grace of God and the loss of Christian status.

The positions taken up by Paul on the one side, and by the
Jewish Christians on the other, were plainly irreconcilable, and
had they been maintained the unity, and possibly the very
existence of the Church, would have been imperilled.   Had the
two sections of the Church been suffered to grow up together,
and to become consolidated each for itself, they would have
been parted as by an invisible but impassable wall, like that
which separates Mahometans and Hindoos in India at the
present day, and would sooner or later have engaged in an
internecine conflict.   The tolerance with which even Paul
seems latterly to have regarded the Jewish section on the score
of its weakness in the faith, was a species of intolerance—and
was necessarily felt to be so by the Jewish Christians, who
clung to their ancient forms of worship, and could have no
other effect than either to compel them to go over to the
Gentile majority or to widen the breach between it and them.
The former alternative was that aimed at by St. Paul, who felt,
with statesmanlike instinct, that it was absolutely necessary
that the section in which the free principle of Christianity had
come into play, should, for its own self-preservation, or for the
preservation of its principle, expel in some way the other
section from the Christian communion.   To have forced this
alternative upon the Church, even at the risk of widening the
breach, was the achievement of St. Paul.   From St. Peter, who
was at once the most enlightened and commanding of the
original disciples, he certainly got no assistance.   If St. Peter
ever rose to the full height of Christian liberty, as perhaps
might be inferred from what is said of the part he took in the
conversion and baptism of Cornelius, it was only for a moment,

and after a period of wavering and indecision he seems to have fallen away from it again. Either he never attained to a clear intellectual conviction on the subject, or he had not the courage of his conviction. And of these alternative explanations of his conduct, the latter, it seems to us, would do him an injustice. We subscribe to the opinion of Weizsäcker, that the apostle's vacillation and apparent duplicity at Antioch, with his ultimate retreat from the Catholic point of view, which for a time he almost seems to have attained, was due not so much to want of courage, as to the want of the full insight enjoyed by St. Paul into the nature and principle of Christian liberty ; or, as we should say, to his want of insight into the evangelical principle, the ground of Christian liberty. His deficiency, in this respect, made it impossible for him to take up a decided and resolute position, and placed him under the sway of the narrow zealot faction which insisted on the prescriptive or divine right of the Jewish law. In analogous cases it is always so.

St. Paul's consciousness of Christian liberty was founded on his immediate insight into the religious relation, and was really independent of any reasoning upon the subject. But the grand difficulty remained for him to impart the same consciousness to the minds of others, but especially his Jewish countrymen, or to justify it to himself and to them on rational or quasi-rational grounds. This difficulty arose from the fact that the liberty claimed by him was liberty from the law, which had been given by divine authority, and which rested, therefore, on a sanction presumably immutable. The real justification of his doctrine lay in that evangelical view of the religious relation which had revealed itself to his mind. But even if the Apostle was fully conscious of this, he felt that for those who had not clearly apprehended that relation he required to find another explanation more level to their apprehension. With this in view, he called to his aid the allegorical, or, let us say, the rabbinical use of the Old Testament, by which, as every one knows who is familiar with his epistles, he made out a case to show that the law had come between the promise given to the fathers and its fulfilment in Christ, and was therefore of temporary validity ; that it had been added because of trans-gressions, to provoke the lusts and to shut men up to the gospel ; and that its function was gone when, as the fourth

Evangelist expressed it, " Grace and truth had come by Jesus Christ."

This apology for Christian liberty was evidently suggested to the Apostle by his own peculiar experience under the law, and might appear to himself to be satisfactory and serviceable in his controversy with the Jewish Christians ; but it could not but appear to be very questionable and unsatisfactory to men who had no such experience, and did not understand what he meant when he said that the strength of sin is the law. Many of those, therefore, who shared with St. Paul in his sense of emancipation from legal bondage could not but cast about for another solution of the difficulty. Accordingly, we find another such in the Epistle to the Hebrews, which may be regarded, and was possibly intended, in part at least, as a defence of Christian liberty from another point of view than that which was taken by St. Paul. This epistle, as its superscription seems to imply, is addressed to Jewish Christians ; and the writer, who was certainly a Jewish convert, devised his solution by calling to his aid the great and catching idea—confessedly of Hellenistic derivation—that finite things are images of the divine ; that, corresponding to the world of sense, there is the world of spirit, of which that other is only a shadow or a prophecy ; the same idea as is expressed in Goethe's words, " Alles vergängliche ist nur ein Gleichniss." The argument is, that the law belonged to the lower, imperfect, or faulty system, and had been ordained as a shadow of heavenly things yet to come ; so that its obligation and *raison d'être* vanished in the presence of those better things under the gospel. And there can be no doubt that, granting his philosopheme, this method of disposing of the Jewish law, and demonstrating the cessation of Jewish privilege, is more simple and intelligible than the highly subtle, complex, and over-ingenious method of St. Paul. With the reservation just made, we may say indeed that it addresses itself to the general reason and common mind of man, which delights in tracing grand analogies or correspondences between different systems, and finds in such correspondences an evidence of a divine, all-comprehensive plan. And to Jewish minds especially, this view of the law, as containing a mystical, symbolical, and prophetic reference in many or all of its arrangements and details, to analogous parts of the higher dispensation of the gospel, could not but appear to be more respectful or, so to speak, more complimentary to the law, than the view of it taken by St. Paul ; and therefore more fitted to reconcile the Jewish converts to the thought of its transitory nature.

The difference between St. Paul's point of view and that of Apollos, or whoever was the writer of the Epistle to the Hebrews, is conspicuous in their diverse treatment of the atonement made by Christ on the Cross. By summarily setting law aside, as St. Paul does, that Apostle debars himself from any but a very general appeal to its sanctions and provisions, though atonement was part of its requirements, and had its sanction. We find accordingly that he nowhere enters into legal details, and that he sees a counterpart of the atonement offered by Jesus, not in the animal sacrifices prescribed by the law, but in the prophetic or Pharisaic idea, that the sufferings of righteous men atone for the sins of the community—the idea which receives its classical expression in Isa. liii. On that idea he rests, and from it he ascends to the atonement offered on the Cross. The writer to the Hebrews, on the contrary, regards that atonement as having its divinely ordained type and counterpart or pattern in the legal sacrifices. He thus pays a certain homage to the Mosaic ritual, which St. Paul goes near to ignore or set aside. But while he thus assigns to the law a well-defined and honourable office, and seems to be more zealous or careful of it than St. Paul is, he at the same time, as we have seen, contrives by means of his Hellenistic philosopheme, to make out its temporary obligation, and to vindicate the emancipation of believers from its requirements. To him the atoning virtue of the Cross was a postulate of the legal rites, which, as belonging to the world of sense, necessarily pointed to something higher and beyond themselves ; and *that* could only be the Cross of Christ. In the height of his devotion a prophetic soul had exclaimed, " I will offer bullocks and goats" (Ps. lxvi. 15). But the interpreter of the new era says, " It is not possible that the blood of bulls and goats can take away sins." The blood of a nobler victim is required for that ; and what nobler victim could there be than the Son of God ?

It must be confessed, however, that the problem which Christian liberty presented to the Church was completely solved neither by St. Paul nor by the writer to the Hebrews. Neither St. Paul's view of the provisional and temporary nature of the law, nor the Hellenistic philosopheme could lay claim to a divine sanction. The roundabout dialectic by which St. Paul (Gal. iii.) and this other writer (ch. viii.) seek to establish a claim to such a sanction for their respective views, is as inconclusive as it can well be, except for those who, being otherwise imbued with the idea of Christian liberty, were disposed to be satisfied with it. And if we bear in mind that, for the Jews generally, the Mosaic ritual was an ordinance of heaven and the Old Testament an inspired volume, and that the claim of the Mosaic dispensation, to "unchangeableness" and perpetuity, was for them neither "economical" nor "simulated," as Newman in his work on the Arians declared it to be, but absolute and *bona fide*, we cannot conceal from ourselves that, in the controversy which St. Paul waged, the logic was all on the side of his opponents. The new spirit and the higher truth were indeed on the Apostle's side. But, while he affirmed the higher truth, he did not trust to its native force alone, as Jesus had done, but endeavoured, not very successfully as we have seen, by the allegorical interpretation of the Old Testament, common among the Jews of that day, and by an ingenious but perplexing dialectic, to carry conviction to the minds of his converts. We do not mean to insinuate that this was a sophistical artifice on the part of the Apostle, for it reflected his own experience and satisfied himself ; nor was it altogether a *brutum fulmen*, for it served, in the immediate emergency, to gainsay and nonplus the adversaries by meeting them on their own ground, and answering them in a way to which they could not consistently object. Yet, though the Apostle's appeal to the law itself might gainsay or silence such of the Jewish converts as desired to be under the law (Gal. iv. 21), it is very doubtful whether it was calculated to tell upon *their* convictions; while it could not possibly tell upon the mind of the Gentile converts generally, to whom the Jewish law was nothing, and who took little or no interest in Jewish modes of thought, or in questions about the law (Acts xviii. 15, xxiii. 29), but had been won over to Christianity by its appeal to their higher nature, and by the confident report of the resurrection of its Founder.

The principle of Christian liberty was involved in the evangelical consciousness of the religious relation, but wherever that consciousness was not fully developed the legal yoke, unlifted, still remained to burden and to fetter the soul. And, as is invariably the case, where a principle lying in the background is not apprehended, mere reasoning and dialectic were unable to break that yoke, and so to avert the danger of schism. Under the circumstances, we might be sure that that danger would arise. And the critical study of the New Testament and other primitive documents which shed light, more or less dim, upon the early history of the Church, has, we think, demonstrated that this danger was much more serious and of longer duration than can be gathered from a superficial and uncritical perusal of these documents. In the end the danger was, we believe, averted partly by the expulsion of the Jewish-Christian element, and partly by the growth of conciliatory relations between the Jewish-Christian section and the Gentile section of the Church, as represented by St. Paul, and by the involuntary resort on both sides to compromise. In the New Testament, critics have imagined that they find indications of a desire on both sides to avert, by mutual concessions, the disruption which seemed to impend : concessions made, it may be, with reluctance, and as it were, with an *arrière pensée*, but still made, though in a covert and undemonstrative way, with the desired effect of building up a communion in which Christians of Jewish and Gentile extraction were welded into unity, and which in due time became recognized as the orthodox and catholic Church, from which no section or individual could dissent or stand aloof without incurring the charge of heresy.

Let it here be observed that wherever an irenical, conciliatory, or catholicizing tendency is visible in the books of the New Testament, it need not be traced to a deliberate intention on the part of the writers to effect a compromise between contending parties, or to restrain the centrifugal forces in the Church. The more probable explanation of such indications is that the various parties in the Church were coming gradually to a better understanding, and drawing nearer to each other ; and that the writers only presented the Christian doctrine in the light in which it was coming, more or less generally, to be viewed, either in the Church at large or in the circle to which the writers belonged. This qualifying remark on the tendency-theory applies, to some extent, probably to the section of the Epistle to the Romans (ch. xiv.) in which St. Paul seems to intend a compromise with his Jewish opponents, and to hold out to them the hand of fellowship. He nowhere ceases to vindicate the liberty of the Gentile converts ; but in that chapter he departs from his generally extreme and unconciliatory ground, and seems to admit, in a spirit of larger charity and consideration, that Jewish Christians may still adhere to the forms of worship inherited by them, even though he cannot help regarding it as a mark of the weakness of their faith (verse 1) that they should yet attach value to these forms. It is conceivable that, in the interval between the letter addressed to the Galatians and that addressed to the Romans, there may have been years, crowded no doubt with manifold experience of the ways and thoughts of men, in which his own dogma may have lost for himself somewhat of its angularity ; and that that section of the latter epistle was in full accord with his own matured conviction, though written also with an ulterior and far-off view to the consolidation of the Church.

Be this as it may, one thing is obvious, viz., that so far as any compromise was arrived at, it was effected not by means of such formal compacts or agreements as those of which the 15th chapter of the Acts gives a specimen, but in an informal and gradual manner, hardly confessed or observed by the parties themselves. The narrative in that chapter is almost certainly not strictly historical, but may be regarded as a proof that some attempts at compromise and conciliation were made on both sides; or at least that a feeling prevailed in the Church that it was desirable that such attempts should be made to come to an understanding. When great interests are felt by all parties to be at stake, the friction of opinion often leads to mutual understanding and to a settlement of differences for the common welfare. That this was the case here, and that the *rapprochement* was effected naturally rather than by such formal compacts as that just mentioned, may be inferred from the circumstance that that particular compact not only remained inoperative, but is rendered historically doubtful by the fact that it is never even alluded to on subsequent occasions ; whereas, had its provisions been really arrived at, they would have been afterwards appealed to for the settlement of the points in dispute. The historical data which bear on the subject are few, and sometimes conflicting ; but indications have been preserved that some of the Jewish-Christians, notwithstanding the compromise which may have been generally accepted, continued to cling so tenaciously to their supposed privileges as sons of Abraham, and to their Mosaic institutions, as to incur the risk of losing hold of all that was distinctive in Christianity, and of falling back into their old position, and so of being merged once more in orthodox Judaism.   Certain well-known passages in the Epistle to the Hebrews (*vide* vi. 6) and elsewhere are supposed to refer to the danger of such apostasy.   On the other hand, we may suppose that, even among the Jewish converts, many like Paul himself, and under the influence of his teaching, may have risen to the level of true Christian liberty ; while others may have been conciliated by concessions made by the Gentiles to the spirit, if not to the forms of Judaism, and so been retained in catholic communion.   At all events, in one or other of these ways, Jewish Christianity as a separate and irreconcilable form, ceased in process of time to create alarm and division in the Church.

The only other remark to be made here is that the way to compromise may have been paved and facilitated, if it be the case, as suggested by Weizsäcker, that the early Church was at no time composed entirely of Paulinists and anti-Paulinists ; that great numbers of the converts from the first occupied a neutral ground between these two sections, and by holding to Christianity in its broader aspects became spontaneously and insensibly indifferent to the remnants of Jewish forms.   Indeed, the distinctive Pauline doctrine may be regarded as a polemical or controversial makeshift, and never seems in that age to have struck deep root into the general Christian consciousness.   The dialectical form in which it was served up was too artificial and fine spun for general comprehension ; and what is still more, the spirit of legalism, which under diverse forms was common to Jews and Gentiles, was too deep-seated to be eradicated by any dialectic, however keen.   We find, accordingly, that the Church which emerged from the spiritual ferment and asserted itself as orthodox and catholic, held to a belief and practice which may be described as a compromise between the purely evangelical and the legal standpoint.   In the canonical post-Pauline epistles there is evident a very considerable relaxation of the doctrinal formulæ by which the Apostle sought to fence the evangelical idea.   And while the Jewish restrictions were discarded more and more, the legal spirit survived and devised for itself new forms, less unsuitable for symbolizing the universal-

istic spirit, under which forms, moreover, the reviving spirit of
legalism again reared its head, till it received a check at the
Reformation, and a new episode began in the eternal warfare
which goes on between the religion of the spirit and the
religion of the letter.

We give the above as an approximate representation of the
course of development in the primitive Church. But without
dwelling on such considerations, or laying stress on the highly
probable conjecture of Weizsäcker which has led to them, we
satisfy ourselves with presenting St. Paul as the representative
figure and prime agent in the great evolution of thought by
which the first century of the Christian era was distinguished.

It has now been shown that the unity of the Church was
imperilled almost from the first by the attitude which the
Jewish section of the converts assumed towards the Gentile
section. The former stood upon their national privileges and
sought to impose the yoke of the law upon the non-Israelitish
converts. Had they been successful in carrying their point,
i.e., in excluding from the Christian community all who refused to
comply with Jewish observances, the effect, as already observed,
would have been to reduce the community to the position of a
Jewish sect, to efface its distinctive character, and to arrest its
further growth. And had they been partially successful, the
Church would have been rent in twain, and its energies dissipated in internal conflicts. But this peril was averted by the
substantial triumph of Paulinism, a result due not so much to
the powerful dialectic of the Apostle, which was probably understood and accepted only by a few of his intimate associates, as
to the intrinsic superiority and inherent force of the new view
of the religious relation which he advocated, aided as it was by
his commanding personality and by the energy with which he
gave utterance to his own sense of spiritual emancipation,
together with the timely concessions which he and his party
made to Jewish feelings. The result was also contributed to
by observation of the conspicuous fact that the gospel as
preached by St. Paul to those of the uncircumcision produced
in them all its best fruits and imbued them with its spirit
(Acts x. 47, xv. 8-11). The grand spectacle of Gentile
multitudes " flocking and trooping to the standard of the
Cross," and without paying homage to the law of Moses, submitting to the restraints of a purer faith, could not but astound

the Jewish Christians and shake their confidence in the obligatory nature of their national rites. More than one passage in the Acts of the Apostles seems to show that this spectacle had made a profound impression, as well it might, on their minds. It was probably the argument which weighed most with them in restraining their schismatic tendencies and in overcoming their repugnance to an association with Gentile believers.

And, finally, the various causes operating to this end were in all probability powerfully reinforced by the logic of a great event, viz., the destruction of the Temple at Jerusalem by the Romans and the compulsory cessation consequent on that catastrophe of many of the greater ritual observances. Happening at that conjuncture, this catastrophe could not but be regarded by many of the Jewish Christians as stamping the divine imprimatur on the Pauline view as to the temporary validity of the Mosaic law and as to the extinction of Jewish privilege.

CHAPTER XVIII.

POST-PAULINE OR GNOSTIC PERIOD.

HARDLY had the obstacle presented by the conceit of Jewish privilege to the growth and stability of the Church been substantially overcome before a new obstacle arose, which did not indeed grow out of that other, but, as will appear, stood to it in some obscure relation of action and reaction. This time the obstacle arose in the Gentile section of the Church (though not wholly confined to it any more than that other was confined to the Jewish section), and consisted in the survival or reimportation of habits of life and modes of thought, which were essentially Gentile and anti-Christian in character and tendency. That, in the rapid propagation of Christianity among the Gentiles, such a complication should arise and should early become manifest was, in the nature of things, inevitable. Lest it should seem, however, that we ante-date the rise of Gnosticism, to which we here allude, let it be observed that while the great Gnostic writers belonged to the middle of the second century, or later, it stands to reason that Gnostic tendencies must have prevailed in the Church for many decades before they could have been thrown into systematic form, and have incurred the censure of heresy. But the whole Gnostic movement forms an obscure episode in the history of the Church, and will be entered upon here only in so far as may be necessary in tracing the contemporaneous development of what came to be regarded as the orthodox dogma.

The leading features of Gnosticism stood in intimate genetic connection with the dualistic theory of the universe. According to that theory matter was eternal, self-existent, and the source or principle of evil, and could be brought under the control of

God only by the agency of angelic, semi-divine, or intermediate spirits ; emanations from the absolute, who would have been defiled by immediate contact with matter. As a mode or form of theosophic speculation, Gnosticism, in germ if not in name, seems to have existed in the east prior to the Christian era, and is supposed with reason to have supplied the foreign element which gave birth to that sectarian form of Judaism which is known as Essenism. And if it be the case, as Bishop Lightfoot supposes, that after the destruction of Jerusalem the larger number of the Essene profession joined the Christian community, they may have carried Gnostic elements with them into the Church. This supposition, however, is not necessary to account for the entrance of Gnosticism, for we may easily believe that the relics of Zoroastrian ideas, which still lingered in eastern lands, may have been carried by converts from the east into the new faith. But the dualistic thought, which may have lain as a germ in pre-Christian Gnosticism, became a developed system of thought by the absorption of such elements of Christianity as could enter into combination with it. A compromising alliance was thus formed between it and Christianity, inimical to the purity and even to the existence of the latter, and suggesting to Pauline Christians the necessity of a restatement of Christian doctrine to ward off the danger.

In practice the dualistic theory led very intelligibly in the first instance to asceticism. For, as according to it, matter is the principle of evil, the infection of evil can be escaped only by avoidance of all contact with matter, and by the mortification, if not the annihilation, of the fleshly nature. But experience is hardly needed to show that effort in this direction can only be very partially successful, and that, as Bishop Lightfoot says, such effort can only "touch the fringe" of the evil ; and hence the temptation to fly to the opposite extreme. That is, to regard matter as a mere negative ; to treat it with indifference as something which is of no concern, and to follow the fleshly impulses of nature without scruple or hesitation. It is thus apparent that when matter is regarded as the principle of evil there may be but a step from an ascetic to a licentious habit of life. It is indeed conceivable that one or both of these mischievous extremes might have made their appearance in the Church apart from any connection with the dualistic theory, or any knowledge or recognition of it. But it is obvious that the prevalence of such a speculation would immensely strengthen and aid the diffusion of any tendency in these directions that might otherwise exist; and make it a conspicuous and formidable evil. It was a startling phenomenon of this nature in the Church which the post-Pauline epistles seek to counteract by what may be called an indirect re-statement of the Pauline doctrine.

We adopt here the expression " post-Pauline," or " deutero-Pauline," as applied to certain books of the New Testament, viz., the Epistles to the Ephesians and Colossians as well as the pastoral Epistles which bear the name of St. Paul, but for various reasons are supposed by many not to have been written by him, at least in their extant form. The expression is so employed by such critics as C. Weizsäcker and O. Pfleiderer, and others who have satisfied themselves that these epistles were written, not by Paul himself, but by men of his school of thought, who in post-apostolic times wrote in his name and in his spirit, and as much as possible in his style of language. But the question may be regarded as still an open one. For while the leading living authorities of Germany declare in favour of the post-apostolic authorship, the leading authority in this country (Lightfoot) takes the opposite view. We agree with the former in thinking that this is pre-eminently a question in which external evidence or ancient testimony goes for little : and in applying the rules of criticism to the internal evidence in this investigation, it should be remembered what is often forgotten, that far more stress should be laid on the facts which tend to show that these epistles are not authentic, than on those which point to the Pauline authorship. The pseudonymous writer, if such he was, must evidently have been a Paulinist of high intellect, familiar with St. Paul's style of thought and language, who did his utmost to imitate that style and to enter into the conditions and circumstances under which the Apostle wrote. This, by no means improbable supposition, is of itself sufficient to account for many Pauline features or touches in these epistles. Whereas, in the case of a man so strenuously individualistic as St. Paul was, both in thought and expression, it is hard to conceive that he should have penned a single sentence without stamping it with the impress of his mind ; so that any lapse or departure from his style may fairly be held to form a presumption that he was not the author.

Further, it may be observed that the polemic in these epistles is directed not against the legalism against which St. Paul waged war, but partly against asceticism and partly against lawless license, to both of which the Gnostic sects were addicted, and both of which were inconsistent with the principles of Christianity. That, in view of these Gnostic tendencies, these epistles, if they do not exhibit a change of front, yet occupy a position different from that occupied by St. Paul in his great epistles, is plain. And the question whether it was the Apostle himself, or men of his school at a later period, who made this advance, depends for its answer partly on the verdict of the literary criticism applied to these epistles, but mainly on the chronology of the Gnostic systems against which their polemic is directed. This chronological question may not admit of being conclusively settled ; but the probability seems to be that the Gnostic element intruded itself into the Christian sphere and became a flagrant evil, so as to postulate an advance in doctrine on the ethical side, or rather another form of its statement, only after the first enthusiasm of the Church had cooled down and the terms of Christian member-ship had become relaxed ; by which time St. Paul had dis-appeared from the scene. The supposition that men of the Apostle's school might write in his name will not appear strange to those who take into account the many instances of a similar procedure in the literary history both of Jewish and of Christian antiquity. Still less will it appear strange if we also take into account the unsatisfactory condition in which St. Paul had left his doctrine in his authentic epistles, and which the rise and spread of Gnosticism must have brought sensibly and painfully under the observation of some of the more clear-sighted among his disciples. At the risk, therefore, of some repetition of what has been already said, we shall here endeavour to show that St. Paul's doctrine was open to mis-construction, so as to form a motive and inducement to the composition of post-Pauline literature, in which a warning against the errors of Gnosticism should have a conspicuous place.

And first, in regard to the ascetic habits of the Gnostic sects. It is obvious that no reproof or correction of these was administered by anything which St. Paul had said against Pharisaic restrictions ; for such restrictions were based on the obligation of obedience to the statutory law of Israel; whereas the asceticism of the sects not only went far beyond the legal observances, but were based on the dualistic idea, with which the Jew had no sympathy; besides that it "condemned the gratification of the natural cravings in every form, as if these were evil in themselves." It may even be affirmed that some expressions in St. Paul's epistles might be understood or misunderstood, as giving countenance to ascetic doctrine, as, for instance, what he says in regard to virginity and the married state; whereas no loophole is left for any such misunderstanding in the deutero-Pauline epistles, which expressly declare that "every creature of God is good, and nothing to be refused, if it be received with thanksgiving" (1 Tim. iv. 4). These and many other words in these epistles condemn, as contrary to the spirit of the gospel, every requirement that would unnecessarily curtail the liberty of the Christian; and every doctrine that would substitute asceticism for self-discipline, or confound the one with the other. *

In these same epistles there is an obvious purpose of protesting against that other and far more flagrant evil, the unbridled license to which there was a tendency in the Gnostic sects. If asceticism was due in part to an imperfect apprehension of Pauline Christianity, the doctrine which gave encouragement to licentiousness was a complete perversion of the liberty which St. Paul proclaimed: yet it can hardly be questioned that the Apostle's doctrine of justification, by faith alone, invited, or at least gave opening to this perversion. Much of his argumentation on the subject of Christian liberty was hardly intelligible, or, so far as intelligible, not very convincing either to Jew or Gentile, and witnessed more to the might and ardour of his genius than to the lucidity of his thought. His dialectic was not calculated to make clear the nature of that deliverance from the Mosaic or statutory law, of which he was in-

---

* In his dissertation on the "Colossian Heresy," Bishop Lightfoot treats of this subject with admirable clearness; and his remarks (from which we have derived much assistance) are all well deserving of attention, if we except the distinction which he draws between the "asceticism of dualism" and the "asceticism of self-discipline." This does not seem to be a happy distinction. What he understands by the latter is not asceticism at all, but simply self-discipline or self-denial; and his language is calculated to confound things which are essentially distinct.

wardly conscious, and for which he so resolutely contended. His manipulation of Old Testament history, in order to find in it a proof of the temporary obligation of the law, and to represent the law as blocking the way to the fulfilment of the promise made to the fathers, is not very satisfactory. His endeavour to combat Judaism with weapons drawn from its own armoury could only be partially satisfactory even to those who, like himself, were acquainted with Pharisaic theology, or satisfied with the current Rabbinical dialectic, by which his own mind had been saturated. Indeed, it could only satisfy the scruples or silence the objections of those who, like himself, had reached the idea of Christian liberty by quite another avenue; who, in a manner, did not need to be convinced, but accepted his argument as a good answer to those who were contentious, and pragmatically captious.

The doctrine by which the Apostle sought to explain, to himself and to the Church at large, that freedom from the Mosaic law of which he was instinctively conscious, was, as already said, the doctrine of justification by faith alone, which was but the necessary deduction from vicarious atonement and imputed righteousness. Now it is obvious that this doctrine, literally understood and carried out to its consequences (whether legitimate or not, we need not say), involved a danger to the cause of religion, as being apt to bring about its divorce from morality; and it may have been owing to the two causes now mentioned, viz., the obscurity of the Apostle's reasoning, and the ethical danger to which it was apt to give occasion, that this Pauline doctrine was laid aside, or thrown into the background in the Epistle to the Hebrews and in the deutero-Pauline epistles, which represent the post-apostolic phase of theological thought. No one can read these epistles with anything like attention without being struck by the fact that, to say the least, the accent is removed from that doctrine; and, omitting other points, that love and other Christian graces divide the field with faith in the mind of the writers, as being co-ordinate in value and alike essential to a justified state. The explanation given of this very noticeable fact by some of the Protestant theologians, who have discriminated between the doctrinal conceptions of the various writers of the New Testament, is that it is the sign of a falling away from the high idealism of the great Apostle of the Gentiles : a sort of relapse into the Judaistic form of doctrine, which, though assailed by him, yet gained ground, and finally established itself in the Catholic Church. But others, such as C. Weizsäcker and O. Pfleiderer, regard this difference as due to a natural and necessary development or correction of the Pauline doctrine, in which the Pharisaic-juristic element has fallen into the background, and the ethical, Hellenic element of the doctrine is accentuated. To ourselves, it seems as if these two explanations may be brought together and reconciled by taking into account a tendency of all striking and original thought, or of what is sometimes called " high doctrine," such as that of the Apostle. The tendency of all such thought is to assert itself at first without qualification; to assume a polemical or antagonistic attitude towards antecedent or current thought in the same walk, and to allow no weight to the latter ; whereas afterwards, under the teaching of experience and the ordeal of criticism, or on better consideration, it yields to the necessity of observing a more conciliatory and moderate tone, so as to square with the realities of life, and to fall into its proper but more unobtrusive place in the general system of thought. Be this as it may, it would certainly seem that the specific, polemical form of the Apostle's doctrine had lost for the post-apostolic Church whatever interest or significance it had ever had, and that the Gentile section, being now the larger and ever increasing majority, had laid aside its deference for the Jewish minority, and felt itself freed from subjection to the law, independently of St. Paul's controversial dialectic. His special form of doctrine thus gave way to a less antinomistic, but more intelligible, popular, and guarded form, which is presented in the deutero-Pauline epistles, and in several non-canonical writings of the same period.

According to the theory or conjecture advanced in a former part of this discussion, St. Paul, in his first enthusiasm, adopted the idea of justification by faith alone, but before writing his epistle to the Galatians, he had been taught by his pastoral experience the necessity of qualifying this doctrine, and, while still retaining the formula, had made it to square with that experience, by giving such an extension to the word " faith " as to include something more than a historical or intellectual persuasion of the truth of the evangelical doctrine, viz., a self-surrender to the method of Jesus, and a self-conformity to his life. By this extension of the word, the formula of the Apostle did, indeed, lose much or all of its paradoxical signi-ficance, inasmuch as " faith " so extended is presumptive, or, as we have already said, inclusive of the entire Christian life. But by such extension of it, the Apostle showed, at least, that he recognized and sought to obviate the danger which was involved in the literal acceptation of his formula.

This expedient, however, was not sufficient. So long as the formula was retained, there was ever a danger that the word " faith " would revert to its original and literal meaning, and hence we find that, effectually to obviate the danger from this source, the deutero-Pauline writers (in this, no doubt, giving expression to a general feeling in the Church) drop the formula entirely, and speak of faith as " the evidence of things not seen " (Heb. xi. 1), that is, a persuasion of the existence of the spiritual world in opposition to the materialistic habit of mind, or simply as a moral intellectual trust in God, and, therefore, as only one of many graces, all equally necessary to the Christian life. In this way faith lost its pre-eminence, or, at least, its sole-sufficiency for justification. In these same epistles Christ is represented as an object of meditation and affection, and an ideal of human endeavour, more than as an object of faith; and his person rather than his death becomes for the disciple the point of vision and the centre of regard. The dangerous consequences or tenden-cies of St. Paul's doctrine were thus averted, and the Church was gradually prepared for the reception of the later or Johannine theology; that is, for the representation of Christ as a personal revelation of the divine mind, and an embodiment of the human ideal.

But neither the formula of St. Paul, as qualified by himself, nor the more guarded doctrine of the deutero-Pauline epistles, sufficed to obviate the antinomian interpretation of Christian liberty, nor to create a barrier to the Gnostic movement, which took up into itself, and sought to give theoretic expression to the antinomian tendency to pervert that doctrine. The tendency in that direction had its deeper root indeed in common human nature, but was, without doubt, very much encouraged by the circumstance that in one of its aspects it was eminently anti-Judaic, a reaction against Jewish Christianity. The attitude of exclusiveness and of assumption on the part of Jewish Christians, while powerfully calculated to impose upon the minds of some among the Gentile converts, as we see in the early case of the Galatian Church (Gal. iii. 5, v. 1., etc.), would be resented by others as obstructive, and call forth a feeling of antagonism, and an over-emphatic assertion of evangelic liberty. The Pauline assertion of this principle would be misunderstood and carried to excess. And though the evangelic principle which differentiated Christianity from Judaism might in many minds be not less powerful and energetic, though it was not theoretically understood ; yet, just because of this defect of understanding, many in the Church would be disposed to adopt the most violent means to prevent a relapse into Judaism ; to rid themselves of a troublesome, irritating and embarrassing controversy, and to make the breach between the Church and the synagogue as wide as possible.

From the preceding remarks we may see that the doctrines of justification by faith alone, and of Christian liberty, which to the Apostle seemed to be legitimate inferences from the death of the Messiah, viewed in the light of his own personal experience, were not, even as expounded and safeguarded by him, adapted to the comprehension of an ordinary judgment, and invited, or at least admitted, of a construction which men of speculative, and still more, of licentious minds, were ready to put upon them ; and such interpretation was also recommended by its seeming to cut the knot which the Apostle had but partially succeeded in untying. It was no easy matter, after all he had urged, to understand in what relative sense the obligation of a God-given law could be done away ; or wherein the difference lay, which St. Paul had laboured to point out, between that " lawlessness which was moral, and that lawlessness which was immoral." To make this clear, there was required an amount of explanation and an expenditure of reasoning which was too subtle and involved, for the comprehension of common minds : a fact which probably drew forth the remark made in the Gnostic era, that there were in his epistles " some things hard to be understood, which they that are unlearned and unstable wrest, . . . unto their own destruction " (2 Peter iii. 16). That freedom from the limitations of the statutory law which the Apostle asserted was apt to be regarded as an absolute emancipation from all law whatever. And even those who had little leaning to Gnosticism might be inclined to adopt some short and easy method, such as it

afforded, of severing the connection between Judaism and
Christianity, betwixt law and gospel ; and to get rid of dialectical subtleties, by pushing the Pauline doctrine to an extreme,
and so to fall into that antinomianism in theory, and that
libertinism in practice, which (sometimes strangely but intelligibly enough varied with asceticism) were more or less
characteristic of the Gnostic sects.   This was a very natural
issue for men who had been accustomed to Gentile looseness of
life, and was exactly what took place in other spiritual crises of
a similar kind, as for example at the period of the Reformation
in the 16th century, when the excesses of the Anabaptists
and other sectaries were indirectly due to those same doctrines
of Christian liberty, revived in the Church by Luther.
Neither the Reformer nor the Apostle was able to give lucid
expression to a distinction of which both were yet profoundly
sensible ; and neither the one nor the other is responsible for
the excesses which followed his teaching.

Attention has thus been called to the modification which the
Pauline soteriology underwent in the deutero-Pauline or post-
apostolic epistles.   And we proceed now to call attention to
the development which St. Paul's Christology underwent, as
against the Gnostic doctrine in these same epistles.   As
notwithstanding his earnest ethical spirit, St. Paul's prominent
principle of justification by faith alone was so involved in
controversial subtleties as to be liable to perversion, so his
Christology was left by him in a state so unfinished and
indefinite as to call imperatively, not indeed for correction like
his soteriological doctrine, but for further definition.   And this
definition was undertaken or carried out in diverse directions ;
the one of which, as we shall yet see, led on ultimately to the
Christology of the fourth Gospel, and came to be regarded as
orthodox, while the other or Gnostic definition was early
stigmatized as heretical.   And if it here be asked in passing
how we are entitled to use such epithets, or, which is the same
thing, how a section of the Church was able to vindicate its
claim to be considered orthodox ; or yet again, how the
doctrines called orthodox got the upper hand in the Church ;
we may answer shortly that the triumphant doctrines were
those which appealed most powerfully to the sentiment or
consciousness awakened among men by the gospel, and were
most in harmony with its leading principles.   We shall find

that that doctrine which aggrandized, not that which derogated from the name and nature of Christ ; that which added to his glory, and exalted the enthusiasm of his followers, was that which prevailed, because it possessed the strength derived from consistency with the evangelic principle in the dogmatic form impressed upon it by St. Paul. This, after contending for a longer or shorter period on apparently equal terms with the competing doctrines, would at length inevitably prevail, and be confidently stamped as orthodox by its adherents.

That period in the history of the early Church, which witnessed the further definition of Pauline Christology, may best be introduced to the notice of the reader by adverting to a very notable circumstance connected with the conversion of the Gentiles, viz., that wherever the Gospel was received by them, the old polytheism disappeared, almost without a blow being directly aimed at it, or without an attempt being made to demonstrate its irrationality and folly. The doctrine of St. Paul was not of a negative nature ; he did not lay himself out to impugn the polytheistic system. His discourses at Lystra and at Athens, as recorded in Acts xiv. and xvii., and his language in the opening of his Epistle to the Romans are exceptional ; but we may infer even from these that he impugned the polytheistic doctrine and worship only in a cursory and incidental fashion. The " Word of the Cross," which formed his main and primary, if not sole, topic of address (1 Cor. ii. 2), was a call to the Gentiles to change their mode of life, and to believe that the Son of God had died for the sins of men. This was the true and only instrument of their conversion, and it seemed as if they could not embrace or give " an entrance " to this message, without " turning from idols to serve the living God " (1 Thess. i. 9). The doctrine which was sufficient for the conversion of the Jews was also sufficient for the conversion of the Gentiles.

The explanation of this remarkable circumstance may be found in the historical fact that, at the introduction of Christianity and for many preceding ages, faith in the heathen pantheon had been undermined by the corrosive effect of ideas which had been set afloat far and wide by the schools of Greek philosophy. That faith still retained its hold of the great masses of the people as a superstition or survival of a past phase of thought, but had lost its living power over their minds, while the cultured classes only observed its forms by way of paying respect to popular feeling. The whole fabric of superstition and of expediency combined was ready to dissolve at the first contact with a living faith. The Jewish people had, it is true, for many ages been possessed of the monotheistic belief, and it might have been expected that the faith of which they were the not unfaithful guardians might have spread to other people ; but in spite of their proselytizing zeal, little comparatively seems to have been effected by them in this direction. The monotheistic faith as presented by them to the Gentiles had somewhat of the weakness of a mere negation ; and the particularism and legalism with which it was associated in their minds was an obstacle to its diffusion through their means. It needed to be detached and set free from the limitations of Judaism before it could make way among surrounding nations. For these could not possibly be attracted by a faith which was seen to be consistent with a narrow exclusiveness, besides being connected with a peculiarly burdensome ceremonial and a repulsive rite of initiation.

Jesus it was who, by his direct appeal to the moral instincts, by his doctrine of the Heavenly Father, and of the better righteousness, first broke through the limitations of Judaism. By the necessity of his situation, however, or by a wise accommodation to circumstances, his personal teaching was confined chiefly, if not entirely, to his own countrymen.

But St. Paul, to whom a wider field was laid open, discerned the universalistic possibilities and significance of the doctrine, and brought it to bear in its dogmatic form upon the Gentile peoples. He appealed directly to their moral sense and to that craving for deliverance from evil which is common to all men ; and instead of entering upon a laboured refutation of their polytheistic ideas, and upon the evidences of the divine unity by way of laying a foundation for the doctrine of redemption, he proceeded on the directly opposite method of commencing at once with the latter doctrine. In listening to the Apostle's appeal, the individual heathen came to himself, touched the deepest ground of his being, and was placed face to face with his own higher nature—the essential divinity within him. This was felt by him instinctively to be the highest authority to which he was amenable, and he was thereby released from allegiance to all authority lower than this, the highest.

In his worship of the gods, the Gentile was always more or less conscious that these beings, merely because they were many, could not be supreme ; that there was a mysterious power or fate over and behind them ; and we have the testimony of an ancient author that in moments of supreme danger or sudden alarm, men turned involuntarily and instinctively from these inferior deities to address that awful Power. This observation makes it intelligible how the simple announcement of the gospel, that, in God over all, men had a common Father in heaven, might be all that was needed to produce a crisis in their spiritual life and to satisfy them at one and the same moment of the vanity (Acts xiv. 15) of all worship not addressed to the One God.   This effect of St. Paul's preaching upon the Gentiles is well illustrated by the experience of the Moravian missionaries in Greenland, where little or no effect was produced so long as they continued to discuss preliminary themes, such as the unity of God, the evidences of religion, and the facts of Bible history ; but where success began to attend their efforts so soon as they appealed directly to the consciences of their hearers and made to them the offer of salvation in the name of the crucified Son of God.

It might now have been expected that, as time went on, this same result would continue to follow the spread of the gospel. And such, we may be sure, was the case with individuals and with populations in which polytheism had been previously discredited by the influence of Greek philosophy and other dissolvents of superstition.   But in the case of others who had had the benefit of no such preparatory discipline or disillusionment, an instantaneous revolution of opinion could hardly be expected.   It is possible that individuals here and there who had been profoundly touched by the message of the gospel, even though they had had the benefit of no such experience, might yet undergo a sudden and complete revolution of opinion and character.   But nothing of the kind could possibly take place either actually or seemingly in the case of great masses of men.   Old habits of thought and action would still survive and reassert themselves after the new principle had taken root, and would long maintain their ground in spite of it, and alongside of it.   The new would for a time enter into combination with the old and would gradually overpower it, or be overpowered by it ; or a resultant form of faith would be evolved, which for a time would satisfy men's minds. It has been said by Professor Huxley, and we believe with truth, " that there is probably as much sheer fetichism among the Roman populace (of Southern Italy) now as there was 1800 years ago." In Southern Europe the pagan form of idolatry has been succeeded by what may be called a Christian form of idolatry, and the lands there have not been perfectly Christianized to this day. The ancient polytheistic ideas have survived under a Christian mask. We suppose, indeed, that to thoroughgoing Roman Catholics, such as Cardinal Newman, for whom " the religious character of Catholic countries was no prejudice to the sanctity of the Church," this circumstance will give little concern. But the fact that such a state of things has continued for so many ages, enables us the better to understand how it was possible for pagan ideas and practices to enter into combination with Christianity so soon after its birth, or at the very moment of its birth, into the world. On a retrospect of Church history it becomes evident that what is called the Catholic Church was founded on a compromise between Christian and ethnic principles, as well as between Jewish and Christian principles ; and that in the end it was moulded by fusion with the ideal principles of Christianity of many foreign and disparate elements, Jewish and Gentile. But at the outset, or at the post-apostolic period of which we now speak, this combination on the part of the converts was attempted in a manner and to an extent so wholesale and unrespecting as to threaten to subvert the character of the Church entirely, and to hurl it back into the gulf of heathenism. The Church grew and multiplied so rapidly that the influx of Gentile elements could only be imperfectly assimilated, and for a time it almost seemed as if in some regions these elements would prevail over those which were distinctively Christian.

Besides the anti-Judaic aspect of the Gnostic heresy, to which reference has been made, we have also to consider what may be called its polytheistic aspect, by which is meant the revival in it of a tendency common to all the Gentile nations, and of which many of the Gentile converts had not got rid, the tendency towards dæmonism—that is, to conceive of the interval between the finite and the Infinite as peopled with ranks of intermediate spirits or angelic beings, executants of the divine purposes ; partakers, more or less, of the divine nature and objects of popular worship. This tendency revived among the Gentile converts, no doubt mainly by virtue of the force of heredity; but its revival may also have been owing in part to the anti-Judaic bias, already mentioned, of these converts, or to the fact that it seemed to them to suggest a proof of the transient nature of the Jewish dispensation, more intelligible than either St. Paul or the writer to the Hebrews had been able to give; a ready means, therefore, of cutting away the ground from under Jewish assumption, and of quashing an inconvenient and embarrassing controversy which threatened to be otherwise interminable. For after all that had been said in vindication of Christian liberty, the Jewish Christians could still take their stand upon the fact, if it were the fact, that their law had been given by God Himself, and must be eternally valid. This was a consideration which was difficult to meet, and it was only by resorting to some violent expedient that it could be set aside. The Gnostic expedient for this purpose could only have recommended itself to men in whom the tendency towards dæmonism was yet strong. It consisted in the position that the God of Israel, who had created the world and given the law from Mount Sinai, was not the Supreme God or the Heavenly Father whom Jesus had revealed, but an inferior divinity, who, if not positively evil, was at best a just and righteous, or, it might be a severe and jealous Being, according to many of the representations given of Jehovah in the Old Testament. He was the demiurge, one of a countless number of æons, or angelic semi-divine ministers of the Supreme Power, whose law was no longer binding upon men; while Christ as Redeemer was regarded as one of the same order of Beings, whose office was to declare the will of the Heavenly Father, and to deliver mankind from the evil inherent in the imperfect creation of the demiurge.

In practice the combination of the dualistic principle with Christianity led, as we have already seen, to the introduction into the Church, by alternate lines of thought, of asceticism and unbridled license. But doctrinally it led to highly derogatory views of the person and work of Christ; for Gnosticism could find a place for these in its various systems only by regarding him as one of those intermediate spirits, and his work of redemption as a cosmical or metaphysical rather than a moral process. This was the form of false doctrine which the deutero-

Pauline writers have in view. Of allusion to such speculative errors not a trace is to be found in St. Paul's great epistles. But the writers just mentioned could not but know that in condemning such doctrines they " had the mind" of Paul. Not that the Apostle actually excluded all speculation from his system ; for, if we lay aside our preconceived notions, we must admit that his dogma is neither more nor less than a speculation grounded on the death and resurrection of the Messiah. But these writers knew that, had the Apostle lived to see speculations, not so grounded, but resting on quite other foundations, mixing themselves with Christianity and claiming to be received as Christianity, he would not only have resolved to know nothing of them (1 Cor. ii. 2), but would also have pronounced upon them his anathema. For of such speculations it might be said that they did not " hold the head from which all the body (of Christian doctrine) . . . increaseth with the increase of God." Such an increase or development on the other hand did the deutero-Pauline writers deem that they gave to Paul's doctrine (Col. ii. 19 ; Eph. iv. 15-16). And this persuasion on their part was probably what seemed to them and to their school, or section of the Church generally, to justify them in prefixing St. Paul's name to their epistles.

To conceive how the fantastic systems of Gnosticism could possibly spring up, it has to be borne in mind that the age was eminently eclectic. Ideas of the most heterogeneous character were afloat in the intellectual atmosphere, as mere *membra disjecta*, without any tendency in that empirical and uncreative age to coalesce into organic unity. And the appearance of Christianity as a new power in human life and a new element of thought was what drew these materials together, and supplied a cementing principle. Some of these, derived from Greek philosophy, were more or less consonant to the genius of Christianity, and helped its dogmatic construction. But Christianity had begun to attract general attention as a phenomenon of world-wide significance, so that it could not be ignored, and even ideas that were alien to it in character sought to place themselves in connection with it. In this way we explain to ourselves the rise of the Gnostic systems. To many more or less cultivated minds, weary of the intellectual monotony and uncertainty, Christianity seemed to be of the nature of a new datum, which might possibly supply the solution of cosmological problems, hitherto insoluble. Its facts and dogmas would be eagerly laid hold of by many, as new factors of thought; combined with pre-existing elements, and formed with them into strange compounds, all of them having a family likeness of a dualistic-theosophic character.

Many in that age would be attracted by the religious ideas involved in Christian dogma without being deeply penetrated by their spirit, and without that true insight into their nature which can be gained only from within by those who adopt them as a rule of life and experience their renovating power. In such individuals the speculative and intellectual interest would predominate over the practical and religious, and the great soteriological and Christological ideas would be valued, chiefly in the hope that they would be found to shed new light and bring order into the existing chaos of thought. Others, again, there would be, in whom the religious or Christian interest would be more pronounced; and who would seek, by means of independent thought, to reach a speculative Gnosis or higher insight into Christianity than was derivable from Pauline dogma; and to draw out of it some universal theory of life or to assign to it its proper place in the general system of human knowledge; in a word, to gratify a curiosity which Pauline dogma had left unsatisfied, and to supply the speculative relations of doctrines which interested the genuine Christian consciousness only in their practical aspects.

Christianity was presented to the Gentiles at the first only as a soteriological intervention in the affairs of men, of which Christ was the instrument and agent. The great Apostle had said little or nothing as to the functions, if any, which Christ discharged with respect to the general order, or to the universe at large. According to him, Christ was indeed Son of God, as well as Son of Man. He had also been pre-existent (Phil. ii. 6, 7; 2 Cor. viii. 9), and his mission was to reveal the will of God and to reconcile the world to God. But all the powers entrusted to him for this purpose were limited in extent and in duration. As if afraid that the monotheistic idea might be compromised by the dominion and authority which he ascribed to Christ, the Apostle, in a well-known passage (1 Cor. xv. 24), declares, somewhat to the surprise of his readers, that the high estate and authority of Christ is only provisional and temporary, that his dominion will come to an end, and he himself be openly reduced to that state of sub-ordination which is common to all beings. The Apostle conceives of Christ as the divine plenipotentiary with delegated powers for the present æon; but when his great redemptive work is accomplished he will lay his authority down that God may be all in all.

The Christian consciousness could not be satisfied with the idea that the divine functions exercised by Christ should thus be confined to the affairs of men or to the accomplishment of the work of redemption. It could hardly but be felt, as time went on, that even to perform these functions satisfactorily and without fail, Christ must be endowed permanently with the powers of universal regiment. A feeling of this kind probably found expression in the concluding words of the Lord's prayer which originally formed no part of it, and were probably added in post-apostolic or Gnostic times, when the feeling prevailed that nothing short of cosmical functions could carry out the soteriological purpose of God. Beyond the domain of re-demption in its more restricted sense there was a province in which thought might expatiate, and by penetrating to the depths of this region, *i.e.*, to the universal and metaphysical relations of Christianity, a deeper Gnosis of its nature might be reached. A problem was thus evidently presented, which demanded a further definition than St. Paul had given of the Christological dogma. It seems, indeed, as if the Apostle himself had a presentiment that his converts might call for some definition beyond that which he deemed sufficient for practical need. So much may be inferred from his accom-modation of Deut. xxx. 12-14 to describe the righteousness which is of faith : " Say not in thine heart, Who shall ascend into heaven ? (that is, to bring Christ down from above :) Or, Who shall descend into the deep ? (that is, to bring up Christ again from the dead.) But what saith it ? The word is nigh thee, even in thy mouth, and in thy heart ; that is, the word of faith, which we preach : That if thou shalt con-fess with thy mouth the Lord Jesus, and shalt believe in thine heart that God hath raised him from the dead, thou shalt be saved " (Rom. x. 6-9). With much else that these words have been thought to imply, this may be ranked, that to inquire into matters beyond the gospel as preached by St. Paul was a thing of trespass and of dangerous consequence, to be carefully abstained from. But it was hardly to be expected that all the Apostle's converts would agree to respect the limit which he wished to impose upon their search into the deep things of God. And the fact was that many did soon break through that limit and embark in speculations which were necessarily fantastic, because wholly divorced from the ground of Christian experience, and wholly at variance with the sober practical spirit of religion as it appeared in the simple doctrine of Jesus, or even in the circumscribed and self-restrained dogma of St. Paul. While the latter ran parallel with the Apostle's personal experience, and was thus kept free from everything in the shape of unpractical and extravagant speculation, the Gnostic doctrine on the other hand ran riot, just because it acknowledged no such limiting guidance or control, and gave the rein to polytheistic fancies. A nomenclature was even invented or adopted from oriental mythologies for those imaginary spirits which were supposed to surround the Throne of the Eternal, and a place among them was assigned to Christ. For Gnostic thought, Christ was one of an intermediate order of beings, godlike in nature, and ministers of the divine purpose; a docetic representation in human form of a shadowy divine energy; or he was the temporal double of a godlike being who had existed in the spiritual world along with countless others in the depths of eternity. By placing him on a level with such beings the sects no doubt thought to exalt him : it was their mode of defining his nature ; but in reality this " co-ordination " of him with a crowd of such beings had the effect of " derogating " from his dignity and depriving him of pre-eminence for the Christian consciousness, and of that exclusive claim to adoration which was assigned to him by St. Paul and the early Church. For, in apostolic Christianity, though his nature was not defined, and was to some extent limited, he yet stood alone and supreme to the Christian consciousness by reason of his redemptive function, so that the Gnostic solution could not satisfy its requirements. And yet, while for Gnostic thought, Christ lost his supremacy for the religious consciousness, extension was given to the functions which he was supposed to discharge. The fruitful idea of redemption was retained, but transformed from an ethical into a cosmical process. And the practical spiritual aspect of that idea, if not entirely lost sight of, was at least thrown into the background, and the religious relations of humanity were absorbed or merged in the metaphysical.

The Gnostic systems seem to have greatly differed in details. But the tendency common to all of them was to generalize and to refine away the positive contents of Christianity, to set aside Pauline Christology by substituting in its place a fantastic purely imaginary scheme of the invisible world, and to represent Christ not so much as the author of human salvation, as the restorer of the world order, and so to distract the mind of the Church, to shift and unsettle the foundations of the faith, and to remove Christianity further and further from the practical into the speculative sphere.   Yet these systems, fantastical as they were, and absolutely destitute of any real basis in the Christian consciousness and the ethical nature of man, were so fascinating to large numbers, who, though included in the Christian pale, were only semi-Christian, as to spread rapidly over Asia Minor, Syria, Egypt, and other provinces, and threaten to prove disastrous to the infant Church by destroying its moral influence, effecting its disintegration, and causing it to subside or to revert into a new form of polytheism or dæmonism.   The danger from this cause was so imminent that a feeling of universal alarm was created in those sections of the Church which held fast to the dogmatic form in which Paul and his disciples had cast the doctrine.

We have hitherto spoken of Gnosticism as due to the intrusion into Pauline doctrine of foreign and disparate elements of thought; but we may here remark, that it may also have been due in some measure to the endeavour to follow up Pauline ideas beyond the limits within which the interests of practical religion and the Christian consciousness could act as guides to thought.   According to one mode of viewing it, indeed, Pauline dogma is itself a species of Gnosis or speculation on the facts or experience of Christian life.   But, without entering upon this view, we may say at least that, in the best authenticated epistles of St. Paul, there occur modes of reasoning, and germs of thought, which in a developed or exaggerated form reappeared in the heretic Gnostic systems, and possibly gave to these a cue, and contributed to their rise.   In the Second Epistle to the Corinthians, and in that to the Galatians, and elsewhere, there are striking examples of that so-called spiritual or allegorical mode of interpreting the Old Testament, which consists in setting aside the historical connection and the grammatical sense, to make way for a less obvious and deeper sense, of which the words may admit. See Gal. iii. 16, iv. 22 ; I Cor. x. 4, etc. In these and a few other cases, the exegesis of the Old Testament is arbitrary, far fetched, and fantastic in the highest degree ; or is such, at least, as would not be tolerated at the present day. Apostolic sanction was thus given to a so-called spiritual or mystical use of Scripture, to which theologians in all ages are naturally prone, and of which the Gnostic system-mongers largely availed themselves.

Further, there occur in St. Paul's epistles, certain isolated and cursory statements which these same teachers worked into their systems, and carried out to their natural consequences, with the result of well-nigh subverting the essential principles of the gospel. According to the Apostle, the law was or-dained by angels in the hand of a mediator (Moses): a proposition which, as understood by Gnostic teachers, was extended to the creation and government of the world, so as obviously to lend countenance to dæmonism. In this con-nection it may be noted, that the Pauline epistle to the Hebrews set a grand example of typological interpretation, which was not lost upon the Gnostic teachers : the government of the present world by angels and intermediate spirits which that epistle seems to imply, must also have served to give impulse and suggestion to kindred ideas in their systems. The distinction which is drawn in this same epistle (v. 11-vi. 1) between the saving and elementary faith which is common to all Christians, and that Gnosis which characterizes and distin-guishes a more perfect state, was an idea which came largely into play in Gnostic doctrine. The typological interpretation of Scripture which the writer apparently had in view, when he exhorted his readers " to leave the principles of the doctrine of Christ, and to go on unto perfection," might naturally be regarded as a direct encouragement to them in the construction of their fantastic pictures of the invisible world.

In a word, Gnosticism may be regarded as a collateral episode, errant and digressive, yet possibly to some extent stimulative of a better and more legitimate development of the Pauline dogma. In this latter, Christianity appeared to be somewhat of the nature of a temporal and isolated intervention in human affairs, not clearly and organically connected with the great cosmic system. This limitation of the sphere was due, in some degree, to its intrinsic supernaturalistic character; yet, as already hinted, a necessity could not but be felt, even in an age in which supernaturalism gave no offence, of finding for Christianity a prominent and essential place in a theosophic construction of the world-system. A solution of this urgent problem was attempted by the Gnostic sects in a direction which ran counter to the Christian consciousness, and to the fundamental monotheism of Christianity; whereas the orthodox Church, as represented by the writers of the post-Pauline epistles, and ultimately by the fourth Evangelist, reacted against the Gnostic tendency, and sought and achieved a further definition of Pauline Christianity, which, because it was more in keeping with the monotheistic principle, has proved determinant of all subsequent development of Christian theology.

The epistles which represent this other development are those to the Hebrews, the Colossians, and the Ephesians. In the Epistle to the Hebrews, which comes first in chronological order, it is observable that a style of language is applied to Christ which is not to be found in those epistles which are undoubtedly Pauline. At the very opening of this epistle, Christ, as Son of God, is called the brightness of His glory, and the express image of His person; and in opposition to the language of St. Paul in 2 Corinthians, his throne is declared to be for ever and ever: he is said to have created the heavens and the earth, in terms more unhesitating than are to be found in St. Paul's writings, while not a hint is given of delegation and still less of demission. In referring to the Christology of this epistle, Professor O. Pfleiderer, in his recent work on *Primitive Christianity*, maintains that through the medium of the apocryphal Book of Wisdom, and the writings of Philo, pre-Christian Hellenism exerted a profound influence on the Pauline construction of Christianity, and still more on deutero-Paulinism; and it is impossible to believe that the many parallelisms of thought and language, which he brings forward in support of his position, are accidental and undesigned. But we venture to think that he has misconceived and exaggerated the nature and extent of the obligation. He goes the length of suggesting that the principles of Christianity were for the most part contained in pre-Christian Hellenism,

and that Christianity added little to the latter, except by supplying it with a historical basis; therefore, as that historical basis
now threatens to become the least secure part of the entire
system, it would thus be made to appear as if the novelty of
Christianity and the value of its contribution to the religious
idea were approaching to the vanishing point. Professor
Pfleiderer has not taken into consideration that the *impulse*
to exalt the person of Christ proceeded wholly out of the
Christian consciousness, and that every side light or speculation, from whatever source, was welcomed, which could help that
impulse to an adequate or suitable expression. It has been
our endeavour to show that religious elements were brought to
light in the life and teaching of Jesus, of which there is little or
no trace in Greek or Jewish literature : that the evangelic
sentiment or *consciousness* of St. Paul was formed, independently
of Hellenistic, or for that matter, of prophetic or Pharisaic
thought, simply by the teaching and death of Jesus acting on
his own experience under the law. The inception of his *dogma*
on the other hand, was owing to the consciousness thus formed,
placed in the re-admitted light of the current or Pharisaic
doctrine of his time. Hellenistic ideas, so far as they came in
at all, could only have come in at a logically later period, not
to found or to mould his dogma, but only to rationalize or
buttress his conception, already formed, of the universal incidence of the atonement. No doubt the deutero-Paulinists
had recourse to the Hellenistic quarry for modes of expression
by which to indicate, without trespassing on the monotheistic
idea, the divine status which the Christian sentiment willed to
confer on Christ; modes of expression which had been coined
by the ranging speculation and subtle ingenuity of the Greek
intellect, but were foreign to the more realistic mind of the
Jew, as well as to the crude phantasy of oriental peoples.
There was thus supplied an important but still subordinate
ministrant contribution to the post-apostolic form of doctrine.
The comparative denationalization of Judaism under the influence of Hellenic thought, of which abundant evidence is
found in Jewish-Alexandrian literature, never got beyond the
stage of an academic flight, and was never likely to become
popular on Jewish soil, or to influence the theology of the
synagogue. Apart from the fructifying ideas of Christianity,
pre-Christian Hellenism would have had no better fate than the

later Platonism of the succeeding age. But we may admit without hesitation, that in this post-apostolic period, the philosophic thought and language of the west came to the aid of Christianity in its conflict with oriental ideas.

While, as already said, the Gnostic minority sought to exalt the conception of Christ, by ranking him with celestial agents of the divine will, and by extending his redemptive function to the universal order ; the Church, as represented by the deutero-Paulinists, especially by the writers of the Epistles to the Colossians and Ephesians, sought the same end, by claiming a place for him above the rivalry of all such agents, and by attributing a wider and more universal significance to his person and office. So far from denying the existence of such intermediate agents, they speak of them as principalities and powers in heavenly places; and of Christ as raised far above them all : as standing on an unapproachable height, and having pre-eminence in all things. While the Gnostic teachers regarded the pleroma or fulness of the divine nature as represented by an infinity of angelic beings, or intermediate spirits, who executed the divine purposes, the deutero-Paulinists, on the other hand, declare that the pleroma dwelt bodily, that is, exclusively or entirely, in the person of Christ (Col. ii. 9) : and also that creation and redemption are alike his work. In the Gnostic systems, that æon, of which Christ was the temporal representative, might be the highest of the powers which mediated between the primal cause and the universe, material and spiritual; but he was still one of them. Whereas, these writers represent him as altogether peerless.

Let it here be observed that we leave it undetermined whether these writers had the incipient Gnosticism in view and wrote with a polemical interest to counteract its influence. The two developments of Pauline doctrine were contemporaneous, so that in all probability they acted and reacted on each other, and if chronological precedence is to be adjudged to either the one or the other, we must probably adjudge it to Gnosticism in its obscure beginnings. According to a general law which a survey of ecclesiastical history seems to suggest, it is the prevalence or growth of false doctrine which induces the conservative Church reluctantly to define its position, and certainly it gives force and meaning to many expressions in the post-Pauline epistles to suppose that they have an anti-Gnostic reference. At the same time the hyper-Pauline definitions in these epistles may have been quite spontaneous, and may have arisen independently of any such reference out of a felt necessity to satisfy the Christian consciousness. That section of the Church, represented by the post-Pauline writers, may have freely adopted one definition of Pauline Christology considered to be orthodox, because in keeping with the general tendency of the dogma, while the Gnostic sects may have adopted another definition more in keeping with inherited Gentile ideas which the general Christian consciousness stigmatized as heretical. This view makes the two definitions to have been originally independent. But which of the two views we may prefer is of little consequence. And even chronological data, if they could be determined, would go but a little way in settling this question, inasmuch as in the great developments of human thought the chronological sequence is not in all cases strictly concurrent with the logical sequence.

So far as can now be judged there was, in the post-apostolic period, a space in which conflicting developments of Pauline theology circulated freely in the Church side by side in a confused ferment. This state of things lasted until the general Christian consciousness was able to discriminate betwixt the various elements according as they did or did not satisfy its own genius, and until it had the courage to define the difference as that of heresy and orthodoxy. That was the critical period in which the dogma, from being a practical system of thought as it was in the hands of Paul, sought to become a speculative system and to determine its relation to the current thought of the age. Something of the same kind has happened, though on a less cardinal scale, in all the great doctrinal conflicts of subsequent ages, and confirms that view of the post-apostolic period which may be gathered from the few notes of it which have come down to us. For every new definition of dogma has been preceded by a period in which the opinion, which was ultimately decreed to be heretical, was able to maintain its ground and to contend on equal terms with that which ultimately prevailed as orthodox.

In the deutero-Pauline epistles, to which we have chiefly referred, there is no polemic overtly and obviously directed against Gnosticism as a recognized heresy. It may be that the orthodox party, as represented by the writers of these epistles, were seeking to overcome or to absorb the Gnostic movement into itself by means of compromise or concession or forbearing polemic, and so to avoid a breach in the Church; but if so, the veiled polemical conciliatory tone is laid aside in the pastoral epistles which were ascribed to St. Paul and written in his name. These epistles direct a polemic against various heretical tendencies (some of which we have left unnoticed) which were combined in Gnosticism. They abound with warnings against giving heed to fables and endless genealogies and vain babblings and oppositions of science ($\gamma\nu\tilde{\omega}\sigma\iota\varsigma$) falsely so-called, and against doctrines of devils ($\delta\alpha\iota\mu\text{ov}\acute{\iota}\omega\nu$). And if these allusions are not even more pointed and direct, the reason may be, that these epistles being published under the name of St. Paul while Gnosticism was a phenomenon of post-Pauline date, it was expedient that the anti-Gnostic tendency should not be too conspicuous lest the anachronism should be too evident and their apostolic authorship challenged from the first. It may be remarked, however, that the anti-Gnostic tendency is more pronounced and undisguised in the First Epistle of St. John, Second Peter, and Jude, the main difference between these epistles being that in some the ethical aspect, in others the Christological aspect of Gnosticism is more kept in view.

CHAPTER XIX.

THE FOURTH GOSPEL.

IT is evident now that the orthodox position in all these epistles would be satisfactory in the highest degree to all in whom the Christian consciousness was fully developed, but it is as evident that to those who were still under the influence of the Gentile ideas in which they had been educated, and which still prevailed in the society around them, this position would be far less satisfactory and conclusive, just because it might be regarded by them as a merely polemical anti-Gnostic position ingeniously occupied by their adversaries, and on that very account carrying with it very little weight and authority. In fact it had this very unsatisfactory and assailable feature, that it rested on mere assertion. On the one hand the Gnostic asserted that between God and the cosmos there existed innumerable hosts of spiritual beings of a nature akin to God. The Paulinists met this assertion by the counter-assertion that Christ the Redeemer was the sole Mediator, not in the moral sense only, but in the metaphysical as well, and therefore possessed of an undivided claim to human homage. Of these positions the one was, or seemed to be, as defensible, speculatively, as the other, and room remained for a controversy which as yet there was no means of settling. For its settlement there was needed some judge or arbiter, to whose verdict both parties should bow. A great historian says that as each side, by the use of the allegorical interpretation of the Old Testament, could claim its support, there was only one opinion against another, so that the dispute between Paulinist and Gnostic could only be decided by some principle standing above Scripture. And this principle he finds in the tradition

which was fixed by the doctrine received in Churches which
had been visited by apostles. It was, he says, in the conflict
with Gnosticism that tradition was first placed in that relation
to Scripture, which it has ever since maintained in the doctrinal
system of the Catholic Church ; and he points out that the
authority of tradition was greatly promoted and established
by the rise of the episcopate, which was due to several causes,
and among others to the felt need of a counterpoise to the centrifugal tendencies of speculative Gnostic thought.

These views of Dr. Baur must, we think, approve themselves at once to everyone who is at all acquainted with the
historical situation, indistinct as it is, of the Church of the
second century. And we deem it unnecessary to say anything by way of illustration. The three ideas of tradition,
the episcopate, and the Catholic Church, form together an
organic unity, and were mutually helpful to each other.
But it is our conviction that even the appeal to tradition,
backed by the power of the rising episcopate, would not
have succeeded in realizing the idea of the Catholic Church,
or in averting the crisis and deadlock in the development
of Christian doctrine of which we have just spoken, had it
not been for the great achievement of the fourth Evangelist
in setting forth a Christological view which appealed to
Gnostics and to Paulinists alike—to Paulinists, because it
seemed to exalt the Christ to the highest conceivable and
unapproachable pinnacle of glory; to Gnostics, because to
the speculative mind it seemed to be a Gnosis in which
every other was swallowed up ; and finally, to both alike,
because it was represented as receiving the sanction of Christ
himself, whose authority could be disowned by neither.

The Gnostic movement was in an acute stage for many
decades, and it was probably during this period that the fourth
Gospel made its appearance. Beyond this general statement
or surmise, its chronological relation to that movement is,
for our purpose, of comparatively little moment ; for, as we have
already said, in the great developments of human thought the
chronological is not always coincident with the logical sequence,
and it is this latter which most concerns us here. The Logos-
idea or, let us say, the prologue of the fourth Gospel, is of the
nature of a speculative or metaphysical definition of the
orthodox Christological standpoint, and on the principle,

guaranteed by the general course of Church history, that all such definition is thrust upon the Church by the prevalence or growth of heretical speculation, we hold that the Gnostic heresy was the logical antecedent of the fourth Gospel.

To open up the question to which we have thus been led, we remark that practically there are only two theories as to the date and authorship of the fourth Gospel. (1) The first of these is, that this Gospel is what it professes to be—a strictly historical narrative of events in the life of Jesus, of which St. John the apostle was witness; composed or dictated by him towards the very end of his life, about the conclusion of the first century or the very beginning of the second century. (2) The other theory is that it is the work of some Christian, almost certainly a Jew, who thought in Hebrew while he wrote in Greek; a man unknown to fame, but of a boldly creative genius, who composed his book some time between the second and the fourth decade of the second century or even later; a book by no means historical, but designed to illustrate in historical form the idea that the Christ, the Messiah of the Jews, was in reality a manifestation veiled in flesh of the Being who was known in Greek philosophy, or in Jewish theosophy, as the Logos, the living, hypostatic word or reason of God. The variants of these two theories may here be left out of consideration.

Much learned ingenuity has been expended by Bishop Lightfoot and other orthodox apologists in tracing the internal evidence of the authenticity of the Gospel. That there should be many marks of authenticity in such a book was only what was to be expected; though it can hardly be denied that at a few crucial points no conclusive settlement has been arrived at. But, not to enter into details, the weak feature of the orthodox argument is, that whatever strength it has is within the narrow area of mere scholarship. It leaves out of consideration all such criticism as has been suggested by the scientific and speculative reasoning of modern times. For instance, it takes no account of the possibility that all such marks of authenticity, as may be pointed out, may conceivably be traceable to some Christian of the second century, who, with wide intelligence and high power of imagination, had also an urgent motive to make use of these in the composition of a new Gospel. Might not such a motive be supplied by the Church's need of an identification of the Christ with the Supreme Being, more complete than can be gathered from the synoptic Gospels or the epistles of St. Paul, and by means of which the tendency towards Gnosticism might be checked? Might not some Christian who perceived the need, and saw that the current Logos-idea was what was needed in the emergency, be the author of the Gospel? Might not the imaginative insight of such an individual enable him to think himself back into the scenes amid which Jesus lived, and give to him a fine feeling for the situation created in Judea by the appearance within its borders of one whom he regarded as at once the Messiah and the Logos? By his power of realistic presentation might he not also be able, after the manner of other great writers, to make use of such knowledge as he had of the topography of Palestine—of the localities in and about Jerusalem, and of the state of the various parties in the population, to give framing, circumstance, and variety to the really few and monotonous but truly grand ideas which he wished to impress upon his readers.

Taking this possibility into consideration, we are entitled to say that, even if we admit to a large extent the details of the internal evidence which have been summed up by apologetic theologians, nothing very positive is established in favour of the Johannine authorship of the Gospel. But another weakness of their argument is, that they uniformly keep out of sight one great improbability which stands on the very threshold of their theory. That theory requires that St. John should be regarded as having written his Gospel about the very end of the first century, near the close of his long life. This date is assigned to it by the tradition of the early Church, and all but universally admitted by modern apologists. So satisfied with this date is Bishop Lightfoot, that it is given by him as the reason why the uncanonical epistles of Barnabas and Clemens Romanus, which belong, at the earliest, to the last quarter of the first century, exhibit no traces of the influence of the Gospel. He says that no such traces can be expected seeing these epistles were written before the fourth Gospel; thus implying for one thing that this Gospel is the only source from which the view of evangelic history peculiar to it could be derived; or, in effect, that St. John alone of the personal followers of Jesus enjoyed, or at least understood, appreciated, and treasured up those intimate confidences and disclosures on the part of Jesus, of which the rest of the Church knew nothing; that the Evangelist being, as he himself relates, the beloved disciple, who leaned on the bosom of Jesus, he was the sole depositary of those most solemn and mysterious communications which he reports. We say the "sole depositary," because, had the synoptists, or St. Paul, or the writer of the Hebrews, or Barnabas, or Clemens, known anything of these, their influence could not possibly have failed to betray itself in their writings, which, by common consent, it does not.

Now, how is it possible to conceive that, for sixty years or more, the apostle could have kept back those wonderful discourses, or refrained from divulging them to the Church at large; that he could have kept from saying to himself, like St. Paul, "Woe is me, if I preach not this gospel," or not been haunted by the dread of neglecting the most sacred duty of preserving those strange utterances to the Church? The early legend, that the design of imparting these reminiscences to the Church did not originate with himself, but with certain elders at Ephesus, who constrained him by their solicitations to place his reminiscences on record, only heightens the inexplicable nature of his conduct. It will not do to say, as has been said, that the apostle may have deferred the writing of his Gospel because the Church was not prepared to receive its high doctrine; for he represents the discourses of Jesus, which are the distinctive feature of his Gospel, as having been spoken to mixed untutored multitudes. We confess that these considerations alone, though they seem never to have startled the easy faith of the Church of the second century, are yet so obvious to us as to be sufficient to induce us to have recourse to the other theory of the authorship, viz., that some unknown Christian, some mighty mind in the second century, was the author of this great work of theological invention.

Turning now to the external evidence, we remark, that at the first and most critical period the tradition of the Johannine authorship rests mainly, or rather wholly, on the few dubious links which connect Irenaeus, Papias, and Justin Martyr with the apostle; and that, against the consideration just advanced, that evidence is of very little weight. We are thus led to abandon the Johannine origin of the Gospel, or, which is the same thing, to regard it as a work of the second century, and it then becomes of comparatively little or no consequence to what decade of that century it is assigned. On general grounds, however, we should prefer to place it late, rather than early, in the century. For it may be confidently asserted that whatever parallelisms and correspondences to the Gospel in thought and modes of expression may be visible in writings believed to belong to an early period of the century, these coincidences are isolated, in the sense that they have no organic connection with the rest of the writings in which they occur, and that the writers are only feebly, if at all, imbued with the Lehrbegriff of the Gospel—that is to say, with its distinctive form of doctrine—a fact which seems to show that the writers have no familiar, or even general, acquaintance with the Gospel itself. And if it yet be asked how then these coincidences can be accounted for, the answer is, either that the Gospel, though not widely known or accepted as of equal authority with the other three, was yet already in existence, and was beginning to work itself into the thought and language of the Church ; or that certain modes of expression and of doctrinal conception, of a sacramentarian leaning, which were coming independently into currency, were gathered up by the author, and woven into a piece with his Gospel. In our opinion, moreover, the latter alternative is the more likely explanation of the two, in support of which opinion we content ourselves with the following quotation from Mr Lecky's *History of the Eighteenth Century*, iv., 444 : " Like all books which mark an epoch in the human intellect, the treatise of Adam Smith *(The Wealth of Nations)* was in a great measure representative : systematizing, elaborating, and harmonizing modes of political thinking, which had been gathering strength in the community." In this sense, we believe the fourth Gospel to have been "representative," doing the same thing for the religious thought of the second century as the *Wealth of Nations* did for the political thought of the eighteenth.

Our position then is, that the Logos idea, having dropped as a living seed into the mind of that master spirit, where it shot forth into a speculative or idealistic view of Christianity, would tend, according to a principle already stated, to clothe itself in a concrete realistic form, and finally would allow no rest to the imagination of the great but obscure artist till the panorama of the life of Jesus, which, conform to that idea, had risen up before his mind's eye, had transferred itself to the historical canvas, as we find it in the fourth Gospel.

Such, in brief, is our solution of the difficulty as to the authorship of this Gospel. But we do not ask our readers to be satisfied with these summary and somewhat abstract considerations. We propose to call in other considerations by which to incline the balance still more in favour of the theory which we espouse. It may truly be said that that theory bristles with difficulties. Of these the first is, that any man of such transcendent ability as we suppose the author to have been, should have veiled his personality or escaped the notice of his contemporaries ; (2) there is the difficulty of conceiving the state of mind which would induce him to frame an imaginary narrative of the life of one whom he believed to be divine, and to have offered it as a genuine record ; (3) that this work should have got so readily into credit and circulation as the work of the apostle St. John—all which points we shall, as they meet us, have to take up.

Before proceeding further with the consideration of this gospel we encounter the fact (to us strange) that many liberal theologians, including Schleiermacher and his followers, regard it as the greatest and most historical of the four, and as containing a comparatively genuine record at least of many of the sayings and discourses of Jesus. The preference thus given to the fourth Gospel may, we believe, be accounted for in two ways—first, by the fact that it carries idealization to a higher summit ; and secondly, by the circumstance that though it contains supernatural realistic elements like the others, it carries these into the region of metaphysical, theosophical thought, which has a strong attraction to many minds, as throwing a softening veil over the outlines of the definite dogma. Among the writers in this country who have adopted the same attitude towards the fourth Gospel may be reckoned Mr. M. Arnold, who seeks to justify the preference over the synoptics which he gives to it by the observation that the doctrines and discourses of Jesus, as there reported, " cannot in the main be the writer's because they are clearly out of his reach," and must therefore be presumed to be the actual and authentic sayings of Jesus. We confess that we see little or no reason for such an observation, but much to the contrary, and that Mr. Arnold's minute but ingenious criticism (upon which we do not enter), goes but a little way to confirm his view. There is a strong presumption that one and the same person wrote both the First Epistle of St. John and the Gospel. Now, in the former the writer shows himself to be quite at home in that same region of thought in which the discourses of Jesus range in the latter. And it is apparent that a writer who could invent, or even select, the other materials of his Gospel, which are so much in keeping with the discourses to which they form the frame, and reduce all into a confessedly epic unity, gives no uncertain proof that the discourses were quite within his reach, and that he perfectly understood their import. Were we indeed to suppose that the writer was one of the first disciples, according to the representation given of them in the synoptic Gospels, we might well admit that these discourses were beyond his reach ; but we cannot so well admit or affirm this if we suppose him to have been a disciple of a later generation, who may have been acquainted with the development of the dogma in its various stages—Jewish-Christian, Pauline, and post-apostolic—leading up step by step, as we have seen, to the application of the Logos-idea to Jesus. We do not know indeed who the writer was ; we know of no man in the second century who could by any possibility have been the author of the book ; but the fact that such a man as Jesus could arise in his time, affords a presumption that another, though less mighty, genius might arise at a later time, who could perceive to what the dogma tended, viz., to the Logos-idea and all that it involved as applied to Jesus. The view here indicated as to the authorship of the book will be confirmed in the sequel.

The question as to the date of the fourth Gospel is still, and may long continue to be, *sub judice*; but, apart altogether from the presumption created by anything which has yet been advanced, we agree with those critics who have arrived at the conclusion that this Gospel was composed about the time, or not much before the time, at which it comes within the direct light of history. A date is thus assigned to it which harmonizes well enough with a period at which the Gnostic movement had well begun, and falls in with our view as to its literary antecedents. Without entering fully into the grounds of this conclusion we may here state briefly that down to the time of Justin Martyr, inclusive of that father's literary activity (supposed to extend from 140 A.D. to 160 A.D.), no direct mention is ever made of the fourth Gospel, and that the constructive proofs of its earlier existence, which have been collected by apologists from the writings of Clement, Barnabas, Hermas, and Justin himself, are far from demonstrative. Such parallelisms with its terminology and modes of thought as do occur in these writings, even if they warranted a belief in its prior existence, are yet of such a nature as to be far from warranting the conclusion that it was regarded by the writers as a work of the same age and authority as the synoptic Gospels. But, in truth, these parallelisms leave the question as to its priority more than doubtful. Holzmann's verdict is— " Nicht Johannes wird citirt, aber Johanneisches ist im Anzug begriffen." That is to say, that in all non-canonical writings down to those of Justin, and his included, such parallelisms as do occur are not quotations, whether free or verbal, from the fourth Gospel, but only so many proofs that its Christology and general style of thought and expression were in process of growth. To ideas which, as may be seen in the Paulinistic epistles and in early non-canonical writings, were struggling ineffectually for utterance in the Church, the fourth Evangelist did but give adequate expression. The parallelisms alluded to were but germs and anticipations of his maturer thought. And this conjecture of Holzmann falls in with and is strikingly confirmed by the general observation just quoted from Mr. Lecky.

One very decisive fact corroborative of the late date of the fourth Gospel may here be given. Writing some time after 140 A.D., Justin Martyr gives an incidental description of the style of discourse employed by Jesus, which is almost of itself sufficient to exclude the possibility of his having regarded that Gospel as of the same age or authority with the synoptic Gospels. His words are: " βραχεῖς δὲ καὶ σύντομοι παρ' αὐτοῦ λόγοι γεγόνασιν." The language of Jesus was brief and concise—a description strikingly appropriate to the discourse of Jesus as reported in the synoptic Gospels; but so glaringly inappropriate to the diffuse style of his discourse in the fourth Gospel that it can be accounted for only by supposing either that Justin was ignorant of the existence of the latter, or that he did not accept of it as an authority of equal rank or of equal historical value with the others.

But there is a still more remarkable and unaccountable difference between the discourses of Jesus in the fourth Gospel and those in the synoptics. While in the latter Jesus says

comparatively little concerning himself, his whole doctrine in
the fourth Gospel is of a self-referent, self-revealing character,
and on that very account more notable, more memorable, more
likely to arrest attention and to excite surprise, than the impersonal, simply ethical and spiritual teaching of which the
synoptic Gospels contain the record.   Had this self-reference,
this identification of himself with the truth of God, been as
pervading and conspicuous a feature of his teaching as the
fourth Evangelist would have us believe, it would have fallen
with such startling effect on the ears of his followers as never
to be overlooked or forgotten, and as in fact to have engrossed
their attention, and to have left them in not a moment's doubt
as to the nature of his claims.   And even if we were to regard
the composition of all four Gospels as nearly contemporaneous,
we should have to explain how it was, by what curious selection, or rather by what capricious obliviousness, the testimonies
of Jesus to himself dropped out of the synoptic tradition.   On
the supposition of the "substantial historicity" of the fourth
Gospel, the formation of a tradition so blind as the synoptic is
to the grander aspects of the life and teaching of Jesus, so
perversely one-sided and unappreciative, is incomprehensible.
What interest could there be, what end could be served, in
abstracting or sifting from his doctrine an element so singularly
fitted as its self-reference is, either to challenge opposition or to
excite surprise, but in either case to fix attention upon itself as
the most novel and characteristic feature of his doctrine.   Is it
conceivable that this self-referent aspect of his teaching, if
really belonging to it, could ever have dropped from the
memory of the disciples who reported it?   Is it credible that
this most palpable, most prominent, most substantive element
should have escaped the notice of all but a bosom disciple?
The superior insight and sympathy with which that disciple is
credited by himself and by theologians were not at all necessary
to appreciate this aspect of his teaching.   And if the fourth
Gospel contains a true report of his teaching, this feature of it
must have been so palpable as to rivet the attention of the
most obtuse, as well as the most unfriendly of his hearers.   We
confess that the impossibility of explaining this curiously
anomalous circumstance would compel us, in the absence of all
other reasons, to regard the synoptic tradition of the teaching
of Jesus as the more authentic.   In this as in many other

respects there is such a discrepancy between the synoptic and the Johannine records, as to make it impossible for us to combine into "one stereoscopic image" the two pictures of Jesus which they present to us.

By the period, of which, so far as this question is concerned, Justin is the representative, Christianity had long been in living contact with the speculative thought of the age, and especially with that of Hellenism. Evidences of this fact reach as far back as the epistles of St. Paul, and since these had been written there had been a growing disposition in the orthodox section of the Church to connect its doctrines more and more closely with current speculation ; to make use of language and ideas which had resulted from the combination in Hellenistic literature of Greek and Jewish modes of thought. This tendency was partly owing, no doubt, to the pressure put upon the Church by the spread of Gnosticism, or by the necessity of providing a counterpoise to heretical doctrines, which were of Eastern character and origin. The proof of what we say is to be seen in the deutero-Pauline epistles. But the further and most palpable proof and instance of it is to be found in the incorporation into the Pauline dogma of the Logos-idea of Philonism. It is highly probable that the applicability of this idea to the person of Christ, and its manifest importance for the settlement of the Gnostic controversy, may have begun to dawn upon various circles of the Church, whether at Alexandria or in Asia Minor, and to affect their doctrinal phraseology. Its Christological importance may have been perceived by the philosophic Justin and by the fourth Evangelist independently, and may have created for itself a terminology common to both. It is noteworthy, however, that the pregnant and mystical depth of the idea remained strange to the philosopher. At the most, Justin may have had a presentiment of the possible value of the idea in a doctrinal point of view, and made use of the expression ; whereas, in the hands of the Evangelist, it is used to effect a complete metamorphosis of the whole tradition and doctrine of the Church. It is thus that ideas and even modes of expression pass through a prophetic or preparatory stage before their final form and full significance are discovered.

To many speculative minds in that and in preceding ages, there had seemed to be grounds, inherent in the divine nature itself and in the relation subsisting between the finite and the

Infinite, for believing in the existence of an intermediate agent, raised far above and out of the rank of all creaturely ministers of the divine will, however exalted—another self of God, between whom and the great First Cause there was only an economic difference ; an object, therefore, of worship and of superlative veneration, not to men only, but to all " the angels of God." By both Greeks and Hellenists this Being had been called the Logos, the word or reason of God. On the hypothesis now that there was such a Being, it was hardly possible that even Gnostics, in whom survived a vestige of the Christian consciousness, could identify him with any other personality than that of Christ, or could fail to rebel against assigning such a peerless and unapproachable dignity in the spiritual world to any other claimant. The Christian consciousness again, as developed among Paulinists, had all along been struggling, as .we have seen, towards some such conception of the Redeemer, and could rest in nothing short of it; and this very drift of that consciousness must have formed in itself an anticipation and guarantee for the truth of the speculative idea, over and above that which was inherent in it. The application of this idea to the person of Christ was all that was needed to arrest the tendency within the Church to revert to polytheistic worship; enough to consign to the limbo of thought all those purely imaginary ranks of angelic beings with which the heretical sects were, in the height of their caprice, peopling the invisible world ; to stop the dispersion of the religious feelings ; to drive off and expel all alien and incompatible gnosis ; to guide the speculative spirit into a safe channel, and to prevent it from wandering into fields which lay outside the Christian sphere.

We must pause here however by the way, to admit that this observation as to the power of the Logos-idea to arrest the polytheistic tendency in the (Gentile) Church needs to be qualified. For that tendency was all but incurable. The idea sufficed, indeed, to counteract the tendency to recruit the heavenly hierarchy with dim, semi-divine shapes *from outside* the Christian system, with forms of existence which reflected nothing of the evangelic spirit ; but the polytheizing tendency after a pause in its action recovered itself as from a kind of backwater in more guarded and colourable form, in the Mariolatry and saint worship of the Church. Such at least is our reading of ecclesiastical history in its general features.

Newman, indeed, says that the cults of the Virgin and the saints are totally different in principle from religious worship. But it needs a mind very much *predisposed*, to accept the apology of Newman and other controversialists for the idolatrous practices of Catholic countries. The moment the Church, by recognizing the divinity of Christ, abandoned the position of monotheism pure and simple, it placed itself on an inclined plane, or on what a popular preacher has called the " down grade"; and that it should descend sooner or later to the worship of the Virgin and the saints was inevitable. Nothing but the evangelic doctrine in its purity and freshness —the living conception of God as our Heavenly Father—could deliver the soul of man from the spirit of fear and diffidence before the Unseen Power, so as to enable it to dispense with the Logos-idea, and consequently with all inferior and subordinate agents of the divine will. The monotheistic doctrine, in its physical or non-moral aspect, is to this day and always has been the strength of Mahometanism. In the moral and humane aspect of it, as presented by Jesus, it has yet to prove the strength of Christianity by the overthrow of all competing cults and of superstition in every shape.

It was reserved for one who was deeply penetrated by the spirit of Christianity, and had a clear perception of the goal of its dogmatic development, to single out with unerring tact from all the theosophic ideas then afloat that one which, overlooked by the Gnostic sects, and even by the Paulinistic writers, could by its application to Christ confer a unique character upon his person and his redemptive functions, and could best express the dogmatic position which Christian experience and Christian sentiment were impelled from within to assign to him. By an act of supreme genius the fourth Evangelist perceived that the Pauline dogma, being merely reflective of religious experience and therefore indefinite, did not present a sufficient barrier against heretical speculation, and that the dogmatic position was insecure so long as it could only be negatively maintained by anti-Gnostic assertions which lay quite beyond the range of experience. We conceive of him as a man who was impelled, either by native and irrepressible tendency, or by the felt necessity of meeting the Gnostic sects on their own ground and combating them with their own weapons, to supply a super-experiential or speculative basis or presupposition for the dogma. He recognized that the great want of the time—the postulate of the Christian consciousness—was a higher gnosis which might act as a counter-attraction to the gnosis of the heretical sects, and this he found in the application to the person of Christ of the Logos-idea which was widely current as an element of religious thought, popular and philosophic, in that and the preceding ages.

Whoever he was, whether of Jewish or of Gentile extraction, the fourth Evangelist was a man of the deepest spiritual insight, and withal a master of dialectic like St. Paul; not like that Apostle, however, of a predominantly logical and practical turn of mind, but rather of a contemplative and mystical order. St. Paul, as we have seen, exercised his dialectic solely in tracing his own religious experience to a supernatural origin and in building up a Christological and soteriological system by means of the naïve and empirical theory of divine action common to that age, and of categories which were specifically Jewish. He overlooked and left out of sight, or, to speak more correctly, he was unaware of the natural, non-magical, or psychological explanation of the great crisis of his life. His dogma was nothing but the construction or interpretation of his individual experience on the basis of his belief in the super-natural, and in the traditional Jewish theology ; and being on that account not a pure reflection of the facts, but only relatively, figuratively, or symbolically true, in the way at most of a working theory or hypothesis, it could not possibly satisfy the speculative thought which inevitably began to play around it. The Gnostic heresy was the product of this play of speculative thought, and the prevalence of this heresy was the main historical and environing condition which, while it might seem to Paulinists to necessitate an appeal to tradition, and a consolidation of the power of the episcopate, also called forth to the rescue the genius of the fourth Evangelist. The reactionary movement towards Judaism which engaged the polemic of St. Paul does not come much, if at all, into consideration here. For it is obvious, that for the fourth Evangelist himself, and probably for the Church at large, the conquest of that tendency was already to a great extent an accomplished fact. But we shall not fully understand the polemical relations and the environing conditions of the fourth Gospel unless we take into account the probability, or rather the certainty, that, in concurrence with the Gnostic heresy, Jewish Christianity in a new form still survived to cause anxiety to the Church.

The period with which we are here dealing is included in the interval between 70 A.D. and 140 A.D., which is acknowledged on all hands to be the most obscure in all the history of the Church. The historical data are few, and often seemingly conflicting ; so that, by the help of conjecture, various schools of theology have been able to frame such a view of this period as may best fit in with their general systems. We do not profess to dispense with this same instrument of reasoning in dealing with this period, and as little do we profess a confidence greater than we feel in the view which we have adopted. The conjectural construction of this period, which we adopt, derives its probability for us from its seeming to harmonize with our general views. What we say is, that during the period referred to, the opposition of Jewish sentiment, whether without or within the Church, to the evangelic and universalistic character of the new religion had died down, or, at least, had been silenced, in consequence, partly, of the destruction of Jerusalem, partly of the powerful dialectic with which St. Paul combated it on grounds which it was unable to dispute, and partly of the imposing spectacle of the rapid Christianization of the Gentiles, by which Jewish exclusiveness was put out of countenance. As far as mere logic was concerned, the right might be on the side of the Jewish Christians. But the reasoning of the Apostle was reinforced by the moral grandeur of that spectacle, and by the enthusiastic conviction with which he assailed their defensive and conservative position. Owing to these causes, the original phase of Jewish opposition was overcome ; Jewish legalism was seen to be a weapon which had lost its power to stay the progress of the new religion, and was practically discredited. But, while this was taking place, the opposition gradually entered upon a new phase. Jewish, or, let us say, monotheistic, sentiment took alarm, and was once more quickened into life by the advanced and still advancing Christology of the Church. In the Pauline age the practical and theoretic difference between the Jewish and the Gentile communities lay entirely in the soteriological province. In his four great epistles, St. Paul makes no reference to any

difference in the Christological field.   The explanation of
which fact is that, during his lifetime, the Christological
dogma was fluid, vague, and indefinite, and admitted of being
construed even by zealous monotheists as not extending
beyond what might be applied to Christ as Messiah.
But as it advanced beyond this point, and became more
pronounced and more determinate, the feeling arose that
the Christological doctrine had become inconsistent with
the maintenance of the monotheistic principle, and Jewish
susceptibilities took alarm.   There is sufficient evidence of
the strength of this feeling in the controversial writings of
Justin, and in the rabbinical literature of the same age.   It
seemed as if the monotheistic principle, of which the Jews
regarded themselves as the guardians, and of which the
preaching of the gospel had awakened a belief among the
Gentiles, was infringed by the unique and transcendent
position in the spiritual world which was assigned to the
Christ.   Here was a point round which a conflict between
Jewish and Christian sentiment could not but arise.   The
indications of this conflict, which occur in non-canonical
literature, may, indeed, as we have just said, be sufficient,
but it is in the fourth Gospel we perceive the clearest
proof of its existence.   The controversy which that Gospel
represents Jesus as carrying on with his Jewish opponents
could not possibly have arisen in his lifetime.   There was
then no question as to his making himself equal with God,
for the synoptists make it plain that he only claims to be
the Messiah, and his claim in that character to be the Son
of God, if it was made by him, did not encroach upon
the divine prerogative.   Whatever the rank or majesty
expressed by this title, it was delegated or conferred upon him
by God.   The title merely indicated the intimate relationship
which subsisted between God and the Messiah.   But by the
time we now speak of, Jesus had been exalted by the reverence
of his followers to a higher position than belonged to him as
Messiah ; terms were applied and attributes ascribed to him,
which seemed to leave no interval between him and the
supreme God.   Everything which men were wont to say of the
latter was freely predicated of him.   Hence the new phase of
Jewish opposition ; and it was to meet this new phase that the
fourth Evangelist represents Jesus and his opponents as fore-

stalling the controversy of the later time. " This controversy," as remarked by Weizsäcker, " is of quite a different character from that recorded in the synoptic Gospels ; the character which it assumed among the epigoni or men of a later generation."

In the report of this controversy, therefore, we recognize not a fanciful, unhistorical invention, but a passage of early *Church* history, carried back by the Evangelist into *gospel* history. Viewed in connection with the earlier or gospel period, the controversy was not practical, or called for by the time, but one which may be characterized as academic, or a controversy of the school. It assumes a practical character only when viewed in connection with the state of parties in the second century, by which time the dogma had raised Jesus far above the Messianic level, and the question was no longer as formerly, whether Jesus was or was not the Messiah, but whether there was not an aspect of his nature still higher than the Messianic. This question Jesus himself is made to settle in favour of the dominant party in the Church, but without detriment to the monotheistic doctrine, by speaking of himself as one with God; one, that is, in the same sense as the Logos ; as the impersonation of the divine energy, the sole channel of the communication of light and life to the race whose nature he had assumed. To this extent the fourth Gospel is a sort of Apokalypse in which Jesus as another Daniel is represented as settling a controversy, which could only be waged in another age, and amid circumstances which had not arisen in his day.

But this account does not cover the whole polemic position of the Evangelist. By one and the same apokalyptic presentation he sought, not only to conciliate the monotheistic sentiment, but also to cut the nerve of Gnostic speculation. The Jewish controversy, in its later phase, was for him of subordinate consequence, inasmuch as the victory of the Church over Judaistic sentiment was already assured, whereas the Gnostic movement was in that age a thing of perilous and living moment; and we are inclined to believe that the Evangelist fully recognized this distinction, and under the veil of a controversy with the later phase of Judaism, in reality carried on an anti-Gnostic polemic ; for it was necessary that in a version of *gospel history* he should conduct this polemic indirectly and unostensibly, as dealing with a phase of opinion which was of more recent origin. But without pressing this view we may regard the fourth Gospel in its controversial character as having been meant as a defence of the divine prerogative of Christ against invasion from the monotheistic side on the one hand, and from the Gnostic or polytheizing side on the other.

The Gnostic heresy was in full swing, and we conceive of the Evangelist as feeling himself prompted to solve the Gnostic problem, *i.e.*, to determine the position of Christ in the scale of universal being, not in the Gnostic way of co-ordinating him with other spiritual beings, and of thereby " derogating from his dignity," but in the way of adhering to the orthodox or Paulinistic line of development, whose guiding principle was to elevate the nature and function of Christ to the utmost, to raise him to a dignity nothing short of divine, and so to represent him as an object of absolute veneration. The means of accomplishing this, and of stamping out once for all the reaction towards polytheism, and, in general, of bringing to a pause the " dangerous questioning of the systematizing intellect," the Evangelist found, as already said, in the application to Christ of the Logos-idea. By this idea the Evangelist raised him clear above all imaginable ranks of mere creaturely ministers, however exalted, of the divine will; yet, without encroaching upon the monotheistic principle, invested him with functions universal and cosmical, including that of being the light and life of men, the source and ground of the grand moral and spiritual revolution which had attended the preaching of the gospel.

The mental attitude towards the Christ, which prevailed among the early Christians, was one of worship, of intense devotion, and of utter self-surrender, and as the monotheistic idea, in its purity, was intolerant of such absolute homage except towards God, the Church had no alternative but sooner or later to exalt Christ to the Godhead, and to efface every distinction between him and the Supreme Being, except a distinction that was economic or conceptual. This necessity was no doubt widely if not universally felt, and was simply and vividly expressed, for example, in the Second Epistle of Clement to the Corinthians, written in that age :—" οὕτως δεῖ ὑμᾶς φρονεῖν περὶ Ἰησοῦ χριστοῦ ὡς περὶ θεοῦ, ὡς περὶ κριτοῦ ζώντων καὶ νεκρῶν." Nothing can be more evident than that the fourth Evangelist, in his application of the Logos-idea to the Christ, was at once obeying and satisfying an impulse which was common in the Church.

From the first the Christian sentiment or consciousness contained in it an impulse to represent to itself the Christ the ideal man, as also God, and yet not God; as divine in a sense in which no mere creature and no intermediate spirit could claim to be, and yet in some, as yet undetermined sense, subordinate to the ground of all existence. Paul himself, as already observed, experienced an impulse in this direction, and sought to qualify the divine attributes of Christ by the ideas of delegation and ultimate demission. But this solution did not satisfy the Christian consciousness, and did not sufficiently differentiate his nature and functions from those of other ministers of the divine purposes. The solution of the problem which satisfied the Church was only disclosed to the full by the fourth Evangelist and his Logos-idea. In the period which intervened between the epistles of St. Paul and the fourth Gospel, Paulinistic writers had, as we have seen, advanced beyond the Pauline position; had laid aside the ideas of delegation and demission, and spoken of Christ as enjoying pre-eminence in all things, as being the pleroma of the Godhead, and the express image of His person; had, in short, gone the length of investing him with titles and attributes, which found their justification and their counterpart in the doctrine of the Logos. But these writers never applied to him this designation itself. This final step was reserved for the fourth Evangelist, who thus completed the circle of Christological thought, and gave to it a consistency and finality, to which the heretical gnosis had nothing to oppose.

A minor presumption in favour of the course of Christological development here suggested is afforded by the close parallelism between it and the emergence of the monotheistic faith in the religion of Israel. The critical study of the Old Testament has shown that Jehovah, who as the national God of Israel was at first only one among a multitude of gods with a localized dominion, became in the course of time, and for the prophetic spirit, a Being who was above all gods. The others, who had been called gods, it has well been said, " lost first their rank, as they fell below Him, and then their existence," as the conviction grew that there could be but one God, whose dominion was

over all. Even so, by a kindred process, Christ was raised for
the Gnostic, *i.e.,* the speculative Gentile mind, to the peerless
altitude and dignity in which he is presented to us in the fourth
Gospel. To the speculative mind, he seemed at first to be but
one among the many æons or sons of God. Then, as we may
perhaps see from the glimpse we get of a passing phase of
thought in the Epistles to the Colossians and Ephesians, he
rose to a position of pre-eminence among them. Not that the
writers of these epistles, or that Pauline Christians generally,
were satisfied with such a view, but probably that, in combating
the Gnostic tendency of thought, they used in speaking of Christ
a phraseology which, by way of accommodation, met half way
the ideas current among the heretically inclined. And, lastly,
all other divine powers having thus lost their rank, next lost
their existence, as we see in the prologue of the fourth Gospel
and in First Timothy, the conviction being there expressed that
Christ alone sustained the whole mediatorial function ; for that,
by the assignation to him of a place hard by the Throne of
God and of a universal function, there was no room left in the
divine administration for the action of any other divine energy.
He became the one sole link between the great First Cause and
the creature, the one sole medium of communication and of
intercourse between heaven and earth—the sole channel of
divine agency. The monotheistic principle in Israel doubtless
required centuries for its development or general recognition,
whereas the Christological development was, as might be
expected, the work of little more than a generation between the
time at which the Gentile element inundated the Church and
the date of the fourth Gospel.

According to the Logos-idea, the divine nature exists in a
twofold form, in one of which God remains for ever in unbroken
seclusion, at rest within Himself, apart from all contact and
defilement with finite existence. In the other, He proceeds
forth from Himself to manifest His hidden, self-contained, and
self-sufficing nature in the creation and government of the
world. This latter is the Logos, the source of all that is finite,
the hypostasis and impersonation of the power and virtue of
that Being who is the ultimate ground of all existence ; and
who, while He manifests Himself by going forth to create and
govern the universe, yet remains withdrawn within Himself.
The Evangelist adopted this idea, and regarded the Logos as

incarnated in Christ, as personally manifested in Him under the
limitations of humanity ; so that for those who could not discern
the divine presence as manifested in the world at large, it
became bodily visible as manifested in the flesh.   As the incarnation or dwelling-place of the Logos, Christ is for him the
Son of God, in the archetypal sense, and occupies the very
closest conceivable relation to the Most High.   He is, in truth,
the other Self of God, and only economically short of absolute
identification with Him.   He is infinitely raised above all
rivalry and confusion with other celestial powers, however
exalted ; or, rather, his agency is so pervasive and universal as
practically to exclude all such.   It may be a question whether
the Evangelist conceived of the Logos as absolutely merged in
the Christ, but the dwelling-place of the Logos is in Christ in
such a sense that they are practically one ; and all power is
centred in him, who as Redeemer has conferred on man the
highest benefit ; has given to man the best proof of his tenderest
love and goodwill, and is therefore an object of man's profoundest love and veneration.   In him too the human mind
may find a resting-place for its devout imagination, and become
reconciled to the existence of an impenetrable mystery.   He is
the immediate source of light and life to men.   By his all-
pervading virtue and sole mediation, all other members of the
heavenly hierarchy are deprived of consideration ; extinguished,
so to speak, in the blaze of his glory, and rendered superfluous
and irrelevant.   The mind of the individual believer is relieved
from the seductive, idolatrous necessity of filling up the interval
between God and man with intermediate powers ; a bound is
set to the encroachment of the mythological spirit, and an
object is presented to the human soul, of mystical meditation,
on which it may pour forth its emotions and sympathies in all
their depth of fulness, without danger of offending or enfeebling
the monotheistic sentiment.

   Two views may be taken of the mental process, by which the
Evangelist fastened upon the Logos-idea as the solution of the
Gnostic problem.   It may have recommended itself to him
either because it seemed to supply for the Christian sentiment
a form more adequately expressive than the pre-existing
Paulinistic form of the Christological idea, more conservative of
the orthodox spirit, and more fitted to satisfy the speculative
craving for something definite ; or, on the other hand, the

Logos-idea may have determined and moulded his view of the Christology and of Christian doctrine generally. In other words, that idea may have been laid hold of by him, because it seemed to supply the best apologetic form for Christian doctrine ; or, it may have laid hold of him independent of and prior to such a consideration, and so as to revolutionize, *ab initio*, all his previous doctrinal views. Which of these two modes of looking at the Evangelist's mental process best represents it we do not pretend to say. They who are disposed to minimize the difference between the Pauline and Johannine dogma will probably prefer the former alternative. They to whom the difference seems more material will probably prefer the latter. The view of the nature of the Christ thus fixed by the application to him of the Logos-idea was exactly what was needed for the further development of Pauline Christology. The veneration which had gathered round the person of Christ as Redeemer would not allow of his being made to occupy any lower relation to God than the very highest ; and the Logos was the only Being on whom, without dishonour to the Father of all, a devout monotheist, such as the fourth Evangelist, could own himself absolutely dependent for his religious experience. He could feel that his devotion to Christ, considered as the incarnate Logos, did not in any way trench on his devotion to the Supreme God ; and in fact that these were but one and the same devotion. And it is easy to see that a doctrine such as this, clearly and authoritatively stated so as to establish itself in the mind of the Church, would sweep away all speculation as to ranks of intermediate and angelic powers, which necessarily seemed to remove God to an inaccessible distance, inconsistent with the central ideas of atonement and reconciliation, which are the specific and essential elements of the dogmatized Christian consciousness. The definition of the nature of Christ by the Logos-idea may be regarded as, in some sense, a compromise between orthodoxy and Gnosticism : a formal concession on the part of the former, but a substantial or material concession on the part of the latter. It was a speculation which outdid or swallowed up all others on the subject. It foreran the drift, and overtook or determined the goal of orthodoxy, while it satisfied the speculative spirit of Gnosticism.

The great achievement then of the fourth Evangelist consisted in bringing the Christological development to a relatively satisfactory close, or at least in securing a position of pre-eminence to Christ, which the age could accept as conclusive. He raised a barrier against the encroachments of ethnic speculations, which were neither germane nor relevant to the nature of Christianity, and it determined the line of subsequent doctrinal development in the Catholic Church. He supplied the missing keystone to the arch of Pauline dogma by bringing together in Christ the absolute essence of the divine nature with its historical manifestation in human form. To that dogma he gave the necessary coherence and solidity by means of that speculative idea which was laid to his hand by Greek and Hellenistic philosophy. Just as we have seen that St. Paul effected a complete breach between Judaism and Christianity by applying Jewish categories to the interpretation of his own experience, so did the fourth Evangelist save Christianity from a relapse into polytheistic ideas by applying to the person of its founder an idea which he borrowed from the speculative thought of Gentile philosophy.

The Logos-idea was not the only contribution which the Evangelist took from Hellenism. Many of the details in his Gospel evince his leaning towards Hellenistic thought. When, for example, he represents Jesus as saying, " My father worketh hitherto, and I work," this implies that he believed in a ceaseless action of God, which has a prominent place in the theosophy of Philo, but is singularly opposed to the sabbatic idea of the Old Testament. But a much stronger evidence of Hellenistic influence may be seen in the undisguised but restrained dualism which pervades the fourth Gospel, and has continued from this source to taint, more or less, the dogma of the Church to the present time. This strange-visaged element in the Gospel may possibly, yet hardly, be accounted for by regarding it as a popular or literary means of explaining certain phenomena in an age of sudden conversions and sudden apostasies. But certain it is that the Evangelist does not carry out his dualism with the same consequence and to the same dangerous extreme as it was carried out in the heretical Gnosticism. He goes so far as to imply that human beings are divided into two classes—men of the spirit, and men of the flesh ; men who are of God, and men who are not of God ; men from above, and men from below—and that the result of the action and revelation of the Logos varies according to the nature of its subjects. The office of the Logos is not to redeem the evil, or to mediate their translation into the other class. He does not so much bring forth anything absolutely new as bring forth the original and native good or evil into manifestation. This is a view of human nature and its possibilities, which, if carried out, leads to dualism of the most pronounced character, and being common to Greek or Hellenistic thought, and to the fourth Gospel, is a proof of the dependence of the latter upon the former, and of the affinity between them. But upon these and other traces of Hellenistic influence in the fourth Gospel we do not need to dwell. They are only mentioned here because they help, by an accumulation of evidence, to overcome the prejudice in many minds against admitting the Hellenistic source of the Logos doctrine in the fourth Gospel, and the presence of Hellenistic elements generally in the dogmatic structure of Christianity. While in those epistles, to which the term deutero-Pauline is applied, Hellenistic elements are introduced sparingly, covertly, and, as it were, piece-meal and incidentally, without acknowledgment and perhaps unconsciously, the fourth Evangelist appropriates the great Hellenistic idea or philosopheme of the Logos without disguise, and even places it in the forefront of his Gospel as if it were familiar to his readers, besides laying it as the foundation of a conception of Christianity entirely new and higher in its mysticism than that which had previously prevailed.

By the application which it makes of this idea, the fourth Gospel may be said to have given a new complexion to the life of Jesus and to Christian doctrine, while still keeping the Paulinistic line of development; or, rather, to have added a second summit to the dogmatic mass, elevating it to a height on which the mystics of all ages have delighted to fix their gaze. It has never indeed been perfectly incorporated or comprehended in the more practical dogma of the Church, but it has been largely made use of as a canon for the interpretation of Pauline Christology. It is not merely the designation and the general idea of the Logos which the Evangelist has borrowed from Philo; but many of the predicates and figures of speech which Philo has applied to the Logos are reproduced by the Evangelist in reference to Christ. When Philo calls the Logos a second God and a Paraclete, and says that the manna in the wilderness was an allegory of the Logos, the parallelisms in the Gospel make it impossible to doubt that the writer drew his inspiration from the Hellenist. Dr. Cairns says that the Logos doctrine, as set forth by Philo, has "but a scant relation to redemption, or to man's recovery to God"; but so far as this is true he only thereby suggests another, though negative and indirect, proof of the identity of the Logos of the Hellenist and of the Evangelist. For it has been pointed out by Pfleiderer, and by many other theologians, that redemption, in the Pauline sense at least, is not among the functions which the Evangelist ascribes to Christ. According to the latter the death of Christ is not a vicarious sacrifice, but only the highest manifestation of his love and submission to the will of the Father. He takes away the sin of those whom the Father has given to him by purifying them from the evil that is in them, and this he does by the exhibition of the love and gracious purpose of the Father.

It must indeed be admitted that the Logos of the Evangelist differs from that of the Alexandrian in two respects, which may be said to be one. The Logos of the latter is a being of a wholly transcendent nature, whereas the incarnation or descent into the finite nature of humanity is essential to the conception of the Evangelist's Logos. And secondly, the one is presented to us as the moral ideal of humanity, which the other never is nor could well be, until he was conceived of as incarnate. These differences may be said to be fundamental, and indeed are so in such a sense as to lend an air of plausibility to the position of Harnack that the Logos of the Evangelist has "little but the name in common with the Logos of Philo." But this position will be seen to have little to recommend it, if we consider the long and eventful history of the Logos-idea— almost as little indeed as if it had been said that the God of the Old Testament had "little but the name in common" with the God of the New Testament. It was Heraclitus—who lived fully six centuries before the age of the Evangelist, and in that district of Asia Minor where the Gospel is believed to have seen the light—who discovered the elasticity and speculative possibilities of the term Logos, and started it on its long career. Professor E. Pfleiderer directs attention to this fact, and calls Heraclitus the philosophical father of the term. After him it was taken up and largely used by the early Stoic schools of Greece to express a function of the deity. Next it made its appearance in the writings of the Alexandrian Hellenist, who extended and emphasized its application so as to express by its means a hypostasis of the divine energy.   But it has been supposed, not unfairly, that this use of the word had a "double root," and that this fruitful extension of its meaning was suggested to Philo by that highly figurative personification of divine wisdom, which occurs with such striking effect in the canonical Book of Proverbs, and in the apocryphal Book of Wisdom, in which divine Wisdom is represented as speaking and acting as a separate personality.   The poetical Hebrew fancy had only to be understood literally (which it was very apt to be) to bring it together with the Logos.   The two ideas could hardly but be felt to be cognate, or, we may say, identical and suggestive of each other.   By the extension of its meaning thus suggested, the speculative idea was transformed, and it had elasticity enough to undergo yet another extension or another transformation by embracing in itself the Christology of St. Paul, and so to give us the Logos of the Evangelist.   From a merely speculative point of view the transformation which the Logos underwent at the hands of Philo is quite as great and as fundamental as it underwent at the hands of the Evangelist. As the term was enriched and fructified by contact in the mind of Philo with Hebrew poetry, so it was yet further enriched and fructified by contact in the mind of the Evangelist with the Christology of St. Paul.   The one step in the development of the idea was quite as conceivable as the other.   Besides the "name," the Logos of Philo had the idea of a hypostasis of the divine energy "in common with" that of the Evangelist.   The speculative elasticity of the word which admitted of its extension by Philo also admitted of its further extension by the Evangelist.   Indeed, considering the perplexity and helplessness of the Pauline party in the Church when confronted by Gnostic speculation, the wonder is that the Logos-idea was so long of being applied to the Christ.   We may admit that what the Old Testament had said of the Messiah and of the suffering servant of God, together with its personification of the Word and Wisdom of God (1 Cor. i. 24), may have helped St. Paul to his dogmatic interpretation of the life and function of Christ.   But all these together could never have suggested to the fourth Evangelist his distinctive conception of Christianity.   He could only have arrived at *that* by his identification of the Christ with the Hellenistic Logos, in which Greek speculation and Hebrew poetry were already fused in one to his hand. This idea forms the key to the whole thought of his Gospel, and when once disclosed to his mind may almost be said to have created a necessity for the composition of a Gospel, all whose details, down to the most minute, grow out of it and group themselves round it. We are of course aware of the contention of many theologians that in designating Christ as the Logos the Evangelist was anticipated by the writer of the Apokalypse (xix. 13), and therefore indebted presumptively to Jewish thought. Now, there are unquestionably many points of affinity between the Gospel and the Apokalypse. The designations Lamb and Logos are applied to Christ in both, and there are various other ideas and expressions common to both. But it is no less unquestionable that the general spirit and tone of thought are very wide apart, perhaps as much so as in the case of any two books in Scripture. Weizsäcker considers the two books to be so unlike that they cannot proceed from the same hand, but so like as to prove that they proceed from the same school of Christian doctrine. While emphasizing the affinities, this writer contends that they are not due to the Evangelist having borrowed from the Apokalyptist. He may be right in this conclusion, but the reason, which he assigns for it, does not, we think, display that range and critical discernment which are so conspicuous in his recent work. He says that the Gospel is too original and peculiar to be a translation of the materials of the Apokalypse into a higher form of doctrine. This reasoning is not satisfactory, because it might be used also to disprove the Evangelist's obligation to the synoptists, though, if there be anything certain in Biblical criticism, it is that the Evangelist has shown his genius and originality just in adopting many of the synoptic materials, and weaving them into a piece with a conception of Jesus much higher than theirs. We may say of the Evangelist what has in various language been often said of Shakespeare, that he " has refashioned, after a nobler pattern, materials already at hand, so that the relics of other men's poetry are incorporated into his perfect work " (Walter Pater, *Appreciations*, p. 188). And proceeding on the supposition of the prior publication of the Apokalypse in its present form, the probability is that the Evangelist has made the same use of materials in it suitable to his purpose. Indeed, if that supposition be correct he had a manifest motive for dealing with the materials of the synoptists and of the Apokalyptist in the same way. In the synoptists there lay before him a record accepted by the Church of the earthly life of Jesus, and the Apokalypse contained glimpses, also accepted by the Church, of the heavenly life of Jesus. And it being the Evangelist's design to compose a Gospel, in which the heavenly life should shine through or blend with the earthly life, he had the same motive to adapt materials which the one as well as the other laid to his hand. We may readily believe, therefore, that he has followed the Apokalyptist in styling Christ the Lamb and the Word of God. This is one view of the relation in which the fourth Gospel and the Apokalypse stand to each other. But we shall see that quite another and perhaps a more probable view may be taken of their relation. In the meantime, however, we shall keep to the former view.

According to the Apokalyptist, the Christ is known and adored in heaven as the Lamb of God, advanced to the highest rank, and to a seat upon the throne of the universe. And all that the Evangelist does in his adaptation of the title is to give it a new setting, letting it be applied to Christ by his fore-runner, the Baptist, at the very commencement of his ministry on earth, in anticipation of his future glory, as it came to be recognized in the heavenly sphere ; but he dismisses it in a single sentence, as if he felt that, considering the frequent and exhaustive use of it by the Apokalyptist, this solitary reference was enough for his purpose, of connecting his view with that already current in the Church. The other designation again of the " Word of God " being applied by the Apokalyptist to Jesus, only once, and in an incidental manner, gives freer scope to the Evangelist's genius. This, therefore, he takes up, charges it with a new meaning, elsewhere derived, and makes it the key-note or watchword of his whole Gospel. And if so, we have here the most striking example of the imaginative skill and of the artistic method with which he seeks to impress organic unity and mystical elevation upon the whole system of Christian thought, to which the religion of Jesus had given rise. In the Apokalyptist's use of the word Logos there is nothing to show that more is meant than that Christ had revealed the will of God, and was the absolute and infallible authority for Christian doctrine ; that, just as a man's word reveals his thought, so

Christ is called the Word of God, because he had revealed the thought and purpose of God. Used in this sense, the name has nothing in common with the speculative, mystical, or meta-physical idea, which the Evangelist lays as the basis or watchword of his Gospel. There is no book in the New Testa-ment which more evidently than the Apokalypse betrays a leaning to the Jewish-Christian position of legalism and ex-clusiveness; and we cannot easily be induced to believe that the idea which underlies its designation of the Christ as the Word is the Logos-idea of the Evangelist, which carries in it the principle of universalism. A very obvious criticism indeed of the Apokalypse is, that the exclusive spirit is not invariably and consistently maintained by it; and that in some passages it lapses or rises into universalism. But, on the supposition that the book is of one casting, this wavering and unsteadiness of its standpoint are enough to show that the writer has not laid hold of the Logos-idea of the Evangelist. And this other considera-tion is to be taken into account, that had that idea been in the Apokalyptist's mind, some traces of it might reasonably be expected to have found their way into the Paulinistic literature, which holds a position logically at least intermediate between the Apokalypse and the fourth Gospel, whereas of such traces there is an entire absence. While therefore we grant that the Evangelist may have derived the *term* from the Apokalyptist, we say that the meaning or content which he thought into it was his own; or, if not his own, yet derived by him not from the Apokalyptist, but from Greek or Hellenistic speculation, and made his own by the new and personal application which he gave to it. The affinity between the two writers shows itself, as well as in some details, in the general design common to both, of carrying the Christ towards the height at which he ceases to be a creature, without infringement of the monotheistic principle; towards the point at which, while differentiated from God, he is yet one with Him. This design or postulate of the dogmatic consciousness was, however, not peculiar to the Apokalyptist and the Evangelist, but common to the whole Christian Church. What the Apokalyptist failed to supply, and what the Evangelist did supply, was the speculative idea or intellectual form which satis-fied that postulate. And readers will be pleased to observe that, while we deny the obligation of the Evangelist to the Apokalyptist in respect of the Logos, we refer not to the term but to the idea.

In the foregoing remarks upon the derivation of the Logos-idea we have proceeded on the supposition that the Apokalypse could not have borrowed the term Logos from the fourth Gospel. But in view of much of the criticism which has in recent years been directed upon the former, this is far from certain. And we prefer quite another view from that now given of the relation in which Rev. xix. 13 stands to the prologue of the Evangelist. Very strong reasons have been assigned for supposing that the Apokalypse is not of one casting, but the work of many hands at different dates. Chancellor Weizsäcker, in his great work (*Das Apostolische Zeitalter*), gives it as his opinion that while the main portion was in existence before or about the fall of Jerusalem, other portions were probably of thirty years later date. Another critic, Völter, has come to the conclusion that the book did not assume its canonical form till about the year 140 A.D., in which case the verse xix. 13 may be an interpolation or allusion to the prologue of the fourth Gospel. The clause, "his name is called the Word of God," has much the character of an "aside" or marginal note, and suggests the question, "by whom is he so called?" and the reply is at least not un-natural, that the interpolator had the fourth Evangelist in view. A glance at the verse and context is sufficient to show that the sentence interrupts the sequence of the passage in which it occurs, and is out of harmony or connection with the description of the Christ as a warrior whose "garments are dipped in blood," and with "a name known only to himself," seeing that in the very passage itself the name Logos, than which there can be none greater, is divulged. Yet further, the title "Word of God" is made no further use of, and has no affinities with the rest of the book; but is thrown in hurriedly, as it were, into a book already completed, too late to have its character and contents modified by the new idea—a circumstance very noticeable when contrasted with the dominating position which the idea holds in the fourth Gospel. But the main thing to be borne in mind is that the parallelism is merely verbal; and that, as already said, the name as applied by the Apokalyptist to Christ has nothing in common with the speculative, mystical, or metaphysical idea, which the Evangelist lays as the basis and watchword of his Gospel. Want of space will not permit us to dwell upon the most recent theory as to the composition of the Apokalypse, propounded in 1886 by a young German theologian (Bernhard Vischer), according to which it was a Jewish apokalypse transformed, by interpolation and otherwise, into the canonical book of Revelation. But we may briefly say that, in our judgment, after a careful study of it, this theory, if not altogether free from objection, is at least more free from such than any of the innumerable theories that have been started from time to time, in ancient and modern times, to harmonize the strange and seemingly incongruous features of the book ; and that, startling as the theory is, it gains a certain probability from the completeness with which it seems to solve the enigma.

For us, who do not believe in the theory of inspiration or in the special election of the people of Israel, it is a matter of no interest or concern to maintain the purely Hebraic origin and descent of the great ideas which entered into the construction of dogmatic Christianity. On the contrary, it is gratifying to perceive that ethnic elements of thought entered into this great scheme, and that, as Dr. E. Pfleiderer puts it, the middle wall of partition between Jew and Gentile has been taken down, intellectually as well as spiritually. It is thus made to appear that a system of ideas, which has enchained and satisfied so many generations of men in the most civilized nations of the earth, was the outcome of the growing thought and speculation of both sections of the pre-Christian world—a result or conclusion deserving all the attention we are here paying to it. The case is somewhat different with the doctrine of Jesus ; for that doctrine probably came down to him, as was formerly pointed out, from a purely Hebrew or Jewish source, being made up of the elements in it of natural religion, which are more or less common to all nations, only revised by his personal insight, and invested with fresh power by being carried into life, and pathetically illustrated in their noblest aspect by his death. With this explanation, we say that we have no sympathy with those theologians who maintain that the doctrine of the Logos grew naturally and spontaneously out of an exclusively Jewish root ; or that Jewish thought and feeling were sufficient here and elsewhere to determine the course of the development of positive Christian theology.

There are, no doubt, in the canonical and apocryphal literature of the Jews expressions which may be regarded as "early anticipations" of the Logos-idea in its application to the Christ.

In the Old Testament we read that God said, and it was done ; that He commanded, and it stood fast ; that by His word were the heavens made, and by His wisdom was the earth spread out. In such passages the word and wisdom of God are spoken of as the agents and instruments of creation ; and in well-known passages in the book of Proverbs, as well as in Wisdom and Ecclesiasticus, the thought is taken up, and a turn is given to it, of which an important use was made in Hellenistic literature. In these books the word or wisdom of God is spoken of as if it were disengaged from the divine subject, and formed a separate existence with a will and purpose of its own. But this mode of speaking is plainly nothing but a highly poetical personification of the energy by which God created and established the world ; whereas the Logos of the Greek schools was a seriously-meant, speculative, or philosophical idea, expressive of the form in which the great Unseen manifests Himself in the creation and government of the world, and reveals Himself to the soul of man. These two uses of the word, though so materially different, yet superficially bear such a degree of resemblance to each other, that the Alexandrian Hellenist, in the way usual with him of putting a Jewish stamp on philosophic ideas, and bringing the prose of Mosaic legislation and the poetry of Jewish chokmah and prophecy into close relation with Gentile speculation, could treat them as identical, and translate the poetical fancy into a theologoumenon. The distinction between a serious attempt to fathom the depths of the divine nature and a poetic or fanciful description of an accepted theory of the divine action was entirely overlooked or intentionally ignored by him. We may observe in passing that Philo seems, in his treatment of this matter, to have been anticipated, or at least countenanced to some extent, by rabbinical theology, which, probably following out the hint given in the above-mentioned books, applied the designation memra, or word, to a personal organ of the divine will, who mediated between God and Israel, and made atonement for sin. But it was by a stroke of genius that Philo perceived that the Greek Logos, with its double signification, was by its elasticity better fitted than the Jewish Memra or the Greek Sophia, to be of service in the theosophic speculations in which he was engaged. And it was an act of still greater genius by which the fourth Evangelist not only adopted the same idea, but also applied it to the Christ, to represent him as the personal and visible manifestation of that divine energy which the Alexandrian had in view. Philo has thus the merit of evolving and elaborating out of Jewish and Hellenic elements the philosophical and speculative form in which the fourth Evangelist could best express the doctrinal conception which he had formed of the Christ, and lay a deeper basis for the Christology of the Church, if not the merit also of even suggesting to the mind of the Evangelist the very conception itself which he brought to bear on his idealistic construction of gospel history.

Through Greek and Hellenistic literature the Logos-doctrine was widely spread, but it wandered or floated about, like many other speculative ideas, without establishing itself very deeply in the convictions of men, because it was felt to be only one of many competing speculations, without attachment to fact and without historical embodiment. But the fourth Evangelist, by connecting it with the person of Christ, gave it a local habitation, and therefore a new power or hold over men's minds, suggesting to the unconverted on the one hand that Christ might be the very being in whom that idea was realized, and, to Christians on the other, investing him with a unique and specific dignity which justified the payment to him of divine honours, and supplied a want in the region of theological thought, of which both believers and unbelievers, the cultivated and the uncultivated, were sensible; besides cutting away the ground from under the Gnostic propagandism, which in many quarters threatened to efface the ethical character of the new religion and to rend the Church in pieces. If it was a mere speculation like those of Gnosticism, yet it was one which supplanted those others, and in which earnest and devout souls could find rest for their intellect and fancy. The abrupt manner in which the Evangelist, without preface or explanation of any kind, introduces the mention of the Logos is enough to show that he is addressing those who were not unfamiliar with the word ; and that he only intends to define more clearly, and to give concrete form and attachment to the idea, of which up till then they had only a vague and abstract notion.

To assert that the Evangelist did not, or could not, derive his doctrine of the Logos from Greek or Hellenistic speculation, because in his hands it grew to be something very different from the form which it took in Hellenistic theosophy, or

because there are moments of thought involved in the former
which are not to be found in the doctrine of Philo, is not much
to the point. It is rather an example of that formal and
wooden criticism, of which the apologetic theologian is apt to
avail himself. Not long ago it was said by a prominent apologist
in this country (Dr. Cairns), to whom we have already referred,
that the doctrine of Philo as to the personality of the Logos is
wavering and uncertain ; that he sometimes distinguishes the
Logos from God, and sometimes identifies both ; that he speaks
of the Logos as a second god, or a second to God, or as His
only begotten son, and His instrument in making and govern-
ing the world ; but that it is "impossible to develop his hints
into distinctive Christianity," because his Logos doctrine has
but a scant relation to redemption and man's recovery to God.
Now, what, we ask, would this writer have ? What short of
absolute identity would he accept as proof of any connection
between the doctrine of Philo and that of the fourth Evangelist?
How else, except by a great transformation of the philosophic
Logos-idea, and of its significance, could it be incorporated or
brought into harmony with its new relations. The term and
the abstract idea were adopted by the Evangelist to define the
super-angelic elevation of the Christ ; but under his hand the
idea necessarily acquired elements of a novel character. Kindred cases may teach us that such transformations do not
invalidate the fact of connection between two ideas, or the
derivation of the one from the other. The mythologies of all
nations contain striking examples (as pre-eminently was the case
in ancient Egypt) of the transmutation of heroes and demigods by the contraction or extension of their attributes ; and
even the gods themselves frequently change their distinctive
characters, and appropriate those of each other. So, too, there
is not a doubt in the minds of competent investigators that
festivals, originally growing out of nature-worship, were incorporated with the religion of Israel, and gradually moulded by a
process of denaturalization into harmony with its growing ethical
requirements till they assumed quite a new significance, and
underwent such a transformation that the radical identity of the
old and new forms is hardly recognizable by the ordinary
student. And there is, or ought to be, as little doubt that the
Christian system of thought was determined in its line of
development by affluence from speculative systems with which

it had otherwise little or nothing in common. It would not be the only instance in the history of human thought, in which an idea comparatively meaningless and infertile in the system of which it was originally a component member, has started into new life and significance when removed from connection with that system and placed in connection with quite another system of thought.

The "distinctive" feature of the gospel, into which (according to Dr. Cairns) it is impossible to develop the hints of Philo, consists in its representation of Christ the Logos as the ideal and Saviour (Redeemer) of humanity. Now, it seems to us that this is not so impossible as Dr. Cairns asserts. It may be that a redemptive function of the Logos is not much emphasized or dwelt upon by Philo; but there is at least a "hint" of something of the kind in those words of his quoted by Pfleiderer (*Urchristenthum*, p. 676):—"Ὁ αὐτὸς ἱκέτης μὲν ἐστι τοῦ θνητοῦ, πρεσβευτὴς δὲ τοῦ ἡγεμόνος. οὔτε ἀγέννητος ὡς ὁ θεὸς ὤν, οὔτε γεννητὸς ὡς ὑμεῖς, ἀλλὰ μέσος τῶν ἄκρων, ἀμφοτέροις ὁμηρεύων," etc. The hint thus given by Philo of a redemptive function is real, though it may be *scant*, and indeed it could not be more until the Logos was embodied in a historical personage or a human subject. So far as there is a difference here between the Logos of Philo, and the Logos of the fourth Evangelist, it consists in this, that the mediating function of the former is essential to his nature, while that of the latter involves or presupposes his incarnation and death upon the cross. And the alleged difficulty or impossibility of the development is quite imaginary, and is seen to be none at all so soon as we take the dogmatic situation into our field of view. That situation consisted in the fact that the Christ was regarded as the Ideal and Redeemer of humanity for many a year before the Evangelist thought of identifying him with the Logos; but the moment this came into his mind—*i.e.*, the moment he regarded the Logos-idea as descriptive of Christ's relationship to God—he necessarily incorporated the exemplary character of the Christ and his redemptive function with that idea. And finally, the question is not, as Dr. Cairns seems to think, whether *we* can develop the hints of Philo into distinctive Christianity, but whether the Evangelist could do so. And there need be no difficulty in conceiving how he could. When the Evangelist had taken the step of identifying the Christ with the Logos it followed, as a matter of course, that he should also regard the Logos as the Ideal and Deliverer of man ; in other words, develop the hint of Philo into " distinctive Christianity." Dr. Cairns' difficulty arises from his having overlooked the evolution or historical succession of the ideas. In the course of this discussion we have had several opportunities for seeing that much depends upon keeping this succession in view, and that many obscurities are cleared up by this means. Considering the wide circulation and notoriety of the Logos-idea among the educated classes of that day it does indeed require some forti- tude to deny that the Evangelist might lay hold of it and wrest it from ethnic or Hellenistic philosophy for the use and elucid- ation of the Christological dogma, and for the glorification of the Founder of the Church. Only by a great transformation could he make it to fit in with the Christian dogma ; but fundamentally the idea, as employed by him, is identical with that of the schools of Greek philosophy and Alexandrine theology. The genius and originality of the Evangelist were displayed in discovering how, by its means, he could recast the Pauline dogma so as to present Christianity in more imposing form to the intellectual classes of that age, and reconcile the heretical sects which were exhausting the spiritual forces of the Church in internecine conflict, and spreading general alarm and anxiety for its safety among those who held to the Pauline form of doctrine.

Long before the Logos-idea was taken up by the fourth Evangelist it had fascinated many minds and probably cir- culated as widely as Hellenic or Hellenistic thought. But, as already said, it floated vaguely as a mere speculation, which might or might not contain in it an element of truth. The circumstance that it fitted so exactly into the requirements of Paulinistic doctrine and came so opportunely to the rescue in the struggle with Gnosticism must, for many Gnostics as well as Paulinists, have amounted to a demonstration of its truth, giving it a hold which it never had before, and, for the great mass of Christians, turning the balance decidedly in favour of the Pauline or anti-Gnostic form of doctrine. We say here, " to Gnostics as well as Paulinists," for while to the latter the Logos-idea would only seem to be the perfect though hitherto missing articulation of their own dogmatic conception of Christ ;

to multitudes of the former the idea would come as a welcome escape from the sea of doubtful and perilous speculation on which, *nolens volens*, they were tossed.

The Evangelist did not content himself with advancing his great and fruitful idea in a merely cursory, uncircumstantial, or epistolary fashion, as he seems to do in I John i. I. Had he only done so, or had he even introduced it into the prologue of another version of the gospel history similar in character to those of the synoptists, it would have made but a faint impression on the mind of the Church, or might have seemed in that connection to be out of place, and have awakened a sense of incongruity. At most, the term Logos would have appeared to that age to be a literary expression for the ordinary Pauline dogma or only a chance speculation of little special moment, and most certainly would never have exerted that magical power which it seems to have exerted in composing the controversy then raging. That power it seems to have owed in a great measure to its being brought forward in the prologue of a new gospel—another, and yet not another— which took its tone and colour from the idea, and represented Christ not only acting as the Logos might be expected to act under human limitations, but also as bearing testimony to himself in language which fully justified the application of the Logos-idea to his person. By this expedient the Christ is made to invest this application of the idea with an authority which no reader could dispute who participated in that veneration for his person in which all Christians, even the Gnostically inclined, were at one.

Whether the Christological doctrine of the fourth Gospel revealed itself to the mind of the Evangelist, or whether it was communicated to him by some one who went before him, is of no consequence. What we have to do is to trace, if we can, the steps by which the Paulinistic Christology was developed into that of the fourth Gospel. In this attempt we cannot pretend to trace the exact course of thought or train of reasoning by which the Evangelist or others before him arrived at his Christological view ; nor, while offering suggestions on this subject, do we suppose that all the terms and details of the process were consciously present to his mind. By the very nature of the case we must have recourse here to conjecture.

We conceive then that the ground for the application of the

Logos-idea to Christ was already prepared by the Christology of St. Paul, and still more by that which found expression in the post-Pauline epistles to the Colossians and Ephesians. In these latter he is emphatically declared to be of a more godlike nature, and to have more of the divine power delegated to him than to all other members of the heavenly hierarchy. But how far he was superior, or in what his superiority consisted, is not declared. It is said of him indeed that all the fulness of the Godhead dwelt bodily in him. But this was simply an anti-Gnostic statement, which, standing alone without further definition, came near to the suggestion of a dual Godhead, and seemed to be, more even than the Gnostic doctrine, an assault upon the monotheistic principle. Manifestly the Church could not rest on such a formula. What the Church sought was to form to itself such a conception of Christ as would satisfy the Christian consciousness, i.e., justify that absolute veneration and unreserved devotion of which Christ was the object. To represent him as the bodily fulness of the Godhead was rather a statement of the problem than its solution. The difficulty still remained to form a definite, intellectual conception of the Christ, and to find a place for him in the spiritual world. This problem was solved by means of the Logos-idea, which presented him not merely as a godlike Being, but as very God, yet without either obliterating the distinction between him and the Heavenly Father, or doing violence to the paramount monotheistic principle.

Or yet again, we may conceive that the Evangelist, as a Paulinist to whom Christ was all in all, had yet become dissatisfied with the Pauline dogma, because, owing to its vagueness, it did not supply a sufficiently clear and definite expression for his Christian consciousness, and seemed to leave some opening or pretext for Gnostic speculations, which were at variance with that consciousness. Let it not be said that we speak without warrant in imputing vagueness to St. Paul's Christological dogma. If the Church of later ages has not appeared to feel this vagueness of his dogma, and if theologians have been able to extract a high and distinct Christology from his epistles, let it be remembered that these have been read and studied in the light of the Logos-doctrine, and that they stand out in relief upon the fourth Gospel as their background. The important bearing which this circumstance has had on the interpretation of St. Paul's epistles can hardly be overstated. It has even been justified by the theory that the whole of the canonical books are to be treated as the production of a single divine mind—a theory which has given to the orthodox interpreter an undoubting and imposing confidence in his hermeneutic; the aim of which is to demonstrate the harmony of Scripture, and to explain its vague and obscure portions by those that are clear and definite. It is needless to say that this is a canon of criticism which we do not accept ; and we return to the position that the rise of the Gnostic heresy, while it called forth the firm and sharply-defined Christology of the fourth Evangelist, has also to some extent to be accepted as a proof and consequence of St. Paul's vagueness of statement, or, let us say, of the unsettled and unfinished state of the current Christology.

The Evangelist sought to obtain a more adequate and satisfactory Christological construction by identifying Christ with the Logos or Hypostasis of the all-pervasive divine energy. The Christ was thus placed in such immediate apposition to the ground of all existence and to the principle of causation, as to make of no account all those intermediate spirits which figured so largely in Gnostic doctrine, and to justify that sentiment of boundless veneration, of which, for the Evangelist, Christ the Redeemer was the object. To a man animated by that sentiment this Christology seemed to be a postulate of consciousness, and to be its own evidence. But then the question arose how such a faith could be impressed on the minds of others, in whom that sentiment might not be so vivid, and in whom that consciousness might be wanting in depth and lucidity; or, in other words, how the inward and subjective evidence could be converted into an outward and objective evidence. For it must be observed that even the Pauline dogma, from which the Evangelist started, was not only vague, but also without any clear and obvious sanction in the Evangelical tradition. The authority of the Apostle, however imposing, was not sufficient to legitimate a conception of Christ's nature and person, so detached from the ground of history and so independent as his was. The step or leap which St. Paul had taken from the Jesus of tradition to the Christ of dogma was stupendous. A sense of this expressed itself in St. Paul's own words (2 Cor. v. 16), " Though we have known Christ after the flesh, yet now henceforth know we him no more." These words imply that the knowledge

which he or the Church at large had gained of Christ in consequence of his resurrection was utterly different from any
knowledge that could be gained of him from the traditional
memorials of his life in the flesh.   The words as much as say
that the Apostle himself could hardly recognize or find again
the Jesus of tradition in the Christ of dogma.   And there are
indications in the synoptic Gospels that a perception of the same
thing was not confined to his mind, but that a feeling existed in
the Church that some justification was needed for this great
stride in Christian thought ; or, let us say, for this dogmatic
construction of the life and work of Christ ; and that such
justification could only be found in the authoritative declarations
of Christ himself.   This feeling is seen to be at work in the
Paulinistic Gospel of St. Luke, where, in the account of the
apparition of Jesus to the two disciples on the way to Emmaus,
(xxiv. 27), it is said that "beginning at Moses and all the
prophets, he expounded unto them in all the Scriptures the
things concerning himself" ; and where it is added that he appeared the same day to the other disciples, and expounded the
Scriptures to them also, thus suggesting and giving his sanction
to an interpretation of Scripture, which found in it frequent
references to his own death and resurrection.   Nay, as if this
were not enough to account for the novelty of the apostolic
dogma, the same Paulinist in his Acts of the Apostles, extends
the period during which these Christophanies occurred, and
states that Christ was seen of the disciples for forty days after
the resurrection, and spoke to them of the things pertaining to
the kingdom of God (Acts i. 3).   Such representations were
calculated to convey the impression that the disciples had got
their higher knowledge of divine things from Jesus himself; and
were, not improbably, made for that purpose, however unconsciously.   By such mythical representations, the Church was
enabled to account to itself for the apparent chasm or breach
of continuity between the teaching of Jesus in the Gospels and
the doctrine which prevailed in the Church ; and also to obtain
a warrant for the use which was made of Old Testament
Scripture.   Some such warrant was felt to be necessary ; and
this feeling operated no doubt, to some extent, in moulding
in other respects the testimony of the synoptic records, and
especially in introducing into them, here and there, a dogmatic
element, as, *e.g.*, in Matth. xx. 28.

But the important part which this feeling played is to be chiefly seen in the origin and composition of the fourth Gospel, in regard to which the obvious remark has been made that the distinction between Christ in the flesh and Christ in the spirit is obliterated ; and that the historical Jesus has become the Logos in the flesh. In the Pauline epistles the historical Jesus or the Christ in the flesh had fallen into the background ; but so far is this from being the case in the fourth Gospel that the ideal or dogmatic greatness of Christ is carried back into his earthly life, so as to suffuse it with a higher glory. Dogma and history, which in Christian literature had hitherto been kept separate and apart, were in the fourth Gospel blended into organic unity. The object of the writer was to exalt the Christology and to raise a barrier to Gnostic speculation. For this end the experience of the working of the evangelic principle which the Church by that time had accumulated, was represented as foreshadowed in the events of the earthly life of Jesus ; and the dogmatic shape which his doctrine had assumed was anticipated in his teaching. The synoptic tradition had, as has been already pointed out, been enriched by a similar process ; but the fact that the fourth Gospel was so much later of publication, and that the experience of the Church had been so much enlarged in the interval, is sufficient to explain how the process could be carried out in this Gospel so much further than in the others. The discourses in it have for their subject, not, as in the latter, the nature of the kingdom of heaven and the conditions of an entrance into it; but rather the nature and eternal sonship which had been ascribed by the Church to the speaker himself, and the conditions of fellowship with him. He is no longer the mere teacher, but the subject of his own teaching; and his doctrine is transformed into a dogma concerning him. The same transformation had in a manner been already effected by St. Paul, or by the Church at large ; but, besides that the Evangelist contemplated a further or hyper-Pauline transformation, he threw back his transformed doctrine into the teaching of Jesus, so as to invest it with more than Pauline or apostolic authority.

Finally, that this great metamorphosis of the doctrine, whether as seen in the epistles of St. Paul or in the new Gospel, should be received without misgiving by the Church, the Evangelist put into the mouth of Jesus the promise that, after he was gone, he would send the Holy Spirit to guide the disciples into all truth

(John xvi. 13). This promise, which occupies a prominent place in the Gospel, conveyed the idea that Jesus himself had not given utterance to all necessary truth; and prepared the Church for new revelations. Probably it reflected an idea to that effect current in the Church; and the danger of it was that it would not only justify developments in the line of Pauline doctrine, but also open the door to such unlicensed and fantastic notions as those of Montanism and other heresies, and so prepare fresh troubles for the Church, as indeed proved both then and in later ages to be the case. Still the idea gave countenance to the expectation that truths not attested or warranted by evangelic history or tradition, and not accessible to reason, might be conveyed from time to time, by a mysterious channel, to the mind of individuals or to the Church at large. And being profoundly impressed with the conviction that Christ was the divine Logos, the Evangelist, whoever he was, was also persuaded that that and other truths had been revealed to himself by the Spirit of Christ. And the question arose to his mind by what means he could also impress the same conviction on the minds of others, and secure for it a place in the creed of the Church. One thing could not but be obvious to him, that such an impression could not be made by his own authority, or by appealing to a revelation privately made by the Spirit to himself. He could not be unaware of the fact, which may be gathered from St. Paul's epistles and from some of the non-canonical writings, that St. Paul's visions and revelations were scouted and derided by his Jewish-Christian opponents; and the Evangelist might well be afraid that the same treatment would be dealt out by his Gnostic opponents to any claim of his to a private revelation. He would perceive, therefore, that his Logos-doctrine must be presented to the Church, not as a private revelation, by the Spirit of Christ, to him or to any individual, so many years after Christ in person had left the earth, but as a revelation of Christ himself, by word of mouth or some other outward sign, to his disciples, while he was still in their company. It was with this in his view that the Evangelist ascribes to Jesus the words reported (xvi. 12-14): "I have yet many things to say unto you, but ye cannot bear them now. Howbeit when he, the Spirit of truth, is come, he will guide you into all truth," etc. Apologetic theologians, who regard these words as having been actually spoken by Jesus, explain by means of them that rich complex of doctrine in the apostolic epistles, and in the creeds of the Church, of which there is little or no indication in the simple teaching of Jesus. They say that the Spirit promised by Jesus speaks through the apostles and the Church, completing his doctrine and supplying what he left unsaid ; and also, that by these words he prepared his disciples for such revelations. But on our supposition that no such words were spoken by Jesus, we have only to inquire what was the Evangelist's object in putting them into his mouth. And our reply is, that, being aware that his conception of the person of Jesus was far in advance of that which was traditional or current in the Church, he sought by these words to familiarize the Church with the expectation of further disclosures, supplementary to those which Jesus had made *vivâ voce* to his immediate followers, and among the rest, of course, to the disciple whom he loved, in whose name the fourth Gospel is written. But then the revelations here promised, supplementary to those reported by the synoptists and the fourth Evangelist, are, so far as we can see, just those which the Evangelist himself reports, with some inconsistency, as being given *vivâ voce* by Jesus-Logos. The fact is that the Evangelist had two objects in view, which could only be reconciled by a certain degree of inconsistency. He wished to disarm the prejudice which his report of the teaching of Jesus, on account of its novelty, would excite; and at the same time to represent that the Logos-doctrine, though novel to his readers as being over and above all that the ear-witnesses had reported, had yet the *vivâ voce* sanction of Jesus. This doctrine was novel to those who knew only the synoptic Gospels and the Pauline epistles; but it is not very evident what new or what higher doctrine remained to be disclosed to those who read the fourth Gospel. For it is hard to conceive that the practical mind of the great teacher could here have in view the difficult dialectic of St. Paul, or the scholastic subtleties of the later time, though, no doubt, there are minds which can believe even this. Thus much is plain, that when the fourth Gospel was published, or, let us say, when Jesus had uttered the discourses there reported, no cardinal element even of the dogmatic system remained to be disclosed to the Church. And we can see that the Evangelist does not entirely avoid inconsistency, but that he succeeds in doing so in so far as the case admitted.

If any doubt arose in the Evangelist's mind as to the morality of such a representation, he would reflect that the revelation, as thus presented, was in substance the same as that which had been conveyed to his own mind, and only different in its mode of communication. The authoritative word of Christ himself, could it be appealed to, would be sufficient to legitimate that new departure in Christological doctrine which recommended itself to the Evangelist's own mind. That was a sanction which none would dispute, not even those who were Gnostically inclined. And out of the Evangelist's feeling that such was the case arose the project in his mind of a new redaction of the evangelic history, in which Jesus should be represented as claiming to be the incarnate Logos, and as living and acting in harmony with this claim.*

Such a redaction behoved of course to be, to a large extent, unhistorical and untraditional—the vehicle not of a real but of an ideal and imaginary history—seeing that Jesus, in intercourse with his disciples, had advanced no such claim. And, indeed, there are not a few indications that the Evangelist was not unaware of the peculiar, not to say hazardous and critical nature of his undertaking. Of these one may be seen in his manner of descending from the high speculative ground of his prologue to the quasi-historical ground. It is impossible not to be struck with the abrupt and hurried way in which he passes from his statement that the Logos is the Creator of the world, and the source of all light and life to men, to the mention first of the Baptist as the witness to that light, and then to the mention of Jesus himself as its incarnation. It seems as if he hurried on not to commit himself to any statements as to the nature of the connection between the Logos and the human subject. The blank thus left between the

---

* Jesus nowhere in the Gospel expressly claims to be the Logos. Indeed the word is never put into his mouth—a circumstance which Bishop Lightfoot regards as a remarkable testimony to the credibility of the writer, seeing there would be a very " strong temptation to introduce it, which for a mere forger would be irresistible." But surely this is a mistake ; for, whether a forger or not, the Evangelist was certainly an artist of no mean degree, and to have put this word into the mouth of Jesus would have been to offend against that law of propriety, the observance of which is an unfailing mark of the true artist. The Logos is the philosophical idea which the Evangelist himself supplies as the key of the book. But it would have been out of place in the mouth of Jesus, whose language throughout is, and behoved to be, simple and popular.

prologue and the rest of his Gospel is nowhere filled up. He appears to have trusted that his theme would be substantiated to the satisfaction of his readers by the subsequent narrative, which is evidently drawn up for the express purpose of showing that the Logos dwelt in Jesus as in a tabernacle, and realized in him the ideal of humanity. In fact, the Logos doctrine is the key of the Gospel—so much so that while the synoptics exhibit a unity which is more or less common to all biographies, this other exhibits a unity which belongs to the drama with a presiding idea. It may here be noted that there is a blank, or break, at the end of the book, just like that here adverted to, at the beginning of the book. The difficulty for the Evangelist was to connect the Logos idea with the Christ, considered as incarnate, and making atonement by his death. And this difficulty he overcomes, in the one case as in the other, by what can only be called a *tour de force*. Having diverged from the synoptic tradition so far as to represent Jesus as claiming to be the Life and Light of men, the Evangelist then proceeds to re-enter the human current of the synoptic history, ending in the crucifixion ; and leaves unexplained how he who made this claim should yet have to submit to death, or what thus he added to his function. We can understand the death of the synoptic Jesus as that of a witness to the truth which he taught; but no explanation can be given of the death of one who, before death, and by nature, was the Life of men. Of course, we do not mean to say that orthodox theologians cannot give an explanation of this, satisfactory to themselves.

Our proposition, then, is that this Gospel was not designed by its author to be in any sense a narrative of the actual doings and sayings of Jesus, but to be a dramatic and imaginative representation of a life befitting one in whom the Logos had his dwelling. It was intended to place before the Church a new conception of Christianity and its Founder, not in the form of a doctrinal deduction from current tradition, such as St. Paul had given in his epistles, but in the form of an imaginary history. John xx. 30-31 comes near to an admission to this effect. Its unknown author treats the early traditions of the life of Jesus with a freedom unknown to the synoptists. He seeks, not as they did, faithfully (Luke i. 1-2) to reproduce the facts of that life so far as their information went; but to mould them anew, so that a form of Christological doctrine, transcending that of St. Paul, might shine through them as through a closely-fitting, transparent vestment. And as the credit of inspiration enjoyed by the Old Testament had not, up to that time, been conceded to any of the apostolic writers, it was essential to his design that the doctrine should not merely be advanced on the authority of an apostle, real or pseudonymous, but should be authenticated by the witness of Jesus himself, which no believer would call in question.

Various considerations have now been produced which may help us to conceive how the project of constructing such a narrative should have been formed in the mind of the Evangelist. But there is yet another consideration which may help us still further to understand his motive and procedure. Let it be remembered that the new religion from the first, and all along, had proved itself to be a great moral and spiritual power in men's lives. By St. Paul, and no doubt by the Evangelist also, this great outstanding fact was viewed as the consequence of the self-impartation of the divine life which was in Christ to those who believed. And the expectation was natural that this great power resident in Christ should have given some indication of its presence and operation during the earthly life of Jesus. But when the Evangelist turned to the synoptic tradition of that life he could scarcely but feel that it contained a somewhat disappointing record, and gave but few indications of that mighty power. He might account to himself for this apparent defect in various ways. At a time when the theory of the inspiration of the books of the New Testament had not established itself in the mind of the Church, he might suppose that the older evangelists had failed to give an adequate or appreciative report of that wonderful life ; that they had failed to apprehend or reproduce what was most spiritual or characteristic in it, and that what the tradition had not preserved could only be recovered by an imaginative history based on the Logos-idea, which, to his mind, gave the true key to that life. Or, again, he may have explained the defect to himself by supposing that the conditions or environment of his life upon earth did not suffer Jesus to manifest his proper self. A poet of the modern time has told us that " life itself may not express us all," and another has asked, " What act proved all its thought had been?" And if it be true that " a man's spiritual life may fall below the level of his deeds," the reverse is still more obviously true that a man's deeds may fall, or seem to fall, below the level of his spiritual life. There may be a spirit and a virtue in a man beyond his power of self-manifestation; for the power may be conditioned and limited by opportunity and external circumstance. The man may live and work in an inexpressive, stubborn, and impracticable element, just as, owing to the coarseness and intractability of his material, the soul of the artist may never come to full expression in his works. The Evangelist may have felt more or less consciously that this was the case in regard to Jesus, and with the Logos-idea in his view he may have set himself to recast the tradition, and so to reconstruct it as to make it more expressive of the inner spirit and power of the life which formed its theme.

Let it here be observed, too, that the Evangelist must have felt that a dogmatic construction like that of St. Paul did not, and could not, supply what he thought to be wanting in the synoptic Gospels. The Pauline dogma was a connected series or system in germ of propositions evolved from the subjective or mythical tradition of the life, death, and resurrection of Jesus. At the instance of what, in speaking of Keble, Newman calls "the living power of faith and love," and with the aid of a dialectic peculiar to itself, the Pauline dogma had put a meaning into the history greater than could be properly or logically evolved from it; in other words, the dogma had out-run the historical position and taken up a position ahead of it. And in its turn the history was impelled to cover the ground by which it now fell short; to place itself in line with the dogma, of which process we see a palmary example in Matth. xx. 28 and in Matth. xxvi. 26, as already remarked. The like process had now to repeat itself with a difference in the case of the fourth Gospel. The Logos-idea was a speculative advance beyond the Pauline dogma, and it was inevitable that the mythical history should seek to bring itself into line with this new form of the dogma. Only, that while in the former case the process went on unconsciously, and required the co-operation of two distinct subjects—the mythicist and the dog-matist—in the latter case it went on intentionally in one and the same subject, viz., the fourth Evangelist. He it was who both rose to the Logos-idea and brought the history abreast of it in his Gospel. We regard this Gospel therefore as a composition *sui generis*, devised to inculcate in a form resembling the synoptic narratives, a view of the nature and work of Jesus, different from that which was conveyed in these narratives, but already accepted in the Church. In short, we regard it as a sort of extended apologue—a species of composition in which a given moral or spiritual truth is set forth in the form of narrative, and in which it is immaterial whether the narrative be drawn from history or from fancy.

But whether or not the Evangelist sought an explanation of it, *there* lay the fact before him that there was little or no sign or indication, no prefigurement or foreshadowing of the Logos-idea in the synoptic tradition. No doubt Jesus appeared in that tradition as a man " approved of God by miracles, and signs, and wonders"; but even the miracles which he was reported to have done afforded no evidence or warrant for regarding him as one with the Logos, the other self of God, the life and the light of men. Such physical and therapeutic miracles as he was said to have done, or even greater, had been performed by many of the prophets and servants of God in Old Testament times, and therefore they did not suffice—at least to those who were Gnostically inclined—to advance him beyond the rank of a minister or delegate of the divine will. The really novel effects of the gospel, to which no works performed by prophets and other servants of God could be compared, were its great moral and spiritual effects; and from the synoptic narratives it appeared as if few or none such had been produced by Jesus during his lifetime. The nearest approach to such effects was the absorbing devotion to his person with which he inspired his followers. Out of that devotion there was yet much to come ; but, except in a few cases, such as that of those from whom he cast out devils, which is hardly a case in point ; or that of Zacchæus, which is a doubtful case, seeing the great moral change in him had taken place before his encounter with Jesus (Luke xix. 8); or that of the woman who was a sinner—very little of this kind is distinctly apparent in the synoptic records. Indeed, if we think of it, there was little room or opportunity for the manifestation of such effects during the lifetime of Jesus amid Jewish society, where the legal outward and conventional forms of religion were in general so strictly observed. It was only when the gospel moved forward into the festering mass and undisguised corruption of heathen lands that the grand moral miracle—the astounding spiritual power of the gospel—became apparent. This unexampled phenomenon, which was palpable and present, so engrossed the attention of St. Paul that he makes no allusion to physical miracles by Jesus and his followers. The signs and wonders to which he refers in his epistles as wrought by himself were probably, or almost certainly, the spiritual effects of his preaching of the gospel. It is not impossible indeed that examples of moral therapeutic may have accompanied his ministry as they did that of Jesus, not to speak of that curious and inexplicable phenomenon of the gift of tongues, which, in a travestied form, has been repeated and exploded in modern times. But such effects as the sudden conversion and spiritual renovation, in large numbers at a time, of men steeped in superstition and in habits of vice, were certainly regarded by him as a greater thing than any merely physical miracle, and were probably the signs and wonders of which he speaks as done by himself (Rom. xv. 19, 2 Cor. xii. 12). He expressly points to his converts as his "work in the Lord" and the seal of his apostleship (1 Cor. ix. 1, 2). In all probability the circumstance that the traditional accounts of the life of Jesus contained so few illustrations of this surpassing miracle was one reason why the Apostle takes so little notice of these traditions in his epistles. The same grand spiritual phenomenon was what imposed upon the imagination of the fourth Evangelist as it must have done upon all believers in the first ages of the Church, and he saw the explanation of it by regarding Christ as the light and life of men, and in his increasing exercise of these pre-eminent functions of the Logos.

In comparison with this phenomenon, the works of healing and the other visible and physical miracles ascribed to Jesus in the tradition sank for the Evangelist into insignificance—not, however, that he undervalued, far less ignored, the miraculous element or lost sight of its value. While he grounds the divine sonship of Christ on the testimony of Christ himself he does not forget that that testimony seemed to derive its sanction and authority, in part at least, from his command and exercise of miraculous powers. And therefore the Evangelist seeks to make these to yield as much as they can towards the exaltation of him who wrought them. He does not indeed represent Jesus as at any time exercising his miraculous powers in the somewhat indiscriminate manner of the synoptic records, but by the circumstantiality of the few select miracles which he represents Jesus as performing, he impresses the reader with the idea that they are more striking and more wonderful than those recorded by the synoptists. He also magnifies their import-ance, as in the case of the man who was born blind (ch. ix.), by saying that the man was thus born in order that the works of God should be made manifest in him, *i.e.*, that the miracle should be performed on him ; and in the case of Lazarus, by saying that the sickness had overtaken him in order that the Son of God might be glorified thereby, *i.e.*, by the miracle of his resuscitation. In one respect indeed this miracle at Bethany affords the most striking illustration of what we are here saying. On the apologetic side it has been maintained that this was not a greater miracle than that of the raising of the daughter of Jairus from the bed of death, or than that of the raising of the widow of Nain's son from the bier, as reported in the synoptists. And from a modern or scientific point of view this may be justly said. But to the men of that day it must have appeared to be a greater miracle; the superlative, as it has been desig-nated, of which these others were the positive and comparative. For it was at that time a current superstition that the dis-embodied spirit hovers about the place of sepulture for three days before taking its flight to far-off regions from which it cannot return. To recall a spirit from that distance seemed to be an enhancement of the miracle of resuscitation, and hence the emphasis with which it is said that Lazarus had been dead four days.

This, however, only by the way. The enhancement of the miracles was only a subordinate object with the Evangelist. His chief aim in depicting Jesus as a wonder-worker was to give prominence to the symbolical character which he saw that physical miracles, treated as he treated them, were capable of sustaining. For him, as for St. Paul, they were comparatively insignificant, of little or of no intrinsic importance ; or, if they did retain their value for him, it was only because he could discern in them the capability of serving as symbols of the permanent, ever-present, outstanding fact of the great moral miracles which the spirit of Christ was still working in the Church. And just because he viewed the miracles chiefly, if not exclusively, under this aspect of symbols, we conceive that the physical miracles lost for him the solidity, the reality of facts. The symbol has no independent existence of its own ; it is nothing in itself ; it is shaped and moulded to the thing symbolized—a creature and plaything of the imagination. And thus the miraculous element became fluid and plastic under the hand of the great idealist ; a material to be shaped at will to represent the strange phenomenon, which alone riveted his mind and fired his imagination. He felt himself relieved from the obligation of fidelity to the mere external facts, and he availed himself to the utmost of the historical license, which seemed thus to be given to him, for the construction of a new Gospel, whose aim was, not to reproduce or rearrange the actual facts of the life of Jesus, but to symbolize and foreshadow his post-humous agency, or, in other words, the moral and spiritual effects of the Gospel.

The miracles recorded by this Evangelist seem to serve merely as pegs or hinges to the discourses which are founded upon them for the purpose of pointing out their symbolical character. They exhibit an intentionalism which is quite foreign to those in the other Gospels. These latter are generally, or all but invariably, works of mercy and beneficence, called forth to relieve distress, or to meet some emergency ; whereas those others have all the appearance of being performed for the express purpose of presenting an occasion, or furnishing a text for dis-courses, which in the other Gospels flow naturally and simply from the desire to impart instruction. And we may also recall here the observation already made that the purpose of these discourses is not, as in the synoptists, to set forth the kingdom of God and the conditions of obtaining an entrance into it, but to assert the divine sonship of Jesus. He is here no longer the mere teacher, as he is there, but the subject and text of his own teaching. He no longer says that men must enter the kingdom of heaven through self-denial and much tribulation, but through faith in himself as the Son of God. It may be true that the two forms of doctrine admit of being reconciled by means of certain well-worn explanations ; but the style of language, the form of doctrine, and the presuppositions of each belong to different individuals. The original doctrine has taken a different hue, by being passed through another mind. It is the Evan-gelist, not Jesus, who speaks in the fourth Gospel; and he shows his consciousness of this, and justifies his new version of the teaching of Jesus by those words, already quoted, which he attributes to him (xvi. 12-14) : " I have yet many things to say unto you ; but ye cannot bear them now.   Howbeit, when he, the Spirit of truth is come, he will guide you into all truth," etc. The Evangelist is so possessed by his hyper-Pauline Christology that he does not shrink from constituting himself the mouthpiece of Jesus, and advancing it in his name.   Christ is the " truth," and whatever recommends itself as truth to the mind of the Evangelist, he does not hesitate to represent as proceeding from him or from his Spirit.

Of the seven miracles which the Evangelist attributes to Jesus two, or, at the most, three are adopted by him from the synoptic records ; the rest are, we believe, the offspring of his own imagination.   But the symbolical intention, which is altogether unobserved or overlooked in the synoptic narratives of the miracles, is apparent here, and prominent on the surface in all the seven.   And of the three most striking of these, the Evangelist represents Jesus as drawing out the symbolical aspect, and impressing it in long discourses on the multitudes who witnessed them.   It was in these discourses especially, though not exclusively, that the Evangelist had the opportunity of representing Jesus as bearing testimony to himself, and of obtaining his authority and sanction for regarding him as the Logos, the life and the light of men (see especially chapters ix. and xi.). This self-testimony of Jesus supplied that authority which was wanting to the Pauline dogma, and which, if only authenticated as his to the judgment of believers, was sufficient to settle the Gnostic question by placing him on an unapproachable pinnacle.

A great part of the fourth Gospel is devoted to the narration of these miracles, with the discourses founded on them.   Interspersed are various episodes, such as those of the conversations of Jesus with Nathaniel, with Nicodemus, and the woman of Samaria ; the story of the Greeks who desired to see Jesus, and his disputations with the Jews with respect to the Sabbath, and his claim to be the Son of God ; all bearing, more or less unequivocally, on Christ himself as the life and light of men, and on the Evangelist's variant of the Pauline dogma ; and all lending confirmation to the general theme.   These, the new materials of the Gospel, are enclosed in a framework generally similar to that which is common to the synoptic Gospels ;

though even here the Evangelist has by no means adhered closely to the synoptic outline, and, in some important points, to which we shall yet call attention, he deviates widely from it. His omissions, too, are significant, because they show that his design was, as far as possible, to keep out of sight whatever might seem to be incongruous with the Logos-nature, or might disturb the dramatic unity of impression. Such are the absence of any allusion to the temptation of Jesus in the wilderness, to his agony in the garden, and to his exhibition of human frailty on the cross. The references to his family relationship are of the most casual kind, and his advent into the world is described as the shining of a light into the darkness, as if the Evangelist was not able to conceive how the Logos did not " despise the virgin's womb."

After all that can be said upon the subject, it will ever remain a difficulty for the modern mind to understand how a man of deep religious instinct, as the Evangelist obviously is, could take such liberty as we imagine him to have done, with a history of such supreme moment. There are other suggestions besides those which we have already thrown out, that may help towards an explanation. We may say that the sentiment of utter devotion to the memory of Christ which had sunk deep into his mind, and had melted into one with his God-consciousness, may have been regarded by him as the breathing or witness of the spirit of Christ in him. In representing Christ, therefore, as testifying during his lifetime, by word and deed, to his own divine sonship, the Evangelist may have regarded this testimony as but the articulation of that spiritual witness; or as the setting of it forth in outward and historical form, by way of accommodation to the sensuous or popular understanding. It is conceivable that a devout idealist might think such a procedure to be perfectly legitimate. Or, yet again, the Evangelist may have seen that the high ideal presented in the life and person of Jesus was the most precious possession of humanity, the best guarantee for all spiritual progress ; and that the impersonation of that ideal in Christ offered the best means of keeping it as a visible and living canon before the eye of man ; and he may have felt himself called upon to remodel the Gospel narrative, to make it a more perfect vehicle for that purpose. For, if it be objected that Christ was already presented as such a visible and living canon in the synoptic Gospels and in the Pauline dogma, the Evangelist may yet have felt that in neither the one nor the other was he invested with that mystical and transcendent character which was best fitted to take hold of the human mind, and to give boundless play to the devout imagination. He may have thought to give a higher pitch to the ideal by identifying the personal canon with the Logos. And this idea, being laid down as a theme and basis, necessarily communicated a completely new and idealistic character to the pragmatic and historical elements of his Gospel. But if none of these suggestions are quite satisfactory, we have no alternative but to fall back on the hypothesis that the Evangelist, being possessed by an absolute conviction of his Christological view, thought himself at liberty to adopt the only means by which he could hope to impress the Church at large with the same conviction, and that he can hardly be acquitted of acting upon the maxim that the end justifies the means. All such suggestions are made under reservation of the remarks that genius like that of the Evangelist does not act by rule, but is guided many times by principles of which it may not be conscious; and that a man of genius may be, and often is, so completely possessed by an idea as to become oblivious of the finer considerations of right and wrong.

It is a noticeable fact, not without significance, that in all the testimony which Jesus bears to himself in the fourth Gospel he nowhere styles himself the Logos or the Word. That was the theme which was to be proved by his own testimony, or it was the key which the Evangelist put into the hands of his readers for their proper understanding of his Gospel. It gave them from the outset and at once to understand that a more absolute significance was to be claimed for the person of Jesus than had yet been claimed for him. It showed that he came not merely to reveal the Heavenly Father and the method of salvation, but also to bear testimony to himself as identical with the religious principle in men, or with that divine energy which stirs within the soul of the believer. The nearest approach to such a view of his nature and function in the synoptic Gospels is to be found in Matthew xi. 28, where Jesus is represented as saying, "Come unto me, and I will give you rest." But there the blessedness of which he speaks is in the shape of a boon which he bestows, a gift which is not himself. A still nearer approach to it occurs frequently in St. Paul's epistles, as, *e.g.*, where the Apostle says that Christ is made unto us complete redemption, and that the new life of which he is the author is the living of Christ in us ; or that that life is imparted to us by our being engrafted upon his life. But all such forms of expression admit more or less of being interpreted as figures of speech to represent the intimate sympathy and fellowship between Christ and believers. According to the fourth Evangelist again, the identification of the spiritual life in believers with the life of Christ is meant literally, if mystically, and forms the very theme and nerve of his Gospel, and imparts a new aspect to the soteriological process. In the synoptic Gospels Jesus points out the way to the better life ; but in the fourth Gospel he declares that he himself, he in person, is the way. Instead of saying that he shows the way and declares the truth, and manifests the life, he says, " I am the way, the truth and the life." It is made to appear to the readers of the Gospel that the Logos has united himself to humanity in the person of Christ, and, by receiving believers into his fellowship, he effects the same union of divine and human nature in them. The inward process of the spiritual life in believers is thus made to depend upon the mystical transfusion of his life into theirs: and it has been truly observed that the subject of the fourth Gospel is not the death of Christ and its efficacy for forgiveness, as in St. Paul's epistles ; but the person of Christ himself, " What he is, is the main thing," and they who receive him for what he is are thereby made partakers of his salvation, and inoculated, as it were, with the divine principle which is in him. Here is a point at which two extremes seem to meet in this Gospel. The apparent spirituality of its mysticism runs into a species of materialism, just as is the case in the Pauline doctrine. Here indeed is one of those deeper-lying affinities between the " Johannine" and Pauline doctrines. The fourth Evangelist might say with truth that he had written his Gospel, " not to destroy, but to fulfil" St. Paul's doctrine. The two doctrines are but one, under different aspects ; and, however much they may differ, they agree in this, that they transform the purely spiritual autosoteric doctrine of Jesus into a heterosoteric, somewhat materialistic, doctrine.

If the fourth Evangelist never represents Jesus as claiming to be the Logos, he represents him (viii. 12) as claiming to be the

" light of the world," which is the next thing to it, and this also
deserves attention.   Few can have read the Sermon on the
Mount, where Jesus says to his disciples, " Ye are the light of
the world" (Matth. v. 14), without a feeling of the incongruity of
such an address to the time and situation.   For, even admitting
the apologetic position that in the spirit of prophetic prescience
Jesus might foresee the great part which his disciples were to
play in the world, what were they themselves to make of such
language addressed to them in the very beginning of their
discipleship ?   What effect could it have but to bewilder them,
or to puff them up with a spirit of conceit and self-consciousness, fatal to all genuine growth and discipline.   The words in
the mouth of Jesus at that time are inconceivable.   But it is
easy to understand how, in a short time after the resurrection,
when the Church had become alive to the fact that the gospel
was a new power in the world, the mythicist who dramatized
the thought that was stirring in the mind of the Church might
put these words into the mouth of Jesus as a forecast of what
was to be.   The words expressed a fact with regard to the
Church already patent and obvious.   But behind that fact there
was the other fact that Jesus was the source of all that light
from which the Church derived hers.   Yet, in the face of the
general and well preserved tradition that Jesus had been simply
a teacher of righteousness, and had not discoursed of himself,
the mythicist could not put that ultimate fact into his mouth.
To do this was reserved for the fourth Evangelist.   The Logos-
idea, with which this Evangelist started, necessitated the adoption of a self-referent style of speech on the part of Jesus, and
as a matter of course the ideal Christ was made to utter the
assertion that he himself, and he alone, was the light of the
world.   The one form of words was true in a sense as well as
the other.   But the point of view is different, and the same
teacher could hardly have adopted both.

The result to which we would conduct the reader is, that the
Evangelist proposed to write not a matter-of-fact account of
the life of Jesus as seen by the corporal eye, or observed by the
ordinary intelligence, for he knew, or believed, that such an
account had already been given by the synoptists ; but such an
account as would convey to the Church the impression which,
under the transfiguring light and inspiration of faith and love,
it had made upon himself, as a life of God moving upon earth

in human form, as of the other self of God—the Logos, the life
and the light of men. He had no evidence before him, no
tradition that Jesus had ever summoned the man of Bethany
from the grave ; but he was firmly persuaded that Jesus, in
virtue of his divine nature as the Logos, might have done this
or any other miracle had he chosen to do it, and to impress a
conviction of the same kind upon his readers the Evangelist
did not hesitate to represent Jesus as exercising his miraculous
power in this particular instance. The synoptists had, it is
true, placed on record two occasions on which Jesus had resuscitated the dead, and the Evangelist might have economized
invention and made use of one of these occasions to represent
Jesus as claiming to be the resurrection and the life ; but the
environing circumstances in these other cases were not adapted
to his design, and he preferred to create a new scene and a new
situation to give a more free and effective play to his imagination, and to impress the lesson which he meant to teach by a
more life-like drama. While these other acts of power might
show that Jesus had come as a delegate from God, this miracle
at Bethany was so arranged as to call forth a testimony
respecting himself as more than a delegate, as allied by nature
to God ; and for the express purpose of manifesting His glory.
The impression which the life of Jesus had made upon the
mind of the Evangelist was absolute truth to himself, and he
had become possessed with an irresistible impulse to inculcate the
same truth upon the mind of the Church. The literary means
employed by him for this purpose, though not according to the
scrupulous notions of modern times, were not unfamiliar to the
practice of the ancient world. Witness the practice of the
great historians of antiquity of putting speeches into the
mouths of their leading characters, to give to their own views of
the situation the sanction of the principal actors ; and witness
also the wide extension of pseudonymous and apocryphal
literature in the ancient world, to promote ends which seemed
desirable to the writers themselves, or to throw into circulation
among their contemporaries their own opinions and judgments
of passing or past events.

From what has now been said it will be seen that we regard
the fourth Gospel, as designed by its author to set forth Jesus
as the Logos, and to establish or vindicate Pauline or dogmatic
Christianity chiefly by the testimony which he represents Christ

as bearing to himself. The object of the Gospel is not to place
on record a narrative of events as they occurred, or as the
writer believed them to have actually occurred, but to dramatize
in the form of a historical narrative the eternal nature and
spiritual truth of Christianity. It is perhaps too much to suppose that he may, however darkly and dimly, have caught sight
of the philosophic doctrine, that the true power which moulds
human life resides in the idea; that events are nothing except
in so far as they are manifestations of the idea, and that any
history, real or unreal, which conveys the idea to the mind, has
a truth and a value of its own. But we can well imagine that
neither the synoptic Gospels, with which the Evangelist was
perfectly familiar, nor the authority of St. Paul, seemed to him
to supply a satisfactory basis for Pauline theology; and yet less
for that Christology, to which—partly on speculative, partly on
controversial grounds, and partly on his own experience and
observation of the marvellous effects of Christianity—he himself
had risen. It had become apparent to him that such a basis
could only be supplied by the declaration or testimony of Christ
himself; for which place could be found only in a new version
of the Gospel history. As he proceeded to the composition of
such a Gospel he would perceive that such a revision must be
radical, and that many deviations from the synoptic versions
which were helpful and auxiliary to his main design besides
those which were more essential to it, would be requisite. And
we conceive of the Evangelist as a consummate artist, every
stroke of whose pencil contributes to the oneness of the effect
of his picture; we should even hesitate to say that his Gospel
could have differed materially from what it is, even in subordinate details, without loss to its presiding thought. Apart
from one or two interpolations and the twenty-first chapter,
which is probably added by another hand, the Gospel is, unlike
the Apocalypse—a work of one casting, a web of one piece—
organically unified by the artistic, and therefore not too obtrusive bearing of all its parts on the Logos-idea, for which, to use
an expression of its own as remarked by Holzmann, it forms
the "seamless" vestment.

This theory of the design and origin of the Gospel recommends itself to our judgment, because it explains the surprising
incongruities or contradictions in details between it and the
earlier Gospels. These will ever remain irreducible, however

much apologetic theologians may endeavour, by the utmost extravagance of conjectural ingenuity, to minimize or explain them away.   Instead of attempting anything in this direction, we find an explanation at every point of these discrepancies, by regarding the Gospel not as a historical document, but as the imaginative vehicle of the Evangelist's Christological conception.

The salient peculiarity in this Gospel, which produces a sense of its fundamental and irreconcilable difference from the other Gospels, is its representation of Christ as uttering long discourses, which stamp with his authority those dogmatic views concerning himself which only came up after his death.   Instead of being utterances of his God-consciousness, as in the synoptists, these discourses are utterances of his self-consciousness, as the Son of God ; and instead of directing attention to practical religion, they direct attention mainly to himself as the object of faith and devotional sentiment.   A purely dogmatic, personal, and self-referent complexion is thus given to the teachings of Jesus, of which there is hardly a trace in the more historical synoptic records.   We have already observed that the Evangelist betrays his sense of the awkwardness of this self-testimony, by his endeavour to show that the objection to such a partial testimony does not apply in the case of Jesus.   He expected that, in spite of the suspicion attaching to a man's professions respecting himself, those by Jesus, as reported by him, would receive credence from his *readers*.   For, it will be observed, that his Gospel is evidently addressed to those who already believed with unbounded faith in Jesus, and were prepared to believe whatever Jesus might say regarding himself, provided the reporter was a credible ear-witness ; and the consummate art of the Evangelist gained its highest triumph, as we shall yet see, in conveying that impression to his readers.

Another irreconcilable incongruity between the fourth and the first three Gospels may be seen in the entire absence in the former of all growth in the consciousness of Jesus ; and this also may be readily accounted for by its design to bring all the details of the life into harmony with the Logos-idea.   In the synoptic Gospels there are various indications that the Messianic consciousness of Jesus unfolded itself gradually and grew clearer to his mind; and also that his Messianic character was a late disclosure to his disciples.   Everyone must feel that these indications, undesigned and unobtrusive as they are, lend an air of historic reality to these records. But in the fourth Gospel this note of genuine history is altogether lost or discarded. That Gospel shows no gradation either in the consciousness of Jesus himself or in the faith of the disciples. He unveils his true character from the very first, and is recognized for what he is by Nathaniel, John the Baptist, and others; and his relations friendly or hostile, with those around him, remain the same from first to last. At the very commencement he drives the money-changers from the temple, and provokes hostility before he has made any attempt to instruct or conciliate. This timing of the event may be in full accord with his character as the Logos. But, assuredly, there is in it, according to all ordinary standards of conduct, less of decorum than in the incident as recorded in the synoptic Gospels, which place it towards the end of his ministry, after he had tried and exhausted every method of conciliation without effect.

Indeed the entire exclusion of growth or gradation in the consciousness of Jesus is involved in the Evangelist's conception of his nature. Nay, the Evangelist feels it to be so important and so essential that he takes care that it should not be overlooked by the readers of his Gospel. In the sixth chapter he says, " For Jesus knew from the beginning who they were that believed not, and who should betray him." He feels it necessary, by such a statement, to forestall, and by forestalling to obviate the suspicion that, in selecting Judas as one of his disciples, Jesus had mistaken the character of the man, or did not foresee what was to come of it. According to the Evangelist Jesus foresaw all, and did not commit himself to Judas and to others who seemed to believe in him, though he allowed them to swell his train. Knowing the treacherous nature of Judas, and that he had a devil in him, Jesus yet chooses him to be one of his most intimate associates, that by this means a hidden and mysterious purpose, which afterwards comes to light, may be accomplished. By this pragmatic construction, the Evangelist raises Jesus so high above human ignorance and infirmity as to merge his humanity in his divinity, and to land himself in a view of his nature, which can hardly be regarded as else than docetic.

The theory of the origin of the Gospel which we advocate throws light not only upon its more general peculiarities, of

which we have now singled out two, but also upon many of
its separate incidents and details.   Let us take the miracle at
Bethany as an example.   This miracle is found only in the
fourth Gospel, and, apart altogether from the general objection
to all miracle, we see many grounds for holding this one to
be altogether unhistorical.   In the first place, to any one
who will candidly compare the parable of the rich man and
Lazarus, in the Gospel of St. Luke, it will be apparent that
the narrative of the miracle is founded upon the parable,
and has been suggested by it.   In the latter, Abraham is
represented as saying of the rich man's relatives, " Neither
will they believe, though one rose from the dead," which
words it was the object of the Evangelist to illustrate by
his narrative of the raising of Lazarus.   For, from the sequel,
it appears that the miracle, so far from awakening belief
in the great mass of the Jewish people, was the more immediate incentive to their crucifixion of the wonder-worker,
and furnished a proof of their invincible hostility to the
Prince of Life.   The Evangelist thus contrives to discredit,
and to break down, the spirit of scepticism with which this
narrative, or his Gospel in general, might be regarded, by
suggesting that that spirit was so virulent that it would
not believe even though it saw.

In contrast to such a spirit, the Evangelist manifests an
evident anxiety to attach peculiar merit to those who believe
without having seen the risen Saviour (xx. 29).   The incident
of Thomas' scepticism seems to be introduced in order to
impress this idea on his readers.   While, in the synoptic
Gospels, Thomas is mentioned only by name in the list of
the apostles, and, like the majority of his colleagues, is quite
inconspicuous; he is, in the fourth Gospel, singled out and
brought into prominence as the representative of doubting and
hesitating believers, of whom there may have been many in
the early days of the Church, and to afford occasion for the
remark of Jesus, that it was a high merit to stifle doubt,
and to believe in him on slender evidence, or even in the
absence of any evidence beyond his own word of asseveration
(compare John iv. 41 and xvii. 21).   A doctrine of this kind
was well calculated, as by a sort of moral compulsion, to
carry a soul over whatever doubts might possess it, not only
as to the fact of the resurrection itself, but also as to the

historical value generally of the new version of the life of Jesus.

Among the *dramatis personae* of the Gospel there were those who saw and believed not. These are classed by the Evangelist as "Jews" (xx. 19 and *passim*). There were those again who believed because they had seen the Christ. These were his personal disciples, including Thomas. But who are they who believed without having seen? Evidently not those of that company, but those who joined the band of the disciples after Jesus had ceased to be an object of sight; and the mention of these is an indication, however slight, that the words were not spoken by Jesus, but are the words of the Evangelist himself, put by him into the mouth of Jesus, and written at a time when all who joined the Church had only the testimony of the personal disciples to rely upon; and it is implied in xx. 29, that while these were excluded from the privilege of seeing the risen Christ, their belief in him was all the more blissful and meritorious.

Apologists have endeavoured to raise a presumption in favour of the historical value of the raising of Lazarus by claiming that it affords an explanation at once of the transient enthusiasm of the populace, and of the deadly rage of the Rulers, which led to the crucifixion, better and more intelligible than can be gathered from the current of events in the synoptic version of them. Now, it is perhaps, though hardly, credible, that the fury of the Rulers might only be exasperated by the proof he had afforded of his being the Lord and Giver of Life, and by the danger in which their authority was thus placed. But it is not easy to see how the multitude could so soon have forgotten such a miracle. Putting this consideration out of sight, however, we say that the explanation of the catastrophe thus given is only too vivid and too dramatic for the pragmatism of real history. All is sufficiently explained without this miracle by the simple fact to which the synoptists confine themselves, that Jesus had come *at last* to Jerusalem. He had often been there, no doubt, in his youth and early manhood, but never before, since he had begun to preach, and to draw upon himself the hostility of the Pharisees. He had purposely avoided the vicinity of the city, and had thus been able in the remote parts of the country to escape the fury of those in authority. A certain degree of incredulity,

especially in Jerusalem, as to his claims was, we may believe
occasioned by this circumstance. But when he was seen at
length calmly and courageously advancing to the city to
brave his enemies in the stronghold of their power, all doubt
was for the moment dissipated ; his apparent confidence
communicated itself to the people. It was believed that
he was about to assert himself, and to erect the kingdom
of God, which he announced (Luke xix. 11). But the enthusiasm cooled as suddenly as it had been excited. When
it was seen that he still continued his office as a mere teacher,
that he offered no demonstration of superhuman power,
and that nothing was to come of all that excitement, the
crowd felt itself befooled, and was infuriated by the disappointment of its expectations, ready to be the tools of the
Rulers, who, at the same time, had regained their confidence,
and all that remained for Jesus was to die, with the reputation
of an impostor and blasphemer.

In this connection let us advert once more to the fact that
the Evangelist places the cleansing of the temple in the very
early period of the ministry of Jesus, whereas the synoptic
tradition places it at the very end, when the relations between
Jesus and the Rulers had become strained to the utmost, and
when he had begun to give vent to his indignation at their
desperate hostility to the truth. Now it has been generally
felt that there is a certain indecorum in representing Jesus
as acting thus violently at the very beginning of his ministry,
before he had exhausted or even tried the means of persuasion
and conciliation. But there were reasons which may have
weighed, unconsciously it may be, with the Evangelist in
deviating here from the synoptic tradition. The incident in
the temple, as recorded by the synoptists, was one which
the Evangelist could neither omit nor reproduce with the same
setting of time and circumstance. Many incidents in the
synoptic narratives, which were no less striking and important,
he does omit, as, *e.g.*, the temptation in the wilderness and the
agony in the garden, and the cry of despair upon the cross.
Such incidents he omitted, because he felt instinctively, as we
feel to this day, that they would interfere, as so many disparate
elements, with a life which was the self-manifestation of the
Logos. But he retained this incident in the temple, because it
seemed to harmonize with such a life, and to be a momentary

revelation to his enemies of the divine power which was at other times latent in that humble exterior.* At the same time it was necessary for his general plan to remove this incident as far as his extended canvas would allow, from proximity and connection with the closing scene, in order that the attention of his readers might be concentrated upon the raising of Lazarus as the final and proximate irritant of the murderous design of the Rulers. To attach this consequence to the grandest of all the miracles of Jesus fell in with one of the main objects, which he keeps before him in his Gospel, viz., to intensify the desperate wickedness of the Jews in rejecting Jesus. Had the incident in the temple been the immediate cause and provocation of their deadly resentment, their resentment might have seemed to be natural, or even venial; for the act which provoked it was done in defiance and contempt of the authority of the Rulers, by whom the worldly traffic in the sacred precincts must have been sanctioned. But if the Jews and their Rulers were instigated and spurred on to their crime by an act of power and beneficence on the part of Jesus, which was truly divine, the reprobate state of their minds was thereby placed in a light the most glaring.

There is, as every one knows, a conspicuous and startling discrepancy between the first three Gospels and the fourth, in their chronology of the life of Jesus, and we decidedly regard the chronology and general outline of the history as given by the synoptists as more true to fact than those given by the latter. No valid reason can be given why the synoptists should have departed from the true chronology (as we have elsewhere shown), whereas a highly probable reason can be shown for such a departure on the part of the fourth Evangelist. St. Paul's silence with regard to the events in the life of Jesus was probably due in part to the fact that there was little to be said, few salient details—only the daily routine of his work as a teacher of righteousness, and the opposition which he encountered, as may be seen in the synoptists. But this did not suit

---

* The Evangelist, it may be observed, had not the same motive for preserving the synoptic record of the Transfiguration, though in it, too, the latent glory of Christ was manifested. It was a manifestation only to those who "were with him in the holy mount," so that the Jews and their Rulers were not cognizant of it, and their guilt in rejecting him was not thereby heightened.

the fourth Evangelist, who had to find motive and opportunity for discourses of a novel kind, not delivered by Jesus himself; in which he could turn about the Messianic and Logos-ideas on every side ; and for this purpose he had to protract the time of the public ministry from little more than one to nearly three years, so as to place the central figure in various new situations, and exhibit him in converse and contact with imaginary persons, unknown to the synoptic tradition.

The most surprising deviation, however, from the synoptic tradition which the fourth Gospel exhibits is the transference of the date of the crucifixion from the 15th to the 14th of the month.   And this deviation will be found also to stand in no distant connection of dependence upon the Logos-idea and the general scope of the Gospel.   The necessary effect of this great idea upon the Evangelist's mind was to heighten and intensify his dogmatic interest.   For we may remark, in passing, that it is a pure misapprehension to suppose, as some seem to do, that because his doctrine is mystical it cannot also be dogmatic.   But without dwelling on this, we say that the Logos-idea, which had taken hold of his mind, inclined him to find a dogmatic and symbolic significance in all the events of the earthly life of Jesus ; and even to retouch and alter these events, so as to make them pat and striking in their dogmatic aspect.   The interest in this instance was to supply a historic basis to the Pauline dogma that Christ was the true Passover or Lamb of God ; to demonstrate that his death on the cross came in the room of the Jewish Passover by alleging that it had taken place on the very day of the Passover, and to exalt the significance of that event by thus making it to appear to be not a mere fulfilment, but a fulfilment which was also an abolition or supersession of the Law.   The fact of the transposition of the date we do not need to prove.   It is acknowledged by the critics of highest eminence even on the apologetic side, and indeed the evidence of the fact is so clear, that no one could or would entertain a doubt of it for a moment, except for the orthodox interests which seem to be at stake.   The manifest variation in the dates assigned to this event is very suggestive of the presumably unhistorical character of many of the details of Gospel history, and deserves all the attention which has been given to it by critics of every school of theology.   Let it be borne in mind that the first evidence in point of time to the date of the crucifixion is that which may be derived from what St. Paul says as to the Last Supper in 1 Cor. xi. In that reference the remarkable thing is that the Apostle does not in any way connect the Last Supper with the Passover. All he says is that it took place on the night on which Jesus was betrayed ; and, if the crucifixion really did take place on the 15th, i.e., within the period during which the festival lasted, and on the day to which the greatest solemnity was attached, the oversight or omission on the part of the Apostle seems not a little curious. For it was clearly in the interest of his doctrine of atonement to point out, allusively at least, this connection. His doctrine, that Christ was the true Passover, would have received a strong confirmation from the coincidence. Indeed the omission seems to us to afford some presumption, however faint, that the coincidence in point of time between the Passover and the crucifixion cannot have been so striking as it came to be afterwards represented. And, if we combine this presumption with the circumstance of the discrepancy between the synoptic and Johannine dates, it becomes an open question whether the crucifixion happened on either of these dates, and not rather on the 13th. Two of the synoptists make it certain that the Sanhedrim had formally resolved, two days before the Passover, i.e., on the 12th, upon the death of Jesus ; and resolved also that the sentence should not be carried out during the feast, lest there should be an uproar of the people. To understand the significance of the latter part of the resolution we have to remember the fact that by way, we suppose, of edifying the crowds then assembled, and exhibiting to them the sanctions of the law, criminals were often reserved for execution during the Passover. The existence of such a custom rendered it necessary to make the express provision that, for the reason stated, it should not be followed in the case of Jesus. The execution of the sentence had in his case either to be postponed or to be precipitated ; and the latter alternative was clearly to be preferred, so that no opportunity might be given for him to work upon the fickle and excitable crowd during the festival.*

---

* It may indeed be said that Judas, by his treachery, created an opportunity unexpectedly, and, as it were, forced the hands of the Sanhedrim. But the whole episode of Judas and the part which he played on the occa-

Prompt action was requisite, and the likelihood is that Jesus was secured that very night, and executed on the 13th. For, if this were not the case, we should have to account for the fact that the Sanhedrim departed from its resolution, and allowed the crucifixion to take place during the Passover ; and also for the circumstance that tradition should have preserved the memory of an abortive resolution. To us this incidental notice of St. Mark seems to be a fragment of genuine history, and remains to throw doubt upon the mythical date which may have crept in at a later period. The circumstance that the two days before the Passover are represented as being filled with other incidents is of no consequence. The mythical fancy could easily provide for this by the re-arrangement of existing materials ; and other data seem to render it probable that the mythical fancy was particularly busy with the events of this period, as indeed is antecedently likely. But upon these we do not enter. Suffice to say that the 13th of the month did not satisfy the dogmatic or mythical tendency, which required that the facts of history at that critical con-juncture should be adapted to preconceived ideas. There must have existed in Jewish-Christian quarters a strong disposition to represent Jesus as having on this occasion given countenance by his presence to the great legal festival ; and besides this,

sion is rendered doubtful by many circumstances, and especially by the fact that St. Paul seems to have been ignorant of it (1 Cor. xv. 5), where it is said that, after Christ rose from the dead, he " was seen of Cephas, then of the Twelve." Besides, it is difficult to understand how the action of the Sanhedrim could have been in any respect determined or precipitated by the treachery of Judas. We know, otherwise than by the testimony of the fourth Evangelist, that Jesus "showed himself openly to the world." His movements, we may be sure, were watched ; his times of going and coming to Jerusalem ; the route which he followed morning and evening, and the periods of the day or night, at which he and his disciples were left alone by the multitude, were well known. The Sanhedrim could not but know the opportunities for seizing him without creating a tumult. Or, if they did not, but were indebted for this knowledge to an accidental informant, they must have been singularly negligent in procuring the intelligence necessary for their design. Under all the circumstances, an offer on the part of a disciple to betray his Master was a wholly gratuitous service, for which even thirty pieces of silver was too high a price. The detail is probably to be explained by the eagerness of St. Matthew, which he elsewhere betrays, as well as here, to make out a correspondence between the life of Jesus and the language of the Old Testament (see Zechariah xi. 12).

Jesus had presumably gone to Jerusalem to keep the Passover, and if he died on the 13th it was evident that his intention had been frustrated, and that he was thereby convicted of a want of that prevision which was conceived to belong to his Messianic character. To do away with such a stumbling-block to faith it was requisite that he should be held to have participated in the Passover on the 14th, and to have been crucified on the 15th.

To show that the early Church may have been alive to a consideration such as this, we have only to point again to the evident anxiety manifested by the fourth Evangelist (ii. 24, vi. 64, xiii. 11), to obviate the very natural suspicion that, in choosing Judas to be an apostle, Jesus-Logos was deceived, and did not know from the beginning that he had made choice of a traitor. Is it too much to conjecture that a kindred consideration may have made itself felt in the mythicizing process, and have contributed insensibly to remove the crucifixion from a date immediately prior to the Paschal feast to a date within it?

Be this as it may, the fourth Evangelist was not satisfied with the date assigned to the crucifixion by the synoptists, and did not hesitate to depart from it. The difficulty which we experience in conceiving how the Evangelist could put forth as genuine history a delineation of the ministry of Jesus, which was largely drawn from his own imagination, here reaches its culminating point. It is true that in that age and in antiquity generally, the obligation of strict fidelity to historical fact was not felt as it is in modern times; and, that in any age, a man animated by an absorbing devotion to a cause of supreme importance to human welfare, might be tempted to think that the promotion of such a cause was an end which justified the use of means which were otherwise questionable. Rightly or wrongly it is generally believed that the Jesuit Order is able to combine such a principle in theory and in practice with a profound religious sentiment. We can, therefore, conceive how the Evangelist, possessed by an ardent conviction that Christ was the Life and the Light of men, but not satisfied with the expression which had been given to this faith in the synoptic Gospels, might deem it both lawful and expedient to impress the same conviction on the mind of the Church by a version of the gospel history expressly constructed

for that purpose, without regard to the pre-existing records,
however authentic.   We can imagine how, with such a design,
he could put discourses into the mouth of Jesus, which were
entirely different from those in the synoptic Gospels, and
ascribe miracles to him, of a more striking order than any
there reported.   But how he could have ventured to alter, *i.e.*,
to contradict the date of the crucifixion expressly indicated in
the Gospels, and accepted as authentic by the Church, it is
more difficult to imagine.   Here we must resort to conjecture,
for we have no historical data to guide us in such an inquiry.
We may, therefore, remember that at the time at which the
fourth Gospel made its appearance, canonical authority was not
enjoyed by any of the books of the New Testament, and that
the statements of the previous Gospels, as to dates and other
facts, might still be questioned, and, no doubt, often were
questioned by Gnostic teachers ; and were, at least, not fully
and definitively binding on the faith of the Christian community.
It is then conceivable that some uncertainty might yet exist as
to the date of the crucifixion, which even the existing written
documents did not wholly dispel; more especially would this be
the case, if there yet lingered some faint echo of a tradition
that the 13th was formerly regarded as the true date.   We
must also take into account that the writer of this Gospel
was an idealist of a daring and speculative imagination, to
whom facts of any kind were of little value except as symbolical
of the relative ideas.   Absorbed in the contemplation of the
idea, intent only on conveying spiritual truth, the Evangelist
was careless of fact, and did not feel himself bound by historical data.   Whether Jesus actually raised Lazarus from the
tomb, or gave sight to a man born blind, or himself submitted
to death on the 13th or 15th rather than on the 14th, was to
him of no moment ; quite subordinate to the indubitable fact
that Jesus Christ exercised the power of quickening the soul to
a new life, and by his death superseded all sacrificial rites, and
the dispensation to which they belonged.   With the mere facts,
therefore, he dealt with freedom, so as to mould them to his
purpose of symbolizing and confirming, by means of them, his
main idea ; and he even goes the length of bodying forth this
idea in facts which were the creatures of his pure imagination ;
his object not being to falsify the history, but rather to charge
it with a higher meaning than could be thought into it in its

synoptic form.   Such an attempt could only have been dreamt of in an age in which the historical sense was in almost total abeyance, and the Evangelist may have been emboldened to it by the presumption that the heightened dogmatic significance, which might be lent by this means to the death of Jesus, would readily suggest itself to his readers ; and to them, dominated as they were by that dogma, would amount to a demonstration or conclusive evidence of its truthfulness.

In this connection the strangest and most unaccountable thing of all is, that the discrepancy between the date of the crucifixion as given by the fourth Evangelist and that given by the synoptists, though, as we now think, so apparent, yet for many ages attracted little or absolutely no attention.* It has, indeed, been asserted that the discrepancy cannot have been real, and that the early Church must have been able, to her own satisfaction, to explain it as only an apparent discrepancy.   But the fact that the Church of later ages had lost this explanation and let both dates stand, leads to quite another conclusion, viz., that from first to last the Church was blind even to the appearance of discrepancy, or slurred it over because she was confident of the substantial truth of gospel history, and so shy of manifesting a captious or lukewarm spirit, as to be ready to receive both dates in the most naïve and uncritical spirit.   In the early period of her history the Church could not afford to lose the tide which was flowing in her favour by engaging in a critical investigation of the exact facts.   Nothing could have done more to arrest the movement than to let herself be involved in disputes about such, to her, apparently trivial matters.   The discrepancy here referred to is of a piece with others which exist generally between the fourth and the other Gospels : and when we see in this instance the metamorphosis which the Gospel underwent in its latest stage thus passing under our eyes, we can the more readily believe in the first or mythical stage of the metamorphosis which the evangelical tradition underwent before it reached the form in which it was fixed by the synoptists.   A metamorphosis which was accomplished intentionally, and at a single stroke by the force of genius in the one case, went on unconsciously and gradually by

---

* If we except the language of Apollinaris, Bishop of Hierapolis, who insists that the crucifixion took place on the 14th, because otherwise the Gospels would appear to be at variance.

slow increments in the other, at the hands of a multitude who were as one man, and swayed by the same great ideas.

According to the view here adopted, there were several stages in the metamorphic process. The starting point for the process was furnished by the actual facts of the life of Jesus, and the immediate impression made by these upon the minds of his disciples. These, however, have been so overlaid by mythical accretions that it is impossible for us now perfectly to recover them. The mythical, oral tradition of the life, was arrested in the course of its growth, and committed to writing by the first three Evangelists. Simultaneously with the mythical growth, came the Pauline-dogmatic conception of Christ's person and work, which may have indefinitely modified and coloured the oral tradition as it grew, and may have been a factor in the redacting process. For, there is a probability that even the *records* underwent revision ; and that they settled down into their canonical form many years after Paul had disseminated his doctrine far and wide. At the same time, we may remark, that the comparative absence of dogmatic elements in the synoptic Gospels is, to our mind, a proof that we have there a substantially correct reproduction or reminiscence of the *teaching* of Jesus at least ; a reminiscence of it, as of a thing so sacred and apart, and also so definite, as to resist the importation or intermixture of alien, or even of apostolic elements ; a proof also that the mythicizing process went on, to a large extent, independently of the dogmatic process, and was but little used as a vehicle for Pauline teaching. The attempts which have been made to show the contrary are highly ingenious, but not very convincing. The probability is, that the mythicizing and redacting tendency found room to play, chiefly, though not entirely, in imparting a transcendental or miraculous character to the *events*, and in making them typical of the religious experience with which the time was rife. The inimitable gnomic and parabolic form of the teaching would go far to protect its integrity. Interpolations, if made, would be merely illustrative, or paraphrastic; variations of words which Jesus had actually spoken ; and such variations, comparatively few in number, might be suggested partly by the dogma, in its attempt to secure a foothold or warrant in the authority of Jesus, and partly by the novel experience made by the

Church in apostolic and post-apostolic times of the working of the evangelic principle. The admitted facts of Christian experience would seem to warrant the anticipation of them in the teaching of Jesus, which may thus have been amplified and enriched. And lastly, after this revision of the tradition had run its course and come to a pause, the fourth Gospel made its appearance, as a reconstruction in one, both of the evangelic history and the Pauline dogma. For, while, as we have said, there is, in the synoptists, a comparative, if not a total absence of Christian dogma, the dogmatic or mystical element is, on the other hand, as conspicuous in the fourth Gospel as it is in St. Paul's epistles; and it is quite obvious that this Gospel is the composition of a man who, thoroughly acquainted with the Christology of St. Paul, and taking it for granted, has yet risen upon it as a stepping stone to another and higher Christology of his own. For the truth of this Christology he provides a warrant in a revised edition of gospel history, of which St. Paul knew nothing. It was thus made to appear, that this "great doctrinal gospel had been reserved to meet a later need of the Church, after men had been toned anew by the morality, and, above all, by the life of Jesus"; or, in the language of the Gospel itself, that the better wine had been kept until men had well drunk of the inferior wine of the new vintage.

For this, it appears to us, comes near to the real significance of the miracle at Cana of Galilee. In ancient and in modern times commentators have found in this miracle, a symbol of the novelty and of the renovating influence of Christianity which had come in place of the pithless elements of Judaism. But, without excluding such reference, it seems to us that, in this narrative, the Evangelist glances at the fact, notorious to all at the time, of the late *publication* of this Gospel, and of its late addition to the treasury of evangelical literature. He endeavours covertly to forestall or remove the suspicions to which this fact might give rise, by hinting that in this, as in other respects, the Gospel reverses or overturns the natural order of things. The miracle consisted in converting the water into wine, but the master of the feast knew nothing of the miracle, and only expresses his surprise that the wine served up at the end of the feast, being better than the wine already drunk, should, contrary to what was usual, have been kept " until now." These things are plainly an allegory. The wine first drunk was the synoptic version of Gospel history. The better wine that came last was the fourth Gospel. The former had not fully supplied the want of the Church. The wine which was " wanted " to supply the needs of the company had not been provided in time, because the " hour " for it was " not yet come "; but, unknown to the master of the feast, it had been provided in secret, and, when " set forth," had taken him by surprise. The narrative of this beginning of miracles is plainly a parable or allegory designed to answer beforehand any doubts to which the late appearance of the Gospel might give rise. The suggestion meant to be conveyed by the parable, that the Gospel had been reserved or " kept " for the later need of the Church, and only set forth when the need arose, was not the true account of it, though necessary to its reception. The simple truth concerning it was, that the need which had arisen to satisfy the Christian consciousness, or to smite down the prevailing Gnosticism, had called the Gospel into existence.

When not dominated by an apologetic spirit, historical criticism has been unable to assign for the publication of the fourth Gospel an earlier date than 120 or 130 A.D., and the difficulty is to conceive how a work, so remarkable in itself, presenting points of so much difference from the other records of the life of Jesus, and these so significant in their doctrinal bearings should, if it were of apostolic origin, have remained for so long in total or even comparative obscurity ; or how, on the other hand, if not adequately authenticated as apostolic, it could, at so late a date, have been accepted as such. Into this deeply interesting, but difficult inquiry, we shall not enter further than we have already done. Indeed, we shall leave the former alternative out of consideration, and, taking for granted that the Gospel was post-apostolic, produced in the age or decade during which it was published, or obtained notoriety, we shall only seek to account shortly for its all but unanimous reception as an apostolic work.

In the composition of his Gospel the Evangelist must have calculated and hoped that, notwithstanding the novelty of many of its materials and the lateness of its publication, this offspring of his genius would be received in the Church as a genuine record, by one of the original disciples, of the life of their Master. Nor is it difficult to condescend upon some of the grounds on which he may have based such an expectation. For example, it is probable that he may have calculated on the uncritical spirit of his fellow Christians, who were little curious as to the origin and authorship of any work which fell in with their dogmatic prepossessions and tended to the good of the Church, *i.e.*, to its consolidation and unity. It was only where the tendency of a work seemed to lie the other way that anything like criticism would be brought to bear upon its authorship. An abstract, dispassionate interest in such a question seems to have been wholly unknown. Indeed, the indifference of the ancient world generally to all questions of historical and literary criticism, and its apparent inability to discriminate between genuine and spurious writings, are, to the modern mind, almost inconceivable. The illustrations of this general indifference or inability that have been collected by German scholars are truly astounding. And there is abundant evidence that the Church of the second century shared to the full in this common failing. The one or two cases which have been made use of to prove the contrary are quite exceptional, and may be said rather to prove the rule. What little interest the Church took in critical questions was overpowered by the prevalent dogmatic bias. This bias was so strong as to create an indisposition to look very inquisitively into the authorship or historical accuracy of any work which made for the orthodox faith and fell in with the doctrinal tendencies of the age. When its contents, historical or doctrinal, appealed to the taste of the Church, no serious attempt was made to dispute its genuineness or its statement of facts, and, indeed, the principles of criticism were so little understood, and the critical apparatus was so limited, imperfect, and difficult of access, that a satisfactory investigation as to the age, authorship, and historical fidelity of a work was hardly possible to any, or only possible to a few ; and this circumstance went far to encourage the publication of pseudonymous writings and of narratives more or less coloured or fanciful, as a means either of recommending or discrediting views that were current. One of the great doctors of the age (Tertullian) laid down the principle, " a nobis quidem nihilominus rejiciendum est, quod pertineat ad nos," and this principle was so generally observed that its action might be counted upon by the writers of such works as we are speaking of. The fourth Gospel is not, there is reason to believe, the only book which, about the same time, gained credit in the Christian community under an apostolic pseudonym ; and it is not unlikely that the Evangelist may have been cognizant of this fact, and may have trusted that the same good fortune might befal his own work, as also, that any objections to it on the part of a small minority—such as were actually raised to it very soon by the Alogi—would be drowned in the general acclaim with which it would be welcomed.

But while the Evangelist might with reason calculate upon the uncritical spirit both without and within the Church, he took care to exercise his great powers of invention in order to impart that air of picturesque realism to his narrative, which is often of itself sufficient to invest the creations of fancy with the repute of history. He employs consummate art in obviating or overcoming the prejudice against his book, which might be stirred by those features of it, in which his Christological views had induced him to traverse the synoptic tradition. For this purpose he poses as a beloved disciple, who had enjoyed the most intimate confidences of his Master, and might be supposed to have had opportunities of information which none of the other disciples had enjoyed. And in this character he contrives to surround himself with an air of mystery which materially aids his design of imposing on the reader. The latter could hardly fail to surmise, or at least to have the suspicion suggested to him, that the author of the book is immediately or remotely identical with that " other disciple," who figures largely in it in company and in contrast with St. Peter, and that this disciple whom Jesus loved is the same as the St. John of the synoptists. John is never once mentioned by name, and the author studiously and meaningly keeps up his anonymity. But the veil is quite transparent, and there is a certain affectation and unreality in the seeming reserve and assumed coyness, which yet, however, served to stimulate curiosity and to impose upon the uncritical credulity of the reader. There is something like dexterous mystification. The Evangelist generally speaks of himself in the third person ; and once at least in the first ; at times it is left in doubt whether the beloved disciple is the writer, or is only the voucher for what is written by the

Evangelist. It is impossible not to think that this is done intentionally to wrap the nameless authorship in mystery and to defeat the objections, which might be drawn from the late publication of the work, to its apostolic authority. It was gratifying to every reader to be able, as he might suppose, to penetrate that reserve, to unravel that open secret, and to attribute the Gospel to one who seemed so little anxious to reveal himself. He was prepossessed in favour of the Gospel by observing that the author did not wish to intrude himself into notice, to put forward a claim to be an apostle, or to boast of his superior acquaintance with the less known, and hitherto unreported, unrecorded passages in the life and teaching of Jesus. His apparent reserve, or his seeming desire to conceal his personality, might even be construed as having some bearing or some probable, though obscure and intangible, connection with the late appearance of his Gospel and with its mysterious origin. And to readers such as those were, for whom the Gospel was primarily intended, who were already acquainted with the synoptic Gospels, the materials selected from these by the Evangelist, and freely but skilfully adapted to his purpose, and woven into a piece with the new materials supplied by his invention, would seem to impart a life-like reality and a character of historical fidelity to these latter, and would even stimulate the imagination of such readers to the congenial task of establishing to their own satisfaction the pragmatic unity of the several component elements, synoptic and original, of the new Gospel.*

* Much stress is laid by Bishop Lightfoot (*Biblical Essays*, p. 40) on the circumstance that the Evangelist never once mentions the Apostle John by name, and he regards it as affording a presumption that the book is the genuine production of that Apostle. For, he says, that on the supposition of forgery, it was a matter of vital moment that the book should be accepted as the work of its pretended author. But to this curious argument there is the obvious objection that the Gospel is only quasi-anonymous. It is the writer's manifest intention to be regarded as the Apostle, and he was probably led to adopt a quasi-anonymity because he saw that the previous Gospels were really anonymous. There is nothing in these themselves to betray their authorship—no claim to be written by those whose names were given to them by the Church. The Evangelist may have felt it to be expedient not to depart from the example thus set. But the anonymity in his case is not genuine, as in the case of the other three. And he betrays an anxiety to be taken for the Apostle which indirectly casts suspicion upon the apostolic authorship which he suggests.

Thus it may be seen that the Evangelist, in many ways, did all that consummate art could accomplish to secure the reception, by the Church, of his Gospel as a genuine record. And there were conditioning circumstances at the time, upon whose operation the Evangelist may or may not have calculated, which yet promoted his design. To some such we have already adverted, and need not do more here than refer to them. Such, for example, was the indisposition of the Church to question the genuineness or apostolic origin of any book which fell in with the current of its own thought and feeling, and the pressing urgency of the situation which made the recognition of some such book as this Gospel a necessity. Besides these, there has to be considered, the non-existence of any central authority within the Church, to which final appeal could be made in any case of disputed authorship, as well as the absence of all hostile criticism or censorship outside the Church; the difficulty of tracing to its author any book which was circulated privately for a time, and passed from hand to hand ; the wide dispersion of the Church through the Roman empire, in any province of which a new book might have had its origin without the cognizance of it in other provinces ; and the dread upon the mind of individuals of incurring the reproach of a lukewarm or sceptical spirit if they hesitated to receive as authentic a book which uttered the word for thoughts astir in the Church, and was helpful to the development of doctrine which was already in process. The natural effect of such conditioning circumstances would be that the book would be tacitly received without demur and be launched upon the world as the genuine work of the apostle whose name, if not prefixed to it, was yet suggested by it from beginning to end.

The specific feature of the fourth Gospel which, in spite of any misgivings to which its late and sudden appearance may have given rise, most of all disposed that generation to receive it as an authentic work of the Apostle John and a genuine record of the ministry of Jesus—the feature which most of all displayed the marvellous skill of its author, whoever he was, and contained the secret of its influence was, undoubtedly, the fact that it met the needs of the Church all round and supplied a common basis or platform on which Pauline and Gnostic Christians could unite, so as to avert that fatal disruption of the Church otherwise imminent. The Gnostic section was satisfied and reconciled to the orthodox or Pauline view by its presentation of this latter in the form of a higher gnosis. The Paulinists were more than satisfied with the form, at once more precise and mystical, which it gave to their Christological doctrine. To a Christological idea which, as may be seen from the Paulinistic epistles and from the earlier non-canonical writings, was struggling ineffectually for utterance in the Church, the fourth Evangelist was able to give adequate expression ; and it was because he did this, because he gave clear expression to an idea towards which the mass of Christians were feeling their way, that his Gospel found such ready welcome in the Church. They did not inquire critically or sceptically into the apostolic authenticity of a Gospel which, dropped opportunely, as it seemed, into their midst as by an invisible hand, supplied an evidence of what to them was a supreme truth, and put an end to all controversy about it. The astounding indifference and carelessness, or, may we not say, vehemence, with which society, or sections of it, accept and champion as truth, and without examination, whatever falls in with their preconceived ideas, or passionate prepossessions ; as well as the difficulty of arresting the circulation of false reports, and establishing the true version of current events, admit of illustration from the history of all ages, and not least from the history of the present time, notwithstanding the vigilance of the press and the rapid communication between one place and another. The higher intelligence, or better information of the few, is completely borne down by the weight of prejudiced, ill-informed, or interested popular opinion. And the application of this observation to the case now before us is obvious.

The revising process to which the Evangelist has subjected the gospel history, besides being radical and opportune, was conducted with a literary skill and an imaginative power, to which, confessedly, none of the known Christian authors of the second century can lay the slightest claim ; and many critics have considered it to be the very height of improbability that, in an age so comparatively barren of literary and artistic productiveness, there should have lived any unknown and nameless individual who could have composed this Gospel. They have

thus sought to add weight to the presumption that the authorship must be referred either directly or ultimately to St. John,
or to some other disciple who had enjoyed the benefit of divine
guidance through personal intercourse with the Founder of our
faith, or with some one of his immediate disciples. From what
has been said it will be seen that we are by no means disposed
to undervalue the marvellous character of the Gospel. But we
cannot go the length of regarding it as a more than natural
product of the human mind. It is not the only work whose
execution we should have deemed impossible, except for its
actual accomplishment. To impair the force of some of the
considerations just referred to, which have been advanced on
the apologetic side, it will be sufficient to name Tacitus and
Lucian, men of great genius, whose literary activity belongs to
the end of the first and the beginning or middle of the second
century, comparatively barren as that period otherwise was of
literary talent. We agree, besides, with a living writer in the
opinion that "any one generation has just the same chance of
producing some individual mind of first-rate calibre as any of
its predecessors" (Ruskin).

The freshness of the thought thrown by Christianity upon
the world was likely to call forth literary talent in isolated
individuals among its professors, more even than among the
non-Christian populations; and it is easy to believe that literary
genius, if it did awake, might not be eager to claim credit for
itself; might even be eager to remain in obscurity, satisfied
simply to contribute to the victory of the cause which it had at
heart. Of the ancient world generally we may assert that
literary fame was not an object of its ambition to the same
extent as it is in the modern world. An evidence of this
indifference to such fame may be seen in the fact that the
pseudepigraph was a form of composition so very common in
ancient times, and that men took little or no trouble to inquire
into the authenticity of the works which were in circulation.
And, if we may judge from such specimens of the pseudepigraph as the apocryphal book of Wisdom and the canonical
book of Daniel, it would seem as if men of a deeply religious
spirit had no scruple in employing their time and talents in the
composition of such works. Like many practices and habits
which the modern conscience condemns, this passed unchallenged in those ages. For conscience is a variable light;

and no more can in general be expected of men, however religious, than that they should be faithful to the light which they have, and act up to the standard of right which prevails around them.   The men who rise above this standard are the rare exceptions.   And one of the startling lessons which history teaches, is that men whose moral sense is not highly enlightened may yet be deeply conscientious, and that men may be capable of entire fidelity and devotion to some great cause before they have acquired a punctilious regard to truth and justice.   In an age which had loose notions as to the ends and objects of literature a man otherwise deeply moral and religious might not scruple to write under the disguise of a mask, and to recommend his work to the public by prefixing to it the name of some distinguished personage.   Certain it is that a considerable proportion of ancient literature seems to have been apocryphal or pseudonymous.   Not a few of our canonical books, both in the Old and the New Testaments, fall under this designation. And we regard the fourth Gospel as the most important and world-historical of all this species of literature.   In this connection, it should not be forgotten that the writer of the Epistle to the Hebrews, though hardly inferior in genius, is quite as unknown to us, even by name, as the fourth Evangelist himself. In assuming a disguise the Evangelist was actuated not merely by indifference to literary fame, but also by the fact that the avowal of his name as that of an unapostolic author removed from the events which he narrated, would have deprived his Gospel of that authority which was essential to the attainment of his object.

Whoever was the author of the Gospel, neither his literary skill nor the originality of his genius can be questioned.   He has at command an art which is above rule and defies imitation.   He has succeeded perfectly in his purpose, which was to invest the person of Christ with a mystical and transcendent character, fitted to take hold of the human mind, and to give boundless play to the devout imagination.   He has transfigured the tradition of the life of Christ from first to last, without blurring its features, and contrived to give a realistic air to the most ideal touches of his creation. The mystical or speculative background which gives the prevailing tone to the whole conception, only serves to throw up into higher relief the human traits which remain.   In achieving this result the Evangelist gives a proof of genius worthy of one who bears the highest name in literature. It has been remarked by Lessing that the heroes of Homer are represented by him as beings of a higher order by their actions, but as true men by their feelings; and just so is it with the Jesus of the fourth Gospel, divine and human nature being blended in him by a literary expedient of a like kind. In the raising of Lazarus his godlike nature is revealed, but his tears at the grave show him still to be very man. The Gospel is a unique creation, for which the elements were extant indeed in the concurrent or contemporaneous phases and tendencies of religious thought. But it was only a profoundly religious personality, a grandly imaginative mind, which could have discerned the possibilities of the situation, and have given organic unity to elements lying so far apart; and, without startling the judgment, or awakening the sense of incongruity, could have combined all these elements into a picture of such sober yet mystical beauty, and of such imposing verisimilitude; one too, so observant of all the requirements of the problem. We cannot but regard it as a supreme stroke of genius by which he has achieved the feat, which we should otherwise have deemed impossible, of combining " fundamentally different portraits into one stereoscopic image." Given the postulate of the supernatural, together with the Logos-idea, and that composite figure might have passed without challenge to the end of time. It is only in an age like the modern, which no longer grants that postulate, and no longer suffers its critical faculty to be curbed by allegiance to a merely speculative idea, that men have had the courage to face the problem, and to question whether such a combination could exist anywhere but in the realms of fancy, in the chambers of devout imagination, and whether, in fact, the portraiture of the Christ be not a creation of the same kind as the heroes and demigods of antiquity, though of a more deeply ethical and profoundly spiritual cast, and therefore better calculated, permanently, to enchain and sway the minds of men.

The Evangelist could not indulge his speculative and idealizing tendency of thought—which is but another name for the impulse to reach towards the universal and absolute idea, without at the same time seeking to remove from Christ the last remaining vestiges of the limited and specifically Jewish character of his Messiahship or divine mission. The Evangelist saw in him, personally and visibly concentrated, the manifestation of God, which is otherwise so dispersed and diffused through all creation as to be, for most men, inappreciable. Hence he assigns to him a position of absolute significance, independent of, and prior to, all Jewish relations, " Before Abraham was, I am " ; and represents him as the divine agent in the creation of the world ; as the source of reason and of prophecy, wherever these had existed among men ; and as the Light and Life which lightened every man, Jew or Gentile, who came into the world. By his dogma of the incarnated Logos, the Evangelist thus laid a speculative and deeper foundation for the universalism of Christianity than could be laid by St. Paul from his practical point of view. The universalism of the Evangelist rested on a speculative, *i.e.*, a hypothetically objective basis; that of St. Paul on a subjective, and, therefore, precarious basis. Modern theologians have seen this, and when they would vindicate the universalism of Christianity, they dwell less upon the Pauline doctrine of the unconditional freeness of the gospel invitation, than upon the grand Johannine doctrine of the Light which lighteth every man, and of that spirit of good which stirs in every bosom. The Logos-idea may be regarded simply as a higher gnosis which was needed to prevent the men of that age from indulging in the " dangerous questionings of the systematizing intellect," from deviating into fields of speculation abhorrent to the nature of Christianity and intruding, beyond what was necessary for Christian faith, into things which they had not seen, *i.e.*, things of which they knew and could know nothing from experience, or from any other source (see Colossians ii. 18).

By its application to Christ, this idea invested his person with a surpassing and transcendent mystery, the reason why men of a mystical and contemplative turn of mind have in all ages had recourse to the fourth Gospel for satisfaction ; whereas the means for supplying the practical religious needs of men have been sought by the Church at large rather in the teaching of Paul. And if the corrosive action of free thought, and the dissolving power of the idea have not, as yet, been able to turn away men's minds from Christianity in its supernatural aspect, and from the heterosoteric doctrine, common both to Paul and John, it is greatly owing to the mystical theological haze in which the latter has wrapped up the whole subject, and which, while obscuring its outlines, has also raised it into a region which baffles thought in all attempts to examine it more carefully. The effect of this supreme gnosis seems to have been magical, for if the Gnostic sects did not immediately disappear before it, they at least very soon ceased to be a source of alarm to the Church.

To understand how the conception of this remarkable book could have originated in the mind of a Christian of the second century, we have only to take into account the very serious conjuncture in the history of the Church, which synchronized with its appearance. The application of the current Logos-idea to the Christ was an opportune development, or, let us say, an emended edition of the Paulinistic Christology; which, to a prophetic, wakeful mind, imbued with that Christology, but alarmed by the progress of the Gnostic heresy, was already at the door—an urgent necessity of the hour. The Gospel was but the outcome of an impulse to take a final step of doctrine, by which the Paulinistic, *i.e.* the anti-Gnostic dogma might acquire secure and undisputed possession of the mind of the Church. In working out his conception, the Evangelist represents Jesus as advancing claims to be the Life and Light of men—claims never attributed to him in the synoptic tradition, but which were readily accepted as utterances of his, because they so perfectly expressed, or foreshadowed, the marvellous experiences of the early Church; and, being so accepted, were calculated ultimately, if not immediately, to arrest the Gnostic movement. And the miracles, which he represents Jesus as performing, were so manifestly symbolical of his claims, that they might be regarded by him as spiritually, if not literally, performed. And might not such representations seem to be lawful to the Evangelist himself, who, doubtless, expressed his own view of this matter in those words of his Christ: " It is the spirit that quickeneth ; the flesh profiteth nothing : the words that I speak unto you, they are spirit, and they are life " (John vi. 63).

All along, the factor in the Christian consciousness which was most powerfully operant and determinant of the line of dogmatic development, was the tendency or craving to exalt and glorify the person of Christ. This tendency formed a point of union for the entire Christian community, however divergent might be the views held among them on some points. And now, as if satisfied that the faith once delivered to them admitted of no better definition than was given to it in the fourth Gospel, and that the Christian sentiment had there found its adequate expression, the great majority sought to intrench themselves in the position thus acquired, and to establish, as the rule of faith for themselves, and their successors in all time coming, those Scriptures which were in the line of this development, and had led up to this point. The formation of the canon and the emerging idea of the Catholic Church thenceforth went on together. All internal conflicts were decided more and more by appeal to Scriptures, which were thus rising to be canonical. The limits of speculation were drawn closer : confined, as it were, to circumscribed and consecrated ground. In fact, the fourth Gospel is manifestly so fitted to effect these results as to afford a strong presumption that, had it been in existence at the earlier date which has been assigned to it, the Gnostic heresy might never have arisen to trouble the peace, or to disturb the equanimity of the Church. The proposition that the Catholic Church was founded on a compromise between conflicting sects or conflicting interpretations of the Christian consciousness, receives confirmation from the course of our remarks. The unity of the Christian world was preserved, first of all, by a compromise between the Jewish and Gentile sections of it, or, we may rather say, by the growth of a form of doctrine less antinomistic than that of St. Paul ; of a form which may be traced in the later or Paulinistic epistles; and we have just seen that it was once again preserved by the compromise between Paulinism and Gnosticism effected by the fourth Gospel, but a compromise which, in reality, was also a development of the Hellenistic elements of the Pauline doctrine. It was only opinions or practices which were thought to be so eccentric and out of harmony with the Christian consciousness as to be incapable of being assimilated or taken up by it, that were declared heretical, and the adherents of which were excluded from the great Christian communion.

Before quitting our remarks on the fourth Evangelist, we have yet to note that as he conceived the divine energy to be hypostatized in the Logos, and incarnated in Christ, so also he conceived of the spirit of Christ, the God-man, in its self-impartation to the believer, as impersonated in the Holy Spirit, thus laying the foundation for the metaphysical trinity of Catholic dogma. It appeared to him as if the sympathy awakened in believers with the sufferings of Christ, and the powerful attraction exerted on them by his manner of life, was the overflow of the spirit of Christ, disengaging itself from him and imparting itself as a personal energy to them. The idea thus arose of a Holy Spirit as a distinct personal entity, so as to constitute with the Father and the Son a triad or trinity. Of St. Paul it may be said 'that he has the germ of this doctrine of a personal spirit in his epistles; in which orthodox theologians have been able to trace many indications of it. Certainly, however, he speaks of the Holy Spirit with apparent indecision, and, at the most, presents the orthodox doctrine in an inchoate or embryonic stage. The probability is, that the Apostle himself was quite aware of his uncertainty on the sub-ject, and quite satisfied to have it so. The same uncertainty concerning the spiritual agents of the divine will was a feature of the rabbinical teaching with which St Paul was familiar. According to that teaching, as set forth by Weber, there were ministering or angelic spirits of a personal and self-subsisting nature ; and there were others of a semi-personal order, which came and went, appeared and vanished, with the special missions on which they were sent, and apart from which they had no separate existence. There were spirits who could assume a visible shape and lay it aside at pleasure. And there were beings who hovered on the confines of reality, emanations from the divine power, which never enjoyed an independent existence. The conception of such agencies seems to have been common to oriental, classical, and Scandi-navian mythologies, as well as to rabbinical theology ; and it appears to us that St. Paul's conception of the Holy Spirit partook of the same character, for it cannot be gathered from his epistles that he distinctly recognized the Holy Spirit as a personal being. But the fourth Evangelist states broadly and explicitly what St. Paul's language may suggest. He repre-sents Jesus as speaking of the Spirit as another comforter like himself, but a better ; to admit of whose coming it was expedient that he himself should go away and absent himself from the company of his disciples ; another like himself and, therefore, a person, and not an impersonal energy. According to John xiv. 16, Christ himself is the Paraclete first in order, a designation which had been originally applied to the Logos by Philo, so that it affords a striking proof, among the many others, of the derivation by the Evangelist of the Logos-idea from the Hellenistic source. The Holy Spirit, being the other or the second Paraclete, ranks with the Logos, and becomes a third member of the heavenly hierarchy, distinct and personal like Christ himself. But of this distinctive doctrine of the Evangelist there is no hint or trace in Philo. That living, personal spirit, remains henceforth in the faith of the Church, the source or medium of an incalculable force or energy in the spiritual life and experience of all whose faith brings them within the sphere of his influence. He is the channel through which divine help descends to reinforce the efforts of the believer in his conflict with evil; the heavenly messenger whose office is to guide believers into all truth, *i.e.*, into the proper understanding of the truth already revealed, and into the discovery of new truth ; a view of his office which might be understood to explain the transformation which the evangelical tradition had undergone in the new Gospel.*

This doctrine of the personality of the Holy Spirit was in keeping with the general tendencies inherent in the growing dogma, and took immediate effect in Montanism, which, however, is a development, or phenomenon, which we choose to consider as lying beyond the limits of this discussion. For it seems to us, that the uncertainty which still rests upon the date of the Gospel makes it hazardous to say

---

* It is not easy to reconcile what Jesus is made to say respecting the dependence of the coming of the Spirit upon his own going away (John xvi. 7, comp. vii. 39) with what is said in Luke xi. 13, that God will give the Spirit without restriction to them that ask Him. We are inclined to see here an example of the advance of the fourth Evangelist beyond the synoptic tradition, and of the freedom with which he sets aside the latter in order to impart significance and consistency to his own doctrine. Chapter vii. 39 may be an interpolation, and seems to show that the writer of it was aware of the difficulty, and sought to overcome it by drawing a distinction between the spirit in general and the Holy Spirit, the Comforter which should be given after Christ was glorified. "This spake he of the spirit, which they that believe on him should receive ; for the Holy Ghost was not yet given because that Jesus was not yet glorified."

what view is to be taken of certain affinities which exist between it and the Montanistic movement. The operation and indwelling within us of a spirit, which is not of us, is an idea which we may, or may not, be able to reconcile with the inviolable autonomy and individuality of the human spirit. But we have here, at least, all the elements of the complete orthodox or trinitarian system laid ready to hand for patristic and scholastic manipulation. In the resulting orthodox theology it was made to appear that Pauline doctrine was an anticipation of the " Johannine," and that the latter supplied a canon for the interpretation of the former; in other words, that they were the complementary parts of one organic whole, which had gradually unfolded itself. The affinity between the trinitarian system and what is called the philosophical trinity is an imagination of modern theology which has little to recommend it. Indeed, these two have as little affinity as can well be imagined, and we may truly say of them that they have " nothing but the name in common."

CHAPTER XX.

CONCLUSION.

HAVING arrived at this point, it is unnecessary to trace the development of Christian doctrine further. It does not lie in our intention, or within the scope of this essay to do so. In conceiving of the death of Jesus as an atonement for the sin of the world—as the inauguration of a great redemptive process, St. Paul took an irrevocable step, far-reaching in its consequences, and broke away from the autosoteric doctrine of Jesus himself. Of this central doctrine all his other dogmas were but inevitable corollaries. By this same doctrine, he supplied a starting point for the symbolism of Christian worship, and an object round which all devout sentiments and emotions, all feelings of awe and tenderness, could play without reserve, so that human sympathies could be enlisted and consecrated to the service of religion. The fourth Evangelist did little beyond supplying, by means of the Logos-idea, a needful definition, a speculative basis, and a mystical character to the practical dogma of St. Paul. The eschatology of the New Testament, not being deduced or deducible from the *experience* either of Jesus or Paul, or of any human being, was probably very much determined or suggested by the inherited and current eschatological views of the age ; * and the doctrine of the sacraments of the

---

* The vulgar, orthodox idea of the occupations in a future state of those who die in the faith is chiefly drawn from the Apokalypse, which there is considerable reason to believe is mainly a Jewish writing. In all that is said on the subject in the gospels and epistles, the ethical element predominates, and heaven is represented generally as a state of bliss. But in the Apokalypse the limits of a wise decorum are passed and exceeded by the sensuous and ritualistic aspect of the state.

Church probably grew up in apostolic times, and in the succeeding age, in the light of practical needs and requirements. They were autochthonic rites or observances for which the mythicizing fancy, after its nature, invented a historical institution and a symbolical meaning. The Church itself, radically considered, was but the association of men who were naturally drawn together for mutual support and by the bond of the common faith, and may be regarded as a divine institution, in the sense that all things really founded in human nature are also divine. The genesis of doctrine becomes more uncertain as we recede from the central doctrine, round which it all gathered and arranged itself with more or less consequence. And the successive steps by which Pauline dogma gradually took the more and more definite and orthodox shape, is matter of ecclesiastical history, in whose records we see human reason and unreason at work to produce the result.

As the difference is great between the teaching of Jesus and the dogma of St. Paul, so also is the difference great between the latter and the patristic and scholastic theology of later times. The difference between Pauline and scholastic dogma may here be briefly indicated. (1) The dogma of St. Paul was the interpretation of his own religious experience, mainly by means of Jewish categories of thought, and in a less degree by Hellenistic speculation. In a manner relevant to the thought of the age, St. Paul constructed and developed his dogma only so far as was necessary to explain, reflect, and symbolize his own personal experience considered as the effect of the death and resurrection of Christ, and of his interposition generally in behalf of guilty man. So constructed and developed, the dogma was fitted to be an engine for producing a like experience in the minds of others. And by his powerful dialectic the Apostle so deepened the channel of thought, by which these two, the dogma and the spiritual experience, were connected, that the passage from the one to the other becomes easy, and all but inevitable. Beginning with a like experience, men fall almost inevitably into the dogma ; or beginning with the dogma, they may end with the experience. The terminus *ad quem* of the Apostle, becomes the terminus *a quo* of the Christian people, or *vice versa*. Pædagogically, the advantage of the dogma is great; for while it veils the thought, it also renders the thought more level to popular apprehension, and for many minds, perhaps, more impressive. Paul made no attempt to construct a complete and consistent system of theological thought. The practical bearing of his theology absorbed his entire interest, and he did not, any more than Jesus, examine the presuppositions on which it was built. His dogma was fluid and his thought abounds with antinomies, which find their solution not in the thought, but in the experience of believers. But (2) scholastic theologians, overlooking these facts, took his doctrines as so many counters of thought, and made it their endeavour to construct, by deduction and combination, a rigid system, a complete theory of the universe; a key by which to decipher the intentions of Providence, to read its secrets, and to explain human life and destiny—in short a system, much of which had no traceable, or only a conventional bearing on life and practice, and which in the end, from its manifest collision with psychological law, and the growing experience and speculation of the race, the present age has found to be no longer tenable. Still the Christian consciousness and experience, founded on the few simple ideas of Jesus which suggested, and still underlie the dogma, is the main thing, surviving, more or less, under all the conflicting systems which have been built upon the Pauline foundation. And it is in virtue of that consciousness alone, so far as it does survive, and not in virtue of either this or that form of the dogma, and least of all in virtue of our faith in the supernatural nature of Christianity, that we are still justified in calling ourselves Christians. We agree with Dr. Reville, in expressing a conviction that religion among civilized men is for ever destined to advance in the same direction which the gospel gave it, eighteen hundred years ago, "Either man will cease to be religious, or he will find himself compelled to be, in a certain measure, Christian." The conclusion here expressed by Dr. Reville may seem to be very indefinite, but not a few who are qualified by an extensive study of the critical data, for forming a judgment on the subject, will duly appreciate the mingled caution and decision with which he forecasts the religion of the future.

In tracing the genesis of Christianity and endeavouring to
show that it almost immediately assumed a form not
contemplated by its founder, we have not, as much as we
might have done, fortified our various positions, by pointing
out the correspondences presented in the history of other
religions. By way of making up for this omission, we may
here briefly call attention to the very striking analogies
between the genesis and history of Islam, and those of
Christianity, analogies all the more striking by reason of
the very different levels on which the two religions stand.
Like the latter, the former, according to the most competent
authorities, was to a large extent " the product not of the
time, or of the people, but of the personality of its founder,"
though neither of the two founders professed to be the
author of a new religion. The Arabian prophet did not lay
claim to supernatural rank, or to a mediatorial office ; indeed
he protested against anything of the kind strongly, because
he knew that a danger lay in that direction, owing to the
polytheistic tendencies of his countrymen. But hardly was
he in his grave before his followers began to pay him
adoration, and to supplicate his intercession with Allah in
their behalf; and in due time, this was followed up by two
phenomena or developments : Cufism or the Mahometan
form of mysticism ; and a dogmatic system, which was
carried out, it is said, with as much elaboration and acumen
as the dogmatic system of the Catholic Church itself, and
dealing very much with the same questions, metaphysical,
soteriological, and theological. The analogy with the
development of Christianity seems to be complete. And
if Jesus did not, like Mahomet, warn his followers against
the idolatry of himself, it was simply because he, a pure
monotheist, living in the midst of pure monotheists, saw no
need for such a caution. Islam is still a vital force
in the world ; but so far as we know, both Cufism and
Mo'tazilitism have long lost their hold, being no true developments of Islam and foreign to its nature. And the same
fate seems surely to await the corresponding developments
in the Christian Church ; no true and living interest attaching
to either of them ; while the influence of Christianity, as the
religion of Jesus, shows no signs of abatement.

If it shall appear to the reader, that we have treated the

historical data of the New Testament with unbecoming or unwarrantable freedom, let us remind him, that the synoptic Gospels are the only records which so much as profess to furnish materials for the life of Jesus ; for, besides other reasons for saying so, even the fourth Evangelist himself, in acknowledging (xx. 31) that he has another and a dogmatic object in view, goes far to withdraw any profession of the kind : and the synoptic Gospels are of such a nature, that they do not enable us to construct the actual life of Jesus. We cannot handle them as inspired records, or even as historical documents ; but simply as mythical histories, from which we may, at most, deduce the general outline of his life, as well as that system of morality and religion which has been the possession of humanity since his time, and which, as we have plainly shown that St. Paul cannot have been its author, we cannot but ascribe to Jesus. The supernatural element, which enters so largely into the synoptic narratives, cannot possibly be eliminated, except by a sifting process involving an extensive dislocation and disturbance of the general history. This eliminating process we have sought to carry out faithfully and thoroughly ; for we do not belong to the mediating or " half and half " school of theologians, who, to state it shortly, endeavour to effect a compromise with the scientific conscience by minimizing that element, leaving Jesus in possession of miraculous powers, but within narrow and indefinite limits ; or ascribing to him a certain superhuman personality, while denying to him the power of performing superhuman acts : confounding in him the human and the divine, the finite and the infinite, and attributing to him the function of bringing to pass in his disciples a like blending of the human and divine. By thus seeking to mediate between the natural and the supernatural view of Christianity, this school only betrays the weakness of its convictions, and its endeavour to sit upon two stools.

No permanent advantage is ever gained by adopting a principle and then evading its consequences. Under pretext of disengaging the inward meaning from the outward form of dogma, or by way of making the latter less obnoxious to modern thought, some of the advanced schools of theology seek to get rid, or in reality lose hold of what is essential to the dogma, without apparently perceiving or without acknowledging the fact. In stretching the dogma to meet the modern thought, it has somewhere been said that they snap the connection with the supernatural ground. No doubt the dogma has an inward meaning, for it is the form in which the Christian consciousness or religious experience seeks to express or explain itself; but to fall back upon that inward meaning and to retain it alone is not only to discard the dogmatic form, but to let go the supernatural sanction. And all attempts of this kind do but furnish a proof that this same supernatural element, which, in the first and for many succeeding ages, served to inspire men with awe, and even to strengthen the claims of Christianity upon their belief, not only is, but is felt to be an insurmountable objection to it for the modern mind. On the other hand, if we deny the supernatural origin and character of Christianity, it is incumbent on us to show, as we have attempted to do, that natural laws and historical conditions are sufficient to account for both. And if we believe that nature itself is divine, Christianity will lose nothing by such a construction.

That the divine power was present, immanent in the life of Jesus, as well as in that long line of lawgivers, prophets, and sages, who prepared the way before him : that it is mysteriously present in all history, ancient and modern, secular and religious, we do not question. We believe that in Jesus that divine power found its most polished instrument and reached its highest and purest expression ; but that is a true observation which some one, we think, has made, that of not one moment of his life, of not one of his acts can it be said, " Lo, here is something above nature." It is only through nature without or within us that God manifests Himself. That, in this divine immanence, there is a great mystery, transcending all human or finite thought, conception, or power of representation, we admit. And we have a strong suspicion, that it is the irrepressible endeavour to form to ourselves some sensuous representation, some intellectual conception of this great mystery : to comprehend the incomprehensible, and to utter the inexpressible, which has given rise to the dogmatic systems of all the great religions of the world. These, wherever thought is active, have necessarily only a transient hold upon men's minds.

The intellect may shift uneasily from one form of dogma to another, and may oscillate between competing systems ; but in the end it will throw all aside and find repose in a more simple faith, such as glowed in the mind of Jesus ; a faith whose proof does not lie outside, but in the depths of the human consciousness. The only mystery of which men will never get rid, is the all-encompassing mystery of the universe, which we cannot penetrate : the mystery which has defied, and will for ever defy all the efforts of human intelligence to solve : a mystery which exhibits no tendency even towards solution, but grows and deepens upon us the more we reflect and ponder over it. In the presence of this mystery, we can only bow the head and say, " Verily, thou art a God that hidest thyself." Of the presence and action of this mysterious power, we regard the evolution of the religious idea, through the long history of Judaism and Christianity, as the most signal proof. And it is by the purification of this idea, and especially, by its disengagement from the supernatural hypothesis, that this proof will gain in strength.

If we conceive of the divine power as entering as a distinct, supernatural element into Christianity, or into the person of its founder and of his disciples, the character of mystery would for us be gone. In becoming distinct and separate, it would become a finite factor along with others without being mysterious ; which is something inconceivable. We believe, on the contrary, that mystery is common to all existence ; and that the pre-eminent glory of Christianity consists, not in clearing the area of religion from mystery in the sense now indicated ; but in revealing to us that ideal of humanity which our own deepest instincts recognize as the true ideal, and in giving us practical helps and encouragements to choose it as the earnest and not wholly fruitless aim of our life and aspirations. We do not seek by our view of its genesis to banish mystery from the origin of Christianity. We say, that the mystery consists in that self-subsisting independence which enabled Jesus to rise above his surroundings, so that the religious element into which he was born could not vanquish it ; and in the spontaneous generation in his mind of a higher view of the religious relation than that which prevailed among his countrymen.

But this is a mystery, which, however great, is yet the same in kind as that which obtains more or less at every point of human progress and development; unique, but not exceptional in the history of religion. After we have put aside the supernatural element of the evangelical history, Jesus still rises before us as the teacher and finest model of humanity, and the value of his doctrine is unimpaired. He remains for all time the living canon of humanity, by which the religious man has to shape and mould himself. We have seen how this living canon grew by the fashioning of many hands, and it still lives and grows; hardly an age but has added some touch to its perfection, and few will doubt that a new touch has been given to it in these latter days by the author of *Ecce Homo*, in attributing to him "the enthusiasm of humanity." The advancing thought of man gathers round that august figure, and exalts it ever more to the soul, so that it fashions the generations by which it is fashioned, and gathers into itself all the growing thought and experience of man, and conserves it for generations yet unborn. Jesus appears to us not less great, not less fitted to awaken our sympathy and veneration, though we see him working no miracle, and though our view of him as suspended on the cross were the last that was seen of him. It was, we conceive, the memory of his teaching, and the contemplation of his dying moments, in which he gave the supreme proof of his devotion to the will of God, and to the good of man, that revived the faith of the first disciples; that convulsed the soul of Paul, and conjured up to his inner eye, the vision of him as once more alive, encompassed with a light above that of the sun at noon; and we believe also that the moral greatness and beauty revealed in him is the sight, which, above all others, sustains the hope of man. For, above all the spectacles which this earth has ever presented, it is that which confirms our hope, as it did that of St. Peter and his companions, that the plant of humanity, which could put forth such a "consummate flower," is not meant to perish.

In attempting to offer a modern view of the genesis and early development of Christianity in place of the canonical view of it, we have been obliged to introduce a pragmatism which may be wearisome to most, and at many points not

satisfactory to any of our readers.   But we would ask them to
remember two things—first, that this is pre-eminently one of
those cases in which, as Dr. Baur points out, the separate
members of a construction, when looked at in themselves, may
appear to be doubtful, or unimportant, or not very cogent, but
may derive support and significance from the unity and consistency of the whole ; and secondly, that we do not insist on the
exclusive validity of this pragmatic element.   We only present
it as that which best satisfies, or most readily suggests itself to
our own mind.   Much of the ground over which we have
travelled may be debatable, in regard to which the critics
have not yet spoken the last word ; but the book may stand as
a whole, and the same general result may be arrived at, though
some of the minor details may be differently stated.   It
may be that some other recast or reconstruction of the evangelical history may approve itself to others, who may adopt the
same general point of view with ourselves.   But one thing is
certain, that if the supernatural element, according to our
hypothesis, did not enter as an integer into the actual current
of that history, but was introduced or inwoven by the mythicizing tradition, the genesis of Christianity must have differed
widely, nay, enormously, from that which can possibly be
gathered from a literal or textual exegesis, and an unsceptical
study of the New Testament.   The genesis, as we endeavour
to trace it, can only be regarded as a theory or hypothesis to
explain the outstanding facts, or as an approximation more or
less to the secret underlying history.   In the nature of the
case, and in the absence of documentary records of such a
history, it can be nothing else.   It can only be offered as the
possible, more or less probable or conjectural, but hardly as the
actual history.   Still, for the intelligent and scientific reader
this will be no objection to the attempt here made, provided
the theory or conjecture suffice to take up and to account for
all the outstanding facts, including what has been called the
great "posthumous miracle of Jesus," viz., the beneficent and
permanent results of his life-work.   Let it be our apology for
this undertaking that the state of modern thought regarding the
supernatural seems to demand that some such attempt should
be made.   The genesis of Christianity is a fact of which the
supernatural explanation is assailed on all sides, but the fact
in all its gravity remains, and if we refuse to accept the

orthodox explanation, we are bound to offer another. And
even if this task, to which we have addressed ourselves, be not
only unskilfully executed, but even erroneous in its conception,
yet the toleration of such hypotheses, and their candid consideration is, as has been often remarked, the price which the
Church has to pay for the preservation of a scientific interest in
the history of our religion, and for a deepening acquaintance
with its spirit.

By many it may be regarded as a great moral delinquency,
or daring impiety, to shock or unsettle, by such a criticism as
has been applied in this volume, the minds of simple Christians who live by it, and find it to be the great source of
strength for the duties, and of consolation under the trials of
life. But it has to be borne in mind that something is due to
the inquiring and educated classes of the community, to whom
religion is not a mere luxury, but as much a necessity as it is
to the ignorant and credulous. There is no doubt that a
deeply religious sentiment may even yet be fostered both by
Catholicism and by orthodox Protestantism; but they will
cease more and more to serve this purpose, in proportion as
men are compelled by the advance of science and of scientific
criticism, to abandon the naïve or ancient theory of divine
government; and there are many ominous signs that this process is already far advanced. " Outside the pale of the so-
called religious world, and firmly resolved never to enter it,
there are thousands of men, not inferior (to those inside the
pale) in character, capacity, or knowledge of the questions at
issue, who estimate the purely spiritual elements of the Christian faith as highly as these do, but will have nothing to do
with the Churches, because in their apprehension, and for them
the profession of belief in the miraculous, on the evidence
offered, would be simply immoral." Such is the testimony of a
man (Professor Huxley) who is entitled to speak for the large
class to which he belongs. For them the offence of the cross
is not moral, but, what is still more insurmountable, intellectual.
Their objection is to the gospel regarded as a supernatural
system. Whether this offence—this objection, can be removed
and the gospel yet remain a power of God for the higher
education of the race, is a question which ought not and
cannot be set aside; for if it be set aside, nothing can thereby
be gained for the cause of religion. According to the same

authority, scepticism and unbelief are advancing " with continually accelerated velocity" among the educated and scientific
classes, and are from them rapidly " descending to the uneducated, or those who have but a smattering of science and
theology." The evil day, if such it be, is already upon us, and
can no longer be averted, and there is little or no prospect of
an age of faith ever returning. Periods of scepticism and
unbelief in the past have doubtless been succeeded by a general
and perceptible return to orthodoxy; but this was owing partly
to the fact that the constancy of the natural order was not
generally accepted, and that sceptics and unbelievers, being in a
small minority, were unable to maintain their ground against
the overwhelming mass and power of vulgar pathos and prejudice in favour of orthodox opinion : whereas in this age, for
the first time these eighteen hundred years, all is changed—
the scientific idea has permeated popular literature, and both
together are at work in almost every household, spreading
doubt and scepticism on every side; so that the cause of
orthodoxy, in the widest sense of the word, will soon cease to
have the power of numbers on its side, and be " deprived of the
support to the imagination which an age of faith afforded."
The time has come when, as was recently declared by a great
Conservative statesman, reaction or stationariness in political
affairs is no longer possible; and the same may be said in
respect of theological thought. Were the spread of views such
as those here expounded to call forth a reaction towards orthodoxy, it would only be as the reflux of the wave in the flowing
tide; and it seems as if the only means of saving the Christian
profession—of making good its claim to the continued allegiance of men, and of preserving those moral and spiritual
elements with which it is instinct, is to sacrifice its miraculous
elements, and to recognize it as the absolute form of natural
religion, with Jesus Christ as its High Priest and bright
Exemplar. When this is accomplished, religion will become
a very simple matter; and he will be seen to be the true Christian who, believing in God as his Heavenly Father, confides in
His forgiveness of the sins that are past, and in this confidence
aims at the ideal life of Jesus, leaving the rest to the disposal
of God.

Our endeavour has been to present a view of Christianity
alternative to the orthodox or canonical conception of it as a

supernatural system.   We have done our best to be just to this alternative view—that is, to state the case for it as well as we could, hardly, indeed, in the hope of carrying conviction to many minds, but trusting, at the most, that we have succeeded in showing that, if this be the true view of it, Christianity does not forfeit its claim to be, in a very proper sense, a revelation to the mind of man, entitled to man's reverence as a directory of human life on its moral and religious side.   If we have presumed to undertake a great task with inadequate resources, it may at least be said that the task has not been self-imposed, but imposed, as we have shown, by the circumstances and necessities of the time.   And if, in the performance of this task, we have relied upon certain conclusions of modern criticism, literary and historical, which have not commanded universal assent, we have done so, at least not blindly, nor without discrimination, inasmuch as we have tested them to the best of our ability.   All or most of these results have been arrived at by specialists, without immediate reference to the general question of the origin and nature of Christianity; and the remark is obvious, that the fact, if it be the fact, that by their means we have succeeded in establishing a coherent and not unworthy conception of Christianity, different from that to which the uncritical or pseudo-critical study of the Scriptures has led men, affords of itself a strong presumption that these results are in the main trustworthy.

APPENDIX.

APPLICATION OF THE THEORY OF ANTI-SUPERNATURALISM TO THE CHRISTIAN DOGMA.

HAVING, in the second chapter of this volume, discussed the anti-supernatural hypothesis or theory of the divine action, it behoves us to determine how much of the orthodox or scriptural system must be sacrificed to conciliate the modern, *i.e.*, the scientific spirit. And it is clear that if we really and seriously accept of that theory, we have no choice but to discard, one by one, what are usually styled the distinctive, cardinal dogmas respecting the person and functions of the Founder of Christianity. And, first of all, we must discard the dogma of the incarnation, which lies at the base of the orthodox system. We must take Jesus to have been by nature, and to have remained, from first to last, a member pure and simple of the human family: a link of the human chain, just as any of ourselves are, having all the properties of human nature, but those of no other: one whose native faculty and character were, to the same extent with those of other men, the product of his ancestry and of his surroundings, and whose life and work went to determine and to influence the life and history of subsequent generations. We take him to have been a man and the son of a man; and if we adopt the phraseology of calling him a divine man, we do so, not as implying that he is exclusively entitled to that designation. We may hold, and we do hold, that by his spiritual and ideal nature, man is kin to the divine; that there is a spark or germ of divinity in each member of the race, and that that germ is part of his natural constitution. We may also hold that in the man Jesus this germ reached a conspicuous manifestation or high development, so high and so conspicuous as to arrest the attention and draw the veneration of many who witnessed his manner of life. But we may hold so much without admitting that he was divine in any exclusive superhuman, or supernatural sense. We say that he was a man in all respects, and nothing but a man—a member of the great human brotherhood. And in saying so we do not feel that we do injury to our religion, or shake our faith in God. It is impossible for us to enter into the feeling of one of our present-day theologians, who has said, " As regards the divinity of Christ, I can only say that without that I have no religion and no God." A more wild and hazardous avowal can hardly be conceived, and can only be explained as the utterance, on the part of a truly Christian man, of a passing phase of feeling. For, unless Christianity rests upon the doctrines of natural religion, what is it but a baseless fabric floating in the cloudland of human fancy? Very different, indeed, was the view of so old a divine as Richard Baxter, who, if we remember aright, somewhere says that the truths of natural religion are more certain to his mind than those of Scripture; as indeed they must be for us all, if they are, as they are, the presuppositions of the latter. Whatever becomes of the distinctive doctrines of Christianity, let us at least hold fast, on independent grounds, the truths of natural religion.

While we readily acknowledge the relative innocence or sinlessness of Jesus, we are also compelled to deny his absolute innocence; because the latter is incompatible with the theory of moral development through the consciousness and experience of evil, and with the nature of a finite being such as we believe him to have been. We cannot say of one who was liable to temptation, as he was, that he was also absolutely sinless. We may unite the two predicates in words, but not in idea, nor in fact. If Jesus was absolutely without sin he was not a true man; just as, if liable to temptation, he was not true God: for it is irrefragable that God can neither be tempted, nor can He tempt any man. And if we make him two in one, it is as much as to say that he is neither God nor man, but by all analogy a *tertium quid*—something different from both; a conclusion to which we are also led by the doctrine that he was sprung from a divine father and a human mother. The origin of these doctrines of the divinity and sinlessness of Jesus may easily be accounted for by the remarkable and overwhelming experiences of his first disciples; but the scholastic reasoning which has been expended to overcome the instinctive feeling with which the reflecting mind rejects them can only be regarded as unintelligible jargon, or as an effort put forth by vigorous minds for many generations to solve an insoluble question, to explain what seems inexplicable, to believe what satisfies curiosity, or to uphold traditional beliefs.

In denying to Jesus the attribute of absolute sinlessness, we do not feel that we much, if at all, disperse the aureole which surrounds his person, or detract from that feeling of veneration with which we have been accustomed to regard his character. To invest him with that attribute is to remove him from the level of humanity. For to err is human, and natures which are most highly endowed are not necessarily those which commit the fewest or the smallest mistakes. The man who, being highly endowed, yet escapes all visible or appreciable shortcomings, can gain little by being called divine. He is the true, the model man, in whose life the development of the divine or better nature within him proceeds by a course which approximates to the normal; and who, being susceptible of temptation, as God is not, yet approaches within a measurable, not to say infinitesimal distance of the ideal of humanity. Such an one is little less worthy of veneration than a being who, by his very nature, is impeccable. The life and character of Jesus were idealized in the evangelical tradition. But the honour and distinction cannot be denied him of having, by his life and doctrine, suggested the ideal after which the narrative of his life was shaped. And the fact that men who were in hourly intercourse with him, while placed in the most trying and testing circumstances, could discern no evil in him, could even derive from his behaviour the strangely novel idea of a perfectly sinless being, is enough to establish his claim to a position in the history of mankind absolutely peerless, if we except the dim and doubtful figure of Buddha; but far indeed from establishing his claim to the possession of absolute sinlessness; enough to constitute him an object of profound reverence and of earnest imitation, but not of that entire prostration of spirit, or of that worship which is due to Him only of whom we can predicate the *non posse peccare.* It is not surprising that the disciples should have paid honours little short of divine to one who so fully satisfied their moral sense. But they can hardly be accepted as competent witnesses to his absolute innocence. If already during his lifetime they formed such an estimate, it can only be regarded as a confession that there was in his character and conduct a phenomenal depth and beauty which baffled comprehension and rivalry. But if the idea grew up subsequently in their minds there are other explanations which can be given of it.

We do not here enter into the consideration of exceptions which have been taken by Francis Newman and others to some of the words and actions of Jesus; because we regard these for the most part as examples of a minute, not to say captious criticism, to which we attach little value. When a manifest flaw is detected in the action attributed

to him by a synoptist, as in the miraculous narrative of his commanding
the devils to enter the swine, we, as a matter of course, regard it with
Professor Huxley, as a slip, or proof of moral bluntness on the part
of the mythical tradition on its own ground. But we rest upon this,
that the spiritual senses of fallible men cannot suffice to certify the
fact of absolute sinlessness, any more than their bodily senses can
certify the perfect sphericity of a ball. Moreover, it is evident, that
the disciples derived their highest notions of morality from the life
and conduct of Jesus, and that, beyond that, they neither could nor
did go. While then, their general testimony to the absolute perfection
of his moral character cannot be accepted, the high ideal which they
derived from his life may fairly be accepted as a proof of its in-
comparable beauty and its relative innocence. It may also be said
with some confidence, that, if the conviction of the absolute sinlessness
of Jesus was impressed upon the disciples before his passion, that
impression was made involuntarily on his part, if not against his
remonstrance. For, omitting the testimony of the fourth Gospel, which,
for reasons assigned in this volume, we do not regard as authentic,
we may say, that Jesus was habitually reticent with respect to himself :
and on the one occasion on which he was addressed by a title which
implied his sinlessness, he is made to decline the title as a trespass
upon a divine prerogative (Mark x. 17), though, of course, orthodox
interpreters have no difficulty in putting another meaning upon his
words. The original, and probably the most authentic version of the
answer which Jesus made to the young man who called him "Good
Master," and asked "what (good) thing shall I do, that I may inherit
eternal life," is given by St. Mark (who, by consent of many recent
and distinguished critics, is now regarded as the earliest of the
evangelists), and is, "Why callest thou me good? There is none
good but one, that is God." The answer here is a rebuke to the
man for so addressing him, and may naturally be understood, as if
Jesus intended to decline the application of the epithet "good"
to himself. According to the best authenticated reading of the
narrative in St. Matthew's Gospel, again (xix. 17), the answer of Jesus
is, "Why askest thou me concerning that which is good," an answer
which is a rebuke to the man for putting the question, not for his
manner of addressing Jesus : a rebuke too, which is wholly undeserved and inappropriate, inasmuch as the question was one which
might very properly be put to Jesus as a professed teacher of righteousness, and to which, therefore, he might justly be expected to give a
direct unevasive answer. Now, this departure from the original form
of the answer, even though it may have been due, not to the Evangelist

Matthew himself, but to a redactor, affords evidence of a tendency in the church to eliminate from the teaching of Jesus whatever might seem to conflict with the dogmatic view of his person as a son of God, and therefore perfectly sinless.

Once more, Jesus told men to "follow" him, as a "compendious direction to those who desired to practice true righteousness." But St. Paul also said something of the same kind: "Be ye followers of me, even as I am of Christ." And if it cannot be inferred from this counsel that the apostle claimed to do more than follow Christ at a distance, as little can we infer from the words of Jesus that he offered himself as the absolute ideal. There is, in the synoptists, abundant evidence that Jesus was far and away superior to the frailties that are common, and all but universal in humanity. It is not too much to say, with Dr. Bruce, that "it came as natural to him to love and labour and suffer and deny himself for others, as it comes to most men to be selfish." But there is no unchallengeable proof anywhere that he claimed in so many words to be sinless. Even that saying reported as his by the fourth Evangelist, "Which of you convinceth me of sin," admits obviously of quite another meaning. And the language that he is elsewhere made to use, which seems to demand such a construction, only serves, with much else, to cast suspicion on the credibility of that Gospel.

The reverence with which the person of Jesus is justly regarded prevents many of us from giving free play to our thoughts on this subject, and, even when we feel constrained at the bidding of science and the growing thoughts of men to abandon the dogmatic view of his person, it gives a wrench, if not to our moral nature, yet to our cherished feelings and associations, which, at times, is almost more than heart can bear. But the truth of things must ever form the soundest foundation for the ultimate good of man, and in that we must acquiesce, cost for the present what it may to personal feelings, and to sentiments which are not so much personal as rather the legacy of ages. And we repeat what has been already said, that it is no disparagement to Jesus to regard him as a mere man, if, at the same time, it be admitted that he realized the ideal of humanity, so approximately as to kindle the idea of true humanity in the world. Is a man who comes within a measurable distance of fulfilling the law of man's higher being the less worthy of our esteem because he is not also, in some inexplicable sense, divine? In being a perfect man, or only separated from that height by an interval that is invisible to us, and so realizing a divine idea, may he not be said to be in this sense, divine? We can easily understand how his disciples came upon the thought of ascribing to him divine attributes in a sense beyond this, and yet we have a suspicion, that in so doing, they took the wrong way to exalt him. Which is the more adorable spectacle? A man equipped with supernatural powers, conscious of a call and mission to a great work, and doing it by an effort, which seems gigantic and exemplary only by excluding the thought of these powers? Or, a simple man, emerging from the multitude, fired by a desire to show a better way to his fellows, and to erect a higher standard of life, awakening deadly enmity by his teaching, and exemplifying it by his patience under wrong, so kindling an enthusiasm of discipleship, and accomplishing a greater work than perhaps he ever dreamed of? If the former spectacle presents a picture of greater condescension, does not the latter excite a more truly human interest? Does not the supernatural endowment go far to destroy the exemplariness of the life? Our forefathers seem to have enjoyed the recital of feats performed by the heroes of romance, clothed in impenetrable steel, and armed with weapons of magical virtue. But, for the men of this age, the felt unreality of such feats has deprived them of all genuine interest. The application of this remark does not need to be dwelt upon, and though the criticism thus suggested may be very hackneyed and commonplace, it is none the less to the point, notwithstanding the many subtle distinctions which have been made use of to evade its force. And, yet again, if Jesus was equipped with supernatural power, which, in a measure, he transmitted to the Church, must it not for ever remain a wonder that so little has been effected by means so extravagant; while, on the other supposition, must not the wonder be that so much has been effected? But enough has been said to show that nothing here advanced is calculated to dim the lustre which, for so many ages, has surrounded the head of Jesus. To all who come within touch of his spirit he must ever remain a son of God, κατ᾽ ἐξοχήν, if not by the evidence of miracle and resurrection, yet by virtue of that essentially human sentiment which ever craves for some finite impersonation of infinite goodness, and has decreed the apotheosis of him in whom the craving was best satisfied.

As to those narratives in the Gospels which represent Jesus as exercising, at will, miraculous powers over nature, animate and inanimate, we decline of course to receive them as literal history, and we have to account for the origin of such narratives, and for the credence attached to them, in some other way than by supposing them to be the literal records of events or incidents that actually occurred. But theologians, even of the most negative school, have never denied that some very remarkable phenomena may have signalized his public life, and have exercised a very important influence upon the mind of his disciples, and, perhaps, even upon his own. He may have cured or alleviated nervous and hysterical complaints and mental derangements of various kinds by a certain "moral ascendency" which he gained over many who came within the sphere of his influence. There may have been enough exhibited of this nature to *suggest to his disciples* the possession by him of some more than human powers, and to give a hint and an impulse to the mythopœic process which, as we shall yet see, invested his history with much of a mysterious and miraculous halo. Well authenticated phenomena of this description have occurred repeatedly, even in modern times, in alliance with an exalted state of religious feeling. And if we take into account the state of religious excitement, which the teaching of Jesus was calculated to produce, and the sympathy which was drawn out towards him personally, we shall find it not impossible to believe that a species of "moral therapeutic" might be exercised by him; and also that without his, in the first instance, even intending or foreseeing it, physical sufferings and mental disorders might disappear in those who felt the mild but imposing influence that emanated from his person.

From the Gospel narrative it is apparent that men were astonished at his doctrine, and powerfully wrought upon by the authority and confidence with which he appealed to their consciences: that faith was kindled and veneration inspired, *before* he had wrought any seeming miracle, and that in villages and districts where his teaching had made no such impression, and a captious, stolid and unsympathetic spirit still prevailed, his progress was marked by no extraordinary phenomena. The same observation, or something akin to it, has been made in many other cases in which miraculous powers were thought to have been exercised: and what is the inference in the case before us, as well as in those others of a similar kind, but that the faith of the patient was the co-efficient cause of the apparent miracle? In other words, it was not any supernatural virtue exerted by Jesus, or going out of him, but the energy of faith exerted by the ailing person himself, which made the latter for the time forgetful of his ailment, or enabled him permanently to cast it off. What Jesus appears frequently to have said was thus literally true, that it was their faith alone which made whole the sick who came to him; not that their faith had set free or evoked a divine power on his part to heal, but that faith itself was the actual wonder-working power.

In some cases of this kind we are told that the cure was effected before the attention of Jesus had been called or directed to the sufferer, and without his having to help the faith of the sick person by saying, "I will, be thou clean," as he sometimes did when he saw the struggle going on in the man's mind. In such cases he saw that the cure had already taken place without his intervention, without the interposition even of a word or a look on his part, and it only remained for him to say, "Go in peace, thy faith hath made thee whole." The exalted state of feeling, the sense of blissful awe produced in sensitive minds by the voice and aspect of one whom they believed to be a teacher sent from God; "the mysterious shiver," "the sudden shock of emotion," sent through their minds by his passing shadow, or even by the touch and rustle of his garment, were enough to produce wonderful effects within the area in which the moral and physical nature of man act and react on each other. In all such cases, however, the witnesses and bystanders, and even the persons themselves who were the subjects of the influence, ascribed the effects, as a matter of course, to a power which Jesus had put forth, to a virtue which had gone out of him. And we need not wonder that the evangelists who report these occurrences should, in doing so, merely reflect or reproduce the popular belief; and, in reference to some occasions of the kind, give such a turn to the language and action of Jesus as to represent that belief as having his sanction.

We can also conceive that when the fame of such events went abroad, the minds of many would thereby be laid hold of; faith would wax strong, and the phenomena would, in consequence, become both more frequent of occurrence and more striking in character. Nay, it is even conceivable that Jesus himself, sharing as he did in the theories of spiritual influence common to his age and country, might come to regard them as manifestations of a divine power resident in himself, and exerted in confirmation of his mission and authority, of which he was deeply convinced. It is not more difficult, for instance, to conceive this of that pure heart and lofty intellect, than to conceive how he could share in the belief, common to that age, in demoniacal possession. It is also natural to suppose that while Jesus might be fully conscious that whatever power of this kind he possessed was limited to the area or class of disorders in which faith could operate, bystanders, on the other hand, might overlook this limitation of his power, and ascribe to him a power of working cures which were wholly beyond his scope and faculty. It was inevitable that if he were credited with miraculous powers at all, it would come to be imagined that these powers were not confined to a small class of bodily and mental disorders of a nervous and hysterical character, including the phenomena which were regarded as due to possession, but extended also to organic derangements and defects which lie far beyond the range within which the will and the emotions can possibly take effect, and even to vegetable and animal life, and to the elements of external nature (Mark iv. 39, Matth. xxi. 19). That mind can act upon mind is unquestionable. And, in view of the phenomena of mesmerism and hypnotism, physiologists now tell us that it is "impossible to assign any limit to the influence of mind upon body." No one can doubt, however, that the influence of mind is limited to the body with which it stands in mediate or immediate organic connection, and that the synoptists go far beyond that limit when they represent the will of Jesus as extending its influence to the motions of external nature, and to material elements between which and his mind there could be no possible rapport. And the high probability is that they much exaggerate the influence of his will, even in the sphere within which such rapport is conceivable.

There are not wanting indications in gospel history itself that the exhibition of powers regarded as miraculous by his disciples was involuntary on the part of Jesus : the unavoidable accompaniment or result of the enthusiasm or expectancy created by his doctrine and personality, and more or less embarrassing to himself in the prosecution of his main design, which was to lay the foundation of an ideal kingdom, whereof he declared emphatically that it should come without observation, *i.e.*, without the accompaniment of signs and wonders : a kingdom, therefore, whose very nature was contradicted, and in danger of being compromised by association with such abnormal phenomena. His loving and compassionate nature would not suffer him, indeed, altogether to withhold his helping hand : to discourage the budding faith, or to defeat the healing power, that resided in the faith which sprang up around his path : he could not refuse to meet half-way the struggling principle which carried in it the blessing of bodily health and mental composure. The faith, which thus, as it were, appealed to him, was already operating sensibly as a virtue, to which his mildly authoritative encouragement did but give its full effect. But his frequent injunction to those who had experienced its healing power, to tell no man what had befallen them : his repeated disapproval of his countrymen, who demanded that he should give them a proof of his miraculous powers, "a sign from heaven," *i.e.*, that he should work a miracle in cold blood, and in the absence of that faith which was the indispensable instrument and medium of such phenomena : or, perhaps, according to another conjecture, that he should gratuitously light up some such bright effulgence in the sky as was expected by the Jews to accompany and legitimate the advent of the Messiah—such a miracle, in short, as should satisfy a scoffing, or at least a sceptical, and uninterested judgment: his declaration that the generation which demanded and expected such a sign was an evil and adulterous generation to which no sign should be given but that of the prophet Jonah, viz., the sign contained in the nature of the teaching itself—these are so many converging proofs, either that he was conscious of possessing no such powers, or that the phenomena, which did occur, and which gave countenance to such an idea, if not at variance with the nature of his mission, were yet considered by himself either as not essential to it, or as not materially advancing, if they did not even obscure its nature and form an impediment to its successful prosecution.

The truth seems to be that the powers of healing and of exorcising, which were, or were thought to be possessed by Jesus, depended for their successful exercise, or, let us say, their manifestation, on the profound impression made by his doctrine and personality on the circle around him; but, that the phenomena suggested to his followers the possession by him of objective miraculous powers which he could put forth at will, or by an act of volition; and this suggestion, being once taken up, was enough to enhance his reputation, to excite a feeling of expectancy, and to contribute with other factors to give an impulse to the mythopœic process.

The wonderful works, or so-called miracles, which Jesus is said to have performed, were by their nature fugitive—such as to leave no visible effect behind them which can be traced to him, and investigated by us, so as to furnish a direct proof of their historical reality. Our faith in them has to depend on the testimony of those who are said to have witnessed them; and many exceptions may, as is well known, be taken to that testimony, and the media through which it reaches us are many; and hence apologists, with this in their view, have appealed to a standing miracle—to a miracle which is still extant, still passing under our eyes, so that we ourselves at this late age are witnesses of it, viz., the great and lasting success which has attended the preaching of the gospel, the "posthumous miracle" of Jesus, as it has been called, as that one which renders all the others which were transient in their nature credible. But this appeal only serves to confuse the true issue by the loose application of the word "miracle." The rapid propagation of the gospel and its grand permanent results may no doubt be called miraculous in a figurative sense, and will even appear to be so in a literal sense if we overlook all the spiritual forces of humanity which the gospel has brought into play; but, if we observe these spiritual forces closely, we shall see that, being themselves included in the natural sphere, they account for that success in a natural way. It can only be said in a popular, literary, and unscientific sense that this posthumous achievement of Jesus "contradicted the probabilities or uniform sequences which men call laws of nature and of history." This can seem to be true only when we take a narrow and partial view of these laws—a view which excludes those of our social and spiritual nature. It is only, if we leave these latter out of our calculation, that we have to supply their place by the interposition of supernatural agencies.

A species of apology for the purely physical or nature miracles recorded of Jesus in the Gospels, allied to that just mentioned, is founded on what are termed his moral miracles. The ingenious writer just quoted has said (Fairbairn's *Studies*, p. 158): "It was no more extraordinary to have miraculous powers over nature than to have miraculous powers over men. To be the moral being Jesus was, to live the life he led, to die as he did, to achieve in man and in society the change he has achieved, is to have accomplished miracles infinitely greater in kind and quality than those of multiplying the loaves and walking on the sea, or even raising the dead." Had Principal Fairbairn said that the former achievements were more valuable in themselves, and more worthy of the founder of a great religion, we should have assented at once to his proposition. But to say that they were greater *as* miracles than the latter, and to say so, in order to suggest that they afforded a reason for believing the latter, derives its whole force from the equivocal and *schillernd* use of the word "miracle." The works of the one description, if they really occurred, were miracles pure and simple, done without mediation between the will of Jesus and the physical effect, "alterations of the ordinary successions of natural phenomena due to the power exerted by spiritual will over that order" (*Spectator*, March 31, 1888). The others were accomplished according to the operation of psychological law, and can be accounted for by the action of mind on mind, by the power of sympathy and of the idea. As to the reality of the miracle in the one case, if it took place as represented, there can be no doubt; in the other case, the presence of a miraculous element is more than doubtful.

These remarks on the miraculous works narrated in the Gospels are incomplete and fragmentary, intended only to define our general position in regard to them. The subject is discussed more fully when we endeavour to explain how such works came to be attributed to Jesus by the early Church. We proceed now to state our views as to the prophetic utterances which the evangelists place to his credit. Some of these, if delivered by him, would go far to indicate his possession of a supernatural foreknowledge, but were, doubtless, the product of a period subsequent to the events predicted, and were only put into his mouth by disciples who regarded the prescience of future events as part of his divine equipment, and who, consciously or unconsciously, "personated" him under that supposition. That he did foresee, and may have foretold, in language more or less obscure, some events which lay beyond the ken, and contradicted the expectations of his followers, is by no means improbable. Amid the plaudits of the impulsive but fickle multitude, he may have had the presentiment of a violent death at their hands; and by his deep acquaintance with the spiritual forces which slumber in the heart of humanity, but which at his call had been awakened into activity, he may have anticipated that the seed of the word which he had cast into the hearts of his disciples would bring forth an abundant harvest, or even that their faith in him would secure to them the victory over the world. With prophetic eye he may have discerned the general drift of the time, and have predicted disasters which were in store for the Jewish nation. But the probability is that some of the utterances reported as his by the synoptists, which went beyond this and yet were fulfilled, were really *vaticinia post eventum* ascribed to him by his disciples. It has yet further to be noted in this connection that the scenery and symbolical apparatus of certain of the apparently prophetic passages, as they occur in Mark xiii., Matth. xxiv., and Luke xxi., seem to warrant the conjecture that they were in part drawn from later Jewish apocalyptic writings which have not come down to us. These may be supposed to have been written at a time when, if the final catastrophe which befel the Jewish state had not arrived, the events which led up to it were in progress, and the portents of coming evil were much more legible than during the lifetime of Jesus. The class of Jewish writings to which we here refer enjoyed a certain prestige of inspiration among the early Christians as well as among the Jews themselves, and were much studied by those who searched their mystic phraseology to obtain some insight into coming events. And as we know that several of these Jewish apocalypses were interpolated with Christian materials, so it is highly probable that the Christian records may have been interpolated with Jewish apocalyptic materials. In an often quoted passage, Papias, who wrote in the earlier part of the second century, attributed to Jesus the curious and highly fantastic prediction that in Messianic times "the earth will bring forth fruit, one producing ten thousand; in the vine there will be a thousand branches, and every branch a thousand clusters," and so forth. But about thirty years ago, on the discovery of the Apokalypse of Baruch, the prediction was found to be a quotation from that Apokalypse: a fact which seems to prove that there was a tendency among Christians to attribute to Jesus those dreams of the future which had established themselves in current belief, how or from what source no one could tell. And if we combine with this tendency that other tendency to ascribe to Jesus the prediction of events which took place after he had left the world, we can easily account for any of the prophecies ascribed to him in the Gospels, without calling in the idea of supernatural foreknowledge.

We have said that Jesus must have had a deep insight into our spiritual nature, and into the effects which his teaching would produce upon it, and, in virtue of this, a prescience of the future development of the kingdom of God upon earth. That in saying so we occupy safe and unassailable ground is made manifest by that parabolic teaching of which he possessed such unique and inimitable mastery. His parables bear the unmistakable stamp of genius, and show him to have been possessed of an unrivalled gift of insight, prior to experience, except indeed it were the inward experience of his own soul, or the experience gained in the limited area of his own personal surroundings, enabling him to divine the whole future course and development of the kingdom of God upon earth, an insight to which little has been added by the critical study of intervening history. Without exaggeration, we may affirm that the general course of Church history, and even most of its salient incidents, are little else than illustrations of that teaching. Indeed, so much is this the case as to have helped to suggest that while some of the parables, such as that of the sower, of the grain of mustard seed, and of the leaven, are, so to speak, root parables, having all the marks of originality and of actual reminiscence of the discourses of Jesus; others again, such as that of the tares, and of the net, are derivative, the embodiment of materials drawn from the experiences of the early Church, after it had, to hasten its self-extension, relaxed its discipline and become a mixed society, not differing in many respects from the society around it. These materials may be supposed to have been thrown by the tradition into the parabolic form, of which Jesus had set the example. This may or may not have been the case. But that Jesus should have anticipated much of that experience, and have had presentiments of events in the near and distant future, relating to himself personally and to the fortunes of his disciples—presentiments which, when recalled to memory by those to whom they were communicated, were sufficient to suggest to them that he was possessed of an intimate and detailed knowledge far beyond all that he could lay claim to: all this we can readily conceive. We can conceive too how his disciples would put into his mouth distinct prophecies of events, of his knowledge of which they had no doubt; or that they might amplify and give definite and precise form to vague hints which he had thrown out respecting what was to come. But beyond this we can hardly go. The foreknowledge ascribed to him by the evangelists was really, to a great extent, the after-knowledge of the evangelists themselves, a knowledge after the events, and was at fault, or couched in vague and ambiguous language, whenever it went beyond the knowledge which they themselves had gained through the intervening history and experience of the Church. The predictions regarding his second coming on the clouds of heaven, which he is reported to have uttered, as they were not fulfilled, so were probably never uttered by him, but put into his mouth by the Church at a period when there existed a confident assurance, on other grounds, that he was so to come again.

Against the historical evidence for the bodily resurrection of Jesus we content ourselves at present with placing the consideration of its supernatural character. The constructive disproof of it, involved in the discrepancy of the several accounts of it, and in the fact that the faith in it which arose in the Church, can be accounted for otherwise than by the supposition of its actual occurrence, receives further consideration elsewhere. This is the more necessary, because the resurrection of Jesus is not, like atonement or incarnation, a mere doctrine resting on authority, or a dogmatic interpretation of facts which claims to be inspired, but offers itself to our acceptance as itself a fact which fell within the experience and observation of many eye-witnesses. On this account, it is by orthodox theologians regarded as the key to the apologetic position of Christianity, serving to lend credibility to facts and doctrines, of which the independent evidence is not so cogent. Such is the opinion of Mr. Hutton, who, concurring with Cardinal Newman, says, " It is irrational in the highest degree for any man who is absolutely convinced of the resurrection of our Lord, to ask for legal proofs of other miracles of the same class, and manifesting the same character." The justice and force of this reasoning we do not deny. But the question here arises whether the proof of the resurrection is so very cogent? Giving expression to his own views on this point, as well as to those of Cardinal Newman, Mr. Hutton says that the resurrection of our Lord is "supported by an overwhelming amount of proof, at all events to all those who begin with a belief in God, and an expectation therefore of some manifestation to men of His character and purposes." These last qualifying words claim careful attention. They cover the silent assumption that this expectation can be satisfied only by a supernatural manifestation ; that, not being able to find a manifestation of God's character and purposes in the slow and regular operation of His laws, religious men expect and long for some manifestation by the short cut of supernatural action. Now, the expectation and craving for "some" manifestation is, we admit, natural, or we may say, intrinsic to the religious instinct. But may not that instinct overstep its province, and misread its own contents, when it expects or demands a supernatural manifestation ? In its inexperience or impatience, that instinct may long or clamour for some such, and it may even seem to find what it thus seeks. But in its maturity, and in the light of science, it expects to find the manifestation which it seeks, only in and through the natural laws of the world without, and the world within us ; and when, as is *now* the case, it has arrived at this stage, the proof of the resurrection, so far from being overwhelming, may by no means be sufficient to overcome the antecedent improbability. A less known but far more liberal apologist than Newman has courageously asserted that, "for the resurrection of Jesus, there is a greater weight of evidence than for almost any other received historical fact, and that it is here, and nowhere else, that the battle (of Christianity) must be lost or won." Elsewhere we state our reasons of dissent from this opinion, and endeavour to show that the evidence for the resurrection is by no means conclusive ; and also, that the cause of Christianity is not "lost," though Jesus did not rise from the dead. Meanwhile we content ourselves with acknowledging that whatever may have been the fact, the *faith* in the fact, if it did not lay the foundation of the Christian Church, did certainly give stability and distinctness to religious convictions which would otherwise have remained vague and fluctuating.

To reduce, as far as possible, the improbability of the bodily resurrection of Jesus, some curious modes of reasoning have from time to time been resorted to by apologists. To one of these, not so much because it is plausible, as because it has recently been brought into prominence, we shall here devote a few words. It has been said (see *Spectator*, April 4th, 1891) that "the spiritual miracle of the crucifixion (regarded as a proof of the supreme self-devotion of Jesus) was an indefinitely greater miracle than the physical miracle of the resurrection—a much more impressive evidence of the actual mingling of the divine with the human." Now, it would be somewhat difficult to put this reasoning into the syllogistic form, and to make it bear upon the credibility of the resurrection. But the meaning is plain, viz., that as we believe in the greater miracle of the crucifixion, the lesser miracle of the resurrection should give us no difficulty. But we cannot admit the force of such reasoning, and we dissent entirely from the premiss. No phenomenon like or approaching to the resurrection has ever come within human experience. But there are on record many examples of heroic devotion akin to that displayed on Calvary. Absolute devotion to any cause, good or bad, is not "Jedermann's Sache." But every creed has had its martyrs. And we have only to think of Paul (Rom. ix. 3), of Francis of Assisi, and of General Gordon, to be sure that any of these men would, rather than withhold his confession to the truth, have, like Jesus, ascended the cross. And every day we may see examples of moral qualities, the same in kind with those displayed by Jesus in that terrible ordeal, though incalculably lower in degree. His death, voluntarily undergone, we regard as an evidence, not of superhuman virtue, but of the grandeur and capabilities of our common humanity. That recourse should be had to an argument such as the above only bears witness to the anxiety which the resurrection causes to the apologist. And the argument itself is but a specimen of a form of reasoning against which we have to protest elsewhere in this discussion.

It will be said that by surrendering our belief in the historical fact of the resurrection we let go the only decisive and palpable evidence for the survival of the human consciousness after the dissolution of its material vehicle, for the immortality of the soul, or even for the existence of an unseen world—the only evidence which turns the balance in favour of the affirmative, and lifts the existence of a future state out of the class of questions which admit neither of proof nor of disproof. It will be said that the mystery and uncertainty which hover over these subjects, after being, to all appearance, dissipated for many generations by the Gospel narratives, will again descend upon them and invest them with a gloom all the deeper because of the withdrawal of the light to which the Christian world had grown accustomed; and that we should once more have to fall back upon that hope which has never been extinguished in the human breast—a hope, it may be, not a little fortified by the fact that it glowed in the soul of him who, of all men, had the deepest religious insight, and read, as with open eye, the mind and will of God in regard to His children. It may be, indeed, that the religious consciousness of Jesus had for its immediate content not so much a belief in the continuance of life beyond the grave, as rather the perception that the life in God was his present possession. But as no degree of submission to the will of heaven could ever reconcile him thoroughly to the loss of such a life, he had herein the best possible proof that he should never be called upon to resign its conscious enjoyment. Yet even for us that loss, great as it may be, would not be altogether without compensation, inasmuch as we should thus escape the temptation to that "other worldliness" which is apt to withdraw our interest from present duties, and, above everything else, to divert the religious development from its proper course, and to confuse or defile the love of righteousness for its own sake with the love of it for the permanence and eternity of the rewards which follow in its train. The deeply and unfeignedly religious man is one who would love righteousness none the less though its blessedness were to be consciously enjoyed only for the present life, and though eternity were a qualitative not a quantitative predicate of its nature. Respect to a future recompense of reward is, not less than respect to a present recompense, a subordinate motive for a religious life. And the proper feeling for a righteous man is, that if the divine order permit him to live beyond, and to retain, after this life is spent, a consciousness of the bliss of righteousness and the vision of God, it is well; but if not, then he will be content to enjoy it while he may in the present life, satisfied with the brief and transient taste and vision of it, and, if necessary, rather to lose life itself than live without the enjoyment of such a consciousness. To be absorbed in the discharge of present duty without meditating much on the unknown future, may be no mean token of the reality and genuineness of the religious life. And if it be true that we can neither prove nor disprove a future life; that God has spread a veil over it, impenetrable by the highest efforts of human reason, it can appear credible only to those who believe that human reason has been enfeebled by a primeval fall, that He has yet lifted that veil by a special act of Providence; that He has had recourse to extraordinary expedients to make up for a lost capacity—for a lapse, of which we can see no evidence.

It has also to be considered that evidence for a future life might only be too strong, going far to destroy the nature of that hope which points beyond the present, making it of the nature of sight, and tending besides to overpower our interest in the present life, which is the proper scene of duty and of trial. The Christian has well been compared to a soldier who has to remain at his post, and to engage in the fight without knowing the plan of battle or foreseeing its issue.

And though in the long course of Christian history a confident belief in the resurrection has had an ennobling and hallowing effect on many minds, yet it is a question whether on the average of men the effect may not have been prejudicial by shifting the central weight of the religious life, and giving an indirect bent to the religious sentiment; estranging the minds of not a few, and puzzling the vast majority of men to whom religion is a necessity. Yet, though the confident belief may be shaken, the undying hope, with its accompaniment of quenchless awe remains, carrying with it, just because it is undying, an evidence of itself, which waxes as the heart grows in purity. For those who have entered into the idea of the Fatherhood of God, and have through the Christian belief in the forgiveness of sin submitted to the "discipline of heart and soul which are needed for the apprehension of things spiritual," the hope of a future life will receive a new confirmation, going far towards its conversion into a steadfast assurance. If the idea of that life may no longer be included in the region of faith, it need not be excluded from the region of hope. For if, through the cosmic and evolutional process, the Great Unseen has been able out of the primordial elements to bring beings into existence akin to Himself, endowed with the spiritual attributes of conscience and a moral sense, may it not be hoped that these same beings may be fitted for a life beyond the limits of a finite duration? It is elsewhere shown that the inexplicit sense of the manifestation of that higher nature in their Master was what led the first disciples to believe in his resurrection from the dead. But one thing is certain, that the future life, which thus became the object of Christian hope, must depend not on a supernatural action on the part of God, but on the divine nature of the soul itself, sustaining its life through the strait of death.

THE END.

GLASGOW : PRINTED AT THE UNIVERSITY PRESS BY ROBERT MACLEHOSE.